Brett R. Turner and Laura W. Morgan

Attacking and Defending Marital Agreements

Second Edition

Library of Congress Cataloging-in-Publication Data

Turner, Brett R.
    Attacking and defending marital agreements / By Brett Turner and Laura Morgan. — 2nd ed.
        p. cm.
    Includes bibliographical references and index.
    ISBN 978-1-61438-385-7 (print : alk. paper) — ISBN 978-1-61438-386-4 (ebook : alk. paper)
    1. Prenuptial agreements—United States—Interpretation and construction. I. Morgan, Laura W., 1958- II. Title.
    KF529.T87 2012
    346.7301'6—dc23

                                    2012008332

Contents

About the Authors

The authors of this volume, Brett R. Turner and Laura W. Morgan, both earn their living as professional research attorneys, providing research, analysis, and writing services to practicing attorneys. Every day, Brett and Laura communicate with practitioners all over the country, performing research for them on family law issues that arise in their practice. Our work encompasses a broad range of products, from short telephone reports on the eve of trial to full drafts of trial and appellate court briefs. We each write multiple appellate court briefs each year, some of which have resulted in major published decisions. We do not know of any other position that gives an attorney the ability to work on so many different family law issues, for such a wide variety of clients, in such a large number of states. In a very real sense, we have a nationwide family law practice.

In addition to completing research and writing projects for attorneys across the country, we have also published extensively in the family law area. Each of us has already written a major family law treatise; Laura Morgan writes *Child Support Guidelines: Interpretation and Application,* published by Aspen, and Brett Turner writes *Equitable Distribution of Property,* published by West Group. If you are not already familiar with these volumes, we encourage you to review them. We also served for many years as editors of a monthly family law journal called *Divorce Litigation,* which covered the entire field of family law. *Divorce Litigation,* alas, ceased monthly publication in April of 2007. Laura is also a member of the Board of Editors of *The Journal of the American Academy of Matrimonial Lawyers* and of the Publications Board of the Family Law Section of the American Bar Association.

Our positions as professional research attorneys require us to read a great deal of appellate case law, addressing not only marital agreements but also a broad range of other family law issues. In addition, our regular involvement with practicing attorneys across the country, in both our research work and our speaking activities, gives us a good awareness of the types of issues that practicing attorneys actually face. We sit literally between the world of the practicing attorney and the world of family law academics.

Our specific detailed credentials are as follows. Brett R. Turner is a Senior Attorney in Family Law with the National Legal Research Group (NLRG). He started working for NLRG in 1984, and has been the lead attorney on the family law team since 1985. He is author of the leading treatise on equitable distribution, *Equitable Distribution of Property* (3d ed. 2005), published by West Group. He has written for *Journal of the American Academy of Matrimonial Lawyers, The Family Advocate, Virginia Lawyer, Washington & Lee Law Review, Equitable Distribution Journal,* and *Divorce Litigation.* Brett speaks regularly at seminars for attorneys and judges, and has served on study committees drafting equitable distribution and spousal support legislation. He is a graduate of the University of North Carolina, and a member of the North Carolina State Bar. His telephone number is (800) 727-6574; his fax number is (804) 817-6570; and his e-mail address is bturner@nlrgom.

Laura W. Morgan is owner and operator of Family Law Consulting, which provides appellate argument and brief writing to family law attorneys nationwide. Family Law Consulting also provides legal research and writing for websites, client newsletters, and trial. Laura is the author of the leading treatise on child support, *Child Support Guidelines: Interpretation and Application* (Aspen Law & Business, 2d ed. 2011). Laura has also written extensively on family law, as Executive Editor of *Divorce Litigation,* and for *New Mexico Law Review, The Family Law Quarterly, Journal of the American Academy of Matrimonial Lawyers, South Carolina Law Review,* and *Canadian Journal of Family Law.* Her articles have also appeared in *American Journal of Family Law, Trial Magazine, The Practical Lawyer, The Journal of the Virginia Trial Lawyers' Association,* and *Florida Bar Journal.* Laura currently serves on the Board of Editors of *Journal of the American Academy of Matrimonial Lawyers* and *American Journal of Family Law,* and she is a member of the Publications Board of the Family Law Section of the American Bar Association. She has lectured extensively and has acted as a consultant to numerous state governments and the federal government of Canada on the issue of child support guidelines. Any comments can be directed to Laura at Family Law Consulting: (434) 817-1880; her e-mail address is goddess@famlawconsult.com.

Acknowledgments

Many persons other than the authors played important roles in creating the volume you now hold in your hands. Some of these people contributed so substantially that their efforts should be acknowledged publicly.

Brett Turner wishes to thank his current colleagues on NLRG's family law team, Sandra M. Thomas and Karen M. Villemaire. Important contributions were also made by former team members David M. Cotter and Nadine E. Roddy, and by the late Dennis T. Burns. Significant contributions to the first edition were made by Edward B. Borris, Margaret B. Barrett. Amy G. Gore, and Richard J. "Jake" Washburne. NLRG's management, in the form of Edward B. Gerber and Stephen Hart, have also extended significant support to writing of this treatise.

Laura Morgan would specifically like to thank Professor Brian Bix of Quinnipiac College of Law in Connecticut for the insights expressed in his writing on antenuptial agreements, and for his advice on agreement-related issues.

On a personal level, we must acknowledge the many contributions made by our families. Brett and Laura wish to thank Michele Turner, Karin Turner, Daniel Morgan, and Hannah Morgan, for tolerating unusually long periods of absence.

Finally, our accumulated experience in family law is a product of the many practicing attorneys with whom we have worked over the years. We wish that we could name them all, for their total contributions to this volume are greater than those made by any persons other than the author. Special thanks for unusually significant contributions are due to the late Louis I. Parley and Monroe Inker; Robert N. Rosen of South Carolina; Mark Bank of Michigan; and Lawrence D. Diehl and Cheryl Smith of Virginia.

Introduction

General Purposes

Why write another book on marital agreements? The subject has already been addressed in a large number of works. Some of these works cover the entire field of marital agreements from a nationwide perspective.[1] Other works cover marital agreements from specific state's viewpoint, often as part of a broader discussion of that state's domestic relations law.[2] Taken together, the existing body of legal literature covers marital agreements with both breadth and depth. Why are the present authors venturing upon ground that has been so well trodden by others?

The answer lies in the viewpoint from which the existing works are written. These works generally approach marital agreements from the viewpoint of the attorney who must negotiate and draft a marital agreement. They provide much practical guidance for negotiating, and a large volume of sample clauses for insertion into draft agreements. In the case of the state-specific works, these sample clauses are consistent with local practice, and they often have a very well-settled meaning under local law. Readers seeking to draft a marital agreement will probably find more guidance in such works than in this one.

---

1. *See* 2 Homer Clark, The Law of Domestic Relations in the United States ch. 19 (2d ed. 1987); Alexander Lindey & Louis I. Parley, Lindey on Separation Agreements and Antenuptial Contracts (1994); Stephen W. Schlissel, Elena Karabatos, & Ronald E. Poepplein, Separation Agreements and Marital Contracts (1997); Gary N. Skoloff, Richard H. Singer, Jr., & Ronald L. Brown, Drafting Prenuptial Agreements (1994).

2. *See, e.g.*, Peter Swisher, Lawrence D. Diehl & James Cottrell, Virginia Family Law: Theory and Practice ch. 3 (2d ed. 1997 & Supp. 1998).

The existing literature on marital agreements, however, tells only part of the story. Negotiation and drafting are important, but they are not the only relevant concerns. Parties who agree on Monday frequently have second thoughts on Tuesday, and then seek to convince the court that their agreement is invalid. Moreover, even if both parties continue to agree on Tuesday, they may still have very different views on what their agreement actually provides. The existing works provide considerable guidance to the drafter, but they provide very little guidance on questions of validity or construction. Since it is a rare practitioner who does not face questions of validity and construction on a regular basis, the limited scope of coverage of the existing literature is unfortunate.

As professional research attorneys, the authors of this work learned early in their careers of the lack of literature on validity and construction of marital agreements. After struggling for several years to use drafting-oriented treatises for guidance on postdrafting issues, we decided to address the need ourselves. Since we served for many years as editors of the monthly journal *Divorce Litigation*, our initial efforts took the form of articles for that publication.[3] Those articles were well received by others, and we ourselves found them much more useful in answering questions of validity and construction than other works. We therefore decided to expand the articles into a full-length book—the first edition of the current treatise.

This treatise, now in its second edition, continues to primarily address what happens *after* a marital agreement is signed by the parties. While we offer drafting tips at appropriate points, our primary focus is upon the twin issues of validity and construction. In addressing these issues, we will mostly assume that the reader has no independent knowledge of what took place during negotiation. This will not be true in many cases, of course, but in almost all cases the court itself will lack such knowledge. It is therefore generally true to note that this work approaches questions of validity and construction from the same viewpoint the court will stand at when it resolves these questions.

The primary purpose of this work is to provide practical guidance to attorneys who are faced with questions of validity and construction. We have tried to keep the text as readable as possible, and have banished most of the citations to the footnotes. To assist the attorney who must argue a particular question of validity or construction, we have tried to describe all of the arguments that find minimum support in the available case law. To assist the attorney who must objectively evaluate the chance that these arguments will prevail, we have tried not only to describe the possible arguments, but also to discuss their general strengths and weaknesses.

---

3. *See* Brett R. Turner, *Attacking and Defending Separation Agreements*, 3 DIVORCE LITIG. 61, 73 (1991); Brett R. Turner, *Attacking and Defending Separation Agreements: A 1995 Update*, 7 DIVORCE LITIG. 225, 245 (1995); Brett R. Turner, *Recent Case Law on Construction of Separation Agreements*, 4 DIVORCE LITIG. 25 (1992); Brett R. Turner, *Recent Case Law of Modification and Enforcement of Separation Agreements*, 4 DIVORCE LITIG. 45 (1992); Brett R. Turner, *A Mini-Encyclopedia of Ambiguous Separation Agreement Provisions and Their Construction by the Courts*, 4 DIVORCE LITIG. 51 (1992); Laura W. Morgan & Brett R. Turner, *Attacking and Defending Antenuptial Agreements: A 1993 Update*, 5 DIVORCE LITIG. 129, 149 (1993).

It has been our general observation over 20-plus years of family law research practice that many practitioners are too quick to argue positions that they have not yet fully evaluated. These practitioners often find themselves making unsuccessful arguments for a "home run" result, while missing much stronger arguments for a lesser result that will still be of substantial benefit to the client. To identify and make the best arguments possible, the attorney must be able to evaluate objectively the strength or weakness of his or her own position. Assisting the practicing attorney in making and evaluating arguments on the validity and construction of marital agreements is the core purpose of this volume.

In addition, we have attempted to accomplish two secondary purposes. First, in the course of reading thousands of cases on marital agreements, we inevitably observed areas in which law either needs clarification or is unusually difficult to explain clearly. The authors are strong believers in the tradition of resolving most family law issues at the state level, but the states cannot function as test laboratories for new rules of law unless someone compares the results, highlighting those rules that experience shows to be unworkable or unsuccessful. An important secondary purpose of this work is to make note of these areas, in the hope that courts and legislatures might be led to address some of the problems we have identified.

Second, in reading marital agreement cases, we also observed various different types of provisions that tend to cause problems for one or both parties. In many instances these provisions were not an essential part of the agreement, and one or both parties were left wishing that the agreement had been differently drafted. There is an obvious benefit to highlighting these provisions, so that future drafters are alerted to think long and hard before including them in an agreement.

Our discussions of these problematic provisions should be read with awareness of the limited expertise of the authors. Most drafting advice is given by experienced practitioners, based upon their own valuable but anecdotal experience of what provisions work best. As research attorneys, the present authors have essentially no personal experience in the negotiation or drafting of agreements. What we do have is a substantial knowledge of the reported appellate case law, and in particular a clear awareness of what types of provisions have ultimately resulted in more harm than benefit. Since research attorneys are sometimes the remedy of last resort when an unwisely drafted agreement calls for a harsh result, we also have a body of personal experience dealing with the consequences of poor drafting.

As a result of our position in the legal system, we feel well qualified to discuss what types of provisions are likely to cause serious problems for one or both parties. The reader will find that we are strongly against clauses preventing the parties themselves from modifying their agreement (§ **6.07**), and strongly in favor of verifying informal financial disclosure through the formal discovery process (§ **4.053**). We cautiously support provisions terminating spousal support upon proof of cohabitation alone, where they are an attempt to avoid the practical problems of proving financial dependency or similarity of the relationship to remarriage, and not a device to control postmarital sexual behavior (§ **3.05**). We confess to particular distaste for nonmodifiable spousal support provisions, which we liken to playing Russian roulette with the parties' financial futures (§ **6.032**).

When the issue becomes what types of provisions work particularly well, however, our base of knowledge is less substantial. Appellate cases are most often heard, and research attorneys are most often consulted, when at least one party is unhappy with the agreement. When a provision works well, the parties never come back to court, and the authors of this volume are unlikely to encounter them. Thus, it is generally accurate to say that we have much knowledge of provisions that failed, and only some knowledge of provisions that succeeded. The reader should keep this fact in mind when reviewing our drafting advice.

Part I

Separation Agreements

Introduction to Separation Agreements 1

§ 1.01 Marital Agreements in General

This is a treatise about marital agreements. We should begin, therefore, by stating our definition of a marital agreement.

In all fifty states, a court must complete certain basic tasks when it divorces two married persons. It must determine whether grounds for divorce exist;[1] divide the parties' property;[2] and award spousal support and attorneys' fees, if required.[3] If the parties have children, the court must also determine custody and visitation,[4] and award child support.[5]

There are, in general, two methods by which these tasks can be accomplished. First, the court can complete the tasks itself, using the rules and procedures established by statute and case law. Second, the parties themselves can agree upon the proper completion of any or all

---

1. *See generally* 2 HOMER CLARK, THE LAW OF DOMESTIC RELATIONS IN THE UNITED STATES, ch. 14 (2d ed. 1987).

2. *See generally* BRETT R. TURNER, EQUITABLE DISTRIBUTION OF PROPERTY (3d ed. 2005 & Supp. 2007).

3. *See generally* MARIAN C. DOBBS, DETERMINING CHILD AND SPOUSAL SUPPORT (rev. ed. 1995); Brett R. Turner, *Rehabilitative Alimony Reconsidered: The "Second Wave" of Spousal Support Reform*, 10 DIVORCE LITIG. 185 (1998); CLARK, *supra* note 1, ch. 17.

4. *See generally* Jeff ATKINSON, MODERN CHILD CUSTODY PRACTICE (1986); LINDA D. ELROD, CHILD CUSTODY PRACTICE AND PROCEDURE (1993 & Supp. 1999).

5. *See generally* LAURA W. MORGAN, CHILD SUPPORT GUIDELINES: INTERPRETATION AND APPLICATION (1996 & Supp. 1999).

of these tasks.[6] Our definition of a marital agreement is *a contract that resolves some or all of the issues that the court must consider in a divorce action.*

Marital agreements fall into three distinct classes. In this book, agreements signed before the marriage are referred to as *antenuptial agreements.* Agreements signed during the marriage that are in contemplation of imminent separation and eventual termination of the marriage are referred to as *separation agreements.* Agreements signed during the marriage that are not in contemplation of imminent separation are referred to as *midnuptial agreements.*[7]

Apart from time, the major difference among these three types of agreements is the nature of the parties' relationship when they are signed. Antenuptial and midnuptial agreements are signed when the parties are either engaged or married. Their relationship is confidential, and each is charged with a duty to watch out for the other's interests. Separation agreements, in the great majority of cases, are signed after the marital breakdown, at a time when the parties have retained counsel to negotiate at arm's length the terms of their divorce settlement. Because the parties' relationship is adversarial, parties to separation agreements do not generally have a duty to watch out for the other party's interests.

§ 1.02 Separation Agreements in General

Definition of "Separation Agreement"

A *separation agreement*, for purposes of this work, is a marital agreement signed at a time when the parties anticipate the termination of their marriage.[8] It may or may not be signed after the parties actually separate, but it must be signed at a time when the parties anticipate that their marriage will actually end, either by divorce or by annulment.[9]

Since an antenuptial agreement is signed before the marriage starts, it is easy to distinguish antenuptial agreements and separation agreements. The difference between a midnuptial agreement signed late in the marriage and a separation agreement signed before actual separation can be difficult to discern. For purposes of this book, if the parties anticipate that their marriage might or might not continue—in other words, if they do not believe that their marriage is finally and irrevocably broken—then the agreement is a midnuptial agreement. If the parties believe their marriage is broken

---

6. *See* §§ **3.03–3.04** (court is generally bound by parties' agreement on division of property and spousal support). The parties' agreement is less binding on questions of child custody and child support, but even in those areas the agreement is controlling unless the court finds that it is not in the best interests of the children. *See* § **3.07**.

7. *See generally* Combs v. Sherry-Combs, 865 P.2d 50 (Wyo. 1993).

8. *See In re* Marriage of Bisque, 31 P.3d 175 (Colo. Ct. App. 2001).

9. An agreement signed to settle a pending annulment action is not technically a separation agreement, but it is generally governed by the same rules of law as an agreement signed to settle a divorce action. *See In re* Estate of Lundahl, 332 Ill. App. 3d 646, 773 N.E.2d 756 (2002); Pittman v. Pittman, 909 So. 2d 148 (Miss. Ct. App. 2005).

when they sign the agreement, it is a separation agreement, even if the parties do not physically separate immediately upon signing.[10]

Types of Separation Agreements

Some states use different terms to refer to different types of separation agreements. For example, some states limit the term *separation agreement* to an agreement for future support, and use the term *property settlement agreement* or *marital settlement agreement* to refer to an agreement to divide property. The authors agree with Professor Clark that this variation in terms creates needless confusion:

> Some cases and authorities produce unnecessary confusion by attempting to draw distinctions between separation agreements, property settlements, stipulations, consent judgments or other forms of agreement in divorce actions. None of these is a technical term. They all refer to method of compromising divorce litigation. In this chapter only one term will be used: separation agreement.[11]

This treatise will generally use the term *separation agreement* to refer to any and all agreements that are signed at a time when the marriage has already broken down and for the purpose of resolving issues expected to arise in divorce or annulment proceedings.

General Policies

Negotiation and drafting of separation agreements are core functions in any modern family law practice. Periodic surveys of *Divorce Litigation* subscribers reveal that over 75 percent of all divorce actions are settled out of court.[12] Because so many divorce cases settle out of court, the law of separation agreements is essential to the final outcome in a large majority of divorce cases.

Separation agreements are merely one specific category in the general field of contracts, and they are therefore subject to the same rules of law that apply to contracts generally. *See* § 5.02. The specific application of these general rules, however, is strongly influenced by two competing public policies. First, as a general rule, courts

---

10. *See In re* Marriage of Bisque, 31 P.3d 175, 179 (Colo. Ct. App. 2001) ("when an agreement between present spouses is entered into 'attendant upon' separation or dissolution, the agreement must be considered a separation agreement, even if it was signed prior to filing for dissolution or legal separation"); *In re* Pond, 700 N.E.2d 1130 (Ind. 1998) (agreement signed during the marriage, on assumption that marriage was over, and at a time when a legal separation action had been filed, was a separation agreement and not a midnuptial agreement).

11. CLARK, *supra* note 1, at 409.

12. For example, a 1992 survey of *Divorce Litigation* subscribers showed that 75.31 percent of subscribers' cases were settled by agreement, and that another 6.16 percent were settled by mediation. Survey Results, 4 *Divorce Litig.* 151 (1992). The data are generally consistent over time; a 1998 survey showed that 76 percent of all cases settled by agreement or mediation. These figures are probably conservative, as the *Divorce Litigation* subscriber base includes a disproportionate number of advanced specialists whose practices are more litigation-oriented than the norm. *See also* CLARK, *supra* note 1, at 408–09 ("probably about ninety percent" of all divorces are uncontested, and "certainly greater than fifty percent" are disposed of by separation agreements).

favor negotiated settlements of private disputes. This rule applies with special force to divorce cases. The issues in a divorce case are heavily fact-specific, and they are often intertwined with personal emotional disputes, which are not susceptible to judicial resolution. As a result, the parties themselves can create a much better divorce settlement than any court could decree for them. When the parties agree to such a settlement, the courts are highly reluctant to set it aside. A Mississippi court has noted:

> The law favors the settlement of disputes by agreement of the parties and, ordinarily, will enforce the Agreement which the parties have made, absent any fraud, mistake or overreaching. . . . This is as true of agreements made in the process of termination of the marriage by divorce as of any other kind of negotiated settlement. . . . They are contracts, made by the parties, upon consideration acceptable to each of them, and the law will enforce them. . . . With regard to the property of the parties, this is a strong and enforceable rule with few, if any, exceptions.[13]

At the same time, courts also recognize that divorce is an emotionally difficult time in the lives of almost all litigants. Many rational persons have difficulty exercising reasoned judgment while their marriage is breaking down, and dishonest spouses are all too aware of this unfortunate fact. Almost every divorce practitioner has seen at least one case in which an emotionally troubled client insists upon signing an obviously unfavorable agreement. The possibility of overreaching is especially troubling because the disadvantaged spouse is frequently the one who is willing to give the most in order to preserve the marriage. If the rule of caveat emptor were strictly applied to these spouses, the law would violate its own policy of encouraging marriage. A Virginia court has noted:

> [M]arriage and divorce create a relationship which is particularly susceptible to overreaching and oppression. . . . [T]he relationship between husband and wife is not the usual relationship that exists between parties to ordinary commercial contracts. Particularly when the negotiation is between the parties rather than between their lawyers, the relationship creates a situation ripe for subtle overreaching and misrepresentation. Behavior that might not constitute fraud or duress in an arm's-length context may suffice to invalidate a grossly inequitable agreement where the relationship is utilized to overreach or take advantage of a situation in order to achieve an oppressive result.[14]

The tension between these two competing public policies underlies the entire law of divorce settlements. On the one hand, courts recognize the many advantages of private settlement of divorce cases; but on the other hand, courts are also aware that divorce cases present a dishonest spouse with a unique opportunity for unjust enrichment.

---

13. McManus v. Howard, 569 So. 2d 1213, 1215 (Miss. 1990).
14. Derby v. Derby, 8 Va. App. 19, 378 S.E.2d 74, 79 (1989).

Formation of Separation Agreements | 2

§ 2.01 Formation in General

Separation agreements are contracts, and they are governed by the same rules of law that apply to contracts generally.[1] Since this is not a general treatise on contract law, we will not restate in great detail rules of contract law that are familiar to first-year law students. Instead, we will recite those rules in summary fashion, and then provide examples of how the courts have applied rules of contract law in the specific context of separation agreements.

The reader seeking detailed guidance on general rules of contract law would be well advised to consult one of several leading multivolume treatises in the area.[2] These sources should be used carefully, however, for courts in domestic relations cases tend to apply common law contract rules with a particular bias toward reaching an equitable result. This distorting effect is particularly noticeable on questions of validity. "Equity is so zealous in this respect that a separation agreement may be set aside on grounds that would be insufficient to vitiate an ordinary contract."[3] On questions of contract formation, however, and to a lesser extent on questions of contract construction, the courts tend to apply traditional contract law principles without substantial modification.

---

1. *See, e.g.*, Luber v. Luber, 418 Pa. Super. 542, 614 A.2d 771 (1992).

2. *See, e.g.*, RICHARD A. LORD, WILLISTON ON CONTRACTS (4th ed. 1990); SAMUEL WILLISTON & W. JAEGER, A TREATISE ON THE LAW OF CONTRACTS (3d ed. 1961); A. CORBIN, CORBIN ON CONTRACTS (1962); RESTATEMENT (SECOND) OF CONTRACTS (1981).

3. Christian v. Christian, 42 N.Y.2d 63, 365 N.E.2d 849, 396 N.Y.S.2d 817, 824 (1977).

§ 2.02 Capacity to Contract

In order to make a valid separation agreement, both parties must have the capacity to contract.[4] The test for capacity to contract is whether or not a party is able to understand the substance of the transaction:

> [T]he dispositive question is the individual's mental capacity to understand the nature of the agreement and the consequences of his or her act at the time the agreement is executed. . . . The party must have "sufficient mental capacity to understand the nature and effect of the transaction."[5]

The standard for incapacity is a high one, and most of the cases find the parties were capable. At a minimum, the attacking spouse must show more than an inability to drive the best possible bargain. "[A] party is not required to exercise good judgment or to make wise decisions so long as he or she understands the nature and character of the agreement and consequences of entering into it."[6]

In addition, even if the attacking spouse can show strong evidence of unusual mental problems, incapacity is still difficult to prove. The motion to set the agreement aside must explain with some specificity why and how the attacking spouse was unable to understand the effect of the transaction. A mere allegation that the attacking spouse suffers from some form of mental impairment is not alone sufficient; that spouse must explain how the impairment actually prevented him or her from understanding what was transpiring.[7] As a practical matter, strongly favorable expert testimony is almost always required.[8] Moreover, even if expert testimony is presented, the court still has

---

4. RESTATEMENT, *supra* note 2, § 12.

5. Drewry v. Drewry, 8 Va. App. 460, 383 S.E.2d 12, 15 (1989) (quoting Price's Ex'r v. Bonham, 147 Va. 478, 137 S.E. 511, 512 (1927)); *see also* Wagner v. Wagner, 156 A.D.2d 963, 549 N.Y.S.2d 256 (1989) (spouse must be wholly unable to comprehend the nature of the transaction).

6. *Drewry*, 8 Va. App. 460, 383 S.E.2d 12, 15.

7. *See In re* Marriage of Gorton & Robbins, 342 Mont. 537, 182 P.3d 746 (2008) (trial court did not err in finding capacity to contract, where no evidence showed that wife was unable to understand the agreement, and indeed had proposed some of the agreement's terms); Towner v. Towner, 225 A.D.2d 614, 639 N.Y.S.2d 133 (1996) (rejecting wife's claim that her chronic alcoholism left her without capacity to contract; wife alleged no specific supporting facts and introduced no expert medical testimony); *Wagner*, 156 A.D.2d 963, 549 N.Y.S.2d 256 (finding that mentally retarded spouse was able on the facts to understand the transaction; refusing to set the agreement aside); Dwyer v. Dwyer, 190 Misc. 2d 319, 321–22, 737 N.Y.S.2d 806, 808–09 (Sup. Ct. 2001) (incapacity not established by husband's claim that he was "'a psychological mess,' 'suffering from extreme depression and anxiety,' 'felt like a complete failure,' 'could not concentrate or focus,' 'was extremely sad,' 'cried constantly,' 'guilt was forever present,' 'felt that life was not worth living,' and 'was broke-destitute and a psychological mess'"; statements did not show that husband was unable to understand the transaction).

8. *See* Bailey v. Assam, 269 A.D.2d 344, 344, 702 N.Y.S.2d 639, 640 (2000) ("the defendant's cross motion to vacate the stipulation was properly denied because he failed to adduce medical evidence to support his claim of mental incapacity"); Nasifoglu v. Nasifoglu, 224 A.D.2d 504, 637 N.Y.S.2d 792 (1996) (wife's simple allegation of incapacity, unsupported by expert testimony, was not sufficient); Roth v. Evangelista, 248 A.D.2d 369, 669 N.Y.S.2d 644 (1998) (husband testified that he was under influence of methadone, but his testimony was inconsistent and refuted by the

its normal power to find that testimony not credible.[9] Only strong and credible expert testimony is likely to convince the court that the attacking spouse lacked capacity to contract.[10] Given this fact, a spouse seeking to prove incapacity always faces a difficult uphill struggle.

A good example of the facts necessary to establish incapacity to contract is *Bailey v. Bailey*.[11] The agreement in that case was signed while the husband was home on a temporary furlough from the psychiatric ward of a hospital. He had "a decades-long history of chronic and severe schizoaffective psychosis, a condition causing him to be totally disabled."[12] He had been admitted to the hospital "after hearing homicidal and suicidal voices, experiencing hallucinations, and being generally 'out of control.'"[13] His treating psychiatrist testified that he was "'helpless' and 'not competent' because he lacked 'capacity to manage his affairs and make decisions in his best interest.'"[14] A long-time friend described him as "living in 'an inward catatonic state'—a situation in which he was not 'really functional' but rather 'totally dependent' and 'helpless.'"[15] The husband erroneously believed that if he did not sign the agreement, he would be divorced and homeless. A trial court decision setting the agreement aside for lack of capacity to contract was affirmed on appeal.

In the authors' experience, many attempts to argue incapacity to contract are probably doomed from their inception. Incapacity is a defense only where the attacking spouse's mental deficiencies are so severe that he was actually unable to understand

---

testimony of his own doctor; error to find incapacity); Eberle v. Eberle, 766 N.W.2d 477, 485 (N.D. 2009) (trial court did not err in rejecting wife's "claims that she was on medication that affected her ability to think and to resist [husband's] demands," where wife's "statements that the medication affected her were the only evidence supporting her claims").

9. *See* Sidden v. Mailman, 137 N.C. App. 669, 676, 529 S.E.2d 266, 271 (2000) (wife's claim that she "was under a drug induced mania that impaired her judgement" was sufficient to show incapacity to contract, but trial court did not err by accepting contrary evidence that wife was capable of understanding the transaction); Vann v. Vann, 767 N.W.2d 855, 862 (N.D. 2009) (trial court did not err in rejecting husband's claim that alcoholism deprived him of capacity contract; court was permitted to accept wife's testimony that husband "had not consumed any alcohol for three full days and he was coherent and not impaired when he signed the agreement"; husband's mental health counselor did not see him until seven weeks after agreement was signed, and therefore lacked knowledge of husband's mental condition at the time of signing); *Drewry*, 468 Va. App. 460, 383 S.E.2d 12, 15 (disregarding expert psychiatric testimony that the wife was unable to reason through any important document; wife had not proven that she was unable to understand the transaction).

10. *See* Young v. Anne Arundel Cnty., 146 Md. App. 526, 543, 807 A.2d 651, 661 (2002) (where evidence showed that husband was suffering from severe dementia, "lacked the ability to communicate, and could not remember significant family dates or names," error to grant summary judgment that agreement was valid); Eubanks v. Eubanks, 273 N.C. 189, 159 S.E.2d 562 (1968) (where wife was mentally disturbed and under care of psychiatrist, trial court did not err by finding that she lacked the ability to understand the transaction).

11. 54 Va. App. 209, 677 S.E.2d 56 (2009).

12. *Bailey, id.* at 217, 677 S.E.2d at 60–61.

13. *Id.*

14. *Id.*

15. *Bailey, id.* at 217, 677 S.E.2d at 61.

what was transpiring. If the attacking spouse was physically capable of comprehending the transaction, but simply made a poor judgment, incapacity is not present. This is true even where the bad judgment at issue was egregious, so long as there was no overwhelming medical or psychological problem that rendered bad judgment essentially inevitable.

It is especially unwise to argue incapacity in a bad judgment case when the acts of the defending spouse contribute to the attacking spouse's bad judgment. In this case, there is often at least a makeable argument for undue influence. *See* § **4.052**. If an incapacity argument is made as well, the weakness of the incapacity argument may taint the attacking spouse's entire case, causing the court to pay insufficient attention to a much stronger undue influence defense. In short, incapacity should be reserved for those very few cases in which a serious physical or mental problem interfered substantially and directly with a spouse's ability to understand the entire nature of the transaction.

Minority

A general rule of contract law permits minors to disaffirm any agreement made before they attained majority. This power must be exercised while the signing spouse is a minor, or within a reasonable time afterwards.[16]

Since few spouses are divorced before majority, courts have not often had occasion to consider whether the common law rule applies to separation agreements. Nevertheless, the only case to consider the point in recent times held that the power applies.[17]

§ 2.03 Offer

Under normal rules of contract law, there are three main elements that must be met before a contract is formed.[18] First, one party to the transaction must *offer* to enter into an agreement. Second, the other party must *accept* the offer. Third, *consideration* must be present on both sides of the bargain. This section considers the first element, the offer.

The normal rules governing offers apply to separation agreements. In *In re Marriage of Dalley*,[19] the Montana Supreme Court defined an offer as follows:

The manifestation of willingness to enter into a bargain, so made as to justify another person in understanding that his assent to that bargain is invited and will conclude it.[20]

---

16. Restatement, *supra* note 2, § 14.

17. *Eubanks*, 273 N.C. 189, 159 S.E.2d 562.

18. *See generally* RESTATEMENT, *supra* note 2, § 12; *In re* Marriage of Masterson, 453 N.W.2d 650 (Iowa Ct. App. 1990).

19. 237 Mont. 287, 773 P.2d 295 (1989).

20. *Id.* at 290, 773 P.2d at 297 (quoting RESTATEMENT, *supra* note 2, § 24).

On the facts of *Dalley*, the wife stated that she would transfer certain stock to the husband. The statement was made during negotiations on how the wife would pay the husband his share of the marital property (as determined in a prior agreement). Given the context of the statement and the sizable amount of stock involved, the court had no difficulty holding that the statement constituted an offer.

One of the most common types of offers is the submission of a proposed contract. In *Muchesko v. Muchesko*,[21] the wife mailed an unsigned proposed agreement to the husband, who signed it and mailed it back to her. The wife put the agreement in a drawer, without signing it. She did not communicate any form of rejection to the husband, and she accepted later payment of a monetary award due under the agreement. The court held that the wife's mailing of the contract constituted an offer, and that a binding contract came into existence when the husband signed the proposed agreement.

An offer must normally be made with the understanding and intent that a contract is being proposed. When one party makes a statement during court testimony, not intending to make an offer but simply responding to a question, and the other party gives a similar response to the same question, the similarity in responses does not automatically constitute an enforceable contract.[22] The parties agreed on the same matter, but neither did so with the understanding or expectation that an enforceable contract would result.

Revocation and Rejection

An offer can generally be revoked by the offeror at any point before acceptance becomes effective.[23] Where the offer is not revoked, it remains open only for a reasonable period of time, unless the offer itself states otherwise. Applying this rule, one court held that an offer could no longer be accepted six months after it was made.[24] Along similar lines, an offer to settle an existing divorce claim cannot be accepted after the divorce action has been dismissed.[25]

If the offer is rejected by the offeree, it loses all legal effect, and the offeree cannot subsequently change his mind and accept it.[26] This applies not only where the offeree rejects the offer directly, but also where the offeree rejects the agreement indirectly by submitting a counteroffer.[27]

---

21. 191 Ariz. 265, 955 P.2d 21 (1997).

22. *See* Woods v. Woods, 788 N.E.2d 897, 901 (Ind. Ct. App. 2003); Morse v. Morse, 80 S.W.3d 898, 905 (Mo. Ct. App. 2002) (parties agreed in their testimony that certain assets would be awarded to wife, but "[n]either party, however, testified that they understood or agreed to a specific agreement for division of the property" and "[n]o agreement between the parties existed for consideration by the trial court").

23. RESTATEMENT, *supra* note 2, § 42.

24. *In re* Marriage of Masterson, 453 N.W.2d 650 (Iowa Ct. App. 1990).

25. Nicit v. Nicit, 160 A.D.2d 1213, 555 N.Y.S.2d 474 (1990).

26. Morange v. Morange, 722 So. 2d 918 (Fla. Dist. Ct. App. 1998) (wife rejected husband's proposed stipulated order, then attempted to accept it; no contract, because offer was terminated by wife's initial rejection); *Masterson*, 453 N.W.2d 650.

27. *See* § **2.04**, note 45.

§ 2.04 Acceptance

Under common law contract principles, an offer is accepted when the offeree clearly and unconditionally agrees to each and every one of the stated terms.[28] The key element of this definition is intention to be bound. Where the husband stated that "although the offer appeared all right, he would first have to consult with his attorney," one court found that the offer had not been accepted.[29] Likewise, another court found that no contract existed when the husband told the wife that he had "no objection to any of the material provisions" of her proposed agreement, but then requested certain minor changes, including a period of one week rather than one day in which to vacate the marital home.[30] Conversely, where the wife stated that the husband's proposal was not satisfactory, but also said that "it seems like the best we can do under the circumstances," another court found that she had consented to the agreement.[31]

Informal Agreements

An offer and its acceptance need not be made in formal written documents. One court held that a settlement can be made through exchange of letters:

> We recognize that a contract may be made by correspondence and, aside from the statute of frauds, may be partly oral and partly in writing. . . . In this respect, if a contract is to be made by letters the letters must contain all that is necessary to form a contract. . . . The terms of the agreement must be definitely fixed and complete so that nothing remains except to reduce the agreement to a formal written contract.[32]

Preliminary Agreements

If negotiations or other informal contacts are to result in a contract, however, the parties must have intended to create an enforceable agreement without the signing of a formal document. "[I]f parties intend their correspondence or oral negotiations to be merely steps leading to a binding contract, no contract is made until final consummation of the negotiations through execution of the formal written agreement."[33] A Vermont court listed several factors to be considered in determining whether the parties intended to be permanently bound by a preliminary agreement:

---

28. *See, e.g., In re* Marriage of Dalley, 237 Mont. 287, 773 P.2d 295 (1989); RESTATEMENT, *supra* note 2, § 58.

29. *Id.*

30. King v. King, 208 A.D.2d 1143, 617 N.Y.S.2d 593 (1994).

31. Flynn v. Flynn, 232 Ill. App. 3d 394, 597 N.E.2d 709 (1992).

32. *Id.*

33. *Masterson*, 453 N.W.2d at 654; *see also In re* Marriage of Rolf, 303 Mont. 349, 16 P.3d 345 (2000) (informal handwritten agreement suggested on its face that parties did not intend it to be a final settlement); Bryant v. McDougal, 49 Va. App. 78, 85, 636 S.E.2d 897, 901 (2006) (where husband's assent to oral agreement in open court was expressly made "subject to" execution of formal written agreement, on which parties never agreed, oral agreement invalid due to failure of an express condition).

First, we consider whether either party has expressly reserved the right not to be bound before the agreement is written down and executed; second, whether either party has partially performed the contract; third, whether all "substantive" terms have been agreed upon; and, fourth, whether the agreement is of a sort that is typically committed to writing. Each of these factors, while not independently dispositive, provides "significant guidance."[34]

When the language of the agreement and terms of the negotiations suggest that the parties did not intend to be immediately bound, a preliminary agreement is not enforceable. For example, where "each party was hedging its bets as they knew the settlement was precarious and could not take place without a final written document," one court found that no contract existed.[35] Another court found no agreement where the wife insisted upon negotiating during a dinner at a crowded restaurant. The majority of the parties' bargain was not written down, and the husband expressly testified that he said "okay, okay" to some of his wife's requests merely in order to avoid an embarrassing scene.[36]

Another important factor is how the parties acted *after* the signing of a preliminary agreement. If they did not perform their obligations under the agreement, and instead continued negotiating on matters already addressed, it is unlikely that the parties intended to be bound by the preliminary agreement.[37]

Conversely, where the parties do intend to be bound at the time they reach an oral or informal agreement, the agreement is enforceable. For example, in *Breyan v. Breyan*,[38] the parties signed a rough handwritten memorandum of understanding. They intended that the memorandum be restated as a traditional written agreement, but before such an agreement was prepared, they reported to the arbitrator that the case had settled, and partly performed their obligations under the memorandum. The final draft agree-

---

34. Willey v. Willey, 180 Vt. 421, 426, 912 A.2d 441, 445 (2006) (quoting Ciaramella v. Reader's Digest Ass'n, 131 F.3d 320, 323 (2d Cir. 1997)).

35. *In re* Pattie, 107 B.R. 370 (M.D. Fla. 1989); *see also* Wear v. Mizell, 263 Kan. 175, 946 P.2d 1363, 1365 (1997) (mere "tacit understanding" that spouses would not change beneficiaries on their life insurance was not an enforceable contract).

36. Walz v. Walz, 652 So. 2d 929, 930 (Fla. Dist. Ct. App. 1995); *see also* Matos v. Matos, 932 So. 2d 316 (Fla. Dist. Ct. App. 2006) (where parties resumed marital cohabitation after oral agreement, and wife's consent was coerced by the husband's physical abuse, parties' failure to agree upon formal written contract suggested that the oral agreement was not alone binding); *In re* Marriage of Frey, 258 Ill. App. 3d 442, 630 N.E.2d 466 (1994) (wife wrote down a proposed division of assets dictated by the husband, requesting no changes and writing "no" next to at least one of the items; some suggestion that the husband's conduct in dictating the proposal was so domineering as to approach undue influence; finding no agreement).

37. *See* Morrison v. Morrison, 837 So. 2d 840, 843 (Ala. Civ. App. 2001) (after parties signed preliminary agreement, discovery and negotiation continued on matters addressed in the agreement; agreement was accordingly not intended as a final settlement); Sword v. Sweet, 140 Idaho 242, 92 P.3d 492 (2004) (applying Indiana law; both parties testified that they intended to return to present a formal written agreement to the court for approval; preliminary oral agreement not binding).

38. 54 Mass. App. Ct. 372, 765 N.E.2d 783 (2002).

ment differed on a series of points from the memorandum of understanding, but the differences did not involve terms essential to the bargain. The trial court held that the memorandum of understanding was an enforceable agreement, and the appellate court affirmed.

Other courts have likewise found that the parties intended to be bound by an informal agreement, based upon the language of the agreement,[39] statements made to the court or a similar neutral party,[40] and partial performance by the parties.[41]

Once in a great while, issues involving the intention to be bound will arise involving formal agreements. In *Espenshade v. Espenshade*,[42] the parties signed a "paper agreement" to reduce the husband's support obligation from $350 per week to $600

---

39. *See* Granger v. Granger, 804 So. 2d 217, 219 (Ala. Civ. App. 2001) (where informal agreement stated in capital letters that "THIS MATTER HAS BEEN RESOLVED," agreement was immediately binding, even though parties expected to sign a more formal writing at a later date); Ford v. Ford, 68 P.3d 1258, 1265 (Alaska 2003) (where both parties' counsel and mediator stated in oral agreement transcribed by court reporter that settlement was immediately binding, agreement was enforceable despite failure of parties to sign anticipated formal written contract); Duffy v. Duffy, 881 A.2d 630, 634 (D.C. 2005) (letter to wife's attorney signed by both parties, setting forth terms of settlement, was an enforceable agreement, even though parties anticipated drafting of a formal written agreement; letter addressed all essential terms of parties' bargain, and its language "shows that the parties understood themselves to have 'agreed upon the basic terms of the divorce settlement'"); Barranco v. Barranco, 91 Md. App. 415, 419, 604 A.2d 931, 933 (1992) (oral agreement was immediately binding, even though parties anticipated formal written contract, both parties "clearly agreed that the agreements they had reached were to be binding, notwithstanding the fact that there were other issues in the case yet unresolved"); Weissman v. Weissman, 42 A.D.3d 448, 449, 839 N.Y.S.2d 798, 800 (2007) ("although the terms of the stipulation of settlement provided the parties 90 days within which to enter into a superseding written agreement, the parties expressly agreed that, in the absence of such an agreement, the terms of the stipulation of settlement would become binding"; stipulation was a contract even though parties never entered into superseding written agreement).

40. *See* Luber v. Luber, 418 Pa. Super. 542, 614 A.2d 771 (1992) (where court asked each party if they consented to the agreement, and each party answered yes, an immediate contract existed); Hollaway v. Hollaway, 792 S.W.2d 168, 169 (Tex. Ct. App. 1990) (oral agreement was recited on the record, and the judge stated without objection that the case was "over with and done," agreement was enforceable).

If a court or mediator states in a party's presence that the case has settled, failure to object may be viewed as an implied representation that the statement is correct. *See In re* Marriage of Lorton, 203 Ill. App. 823, 561 N.E.2d 156 (1990) (oral agreement recited on the record was intended to be final; terms were recited in great detail, and neither party objected when court ordered preparation of order incorporating terms of agreement).

Where a party facially accepts an agreement, but states in passing that he or she is unhappy with it, the agreement is binding. In other words, a statement that one is unhappy with an agreement does not indicate any lack of intention to be bound by it. *In re* Marriage of Steadman, 283 Ill. App. 3d 703, 670 N.E.2d 1146 (1996).

41. *See* Willey v. Willey, 180 Vt. 421, 912 A.2d 441 (2006) (oral agreement binding even though anticipated formal written agreement was never signed, where agreement was partly performed, and oral agreement resolved all of the essential terms of the settlement); Kanaan v. Kanaan, 163 Vt. 402, 659 A.2d 128 (1995) (enforcing oral agreement to pay maintenance; husband had made at least some payments under agreement).

42. 729 A.2d 1239, 1241 (Pa. Super. Ct. 1999).

per month. They agreed that the agreement was only for the purpose of convincing the bank to grant the husband a certain mortgage, and that the agreement would have no real effect on the husband's liability. As soon as the husband received the mortgage, he sent his only copy to the wife, who promptly destroyed it. The court held that the parties had never had any intention to be bound, so that they never had an enforceable contract. *Espenshade* is obviously an extreme case; in most situations, the mere existence of a formal contract would almost certainly be conclusive evidence of an intention to be bound by the agreement.

The question of whether the parties intended to be bound immediately by an oral or informal agreement is a difficult issue of fact. Accordingly, it is generally error to decide the question without holding a factual hearing.[43] The burden of proof is always upon the party who seeks to prove that an enforceable agreement existed.[44]

It should be noted that the discussion in this section considers only whether the parties have formed an oral or other informal agreement under the law of contracts. Even where such an agreement has been formed under contract law, some states hold for public policy reasons that informal agreements will not be enforced. These rules of policy are discussed in §§ **2.06–2.07**.

Meeting of the Minds

Under the common law of contracts, a contract exists only if the offeree accepts each and every term of the offer exactly as stated.[45] This point is often known as the *mirror image rule*, because it holds that the acceptance must be a mirror image of the offer. Thus, if the offeree accepts most but not all of the terms of the offer, there is no acceptance. The offeree's purported acceptance is instead a counteroffer to enter into a contract with different terms.[46] Only if the offeror accepts the counteroffer will an enforceable contract exist.

A good example is *Espenshade*,[47] discussed *supra*. There, the husband had originally proposed an agreement immediately reducing his spousal support to $600 per month. The wife agreed, on the condition that the husband pay the higher amount for two more months. The court held that the husband's offer had not been accepted and that no agreement existed, because the wife had expressly refused to agree to one term of the offer: the effective date of the reduction. The wife's actions therefore constituted a counteroffer to accept a reduction in support, effective in two months. Because the

---

43. *See* Harrington v. Harrington, 281 N.J. Super. 39, 656 A.2d 456 (1995) (reversing summary finding that oral agreement was binding, and remanding with instructions to hold a factual hearing).

44. *See* Walz v. Walz, 652 So. 2d 929 (Fla. Dist. Ct. App. 1995).

45. *In re* Marriage of Masterson, 453 N.W.2d 650 (Iowa Ct. App. 1990); *see generally* RESTATEMENT, *supra* note 2, § 58.

46. *See generally* RESTATEMENT, *supra* note 2, § 59.

47. 729 A.2d 1239 (Pa. Super Ct. 1999); *see also* Kellogg v. Kellogg, 827 So. 2d 1178 (La. Ct. App. 2002) (where wife's offer waived her right to permanent alimony, and husband's acceptance waived both permanent alimony and interim periodic support under a prior order, acceptance was a counteroffer and no agreement existed); Autin-Germany v. Germany, 789 So. 2d 608 (La. Ct. App. 2001) (acceptance that varied from terms of offer was a counteroffer, not an acceptance).

husband did not pay the higher amount of support for the two months in question, the court concluded that the counteroffer had been rejected, and that there was no enforceable agreement to reduce the husband's support obligation.

Likewise, in *Rennie v. Rennie*,[48] the wife's attorney mailed an unsigned proposed separation agreement to the husband. The husband signed the agreement and returned it, but before the wife signed, he called the wife's attorney and made various changes. The wife refused to agree to the changes. The husband argued that an enforceable contract existed, but the court disagreed. Because of the husband's changes, the contract that he agreed to sign was different from the contract the wife proposed. The husband's actions therefore constituted a counteroffer rather than an acceptance. Since the wife expressly rejected the counteroffer, there was no agreement between the parties.

There is a common misconception that under the mirror image rule, the intent of the offeree must exactly match the intent of the offeror. This point is sometimes stated as a purported rule that the minds of the parties must meet on each and every term of the contract. Upon close examination, however, one discovers that the minds of the parties need not meet on each and every issue involved in the case. On the contrary, there are two aspects in which the parties' minds need not meet.

Objective Language versus Secret Intent

First, the parties must agree only on the objective *language* of the offer and acceptance; they need not agree on meaning of that language. If the rule were otherwise, all ambiguous contracts would be invalid. Where the parties agree to specific objective written or oral terms, but disagree as to the subjective meaning of those terms, a valid contract nevertheless exists:

> The mental assent of the parties is not requisite for the formation of a contract. If the words or other acts of one of the parties have but one reasonable meaning, his undisclosed intention is immaterial. . . .
>
> . . . [T]he law imputes to a person an intention corresponding to the reasonable meaning of his words and acts. If his words and acts, judged by a reasonable standard, manifest an intention to agree, it is immaterial what may be the real but unexpressed state of his mind.[49]

A good example of the objective language rule is *Reno v. Haler*.[50] The wife in that case signed a written document agreeing to joint custody. After signing, she attempted to void the agreement, claiming that she did not remember agreeing to joint custody. She also claimed that she never agreed to a provision in the final judgment requiring her to notify the husband if the child suffered a serious injury. The court held that her

---

48. 718 So. 2d 1091 (Miss. 1998).

49. Lucy v. Zehmer, 196 Va. 493, 84 S.E.2d 516, 522 (1955); *see also* Allen v. Allen, 903 So. 2d 835 (Ala. Civ. App. 2004) ("Almost never are all the connotations of a bargain exactly identical for both parties; it is enough that there is a core of common meaning sufficient to determine their performances with reasonable certainty[.]"). RESTATEMENT, *supra* note 2, § 20 cmt. b.

50. 734 N.E.2d 1095 (Ind. Ct. App. 2000).

signature on the document was conclusive proof that she had agreed to its terms. The notification provision did not appear on the written document, but it was a settled part of the statutory definition of joint custody. By agreeing in writing to joint custody, the wife had also agreed to all of the benefits and obligations of joint custody as that term is objectively understood, including the duty to notify the other parent in the event of a serious injury to the child.

While mutual consent to the objective language of a written agreement is sufficient to create a contract, disagreement on the meaning of that contract can be considered in deciding other issues. If the parties disagree as to the meaning of language that they both agreed to accept, the disagreement might give rise to a claim to reform or rescind the contract under the doctrine of mistake. *See* **§§ 4.054, 5.09**. If the language chosen does not have a single clear meaning, there is obviously a construction issue for the court, and the parties' subjective understanding of that language might be relevant extrinsic evidence. *See* **§ 5.054**.

Partial Agreements and Essential Terms

Second, while the parties must both agree to the objective language of every term of the contract, it is not necessary that the objective language of the contract cover every possible source of disagreement between the parties. Thus, if the parties agreed on the terms of contract, but disagreed as to other matters not addressed in the contract, the contract is still valid.[51]

As an exception to this point, the law does require that the parties' minds meet on all *essential* terms of the contract. Phrased differently, this rule states that no contract exists unless the express language of the agreement covers all essential terms of the underlying dispute. The most common example of this rule in common law contract theory is a sales contract that has no price or quantity term. Even if the parties' minds actually met as to every term of the contract, an enforceable sales contract still cannot exist unless the parties have agreed on how many goods will be sold at what price. Thus, if the parties fail to agree on these essential points, they have not made an enforceable contract.[52]

---

51. *See* Wyrick v. Wyrick, 722 So. 2d 914 (Fla. Dist. Ct. App. 1998) (enforcing handwritten agreement; agreement was incomplete, but not on essential issues); Barranco v. Barranco, 91 Md. App. 415, 604 A.2d 931 (1992) (incomplete oral agreement held binding on issues within its scope, even though other issues were not addressed); *In re* Marriage of Carter, 862 S.W.2d 461 (Mo. Ct. App. 1993) (where parties each consented to essential terms of oral agreement, an enforceable contract existed, despite minor differences between the proposed written agreements thereafter drafted by the parties); Shearer v. Shearer, 270 Neb. 178, 700 N.W.2d 580 (2005) (where agreement divided all marital property except for husband's retirement benefits, which were reserved by division by the court, court's division of retirement benefits was not a breach of the agreement); Brawer v. Brawer, 329 N.J. Super. 273, 747 A.2d 790 (App. Div. 2000) (parties agreed to settle economic issues independently from ongoing dispute over custody and visitation); Luber v. Luber, 418 Pa. Super. 542, 614 A.2d 771 (1992) (contract was enforceable even though parties intended to resolve certain supplemental issues at a later date; parties' minds need not meet on nonessential terms of contract).

52. *See generally* RESTATEMENT, *supra* note 2, § 33.

In the domestic relations context, the clearest example of an essential term is the value of an asset included in a property division provision. In *Moss v. Moss*,[53] the contract provided that a certain piece of property would go to the husband, with the wife apparently receiving a share of the asset's value. The agreement did not, however, specify the value, providing only that the parties' attorneys would agree upon the issue. The court held that there was no agreement upon an essential term, and thus held that there was no enforceable agreement.

The essential terms rule was also applied to a separation agreement in *In re Marriage of Masterson*.[54] The issue in that case was whether the parties made a contract with a mutual exchange of settlement letters. The court had no problem with the concept that an exchange of letters could create a contract. The court found, however, that the letters omitted essential terms of the underlying bargain: "when the alimony was to cease and when the property settlement payments were to commence."[55] Therefore, the court held that no enforceable agreement existed.

Likewise, in *Burkart v. Burkart*,[56] the parties' oral and written agreements both failed to specify who would be responsible for the mortgage after the wife purchased the husband's interest in the marital home. The wife thought the parties would pay the mortgage equally; the husband thought the wife would alone be responsible. The court found that the allocation of the mortgage was a "key element" of the underlying dispute,[57] and it therefore held that no contract existed.

Terms that merely provide incidental details for implementing the main provisions of the agreement are generally not essential.[58] Thus, a binding agreement exists even though the parties have not specified the manner in which a monetary award should be paid,[59] or the specific stocks that should compose each party's share of a retirement account that the agreement divides equally.[60]

---

53. 265 Ga. 802, 463 S.E.2d 9 (1995); *see also* Davis v. Davis, 107 S.W.3d 425, 431 (Mo. Ct. App. 2003) (stipulation of value not binding, as parties "did not make the stipulation clear as to purpose and intent or clearly state the agreed-upon value").

54. 453 N.W.2d 650 (Iowa Ct. App. 1990).

55. *Id.* at 654; *see also* Williams v. Dietz, 999 P.2d 642, 645 (Wyo. 2000) (husband's alleged promise to wife that he would "help her" was not an enforceable contract, as the language "does not definitely establish any of the essential terms of the alleged agreement").

56. 182 A.D.2d 798, 582 N.Y.S.2d 783 (1992).

57. *Id.* at 798.

58. *See* Haynes v. Haynes, 180 S.W.3d 927, 930 (Tex. Ct. App.—Dallas 2006) ("Terms necessary to effectuate and implement the parties' agreement do not affect the agreed substantive division of property and may be left to future articulation by the parties or consideration by the trial court[.]").

59. *See* Granger v. Granger, 804 So. 2d 217, 219 (Ala. Civ. App. 2001) (agreement required husband to pay $30,000 monetary award to wife, but did not specify manner of payment; missing term was not essential and contract still existed, with court determining manner of payment on a motion to clarify).

60. *See* Kreimer v. Kreimer, 274 Ga. 359, 363, 552 S.E.2d 826, 829 (2001) (parties agreed to divide value account equally, but did not agree which specific shares of stock within the account each spouse would receive; "the decision which particular shares of stock will actually be transferred is a non-essential element of the settlement agreement, and the fact that the agreement does

When essential terms of an agreement are ambiguous, and the ambiguity cannot reliably be resolved from extrinsic evidence, principles of construction, or other rules of law, the agreement may be unenforceable for vagueness. *See* § **5.07**. As noted in that section, however, an agreement will be unenforceable for vagueness only in the most extreme cases, when the language is not clear on its face and there is no way to resolve the ambiguity. The great majority of all ambiguous agreements are successfully construed by the court, and therefore held to be valid.

Authority to Settle

When an offer is accepted directly by a spouse, a contract has obviously been formed. In some cases, however, an offer to settle will be accepted by one spouse's attorney. The mere fact that a client retains an attorney does not give that actual authority to settle the case; authority to settle must come from the client.[61]

Whether a client gave an attorney actual authority to settle is normally a question of fact.[62] Some states will presume that an attorney representing a client in open court has authority to settle the case unless the evidence positively shows otherwise.[63] If a client is present while his or her attorney accepts an offer, and fails to express an objection, the client's silence normally constitutes implied consent to the attorney's actions.[64]

---

not identify those shares does not render the agreement void for failing to set forth a material term"); *In re* Marriage of Thompson, 27 S.W.3d 502, 506 (Mo. Ct. App. 2000) (where parties agreed that accounts would be divided "in kind," with wife receiving 30 percent share, agreed was enforceable even though "in kind" was not defined; extrinsic evidence showed parties' intent that wife receive 30 percent of all stock held in the account).

61. *E.g.*, Szymkowski v. Szymkowski, 104 Ill. App. 3d 630, 633, 432 N.E.2d 1209, 1211 (1982) ("an attorney's authority to settle must be expressly conferred").

62. Cummings v. Cummings, 104 Ark. App. 315, 325, 292 S.W.3d 819, 826 (2009) ("Whether the parties intended to enter into a binding agreement, and whether the husband's attorney was authorized to do so without the approval of his principal, are questions of fact best resolved by the circuit court[.]"). For an overview of the law on the power of an attorney to settle the client's action, *see generally* Annotation, *Authority of Attorney to Compromise Action—Modern Cases*, 90 A.L.R.4th 326 (1991 & Westlaw 2008).

63. *Szymkowski*, 104 Ill. App. 3d at 633, 432 N.E.2d at 1211 ("the existence of the attorney of record's authority to settle in open court is presumed unless rebutted by affirmative evidence that authority is lacking").

64. *See* Elwell v. Elwell, 947 A.2d 1136, 1141 (D.C. 2008) (where counsel stated agreement on the record with wife present, and "[t]here is no indication in the record that appellee objected to her counsel's statements," terms as stated were binding upon the wife); Ford v. Ford, 68 P.3d 1258, 1264 (Alaska 2003) (husband did not object when attorney agreed to final settlement; "in light of Henry's active participation, particularly at the end of the day when he now alleges he was exhausted and unable to understand the process, the superior court's finding that Henry intended to settle the case" was affirmed on appeal); *In re* Marriage of Gibson-Terry, 325 Ill. App. 3d 317, 322, 758 N.E.2d 459, 464–65 (2001) (where husband "sat silently and permitted his attorney to enter into the property settlement agreement on his behalf, [husband] is estopped from denying the existence of the property settlement agreement"); *In re* Marriage of Marr, 264 Ill. App. 3d 932, 638 N.E.2d 303 (1994).

An attorney that does not have actual authority may still have apparent authority. Where apparent authority exists, the client is bound by the agreement,[65] but may have a remedy against an attorney who settled the case without actual authority.[66] Some states hold that an attorney inherently has apparent authority to settle a case for a client.[67] Other states hold that an attorneys do not automatically have apparent authority, but rather must be given that authority by some action on the part of the client that reasonably led the enforcing party to believe that the attorney had authority to settle. Some states that nominally follow this rule will hold that an attorney acquires apparent authority by the mere act of negotiating an agreement with the client not present, so long as the attorney is authorized to negotiate.[68] Other states require some positive act on the part of the client giving the attorney not only the power to negotiate,[69] but also the power to agree upon final settlement.[70]

Of course, if the attorney does have authority and settles the case on the client's behalf, the attorney's authority cannot be retroactively revoked by the client.[71]

---

65. *E.g.*, Lynch v. Lynch, 122 A.D.2d 572, 573, 505 N.Y.S.2d 739, 741 (4th Dep't 1986) ("A stipulation of settlement made by counsel may bind a client even where it exceeds counsel's actual authority if counsel had apparent authority to enter into the stipulation[.]").

66. *E.g.*, Brumbelow v. N. Propane Gas Co., 251 Ga. 674, 675, 308 S.E.2d 544, 546 (1983) (where attorney has apparent authority but no actual authority, "[t]he client's remedy . . . is against the attorney who overstepped the bounds of his agency, not against the third party" who relied on the apparent authority).

67. *E.g.*, Ray v. Ray, 263 Ga. 719, 719, 438 S.E.2d 78, 79 (1994) ("An attorney has apparent authority to enter into a binding agreement on behalf of a client[.]") (quoting Brumbelow v. N. Propane Gas Co., 251 Ga. 674, 676, 308 S.E.2d 544 (1983)); Bossi v. Bossi, 131 N.H. 262, 264, 551 A.2d 978, 980 (1988) ("The reasoning behind our 'liberal' rule 'regarding the power of an attorney to bind his client by settlement,' is that the 'authority of attorneys to make [settlement] agreements . . . is essential to the orderly and convenient dispatch of business, and necessary for the protection of the rights of the parties.'") (quoting Ducey v. Corey, 116 N.H. 163, 164, 355 A.2d 426, 427 (1976), and Beliveau v. Amoskeag Co., 68 N.H. 225, 226, 40 A. 734, 734 (1894)).

68. *See* Walson v. Walson, 37 Va. App. 208, 216, 556 S.E.2d 53, 57 (2001) (no apparent authority had been given to attorney on the facts; "[i]t was unmistakably evident at the second negotiation meeting that [wife's attorney] had no authority to act on his own. He could not accept husband's counteroffer without first calling wife to obtain her assent").

69. *E.g.*, *Lynch*, 122 A.D.2d at 573, 505 N.Y.S.2d at 741 ("counsel's presence at the morning [negotiating] session constituted an implied representation by defendant to plaintiff that counsel had authority to bind him to the settlement").

70. *E.g.*, *Walson*, 37 Va. App. 208, 556 S.E.2d 53 (attorney had authority to negotiate but no apparent authority to settle; over a strong dissent, arguing essentially for the New York rule discussed *supra* note 69).

71. *See* Gravley v. Gravley, 278 Ga. 897, 608 S.E.2d 225 (2005) (where attorney had authority to settle, client was bound by the result, even if client later disagreed with it); Pfleiderer v. Pfleiderer, 591 N.W.2d 729, 733 (Minn. Ct. App. 1999) ("The letter appellant sent to her former attorney stating that she would not agree to anything until she had a chance to review the documents was dated four days after she had already agreed to the terms of the agreement at the pretrial conference[.]"; agreement was valid); McGee v. McGee, 168 Ohio App. 3d 512, 860 N.E.2d 1054 (2006).

If the attorney lacked authority to settle the case, any agreement reached by the attorney is not binding upon the client.[72]

§ 2.05 Consideration

Like all other contracts, separation agreements are valid only if there is valid consideration on both sides of the bargain.[73]

Nevertheless, courts have generally had little difficulty finding mutual promises in most separation agreements. For instance, a Minnesota court stated that the agreement would fail for lack of consideration only if one party received nothing whatsoever from the agreement.[74] The authors have rarely seen a separation agreement that gives one of the parties nothing at all. In addition, several cases hold that the separation itself is sufficient consideration for a separation agreement.[75] As a practical matter, therefore, separation agreements never fail for lack of consideration.

Of course, agreements drafted by one spouse will frequently award that spouse much more consideration than the other. The amount of benefit received is irrelevant to the question of consideration; the law requires only that some benefit, however small or disproportionate, be present on each side of bargain.[76] Where the bargain is substantially unequal, however, the disadvantaged spouse may be able to establish the defense of unfairness or unconscionability. *See* § **4.06**.

§ 2.06 Oral and Other Informal Agreements

In all states, the best type of separation agreement is a formal typed document signed by both parties. Such a document has important advantages over less formal agreements:

---

72. *See* Cummings v. Cummings, 104 Ark. App. 315, 325, 292 S.W.3d 819, 826 (2009) (trial court did not err in refusing to follow agreement singed by husband's attorney, where court concluded that attorney lacked authority to bind his client); *Walson*, 37 Va. App. 208, 556 S.E.2d 53.

73. *See generally* Restatement, *supra* note 2, § 71. *But see* Guthrie v. Guthrie, 259 Ga. App. 751, 752, 577 S.E.2d 832, 833 (2003) ("it is well settled that 'the termination of family controversies affords a consideration which is sufficient to support a contract made for such purpose'") (quoting Fulford v. Fulford, 225 Ga. 9, 17, 165 S.E.2d 848, 854 (1969)).

74. Kornberg v. Kornberg, 542 N.W.2d 379 (Minn. 1996); *see also* Kielley v. Kielley, 674 N.W.2d 770, 777 (Minn. Ct. App. 2004) (contract reducing maintenance was supported by consideration, where it "eliminated the uncertainty of the result inherent in litigating modification of maintenance as well as the certainty of incurring the considerable attorney fees and other costs associated with doing so"); DeAngelis v. DeAngelis, 923 A.2d 1274, 1279 (R.I. 2007) ("Laureen's promise to allow Peter to return to the marital home was more than adequate consideration").

75. *See* Brown v. Brown, 90 Ohio App. 3d 781, 630 N.E.2d 763 (1993); *see generally* 2 Homer Clark, The Law of Domestic Relations in the United States § 19.1, at 412–13 (2d ed. 1987); *cf.* Sheppard v. Sheppard, 229 Ga. App. 494, 494 S.E.2d 240 (1997) (divorce itself was sufficient consideration).

76. *See generally* Restatement, *supra* note 2, § 79.

Clearly, a prudent attorney would make certain that a separation agreement was in writing and signed by the parties to indicate their approval of its terms. Such a precaution would avoid any claim that the agreement was not valid from a technical standpoint. A written agreement would also substantially diminish any claim that the agreement was unenforceably vague or could not be understood. Finally, requiring the parties to sign a written agreement would militate against a later claim that the agreement was coerced or inequitable.[77]

Despite this preference for formal written agreements, courts have enforced a number of types of agreements that are less documented.

Handwritten Agreements

Courts generally treat handwritten agreements in the same manner as typed or printed agreements.[78] Handwritten agreements can create opportunities for abuse by dishonest parties. In *Naples v. Naples*,[79] the parties created a handwritten settlement document. The wife did not sign, but initialed specific terms. Before the agreement was presented to the court, additional terms were added, in lighter ink, and initialed only by the husband. The wife did not review the document again, but told the court she had initialed its terms, and the court then told her she did not have to sign again. The trial court held that the wife was bound by the entire document. Fortunately, the appellate court reversed, holding that the wife was bound only by the terms she initialed. But the husband's additions could easily have gone undetected, especially if he had not used lighter ink to make the additions. Parties to handwritten agreements should take special care to ensure that the document is not modified before presentation to the court.

Oral Agreements

Statutory Writing Requirement. Many states require by statute that separation agreements be in writing.[80] In these states, an oral separation agreement is generally not

---

77. Gangopadhyay v. Gangopadhyay, 184 W. Va. 695, 403 S.E.2d 712, 715 (1991) (footnote omitted).

78. For sample cases enforcing handwritten agreements, *see In re* Marriage of Goldin, 923 P.2d 376 (Colo. Ct. App. 1996); Mathes v. Mathes, 267 Ga. 845, 483 S.E.2d 573 (1997); Wyrick v. Wyrick, 722 So. 2d 914 (Fla. Dist. Ct. App. 1998); Reno v. Haler, 734 N.E.2d 1095, 1099 (Ind. Ct. App. 2000) ("both parties and their attorneys signed the mediator's handwritten notes of the agreement after the mediator and all parties fully reviewed the terms"; agreement enforceable); Clanin v. Clanin, 918 S.W.2d 673 (Tex. Ct. App. 1996). *See also* Morris v. Morris, 251 A.D.2d 637, 676 N.Y.S.2d 702 (1998) (rejecting proposed rule that every handwritten addition to typed agreement must be separately initialed by the parties).

79. 2009 WL 806796 (Ohio Ct. App. 2009).

80. *See, E.g.,* IDAHO CODE ANN. § 32-917 (Westlaw 2008); KY. REV. STAT. ANN. § 403.180 (Westlaw 2008); VA. CODE ANN. §§ 20-149, 20-155 (Westlaw 2008); R.I. FAM. CT. R. 1.4 (Westlaw 2008); *see also* CAL. FAM. CODE § 2550 (Westlaw 2010) (agreement to divide community property unequally must be in writing, unless made in open court).

enforceable.[81] Oral agreements stated on the record in open court are a special case; they are discussed later in this section.

No Statutory Writing Requirement. Where no statute specifically prohibits oral agreements, courts have generally held that there is no per se rule against enforcement of an oral agreement.[82]

In states that generally enforce oral separation agreements, those agreements are still subject to the normal requirements of the statute of frauds.[83] Thus, an oral separation agreement could not contain an enforceable promise to convey title to real property.[84] Likewise, a promise that cannot be completely performed within one year or until the end of a party's lifetime is invalid if not in writing.[85] In specific states, other types of provisions may fall within unique additions to the traditional common law statutes of frauds.[86]

Of course, in states that enforce oral agreements, the evidence must still be sufficient to prove that an oral agreement actually exists.[87]

---

81. *See In re* Marriage of Dellaria, 172 Cal. App. 4th 196, 201, 90 Cal. Rptr. 3d 802, 806 (2009) ("If the parties themselves want to agree upon [an unequal division of community property], they must do so either in writing or in open court[.]"); Stevens v. Stevens, 135 Idaho 224, 16 P.3d 900 (2000); Pike v. Pike, 139 Idaho 406, 409, 80 P.3d 342, 345 (Ct. App. 2003) ("Because any agreement regarding the division of the retirement accounts is not in writing, it is unenforceable by either party[.]"); Bratcher v. Bratcher, 26 S.W.3d 797, 799 (Ky. Ct. App. 2000) ("Charles and Sheila's agreement was oral, neither written nor signed by the parties, so it was not a valid separation agreement"); *In re* Marriage of Franks, 275 Mont. 66, 909 P.2d 712 (1996); *In re* Marriage of Simms, 264 Mont. 317, 871 P.2d 899 (1994); Ruffel v. Ruffel, 900 A.2d 1178 (R.I. 2006) (oral stipulation not recited in open court was not enforceable); *In re* Marriage of Allsup, 926 S.W.2d 323 (Tex. Ct. App. 1996); Smith v. Smith, 794 S.W.2d 823 (Tex. Ct. App. 1990); Flanary v. Milton, 263 Va. 20, 556 S.E.2d 767 (2002); Squirts v. Squirts, 201 W. Va. 30, 491 S.E.2d 30 (1997).

82. *See, e.g., In re* Marriage of Takusagawa, 38 Kan. App. 2d 401, 166 P.3d 440 (2007); Harrington v. Harrington, 281 N.J. Super. 39, 656 A.2d 456 (1995).

Oral agreements can still be attacked, of course, on grounds that the parties did not intend to be bound before signing a formal written contract. *See* § **2.04**.

83. *See Takusagawa*, 38 Kan. App. 2d 401, 166 P.3d 440 (2007); *see generally* RESTATEMENT, *supra* note 2, § 110.

84. *See Takusagawa*, 38 Kan. App. 2d 401, 166 P.3d 440 (2007). After stating that an oral separation agreement could not transfer title to real estate, the court then avoided the rule on the facts by holding that the agreement in question, stated in open court with a court reporter present, was a sufficient writing to satisfy the statute.

85. *See* Yedvarb v. Yedvarb, 237 A.D.2d 433, 655 N.Y.S.2d 84 (1997) (promise to provide lifetime support); *see also* Walz v. Walz, 652 So. 2d 929, 931 n.1 (Fla. Dist. Ct. App. 1995) (dicta that promise to pay alimony for five years would violate the statute of frauds).

86. *See, e.g.,* Albrecht v. Albrecht, 19 Conn. App. 146, 562 A.2d 528 (under specific statute, statute of frauds applies to promises to support children after majority), *cert. denied*, 212 Conn. 813, 565 A.2d 534 (1989).

87. *See* Clemens v. Clemens, 2008 WL 4278216 (Ohio Ct. App. 2008) (oral separation agreements are generally enforceable, but uncorroborated testimony of one spouse alone was not sufficient on the facts prove that oral agreement existed).

Defining a Writing. While writing requirements are most commonly met with formal signed contracts, lesser writings may be sufficient as well. The most common example is the substantial body of case law holding that when an oral agreement is recited in open court, the transcript of the hearing in which the agreement is recited constitutes a sufficient writing.[88] Other forms of court testimony have also been found sufficient to meet writing requirements.[89]

Partial Performance. Partial performance is a long-recognized exception to the statute of frauds. If an oral agreement has been partly performed, the statute of frauds may not prevent enforcement of the agreement.[90]

Does partial performance prevent application of a statutory writing requirement? There is at least some authority holding that it does.[91] Refusal to enforce a partly performed agreement could result in serious inequity if the parties were permitted to retain the benefit of the provisions already performed. The already-performed provisions would probably not benefit both parties equally, and indeed the unperformed provisions might well be inseverable from the performed provisions.[92] In most situations, therefore, partly performed agreement should probably be either enforced as a whole or entirely rescinded. But rescission has its own problems, as it may be difficult to restore the status quo ante if the agreement has been performed for any length of time.

The best option may therefore be to extend the partial performance exception to cover statutory writing requirements. Such application is not necessarily inconsistent with the writing requirement itself, as that requirement does not render the agreement absolutely void; an oral agreement is surely a contract if both parties wish it to be so. But if an oral agreement is only voidable and not void, then equitable doctrines such as estoppel can be used to prevent a party from exercising the right to set it aside. At least one court has held that where the attacking spouse has received benefits under an oral agreement—that is, where the agreement has been partly performed—that spouse can be estopped for raising a statutory writing requirement.[93] The result is consistent with the nature of writing requirements, which are aimed mostly at hasty agreements disavowed by one party reasonably soon after they were made, and not at oral agreements performed by both parties for a substantial period of time.

Other Limitations. A number of states have adopted other special requirements that apply specifically to oral agreements. For instance, Ohio law provides that oral agree-

---

88. *See* § **2.06**, note 98.

89. Baranco v. Baranco, 91 Md. App. 415, 604 A.2d 931 (1992) (sworn testimony reciting the essential elements of an oral agreement was sufficient to satisfy the statute of frauds); *cf.* Herrera v. Herrera, 126 N.M. 705, 974 P.2d 675 (Ct. App. 1999) (relying on express exception to statute for cases in which the agreement is admitted in court testimony).

90. *See generally* 37 C.J.S. *Statute of Frauds* § 137 (Westlaw 2008).

91. *See* Carter v. Carter, 862 S.W.2d 461 (Mo. Ct. App. 1993).

92. *Cf.* § **3.09**.

93. *See Carter*, 862 S.W.2d 461.

ments must be proven by clear and convincing evidence.[94] Illinois will not enforce an oral agreement if either party challenges its material features before entry of the final decree.[95]

Policy Concerns. An Idaho court explained concisely why most courts require that separation agreements be in writing:

> Public policy favors requiring divorce settlement agreements to be in writing. One of the major purposes for requiring life-changing documents to be written and executed is to impress upon the parties the importance of the legal consequences of the document. For example, prenuptial agreements and wills must be written, signed, executed, and acknowledged. *See* I.C. § 32-922; I.C. § 15-2-502. Dividing the property of a community that may have lasted for decades has consequences at least as important as distributing the assets of the deceased. Indeed, the process of drafting an agreement often shows the parties that they omitted major issues or made hasty assumptions while negotiating. In addition, the requirement of writing and execution substantiates that the parties actually did come to a meeting of the minds in a vitally important area.[96]

A West Virginia court addressed the same issue from a more practical perspective:

> [Oral separation agreements are] fraught with the potential for misunderstanding and abuse. If the agreement is the product of eleventh hour negotiations or is agreed to on the eve of hearing, it may not bear the deliberateness and informed consent of a prior written agreement. The first time the court will hear the agreement is when it is dictated into the record. If the agreement is of any length, both the court and the parties may have difficulty remembering and understanding its terms. Finally, the potential for fraud, duress or coercion is much greater where the agreement is not reduced to writing before being presented to the court.[97]

While the risks identified by the West Virginia court certainly exist, they are not at all unique to separation agreements. Difficulties of proof and increased potential for abuse accompany any oral contract. As the Idaho court suggested, however, the divorce situation is unusual, as separation agreements are extraordinarily important contracts, the parties sometimes have very unequal bargaining ability, and their emotions often interfere with rational thinking. Given these problems, the dangers of oral contracts are especially acute in the matrimonial setting.

If courts were more willing to enforce oral separation agreements, the number of fair divorce settlements would increase. Along with this increase, however, would come a similar increase in the number of unfair or ambiguous settlements. The wisdom of the writing requirement therefore depends upon whether the benefit from the increased

---

94. Pawlowski v. Pawlowski, 83 Ohio App. 3d 794, 615 N.E.2d 1071 (1992).
95. *In re* Marriage of Lakin, 278 Ill. App. 3d 135, 662 N.E.2d 617 (1996).
96. Stevens v. Stevens, 135 Idaho 224, 229, 16 P.3d 900, 905 (2000).
97. Gangopadhyay v. Gangopadhyay, 184 W. Va. 695, 698–99, 403 S.E.2d 712, 715–16 (1991).

number of good settlements would outweigh the harm done by the increased number of bad settlements. The clear consensus of the legislatures and courts is that the risk of a bad settlement is substantial, and that is why most states require that separation agreements be written.

Oral Agreements in Open Court

The strong general rule is that an oral agreement stated on the record is open court is fully enforceable. Where a writing requirement exists, the requirement is satisfied by the court reporter's transcript of the words spoken on the record.[98] To the extent that a *signed* writing is required, one court held that a party's solemn affirmation of the agreement on the record was sufficient to constitute a signature.[99]

An agreement is stated in open court when it is orally recited, in the presence of both parties (or their counsel) and the trial judge, with the recitation subscribed by a court reporter. If the opposing party is not present to consent to the agreement on the record, there is no stipulation to begin with.[100] If the parties and a court reporter are present, but a judge is not present, the agreement is generally not deemed to have been

---

98. *See, e.g.*, Jenkins v. Jenkins, 103 Ark. App. 21, 23, 285 S.W.3d 704, 706 (2008) ("oral stipulations dictated in open court have the force and effect of a binding agreement"); *In re* Marriage of Weck, 706 P.2d 436 (Colo. Ct. App. 1985); *Stevens*, 135 Idaho at 229, 16 P.3d at 905 ("Stipulations taken by oath are of a different character than self-serving testimony by one spouse, contested by the other spouse, that the parties at a former time reached an oral agreement[.]"); Gigantelli v. Gigantelli, 992 So. 2d 825, 826 (Fla. Dist. Ct. App. 2008) ("an oral agreement reached by the parties and announced to the trial court is a fully enforceable settlement agreement"); *In re* Marriage of Lorton, 203 Ill. App. 823, 561 N.E.2d 156 (1990); Reon v. Reon, 982 So. 2d 210 (La. Ct. App. 3d Cir. 2008); Page v. Page, 671 A.2d 956 (Me. 1996); Dominick v. Dominick, 18 Mass. App. Ct. 85, 463 N.E.2d 564, 569 (1984); Bougard v. Bougard, 991 So. 2d 646 (Miss. Ct. App. 2008); Dahn v. Dahn, 256 S.W.3d 187 (Mo. Ct. App. 2008); Peirick v. Peirick, 641 S.W.2d 195, 197 (Mo. Ct. App. 1982); Wilson v. Wilson, 35 A.D.3d 595, 596, 826 N.Y.S.2d 416, 417 (2006) ("where an open court stipulation contains all of the material terms of an enforceable agreement, it will be enforced" if otherwise valid as a contract); Ashcraft v. Ashcraft, 195 A.D.2d 963, 601 N.Y.S.2d 753 (1993); McIntosh v. McIntosh, 74 N.C. App. 554, 328 S.E.2d 600 (1985); Luber v. Luber, 418 Pa. Super. 542, 614 A.2d 771 (1992); *Gangopadhyay*, 184 W. Va. 695, 403 S.E.2d 712.

The same result can also be reached by holding that the parties are judicially estopped to deny that they consented to an oral agreement in open court. Paxaio v. Paxaio, 429 Mass. 307, 708 N.E.2d 91 (1999).

99. The transcript shows that the judge asked Mieko, "Ma'am, is that your understanding of the agreement?" She replied, "Yes." That response was her sign or symbol authenticating the agreement that had just been recited to the court. As the court recognized in *Whitlow*, the authenticity of that sign or symbol is not lessened when it is accurately taken down by a public official whose duty it was to record the proceeding rather than being handwritten by the party.

In re Marriage of Takusagawa, 38 Kan. App. 2d 401, 410, 166 P.3d 440, 445 (2007).

100. *See Jenkins*, 103 Ark. App. 21, 285 S.W.3d 704 (stipulation dictated to court reported by one attorney alone, without presence of the opposing attorney or the opposing party, before a court hearing, was not an open-court stipulation).

read onto the record in open court, so that special rules relating to open court agreements are not applicable.[101]

An agreement is made in open court only if all essential terms of the agreement have been stated on the record.[102] In addition, the record must clearly show that both parties consented on the record to the stated terms.[103] If a written judgment is prepared to incorporate the terms of an open-court stipulation, the judgment cannot include terms beyond those stated in the stipulation.[104] If material issues are not resolved by the stipulation, the court would of course retain the power to decide those issues under normal law, but the court cannot hold that the additional issues were resolved by the stipulation.

When an oral agreement is read into the record, many states require that the trial judge must independently ask the parties on the record whether they understand the agreement and voluntarily consent to its terms.[105] The review must be a "reasoned and thorough inquiry," and not merely a summary review, particularly where the agreement is unfair on its face.[106] Where the husband had consented off the record but his consent

---

101. *See* Ledbetter v. Ledbetter, 163 S.W.3d 681, 685 (Tenn. 2005) (audiotaped oral agreement stated before mediator was not stated in open court, as mediator was not a sitting judge); Carter v. Carter, 862 S.W.2d 461 (Mo. Ct. App. 1993) (oral agreement reached in attorney's office was materially different from one reached in open court).

102. *See* Loss v. Loss, 608 So. 2d 39 (Fla. Dist. Ct. App. 1992) (where essential terms were stated in conversations off the record, and trial court's final judgment contained terms to which the parties did not stipulate at any point in the transcript, error to enforce stipulation).

103. *See Loss*, 608 So. 2d 39 (where trial court's final judgment contained terms to which the parties did not stipulate at any point in the transcript, error to enforce stipulation); O'Donnell v. O'Donnell, 288 A.D.2d 452, 453, 733 N.Y.S.2d 495, 496 (2001) (error to enforce stipulation; "the record does not reflect that the defendant or her attorney consented to the terms placed on the record by the plaintiff's attorney"); Stern v. Stern, 273 A.D.2d 298, 298, 708 N.Y.S.2d 707, 708 (2000) (error to enforce stipulation; "the record is inadequate to demonstrate that either the defendant or his attorney actually consented to the equal distribution of assets proposed by the plaintiff's attorney"); Chisholm v. Chisholm, 209 S.W.3d 96, 98 (Tex. 2006) (error to enforce agreement; record did not show clear consent to agreement by wife, whose command of English was very limited); Gaffney v. Gaffney, 45 Va. App. 655, 659, 613 S.E.2d 471, 473 (2005) (parties introduced unsigned exhibit "reflecting various terms" of agreement, and gave testimony "describ[ing] some of the terms of that agreement," but did not read agreement into the record or formally agree to its terms upon the record; agreement was not made in open court, as required for enforcement without signatures).

It must also be clear that the parties consented to the stated terms with intent to be bound by a contract. Where both parties agree on the same matter in their testimony, but neither party intends to offer or accept a contract, no enforceable contract exists. *See* § **2.03**.

104. *See* Reon v. Reon, 982 So. 2d 210 (La. Ct. App. 3d Cir. 2008) (striking additional terms from the judgment).

105. *See Loss*, 608 So. 2d 39; McIntosh v. McIntosh, 74 N.C. App. 554, 328 S.E.2d 600 (1985); Gangopadhyay v. Gangopadhyay, 184 W. Va. 695, 403 S.E.2d 712 (1991).

106. Hager v. Hager, 190 W. Va. 399, 438 S.E.2d 579, 581 (1993) (remanding for further review). *But see* Hestek v. Hestek, 587 N.W.2d 308, 310 (Minn. Ct. App. 1998) (summary review was a "deficient practice," but agreement was nevertheless valid).

did not appear on the record, a Florida court held that no contract existed.[107] Likewise, where counsel told a New York court that an oral agreement had been reached but neither the opposing counsel nor the client was present, the court found no agreement.[108]

In New York, an oral stipulation must not only be read into the record, but be signed and acknowledged as a deed. When these requirements are not met, the agreement is invalid.[109] The requirement is satisfied by the recitation of the stipulation into the record, followed by the execution of a written agreement, executed as a deed, that incorporates the stipulation by reference.[110] A postdivorce oral modification is apparently enforceable, at least where it has been performed by the parties.[111] The requirement applies only to contracts made before or during the marriage; it does not apply to contracts signed after entry of a divorce decree.[112]

While an oral agreement stated in open court usually satisfies any writing requirement imposed by law, the parties are still free to provide that their oral agreement will not be permanently binding unless reduced to a formal writing. Since the writing requirement imposed by law is satisfied, a condition imposed by the parties generally exists only where there is express language in the oral agreement requiring consent to a later writing.[113]

§ 2.07 Formalities

The preceding sections of this chapter have discussed whether a separation agreement is valid under the common law of contracts. In all cases, the common law requirements state a minimum that must be met in order for the agreement to be enforceable. There is a strong tradition, however, of state involvement with domestic relations in general and with separation agreements in particular. In keeping with this tradition,

---

107. *Loss*, 608 So. 2d 39; *see also* Paxaio v. Paxaio, 429 Mass. 307, 708 N.E.2d 91 (1999) (where parties did not expressly state their assent on the record to final agreement, no enforceable contract existed).

108. Sheridan v. Sheridan, 202 A.D.2d 749, 608 N.Y.S.2d 582 (1994); *see also* Heath v. Heath, 132 N.C. App. 36, 509 S.E.2d 804 (1999) (stipulation was not read into record, and there is no evidence that the parties understood the terms of their bargain; no contract).

109. Harbour v. Harbour, 243 A.D.2d 947, 664 N.Y.S.2d 135 (1997) (court cannot direct party who consented on the record to sign and acknowledge a writing); Sorge v. Sorge, 238 A.D.2d 890, 660 N.Y.S.2d 776 (1997).

110. Cheruvu v. Cheruvu, 59 A.D.3d 876, 877, 874 N.Y.S.2d 296, 298 (2009).

111. *See* O'Malley v. Baruch, 239 A.D.2d 477, 658 N.Y.S.2d 64 (1997).

112. Hargett v. Hargett, 256 A.D.2d 50, 680 N.Y.S.2d 526 (1998) (contract to settle postdivorce equitable distribution claim); *but cf.* Wetherby v. Wetherby, 50 A.D.3d 1226, 1227, 854 N.Y.S.2d 813, 814 (2008) (where agreement required that future modifications be "in writing duly subscribed and acknowledged with the same formality as this Agreement," acknowledgment requirement applied to future modifications).

113. *See* Bryant v. McDougal, 49 Va. App. 78, 85, 636 S.E.2d 897, 901 (2006) (where husband's assent to oral agreement in open court was expressly made "subject to" execution of formal written agreement, on which parties never agreed, oral agreement invalid due to failure of an express condition).

some states impose special requirements that apply only to separation agreements. This section will discuss those requirements.

This section will discuss only requirements that apply across the board to all separation agreements. Formalities that apply only to oral or other informal agreements are discussed in § **2.06**.

Signature

As noted in § **2.06**, many states have statutes requiring that separation agreements be in writing. Some of these statutes also require that the agreement be signed by the parties.[114] Where the statute requires only that the agreement be in writing, some courts have implied a signature requirement.[115] Other courts have held that a written agreement need not necessarily be signed by parties.[116]

If there is no requirement that separation agreements be written, there is obviously no requirement that they be signed.[117] Be aware that even in the absence of a writing requirement applying specifically to separation agreements, the statute of frauds still requires that certain types of agreements be supported by a writing,[118] and the writing must generally be signed by the party against whom enforcement is sought.[119]

Acknowledgment

A small number of states require not only that a separation agreement be written, but also that consent be acknowledged before a certifying officer.[120] If the necessary acknowledgment is not present, the agreement is not enforceable.[121]

Where acknowledgment is required, the agreement need not be acknowledged at the same time it is created. On the contrary, the agreement can be acknowledged at any

---

114. *See, e.g.*, VA. CODE ANN. §§ 20-149, 20-155 (Westlaw 2008).

115. *See* Heskett v. Heskett, 245 S.W.3d 222, 227 (Ky. Ct. App. 2008); Bratcher v. Bratcher, 26 S.W.3d 797, 799 (Ky. Ct. App. 2000); *In re* Marriage of Killpack, 320 Mont. 186, 189, 87 P.3d 393, 396 (2004) ("[t]he only agreement in the record is the unsigned document drafted by Sara and attached to her motion to enforce the oral agreement"; trial court properly held that document was not an enforceable contract).

116. *See* Stolberg v. Stolberg, 538 N.E.2d 1 (Ind. Ct. App. 1989) (statute requiring that the agreement be "in writing" did not require that the writing be signed).

117. *See* Muchesko v. Muchesko, 191 Ariz. 265, 955 P.2d 21 (1997) (wife mailed unsigned contract to husband, who signed it and mailed it back to the wife; parties then partly performed the contract; contract was enforceable, even though wife never signed the agreement).

118. *See* § **2.06**, note 83.

119. *See generally* 37 C.J.S. STATUTE OF FRAUDS §§ 128–132 (Westlaw 2008).

120. *E.g.*, IDAHO CODE ANN. § 32-917 (Westlaw 2008); N.Y. DOM. REL. LAW § 236B(3) (Westlaw 2008); N.C. GEN. STAT. § 52-10.1 (Westlaw 2010).

121. *See* Tomei v. Tomei, 39 A.D.3d 1149, 1150, 834 N.Y.S.2d 781, 782 (2007) (unacknowledged oral stipulation was not enforceable); Sluder v. Sluder, 198 N.C. App. 401, 679 S.E.2d 435 (2009). *But cf. In re* Estate of Sbarra, 17 A.D.3d 975, 794 N.Y.S.2d 479 (2005) (acknowledgment necessary only for enforcement in matrimonial proceedings; agreement can be enforced in postdivorce probate proceedings even if not acknowledged).

point in time after its creation,[122] so long as both spouses properly state to the certifying officer that they consented to the agreement.

When an agreement is restated or reaffirmed by both parties in open court, it is generally enforceable despite lack of acknowledgment.[123]

The purpose of the acknowledgment requirement is to ensure that both spouses genuinely consent to the agreement. The underlying theory is that duress and undue influence are less likely if consent must be formally manifested.[124]

Presentation to the Court

Some states require that a written agreement reached out of court be presented to the court and entered into the record before it can be enforced.[125] Where the writing had been lost, one court held that the requirement could not be met and the agreement was unenforceable.[126]

The presentation requirement is met if the agreement is presented at any point before the trial court's judgment becomes final. It is generally not required that the agreement be submitted with the pleadings, or even that it be submitted before trial.[127]

Approval by the Court

A significant minority of states hold that a separation agreement is not binding until it is approved by a court. A majority of states hold that a separation agreement is not valid

---

122. *See* Hartloff v. Hartloff, 296 A.D.2d 847, 848, 745 N.Y.S.2d 361, 362 (2002) (husband signed affidavit of acknowledgment certifying he had voluntarily consented to prior oral stipulation); Hurley v. Johnson, 4 Misc. 3d 616, 620, 779 N.Y.S.2d 771, 774 (Sup. Ct. 2004) ("the instant separation agreement is now clearly valid and enforceable since the subsequent acknowledgment complies with the statutory requirements").

123. *See* Herrera v. Herrera, 126 N.M. 705, 974 P.2d 675 (Ct. App. 1999).

The New York cases are divided. For cases holding that an open-court stipulation is enforceable, *see* Rubenfeld v. Rubenfeld, 279 A.D.2d 153, 159, 720 N.Y.S.2d 29, 33 (1st Dep't 2001).; Public Adm'r of Nassau Cnty. v. Wolfson, 282 A.D.2d 730, 725 N.Y.S.2d 48 (2d Dep't 2001); Harrington v. Harrington, 103 A.D.2d 356, 479 N.Y.S.2d 1000 (2d Dep't 1984). For cases holding to the contrary, *see* Harbour v. Harbour, 243 A.D.2d 947, 664 N.Y.S.2d 135 (3d Dep't 1997); Hanford v. Hanford, 91 A.D.2d 829, 458 N.Y.S.2d 418 (1982). Given the strong support nationwide for enforcing oral agreements stated upon the record in open court, *see* § **2.06**, note 98, the First and Second Department cases are better reasoned. Consent to an agreement in open court, with a judge and court reporter present, is a higher level of formality than mere acknowledgment before a notary or other certifying officer.

124. *See, e.g.,* McIntosh v. McIntosh, 74 N.C. App. 554, 328 S.E.2d 600 (1985).

125. *E.g.,* S.C.R. Civ. P. 43(k).

126. *See* Buckley v. Shealy, 370 S.C. 317, 322, 635 S.E.2d 76, 78 (2006).

127. *See In re* Raffaelli, 975 S.W.2d 660 (Tex. Ct. App. 1998) (agreement presented after judgment was announced, but before it became final); Childers v. Childers, No. 2659-98-3 (Va. Ct. App. 1999) (agreement presented at beginning of trial of unsettled case).

Note that a prolonged failure to raise the agreement could constitute evidence of abandonment. *See* § **4.075**. Childers held that the trial court's finding that the agreement was not properly produced was harmless error on this case. It is important to note, however, that the husband in Childers had not only failed to produce the agreement, but also acted as if no agreement existed for a period of over a year.

until it is approved by a court.[128] This rule is mostly a procedural device for facilitating court review of the voluntariness of the parties' consent and the substantive sufficiency of the agreement's terms. It will therefore be considered in § **4.04**.

In states that do not require court approval of separation agreements, an agreement does not cease to be binding merely because the court accidentally or deliberately fails to expressly mention or approve the agreement in the divorce decree. In *Addy v. Addy*,[129] the parties signed an addendum to their separation agreement. The agreement was filed with the court and incorporated into the decree, but the court remained unaware of the addendum. Several years later, the wife sought to enforce the addendum. The court granted her request, on grounds that the original court's failure to approve the addendum did not destroy its validity.[130]

Other Formalities

A small number of states require specific formalities for certain issues within a separation agreement. For example, in Connecticut, all agreements to provide college support must be in writing.[131]

Types of Divorce Actions

A few states draw distinctions between separation agreements signed in different types of divorce actions. In Mississippi, for instance, an agreement signed for purposes of summary dissolution proceedings is invalid as a contract until approved by the court. In addition, such an agreement can be enforced only in dissolution proceedings; it cannot be enforced in a contested divorce case.[132]

Types of Agreements

In some states, the formalities necessary in a separation agreement are different from the formalities required for other forms of marital agreements. In these cases, difficult questions may arise regarding which set of formalities the parties were required to follow.

For instance, in *Langley v. Langley*,[133] the court had to consider whether the agreement was an interspousal contract or a matrimonial agreement. The former requires few formalities under Louisiana law, but the latter requires relatively extensive formalities. The court concluded that the difference between the two was their intended time of effect: A matrimonial agreement governs marital property rights in the future, while an

---

128. *See* Wis. Stat. Ann. § 676.10(1); Knox v. Remick, 371 Mass. 433, 358 S.E.2d 432 (1976); Voight v. Voight, 670 N.E.2d 1271 (Ind. 1996); Funderburk v. Funderburk, 286 S.C. 129, 332 S.E.2d 205 (1985).

129. 456 N.W.2d 506 (N.D. 1990).

130. For additional cases holding that court approval is not a prerequisite to the enforceability of a separation agreement, *see* Arnold v. Arnold, 227 Ga. App. 152, 489 S.E.2d 65 (1997) (agreement not even mentioned in divorce decree is still binding as a contract); Parra v. Parra, 1 Va. App. 118, 336 S.E.2d 157, 163 (1985).

131. Lowe v. Lowe, 47 Conn. App. 354, 704 A.2d 236 (1997).

132. Grier v. Grier, 616 So. 2d 337 (Miss. 1993).

133. 647 So. 2d 640 (La. Ct. App. 1994).

interspousal contract governs marital property rights in the past. Because the contract at issue was signed at separation and dealt with marital property rights acquired during the previous years of marriage, the court held that it was an interspousal contract.

Estoppel

An agreement that lacks required formalities can be enforced on a theory of estoppel or ratification. For example, in *Mahon v. Moorman*,[134] the agreement did not comply with the New York requirement that the agreement be signed and formally acknowledged. The agreement was attacked by the husband, but he had accepted substantial benefits under it. The court held that his acceptance of benefits estopped him from raising the formalities issue.

A party is especially likely to be estopped from arguing that an agreement is unenforceable for failure to comply with required formalities when the party was silent on the issue in the original divorce case and then attempts to raise the issue at some later point in time.[135]

For a general discussion of ratification and estoppel, *see* **§ 4.073**.

§ 2.08 Mediation

One of the great changes in family law practice over the past 20 years has been a substantial increase in the use of mediation. Mediation has been so successful in settling divorce cases that it is strongly encouraged nearly everywhere. In addition, a growing number of jurisdictions are requiring that the parties attempt mediation before proceeding to litigation. Given these changes, a significant body of case law is beginning to consider various procedural issues that arise when an agreement is negotiated through mediation.

While most mediation is done either under mandatory court rules or by joint decision of the parties, agreements to mediate specific issues are enforced by the courts.[136]

The Mediation Process

As used in this section, *mediation* is a settlement technique in which a neutral person (the *mediator*) attempts to assist the parties in reaching an agreed settlement. The mediator is not a sitting judge, but rather a private person chosen by the parties. Different states have different sets of qualifications for mediators; some require more training and experience than others.

---

134. 234 A.D.2d 1, 650 N.Y.S.2d 153 (1996).

135. *See In re* Estate of Sbarra, 17 A.D.3d 975, 976, 794 N.Y.S.2d 479, 480 (2005) (where wife "affirmatively alleged in the divorce action that the separation agreement was valid" and "received the benefit of the separation agreement's provisions for division of marital property in the earlier divorce action," "she is judicially estopped from now challenging its validity"); *see generally* **§ 4.02** (res judicata as a defense to postdivorce attacks upon separation agreements).

136. Indeed, many separation agreements contains provisions requiring mediation of postjudgment disputes. *E.g.*, Edwards v. Poulmentis, 307 A.D.2d 1051, 763 N.Y.S.2d 677 (2003).

The mediator does not have formal power to decide any issue; he or she can only assist the parties in reaching an agreement. (The parties can agree to give the mediator power to decide an issue; this alternative, known as *binding mediation,* is similar to arbitration. *See* § **6.067.**) The mediator is not responsible for giving legal advice to either party, and indeed may not necessarily be trained as an attorney. The parties therefore usually retain their own attorneys to provide legal and practice advice during the negotiations. When mediation results in a binding agreement, the initial agreement is usually preliminary. It is then reduced to a formal written agreement by the parties' attorneys. In some situations the final agreement will be written by the mediator; this can be a risky practice of the mediator is not an experienced drafter.

The ground rules for mediation are normally set forth in a *mediation agreement* signed at the beginning of the mediation process. This agreement at a minimum will name the mediator and define the issues that are being mediated. In many situations, it will also set forth important procedural guidelines. For example, some mediation agreements will state that any agreement reached in mediation will not be binding unless reduced to a signed writing. When contract creation, validity, or construction issues arise regarding any mediated agreement, it is essential that counsel review the mediation agreement early in the dispute resolution process.

Preliminary Agreements

Because the initial agreement reached in mediation is often preliminary, mediated cases are an especially fertile field for disputes as to whether a preliminary agreement was intended to be immediately binding. *See generally* § **2.04**. If the preliminary agreement itself does not address this point, the next logical resource is the mediation agreement, which will sometimes provide that certain types of preliminary agreements will not be binding.

Some states specifically prevent enforcement of oral agreement reached during mediation and not reduced to writing.[137] Even in the absence of such a requirement, an oral agreement before the mediator is likely to violate the general rule that separation agreements must be written unless recited into the record in open court.[138] A writing requirement for mediation-based agreement is sound policy, as it allows more involvement in the drafting process by the parties' attorneys, who may well be more experienced at drafting agreements than the mediator.

If the parties intended to be immediately bound by a written preliminary agreement under the principles discussed in § **2.04**, the agreement is enforceable.[139] Preliminary agreements are especially likely to contain provisions drafted by the mediator and not reviewed by counsel, which makes them especially dependent upon the training and experience of the mediator. The better practice is probably to bind the parties only

---

137. *See* Reno v. Haler, 734 N.E.2d 1095 (Ind. Ct. App. 2000).

138. *See* Ledbetter v. Ledbetter, 163 S.W.3d 681, 685 (Tenn. 2005) (audiotaped oral agreement stated before mediator was not stated in open court, as mediator was not a sitting judge).

139. *See Reno,* 734 N.E.2d at 1099 ("both parties and their attorneys signed the mediator's handwritten notes of the agreement after the mediator and all parties fully reviewed the terms"; agreement enforceable).

by the final written agreement, after full review by counsel. To the extent that some preliminary settlements are lost upon final review, the settlements lost will tend to be those in which the terms were not stated clearly in the preliminary agreement, or in which the preliminary agreement was unfair or involuntary. But the choice is clearly left to the parties; a written preliminary agreement will be enforceable if the parties intended that result.

Mediators as Witnesses

Many mediation statutes and agreements contain specific provisions that statements made in mediation shall be confidential. The extent to which these statutes prevent parties from subsequently calling the mediator as a witness is a heavily disputed issue.

The mediator has a unique role in the process of creating a mediated agreement, as he or she will frequently be the only neutral party present in the negotiations. If one party subsequently raises a claim of bargaining inequity or lack of capacity, the testimony of the mediator may be the only way to resolve the parties' competing factual claims as to what occurred during negotiation.

Because of the importance of the mediator's testimony, some states give the court discretion to permit a party to call the mediator as a witness when the validity of an agreement is seriously questioned. The Georgia Supreme Court explained why:

> Some courts have held that, when a party to a mediated agreement contends in a court of law that the agreement is unenforceable, the party waives any privilege of confidentiality. This case law is consistent with Section 6(b)(2) of the Uniform Mediation Act (2001), which provides that, when a party contends that a mediated settlement agreement is unenforceable, the mediator may testify regarding relevant mediation communications if a court determines that "the party seeking discovery or the proponent of the evidence has shown that the evidence is not otherwise available, [and] that there is a need for the evidence that substantially outweighs the interest in protecting confidentiality." Although neither this Court nor the Georgia Commission on Dispute Resolution has adopted this exception to the confidentiality of a court-referred mediation, we conclude that fairness to the opposing party and the integrity of mediation process dictate that we create such an exception when a party contends in court that he or she was not competent to enter a signed settlement agreement that resulted from the mediation.[140]

Unlimited mediator confidentiality, the court noted, would not necessarily serve the important public purpose of encouraging mediation. On the contrary, it could create potential for abuse, which would discourage mediation:

> [A] blanket rule prohibiting a mediator from being able to testify in such cases might well deprive the court of the evidence it needs to rule reliably on the plaintiff's contentions—and thus might either cause the court to impose an unjust outcome on the plaintiff or disable the court from enforcing the settle-

---

140. Wilson v. Wilson, 282 Ga. 728, 732, 653 S.E.2d 702, 706 (2007).

ment. In this setting, refusing to compel testimony from the mediator might end up being tantamount to denying the motion to enforce the agreement—because a crucial source of evidence about the plaintiff's condition and capacities would be missing. Following that course . . . would do considerable harm not only to the court's mediation program but also to fundamental fairness. If parties believed that courts routinely would refuse to compel mediators to testify, and that the absence of evidence from mediators would enhance the viability of a contention that apparent consent to a settlement contract was not legally viable, cynical parties would be encouraged either to try to escape commitments they made during mediations or to use threats of such escapes to try to re-negotiate, after the mediation, more favorable terms—terms that they never would have been able to secure without this artificial and unfair leverage.[141]

On the facts of the Georgia case, the husband alleged that he was clinically depressed, under medication, and lacked capacity to contract. The trial court called the mediator as a witness. The supreme court affirmed, rejecting the husband's attempt to prevent the mediator from testifying:

It is clear that the only witness to all but about 15 minutes of Mr. Wilson's conduct during the mediation was the mediator, and thus there was no other witness available to offer evidence of Mr. Wilson's mental and emotional condition during the nine hours of mediation. Moreover, the mediator did not testify about specific confidential statements that Mr. Wilson made during the mediation, but only testified about his general impression of Mr. Wilson's mental and emotional condition, thus diminishing the potential harm to the values underlying the privilege of confidentiality in mediations. Finally, if the mediator here could not testify regarding his general impressions of Mr. Wilson's mental and emotional condition, it would be extraordinarily difficult for the trial court to reach a reasoned and just resolution of Mr. Wilson's contention that the agreement is unenforceable, thus undermining the efforts of the parties and the mediator in conducting the mediation and causing a potentially unjust result to Ms. Wilson.[142]

Note that the mediator testified in *support* of the agreement, testifying that the husband did have sufficient capacity to contract. The court reached this result despite the presence of a confidentiality provision in the mediation agreement, holding that the integrity of the mediation process required an exception to the confidentiality provision.

In defining the scope of the mediation confidentiality privilege, many decisions agree with the Georgia court that the Uniform Mediation Act is an appropriate analogy, even in states that have not enacted that act. Section 6(b)(2) of the Act provides:

---

141. *Wilson*, 282 Ga. at 732–33, 653 S.E.2d at 706 (quoting Olam v. Cong. Mortg. Co., 68 F. Supp. 2d 1110, 1137 (N.D. Cal. 1999)); *see also* Kalof v. Kalof, 840 So. 2d 365, 367 (Fla. Dist. Ct. App. 2003) ("The former wife concedes that by making a motion to vacate the mediated marital settlement agreement, she has thereby waived the mediation privilege[.]").

142. *Wilson*, 282 Ga. at 733, 653 S.E.2d at 706–07.

(b) There is no privilege under Section 4 if a court, administrative agency, or arbitrator finds, after a hearing in camera, that the party seeking discovery or the proponent of the evidence has shown that the evidence is not otherwise available, that there is a need for the evidence that substantially outweighs the interest in protecting confidentiality, and that the mediation communication is sought or offered in:

. . .

(2) except as otherwise provided in subsection (c), a proceeding to prove a claim to rescind or reform or a defense to avoid liability on a contract arising out of the mediation.[143]

Section 6(c) of the Act provides that "[a] mediator may not be compelled to provide evidence of a mediation communication referred to in subsection (a)(6) or (b)(2)."[144] Reading both sections together, if the only available evidence to establish a point is a mediation communication, and the need for the evidence outweighs the interest in protecting confidentiality, evidence of a mediation communication can be admitted. If the exception applies, the parties themselves are free to testify as to a mediation communication, and the mediator may testify if he or she desires. The mediator's testimony, however, cannot be compelled.[145]

The comments to the Uniform Act explain subsection 6(c) as follows:

Section 6(c) allows the mediator to decline to testify or otherwise provide evidence in a professional misconduct and mediated settlement enforcement cases to protect against frequent attempts to use the mediator as a tie-breaking witness, which would undermine the integrity of the mediation process and the impartiality of the individual mediator. Nonetheless, the parties and others may testify or provide evidence in such cases.[146]

Mediator Misconduct

Many mediation programs are subject to specific state rules or statutes governing how the mediation process operates. Failure to comply with these mandatory rules may be sufficient cause to set aside an agreement resulting from the mediation.[147] Whether the agreement is actually set aside would presumably depend upon the nature and severity of the violation. The leading case involved a claim that the mediator had coerced a

---

143. UNIF. MEDIATION ACT § 6(b) (Westlaw 2008).

144. *Id.* § 6(c).

145. *See* Addesa v. Addesa, 392 N.J. Super. 58, 919 A.2d 885 (App. Div. 2007) (error to admit mediator's testimony).

146. UNIF. MEDIATION ACT § 6(c) cmt. (Westlaw 2008).

147. "If the required practices and procedures are not substantially complied with, no party to the mediation can rightfully claim the benefits of an agreement reached in such a way. . . . We hold that the court may invoke its inherent power to maintain the integrity of the judicial system and its processes by invalidating a court-ordered mediation settlement agreement obtained through violation and abuse of the judicially-prescribed mediation procedures." Vitakis-Valchine v. Valchine, 793 So. 2d 1094, 1099 (Fla. Dist. Ct. App. 2001).

party into signing an agreement. The trial court refused to consider the claim at all; the appellate court remanded for a factual hearing.[148]

Special Procedures for Mediated Separation Agreements

Some states give special preferences to separation agreements created as a result of the mediation process. For example, Texas allows parties to rescind separation agreements at any point before their approval by the court, but mediated agreements are binding immediately if certain specific language appears prominently in the agreement.[149] California presumes that an unequal agreement is the result of undue influence, but the presumption does not apply to mediated agreements.[150]

Where special rules and procedures apply to mediated agreements, they apply only where the agreement is reached in a mediation session, with the mediator's actual assistance. If parties reach an agreement in a traditional settlement conference, without the presence or assistance of the mediator, the mediation procedures do not apply.[151]

For analogous reasons, deadlines for raising objections or seeking relief before the mediator do not prevent a party from asking the court to set the agreement aside.[152]

Attacks upon Mediated Separation Agreements

A mediated separation agreement is only a contract, and it remains subject to the normal contract law defenses discussed in **chapter 4**. This is an important point, for the presence of a mediator is not an absolute guarantee that an agreement is procedurally or substantively fair. A striking example is *Matos v. Matos*,[153] which set aside a mediated agreement signed under duress by the wife, who had been physically abused during the marriage. "The mediator testified that she did not participate in the formation of the agreement and that her role was merely to reduce it to writing."[154]

A New Jersey court noted along similar lines that a mediator is not realistically able to provide protection against fraud and other asset-related misconduct:

> [A] property settlement agreement resulting from a voluntary mediation, like any privately negotiated PSA, may be reformed where there is unconscionability, fraud, or mistake and concealment. Indeed, there may be more reason to apply the principle in this context, since the mediator has no authority to

---

148. *Vitakis-Valchine*, 793 So. 2d 1094.

149. *See* Mullins v. Mullins, 202 S.W.3d 869 (Tex. Ct. App. 2006); *In re* Marriage of Joyner, 196 S.W.3d 883 (Tex. Ct. App. 2006).

150. *In re* Marriage of Kieturakis, 138 Cal. App. 4th 56, 41 Cal. Rptr. 3d 119 (2006).

151. *See* Lee v. Lee, 158 S.W.3d 612, 614 (Tex. Ct. App. 2005) (where parties reached agreement in session without mediator present, resulting agreement was not subject to special finality rule regarding mediated agreements).

152. *See* Kalof v. Kalof, 840 So. 2d 365, 367 (Fla. Dist. Ct. App. 2003) (where state law gave counsel a 10-day period for raising objections to drafting of final mediation agreement, period did not limit party's right to ask court to set agreement aside under the common law of separation agreements).

153. 932 So. 2d 316 (Fla. Ct. App. 2006).

154. *Id.* at 320.

compel disclosure and the process is dependent upon the candor and forthrightness of the parties.[155]

In the absence of specific contrary authority, mediated agreements are not immune from court review in those states that require court approval of separation agreements.[156] *See generally* **§ 4.04**.

Mediation of Child Custody, Support, and Visitation

As noted in **§ 3.07**, the court is not bound by private agreements on the issues of child custody, visitation, and child support. On these issues, the court has independent power to invalidate any provision in a private agreement that interferes materially with the best interests of the children.

The court's power to act in the best interests of the children applies to all agreements, even those that are a product of voluntary or mandatory mediation.[157] Thus, the court is not bound by the child custody, visitation, or child support terms of a mediated agreement.

As a practical matter, however, courts follow private agreements on these issues when they are consistent with the children's best interests. Some courts have stated that mediated agreement are especially likely to be respected on these issues, as they are more likely to result from a fair bargaining process.[158]

---

155. Addesa v. Addesa, 392 N.J. Super. 58, 75, 919 A.2d 885, 895 (App. Div. 2007).

156. *See* Spencer v. Spencer, 752 N.E.2d 661, 664–65 (Ind. Ct. App. 2001) ("even if a valid agreement had been reached at the conclusion of mediation, it could not bind the Wife until the parties had signed it and it was approved by the trial court"); *cf.* Reno v. Haler, 743 N.E.2d 1139 (Ind. Ct. App. 2001) (where trial court prematurely approved early unsigned agreement, but then later properly approved final signed agreement, final agreement was fully enforceable).

157. *See* Higgins v. Higgins, 945 So. 2d 593 (Fla. Dist. Ct. App. 2006) (error to approve mediated agreement; strong possibility existed that wife had given up custody of son in manner inconsistent with son's best interests); *In re* Marriage of Duffy, 307 Ill. App. 3d 257, 718 N.E.2d 286 (1999); *cf.* Blase v. Brewer, 692 N.W.2d 785 (S.D. 2005) (trial court properly refused to follow mediated paternity agreement that awarded more visitation to noncustodial father than statewide visitation guidelines suggested).

158. *See, e.g.,* Reno v. Haler, 734 N.E.2d 1095, 1101 (Ind. Ct. App. 2000).

Public Policy | 3

§ 3.01 Overview

In the days of fault-based divorce, courts believed that separation agreements were inherently conducive to marital breakdown. Since divorce was disfavored in public policy, agreements that encouraged it were held to be void. Thus, separation agreements were valid only if the parties had already separated or separated immediately upon signing the agreement.[1]

Most restrictions upon separation agreements vanished upon the enactment of no-fault divorce. The modern decisions all agree that separation agreements are favored in the law, as they avoid the need for a contested divorce trial. Accordingly, public policy is rarely a defense to an otherwise valid agreement.[2] There are, however, a few areas in which public policy may still be a problem.

---

1. *See* 2 HOMER CLARK, THE LAW OF DOMESTIC RELATIONS IN THE UNITED STATES § 19.1, at 411 (2d ed. 1987); *see, e.g.*, Rooks v. Plavec, 40 Ill. App. 2d 298, 188 N.E.2d 251 (1963); Costa v. Costa, 192 A.D.2d 1034, 597 N.Y.S.2d 222 (1993); Carlisle v. Carlisle, 123 Ohio App. 3d 277, 704 N.E.2d 39 (1997) (isolated decision holding agreement invalid because parties did not immediately separate); *cf.* Newland v. Newland, 129 N.C. App. 418, 498 S.E.2d 855 (1998) (court did not violate public policy by enforcing separation agreement, where parties did not actually physically separate until 31 days after signing; wife began packing, and couple held themselves out as separated, immediately upon signing).

2. 2 CLARK, *supra* note 1, at 411–12; *see also* Britton v. Britton, 400 Pa. Super. 43, 582 A.2d 1335 (1990) (excellent discussion of public policy restrictions on divorce settlements generally).

§ 3.02 Contracts Requiring Divorce

A clause that obligates the parties to obtain a civil divorce is void as against public policy.[3] While divorce is no longer inherently disfavored, the law will not enforce an agreement that requires divorce at a specific future time, regardless of future events.

Religious Divorces

The agreement may, however, obligate one or both parties to obtain a religious divorce once a valid civil divorce is issued. These religious divorces of are particular importance to those of the Orthodox Jewish and Catholic faiths, as these religions place restrictions upon the spiritual life of members who do not obtain religious divorces. As long as the religious divorce provision becomes effective only upon the issuance of a civil divorce, there is no reason such a provision should encourage divorce. Moreover, since the spouse who opposes the religious divorce is generally only required to appear before the religious court and answer questions, and is not required to participate in any prayer or other religious act, enforcement of a religious divorce provision does not violate the establishment clause of the federal or state constitution.[4]

§ 3.03 Grounds for Divorce

The parties cannot validly agree to the existence of grounds for divorce. For instance, in *Britton v. Britton*,[5] the parties tried to agree that a trial reconciliation period would not be counted as cohabitation for purposes of Pennsylvania's three-year separation no-fault statute. The court found that the parties could not change the three-year rule by contract, and denied the divorce decree.

Can the parties agree that they will not utilize grounds for divorce in the future? An agreement that waives all grounds for divorce is highly problematic; courts tend to hold that parties have an absolute nonwaivable right to obtain a divorce if grounds, especially no-fault grounds, are proven.[6] In other words, public policy prevents a complete waiver of the right to obtain a divorce in the future.

---

3. *E.g.*, Taft v. Taft, 156 A.D.2d 444, 548 N.Y.S.2d 726 (1989); Combs v. Sherry-Combs, 865 P.2d 50 (Wyo. 1993) (contract providing that marriage would automatically terminate unless renewed in writing every three years).

4. *See* Avitzur v. Avitzur, 58 N.Y.2d 108, 446 N.E.2d 136, 459 N.Y.S.2d 572, *cert. denied*, 464 U.S. 817 (1983); *In re* Schnoll, 621 A.2d 808 (Del. Fam. Ct. 1992); *see generally* Marcia Retchin, *To Get a "Get": Enforcement of Contracts Requiring Spouses to Secure or Accept Religious Divorces*, 6 DIVORCE LITIG. 28 (1994).

5. 400 Pa. Super. 43, 582 A.2d 1335 (1990); *see also* Anostario v. Anostario, 255 A.D.2d 777, 680 N.Y.S.2d 279 (1998) (trial court properly refused to accept stipulation that grounds for divorce existed).

6. *See* P.B. v. L.B., 19 Misc. 3d 186, 194, 855 N.Y.S.2d 836, 844 (Sup. Ct. 2008) (provision stating that husband would not pursue a divorce from the wife for five years after signing of agreement without wife's written consent was void as against public policy; "no waiver of a person's right to seek a divorce for longer than the statutory one year after execution of a separation agreement will be enforced by the Court"); *cf.* Coggins v. Coggins, 601 So. 2d 109 (Ala. Civ. App. 1992) (applying a similar policy antenuptial agreements); *see also* **§ 9.01** (discussing the antenuptial agreement cases).

A waiver of specific individual fault grounds, when the marriage has already failed and no-fault grounds remain available, is generally not objectionable.[7] If the marriage has not failed, a waiver of fault grounds might be invalid for encouraging divorce.[8]

§ 3.04 Property Division

There is generally no public policy objection to waiving equitable distribution rights in a separation agreement.[9] The same rule generally holds true in community property states.[10] Some community property courts have been reluctant to accept the agreement, however, where it waives community property rights entirely.[11]

Where the parties do waive property division rights, they are not bound in any way by the property division statutes. Thus, they are free to divide separate property or other assets that would not normally be divisible.[12] In states that presume or require

---

7. *See* McClellan v. McClellan, 52 Md. App. 525, 538, 451 A.2d 334, 342 (1982) (waiver of right to obtain divorce for desertion "is valid under Maryland law").

8. *See id*. at 538, 451 A.2d at 342 ("the waiver provision in the separation agreement does not create a 'license for licentiousness' that would bar a suit for divorce for an adultery committed prior to the running of the statutory period of voluntary separation").

9. *See, e.g., In re* Marriage of Weck, 706 P.2d 436 (Colo. App. 1985); *In re* Marriage of Vella, 237 Ill. App. 3d 194, 603 N.E.2d 109 (1992) (agreement need not cite the statute in order to waive equitable distribution); Stuart v. Stuart, 956 So. 2d 295 (Miss. Ct. App. 2006); Hagler v. Hagler, 319 N.C. 287, 354 S.E.2d 228 (1987); *see generally* BRETT R. TURNER, EQUITABLE DISTRIBUTION OF PROPERTY § 3:14 (3d ed. 2005).

10. *See, e.g.,* Cayan v. Cayan, 38 S.W.3d 161, 166 (Tex. Ct. App. 2000) ("the prohibition against divesting a spouse of separate property applies only to judicial, i.e., unagreed, divestitures and does not restrict parties from dividing separate property by agreement"); Boyett v. Boyett, 799 S.W.2d 360 (Tex. Ct. App. 1990).

11. *See* McBride v. McBride, 797 S.W.2d 689 (Tex. Ct. App. 1990) (rejecting agreement that wife waived all community property rights if she filed action for divorce).

12. *See* Morris v. Morris, 908 P.2d 425, 428 n.2 (Alaska 1995) (separate property in general); Harmand v. Harmand, 931 So. 2d 18 (Ala. Ct. App. 2005) (retirement benefits); Williams v. Williams, 581 So. 2d 1116 (Ala. Ct. App. 1991) (military retirement pay); Hayes v. Wallace, 582 So. 2d 1151 (Ala. Ct. App. 1991) (retirement benefits); Sachs v. Sachs, 60 Conn. App. 337, 759 A.2d 510 (2000) (postdivorce contributions to pension plan); Franken v. Franken, 191 S.W.3d 700 (Mo. Ct. App. 2006) (annuity); Pulaski v. Pulaski, 22 A.D.3d 820, 804 N.Y.S.2d 404 (2005) (disability benefits); Reed v. Reed, 180 A.D.2d 1006, 580 N.Y.S.2d 572 (1992) (retirement benefits acquired after the divorce); Torres v. McClain, 140 N.C. App. 238, 242, 535 S.E.2d 623, 626 (2000) ("Although the parties in this action created rights in the plaintiff which she would not have had under the equitable distribution statute as it was written at the time, it does not follow that this amounts to a violation of North Carolina's public policy[.]"); Matlock v. Matlock, 444 Pa. Super. 507, 664 A.2d 551 (1995) (postdivorce increases in retirement benefits).

The parties can even agree to transfer marital property to third persons, most commonly the parties' children. *See* Smith v. Smith, 281 Ga. 204, 636 S.E.2d 519 (2006).

an equal division, the parties are free to make an unequal division by contract.[13] In states that give the court broad discretion to divide all property, however and whenever acquired, the court's discretion is still bound by the property division provisions of an enforceable agreement.[14] In most cases, property divided by agreement between the parties need not be valued by the court.[15]

In addition to waiving equitable distribution altogether, the parties are free to settle certain equitable distribution issues by contract. Thus, the parties can agree to divide some assets, while leaving others for division by the court;[16] to treat certain stated assets as marital or separate property;[17] or to give a certain asset a stated value for purposes of division by the court.[18] The parties can also agree upon the manner in which their divisible property will be divided, while leaving the definition and valuation of divisible property to the court.[19]

Separation agreements are subject to the normal rules of law governing ownership of property. For example, the parties cannot allocate stock in a professional practice to a nonprofessional spouse.[20]

---

13. *See* Mejia v. Reed, 31 Cal. 4th 657, 74 P.3d 166, 3 Cal. Rptr. 3d 390 (2003) (California law requiring an equal division of community property does not prevent parties from agreeing to an unequal division).

14. *See* Damone v. Damone, 172 Vt. 504, 782 A.2d 1208 (2001). The court may have discretion to refuse to approve the agreement, *see generally* § **4.04**, but that is a different inquiry focused mainly upon the fairness of the agreement. The court is not permitted to disregard the agreement merely because the trial judge disagrees with the manner in which the parties have chosen to divide their property.

15. *See In re* Marriage of Thompson, 27 S.W.3d 502 (Mo. Ct. App. 2000).

As an exception, valuation would be required where the agreement does not divide all marital property, as the court must know the value of the property divided under the agreement in order to fairly divide the property not covered by the agreement. *See generally* TURNER, *supra* note 9, § 8:18 (3d ed. 2005 & Supp. 2007) (amount of separate property owned by each party is a division factor). Also, the amount of property awarded to each property may be a factor to be considered in setting spousal support, if such support is left open by the agreement.

16. *See, e.g.*, Shearer v. Shearer, 270 Neb. 178, 700 N.W.2d 580 (2005). *But see* Dewbrew v. Dewbrew, 849 N.E.2d 636, 646 (Ind. Ct. App. 2006) (agreement failed to divide marital home and husband's businesses; because of ambiguity, trial court erred by refusing to set agreement aside).

It is not completely clear why the parties in Dewbrew did not have a valid enforceable agreement to divide only part of the marital estate. The authors' reading is that the agreement did not divide the existing assets fairly, so that the agreement as a whole was not entitled to court approval. Dewbrew should certainly not be read in future cases to provide that an agreement dividing only some of the divisible assets is unenforceable if the agreement otherwise meets the requirements for court approval. A partial settlement is better for the courts and the parties than no settlement at all.

17. *E.g.*, Lowinger v. Lowinger, 303 A.D.2d 723, 757 N.Y.S.2d 323 (2003).

18. *See, e.g.*, Batty v. Batty, 153 P.3d 827 (Utah Ct. App. 2006); Glass v. Glass, 177 A.D.2d 807, 576 N.Y.S.2d 421 (1991); *see generally* TURNER, *supra* note 9, §§ 3:14, 7:2.

19. *See* Miller v. Miller, 97 N.C. App. 77, 387 S.E.2d 181 (1990); Cleary v. Cleary, 582 N.E.2d 851 (Ind. Ct. App. 1991); *see generally* TURNER, *supra* note 9, § 9:2.

20. Sangiorgio v. Sangiorgio, 173 Misc. 2d 625, 662 N.Y.S.2d 220 (Sup. Ct. 1997) (provision giving nonveterinarian wife 51 percent of stock in veterinary practice was void as against public policy).

Where one spouse receives most of the marital property, there is no public policy objection to a clause requiring one spouse to make installment payments to the other spouse.[21] The payments may be indefinite in amount, but they must stop upon a certain specific event (such as the remarriage or death of one or both spouses).[22]

There is no public policy objection to allocating debts in the nature of restitution for criminal activity, unless the effect of the allocation is to encourage future criminal activity.[23]

Federal Benefits

Once particular type of property that has been the subject of controversy in recent years is retirement benefits provided by the federal government. Federal statutory law expressly permits division of some of these benefits,[24] expressly forbids division of other benefits, and is silent as to others.

When federal statutory law permits division of federal benefits, it does not require that the former spouse be awarded any specific share of the retirement benefit. Rather, it permits state courts to apply state law to determine that amount. Thus, an agreement that merely reserves to the former spouse his or her rights under the statute may actually award nothing.[25] To divide these benefits, the agreement must affirmatively state the portion of the benefits to which the former spouse is entitled.

When federal statutory law expressly forbids division, there is no doubt that the benefits at issue cannot be divided either by court order or by agreement. The clear example is social security benefits, which are universally held not subject to division by agreement.[26]

When federal statutory law is silent on division of federal benefits, the U.S. Supreme Court has tended to hold that division by state courts is not permitted. The leading Supreme Court case is *Mansell v. Mansell*,[27] which held that state courts can-

---

21. Sutton v. Sutton, 28 Ark. App. 165, 771 S.W.2d 791 (1989).

22. *Id.*

23. *See* Loscher v. Hudson, 39 Kan. App. 2d 417, 428, 182 P.3d 25, 34 (2008) ("Unless an indemnity agreement encourages the commission of the illegal act, a contract to indemnify against the consequences of an illegal act that has already been committed has generally been upheld"; "Hudson's agreement to indemnify Loscher occurred after Loscher's criminal acts and did not encourage Loscher's commission of wire fraud[.]").

24. *See, e.g.,* 5 U.S.C.A. § 8345(j)(1) (civil service retirement benefits); 10 U.S.C.A. § 1408 (1996) (military retirement benefits); *see generally* TURNER, *supra* note 9, §§ 6:3–6:20.

25. *See* Meyer v. Meyer, 952 So. 2d 384, 391 (Ala. Ct. App. 2006). *But see* Gilmore v. Garner, 157 N.C. App. 664, 668, 580 S.E.2d 15, 18 (2003) (under agreement, wife "agrees not to make any demand on Husband at the present time," but "each [party] may draw Railroad Retirement benefits in accordance with law when they are eligible to so draw"; trial court properly construed language as a contractual promise to pay wife a share of the pension equal to her rights under state equitable distribution law, even though wife did not invoke that right until long after the divorce).

26. *See* Gentry v. Gentry, 327 Ark. 266, 938 S.W.2d 231 (1997); Boulter v. Boulter, 930 P.2d 112 (Nev. 1997); *In re* Marriage of Hulstrom, 342 Ill. App. 3d 262, 794 N.E.2d 980 (2003); Wolff v. Wolff, 929 P.2d 916 (Nev. 1996); *see generally* TURNER, *supra* note 9, § 6:17 (case law holding that social security benefits cannot be divided by court order).

27. 490 U.S. 581 (1989); *see generally* TURNER, *supra* note 9, §§ 6.3–6:12.

not divide veterans' disability benefits under the law of community property or equitable distribution.

The Supreme Court has not yet decided whether federal law prohibits division of federal benefits by contract when federal statutory law is silent. *Mansell* noted but declined to resolve this issue.[28] A majority of state court cases permit such division.[29] A minority of cases hold that preempted federal benefits cannot be divided by either court order or agreement.[30]

The authors of this treatise believe strongly that the majority rule on this point is correct. Many cases finding division to be prohibited have acted under the misapprehension that the benefits at issue in *Mansell* were not divided. *This assumption is untrue.* The Supreme Court held that the benefits could not be divided under a theory of community property or equitable distribution, and remanded the case back to the courts of California. On remand, however, the California court determined that the benefits could be divided under a theory of res judicata—*Mansell* was a collateral attack upon a final order that actually divided veterans' disability benefits—and the Supreme Court refused a second petition for certiorari.[31] Thus, the end result of the *Mansell* litigation was that the husband's veterans' disability benefits were actually divided.

---

28. *See Mansell*, 490 U.S. at 587 n.6 (refusing to reach the issue).

29. *See* Poullard v. Poullard, 780 So. 2d 498, 500 (La. Ct. App. 2001) (consent judgment, "[n]othing in either the state or federal law prevents a person from agreeing to give a part of his disability benefit to another"); *In re* Marriage of Stone, 274 Mont. 331, 908 P.2d 670 (1995); Shelton v. Shelton, 119 Nev. 492, 78 P.3d 507 (2003), *cert. denied*, 541 U.S. 960 (2004); Hoskins v. Skojec, 265 A.D.2d 706, 696 N.Y.S.2d 303 (1999); White v. White, 152 N.C. App. 588, 568 S.E.2d 283, 285 (2002), *aff'd*, 357 N.C. 153, 579 S.E.2d 248 (2003) (*Mansell* "does not prohibit military spouses from contracting away their disability benefits"); Evans v. Evans, 2003 WL 22053929 (Ohio Ct. App. 2003); Maxwell v. Maxwell, 796 P.2d 403 (Utah Ct. App. 1990) (stipulation dividing husband's gross retirement pay, without making the various deductions set forth in 10 U.S.C.A. § 1408(a)(4) (1996), could be enforced without violating *Mansell*); Price v. Price, 325 S.C. 379, 480 S.E.2d 92 (Ct. App. 1996); McLellan v. McLellan, 33 Va. App. 376, 533 S.E.2d 635 (2000); *see also In re* MacMeeken, 117 B.R. 642 (D. Kan. 1990) (stating in dicta that "this court does not find any Congressional intent in [federal law] to prevent or protect service members from disposing of their disposable retirement benefits as they choose," even if the same division would violate federal law if ordered by a court).

A contractual spousal award is fully enforceable, even if the intended source of the support payments is military disability. *See In re* Marriage of Gurganus, 34 Kan. App. 2d 713, 717, 124 P.3d 92, 95–96 (2005) ("settlement agreement states that Alton's payment of one-half of his military retirement benefits was 'intended to substitute for formal spousal support payments'"; error to treat obligation as property division); Mills v. Mills, 22 A.D.3d 1003, 802 N.Y.S.2d 796 (2005).

30. *Ex parte* Billeck, 777 So. 2d 105 (Ala. 2000); Abernethy v. Fishkin, 699 So. 2d 235 (Fla. 1997); Moon v. Moon, 795 S.W.2d 511 (Mo. Ct. App. 1990); Lutes v. Lutes, 328 Mont. 490, 495, 121 P.3d 561, 564 (2005).

Note that most of these courts are willing to enforce indemnity provisions that require one spouse to compensate the other for divisible benefits lost when preempted federal benefits are elected. Abernethy, for instance, ultimately divided the benefits at issue on this basis. *See* § **6.021**.

31. Mansell v. Mansell, 216 Cal. App. 3d 937, 265 Cal. Rptr. 227 (1989), *cert. denied*, 498 U.S. 806 (1990). The court's action was consistent with footnote 5 in its published opinion, *Mansell*, 490 U.S. at 587 n.5, which stated that whether the California final judgment could be reopened was an

The Supreme Court's refusal to hear the case a second time speaks volumes about its first decision. That decision considered division under only two specific theories, community property and equitable distribution. The court did not reach the question of whether such benefits can be divided by other theories. Moreover, by refusing to reverse the *second* California *Mansell* opinion, the Supreme Court directly accepted one such theory, res judicata. Thus, if a separation agreement dividing military disability benefits is *approved, incorporated*, or *merged* into a divorce decree, the agreement is res judicata and the division of disability benefits is final.[32]

The Supreme Court has not expressly considered whether military disability benefits can be divided by contract, when the contract has not yet been approved, incorporated, or merged into a divorce decree.[33] A federal statute prohibits contractual assignment of disability benefits,[34] but the Supreme Court has held for support purposes that the statute applies only to third-party creditors, and not to family members.[35] The majority of decisions allowing contractual division of disability benefits essentially follow the same reasoning. Whether the Supreme Court will accept that position is not yet certain. It is increasingly clear, however, that the Court is inclined to accept state court decisions refusing to reconsider a contractual division of disability benefits, which has the status of a final judgment.[36]

Note also that when military disability benefits are elected after the divorce, thereby reducing a former spouse's monthly payment of military retirement benefits, many decisions find a breach of the agreement. The clearest cases are those in which the original agreement contains an express indemnity provision, requiring the service member to pay damages if his or her actions reduce the amount of the former spouse's award. These *express indemnity* provisions are enforceable by res judicata if the decree is final, and probably enforceable on contractual grounds even if the decree is not final, especially if enforcement can come from nondisability assets.[37] Many courts have

---

issue of state law outside of the Supreme Court's jurisdiction. The first California *Mansell* opinion assumed for sake of argument that the judgment could be reopened, and nevertheless held that the judgment was correct. The second California Mansell opinion revisited that assumption and held that the judgment, even though erroneous, could not be reopened after it was final.

32. *See, e.g.*, Shelton v. Shelton, 119 Nev. 492, 78 P.3d 507 (2003), *cert. denied*, 541 U.S. 960 (2004); *In re* Marriage of Hayes, 228 Or. App. 555, 208 P.3d 1046 (2009).

Many res judicata cases involve indemnity provisions in litigated divorce decree. *See generally* TURNER, *supra* note 9, § 6:9.

33. *See Mansell*, 490 U.S. at 587 n.6 (refusing to reach the issue).

34. 38 U.S.C.A. § 5301(a) (Westlaw 2008).

35. Rose v. Rose, 481 U.S. 619 (1987).

36. In particular, *See* Shelton v. Shelton, 541 U.S. 960 (2004), refusing to review the broad applications of the indemnity and contract theories in *Shelton*, 119 Nev. 492, 78 P.3d 507.

37. *See* Gatfield v. Gatfield, 682 N.W.2d 632, 637 (Minn. Ct. App. 2004) ("Neither the Supreme Court's holding in Mansell nor the Uniformed Services Former Spouses Protection Act precludes a veteran from voluntarily entering into a contract whereby he or she agrees not to waive retirement pay in favor of disability benefits and to indemnify a former spouse for any loss the spouse might incur should the veteran choose to waive any portion of retirement pay."); Owen v. Owen, 14 Va. App. 623, 419 S.E.2d 267 (1992).

found a contractual breach even without an express indemnity provision, often relying upon the implied duty of good faith and fair dealing.[38] None of these holdings violates the antiassignment provision, as disability benefits are not being assigned to the former spouse. Rather, the service member is being forced to pay damages for breaching an agreement to provide *retirement benefits* to the former spouse. The Supreme Court has not to date shown any interest in interfering with these indemnity-based holdings.

An agreement can obtain an effect similar to an indemnity provision by requiring the service member to pay the former spouse a stated sum per month, without regard to what happens to his or her military retirement benefits. These *sum certain* provisions have consistently been enforced by the courts.[39]

Right to Dissent from Will

There is no public policy objection to a clause that waives the right of either party to dissent from the other's will. Indeed, the agreement can even provide that the parties will use their best efforts to obtain a waiver of dissenter's rights from any persons they should subsequently marry.[40]

---

38. *See* Surratt v. Surratt, 85 Ark. App. 267, 148 S.W.3d 761 (2004); *In re* Marriage of Warkocz, 141 P.3d 926 (Colo. App. 2006); Blann v. Blann, 971 So. 2d 135 (Fla. Dist. Ct. App. 2007); *In re* Marriage of Neilsen, 341 Ill. App. 3d 863, 792 N.E.2d 844 (2003); Allen v. Allen, 178 Md. App. 145, 941 A.2d 510 (2008); Krapf v. Krapf, 55 Mass. App. Ct. 485, 771 N.E.2d 819 (2002), *aff'd*, 439 Mass. 97, 786 N.E.2d 318 (2003); Hodge v. Hodge, 197 P.3d 511 (Okla. Civ. App. 2008); Hayward v. Hayward, 868 A.2d 554 (Pa. Super. Ct. 2005); Resare v. Resare, 908 A.2d 1006, 1010 (R.I. 2006); Hisgen v. Hisgen, 1996 SD 122, 554 N.W.2d 494; Johnson v. Johnson, 37 S.W.3d 892, 896 (Tenn. 2001); *see also In re* Smith, 148 Cal. App. 4th 1115, 1124, 56 Cal. Rptr. 3d 341, 347 (2007) (addition of express indemnity provision by postjudgment order did not impermissibly modify agreement, but rather ensured that wife would receive full benefit for which she had bargained).

For similar case law applying the indemnity theory to divisions of retirement benefits in litigated divorce decrees, *see* TURNER, *supra* note 9, § 6:10.

Some agreements, of course, will expressly or implicitly contemplate that the service member may elect disability benefits without compensating the former spouse for any resulting reduction in retirement benefits. *See* Harris v. Harris, 195 Ariz. 559, 991 P.2d 262 (Ct. App. Div. 1 1999); *In re* Marriage of Krempin, 70 Cal. App. 4th 1008, 83 Cal. Rptr. 2d 134 (1st Dist. 1999).

For insight into the factual issues surrounding a claim that election of disability without compensation was intended by the parties, *compare* Price v. Price, 325 S.C. 379, 480 S.E.2d 92 (Ct. App. 1996) (requiring compensation on the facts), *with* Tirado v. Tirado, 339 S.C. 649, 530 S.E.2d 128 (Ct. App. 2000) (requiring no compensation on the facts).

39. *See* McHugh v. McHugh, 124 Idaho 543, 861 P.2d 113 (Ct. App. 1993); Jones v. Jones, 900 S.W.2d 786 (Tex. Ct. App. 1995).

40. Fell v. Fell, 213 A.D.2d 374, 623 N.Y.S.2d 315 (1995).

§ 3.05 Spousal Support

As a general rule, there is no public policy objection to a waiver of the duty to support an ex-spouse after the marriage has terminated.[41]

The waiver is void, however, to the extent that it would make the ex-spouse a public charge.[42] Of course, this exception only removes the agreement as a barrier; it does not by itself provide any authority not already present under the law of alimony. Thus, where an award of alimony was barred by the wife's fault, one court held that alimony could not be awarded to keep the wife off public assistance, even though the waiver of support in the parties' separation agreement was unenforceable.[43] If the court does rely on this exception to justify a support award, it should award only enough alimony to remove the recipient from public assistance.[44]

In the few remaining states in which marital fault (most commonly adultery) is a complete bar to spousal support, the fault bar does not apply to agreement-based support. Thus, an agreement to pay spousal support to spouse who is guilty of marital fault is enforceable.[45] The parties are likewise free to contract around other statutory limitations on spousal support.[46]

A growing number of jurisdictions are experimenting with some form of statutory or regulatory guideline for spousal support awards. In these jurisdictions, the parties are free to exceed the guideline amount by contract.[47]

---

41. *See, e.g., In re* Marriage of Okonkwo, 525 N.W.2d 870 (Iowa Ct. App. 1994); Knox v. Remick, 371 Mass. 433, 358 N.E.2d 432 (1976).

42. *See* Premo v. Premo, 419 Mass. 1011, 646 N.E.2d 1027 (1995); O'Brien v. O'Brien, 416 Mass. 477, 623 N.E.2d 485 (1993); *Knox,* 371 Mass. 433, 358 N.E.2d 432; Lasky v. Lasky, 163 Misc. 2d 859, 622 N.Y.S.2d 649 (Sup. Ct. 1994); Greenberg v. Greenberg, 175 A.D.2d 18, 571 N.Y.S.2d 731 (1991); Curran v. Curran, 169 A.D.2d 975, 564 N.Y.S.2d 873 (1991).

A public charge for purposes of this rule is a spouse who is unable to support himself or herself without significant continuing public assistance. A New York court held that a spouse is not a public charge where she "had received only a one-time subsidy," but otherwise "was capable of self-support and was not dependent on on-going public assistance." Cole v. Cole, 195 Misc. 2d 908, 912, 761 N.Y.S.2d 822, 825 (Sup. Ct. 2003).

43. *Greenberg,* 175 A.D.2d 18, 571 N.Y.S.2d 731.

44. Broome v. Broome, 43 Mass. App. Ct. 539, 684 N.E.2d 641 (1997) (error to support wife at middle-class lifestyle); *O'Brien,* 416 Mass. 477, 623 N.E.2d 485.

45. *See* Maxwell v. Maxwell, 375 S.C. 182, 650 S.E.2d 680 (Ct. App. 2007).

46. Most of the case law on this point comes from Indiana and Texas, which restrict the duration of spousal support by statute. The restrictions apply only to court awards, and the parties are free to contract for a longer duration. *See* Cox v. Cox, 833 N.E.2d 1077, 1081–82 (Ind. Ct. App. 2005) ("the parties were free to agree to a maintenance provision even though the requirements for court-ordered maintenance were not met"); McCollough v. McCollough, 212 S.W.3d 638 (Tex. Ct. App. 2006). Be aware, however, that the obligation may not be subject to modification, *see Cox,* and it may not be enforceable by contempt after the end of the statutory duration. *See* § 7.031.

47. *See* Ellefson v. Ellefson, 616 So. 2d 221 (La. Ct. App. 1993) (despite statutory rule that alimony cannot exceed one-third of payor's income, parties are free to agree that a greater amount of support will be paid).

Although some states do not allow trial courts to place escalation clauses in spousal support orders, escalation clauses in separation agreements are not void as against public policy.[48] Indeed, some courts have even encouraged the parties to employ escalation clauses, since they reduce the time and effort courts must spend modifying support awards.[49]

The parties are generally free to provide that support shall or shall not be modifiable under certain circumstances.[50] In particular, the public policy against support after remarriage is generally not so strong as to affect private contracts. Agreements to provide spousal support despite remarriage are therefore not void as against public policy.[51] Likewise, an agreement that remarriage shall merely suspend support, and not terminate support completely, is enforceable.[52]

The parties are likewise free to agree to nonmodifiable unitary support—a combination of spousal and child support. Such a provision will not prevent the court from subsequently allocating the support into components and modifying the child support,[53] but it will prevent modification of spousal support.[54]

There is no public policy obstacle to the use of acceleration clauses and other innovative remedies to ensure compliance with spousal support agreements.[55]

Cohabitation

There is broad general agreement that a provision terminating spousal support upon cohabitation does not violate public policy.[56]

In *Melletz v. Melletz*,[57] a New Jersey court appeared to hold that all cohabitation provisions are void as against public policy. The case could probably have been resolved on

---

48. *See* West v. West, 891 So. 2d 203 (Miss. 2004).

49. *See, e.g.*, Wing v. Wing, 549 So. 2d 944 (Miss. 1989); Petersen v. Petersen, 85 N.J. 638, 428 A.2d 1301 (1981).

50. *See* Cason v. Cason, 886 So. 2d 628, 632 (La. Ct. App. 2004) (Louisiana law permits contractual nonmodifiable spousal support); Lipps v. Loyd, 967 P.2d 558 (Wyo. 1998) (agreement for nonmodifiable spousal support was enforceable); *see generally* § **6.032**.

51. *See* Campitelli v. Johnston, 134 Md. App. 689, 761 A.2d 369 (2000); Jung v. Jung, 171 A.D.2d 993, 567 N.Y.S.2d 934 (1991); Sacks v. Sacks, 168 A.D.2d 733, 563 N.Y.S.2d 884 (1990). Be aware, however, that many courts will not construe an agreement to require support after remarriage unless the agreement is clear and express. *See* § **6.033**.

52. Pelfrey v. Pelfrey, 25 Va. App. 239, 487 S.E.2d 281 (1997).

53. *In re* Watson, 149 Or. App. 598, 945 P.2d 522 (1997).

54. *In re* Marriage of Steadman, 283 Ill. App. 3d 703, 670 N.E.2d 1146 (1996).

55. *See, e.g.*, Melnick v. Melnick, 211 A.D.2d 521, 621 N.Y.S.2d 64 (1995) (acceleration clause providing that entire maintenance award would immediately become due if husband missed a single payment).

56. *See* Draper v. Draper, 40 Conn. App. 570, 672 A.2d 522 (1996); Auer v. Scott, 494 N.W.2d 54 (Minn. Ct. App. 1992); Weathersby v. Weathersby, 693 So. 2d 1348 (Miss. 1997); Pesa v. Pesa, 230 A.D.2d 837, 646 N.Y.S.2d 558 (1996); Spector v. Spector, 112 Nev. 1395, 929 P.2d 964 (1996); Beechler v. Beechler, 95 Ohio App. 121, 641 N.E.2d 1189 (1994); *see generally* Wendy S. Ricketts, *The Relevance of Premarital and Postmarital Cohabitation in Awarding Spousal Support*, 7 Divorce Litig. 150 (1995).

57. 271 N.J. Super. 359, 638 A.2d 898 (App. Div. 1994).

grounds that the definition of cohabitation had not been met, *see* § **6.034**, but the court reached beyond the facts to suggest that all such clauses are invalid. Another panel of the same court then receded from *Melletz* in *Konzelman v. Konzelman*,[58] adopting the general rule nationwide that cohabitation clauses do not violate public policy, at least where the relationship at issue strongly resembles marriage. The New Jersey Supreme Court subsequently affirmed *Konzelman*.[59]

Melletz was extremely bad policy, and *Konzelman* was correct to recede from it. It is settled law in New Jersey and other states that spousal support ceases upon remarriage. *See* § **6.033**. Unfortunately, as cohabitation has become more acceptable as a lifestyle, support recipients who desire to avoid this rule have sometimes refused to remarry a long-term romantic partner, for the sole purpose of avoiding termination of support. This practice makes a mockery of the strong public policy that support terminates upon remarriage, and courts that tolerate the practice are creating a real disincentive to marriage—a status that the law is generally said to favor. In fact, when a cohabitation relationship is strongly akin to marriage, some states have provided by statute that support may be terminated.[60] There is certainly an argument that cohabitation creates no permanent legal duty of support, although this is less true today than it once was,[61] and other states have refused to adopt this type of statute. But is the policy that support should terminate only upon remarriage so strong that the parties should not be allowed to contract around it? Are the parties not permitted to create by contract a remedy for the situation in which a spouse refuses to remarry for the sole purpose of avoiding termination of spousal support? Even in states without such a statute, the parties should be permitted to agree that this type of deliberate avoidance of remarriage will not be tolerated.

The case for cohabitation clauses is strongest with regard to "marital cohabitation" provisions—provisions that terminate support only when the relationship looks greatly like a marriage. The question then becomes whether agreements should be permitted to include a "pure cohabitation" provision that terminates support upon cohabitation alone. The law on this point is a compromise between two competing principles. To the extent that one spouse is attempting to control the postmarital sexual behavior of the other, the agreement is being used for an improper purpose, and there are good reasons not to enforce a cohabitation provision. *Melletz* suggested that cohabitation clauses generally are used for this purpose, failing completely to realize the very real difference in the *Konzelman*-type situation where the cohabitation is akin to remarriage. The

---

58. 307 N.J. Super. 150, 704 A.2d 591 (1998), *aff'd*, 158 N.J. 185, 729 A.2d 7 (1999).

59. Konzelman v. Konzelman, 158 N.J. 185, 729 A.2d 7 (1999).

60. *See* Ricketts, *supra* note 56.

61. Spousal support, the postdivorce legal quantification of the marital support duty, is increasingly viewed as a limited-term rather than permanent obligation. *See generally* Brett R. Turner, *Rehabilitative Alimony Reconsidered: The "Second Wave" of Spousal Support Reform*, 10 Divorce Litig. 185 (1998). At the same time, courts are expanding the legal remedies available to cohabiting persons. *See generally* Nadine E. Roddy, *Rights and Remedies of Cohabiting Couples Upon Termination of the Relationship*, 4 Divorce Litig. 209 (1992). The result of these two trends is to narrow the economic difference between cohabitation and remarriage.

problem with the *Konzelman* analysis in the real world, however, is that it is very difficult to prove that cohabitation is actually akin to remarriage.[62] The cohabiting spouse has every incentive to conceal the facts, and whether the relationship is similar to marriage really depends upon events that occur behind closed doors. Supporting spouses who are aware of these practical difficulties have often tried to include pure cohabitation provisions in their agreements, not out of any intent to control anyone's sexual behavior, but rather out of desire to avoid the difficult practical problems of proving that cohabitation is akin to remarriage. It could also be argued that pure cohabitation provisions serve the useful purpose of protecting the privacy of the cohabitation relationship against the intrusive examination needed to determine whether the parties are truly acting as if they were married. Finally, it is important to remember that separation agreements require mutual consent, and very few spouses agree to a provision that is intended to harass them. *Melletz* acted at points as if cohabitation clauses were being forced upon dependent spouses against their consent, when actually every such provision must by definition be a product of mutual consent.[63] Harassment is still possible, but in a greater number of cases the supporting spouse is simply seeking to avoid the practical problems of proving marital cohabitation.

The enforceability of pure cohabitation clauses should therefore depend upon the facts. If the requirement is truly being used only to harass, there is a good argument against enforcement. Also, of course, any agreement that was not signed voluntarily should always be subject to attack under normal principles of contract law. *See § 4.05.* If the purpose of the requirement is to avoid difficult problems of proof, however, and if the supporting spouse made concessions in other areas to obtain the provision, then the provision should be enforceable.

Support during the Marriage

While the parties are free to waive the duty to support each other after the marriage, they generally cannot waive their duty to support each other during the marriage:

> [P]remarital and marital agreements purporting to waive, diminish or alter the statutory obligation of the spouses to mutually support each other are contrary to public policy and are therefore void and unenforceable. . . . The rationale for this rule is the recognition that marriage is more than a mere contract—that it is a social institution impressed with public interest and vital to society's stability.[64]

---

62. There are similar practical difficulties to proving a pure financial change in circumstances by demonstrating financial dependency between the cohabiting parties. Supporting spouses often press for pure cohabitation provisions in order to avoid the difficult task of determining whether cohabiting parties are truly financially dependent.

63. In other words, if such a provision is not produce of true voluntary mutual consent by the parties, then it is invalid under the law of contracts, and the public policy question never arises.

64. *In re* Marriage of Mathiasen, 219 Cal. App. 3d 1428, 268 Cal. Rptr. 895 (1990). For cases applying this rule, *see id.* (agreement to share expenses equally during the marriage was not enforceable); Lang v. Lang, 551 So. 2d 547 (Fla. Dist. Ct. App. 1989) (waiver of spousal support did not bar award of temporary alimony); *In re* Marriage of Sutton, 136 Ill. 2d 441, 557 N.E.2d 869

The parties can permissibly waive temporary spousal support due during the pendency of the divorce case, after a bifurcated divorce decree has been granted.[65]

§ 3.06 Attorney's Fees

The parties are free to agree that the prevailing party can recover attorney's fees in any subsequent action to determine the validity or construction of the agreement.[66]

Where there is great financial inequity between the parties, however, an attorney's fees provision might be unenforceable. In *In re Marriage of Pond*,[67] the agreement required the wife to pay the husband's attorney's fees if she attacked its validity. The wife's income was about $35,000, while the husband's was $463,000. The court held that the attorney's fees provision was unconscionable.

An attorney's fees award is usually treated as an incident of spousal support. Accordingly, one court held that public policy prevents a waiver of the right to recover attorney's fees for services provided during the marriage.[68] A waiver of attorney's fees is particularly suspect where it applies to legal expenses incurred on child-related issues.[69] Also, in states where the dependent spouse's attorney has an independent right to seek a fees award from the other spouse, that right cannot be waived by a contract between the parties.[70]

§ 3.07 Child Support, Custody, and Visitation

The court's duty to act in the best interests of children cannot, of course, be controlled by any private agreement between the parents. Some courts have expressed this principle in public policy terms, holding that private agreements on child-related matters are void as against public policy.[71] Other courts express the principle as a rule of construction, holding that the agreement is valid, but that it does not bind the court on

---

(1990) (agreement that settled legal separation action could not waive spousal support, because legal separation judgment did not terminate marriage).

65. Unkel v. Unkel, 699 So. 2d 472 (La. Ct. App. 1997).

66. *See* Pond v. Pond, 700 N.E.2d 1130 (Ind. 1998); Rauch v. McCall, 134 Md. App. 624, 637, 761 A.2d 76, 83 (2000) ("A provision regarding attorney's fees may be included in the separation agreement[.]"); *In re* Marriage of Caras, 263 Mont. 377, 868 P.2d 615 (1994); Smith v. Smith, 188 A.D.2d 1004, 591 N.Y.S.2d 662 (1992); Bromhal v. Stott, 341 N.C. 702, 462 S.E.2d 219 (1995).

67. 676 N.E.2d 401 (Ind. Ct. App. 1997).

68. Abern v. Abern, 572 So. 2d 927 (Fla. Dist. Ct. App. 1990); *cf.* **§ 3.05** (parties cannot generally waive duty to support each other during the marriage).

69. *In re* Marriage of Joseph, 217 Cal. App. 3d 1277, 266 Cal. Rptr. 548 (1990).

70. Lee v. Lee, 302 Ill. App. 3d 607, 707 N.E.2d 67 (1998).

71. *See, e.g.*, McManus v. Howard, 569 So. 2d 1213, 1216 (Miss. 1990) ("the court simply cannot surrender its jurisdiction and authority [on custody questions] . . . such an Agreement [is] void and contrary to public policy").

child-related matters.[72] The difference between these two lines of authority is probably more semantic than real.

Child Support

Courts uniformly hold that a private agreement cannot limit the size of the court's child support award.[73]

A majority of states nevertheless give weight to private agreement when they are consistent with the best interests of the children. The most common rule is that the court must compute the presumptive amount of child support under the applicable child support guidelines as if no agreement existed. It must then consider the agreement as one relevant factor in deciding whether to deviate from the guideline amount.[74] Some

---

72. *See, e.g.*, Bucholt v. Bucholt, 152 Vt. 238, 566 A.2d 409 (1989).

73. *E.g.*, Wilkerson v. Wilkerson, 719 So. 2d 235 (Ala. Ct. App. 1998); *In re* Marriage of LaBass, 56 Cal. App. 4th 1331, 66 Cal. Rptr. 2d 393 (1997); Solis v. Tea, 468 A.2d 1276 (Del. 1983); Evans v. Evans, 595 So. 2d 988 (Fla. Dist. Ct. App. 1992); Dep't of Pub. Aid *ex rel.* Cox v. Miller, 146 Ill. 2d 399, 586 N.E.2d 1251 (1992); *In re* Marriage of Sheetz, 254 Ill. App. 3d 695, 627 N.E.2d 154 (1993); Tilley v. Tilley, 947 S.W.2d 63 (Ky. Ct. App. 1997); Geramifar v. Geramifar, 113 Md. App. 495, 688 A.2d 475 (1997) (even though husband was not child's natural father, court found that father had equitably adopted child); *In re* Marriage of Widhalm, 279 Mont. 97, 926 P.2d 748 (1996); *In re* Marriage of Franks, 275 Mont. 66, 909 P.2d 712 (1996); Jensen v. Jensen, 275 Neb. 921, 927, 750 N.W.2d 335, 341 (2008) ("public policy forbids enforcement of a private agreement that purports to discharge a parent's liability for child support, if the agreement does not adequately provide for the child"); Pecora v. Cerillo, 207 A.D.2d 215, 621 N.Y.S.2d 363 (1995); Harriman v. Harriman, 227 A.D.2d 839, 642 N.Y.S.2d 405 (1996); Litchfield v. Litchfield, 195 A.D.2d 747, 600 N.Y.S.2d 163 (1993); McDonnold v. McDonnold, 98 Ohio App. 3d 822, 649 N.E.2d 1236 (1994); *In re* Watson, 149 Or. App. 598, 945 P.2d 522 (1997); Ruth F. v. Robert B., 456 Pa. Super. 398, 690 A.2d 1171 (1997); Hyde v. Hyde, 421 Pa. Super. 415, 618 A.2d 406 (1992); Leonard v. Lane, 821 S.W.2d 275 (Tex. Ct. App. 1991); Grimes v. Grimes, 621 A.2d 211 (Vt. 1992); Kelley v. Kelley, 248 Va. 295, 449 S.E.2d 55 (1994) (agreement giving wife home in lieu of child support was not enforceable); Hammack v. Hammack, 114 Wash. App. 805, 60 P.3d 663 (2003) (agreement making highly unequal division of property in husband's favor was void as against public policy, where consideration was husband's oral agreement never to seek child support from wife); Combs v. Sherry-Combs, 865 P.2d 50 (Wyo. 1993); *cf. In re* Marriage of Salas, 868 P.2d 1180 (Colo. Ct. App. 1994) (parties cannot waive duty to support adult disabled child).

Contracts that purport to change specific rules of law for determining child support are likewise unenforceable. *See* Cox v. Cox, 776 P.2d 1045 (Alaska 1989) (parties cannot contract out of child support guidelines); Thompson v. Thompson, 696 N.E.2d 80 (Ind. Ct. App. 1998) (agreement to exclude overtime pay from income under child support guidelines; guidelines were to the contrary); Thomas B. v. Lydia D., 69 A.D.3d 24, 886 N.Y.S.2d 22, 28 (2009) (agreement providing that child would be emancipated upon obtaining full-time employment, where legal definition of emancipation was materially different; "[e]conomic independence from the child's parents is not established by merely working a standard, full-time work week"); Zarrett v. Zarrett, 574 N.W.2d 855 (N.D. 1998) (agreement to give credit against income not permitted by guidelines).

The rule against enforcement of child support contracts does not violate the contracts clause of the U.S. Constitution. *Pecora*, 207 A.D.2d 215, 621 N.Y.S.2d 363.

74. *See, e.g., In re* Marriage of Handeland, 564 N.W.2d 445 (Iowa Ct. App. 1997) (approving agreement setting wife's child support obligation to husband at less than guideline amount; wife had waived alimony in exchange for reduced child support); Wormuth v. Taylor, 251 A.D.2d 806,

states will apply this rule only if the agreement states the guideline amount of child support, acknowledges that the guideline amount is presumptively correct, and explains any deviation.[75]

North Carolina follows pre-guideline law holding that the amount of child support established in an agreement between the parents is presumptively binding on the court.[76]

A few decisions state that private agreements have no effect on child support, and that the court should determine child support independently from the agreement.[77]

---

674 N.Y.S.2d 169 (1998) (child support agreement followed on the facts); *see generally* LAURA W. MORGAN, CHILD SUPPORT GUIDELINES: INTERPRETATION AND APPLICATION § 4.09[b] (1996 & Supp. 2008).

This result holds true even where the contract was drafted before the guidelines came into force. *See* Chesler v. Bronstein, 176 Misc. 2d 237, 672 N.Y.S.2d 82 (1997) (pre-guideline promise to "contribute to [the child's] welfare . . . according to his means" construed to require support according to the guidelines).

75. *See In re* Marriage of Hightower, 358 Ill. App. 3d 165, 830 N.E.2d 862 (2005) (trial court erred by accepting child support provision of agreement without stating the guideline amount and justifying any deviation from it); Clark v. Clark, 198 A.D.2d 599, 603 N.Y.S.2d 245 (1993) (contract must include specific statement that parties were aware of child support guidelines); Elizabeth B. v. Emanuel K., 175 Misc. 2d 127, 667 N.Y.S.2d 1004 (Fam. Ct. 1997) (agreement must compute guideline amount and explain any deviation); *cf.* Blaikie v. Mortner, 274 A.D.2d 95, 101, 713 N.Y.S.2d 148, 152 (2000) (statement in agreement that guideline amount was presumptively "just and appropriate" substantially complied with statutory requirement that agreement state that guideline amount is presumptively "correct").

For New York cases striking down agreements that did not meet these requirements, *see, e.g.,* Cheruvu v. Cheruvu, 59 A.D.3d 876, 879, 874 N.Y.S.2d 296, 300 (2009) (agreement did not state the reason for deviating from the guideline amount); Baranek v. Baranek, 54 A.D.3d 789, 790–91, 864 N.Y.S.2d 94, 96 (2008); Warnecke v. Warnecke, 12 A.D.3d 502, 784 N.Y.S.2d 631 (2004); Schaller v. Schaller, 279 A.D.2d 525, 527, 719 N.Y.S.2d 278, 280 (2001); Klein v. Klein, 246 A.D.2d 195, 676 N.Y.S.2d 69 (1998). At least one court suggested that the agreement must also state the amount of any separately computed add-ons, such as child care or medical expenses. *See* Cardinal v. Cardinal, 275 A.D.2d 756, 757, 713 N.Y.S.2d 370, 372 (2000) (agreement invalid for failure to specify "the amount of child support that would have been awarded under [the guidelines], including the amounts for child care and medical care costs").

The New York rule applies only to basic child support, "which generally does not include college education expenses." Colucci v. Colucci, 54 A.D.3d 710, 712–13, 864 N.Y.S.2d 67, 69 (2008).

76. "[W]here the parties have executed a separation agreement that includes provision for child support, the court must apply a rebuttable presumption that the amount set forth is just and reasonable and therefore application of the guidelines would be inappropriate." Pataky v. Pataky, 160 N.C. App. 289, 301–02, 585 S.E.2d 404, 412–13 (2003).

77. *See, e.g., Widhalm,* 279 Mont. 97, 926 P.2d 748; *In re* Marriage of Syverson, 931 P.2d 691 (Mont. 1997).

These Montana cases hold on their face that the court should determine child support completely independently from the agreement. There is a reasonable argument that Montana law should be otherwise, as a specific statute requires that a child support agreement state the guideline amount and provide reasons for any deviation. MONT. CODE ANN. § 40-4-204(3)(b). This statute would be pointless if Montana law required courts to completely ignore child support agreements in setting child support. In addition, if private agreements are given no weight at all, the law will seriously discourage settlement of child support cases. A better result would be reached under the general

While child support agreements are not technically binding, they are highly likely to be accepted by the court where the amount of support provided is reasonable.[78] Most parents are committed to the best interests of their children, most child support agreements are reasonable, and their enforcement tends to conserve scarce judicial resources.

Where a child support provision is contrary to the best interests of the children, however, it will not be enforced. For example, in *Dewbrew v. Dewbrew,*[79] the agreement did not include child support, but included a sufficiently large sum of alimony to support both wife and children. The husband argued that the children were actually receiving sufficient support, and the agreement was therefore not contrary to the children's interests. The trial court agreed, but the appellate court reversed. Because alimony is taxable income to the recipient, the children did not receive *after taxes* a sufficient amount of support. "Based on the difference in tax treatment between spousal maintenance payments and child support, we conclude that the inclusion of child support within the amount of spousal maintenance is against the welfare and interest of the children."[80]

Courts have also refused to approve child support provisions that vary substantially from the guideline amount of child support without sufficient explanation,[81] limit necessary future modification,[82] or rely upon outdated financial information.[83]

An agreement can vary significantly from the guideline amount of child support if the variance is reasonably explained. For example, in *Lounsbury v. Lounsbury,*[84] the

---

nationwide rule, which treats an agreement between the parties as one significant factor to be considered in deviating from the guidelines.

78. "The notion, that parents who have agreed on how best to meet the needs of their children may expect to have the court ignore their agreement, is an idea too counterintuitive and illogical to be countenanced by this Court. Parents generally are in the best position to determine their children's needs." *Pataky,* 160 N.C. App. at 303–04, 585 S.E.2d at 414 (2003); *see also Wormuth,* 251 A.D.2d 806, 674 N.Y.S.2d 169 (following child support provision on the facts); *see generally* MORGAN, *supra* note 74, § 4.09[b]; *cf. In re* Dissolution of Marriage of De St. Germain, 977 So. 2d 412, 417 (Miss. Ct. App. 2008) (trial court must review the sufficiency of the agreement's child support provisions, but need not make a formal finding using the exact words ("adequate and sufficient") set forth in the statute) (quoting MISS. CODE ANN. § 93-5-2(2)).

79. 849 N.E.2d 636 (Ind. Ct. App. 2006).

80. *Id.* at 643.

81. *See* Kraisinger v. Kraisinger, 928 A.2d 333, 340 (Pa. Super. Ct. 2007) (award smaller than guideline amount); Gorton v. Gorton, 80 Conn. App. 52, 832 A.2d 675 (2003) (award larger than guideline amount).

In computing the guideline amount for purposes of determining whether the agreement materially varies from it, the court may use its own state's guidelines and not the guidelines of the state in which the agreement was signed, where both parties have moved away from that state. Petitto v. Petitto, 147 Md. App. 280, 808 A.2d 809 (2002).

82. *See* Frisch v. Henrichs, 304 Wis. 2d 1, 736 N.W.2d 85, 102 (2007) ("the 1996 stipulation is unenforceable and against public policy because it set a ceiling on the amount of child support for four years of $1050 per month, and prevented Heidi from seeking a modification in child support, even if Ronald's income increased").

83. *See, e.g., In re* Marriage of Bonnette, 492 N.W.2d 717 (Iowa Ct. App. 1992) (seven-year-old agreement provision on child support was out of date, and would be given little weight).

84. 300 A.D.2d 812, 752 N.Y.S.2d 103 (2002).

agreement terminated child support at age 18, well short of the statutory age of majority, which is age 21 in New York. The court nevertheless approved the agreement, noting that it awarded the wife full ownership of the marital home, in which the children resided, and that the father had also agreed to pay a disproportionate portion of the marital debt. "[T]he child support provision of the agreement is fair to the children despite the deviation from the [guidelines]."[85]

In reviewing child support agreements, the court should avoid second-guessing decisions of the parents unless the interests of the children so require. In *Griffith v. Griffith*,[86] the trial court made an award of child support larger than the award made in the agreement, reasoning that a larger award would allow the mother to work less and spend more time with the children. The appellate court reversed:

> The record, however, contains absolutely no evidence that Dr. Griffith has neglected her children or has failed to spend appropriate time with them. The action of the court was based upon facts the parties certainly knew, or should have known, at the time of the settlement agreement, and therefore amounted to an unjustified revisiting of the parties' contract. Although we recognize the trial court's discretion to approve matters involving custody, visitation, and support, our scrutiny of the present matter does not suggest the existence of any sufficient evidence to support the trial court's order disdaining the settlement and reducing Dr. Griffith's child support obligation.[87]

A contractual provision setting child support is valid until and unless a court expressly disapproves it.[88] In other words, the mere fact that a future court might possibly find the support provision to be inadequate or excessive is not an excuse for noncompliance. The obligor's remedy is to obtain a court order rejecting the provision, and not to simply refuse payment. Along similar lines, the mere fact that a court modifies a child support provision does not automatically supplant the entire provision. Those portions of the provision that are consistent with the court's modification will continue to be valid.[89]

---

85. *Id*. at 817, 752 N.Y.S.2d at 109.

86. 860 So. 2d 1069 (Fla. Dist. Ct. App. 2003).

87. *Id*. at 1072.

88. Dillon v. Dillon, 696 N.E.2d 85 (Ind. Ct. App. 1998). The case involved temporary support, but the same concept should apply to any contractual provision regarding child support, so long as a court has not disapproved it.

For a case applying the to rule to the obligor's benefits, *see* Kosnac v. Kosnac, 60 A.D.3d 636, 637, 875 N.Y.S.2d 504, 506 (2009) (agreement that child support would be "reduced proportionately" upon emancipation of each of five children was not ambiguous, and required a 20 percent reduction per child, rather than reduction to the guideline amount for one less child; father had therefore complied with agreement).

89. *See* Curry v. Curry, 716 So. 2d 707 (Ala. Ct. App. 1998) (provision in agreement automatically reducing support on emancipation of first child was valid, even though court had modified agreement by increasing total amount of support). *But cf.* Zerr v. Zerr, 7 Neb. App. 285, 586 N.W.2d 465, 468 (1998) (where agreement provided that it would be null and void if disapproved by the

A provision that awards the custodial parent a lump sum amount, and requires that any future child support liability be met first from that amount, is not against public policy, so long as there is no attempt to limit the payor's overall liability.[90]

While the parties cannot agree to limit the court's child support award, they can agree to pay more support than the law would require. The most common example of this point is the substantial volume of case law enforcing agreements to pay college tuition and other forms of postmajority child support. *See* §§ **6.043–6.044**.

Can the court award a smaller amount of child support than provided for in the agreement? The case law on this point is divided. One line of cases holds that the payor has essentially agreed to pay more support than the law requires, and therefore refused to allow reduction. Another line of cases holds that if the court has the power to increase support, it must likewise have the power to decrease it. This split of authority is discussed in more detail in § **6.042**.

A party can even agree to pay support for a child to whom he would normally owe no duty of support at all. The most common application of this point occurs when the court enforces a contract to support a stepchild.[91]

An agreement to pay more than the required amount of child support can extend not only to the present, but also to the future, so that the minimum amount would apply regardless of future changed circumstances.[92]

A contract can require that a payor make both current payments and payment of arrears covering the same period. Such a provision is unwise, but it is not unenforceable.[93]

Escalator Clauses. Child support provisions in separation agreement may use computation methods that the court cannot normally employ. The most common example is an escalator clause setting support at a percentage of the obligor's income.[94] The

---

court, and the court increased the amount of child support, increase was tantamount to disapproval, and the entire agreement was invalid).

90. *See* Jensen v. Jensen, 275 Neb. 921, 750 N.W.2d 335 (2008) (agreement awarding the wife $14,000, to be used as a prepayment of future child support, was not contrary to public policy; agreement did not purport to limit husband's liability, but merely stated that such liability would be met first from the sum at issue).

91. *See* Dewey v. Dewey, 886 P.2d 623 (Alaska 1994); *In re* Marriage of Dawley, 17 Cal. 3d 342, 131 Cal. Rptr. 3, 551 P.2d 323 (1976) (court could order stepparent to pay support based on contractual obligation); Brown v. Brown, 287 Md. 273, 412 A.2d 396 (1980); Cavanaugh v. deBaudiniere, 1 Neb. App. 713, 493 N.W.2d 197 (1992); Moyer v. Moyer, 122 N.C. App. 723, 471 S.E.2d 676 (1996); Duffey v. Duffey, 113 N.C. App. 382, 438 S.E.2d 445 (1994); T. v. T., 216 Va. 867, 224 S.E.2d 148 (1976); *see generally* Laura W. Morgan, *The Rights, Duties and Responsibilities of Stepparents to Their Stepchildren*, 8 DIVORCE LITIG. 165 (1996); MARGARET MAHONEY, STEPFAMILIES AND THE LAW 27–31 (1994). *See also* Brannon v. Brannon, 261 Ga. 565, 407 S.E.2d 748 (1991) (enforcing agreement to support grandchild).

92. Honore v. Honore, 149 Wis. 2d 512, 439 N.W.2d 827 (1989).

93. Geiger v. Geiger, 632 So. 2d 693 (Fla. Dist. Ct. App. 1994).

94. *See* Karpuleon v. Karpuleon, 881 P.2d 318 (Alaska 1994); Kendrick v. Kendrick, 267 Ga. 98, 475 S.E.2d 604 (1996); Malone v. Malone, 637 So. 2d 76 (Fla. Dist. Ct. App. 1994); *In re* Marriage of Singleteary, 293 Ill. App. 3d 25, 687 N.E.2d 1080 (1997); Cochran v. Rodenbarger, 736

ultimate amount of support provided by such a provision, of course, must still meet the reasonable needs of the children.

A minority of jurisdictions have had problem with escalator clauses.[95] As long as the amount of support provided meets the reasonable needs of the children, it is hard to see how an escalator clause harms anyone, and such a clause offers the positive benefit of reducing the need for future modification actions. The majority rule therefore seems better reasoned.

Method of Payment. A separation agreement can also determine the method by which child support shall be paid, so long as the method chosen is not inconsistent with the best interests of the children being supported.[96]

Federal Tax Exemption. State courts are permitted to order spouses to sign federal tax documents that allocate between them the federal tax exemption for dependent children.[97] Contractual provisions allocating the tax exemption are not enforceable if the court finds, either initially or in a subsequent modification proceeding, that the provision is not in the best interests of children.[98]

Modification. An agreement modifying a prior child support order is not enforceable. Child support obligations are established by court order, and a contract between the parties is not alone sufficient to modify the terms of a court order. *See* **§ 6.042**. In a properly filed action to modify the child support order, however, the court may follow a private agreement between the parties if it is consistent with the best interests of the children.[99]

N.E.2d 1279, 1281 (Ind. Ct. App. 2000) (noting that an escalator provision might not be in the children's best interests under modern child support guidelines, but enforcing an escalator provision drafted under pre-guideline law).

95. *See In re* Marriage of Ingram, 259 Ill. App. 3d 685, 631 N.E.2d 386 (1994) (refusing to enforce agreement that set support at percentage of income; statute required a specific monetary award); Bruce v. Bruce, 687 So. 2d 199 (Miss. 1996) (4–3 decision holding over strong dissent that escalation clause is enforceable only if it considers inflation, both parties' income, and expenses of child).

96. *See* Hosza-Dzielak v. Hosza, 26 A.D.3d 378, 812 N.Y.S.2d 564 (2006) (where agreement called for child support payments directly to the mother, court erred by providing in decree that child support must be paid to the Support Collection Unit).

97. I.R.C. § 152(e); *see, e.g.*, Eppler v. Eppler, 837 N.E.2d 167 (Ind. Ct. App. 2005).

98. *See* Bardes v. Todd, 139 Ohio App. 3d 938, 941, 746 N.E.2d 229, 232 (2000) ("the clause in the parties' property-settlement stipulations that seeks to characterize dependent tax exemptions as property is void as contrary to statutory authority based on public policy, but only to the extent the characterization seeks to avoid the continuing jurisdiction of the trial court").

99. *See In re* Marriage of Smith, 347 Ill. App. 3d 395, 400, 806 N.E.2d 727, 731 (2004) ("parents may create an enforceable agreement for modification of child support only by petitioning the court for support modification and then establishing, to the satisfaction of the court, that an agreement reached between the parents is in accord with the best interests of the children").

Custody and Visitation

Just as the parties cannot settle child support by contract, so are they unable to settle the questions of custody and visitation.[100]

The parties cannot control custody and visitation indirectly. In *Fryman v. Fryman*,[101] the agreement provided that the wife's support payments would cease if she made any attempt to modify the agreement. The wife filed a motion to modify visitation, and the husband argued that support was terminated. The court disagreed, finding that the husband was making an invalid attempt to exert indirect control over the court's power to determine visitation.

The court should, of course, consider any bona fide agreement of the parents as one important factor in making its own independent determination on these questions.[102] In practice, the courts will generally follow a custody or visitation provision, so long as it is facially consistent with the best interests of the children.[103] "The courts recognize that two responsible parents are usually better equipped than a judge to decide what is best for their children. . . . 'No stranger in a judicial robe, however able and well-motivated he or she may be, is equipped to make a decision as valid as the parents working together might make.'"[104]

---

100. *See, e.g.*, Feliciano v. Feliciano, 674 So. 2d 937 (Fla. Dist. Ct. App. 1996); McManus v. Howard, 569 So. 2d 1213 (Miss. 1990); *In re* Marriage of Widhalm, 279 Mont. 97, 926 P.2d 748 (1996); Truman v. Truman, 256 Neb. 628, 591 N.W.2d 81 (1999); Frizzell v. Frizzell, 193 A.D.2d 861, 597 N.Y.S.2d 513 (1993); *In re* Marriage of Thier, 67 Wash. App. 940, 841 P.2d 794 (1992); *see generally* RESTATEMENT (SECOND) OF CONTRACTS § 191 (1981).

The rule applies to questions of modification as well as to initial awards. *See* Mundon v. Mundon, 703 N.E.2d 1130 (Ind. Ct. App. 1999) (refusing to enforce agreement that conditioned mother's custody upon proof that she obtained counseling for alcoholism; mother had complied with spirit if not letter of obligation, and a change in custody would be contrary to children's best interests).

101. 926 S.W.2d 602 (Tex. Ct. App. 1996).

102. *See, e.g.*, Reno v. Haler, 734 N.E.2d 1095 (Ind. Ct. App. 2000) (custody and relocation); Dwyer v. De La Torre, 252 A.D.2d 696, 675 N.Y.S.2d 412 (1998) (visitation); *Feliciano*, 674 So. 2d 937 (visitation); *see generally* JEFF ATKINSON, MODERN CHILD CUSTODY PRACTICE § 4.47 (1986 & Supp. 1998); RESTATEMENT (SECOND) OF CONTRACTS § 191 (1981).

In *In re* Marriage of Arvin, 689 N.E.2d 1270 (Ind. Ct. App. 1997), the court held that a provision awarding custody to the wife was inseverable from a void provision limiting her right to relocate, and struck down both provisions. If the custody provision of the agreement were irrelevant to the court's custody decision, there would have been no reason to consider the severability issue. Arvin therefore suggests strongly that a contract provision regarding custody, when not linked to a void provision restricting relocation, is at least one relevant factor in determining custody.

103. "As a practical matter, however, courts rarely exercise their inherent power to enter orders affecting children that differ from the terms arrived at by agreement between the parties." Sally B. Sharp, *Semantics as Jurisprudence: The Elevation of Form Over Substance in the Treatment of Separation Agreements in North Carolina*, 69 N.C. L. REV. 319, 322 n.12 (1991); *see also* Reno v. Haler, 734 N.E.2d 1095 (Ind. Ct. App. 2000) (noting that it is especially appropriate to give strong consideration to mediated agreements); Patterson v. Taylor, 140 N.C. App. 91, 535 S.E.2d 374 (2000) (parties agreeing upon joint custody should have the same flexibility as a court would have in fashioning the details of the arrangement).

104. Giangeruso v. Giangeruso, 310 N.J. Super. 476, 708 A.2d 1232, 1233 (Ch. Div. 1997) (quoting Tahan v. Duquette, 259 N.J. Super. 328, 613 A.2d 486, 490 (App. Div. 1992)).

When the agreement is inconsistent with the best interests of the children, the court will refuse to follow it. The clearest cases are those where decisions regarding custody and visitation are made far in advance, without any consideration of the best interests of the children.[105] Even where the parties do have the children's best interests in mind, however, the court is free to disregard the agreement when its judgment as to the children's interests is different from the parties.[106] For the reasons stated above, the parties are often the best judge of the interests of their children, and the power to disregard a bona fide agreement on child-related issues should be exercised carefully.

Jurisdiction. Standards for the jurisdiction of state courts over custody and visitation actions are set forth in binding federal and state statutes.[107] These statutes involve subject-matter jurisdiction, which cannot be conferred or denied by consent. Contractual provisions regarding custody or visitation jurisdiction are therefore completely unenforceable.[108]

Pets. The law has traditionally been hostile to agreement that attempt to create visitation rights with the parties' pets.[109] Pets are personal property, not children, and thus not a proper subject of visitation rights. As one court noted in refusing to enforce such

---

105. *See* Combs v. Sherry-Combs, 865 P.2d 50 (Wyo. 1993) (refusing to enforce provision that each parent would receive custody of any children of the same sex); Turman v. Boleman, 235 Ga. App. 243, 510 S.E.2d 532, 533 (1998) (agreement preventing visitation in the presence of an "African-American male" violated public policy against race-based discrimination); *cf.* Palmore v. Sidoti, 466 U.S. 429 (1984) (equal protection clause prohibits race-based discrimination in custody decisions).

106. *See Giangeruso*, 310 N.J. Super. 476, 708 A.2d at 1232 (contract provided that children would have no contact with future boyfriends or girlfriends of parents, if the children "express reluctance" to have such contact; provision placed too much weight upon shoulders of children, ages six and nine, and was contrary to their best interests).

Another problem with the agreement in *Giangeruso* was the inherently vague notion meaning of the phrase "express reluctance." Does one single isolated objection to visitation with the father's girlfriend qualify? What if the children prefer to have a parent entirely to themselves, but have no greater objection to the presence of the mother's boyfriend than they would have to any other third party intruding upon the parent-child relationship? The authors would have no quarrel with an agreement providing that the parents will respect substantial, longstanding, deeply felt objections by their children to visitation with a boyfriend or girlfriend, but the agreement in *Giangeruso* contained much more troubling language.

107. *See* Parental Kidnapping Prevention Act, 28 U.S.C.A. § 1738A (1994 & Supp. 1999); UNIF. CHILD CUSTODY JURISDICTION AND ENFORCEMENT ACT, 9 U.L.A. 649 (1999); UNIF. CHILD CUSTODY JURISDICTION ACT, 9 U.L.A. 261 (1999); *see generally* JEFF ATKINSON, MODERN CHILD CUSTODY PRACTICE ch. 3 (1986); Ron W. Nelson, *The UCCJA and the UCCJEA: A Side-by-Side Comparison*, 10 DIVORCE LITIG. 233 (1998); Brett R. Turner, *Deciding Who Decides: A Critical Review of the Law of Jurisdiction in Child Custody Cases*, 4 DIVORCE LITIG. 177, 197 (1992).

108. *See* Cricenti v. Weiland, 44 Mass. App. Ct. 785, 694 N.E.2d 353 (1998); Steele v. Steele, 978 S.W.2d 835 (Mo. Ct. App. 1998).

109. *See* Desanctis v. Pritchard, 803 A.2d 230, 232 (Pa. Super. Ct. 2002).

a provision, "[a]ppellant is seeking an arrangement analogous, in law, to a visitation schedule for a table or a lamp."[110]

The traditional attitude toward visitation with pets is harsh, and there are a few cases in which the court seemed to adopt a more tolerant position.[111] Pets are living entities, and therefore a special type of personal property. The law recognizes this point in other contexts. For example, while owners of inanimate property are generally free to break it as they will, mistreatment of animals is often a criminal act.

The practical problem with pet visitation, however, is that it would burden the courts with an entire new category of postdivorce litigation. When courts barely have enough resources to resolve visitation disputes involving children, their refusal to consider visitation disputes involving pets is understandable. But there may be ways to draft pet visitation clauses that do not add to the courts' workload. For example, a mediator or other private dispute resolution service could be given exclusive authority to resolve disputes over pet custody and visitation, with the parties sharing the cost in defined percentages. As long as pet visitation provisions do not require court enforcement, there is a reasonable argument that they are consistent with public policy. Pets are not children, but they are considerably more important than tables and lamps.

Relocation

The court is not bound by a contractual provision permitting or preventing relocation of the custodial parent.[112] Case law considering whether such a provision should receive at least some weight is considered in **§ 6.066**.

Paternity

The court is not bound by a provision stating that the husband is not the father of the parties' children.[113]

Other Child-Related Issues

Isolated decisions have held that the court is not bound by the parents' agreement on other issues regarding the welfare of children.[114]

---

110. *Id.* at 232.

111. *E.g.*, Juelfs v. Gough, 41 P.3d 593, 597 (Alaska 2002) (modifying an joint custody sharing agreement with a dog to give sole custody to the husband).

112. *See In re* Marriage of Findlay, 296 Ill. App. 3d 656, 695 N.E.2d 548 (1998); *In re* Marriage of Arvin, 689 N.E.2d 1270 (Ind. Ct. App. 1997); McManus v. Howard, 569 So. 2d 1213 (Miss. 1990).

113. Witt v. Witt, 929 S.W.2d 360 (Tenn. Ct. App. 1996).

114. *See* Lynch v. Unlenhopp, 248 Iowa 68, 78 N.W.2d 491 (1956) (promise to raise child in particular religion); R.H. v. M.K., 254 N.J. Super. 480, 603 A.2d 995 (Ch. Div. 1991) (termination of parental rights); Haimowitz v. Gerber, 153 A.D.2d 879, 545 N.Y.S.2d 599 (1989) (contract cannot waive parent's statutory duty to pay college tuition where certain requirements are met).

§ 3.08 Other Provisions

Arbitration and Mediation

There is generally no public policy objection to arbitration clauses in separation agreements. On issues involving the welfare of children, however, the court must still exercise independent judgment in the children's best interests.[115] Case law construing arbitration provisions is discussed in § **6.067**.

A separation agreement resulting from arbitration or mediation should be treated no differently from any other agreement.[116]

Agreements to Defraud Creditors

Separation agreements drafted collusively for the purpose of committing an illegal fraud upon the parties' creditors are contrary to public policy. For instance, in *Espenshade v. Espenshade*,[117] the parties signed a "paper agreement" to reduce the husband's support obligation from $350 per week to $600 per month. They agreed that the agreement was only for the purpose of convincing the bank to grant the husband a certain mortgage, and that the agreement would have no real effect on the husband's liability. The court held that the contract was drafted for the illegal purpose of defrauding the mortgagee bank, and that it was accordingly unenforceable.

Another example is *Uhl v. Uhl*.[118] The agreement in that case required the wife to file a federal tax form indicating that she was an employee of the husband's business, so that his property division payments could be deducted as a business expense. Because the agreement would "effectively obligate defendant to aid and abet plaintiff in committing employment tax fraud,"[119] a lower court decision invalidating the agreement was upheld on appeal.

Confidentiality

There is no public policy objection to provisions in which the parties agree not to disclose certain details about their marriage or its breakup to third persons, including most notably the media.[120]

In *Perricone v. Perricone*,[121] the court held that a confidentiality clause is not an invalid restraint upon constitutional right to free speech. Interestingly, the court made a point of noting that the purpose of the agreement was to protect the value of the husband's business, and that there was not a strong public interest in the information at issue. "The agreement does not prohibit the disclosure of information concerning

---

115. Faherty v. Faherty, 97 N.J. 99, 477 A.2d 1257, 1261 (1984).

116. *See In re* Marriage of Banks, 887 S.W.2d 160 (Tex. Ct. App. 1994).

117. 729 A.2d 1239, 1241 (Pa. Super. 1999).

118. 274 A.D.2d 915, 711 N.Y.S.2d 271 (2000).

119. *Id.* at 917, 711 N.Y.S.2d at 272.

120. Perricone v. Perricone, 292 Conn. 187, 204, 972 A.2d 666, 679 (2009); Anonymous v. Anonymous, 233 A.D.2d 162, 649 N.Y.S.2d 665 (1996); Trump v. Trump, 179 A.D.2d 201, 582 N.Y.S.2d 1008 (1992).

121. *Perricone*, 292 Conn. at 204, 972 A.2d at 679.

the enforcement of laws protecting important rights, criminal behavior, the public health and safety or matters of great public importance, and the plaintiff is not a public official."[122] A confidential clause might pose public policy issues, therefore, where it prevents disclosure of information in which the public has a strong interest. No divorce case has yet found this exception present on the facts.

Unreasonable Penalties

Public policy permits contractual penalty clauses only where the penalty bears a reasonable relationship to the actual damages suffered by the innocent party. Clauses imposing unreasonable penalties are void as against public policy. These rules are discussed further in § **7.021**.

Right to Appeal

A provision waiving the right to appeal any adverse decision beyond the trial court level is not void as against public policy.[123]

§ 3.09 Severability

The presence of a single void clause does not necessarily destroy an otherwise valid contract. If the void clause is severable from the rest of the contract, the court will simply treat the contract as if the void clause did not exist.

Whether a clause is severable depends upon whether it was an integral part of the parties' overall bargain. Perhaps the best evidence of severability is an express clause in the agreement stating that any void clauses can be severed.[124] If no severability clause is present, the question then becomes a factual matter of determining the parties' intent.[125] "Whether a contract is entire or severable generally is a question of intention, to be determined from the language employed by the parties, viewed in the light of the circumstances surrounding them at the time they contracted[.]"[126]

There is some law suggesting that property division and spousal support provisions are generally severable from provisions involving the welfare of minor children—cus-

---

122. *Id.* at 221, 972 A.2d at 688–89.

123. Burke v. Burke, 52 Va. App. 183, 193, 662 S.E.2d 622, 627 (2008). The quality of decision-making in the trial courts varies greatly, and without the right of appeal, there is a material risk that one or both parties will be harmed by a misconstruction or misapplication of the law. Clauses waiving the right to appeal are therefore significantly unwise. But like many other unwise provisions, they will be enforced when present in an agreement.

124. *See In re* Marriage of Taft, 156 A.D.2d 444, 548 N.Y.S.2d 726 (1989); Christian v. Christian, 42 N.Y.2d 63, 365 N.E.2d 849, 396 N.Y.S.2d 817 (1977); Kraisinger v. Kraisinger, 928 A.2d 333 (Pa. Super. Ct. 2007).

125. *See* Harrington v. Harrington, 281 N.J. Super. 39, 656 A.2d 456 (App. Div. 1995) (if support agreement was unenforceable, property division and support provisions could not be severed, and entire agreement would become invalid).

126. *Christian*, 42 N.Y.2d 63, 365 N.E.2d 849, 396 N.Y.S.2d at 824.

tody, visitation, and child support.[127] But this point is more a general guide than a firm rule, for it is possible to draft an agreement in which provisions involving children are not severable. For instance, in *Zerr v. Zerr*,[128] the agreement contained an express provision stating that "the entire document shall be null and void" in the event that it "is not approved by the Court." The court approved the agreement, but increased the amount of child support. The court held that the increase in child support was tantamount to refusing to approve the agreement. Thus, when the child support provision fell, the rest of the agreement fell with it.

Likewise, in *In re Marriage of Arvin*,[129] the court held that a provision restricting the custodial parent's right to relocate was unenforceable. It then found that the provision awarding custody to the wife was inseverable from the relocation provision. Both provisions were thus invalid, and the case was remanded for a custody hearing without any consideration of the agreement.

Conversely, in *Warnecke v. Warnecke*,[130] the court held that the child support provision in an agreement was invalid for failure to state the guideline amount and explain any deviation. But the court summarily rejected an argument that the invalid child support provision was inseverable from the provisions of the agreement governing spousal support. The spousal support provisions therefore remained valid.

---

127. *See In re* Marriage of Alter, 171 Cal. App. 4th 718, 728, 89 Cal. Rptr. 3d 849, 857 (2009) ("child support orders are always severable from an agreement dividing the marital property"); Baranek v. Baranek, 54 A.D.3d 789, 791, 864 N.Y.S.2d 94, 96 (2008) (child support provisions were set aside, but "it does not appear from this record that the basic child support provision was intertwined with other provisions of the stipulation, which included custody and visitation, equitable distribution of property, and a waiver of maintenance"; these provisions therefore remained valid).

128. 7 Neb. App. 285, 586 N.W.2d 465, 468 (1998).

129. 689 N.E.2d 1270 (Ind. Ct. App. 1997).

130. 12 A.D.3d 502, 784 N.Y.S.2d 631 (2004).

Validity of Separation Agreements 4

§ 4.01 Validity in General

General Policy: The Battle of the Boilerplate Provisions

Court decisions on the validity of separation agreements often begin by reciting a series of standard provisions. The reader can often tell which way the court is leaning simply by noting which standard provisions the court recites.

If the court is inclined to view the agreement favorably, it will note that separation agreements are merely one variety of enforceable contract.[1] As such, they are subject only to those limited defenses recognized under general contract law. The court may also observe that separation are agreements are favored by the law, and that they will not be set aside for trivial reasons.[2]

If the court is inclined against the agreement, it is likely to begin with the proposition that separation agreements have a special status under the law. The state has a strong interest in domestic relations cases, and that interest entitles it to scrutinize separation agreements closely. The law has traditionally recognized that married persons have a confidential relationship, and that contracts between them must be closely scrutinized for evidence of unfairness. "Agreements between spouses, unlike

---

1. *See, e.g.,* Tanner v. Tanner, 57 Cal. App. 4th 419, 67 Cal. Rptr. 2d 204 (1997); Rimkus v. Rimkus, 199 Ill. App. 3d 903, 557 N.E.2d 638 (1990); Bittick v. Bittick, 987 So. 2d 1058 (Miss. Ct. App. 2008).

2. *See, e.g.,* Young Choi v. Young Choi, 167 A.D.2d 217, 561 N.Y.S.2d 724 (1990).

ordinary business contracts, involve a fiduciary relationship requiring the utmost of good faith. . . . There is a strict surveillance of all transactions between married persons, especially separation agreements."[3]

Each of these standard provisions has a degree of truth, but the real state of the law is somewhere between them. At one point in time, the second set of standard provisions was undoubtedly correct. Divorce was disfavored, and any agreement involving divorce was closely scrutinized for invalidity. In particular, courts were very concerned that the agreement not encourage divorce. *See* § **3.01**. Moreover, women as a class were disadvantaged, and the law took strict measures to protect them against overreaching by men with more experience, more property, and generally more rights under the law.

The society that required those strict protective rules, however, does not exist today. Separation agreements no longer partake of the stigma of divorce; on the contrary, courts recognize that agreements serve an important public purpose by resolving divorce litigation quicker, less expensively, and more fairly than any court order. "It would be shortsighted and unwise for courts to reject out of hand consensual solutions to vexatious personal matrimonial problems that have been advanced by the parties themselves."[4] Moreover, while individual women, particularly older homemakers, may still require a degree of special treatment, the notion that women as a class are disadvantaged seems paternalistic and outdated. In the overwhelming majority of modern divorce cases, the wife is as able to protect her own interests as the husband is to protect his, and there is no reason to give special treatment to either.

In short, the modern divorce case does not greatly resemble the divorce case of 50 years ago, when an inexperienced and financially disadvantaged wife needed a measure of special protection. The first set of standard provisions continues the trend, arguing that a separation agreement under current practice is no different from any other agreement between persons of equal bargaining power. As a general rule, when a party with equal bargaining power signs an unwise agreement, the agreement is nevertheless enforced. The task of the courts is not to judge the wisdom of contracts, but simply to enforce certain ground rules of negotiation. No one would ever argue that the court has a special duty to evaluate the fairness of a general business contract. The first set of standard provisions suggests that we should apply the same hands-off notion to separation agreements.

Yet some courts continue to insist that there is something special about separation agreements. If this notion is to be justified, there must be something unique to the divorce setting that justifies special treatment. The second set of provisions reaches in the right direction by claiming the existence of a special state interest in domestic relations, but these courts are relying too much upon the past. Often, the only authority cited in support of this special state interest is dated. For example, the leading New York decision asserting a special state interest relied exclusively upon case law from the early 1900s.[5] The court did not explain how that authority, founded upon a strong

---

3. Christian v. Christian, 42 N.Y.2d 63, 365 N.E.2d 849, 396 N.Y.S.2d 817 (1977).
4. Petersen v. Petersen, 85 N.J. 638, 428 A.2d 1301, 1304 (1981).
5. *Christian*, 42 N.Y.2d 63, 365 N.E.2d 849, 396 N.Y.S.2d 817.

distaste for divorce and a paternalistic need to protect women, retained any current validity. Nor did the court explain why the state's interest in a domestic relations agreement is necessarily greater than its interest in a general business contract involving a similar dollar amount.

Other courts have struggled a step further by suggesting that the need for special protection arises from the confidential nature of the marital relationship. In the case of antenuptial agreements, which are signed when the parties' relationship is almost always truly confidential, this rationale is compelling. *See* § **10.01**. But the parties to separation agreements often do not actually have a confidential relationship. Indeed, in many if not most divorce cases, the parties are highly antagonistic. The law gains little by imposing a confidential relationship upon parties whose actual relationship is adversarial. Courts that emphasize the confidential nature of marriage are ignoring the real conditions under which most modern separation agreements are negotiated.

An objective evaluation of separation agreements in modern practice must begin by acknowledging that women as a class do not need specific protection and that most divorcing parties lack a confidential relationship. These facts provide some support for the concept that separation agreements are "just like" other contracts. It is certainly difficult to find any consistent, systemic bias in the negotiation process in favor of either party similar to the pro-husband bias that existed 50 years ago.

Yet are separation agreements truly ordinary contracts? Common experience suggests that however equal the parties are in bargaining power, equality in process does not always translate well into equality of result. Most persons have at least anecdotal knowledge of a person who signed an unfair agreement under the pressure of a divorce case. Experienced domestic practitioners can tell horror stories of parties who were advised not to sign an unfair agreement, but who nevertheless did so. In short, people seem to sign unfair separation agreements more often than they sign other types of unfair contracts. This is a valid, objective, commonly observed difference between separation agreements and other types of contracts.

Why does the difference exist? Why are unfair separation agreements more common than unfair agreements in other areas? The authors' observation, formed after years of experience in the domestic relations area, is that divorcing parties are at a difficult time in their lives. Most persons build their personal lives around their marriage, and when that marriage breaks up, most persons suffer a substantial amount of emotional distress. Inevitably, this distress interferes with good judgment. In the authors' experience, the situation is not at all unique to either sex; men and women sign unfair divorce settlements with roughly equal frequency. The problem is not any sex-based lack of bargaining power, but rather the commonly observed effect of emotional distress upon clear thinking.

The emotional stress that accompanies most divorce cases also makes divorcing parties unduly subject to certain forms of bargaining pressure.[6] Extremely inequitable

---

6. "The state has an interest in protecting all citizens from bargaining contexts which are peculiarly conducive to overreaching tactics." Sally B. Sharp, *Semantics as Jurisprudence: The Elevation of Form Over Substance in the Treatment of Separation Agreements in North Carolina*, 69 N.C. L. Rev. 319, 349 (1991); *see also* Bromhal v. Stott, 341 N.C. 702, 462 S.E.2d 219,

agreements can result when one spouse is willing to give up anything to preserve the marriage, and the other spouse takes undue advantage of this fact. To throw these parties upon their own resources, with no court protection, would be to penalize those persons most interested in preserving marriage—an institution of unquestioned social value. In addition, in many divorce cases, access to the children of the marriage is an issue. Again, many rational persons will become highly irrational when their custody or visitation rights are called into question. These are only two of the many ways in which the stress of divorce interferes with the normal exercise of rational judgment.

The fact that men and women have generally equal bargaining power does not mean, therefore, that separation agreements are just like other contracts. On the contrary, the inherent stresses of divorce impose unique obstacles to the exercise of rational judgment in the process of negotiating agreements. The existence of these obstacles is confirmed by the observed frequency of unfair agreements in divorce cases.

In addition to their uniquely emotional setting, divorce cases also have a unique financial setting. The amounts at issue in divorce cases, objectively viewed, are not larger than the amounts at issue in contracts or torts cases, but the amounts are much larger in comparison to the net worth of those involved. The amount of property at issue in a divorce case often consists of literally every asset owned by either party. Because of this fact, an unfair divorce settlement can impose substantially more damage upon the parties than an unfair settlement in another type of case. At times, an unfair agreement can actually place the disadvantaged party on public assistance.

These factors do not support imposition of the broad, paternalistic review standard stated in older case law. They do suggest, however, that separation agreements must be reviewed for abuse more carefully than agreements in other areas. Courts would do well to base this enhanced review standard not upon outdated policies or differences between the sexes, but upon the unique emotional and financial setting of a divorce case. Bluntly put, a modest degree of special protection is needed to protect divorcing parties from suffering undue financial injury due to rash, overly emotional acts of misjudgment.

The authors observe in passing that there is no particular reason to expect that this need for special protection will diminish over time. Properly understood, the special rules that apply to separation agreements are a result of the emotional setting in which divorce generally occurs. Well-trained negotiators and mediators can assist the parties in dealing with those emotions, but the emotions themselves are a fact of human nature that is not likely to change. Indeed, the authors would feel concern for the fate of marriage as a human institution if divorce were *not* a difficult, emotionally charged process. As long as human beings continue to exercise poor judgment when falling into and out of love, there will probably remain a need to apply special rules when reviewing marital agreements of all types.

---

221 (1995) (quoting Sharp's statement with approval). The present authors believe that the divorce setting is "peculiarly conducive" not only to bad-faith overreaching, but also to simple good-faith errors in judgment.

Overview of the Law

The various available grounds for attacking separation agreements can be divided into two separate classes: procedural and substantive. Procedural defenses are those that relate to the conditions under which the agreement was signed. This group of defenses includes the "big four" defenses that apply to all contracts: duress, undue influence, fraud, and mistake. *See* § **4.05**. Substantive defenses are those that relate to the fairness of the agreement itself. The primary defense in this group is the traditional doctrine of unconscionability, which is applied to separation agreements in a somewhat stricter form than to contracts generally. *See* § **4.061**. Also, a significant number of states take the point one step further, and permit separation agreements to be set aside for mere unfairness—a doctrine not generally recognized by the common law of contracts. *See* § **4.062**.

Defenses to separation agreements must ordinarily be proven by clear and convincing evidence.[7] As set forth below in § **4.052**, some courts may shift the burden and presume that the agreement is invalid for undue influence where the parties enjoyed a confidential relationship and the agreement is not fair and reasonable.[8]

If neither party proves any of the available procedural or substantive defenses, the agreement is prima facie valid. Conversely, if one or more defenses is proved, the agreement is prima facie invalid. The validity of an agreement, however, can be changed by the parties' actions. Valid agreements can become invalid if they are abandoned or if the parties decide to reconcile. *See* §§ **4.074–4.075**. Invalid agreements can become valid if the relevant statute of limitations expires, or if the attacking spouse sleeps on his or her rights for a significant period of time or knowingly accepts benefits under the agreement. *See* §§ **4.071–4.073**.

The rules described in this chapter are rules for determining the validity of the agreement. If application of the rules indicates that all or part of the agreement is invalid, then the invalid portion is set aside. The court is not permitted, however, to rewrite the agreement; only the parties themselves can do that.[9] If the parties are not able to reach a new agreement, then there is no agreement and the contested issues are decided under the normal principles of law that apply to nonsettled cases.

Courts apply normal choice-of-law rules in separation agreement cases. Thus, if the contract contains an express choice-of-law clause, that clause will be enforced.[10]

---

7. *See, e.g., In re* Marriage of Carlson, 101 Ill. App. 3d 924, 428 N.E.2d 1005 (1981); Nitkiewicz v. Nitkiewicz, 369 Pa. Super. 504, 535 A.2d 664 (1988), *allocatur denied*, 551 A.2d 216 (Pa. 1989); Derby v. Derby, 8 Va. App. 19, 378 S.E.2d 74 (1989); Warner v. Warner, 394 S.E.2d 74 (W. Va. 1990).

8. *E.g.,* Robert O. v. Ecmel A., 460 A.2d 1321 (Del. 1983), *overruled on other grounds*, Sanders v. Sanders, 570 A.2d 1189 (Del. 1990); Hale v. Hale, 74 Md. App. 505, 539 A.2d 247, *cert. denied*, 313 Md. 30, 542 A.2d 857 (1988).

9. *See* Yoell-Mirel v. Mirel, 34 A.D.3d 796, 797, 826 N.Y.S.2d 345, 347 (2006) (agreement was properly held unconscionable, but trial court "erred in re-writing rather than setting aside the provision of the agreement concerning the marital home").

10. Church v. McCabe, 25 A.D.3d 454, 455, 808 N.Y.S.2d 204, 205 (2006) (where parties' "separation agreement is in a format recognized under, and governed by, Hong Kong law," applying Hong Kong law to determine its validity).

Otherwise, the court will look to whatever choice-of-law test has been adopted for use in contract cases generally.[11]

§ 4.02 Res Judicata

Before considering any of the various contract law doctrines for invalidating separation agreements, the court must first consider whether contract law applies at all. If the parties have already been divorced, the divorce decree may represent a binding determination that the agreement is valid. If so, the time for arguing contract law defenses has passed, and the agreement can be attacked only upon principles of law governing the reopening of judgments.

§ 4.021 General Rule

Most separation agreements begin their lives as private agreements between the parties. A separation agreement is inherently part of a divorce case, however, and most separation agreements are therefore ultimately presented to the divorce court. The manner in which the court should treat the agreement is a topic of considerable confusion. *See* § 5.01. Nevertheless, one fact about the issue emerges clearly and uniformly from all of the reported decisions. Regardless of whether the divorce court *approves, incorporates*, or *merges* a separation agreement, the court's divorce decree contains an express or implied finding that the agreement is valid under the law of contracts.[12]

This fact has immense consequences when one party seeks to attack a separation agreement after a final judgment has been rendered in the divorce case. When the court has already held that a contract is valid, the party seeking to attack the agreement has already had one day in court. Accordingly, mere contract law defenses are not sufficient to invalidate the agreement. "[A]s a general rule, contractual defenses are impermissible collateral attacks upon the finality of a trial court's judgment."[13]

For instance, in *Cooper v. Smith*,[14] the husband agreed that he would not amend a certain trust, and he agreed to sell the wife 35 percent of the marital estate for only $100 if he did so. The husband amended the trust, and then sought to argue that the sale requirement was an invalid penalty clause. The court refused to permit this defense, on grounds that it should have been made in the initial divorce proceedings. After the divorce decree incorporated the agreement, its validity was res judicata, and contract law defenses were no longer available.[15]

---

11. *See, e.g.*, Behr v. Behr, 46 N.C. App. 694, 266 S.E.2d 393 (1980).

12. *E.g.*, Barry v. Barry, 409 Mass. 727, 569 N.E.2d 393 (1991); Bracci v. Chiccarelli, 53 Mass. App. Ct. 318, 759 N.E.2d 330 (2001) (judgment that incorporated agreement implicitly found agreement to be fair and reasonable, even though judgment did not say so expressly).

13. Spradley v. Hutchinson, 787 S.W.2d 214, 219 (Tex. Ct. App. 1990).

14. 70 Haw. 449, 776 P.2d 1178 (1989).

15. For additional cases holding that contract law defenses to a separation agreement cannot be raised after the divorce decree has become final, *see In re* Marriage of Alexander, 212 Cal. App. 3d 677, 261 Cal. Rptr. 9 (1989); Jones v. Jones, 280 Ga. 712, 632 S.E.2d 121 (2006); *In re* Marriage of Lindjord, 234 Ill. App. 3d 319, 600 N.E.2d 431 (1992); *Barry*, 409 Mass. 727, 569 N.E.2d

Res judicata may also bar other types of actions, such as an action for fraud[16] or unjust enrichment,[17] which argue that an approved agreement is invalid. Again, the approval of an agreement by the court constitutes a binding determination that the agreement is valid.

Res judicata also clearly applies where the issues raised in one motion to set aside an agreement were resolved against the moving party on a previous motion to set aside that agreement.[18]

Res judicata is an issue only where the agreement has been approved by a final court order. Where issues of validity are addressed in an order that is not final, such as an order awarding temporary spousal support, res judicata does not apply.[19]

While the existence of a divorce decree is often conclusive as to the validity of the agreement, the absence of a divorce decree may or may not indicate that the agreement is invalid. Case law on this subject is discussed elsewhere in this treatise.[20]

§ 4.022 Reopening the Judgment

While mere contractual defenses are not sufficient to overturn a separation agreement after the divorce, it is not by any means true that separation agreements are immune from attack once the court approves them. A court order that approves a separation agreement is a judgment, but it is no more final than a court judgment in any other field

---

393; Mason v. Mason, 873 S.W.2d 631 (Mo. Ct. App. 1994); Reinsch v. Reinsch, 259 Neb. 564, 611 N.W.2d 86 (2000); Hayward v. Hayward, 808 A.2d 232 (Pa. Super. Ct. 2002); Jackson v. Culp, 400 Pa. Super. 519, 583 A.2d 1236 (1990); Green v. Green, 327 S.C. 577, 491 S.E.2d 260 (Ct. App. 1997) (contract law defense of fraud cannot be raised in motion to set aside incorporated contract; validity was res judicata); Crothers v. Crothers, 2001 SD 78, 630 N.W.2d 103; Ellett v. Ellett, 35 Va. App. 97, 542 S.E.2d 816 (2001); Doherty v. Doherty, 9 Va. App. 97, 383 S.E.2d 759 (1989) (contract law defenses of laches and estoppel were not available in action to enforce merged separation agreement); Tudhope v. Riehle, 704 A.2d 765 (Vt. 1997); *but cf.* Spradley v. Hutchinson, 787 S.W.2d 214 (contract law defenses cannot overturn approved agreement, but they are factors to be considered in assessing damages when enforcing the contract).

Of course, contract law defenses clearly cannot be raised after they have expressly litigated and resolved. *See* Falco v. Falco, 247 A.D.2d 426, 668 N.Y.S.2d 715 (1998) (error to find contract invalid on grounds that husband was under influence of Valium and Percocet when it was signed; earlier final order had rejected these defenses).

16. *E.g.*, Gavrilis v. Gavrilis, 116 P.3d 1272 (Colo. App. 2005); *see generally* 3 BRETT R. TURNER, EQUITABLE DISTRIBUTION OF PROPERTY § 9:30 n.69 (3d ed. 2005).

17. *See* Kelly v. Kelly, 887 A.2d 788, 792 (Pa. Super. Ct. 2005).

18. *See* Cheruvu v. Cheruvu, 61 A.D.3d 1171, 1173, 878 N.Y.S.2d 208, 210 (2009) (refusing to allow relitigation of validity of stipulation; "the husband made these arguments in his earlier attempt to set aside the stipulation").

19. *See* Wells v. Wells, 132 N.C. App. 401, 512 S.E.2d 468 (1999) (parties not bound by findings regarding effect of reconciliation on agreement made at temporary spousal support hearing).

20. When divorce fails to occur because the parties reconcile, there is a good chance that at least part of the agreement has become invalid. *See* **§ 4.074**. When divorce fails to occur because of death, lack of jurisdiction, or other reasons, the cases reach different results. *See* **§ 4.08**.

of law. Thus, if the attacking party can show a sufficient basis for reopening a final judgment, the judgment and the agreement can both be set aside.[21]

Grounds for Reopening

The grounds for reopening a judgment vary somewhat from state to state. A majority of states have a state statute or rule of civil procedure that sets forth the grounds, usually based upon Federal Rule of Civil Procedure 60(b).[22] A minority of states follow common law principles.[23] The potential bases for reopening under the statutes and rules are generally similar those available at common law, so the various bases are discussed together in this section.

The bases for reopening a judgment approving a separation agreement are generally similar to the available grounds for attacking the agreement under contract law. Indeed, a fair number of cases resolve attacks on approved agreements without distinguishing between bases for reopening the judgment and grounds for attacking the contract.[24]

Nevertheless, differences do exist between the bases for reopening a judgment and the grounds for attacking a contract. The bases for reopening are universally stricter; indeed, some states formally hold that to reopen a judgment, the moving party first must prove a successful defense on the merits.[25] In the separation agreement context, that means a ground for setting the agreement aside under contract law.

---

21. *See* Morris v. Horn, 219 P.3d 198, 204 (Alaska 2009) ("Generally, if a party to a property settlement seeks relief from a dissolution decree into which the settlement is incorporated, the party must request relief under Civil Rule 60(b)[.]").

22. FED. R. CIV. P. 60(b) (Westlaw 2008).

23. *E.g.*, Ellett v. Ellett, 35 Va. App. 97, 542 S.E.2d 816 (2001).

24. *See, e.g.*, Elliott v. Elliott, 667 So. 2d 116 (Ala. Ct. App. 1995) (setting aside incorporated agreement for fraud and duress); Billington v. Billington, 27 Conn. App. 466, 606 A.2d 737 (1992) (fraud); Cerniglia v. Cerniglia, 679 So. 2d 1160 (Fla. 1996) (judgment can be reopened for duress or coercion, but motion must be filed within one year of judgment); Goodstein v. Goodstein, 649 So. 2d 273 (Fla. Dist. Ct. App. 1995) (duress and undue influence); *In re* Marriage of Shaner, 252 Ill. App. 3d 146, 624 N.E.2d 1217 (1993) (fraud and mistake); Murphy v. Murphy, 212 A.D.2d 583, 622 N.Y.S.2d 755 (1995) (fraud); Peterson v. Peterson, 555 N.W.2d 359 (N.D. 1996) (undue influence); Kelley v. Kelley, 248 Va. 295, 449 S.E.2d 55 (1994) (waiver of child support, which was void as against public policy); *see also* Pate v. Pate, 874 S.W.2d 186 (Tex. Ct. App. 1994) (judgment can be reformed for mutual mistake in incorporated agreement, but not on the facts of the instant case). *Cf.* United States v. Baus, 834 F.2d 1114 (1st Cir. 1987) (citing long line of federal cases holding that material breach of settlement agreement incorporated into court order, in nondomestic litigation, is a sufficient basis for reopening the judgment).

25. *See* Kellman v. Kellman, 162 A.D.2d 958, 559 N.Y.S.2d 49 (1990) (where attacking spouse sought only to reopen judgment, and did not allege that incorporated contract was invalid under contract law, judgment could not be reopened); *In re* Marriage of Rosevear, 65 Cal. App. 4th 673, 76 Cal. Rptr. 2d 691 (1998) (where judgment approving agreement was actually fair, so that court would reach similar result even in the absence of an agreement, judgment could not be reopened).

The following discussion is organized generally along the same lines as the defenses discussed in §§ **4.05–4.06**. For each defense, it lists the *additional* elements necessary to use that defense as the grounds for setting aside a judgment approving a separation agreement.

Duress and Undue Influence. If an agreement was a product of duress, and the attacking party can establish that the misconduct continued through the approval of the agreement by the court, the judgment can be set aside.[26]

Lack of Capacity. If one spouse deliberately took advantage of the other's incapacity, that would be a classic fact pattern showing sufficient undue influence, which is generally deemed sufficient misconduct to reopen a judgment.[27] If one spouse was aware of the other's incapacity and failed to inform the court, the lack of disclosure might well be sufficient to constitute extrinsic fraud to reopen the judgment. If one spouse lacked capacity to contract and the other spouse was unaware of it, reopening the judgment might theoretically be difficult, but the standard of lack of capacity is so high—complete inability to understand the substance of the transaction[28]—that it is very difficult to conceal. The only case to consider the issue in recent years suggested that lack of capacity did not analyze the issue in terms of the traditional basis for reopening, but suggested strongly that a judgment approving an agreement can be reopened if one spouse lacked capacity to contract.[29]

Mistake. Judgments can almost always be opened for a clerical mistake by the court. Judgments can be reopened for a substantive mistake by the parties only if the mistake

---

26. *See* Rothschild v. Devos, 757 N.E.2d 219, 224 n.9 (Ind. Ct. App. 2001) ("Duress and undue influence could presumably be grounds for relief from judgment under T.R. 60(B)(3) as 'other misconduct of an adverse party[.]' "); Lowrey v. Lowrey, 919 So. 2d 1112 (Miss. Ct. App. 2005) (error to deny motion to reopen judgment approving one-sided agreement that resulted from overreaching; husband threatened to take children and run wife out of town if she retained counsel and litigated the divorce).

In *Ellett*, 35 Va. App. at 102, 542 S.E.2d at 818, the court held that "claims based on duress, undue influence and unconscionability, all involve challenges to the agreement that could have been raised during the divorce proceeding, and do not involve 'extrinsic' fraud, or fraud upon the court." This is terribly confused language, for duress and undue influence are independent bases for attack upon a judgment, regardless of whether fraud was committed. If one party signed the agreement at gunpoint, and the innocent spouse was too intimidated to object when the agreement was approved by a court order, did the court really mean to suggest that the agreement could not be attacked? The general rule nationwide is that duress and undue influence are sufficient bases for reopening a judgment.

27. *Id.*

28. *See* § **2.02**.

29. *See Rothschild*, 757 N.E.2d at 224.

was mutual,[30] and not if it was unilateral.[31] Relief is also available only for a limited time period after the judgment was entered.[32]

Fraud. State rules based on the federal model[33] usually allow a judgment to be reopened for any type of fraud for a limited period after the judgment is entered. The period is one year under the federal rule; it can be either longer or shorter under state counterparts. The time period usually runs from the date of the judgment, regardless of whether the victim knew or reasonably could have known that fraud was committed.

After the relevant time period has passed, the judgment cannot be set aside for fraud under the rule.[34] But the state rules do not generally replace the common law of reopening judgments; rather, they supplement that law with additional provisions.[35]

In states that follow the common law, and in states that have a rule of civil procedure where the time limit has expired, the ability to attack a judgment for fraud is limited. One group of states allows the judgment be reopened only for extrinsic fraud.[36] In theory, extrinsic fraud is fraud that denies a party the chance to present an argument to the court.[37] Extrinsic fraud is distinguished from intrinsic fraud, the giving of false

---

30. *See, e.g.*, Nardecchia v. Nardecchia, 155 Ohio App. 3d 40, 798 N.E.2d 1198 (2003) (mutual mistake in valuing both parties' retirement benefits); Richard v. Boggs, 162 P.3d 629 (Alaska 2007) (mutual false assumption that home could be saved from risk of foreclosure only by awarding it outright to husband).

In Peter v. Peter, 262 Neb. 1017, 637 N.W.2d 865 (2002), the court suggested that mathematical error by both parties, their counsel, and the court was not a sufficient basis to reopen a judgment. The court's suggestion is contrary to a significant body of case law nationwide reopening judgments for mutual mistake. On the facts, where the error involved only $2,256 out of a marital estate of over $600,000, a reasonable basis obviously existed for denying relief. But *Peter* should not be read as precedent for denying relief in future cases where the mistake is mutual and the amount involved is material.

31. *E.g.*, Richards v. Richards, 78 Conn. App. 734, 829 A.2d 60 (2003). *But see* Keysa v. Sieber, 113 Ohio App. 3d 572, 681 N.E.2d 949 (1996) (inadvertent mathematical error by one party's counsel was sufficient excusable neglect to justify reopening the judgment).

32. *E.g.*, Salemi v. Salemi, 972 So. 2d 1 (Miss. Ct. App. 2007) (motion to reopen for mistake was untimely more than six months after judgment was granted); Melkerson v. Melkerson, 2009 WL 4547774 (Ohio Ct. App. 2009) (refusing to allow a remedy for mutual mistake in drafting agreement, as time period for reopening a judgment for mistake had expired).

33. FED. R. CIV. P. 60(b) (Westlaw 2008).

34. *E.g.*, Trim v. Trim, 2009 WL 1058630 (Miss. Ct. App. 2009), *cert. granted*, 20 So. 3d 680 (Miss. 2009).

35. *See generally* 3 TURNER, *supra* note 16, § 9:30, at 132–33.

36. *See, e.g.*, In re Marriage of Turner, 803 S.W.2d 655 (Mo. Ct. App. 1991); *In re* Marriage of Doyle, 280 Mont. 429, 929 P.2d 886 (1996) (after time limit, decree can be reopened only for extrinsic fraud); Gainey v. Gainey, 382 S.C. 414, 675 S.E.2d 792 (Ct. App. 2009); *Black*, 166 S.W.3d 699; Ellett v. Ellett, 35 Va. App. 97, 542 S.E.2d 816 (2001).

37. *E.g.*, *Black*, 166 S.W.3d 699; *but cf. Gainey*, 382 S.C. at 426, 675 S.E.2d at 798 (extrinsic fraud is fraud that could not have been discovered in the course of the action itself, which normally requires a least some out-of-court conduct) For extended discussion of the distinction between extrinsic and intrinsic fraud, as applied in property division cases, *see* 3 TURNER, *supra* note 16, § 9:30.

testimony before the court. Intrinsic fraud is generally not a sufficient basis for attacking a judgment under common law principles.

A good example of extrinsic fraud is *Liberoff v. Liberoff*.[38] In that case, the parties signed a separation agreement on March 6. The wife threatened to retain counsel and attack the agreement, and the husband offered to give her additional value if she did not retain counsel to protect her interests. The wife agreed, and the bargain was expressed in a written contract signed March 9. The wife then left for a foreign country, in accordance with longstanding plans. While she was away, the husband presented the March 6 agreement for incorporation, while omitting all mention of the March 9 agreement. The divorce decree became final before the wife discovered the husband's conduct. The trial court granted judgment on the pleadings against the wife's action for breach of the March 9 agreement, but the appellate court reversed. The court expressly held that extrinsic fraud is an exception to the general rule of res judicata, and since the wife had pled a prima facie case of extrinsic fraud, judgment on the pleadings was improper.

Another example of extrinsic fraud is *Ray v. Ray*.[39] There, the wife sold her pharmacy shortly before the divorce. The transaction included a sales agreement and a covenant not to compete, each giving the wife a substantial lump sum. The wife disclosed the sales agreement, but "deliberately concealed [the noncompete agreement] in response to discovery requests and during depositions."[40] More importantly, she instructed the buyer to delay the $130,000 payment under the covenant until after the divorce, an out-of-court action that reduced the ability of the husband to discover the deception. After the decree became final, however, the husband learned the truth and moved to reopen the judgment. The court held that the noncompliance with discovery was intrinsic fraud. The delay in payment was extrinsic fraud, however, and on that basis the decree was reopened.

In addition to permitting reopening for extrinsic fraud, some states permits reopening for fraud upon the court.[41] The precise definition of fraud upon the court varies, but the concept is not taken so literally that any fraud in the court's presence, including mere perjury, is sufficient. At a minimum, the fraud must involve sufficient out-of-court actions to be distinguishable from mere perjury.[42]

The common law extrinsic-intrinsic distinction is coming under increasing attack by commentators on civil procedure generally. The leading treatise on federal civil procedure, for example, argues that the distinction is a product of misread precedent, and

---

38. 711 So. 2d 1333 (Fla. Dist. Ct. App. 1998).

39. 374 S.C. 79, 647 S.E.2d 237 (2007).

40. *Id.* at 82, 647 S.E.2d at 238–39.

41. *See, e.g.*, Wise v. Nirider, 261 Mont. 310, 862 P.2d 1128 (1993) (once time limit passes, judgment can be reopened only for fraud on the court, and not mere fraud on the opposing party). *But cf.* Lopez v. Lopez, 627 So. 2d 108 (Fla. Dist. Ct. App. 1993) (judgment cannot be reopened even for fraud on the court, where fraud was committed by both parties).

42. *E.g.*, Rocca v. Rocca, 760 N.E.2d 677, 681 (Ind. Ct. App. 2002) (husband's out-of-court conspiracy with his father to hide his ownership of two parcels of land was fraud on the court; plan was more than mere perjury, and "prevented Wife from fully presenting her case for a share of the interest in the properties"); Shaw v. Shaw, 985 So. 2d 346, 350 (Miss. Ct. App. 2007) ("Allegations of non disclosure in pretrial discovery will not support an action for fraud on the court[.]").

urges the federal courts to abolish it completely.[43] The trend in federal court is to grant relief for any "grave miscarriage of justice,"[44] without placing controlling weight upon the extrinsic or intrinsic nature of the fraud involved.

The strict extrinsic-intrinsic distinction has reached outrageous results in many areas of law, and family law has certainly been among them. The fundamental problem is that the distinction between extrinsic and intrinsic fraud has very little to do with the seriousness of the underlying misconduct or the harm inflicted upon the innocent spouse. Judgments can be reopened for relatively minor episodes of fraud if fraud occurred outside of the court's presence; judgment cannot be reopened for fraud that wrecks the victim's financial condition if the fraud consists primarily of perjury. In many situations, the net effect of the extrinsic-intrinsic distinction is to reward spouses who commit outrageous acts of fraud, if they are clever enough to prevent the victim from learning of the fraud until after the time period for raising intrinsic fraud has passed.

A good demonstration of the problem is the *Ray* case. As noted above, the wife in that case deliberately concealed $130,000 in marital property in responses to discovery requests. The court held that this fraud was merely intrinsic, and therefore not a sufficient basis for reopening the judgment. The court so held even though the wife had deliberately lied in discovery responses, for the purpose of hiding $130,000 from the husband. The authors suspect that the citizens of South Carolina would react with dismay and outrage upon being told that there is no remedy against a spouse who deliberately lies in discovery responses, if the fraud is not discovered until after the divorce judgment has become final.

Ray had a good ending, as the wife also instructed the buyer to delay paying the $130,000 until after the divorce was over. In a 3–2 decision, the court held that the instruction was extrinsic fraud, and the decree was therefore reopened. The dissent argued that the instruction to delay did not make a difference, and the dissent was probably technically correct. By any standard, the wife's deliberate false statement in discovery was many times worse than her instruction to buyer to delay payment. But this is exactly the sort of situation that the extrinsic-intrinsic distinction encourages: a minor episode of technically extrinsic fraud taking priority over a much more serious episode of technically intrinsic fraud.

To the extent that the majority stretched the law to grant relief in *Ray*, the authors applaud it for doing so. But the better basis would have been to abolish the extrinsic-intrinsic distinction altogether, and hold instead that a judgment can be reopened for any fraud, either extrinsic or intrinsic, when failure to reopen would be a grave miscarriage of justice. It is hard to imagine a graver miscarriage of justice than a deliberate false statement made in a discovery response. Allowing such a statement to go without remedy strikes directly at the fundamental fairness of the entire court system.

A defender of the extrinsic-intrinsic distinction might respond that the courts will be swamped with motions to reopen judgments if intrinsic fraud is recognized. This is

---

43. CHARLES ALAN WRIGHT, ARTHUR R. MILLER & MARY KAY KANE, FEDERAL PRACTICE AND PROCEDURE § 2868 (2d ed. Westlaw 2008).

44. *E.g.*, United States v. Beggerly, 524 U.S. 38, 47 (1998).

a quite a cynical response; it argues that intrinsic fraud is so common and widespread that the law cannot afford to provide a remedy. Very little hard evidence has been cited in support of this belief. In states that do allow motions to reopen for technically intrinsic fraud[45] if the fraud is sufficiently serious, the courts have clearly not found themselves beset with motions to reopen. There is every reason to believe that serious intrinsic fraud is highly uncommon, and that providing a remedy would not unduly strain the courts.

A good example of why the courts would not necessarily be overburdened if a remedy existed for serious intrinsic fraud is *Shaw v. Shaw.*[46] The husband in *Shaw* failed to disclose his 401(k) plan in the correct place on his financial affidavit. But he did mention the plan in another place, and he provided the wife with W-2 forms that clearly showed deductions for the plan. The court summarily held that nondisclosure in discovery was not fraud on the court, but it then held in the alternative that the wife "had ample opportunity to become aware of the 401K account prior to entering the property settlement agreement,"[47] so that no fraud was committed. *Shaw* suggests that in many cases denying a remedy for intrinsic fraud, the record may well be sufficient to deny relief upon a stronger and better ground, including especially the failure of the victimized spouse to utilize the discovery process or take other reasonable measures for self-protection.

Assuming for argument that the courts do not have sufficient resources to provide a remedy for every case of intrinsic fraud, the extrinsic-intrinsic distinction is a very poor way to allocate whatever limited amount of resources are available. If the courts can afford to provide remedy in only some cases, one would think that the most important fact would be the *amount* of harm inflicted upon the victim. It is unacceptably arbitrary to allow a remedy for technically extrinsic fraud that inflicts only limited harm, while allowing no remedy for technically intrinsic fraud that inflicts major damage. One would also think that limited resources should be applied first to those who have taken reasonable measures to protect themselves, as this will encourage all divorce litigants to be on their guard against future misconduct. The extrinsic-intrinsic distinction places insufficient importance upon these factors, and allocates limited judicial resources among multiple motion to reopen in a way that is ultimately arbitrary and irrational.

A growing number of states have accepted this argument and rejected the distinction between extrinsic and intrinsic fraud, by either statute,[48] rule,[49] or court decision.[50]

---

45. *See infra* notes 48–50.

46. 985 So. 2d 346.

47. *Id.* at 350.

48. *E.g.,* Cal. Fam. Code §§ 2100–2129 (Westlaw 2008); Mont. Code § 40-4-253(5) (Westlaw 2008) (extended five-year period for relief based on fraudulent financial statement).

49. *E.g.,* Fla. R. Civ. P. 1.540(b) (time limit on raising fraud in divorce cases does not apply to claims based on fraudulent financial affidavit in divorce cases).

50. *See* Terwilliger v. Terwilliger, 64 S.W.3d 816 (Ky. 2002); Sahin v. Sahin, 435 Mass. 396, 758 N.E.2d 132 (2001); Zaino v. Zaino, 818 A.2d 630 (R.I. 2003).

The distinction is mostly commonly replaced with a standard placing primary emphasis upon the severity of the fraud, in the same manner as the federal standard.

It should be stressed that even in states that allow remedy for intrinsic fraud, one generally cannot allege a case of such fraud simply by making an unsupported claim that a witness testified falsely. Final judgments are entitled to presumption of correctness, and a motion that simply seeks to relitigate the same issues, based on the same evidence, is never sufficient. Most of the cases granting a remedy for intrinsic fraud have involved situations like *Ray*, in which a spouse learns after the fact that a significant asset was deliberately concealed or seriously undervalued, and presents substantial evidence of deliberate and intentional fraud. In these cases, allowing the judgment to stand would inflict grave financial harm upon a innocent spouse. Even where the fraud is intrinsic, the better policy is to provide a remedy.

Unconscionability. It is very difficult, if not functionally impossible, to set an agreement aside for unconscionability alone after the agreement has been approved by a final judgment.[51] Unconscionability will almost always be an argument that could have been raised in the proceedings that led to the final judgment. To reopen that judgment, the moving party must show some valid reason why unconscionability was not argued initially—essentially one of the procedural bases discussed earlier in this section.

Unfairness. For essentially the same reasons as unconscionability, unfairness alone is never a sufficient basis for reopening a final judgment.

Void Judgment. A judgment can be reopened at any time if it contains a defect so substantial as to render it void. This rule has been applied to judgments incorporating agreements that divide benefits that cannot be divided by contract[52] and to a qualified domestic relations order that was plainly inconsistent with the terms of a prior consent order dividing retirement benefits.[53]

---

51. *See* Ellett v. Ellett, 35 Va. App. 97, 102, 542 S.E.2d 816, 818 (2001) (judgment cannot be reopened on basis that approved agreement is unconscionable). *But see* Crawford v. Crawford, 524 N.W.2d 833, 836 (N.D. 1994) ("Just as courts will not enforce an agreement that is illegal, so too courts should vacate judgments that are unconscionable[.]"); Cliche v. Cliche, 143 Vt. 301, 466 A.2d 314 (1983) (likewise allowing reopening of judgment based upon unconscionable stipulation).

52. *E.g., In re* Marriage of Hulstrom, 342 Ill. App. 3d 262, 794 N.E.2d 980 (2003) (social security benefits). The question of whether specific types of benefits can be divided by contract is discussed in **§ 3.04**. Almost all benefits can be so divided, but there are a few critical exceptions, such as the social security benefits at issue in *Hulstrom*.

53. *See* Hayward v. Hayward, 808 A.2d 232 (Pa. Super. Ct. 2002).

For a general discussion of QDROs, *see* BRETT R. TURNER, EQUITABLE DISTRIBUTION OF PROPERTY §§ 6:18-6:19 (3d ed. 2005).

Defenses

Ratification. Where grounds to reopen exist, a spouse who knows or should know of those grounds has a duty to request relief promptly. Where unreasonable delay is present, the delay may render a motion to reopen untimely.[54]

Procedure

Remarriage. If sufficient grounds to reopen a judgment are proven, the financial provisions of the judgment can be reopened even if one spouse has remarried.[55]

Subsequent Modification. Where res judicata prevents an attack upon an original agreement, it obviously does not prevent attack upon a later addendum or other modification to the agreement that has not yet been reviewed by a court.[56] If a subsequent modification is valid under the principles set forth in **§ 6.07**, the modification can be enforced without moving to reopen the original judgment.[57]

§ 4.03 Confidential Relationship

Before determining the validity of any separation agreement, it is important to consider whether the parties had a confidential relationship at the time the agreement was negotiated and signed. The existence of such a relationship does not automatically invalidate the agreement, any more than the nonexistence of such a relationship will automatically uphold it. The various common law contract defenses, however, are applied more strictly when the relationship is confidential. In particular, courts are more prone to find that borderline coercive tactics amount to undue influence; indeed, some jurisdictions will even presume undue influence when the agreement is unfair and a confidential relationship is present. *See* **§ 4.052**. The duty to disclose material facts is also stronger when a confidential relationship is present. *See* **§ 4.053**. Because the existence of a confidential relationship is relevant to a number of different specific defenses, case law addressing the issue is discussed in this section, regardless of which specific defense the court was applying.

---

54. *See generally* **§ 4.073**; *see also* Walker v. Walker, 211 S.W.3d 232 (Tenn. Ct. App. 2006) (where wife alleged that court reporter did not record important provision in agreement read onto the record in open court, but waited four months after decree to raise the issue, trial court did not err in refusing to grant relief).

55. *In re* Marriage of Whitman, 81 Ohio St. 3d 329, 690 N.E.2d 535 (1998). The court did note that remarriage is one factor weighing against the granting of a motion to reopen.

56. Quinn v. Schipper, 180 Vt. 572, 908 A.2d 413 (2006). If the rule were otherwise, a husband "could fraudulently induce wife to enter into an addendum years later and gain the benefit of his fraud, leaving wife with no power to prevent it or seek review by the court because the agreement is not subject to collateral attack." *Id.* at 576, 908 A.2d at 419.

57. *See* Morris v. Horn, 219 P.3d 198 (Alaska 2009).

Majority Rule: Issue of Fact

In the great majority of states, whether a confidential relationship exists is a question of fact.[58] The spouses obviously enjoy such a relationship before the marital breakdown. "Agreements between spouses, unlike ordinary business contracts, involve a fiduciary relationship requiring the utmost of good faith."[59] At some point before the final divorce, however, the parties' relationship loses its confidential status and becomes adversarial. To determine whether a confidential relation existed during negotiation of the agreement, the court must determine whether this point in time had already occurred.

Presence of Counsel

In determining when the parties' relationship changed from confidential to adversarial, the most important evidence is the existence of independent counsel. When both parties begin bargaining at arm's length through such counsel, the confidential relationship generally ends.[60]

One Attorney for Both Spouses. When both parties are represented by the same lawyer, the confidential relationship may or may not continue. A North Carolina court noted:

> [T]he involvement of an attorney does not automatically end the confidential relationship of husband and wife. Where, as here, one spouse alleges and offers evidence that the confidential relationship still existed and that the attorney's role was merely to record the agreement the spouses negotiated, it is a question of fact as to whether the confidential relationship has been terminated.[61]

Thus, where the attorney is a neutral scrivener, the confidential relationship may continue.

Courts disfavor the practice of both parties using a single attorney, and they are quick to find that a confidential relationship existed. For instance, in *Blum v. Blum*,[62] the parties used a single attorney to draft their agreement. The husband was the dominant spouse during the marriage, however, and the evidence showed that he dictated

---

58. Blum v. Blum, 59 Md. App. 584, 477 A.2d 289 (1984).

59. Christian v. Christian, 42 N.Y.2d 63, 365 N.E.2d 849, 396 N.Y.S.2d 817, 823 (1977).

60. *See, e.g.*, Barnes v. Barnes, 231 Va. 39, 340 S.E.2d 803 (1986) (citing the cases); Petracca v. Petracca, 706 So. 2d 904 (Fla. Dist. Ct. App. 1998); *In re* Marriage of Turner, 803 S.W.2d 655, 661 (Mo. Ct. App. 1991) (parties had been separated for 14 months and each of them had counsel; no confidential relationship); Applebaum v. Applebaum, 93 Nev. 382, 566 P.2d 85 (1977); Avriett v. Avriett, 88 N.C. App. 506, 363 S.E.2d 875 (1988), *aff'd mem.*, 322 N.C. 468, 368 S.E.2d 377 (1988) (where wife had her own independent attorney, no confidential relationship).

61. Harroff v. Harroff, 100 N.C. App. 686, 398 S.E.2d 340, 343–44 (1990), *cert. denied*, 328 N.C. 330, 402 S.E.2d 833 (1991); *see also* Sidden v. Mailman, 137 N.C. App. 669, 678, 529 S.E.2d 266, 272 (2000) ("Representation by an attorney does not automatically end the confidential relationship of the spouses if the attorney's role was merely to record the agreement the spouses agreed to while living in the confidential relationship[.]").

62. 59 Md. App. 584, 477 A.2d 289 (1984).

the agreement to the attorney. At no point did the attorney discuss with the wife the possibility of a conflict of interest, or suggest that she obtain independent counsel. The court held that a confidential relationship still existed. The court also suggested that an attorney who represents both parties to a divorce action may be acting unethically.

One Spouse Unrepresented. A similar fact situation occurs when one spouse has counsel and the other does not. This situation presents clear opportunities for abuse, and courts tend to find that a confidential relationship still existed. For example, in *Selke v. Selke*,[63] only the husband was represented by counsel. There was no evidence that the wife was told of the need to retain counsel, and she expressly testified that she believed that the husband's lawyer was representing both parties' interests. The husband did not disclose the value of his retirement benefits to the wife, and as a result she signed an unfair agreement. The court implicitly held that the confidential relationship still existed, and set the agreement aside on grounds of constructive fraud.

Likewise, in *Tenneboe v. Tenneboe*,[64] the wife had counsel and the husband had none. Instead of clearly telling the husband to retain his own attorney, counsel for the wife gave him legal advice that was either oversimplified or erroneous. In particular, the attorney failed to clearly tell the husband that spousal support can be modified only for changed circumstances. The court held that the parties continued to have a confidential relationship.

The key fact in the above cases is that the unrepresented party was not told of the conflict of interest and advised to seek independent counsel. In any one-attorney situation where such advice is not given, the court is likely to find that a confidential relationship still existed. The key to drafting an enforceable agreement in a one-attorney case, therefore, is to preserve clear documentation that the opposing spouse was repeatedly and bluntly advised to seek independent counsel. Such advice should be given in writing, in a letter sent by registered mail. The advice should further be expressly acknowledged, again in very blunt terms, in the agreement itself.

When these precautions are taken, there is a good chance that a confidential relationship will not exist.[65] Otherwise, a party could force the continuance of the confidential relationship simply by refusing to obtain counsel. If there is any possibility that the lack of counsel resulted from ignorance rather than voluntary informed choice, however, the confidential relationship is likely to continue.

When an unrepresented party engages in actual bargaining, some courts will overlook the lack of counsel. In *In re Marriage of Auble*,[66] the wife had moved to another city and was living with another man while the parties negotiated their agreement. The

---

63. 569 N.E.2d 724 (Ind. Ct. App. 1991).

64. 558 So. 2d 470 (Fla. Dist. Ct. App. 1990).

65. *See* Lancaster v. Lancaster, 138 N.C. App. 459, 464, 530 S.E.2d 82, 85 (2000) (no confidential relationship even though wife lacked counsel, where parties argued over terms of agreement, agreement stated that husband's attorney represented only husband, husband's attorney refused to give wife legal advice, and attorney's "paralegal advised [wife] to seek her own counsel before signing the separation agreement").

66. 125 Or. App. 554, 866 P.2d 1239 (1993).

husband had counsel, the wife had none, and there was no evidence that the wife was ever advised to seek an attorney. Indeed, there was some evidence that the husband told the wife she did not need an attorney. In view of the geographical distance and the actual bargaining that occurred, the court held that there was no confidential relationship. The authors are troubled by wife's lack of counsel, which apparently resulted to some extent from the husband's own assurances. If that lack of counsel contributed in any way to the signing of the agreement, the agreement should have been reviewed carefully for unfairness.

Why do divorcing parties persist in retaining a single lawyer to represent both of their interests? The answer is a combination of economics and ignorance. Retaining one attorney is certainly cheaper, and there is notion in the public mind that separation agreements are simple documents that do not require extensive review. *The authors urge every nonlawyer reading this book to abandon that notion.* In our years of family law practice, we have seen a large number of cases where the court enforced an unfair agreement. In the overwhelming majority of these cases, the disadvantaged party either lacked counsel or did not have the agreement fully reviewed. There are literally a thousand ways in which an experienced attorney can slip extremely damaging language into a separation agreement. Support provisions can be set too high and made nonmodifiable; clauses that appear to give enforceable rights can be carefully qualified into an unenforceable agreement to agree; material protective provisions can be omitted entirely. Separation agreements are more complicated that the public understands, and in most cases they establish the very foundation of the parties' postdivorce lives. Because of the complexity and importance of these agreements, there is no substitute for review by independent counsel with experience in the field of domestic relations. It is often said that a lawyer who represents himself has a fool for a client. That conclusion applies even more strongly to a spouse who not an attorney.

Attorney Spouses. The case for a confidential relationship can be particularly strong when one spouse is an attorney and the other has no independent counsel. In *Webb v. Webb*,[67] the husband was an attorney. During the course of negotiating the agreement, he gave the wife legal advice on various aspects of the divorce, and he actively discouraged her from obtaining independent counsel. The court held:

> When husband advised wife on legal matters he acted as an attorney as well as a party. Husband had "superior knowledge of financial affairs" that put him in a "greatly superior" position during the negotiation of the agreement. . . . Husband's position as attorney and advisor placed him in the category of one who continues in a "special relationship" with the wife. As such, husband had an affirmative duty to make a full disclosure to wife as to the value of the [marital assets] and to inform her that she was entitled to have her rights and equities in those assets determined in accordance with [the equitable distribution statute.][68]

---

67. 16 Va. App. 486, 431 S.E.2d 55 (1993).
68. 431 S.E.2d at 60.

The court held that the husband had not met this duty of disclosure, and that the agreement was accordingly invalid.[69]

Other Factors

While the presence or absence of counsel is the most important fact to be considered in determining whether the parties' relationship was confidential, courts look to other types of evidence as well.

Prior Dealings between the Parties. Where one spouse has dominated the other throughout the marriage, the court is more likely to find a confidential relationship. A spouse who has insisted upon the other spouse's blind trust throughout the marriage will have a harder time arguing that such trust was not appropriate during the negotiation of a separation agreement.[70]

Disadvantaged Spouse's Emotional Condition. Courts are more likely to find a confidential relationship when the disadvantaged spouse suffered from emotional weaknesses that hindered his or her ability to be self-reliant. Such weaknesses are not, however, alone sufficient to create a confidential relationship.[71]

Minority Rule: Always Confidential

A small minority of states hold that the husband-wife relationship is confidential as a matter of law.[72] In these states, no matter how adversarial the parties' relationship becomes in fact, the parties still have a duty to act with regard to the other spouse's welfare. Thus, these states generally recognize a duty to disclose at least the major marital assets. *See* § **4.053**. In addition, undue influence is somewhat easier to prove in these jurisdictions. *See* § **4.052**.

The minority rule is inconsistent with reality, and better results are reached under the majority position. There are certainly some cases in which separating parties actually have a confidential relationship. But in a majority of cases, the parties negotiate their separation agreement at arm's length, through independent counsel, in an adversarial manner. It would be safe to say that in many of these cases, if not a clear majority, the parties' relationship is to some degree acrimonious. Why should the law assume

---

69. For additional cases holding that a confidential relationship existed where one spouse was an attorney, *see* Cook v. Cook, 112 Nev. 179, 912 P.2d 264 (1996); Williams v. Waldman, 108 Nev. 466, 836 P.2d 614 (1992); *see also* Nessler v. Nessler, 387 Ill. App. 3d 1103, 1111, 902 N.E.2d 701, 708 (2008) (where nonattorney wife alleged that attorney husband gave her advice regarding Illinois divorce law; case remanded to determine whether confidential relationship existed).

70. *See* Blum v. Blum, 59 Md. App. 584, 477 A.2d 289 (1984) (confidential relationship existed; court noted that husband was dominant spouse throughout marriage).

71. *See* Drewry v. Drewry, 8 Va. App. 460, 383 S.E.2d 12, 17 (1989) (although "wife's emotional condition is, indeed, a factor which the trial court must consider," wife's "emotional condition alone did not give rise to a fiduciary relationship between the estranged spouses").

72. *See In re* Marriage of Bowers, 143 Or. App. 24, 922 P.2d 722 (1996). This rule is particularly common in community property jurisdictions. *See* McCarroll v. McCarroll, 701 So. 2d 1280 (La. 1997).

that the parties in these cases have a confidential relationship, when their relationship in fact is so clearly different? Courts following this rule to date have tended to rely upon a broad assumption that all marital relationships are confidential. When the parties are separated, however, this broad assumption is often untrue. No court has yet explained the cognitive dissonance between the broad presumption of the law and the actual state of the parties' relationship in most broken marriages.

Is there any policy basis for assuming that an acrimonious marital relationship is actually confidential? There are certainly valid reasons for imposing upon both parties a broad duty to disclose marital assets. Those reasons do not, however, depend upon whether the parties' relationship is confidential or adversarial. They depend instead upon the strong policy against concealment of assets in divorce cases. Some states following the majority rule have imposed such a duty by enacting a court rule requiring each party to file a financial statement signed under oath. *See* **§ 4.052**. These rules create a broad duty to disclose, without making the courts pretend that an adversarial relationship is confidential.

The other major practical effect of a confidential relationship is to make undue influence easier to prove. *See* **§ 4.052**. The effect arises from the common observation that undue influence is easier to accomplish in the setting of a confidential relationship. But such influence is not easier merely because the law deems marriage to be confidential; it is easier only in those fact situations where the relationship is *functionally* confidential. Rules of undue influence aimed at functionally confidential relationships should not be applied to marriages that are functionally adversarial. Such application makes undue influence too easy to prove, and therefore invalidates at least some agreements that were signed voluntarily by the parties.

If the point of the rule is to encourage spouses negotiating agreements to act as if their relationship were confidential, the law is standing bravely in the path of an onrushing train. Parties do not initiate divorce proceedings unless their relationship is in serious trouble. A certain amount of dissension and acrimony is therefore inevitable in divorce cases. To expect parties to divorce cases to behave as if they had a genuinely confidential relationship is to impose a burden that most divorcing parties cannot meet.

A better way to handle the acrimony of divorcing parties is to channel it constructively into the settlement process. Through over 100 years of litigating divorce cases, the law has learned that the best resolution to a contested divorce case is a negotiated settlement. The best way to encourage such settlement, without going so far as to enforce unfair agreements, is to empower to parties to negotiate with one another as equals. The arm's-length bargaining process produces much better settlements than any court could ever impose.

The minority rule, however, unduly burdens the adversarial process. When spouses reach a fairly negotiated agreement through adversarial bargaining, the courts should respect that agreement. Any other approach effectively invites the court to second-guess the parties' own judgment as to a fair settlement—a practice that destroys much of the benefit to private agreements. When the court applies confidential relationship rules in the context of a factually adversarial relationship, it is interfering with the parties' ability to reach their own desired bargain.

The authors fully recognize the very real need for court review of separation agreements, but there is no valid basis for presuming across the board that all divorcing parties have a confidential relationship. The better approach is the majority rule, which recognizes such a relationship only where it exists on the facts.

§ 4.04 Review by the Court

§ 4.041 Court Approval

At the very foundation of the law on validity of separation agreements lies a significant split in authority. In a majority of states, separation agreements are presumptively enforceable in the same manner as any other contract. In a minority of states, separation agreements are not enforceable as contracts until they have been approved by the court.

Approval Required

The minority position was first adopted long ago, when women were dependent on men and unable to negotiate contracts as equals. To prevent men from taking advantage of women unfairly, the law often required women to obtain special approval of certain agreements. Some states required approval by a notary or other certification official;[73] that requirement evolved into the modern acknowledgment requirement discussed in § 2.07. Other states required approval by the court; that requirement evolved in the rule discussed in the present section.

The traditional justification for the minority rule is no longer valid, of course, as women are not longer unable as a class to negotiate equally with men. Modern courts tend to justify the rule by citing the important role of the state in overseeing marriage and divorce,[74] or by claiming that the parties cannot by agreement control how the court resolves property division and spousal support issues.[75]

---

73. *E.g.*, N.C. GEN. STAT. § 52-6 (repealed 1978) ("[N]or shall any separation agreement between husband and wife be valid . . . unless [it] is acknowledged before a certifying officer who shall make a private examination of the wife. . . .").

74. *See, e.g.*, Cloutier v. Cloutier, 814 A.2d 979, 982 (Me. 2003) ("This is not a general civil matter where the parties are ordinarily free to enter into any agreement so long as it is not coerced. Rather, this is a family matter, where the court is called upon to exercise its authority in equity, and may be required to act as parens patriae if children are involved[.]"); Gorman v. Gorman, 883 A.2d 732, 737 (R.I. 2005) ("As a result of the fundamental difference between ordinary business contracts and spousal agreements, family courts should and do monitor such agreements with special attention and with a concern for the equities of the situation[.]"); Pouech v. Pouech, 180 Vt. 1, 12, 904 A.2d 70, 77–78 (2006) ("an agreement in anticipation of divorce is not the same as any ordinary contract . . . the family court has a statutorily authorized role to play in divorce proceedings to assure a fair and equitable dissolution of the state-sanctioned institution of marriage"); Hottenroth v. Hetsko, 298 Wis. 2d 200, 216, 727 N.W.2d 38, 46 (Ct. App. 2006) ("a divorce is not a business matter between two people but, rather, a matter in which the state has an interest").

75. Adams v. Adams, 11 P.3d 220, 221 (Okla. Civ. App. 2000) ("The parties may not enter a judgment. Only the court has the power to adjudicate. Only that portion of the parties agreement which is incorporated in and made a part of the divorce judgment by the court is enforceable[.]");

In states following the minority rule, separation agreements cannot be enforced until they are approved by the court.[76] The standard for court approval is fairly high on its face; most states require a positive finding by the court that the agreement is fair and reasonable.[77] If court finds that the agreement is not fair and reasonable, it is not enforceable and the case must be decided as if no agreement exists. The court has the

---

Jensen v. Jensen, 197 P.3d 117, 124 (Utah Ct. App. 2008) ("[A] stipulation regarding property division in a divorce proceeding 'is not necessarily binding on the trial court. It is only a recommendation to be adhered to if the trial court believes it to be fair and reasonable.'") (quoting Colman v. Colman, 743 P.2d 782, 789 (Utah Ct. App. 1987)).

76. *See* Mullins v. Mullins, 770 So. 2d 624, 625 (Ala. Civ. App. 2000) ("Although an agreement may be binding upon the parties, it is not binding upon the trial court and the trial court may accept it or reject it[.]"); Rutherford v. Rutherford, 81 Ark. App. 122, 128, 98 S.W.3d 842, 845 (2003) ("the court is not bound by a stipulation entered into by the parties: rather, it is within the sound discretion of the court to approve, disapprove, or modify the agreement"); *Cloutier*, 814 A.2d 979; Marcovitz v. Rogers, 276 Neb. 199, 204, 752 N.W.2d 605, 609 (2008); *Adams*, 11 P.3d at 221 ("a settlement agreement is not enforceable, absent its approval by the court"); *Gorman*, 883 A.2d at 736 ("The Family Court has broad power to review and to decide whether to approve proposed property settlement agreements[.]"); Long v. McAllister-Long, 221 S.W.3d 1, 8 (Tenn. Ct. App. 2006) ("These agreements, however, are not binding on the courts[.]"); *Pouech*, 180 Vt. 1, 904 A.2d 70; Van Boxtel v. Van Boxtel, 242 Wis. 2d 474, 483, 625 N.W.2d 284, 287 (2001) ("any agreement regarding the division of property entered into between spouses after divorce proceedings have commenced is a stipulation under § 767.10(1) and is therefore subject to the approval of the court").

Texas requires court approval for most agreements. *See* Tex. Fam. Code § 7.006 (Westlaw 2008); Byrnes v. Byrnes, 19 S.W.3d 556, 560 (Tex. Ct. App. 2000). Court approval is not required for certain mediated agreements, if the proper statutory formalities are followed. *See In re* Marriage of Joyner, 196 S.W.3d 883, 891 (Tex. Ct. App. 2006).

A 2001 Oregon statute appears to state that separation agreements are binding unless specific defenses are proven. Or. Rev. Stat. Ann. § 107.014 (Westlaw 2008); *see In re* Marriage of Patterson & Kanaga, 206 Or. App. 341, 352, 136 P.3d 1177, 1182 (2006). Nevertheless, the Oregon courts seem to be holding that court retain the power to approve or disapprove private agreements. *In re* Marriage of Grossman, 338 Or. 99, 106 P.3d 618 (2005). *Grossman* did not disapprove an agreement on the facts—rather, it held that the agreement was inapplicable on its face—so it is not yet fully clear how the statute will be applied in practice. The most likely result is that court approval will still be required, but that the standard of approval will be materially relaxed.

77. *See, e.g.,* Tex. Fam. Code § 7.006 (Westlaw 2008) ("just and right"); *In re* Marriage of Takusagawa, 38 Kan. App. 2d 401, 405, 166 P.3d 440, 444 (2007) ("fair"); *Adams*, 11 P.3d at 221 (agreement "shall not be approved unless it is fair, just and reasonable"); *Pouech*, 180 Vt. at 12, 904 A.2d at 77 ("the question is one of fairness and equity viewed from the perspective of the standards and factors set forth in our divorce statutes"); *Hottenroth*, 298 Wis. 2d at 216, 727 N.W.2d at 46 ("Because [an agreement] is only a recommendation, the court need not accept it, but instead has a duty to decide whether that recommendation is a fair and reasonable resolution of the issues[.]"); Evenson v. Evenson, 228 Wis. 2d 676, 598 N.W.2d 232 (1999); Ayres v. Ayres, 230 Wis. 2d 431, 602 N.W.2d 132 (1999). *But see Marcovitz*, 276 Neb. at 204, 752 N.W.2d at 609 (requiring court approval, but standard is whether the agreement is unconscionable).

power only to approve or disapprove the agreement; the court cannot rewrite the agreement's terms.[78]

Case law addressing whether particular agreements are fair and reasonable is discussed in § **4.062**.

Approval Not Required

A majority of states hold that separation agreements are binding just like other contracts. They need not be approved in advance by the court; they are binding as soon as the parties agree to them.[79] The court is not permitted to second-guess the wisdom of the agreement; that is a matter for the parties alone to decide.[80]

An interesting hybrid is Arizona, which provides by statute as follows:

> [T]he terms of the separation agreement, except those providing for the support, custody and parenting time of children, are binding on the court unless it finds, after considering the economic circumstances of the parties and any other relevant evidence produced by the parties, on their own motion or on request of the court, that the separation agreement is unfair.[81]

Thus, private agreements are presumptively binding, but the court may still refuse to approve them if the agreement is unfair. The key point that makes Arizona less than a full *majority* rule jurisdiction is that the court may disapprove the agreement, on matters not involving the welfare of children, upon its own initiative.[82] The key point

---

78. *Gorman*, 883 A.2d 732. *Gorman* noted that the court did retain the power reform the agreement to correct a mistake under the common law of contracts. *See generally* § **4.053**.

79. *See* Duffy v. Duffy, 881 A.2d 630, 633 (D.C. 2005) ("[A] separation agreement is presumptively valid and binding no matter how ill-advised a party may have been in executing it."); Crupi v. Crupi, 784 So. 2d 611 (Fla. Dist. Ct. App. 2001); Lentz v. Lentz, 271 Mich. App. 465, 471–72, 721 N.W.2d 861, 865–66 (2006) ("We find no reason to rewrite a contract between adults who negotiated their own property disposition in anticipation of separation or divorce. Absent fraud, coercion, or duress, the adults in the marriage have the right and the freedom to decide what is a fair and appropriate division of the marital assets, and our courts should not rewrite such agreements[.]"); Lowrey v. Lowrey, 919 So. 2d 1112, 1120 (Miss. Ct. App. 2005) ("Cynthia is not entitled to special privilege simply because she asks this Court to interpret a property settlement agreement, entered incident to a divorce on irreconcilable differences. Quite the contrary, as '[a] true and genuine property settlement agreement is no different from any other contract, and the mere fact that it is between a divorcing husband and wife, and incorporated into a divorce decree, does not change its character[.]'") (quoting West v. West, 891 So. 2d 203 ¶ 13 (Miss. 2004)); Reinsch v. Reinsch, 259 Neb. 564, 611 N.W.2d 86 (2000); Adams v. Adams, 848 A.2d 991 (Pa. Super. Ct. 2004); Barnes v. Barnes, 193 S.W.3d 495 (Tenn. 2006); Sweet v. Sweet, 138 P.3d 63, 64 (Utah Ct. App. 2006); Campbell v. Campbell, 32 Va. App. 351, 528 S.E.2d 145 (2000).

80. *See Duffy*, 881 A.2d at 633 ("the parties are in a better position than the court to determine what is fair and reasonable in their circumstances").

81. Ariz. Rev. Stat. Ann. § 25-317(B) (Westlaw 2008).

82. *See* Breitbart-Napp v. Napp, 216 Ariz. 74, 163 P.3d 1024, 1029 (2007) (statute "does not limit the court's authority to approve an agreement to instances when the separation agreement is to be merged into the decree").

that makes Arizona less than a full minority rule jurisdiction is the placement of the burden of proof. The minority rule requires the court to take affirmative action and approve the agreement before it is binding; Arizona provides that the agreement is binding unless the court takes affirmative action and disapproves it.

Minnesota law is similar, allowing the court to "relieve a party from the terms of a dissolution stipulation if, before entry of a judgment based thereon, it is determined that the stipulation was 'improvidently made and in equity and good conscience ought not to stand.'"[83] The burden of proof again appears to be on the party who asks the court to disapprove the agreement, but the standard for invalidity is again broader than the ordinary law of contracts.[84]

Policy Concerns

The minority rule that separation agreements require court approval is unwise policy. Divorce cases are resolved more fairly, more quickly, and less expensively in states following the majority position.

The original justification for the minority rule, the dependent status of women, is clearly no longer valid. The modern justification is not much more persuasive. Only courts can decide cases, but court respect private settlements in many areas of the law. Private parties are permitted to settle private litigation. In fact, such settlement is almost universally viewed as desirable, because dispute resolution by private agreement gives better results at less cost in time and money than litigation in court. Even the minority rule states admit the advantages of private agreements. What is the basis, then, for treating such agreements as presumptively invalid, rather than presumptively valid?

Cases stressing the role of state in the law of domestic relations are not on much firmer ground. The state has an interest in issues involving children, of course, but that issue is fully accommodated by the universal rule that the court may disregard any provision that is not in the best interests of the parties' children. *See* § **3.07**. Even then, the great majority of all private custody and support agreements are followed in actual practice.

On property division and spousal support issues not involving the rights of children, what state interest is sufficient to override a private agreement signed by the parties whose rights are at issue? Private persons are normally permitted to settle their

---

83. Toughill v. Toughill, 609 N.W.2d 634, 639 (Minn. Ct. App. 2000) (quoting Shirk v. Shirk, 561 N.W.2d 519, 521 (Minn. 1997)).

84. This reading of Minnesota law is based primarily on *Toughill*, which refused to permit a party to withdraw from an agreement before its approval by the court, and which seemed to speak of disapproval by the court as an affirmative act. A later case seemed to hold otherwise, in a situation in which one spouse died before approval of the agreement. "[W]hat the parties talked about while both were living, and incorporated into a private settlement agreement, is not 'self-executing.' A district court needed to approve the parties' proposed settlement." *In re* Marriage of Rettke, 696 N.W.2d 846, 850–51 (Minn. Ct. App. 2005). But *Rettke* involved an unusual and specific fact situation. *Toughill* certainly did not act as if agreements are invalid unless and until approved by the court, as they are in true minority rule states; on the contrary, the court expressly stated that "an [agreement] not yet adopted by a district court is provisionally binding on the parties." *Toughill*, 609 N.W.2d at 639.

disputes; private agreements do not normally require court approval. Indeed, there is nearly universal recognition that private agreements are *better* for the parties than a decision imposed by a court. There is no reason for believing that the advantages of private settlement are any less in divorce cases than in other types of litigation. Indeed, they may well be greater, because divorce litigation is such an emotionally sensitive area, and consumes such a large portion of most trial court case loads. Parties to divorce cases are grown-ups, and they should be allowed to make their own decisions regarding separation agreements without the need to seek permission from a court.

In addition to giving insufficient weight to the right of grown-ups to reach their own divorce settlements, the minority rule is also not a very efficient use of court resources. When trial courts must review the fairness and reasonableness of all divorce settlements, divorce hearings become longer and more expensive. Even if all contested issues settle, the parties must still convince the court to approve their agreement. This requires significant court time, most of which would better be spent resolving disputes between parties who are in actual disagreement. The majority rule allocates judicial resources more efficiently, as it requires significant court time only when one party actually contests the validity of the agreement.

There is also cause to wonder whether the minority rule discourages settlement. When the court must approve private agreements, the end result of the case is more dependent upon what the court believes, and there is no way to determine what the court believes without holding a hearing. As a result, parties are discouraged from bargaining seriously and encouraged to seek guidance form the court. Providing that guidance uses judicial resources that could more efficiently be used elsewhere. The majority rule, by contrast, gives the parties more freedom to bargain, and thereby encourages them to take the private bargaining process more seriously.

If the minority rule has a strength, the strength is that it encourages courts to take allegations of invalidity seriously. Marital breakdown is a setting that is uniquely conducive to irrational and emotional thinking, and even to various forms of overreaching and fraud. Some majority rule states have taken private contract rights too far, to the point where there is not much of a safety net against unfair or involuntary agreements. *See* § **4.06**.

But the need for a safety net is not too great as to justify treating private agreements as presumptively invalid unless they are approved by the court. Even in the strictest minority rule states, the number of separation agreements ultimately found invalid is not anywhere near 50 percent. In all states, the chances are very good that any given separation agreement will ultimately be approved by the court. This suggests very strongly that separation agreements, like other forms of contracts, should be presumptively valid. Concerns about overreaching, fraud, and substantive unfairness should be handled in the divorce context in the same way they have been handled in other areas of the law: as potential *defenses* that rebut the presumptive validity of the agreement.

§ 4.042 Lack of Consent

When the parties mutually consent to a separation agreement, they create a binding legal document that cannot be destroyed by either party alone. The overwhelming majority rule is therefore that a party cannot simply change his or her mind and walk away from the agreement.[85] This rule holds true even where the change of heart results from recognition that the agreement reflects an unwise bargain.[86] It applies with equal force even where the agreement results from mediation, rather than from more traditional forms of negotiation.[87]

Likewise, the rule applies even where consent was influenced by ineffective advice of counsel.[88] In other words, ineffective assistance of counsel is not a sufficient basis for setting aside a separation agreement. Where counsel gives bad advice, the proper remedy is not an attack upon the agreement, but rather a malpractice action against the lawyer.[89]

Open Court Consent Requirements

A small number of states hold that a separation agreement is effective only if the parties consent to it in open court at the final divorce hearing.[90] Under this rule, if the parties do not consent to the agreement before the court, there is no binding contract, and the contested issues must be decided by the court. Once consent in open court is given, it generally cannot be later withdrawn.[91]

Open court consent requirements are especially common in states that follow the minority rule that a separation agreement is not valid until it is approved by the court.

---

85. *E.g.*, Tanner v. Tanner, 975 So. 2d 1190, 1191 (Fla. Dist. Ct. App. 2008) ("'Buyer's remorse' is not a sufficient basis for overturning a marital settlement agreement freely and voluntarily entered into[.]"); Young Choi v. Young Choi, 167 A.D.2d 217, 561 N.Y.S.2d 724 (1990).

86. Helms v. Helms, 317 Ark. 143, 875 S.W.2d 849 (1994); Tubbs v. Tubbs, 648 So. 2d 817 (Fla. Dist. Ct. App. 1995); Kaffenberger v. Kaffenberger, 228 A.D.2d 743, 643 N.Y.S.2d 740 (1996).

87. *In re* Marriage of Banks, 887 S.W.2d 160 (Tex. Ct. App. 1994).

88. *See In re* Marriage of Rosevear, 65 Cal. App. 4th 673, 76 Cal. Rptr. 2d 691 (1998); Mathes v. Mathes, 267 Ga. 845, 483 S.E.2d 573 (1997); *Tubbs*, 648 So. 2d 817; *In re* Marriage of Cutler, 588 N.W.2d 425 (Iowa 1999); Shirk v. Shirk, 561 N.W.2d 519 (Minn. 1997).

89. *See, e.g.*, Picket, Houlou & Berman v. Haislip, 73 Md. App. 89, 533 A.2d 287 (1987); Ziegelheim v. Apollo, 128 N.J. 250, 607 A.2d 1298 (1992); *see generally* Annotation, *Legal Malpractice in Settling or Failing to Settle a Client's Case*, 87 A.L.R.3d 168 (1978); Annotation, *Attorney Liability for Negligence in Cases Involving Domestic Relations*, 78 A.L.R.3d 255 (1977); L. Allison McKeel, *Avoiding Attorney Malpractice in Drafting Separation Agreements*, 4 DIVORCE LITIG. 57 (1992); Laura W. Morgan, *Update: Attorney Malpractice in Recommending Settlement*, 4 DIVORCE LITIG. 170 (1992).

90. *See* Musser v. Johnson, 914 P.2d 1241 (Alaska 1996); Freeland v. Freeland, 256 S.W.3d 190 (Mo. Ct. App. 2008); Reynolds v. Reynolds, 109 S.W.3d 258, 279 (Mo. Ct. App. 2003) ("the parties were not in agreement at the time the settlement agreement was presented to the court, so the agreement was never enforceable"); Dolan v. Dolan, 107 S.W.3d 438, 441 (Mo. Ct. App. 2003) (not sufficient that agreement had been presented to commissioner, where it had not been presented to the court); Wakili v. Wakili, 918 S.W.2d 332 (Mo. Ct. App. 1996); *In re* Marriage of Brinell, 869 S.W.2d 887 (Mo. Ct. App. 1994).

91. *See* Perryman v. Perryman, 117 S.W.3d 681, 686 (Mo. Ct. App. 2003). Of course, at any point before a judgment approving the agreement is final, a party can ask the court to invalidate the agreement on any basis recognized by the law. But lack of consent, alone and by itself, is not a sufficient defense once consent has been given in open court.

These states often permit consent to be withdrawn by either party at any point before the agreement is approved by the court.[92] Some states following the minority rule, however, do not permit spouses to withdraw from agreements not yet approved by the court.[93] Most majority rule states do not have an open court consent requirement.[94]

Texas generally allows withdrawal of consent at any point before the final judgment is issued.[95] Consent cannot be withdrawn in a motion for a new trial.[96] Consent cannot be revoked if the agreement states in a separate underlined paragraph that it is not revocable.[97] When the provision was present but not underlined, one court held that consent remained revocable.[98]

Tennessee seems to allow a spouse to withdraw from an agreement at any point before approval by the court, unless the other party has detrimentally relied upon the agreement.[99]

Consent Judgments. There is much broader agreement that a consent judgment cannot be issued unless the parties consent to it in open court. Thus, if either party refuses to consent to an agreement, the agreement cannot be approved or adopted *in a consent judgment*.[100]

The agreement can be approved and adopted in a traditional nonconsent judgment, however, if it is otherwise valid under the law of contracts.[101] A true open court consent requirement, as the term is used in this section, exists only when consent before the court is required for enforcement of a separation agreement in *any* form of judgment.

---

92. *See* Hottenroth v. Hetsko, 298 Wis. 2d 200, 216, 727 N.W.2d 38, 46 (Ct. App. 2006).

93. *See* Reno v. Haler, 734 N.E.2d 1095, 1101 (Ind. Ct. App. 2000) ("conferring upon parties an absolute right to repudiate a written agreement prior to court approval would thwart the public policy of favoring amicable settlement of disputes"); Gabriel v. Gabriel, 654 N.E.2d 894 (Ind. Ct. App. 1995) (rejecting open court consent requirement; noting that agreement had been substantially performed by the parties); Toughill v. Toughill, 609 N.W.2d 634, 638 (Minn. Ct. App. 2000) ("even though the district court had yet to adopt the parties' stipulation or incorporate it into a dissolution judgment, appellant could not repudiate or withdraw from the stipulation absent respondent's consent or the court's permission").

94. *See* Barnes v. Barnes, 193 S.W.3d 495, 499 (Tenn. 2006) ("A marital dissolution agreement may be enforceable as a contract even if one of the parties withdraws consent prior to the entry of judgment by the trial court, so long as the agreement is otherwise a validly enforceable contract[.]").

95. Clanin v. Clanin, 918 S.W.2d 673 (Tex. Ct. App. 1996).

96. *Id.*

97. *See, e.g.*, Mullins v. Mullins, 202 S.W.3d 869, 876 (Tex. Ct. App. 2006) ("A mediated settlement agreement is binding on the parties if the agreement states in the appropriate font that it is not subject to revocation and is signed by both parties and their attorneys[.]"); *In re* Marriage of Joyner, 196 S.W.3d 883, 891 (Tex. Ct. App. 2006).

98. Spinks v. Spinks, 939 S.W.2d 229 (Tex. Ct. App. 1997).

99. *See* Altman v. Altman, 181 S.W.3d 676 (Tenn. Ct. App. 2005).

100. *See* Small v. Parker, 184 N.C. App. 358, 646 S.E.2d 658 (2007); Ledbetter v. Ledbetter, 163 S.W.3d 681 (Tenn. 2005).

101. *See Small*, 184 N.C. App. 358, 646 S.E.2d 658 (2007); *Ledbetter*, 163 S.W.3d 681.

Policy Concerns. It is questionable whether courts have authority to adopt this rule as a matter of first instance. An agreement reached before divorce is enforceable under the common law of contracts, even if one party subsequently changes his or her mind. In the absence of legislative enactment, there is no reason why the common law should not control in divorce cases. The court must have the power to reject an invalid agreement, of course, but that power does not justify what is effectively a blanket presumption that all contracts are invalid unless the parties consent to them in open court.

Nevertheless, this rule has solid appeal as a matter of public policy, and it is commended for legislative adoption. Divorce courts spend a significant amount of time and effort litigating cases in which one party or the other seeks to avoid an agreement after it has been signed. If the law requires that consent be manifested in open court, many of these cases will no longer arise. Moreover, by requiring consent before a judge, in a formal hearing, the law can impress upon the parties the utter seriousness of the decisions they are making—decisions that will set the financial foundation upon which they will build their postdivorce lives. Finally, the mere fact that objective, formal consent is required will discourage (although most certainly not eliminate) overreaching by dishonest spouses.

There is some possibility that an open court consent requirement might discourage posthearing attacks on agreements. Judges, having heard the parties affirm the agreement, might be more reluctant to hear attacks upon it.[102] Such reluctance would be unfortunate, for there will still be many cases in which out-of-court pressure drives in-court behavior. Moreover, consent induced by fraud should always be invalid, regardless of how many highly placed officials hear the consent being given. On both of these points, however, a properly worded open court consent statute could preserve the right of either party to attack the agreement upon traditional common law grounds.

The one significant policy reason for disfavoring an open court consent requirement is its effect upon the frequency of settlement. If fewer cases settled fairly under this rule than under the common law of contracts, there would be a solid reason to prefer the common law approach. But under present law, every divorce case requires a hearing on the question of grounds.[103] Thus, every divorce case must at some point come before a judge. It seems unlikely that there would be any strong disincentive to settlement merely because the parties had to formally restate their consent to their agreement before the court, in a hearing that is already required. In cases where a spouse refused to consent, at least some of the agreements would be invalid under the common law in any event. Moreover, at least some of the cases in which consent is initially refused would subsequently settle upon terms more favorable to the nonconsenting party. The question then becomes whether the costs of litigating those cases in which prior consent is consistently rejected exceed the costs of litigating the validity of agreements under the common law approach. The present authors are inclined to believe that the costs of the common law approach are on the whole somewhat greater.

---

102. This fear finds some support in the summary nature of decisions rejecting the notion that consent given in open court was a product of duress. *See* **§ 4.051**, note 431.

103. *See generally* 27 C.J.S. *Divorce* § 328 (Westlaw 2008).

As noted above, however, the policy advantages of an open court consent requirement are not a valid basis for judicial action. Such a substantial change in common law contract procedure should be made only after full consideration by the legislature. At that level, however, an open court consent requirement is well worth considering.

§ 4.05 Procedural Defenses

This section discusses the "big four" affirmative defenses under the common law of contracts: duress, undue influence, fraud, and mistake. These defenses are very actively litigated in states that judge the validity of separation agreements under law of contract. In states that require court approval of separation agreements, these defenses are not litigated quite so precisely, but there is still a body of case law refusing to approve a separation agreement under facts that would probably be sufficient to establish a common law defense.[104]

§ 4.051 Duress

Duress is a defense that is frequently applied without a full discussion of its elements. One court defined the defense as

> that degree of constraint or danger, either actually inflicted or threatened and impending, which is sufficient in severity or in apprehension to overcome the mind and will of a person of ordinary firmness. . . . The requirements of common-law "duress" have been enlarged to include any wrongful acts that compel a person, such as a grantor of a deed, to manifest apparent assent to a transaction without volition or cause such fear as to preclude him from exercising free will and judgment in entering into a transaction.[105]

Thus, a contract is invalid for duress when (1) one party makes a threat; (2) the threat is wrongful; (3) the threat causes the other party to sign the contract against his will; and (4) the threat would have overcome the will of a reasonable person.

There is a considerable overlap between duress and undue influence, and the reported decisions sometimes fail to draw a clear distinction between them.[106] As a general rule, duress occurs when one spouse overcomes the other spouse's free will with a specific wrongful threat. Undue influence, by contrast, occurs when one spouse overcomes the other's free will with a general pattern of coercive conduct. For present

---

104. *See, e.g.*, Rutherford v. Rutherford, 81 Ark. App. 122, 98 S.W.3d 842 (2003) (trial court properly refused to approve contract, where husband's consent was influenced by wife's improper threat to burn down home if it was not awarded to her in the agreement).

105. Warner v. Warner, 394 S.E.2d 74, 78 (W. Va. 1990) (quoting Norfolk Division of Soc. Servs. v. Unknown Father, 2 Va. App. 420, 345 S.E.2d 533, 541 (1986)); *see also In re* Marriage of Baltins, 212 Cal. App. 3d 66, 260 Cal. Rptr. 403 (1989).

106. *E.g., In re* Marriage of Richardson, 237 Ill. App. 3d 1067, 606 N.E.2d 56 (1992) (holding that undue influence is merely one specific form of duress, and defining neither term precisely).

purposes, we will treat any case not involving a specific wrongful threat as an undue influence case, even if the court claimed to be applying the law of duress.

Threat

In order to prove duress, the attacking spouse must first prove that the existence of a specific threat. In *In re Marriage of Baltins*,[107] the court found the following course of conduct sufficient to meet the requirement:

> Husband . . . threatened Wife with bankruptcy and urged her immediate action to prevent dissipation of her share of the property through credits to him of all payments for debt and support. . . . He aimed at her most vulnerable spot when he threatened not to see their child.[108]

Conversely, where the wife did not testify to any threat on direct examination, and made only conclusory allegations on cross-examination that a threat had prevented her from appearing at a prior hearing, another court found this burden not met.[109]

Duress can be present even where the improper threat was made by a third party.[110] If consent is coerced by an improper threat, the origin of the threat is not material. If an innocent party acted in good faith with no knowledge of the threat, however, and gave value in reliance upon the agreement, the agreement may remain valid.[111]

---

107. 212 Cal. App. 3d 66, 260 Cal. Rptr. 403 (1989).

108. 260 Cal. Rptr. at 415. *See also Rutherford*, 81 Ark. App. at 126, 98 S.W.3d at 844 (refusing to approve agreement, where husband "was influenced to consent to the agreement because appellant threatened to burn the house if she did not receive the home in the settlement agreement"; threat was especially credible because wife had set fire to parties' previous marital residence, had undertaken other violent actions, and had been arrested for driving while intoxicated and disorderly conduct).

109. *Warner*, 394 S.E.2d at 78; *see also In re* Marriage of Hamm-Smith, 261 Ill. App. 3d 209, 633 N.E.2d 225 (1994) (rejecting duress on grounds that record contained no proof that wife had threatened husband); *In re* Marriage of Pfeifer, 862 S.W.2d 926 (Mo. Ct. App. 1993) (husband's statement that he was facing bankruptcy was merely an accurate passing comment, and not any form of threat); Young Choi v. Young Choi, 167 A.D.2d 217, 561 N.Y.S.2d 724 (1990) (agreements "should not lightly be cast aside upon conclusory and unsupported allegations of duress"); Gainey v. Gainey, 382 S.C. 414, 429, 675 S.E.2d 792, 800 (Ct. App. 2009) (rejecting wife's claim of duress; "[t]here is no evidence that Husband made any improper threat to Wife that left Wife with no reasonable alternative").

110. "If a party's manifestation of assent is induced by one who is not a party to the transaction, the contract is voidable by the victim unless the other party to the transaction in good faith and without reason to know of the duress either gives value or relies materially on the transaction." RESTATEMENT (SECOND) OF CONTRACTS § 175(2) (1981). *But see* Maury v. Maury, 2008 WL 2609702 (Ohio Ct. App. 2008) (suggesting without authority that duress must come from the other spouse).

111. "If a party's manifestation of assent is induced by one who is not a party to the transaction, the contract is voidable by the victim unless the other party to the transaction in good faith and without reason to know of the duress either gives value or relies materially on the transaction." RESTATEMENT (SECOND) OF CONTRACTS § 175(2) (1981) (emphasis added).

Wrongfulness

A wrongful threat is generally one that the threatening party ought not to have made under the circumstances present at the time. The most common example of a wrongful threat is one that is illegal; for instance, the threat of physical violence.[112]

The illegality must relate to the threat itself, however, and not the threatened conduct. For instance, an agreement is not void for duress because one spouse threatened to commit suicide unless the other spouse signed.[113] Even though suicide may be an illegal act, a threat to commit suicide is not inherently wrongful in the same sense as a threat to commit murder or assault.

While an illegal threat is generally wrongful, a legal threat is not necessarily proper. In particular, section 176 of the *Restatement (Second) of Contracts* expressly states that all threats of criminal prosecution are per se wrongful.[114] The rationale is that such threats are a use of legitimate power for illegitimate ends, and thus that the power to prosecute for criminal charges should not be used for financial gain.[115] For example, in *Warner v. Warner*,[116] the wife forged the husband's name when purchasing an automobile. According to the wife, the husband then threatened to prosecute a criminal complaint against her unless she signed the agreement. The husband claimed that the alleged threat was not wrongful, because the wife was actually guilty of forgery. The court agreed that the wife was guilty, but nevertheless held that the threat was wrongful. "[W]hen a person can establish that a threat to prosecute a criminal claim, irrespective of the individual's guilt or innocence, destroyed her ability to exercise her free will, duress may exist."[117]

Conversely, where the threat is of civil rather than criminal prosecution, the *Restatement* provides that the threat is wrongful only if made in bad faith.[118] For example, in *Beechler v. Beechler*,[119] the wife threatened that she would pursue a contempt motion for discovery violation and continue in force an injunction against transferring marital assets if the husband did not sign the agreement. The court found that the wife had a legal right to take these actions, which involved civil and not criminal prosecution, and that the threat was therefore not wrongful.

A similar analysis applies when one spouse threatens to file a custody claim unless the other signs the agreement. When such a claim is made in bad faith, it can make

---

112. *See generally* RESTATEMENT (SECOND) OF CONTRACTS § 176 (1979); *see Rutherford*, 81 Ark. App. at 126, 98 S.W.3d at 844 (refusing to approve agreement, where husband "was influenced to consent to the agreement because appellant threatened to burn the house if she did not receive the home in the settlement agreement"; threat was especially credible because wife had set fire to parties' previous marital residence, had undertaken other violent actions, and had been arrested for driving while intoxicated and disorderly conduct).

113. Pelfrey v. Pelfrey, 25 Va. App. 239, 487 S.E.2d 281 (1997).

114. RESTATEMENT (SECOND) OF CONTRACTS § 176.

115. *Id.* § 176, cmt. c.

116. 394 S.E.2d 74 (W. Va. 1990).

117. *Id.* at 78. Ultimately, however, the court decided that the wife had not shown sufficient proof that the husband actually made the threat.

118. RESTATEMENT (SECOND) OF CONTRACTS § 176 & cmt. d.

119. 95 Ohio App. 121, 641 N.E.2d 1189 (1994).

the agreement invalid for duress. In addition, since it constitutes generally coercive conduct that takes advantage of the other parent's attachment to the children, it may well be sufficient evidence of undue influence.[120] Of course, the mere fact that a parent seeks custody in good faith should not invalidate the agreement; parties who are litigating custody should not be foreclosed from settling other issues in the case. But a parent who is acting in genuine good faith would not threaten to seek custody unless the agreement were signed; he or she would simply file an absolute claim for custody. The very action of stating an intention to seek custody *only if* the agreement is not signed is in most cases a sufficient wrongful act to constitute duress.

Apart from threats of a custody battle or criminal prosecution, the general trend is to hold that a threat is not wrongful unless the threatened conduct is illegal. Thus, an agreement is not invalid for duress merely because one spouse threatens to leave the other unless the agreement is signed.[121] The threat is not wrongful, because there is no legal requirement that married persons must live together at all times.

---

120. See Lowrey v. Lowrey, 919 So. 2d 1112, 1121 (Miss. Ct. App. 2005) (husband threatened wife that "You will never live in this town again and you will never ever see your children again" if wife retained counsel and failed to sign husband's proposed agreement, which was substantively one-sided; agreement invalid for overreaching); Schneider v. Schneider, 110 Ohio App. 3d 487, 674 N.E.2d 769 (1996) (agreement invalid; relying in part upon fact that husband had threatened to seek custody). *But see* Lyons v. Lyons, 289 A.D.2d 902, 904, 734 N.Y.S.2d 734, 737 (2001) (husband's threat to seek custody if wife did not settle was not duress; "defendant, in the absence of an agreement, had the right to commence litigation, including custody litigation, and the fact that such litigation would be expensive does not convert this lawfully made statement to one which constitutes coercion or duress").

Lyons is questionable, for while the husband had a right to seek custody, he did not have a right to seek custody in bad faith. The court did not address the husband's state of mind, but the mere fact that the husband threatened to seek custody only if the wife failed to sign suggests strongly that he did not have a bona fide desire to have custody of the children, and that his threat was intended to be coercive. Whether it actually coerced the wife, of course, is an issue of fact. But the court should not have held so broadly that a threat to seek custody is never wrongful. That holding encourages the harmful use of custody claims as tactical weapons in property division and spousal support litigation.

An interesting variant on duress and custody claims is Young v. Anne Arundel Cnty., 146 Md. App. 526, 807 A.2d 651 (2002), where an elderly wife alleged that her husband's family told her she would never see him again unless she signed a separation agreement. The husband was also elderly and incompetent as well, and the threat suggests that the family was more interested in the husband's money than in his welfare. In effect, the wife alleged that the husband's family threatened in bad faith to deny the wife custody of and/or visitation with the husband. A trial court decision granting summary judgment against the wife was reversed, and the case was remanded for trial.

121. Rubenstein v. Sala, 137 Ariz. 563, 672 P.2d 492 (Ct. App. 1983); *see also* Sharp v. Sharp, 179 Ariz. 205, 877 P.2d 304 (Ct. App. 1994) (husband told wife that she would get a better deal if she negotiated herself rather than through counsel, and thus implicitly threatened a worse deal if she used counsel; threat not wrongful); *In re* Marriage of Gorman, 284 Ill. App. 3d 171, 671 N.E.2d 819 (1996) (husband threatened not to send funds to wife to close on new home in Atlanta unless she signed agreement, but husband had no duty to send such funds; agreement not invalid for duress); *cf.* Rushing v. Rushing, 724 So. 2d 911 (Miss. 1998) (wife consented to agreement only because certain tapes of conversations between her and her paramour were admitted into evidence,

A threat is particularly likely to be found not wrongful when the threatened spouse essentially consented to it in advance. In *Greenberg v. Greenberg*,[122] the wife consented to submit her divorce case to a beth din, a religious court in the Orthodox Jewish faith. The beth din then threatened to ostracize the wife from the religious community unless she agreed to certain provisions of its judgment. The wife signed a contract agreeing to do so, and then sought to set the agreement aside for duress. The trial court held that the agreement was valid, as the wife had agreed to permit the beth din to hear the case. Having agreed to the beth din's jurisdiction, the wife had effectively consented to enforcement of the beth din's decree by ostracizing, the traditional and accepted method by which decrees of a beth din are enforced.

Intent

Duress generally exists only where a threat was made with intent to obtain an unfair bargaining advantage. In *In re Marriage of Takusagawa*,[123] the husband sent the parties' adult children an e-mail message, asking for their advice in determining the legal consequences of the wife's failure to disclose a large sum of currency when entering the country. Shortly before the agreement was signed, without the husband's awareness, one of the children forwarded the e-mail to the wife. The wife alleged that the e-mail constituted an improper threat that coerced her to sign the husband's proposed separation agreement. The trial court found no duress, as the husband did not send the e-mail for the purpose of coercing the wife. The appellate court affirmed the trial court's decision.

Subjective Causation

Even if a wrongful threat is made, it must still actually cause the other party to sign the contract. "To determine whether a contract . . . was the product of duress, the courts look not so much to the nature of the threats, but to their effect on the state of the threatened person's mind."[124]

In one recent case, the husband threatened to expose the wife's adultery unless she signed the contract. The wife's adultery had been relatively flagrant, however, and it was general knowledge in the community. Accordingly, the court found that the threat of exposure had not actually caused the wife to sign the agreement. "A threat of exposure could not have amounted to coercion sufficient to destroy Mrs. Warner's free will in view of appellant's general openness about the adulterous relationship."[125]

---

but tapes were properly admitted; rejecting wife's argument that agreement was invalid for "fraud," which was essentially an attack based upon duress).

122. 238 A.D.2d 420, 656 N.Y.S.2d 369 (1997).

123. 38 Kan. App. 2d 401, 166 P.3d 440 (2007).

124. *In re* Marriage of Baltins, 212 Cal. App. 3d 66, 260 Cal. Rptr. 403, 414 (1989).

125. Warner v. Warner, 394 S.E.2d 74, 79 (W. Va. 1990); *see also Takusagawa*, 38 Kan. App. 2d at 402, 166 P.3d at 442 (e-mail sent to parties' adult children, asking for advice regarding wife's failure to disclose substantial sum of currency when entering the company, and forwarded to wife by one of the children, did not actually cause wife to sign husband's proposed agreement; agreement therefore not invalid for duress); Bougard v. Bougard, 991 So. 2d 646, 649–650 (Miss. Ct. App. 2008) (rejecting husband's argument that trial court coerced him into signing agreement by

A "no duress" clause in the agreement does not prevent the court from finding that duress actually existed.[126] It is, however, some evidence that the agreement was not signed under duress.[127]

Objective Causation

Even if a wrongful threat actually overcame the free will of the victim, the agreement is still not invalid if the threat would not have overcome the free will of a reasonable person. Accordingly, duress cannot be based on threats that the reasonable person would recognize as hollow or harmless.

For example, in *Kunkel v. Kunkel*,[128] the wife claimed that she signed an agreement only because the husband had threatened that he would not pay child support unless she signed. The court held that duress was not present, for in view of the court's power to enforce child support by contempt, a reasonable person's will would not have been overcome by the husband's threat.

The objective causation standard is applied especially often to stipulations read onto the record in open court. Where the parties hear the stipulation read and each party repeatedly assents to it under the judge's direct questions, courts have generally rejected a claim of duress.[129] The reasoning of these cases is that no reasonable person would repeatedly consent to a stipulation in open court if it were truly a product of duress.

§ 4.052 Undue Influence and Overreaching

Another common defense to separation agreements is undue influence. One court defined undue influence as follows:

> To invoke undue influence as a means of voiding an executed document, an individual must establish that he had no free will when he signed the document in question. . . . [U]ndue influence occurs when "manifest irresistible coercion" deprives [a] person of volition to dispose of property as he desired.[130]

---

threatening to imprison him for nonpayment of temporary support; husband's prior imprisonment had been for civil contempt, so that he could leave prison simply by paying his arrearage, and there was no evidence that the husband's consent was actually coerced).

126. *See* Marjon v. Lane, 995 So. 2d 1086, 1087 (Fla. Dist. Ct. App. 2008) (error not to consider duress, even though agreement stated that it was not a product of duress; "the clause at issue does not bar the trial court's consideration of whether the Agreement was procured by fraud, duress, or coercion").

127. *See* Gaton v. Gaton, 170 A.D.2d 576, 566 N.Y.S.2d 353 (1991); Kazimierski v. Kazimierski, 252 A.D.2d 481, 675 N.Y.S.2d 124 (1998) (treating no-duress clause as persuasive evidence that duress was not present).

128. 547 So. 2d 555 (Ala. Ct. Civ. App.), *cert. denied*, 547 So. 2d 561 (1989). *But see* Jenks v. Jenks, 34 Conn. App. 462, 642 A.2d 31 (1994) (claiming that the modern trend is against strict application of an objective causation requirement).

129. *See, e.g.*, *In re* Marriage of Rosevear, 65 Cal. App. 4th 673, 76 Cal. Rptr. 2d 691 (1998); Roskind v. Roskind, 552 So. 2d 1155 (Fla. Dist. Ct. App. 1989); Cantamessa v. Cantamessa, 170 A.D.2d 792, 565 N.Y.S.2d 895 (1991); Gotard v. Gotard, 165 A.D.2d 824, 560 N.Y.S.2d 204 (1990).

130. *Warner*, 394 S.E.2d at 78 (quoting Nuckols v. Nuckols, 228 Va. 25, 320 S.E.2d 734, 741 (1984)); *see also In re* Marriage of Baltins, 212 Cal. App. 3d 66, 260 Cal. Rptr. 403, 414 n.9 (1989)

The Delaware courts use a four-part test to determine undue influence:

> Though the presence of undue influence depends on the facts of any given case, it consists of four elements: 1) a person who is subject to influence; 2) an opportunity to exert undue influence; 3) a disposition to exert such influence; and 4) a result indicating the presence of undue influence.[131]

The best summary of these various tests is simply to observe that undue influence is present whenever a general pattern of coercive conduct actually overcame the victim's own free will.

There is a considerable overlap between duress and undue influence, and the reported decisions sometimes fail to draw a clear distinction between them.[132] As a general rule, duress occurs when one spouse overcomes the other spouse's free will with a specific wrongful threat. Undue influence, by contrast, occurs when one spouse overcomes the other's free will with a general pattern of coercive conduct. For purposes of this work, we will treat any case not involving a specific wrongful threat as an undue influence case, even if the court claimed to be applying the law of duress.

Some courts recognize a similar contractual defense known as overreaching.[133] Overreaching, like undue influence, involves a coercive pattern of conduct that overcomes the free will of the victim.[134] The distinction between undue influence and overreaching is minimal, and this section discusses case law applying both defenses.

Still another similar defense, recognized in at least one state, is procedural unconscionability. "Procedural unconscionability goes to the formation of the contract."[135] It is therefore distinguishable from substantive conscionability, which involves the substantive sufficiency of the contract's terms.[136] Procedural unconscionability is proven "by showing 'a lack of knowledge, lack of voluntariness, inconspicuous print, the use of complex legalistic language, disparity in sophistication or bargaining power of the parties and/or a lack of opportunity to study the contract and inquire about the contract

---

("a high pressure which works on the other party's weaknesses and approaches coercion"); Knutson v. Knutson, 639 N.W.2d 495, 499 (N.D. 2002) ("the improper use of power or trust in a way that deprives a person of free will and substitutes another's objective") (quoting BLACK'S LAW DICTIONARY 1529 (7th ed. 1999)).

131. Robert O. v. Ecmel A., 460 A.2d 1321, 1323 (Del. 1983), *overruled on other grounds*, Sanders v. Sanders, 570 A.2d 1189 (Del. 1990).

132. *E.g.*, *In re* Marriage of Richardson, 237 Ill. App. 3d 1067, 606 N.E.2d 56 (1992) (holding that undue influence is merely one specific form of duress, and defining neither term precisely).

133. *E.g.*, Cardinal v. Cardinal, 275 A.D.2d 756, 757, 713 N.Y.S.2d 370 (2000).

134. *See* Lowrey v. Lowrey, 919 So. 2d 1112, 1117 (Miss. Ct. App. 2005) ("overreaching is 'the act or an instance of taking unfair advantage of another,'" requiring "a sufficient showing that the settlement agreement resulted from an inequality of bargaining power or other circumstances such that there was no meaningful choice on the part of the disadvantaged party") (quoting BLACK'S LAW DICTIONARY).

135. West v. West, 891 So. 2d 203, 213 (Miss. 2004).

136. *See generally* § **4.06**.

terms.'"[137] The focus again appears to be upon whether an overall pattern of coercive conduct overcame the free will of the victim.

Under any of these theories, whether the victim's free will was actually overcome is a question of fact that is not subject to precise legal analysis. There are, however, a number of factors that the court tend to consider in making the determination.

Conduct of the Parties

Perhaps the most important factor to be considered in determining undue influence is the conduct of the party who proposed the agreement. Where the actions of that party are wrongful, a finding of undue influence is more likely.

The classic example involves a wife who was physically abused during the marriage. If the husband makes a specific threat to strike the wife unless she signs the agreement, the agreement is invalid for duress. *See* § **4.051**. But in many cases, no such threat is necessary. Women who are abused regularly must develop passive behavior patterns to survive, and they often defer to the wishes of their husbands even when no express threat is made. In the absence of a specific threat, it is not possible to invalidate the agreement for duress, but it may very well be possible to attack the agreement for undue influence.[138]

A similar result obtains when the disadvantaged spouse was not subject to regular physical abuse, but was still the victim of specific incidents or threats of abuse in the recent past. If those threats or incidents were directly related to the agreement at issue, the agreement is invalid for duress. If the threats or incidents were not agreement-related, duress is not present, but the abuse is one factor suggesting that the agreement is invalid for undue influence.[139]

In any situation where an undue influence argument is based upon past abuse, it is important to consider the extent to which that abuse has an actual present effect upon the victimized spouse. For instance, in *Putnam v. Putnam*,[140] there was specific evidence that the wife was afraid of the husband at the time she negotiated the agreement and that she was greatly concerned over how he would react to each position she took. If the facts had shown that the prior abuse did not have any particular effect upon the wife's negotiation of the agreement, her position would have been weaker.

As the history of past abuse becomes less substantial, the argument in favor of undue influence generally becomes weaker. There are no reported cases, but the

---

137. E. Ford, Inc. v. Taylor, 826 So. 2d 709, 714 (Miss. 2002) (quoting Pridgen v. Green Tree Fin. Servicing Corp., 88 F. Supp. 2d 655 (S.D. Miss. 2000)). *East Ford* is not a domestic relations case, but it is the leading authority cited in *West v. West*, 891 So. 2d 203, 213 (Miss. 2004), for the concept of procedural unconscionability, which *West* did not otherwise define.

138. *See* Matos v. Matos, 932 So. 2d 316 (Fla. Dist. Ct. App. 2006) (where husband was physically abusive to wife during marriage and did not fully disclose marital assets, error to enforce agreement).

139. *See* Peterson v. Peterson, 555 N.W.2d 359 (N.D. 1996) (husband made general threats to kill wife and children; threats were one factor in court's finding of undue influence); Putnam v. Putnam, 689 A.2d 446 (Vt. 1996) (wife was subject to two prior episodes of physical abuse and many episodes of emotional abuse).

140. *Id.*

authors suspect that it would be harder to show undue influence from a pattern of abuse that terminated several years before the agreement was signed, or from a continuing pattern of abuse that is sporadic rather than regular. It should be stressed, however, that an overall pattern of abuse is very possible even where actual episodes of violence are sporadic, if the abused spouse submits to the abusing spouse's will before a violent stage is ever reached. In other words, the issue is more the effect of the abuse upon the will of the victim than the frequency of actual violent episodes. Where the abuse is so sporadic that it did not actually overcome the victim's will and judgment, undue influence is probably not present.

It should be stressed that not every agreement signed by an abused spouse is invalid for undue influence. When such a spouse has counsel, is not unfairly pressured, and signs the agreement voluntarily, the agreement will be found valid.[141]

Limitations of the Victim

Courts have often found undue influence in cases where the spouse who proposed the agreement somehow took advantage of the personal limitations of the victim.

The easiest cases are those where the victim was on medication or otherwise limited by a serious health care problem. For purposes of this rule, the health care problem can be physical or mental. For instance, in *Weinstock v. Weinstock*,[142] the wife introduced expert psychiatric testimony that the husband had dominated her throughout the marriage. He told her nothing about the family finances, and presented the agreement to her at a time when she was dependent on Valium and alcohol. The court found the agreement invalid.

Similarly, in *Terio v. Terio*[143] the husband had been the dominant spouse during the 35-year marriage, and the wife was in a severe depression requiring professional counseling. Although the agreement was unfair, the husband "continuously pressured, badgered and verbally harassed her until she acquiesced in his demands that she sign the agreement."[144] The agreement was found to be invalid.

---

141. *See* Jenks v. Jenks, 34 Conn. App. 462, 642 A.2d 31 (1994) (mere fact that wife had been battered by husband during marriage did not prove that agreement was invalid; wife had counsel, and agreement was fair and reasonable).

142. 167 A.D.2d 394, 561 N.Y.S.2d 807 (1990); *see also* G.A.S. v. S.I.S., 407 A.2d 253, 257 (Del. Fam. Ct. 1978) (husband was a paranoid schizophrenic receiving inpatient treatment at a mental hospital and receiving "significant amounts of 'anti-psychotic' medication"; treating psychiatrist testified that husband may not have understood transaction; "even if the mental weakness of the [husband] did not rise to the level of contractual incapacity," the contract was invalid for undue influence); Goodstein v. Goodstein, 649 So. 2d 273 (Fla. Dist. Ct. App. 1995) (wife signed agreement against advice of counsel two weeks after the end of a hospital stay for open heart surgery, at a time when she was taking strong prescription medicine; a medical expert testified that she was unable at the time to participate in serious discussions; contact invalid for undue influence).

143. 150 A.D.2d 675, 541 N.Y.S.2d 548 (1989); *see also In re* Marriage of Richardson, 237 Ill. App. 3d 1067, 606 N.E.2d 56 (1992) (agreement signed by wife one week after death of her father held invalid for undue influence).

144. 541 N.Y.S.2d at 549.

One common mental limitation is a strong desire to continue the marriage. Where the opposing spouse takes advantage of such a desire by making a false promise that the parties will reconcile if the agreement is signed, there is a good argument for undue influence. In *Derby v. Derby*,[145] for instance, the wife encouraged the husband to believe that signing the agreement would save the marriage. In reality, however, she had been seeing someone else and had no true desire to reconcile. "While Mrs. Derby is not responsible or accountable for Mr. Derby's emotional problems," the court held, "she took advantage of them in a manner that induced an unconscionable agreement."[146] The contract was therefore held invalid.

Another specific mental limitation is the requirement in certain religious faiths (most notably Orthodox Judaism) that the spouses obtain a religious divorce as well as a civil one. Religious divorces generally require the participation (although not the consent) of both spouses, and the divorce will not be granted without the cooperation of both parties. Where one spouse uses this veto power to coerce an unfair civil settlement, the resulting agreement has been held invalid.[147]

Mental limitations can also result from social and cultural sources. The most common situation involves the foreign-born spouse with only a limited command of English. The reported cases show a trend toward reviewing unfair agreements in this situation closely for evidence of undue influence. For example, in *Notkin v. Notkin*,[148] the wife was a native of Thailand who was not fluent in English. She had independent counsel, but did not fully understand the agreement and signed it against counsel's advice. There was evidence that the wife made a deliberate and knowing decision to accept a smaller sum of immediate cash rather than a larger, deferred award, and there was no evidence that the husband took advantage of the wife's limitations in any way. The facts of the case provide a strong basis for argument that the wife's decision to sign was voluntary, but the court still found the agreement invalid. *Notkin* suggests that the courts are willing to stretch the law in favor of a spouse whose command of English is limited.

---

145. 8 Va. App. 19, 378 S.E.2d 74 (1989); *see also* Hale v. Hale, 74 Md. App. 505, 539 A.2d 247 (husband misled wife into believing that reconciliation was possible if she signed contract; agreement invalid for fraud and undue influence), *cert. denied*, 313 Md. 30, 542 A.2d 857 (1988); *Richardson*, 237 Ill. App. 3d 1067, 606 N.E.2d at 66 (where wife did not desire divorce, and husband told her that signing the agreement would make them "a family again," contract was invalid for undue influence). *But cf. In re* Marriage of Derzay, 312 Mont. 524, 55 P.3d 418, 2002 WL 1969833, at *4–5 (2002) (unpublished table opinion) (husband claimed that wife made promise to reconcile, but agreement stated that parties "shall, from this time forward live separate and apart from each other" and that "in consequence of an irretrievable breakdown in their marriage relationship [the parties] are going to get a divorce"; husband's argument that wife misrepresented her intentions was "disingenuous at best"; agreement upheld).

146. 378 S.E.2d at 81.

147. *See* Segal v. Segal, 278 N.J. Super. 218, 650 A.2d 996 (App. Div. 1994); Golding v. Golding, 176 A.D.2d 20, 581 N.Y.S.2d 4 (1992); Perl v. Perl, 126 A.D.2d 91, 512 N.Y.S.2d 372 (1987); Burns v. Burns, 223 N.J. Super. 219, 538 A.2d 438 (Ch. Div. 1987); *see generally* Marcia Retchin, *To Get a "Get": Enforcement of Contracts Requiring Spouses to Secure or Accept Religious Divorces*, 6 DIVORCE LITIG. 28 (1994).

148. 921 P.2d 1109 (Alaska 1996).

A much clearer fact situation was present in *Tal v. Tal*.[149] There, the wife was a 38-year-old unemployed woman who did not speak English. At the urging of the husband, who earned $171,000 per year and spoke English fluently, she signed a separation agreement. The agreement waived periodic alimony and awarded the husband all of the marital property, although the wife did receive a modest lump sum support award. The wife did not have counsel. The court held that the extreme unfairness of the agreement and the wife's lack of counsel combined to create an inference of overreaching, which the husband had not rebutted. The contract was therefore held invalid. The wife's absence of counsel was a key fact in the court's conclusion that the agreement was invalid.

It should be noted that the crucial fact in the above cases was not the mere fact of disability, but rather the fact that the opposing spouse took advantage of the disability in some unfair manner. Where this element of unfair advantage is not present, mere proof of a physical or emotional disability is not sufficient to show undue influence.[150] Courts are particularly likely to look past a disability that was to some extent self-inflicted.[151]

In addition, the mere fact that a spouse is suffering from emotional distress is not generally a sufficient weakness to satisfy the requirements of undue influence. All parties to a broken marriage suffer from stress, and if the normal stress of the situation were sufficient to question the validity of the agreement, then it would be unreasonably difficult to settle divorce cases.[152]

---

149. 158 Misc. 2d 703, 601 N.Y.S.2d 530 (1993).

150. *See, e.g., In re* Marriage of Steadman, 283 Ill. App. 3d 703, 670 N.E.2d 1146 (1996) (wife was afraid she would lose custody if she did not sign agreement, but no evidence that husband contributed to this fear in any way; agreement valid); Birch v. Birch, 771 P.2d 1114 (Utah Ct. App. 1989) (paraplegic is not inherently more susceptible to undue influence); Lavelle v. Lavelle, 187 A.D.2d 912, 590 N.Y.S.2d 557 (1992) (contract not invalid because husband signed it only to show love for wife; no evidence that wife had taken advantage of husband's continuing emotional attachment).

151. *See* Worland v. Worland, 193 P.3d 735, 740 (Alaska 2008) (mere fact that husband flew in excess of 20 hours to reach settlement discussions not sufficient to invalidate agreement); Lyons v. Lyons, 289 A.D.2d 902, 904, 734 N.Y.S.2d 734, 737 (2001) (wife was a chronic alcoholic, but presented neither medical evidence suggesting incapacity nor an affidavit from her former attorney supporting a claim of bargaining inequity; "her allegations of coercion, duress and overreaching, based on her physical and mental condition, are completely refuted by her return to her attorney, one month after executing the agreement, for . . . institut[ing] the first action for divorce in which she sought to incorporate this very agreement"; agreement upheld); Towner v. Towner, 225 A.D.2d 614, 639 N.Y.S.2d 133 (1996) (rejecting wife's claim that agreement was invalid because she was an alcoholic; no supporting facts or medical testimony); Bristow v. Bristow, 834 S.W.2d 497 (Tex. Ct. App. 1992) (agreement signed while husband was intoxicated was not invalid for undue influence; husband's intoxication was voluntary, and wife had not encouraged it in any way).

152. *See* Allen v. Allen, 903 So. 2d 835, 843 (Ala. Civ. App. 2004) (husband was "under stress when he executed the agreement," but also "with the assistance of counsel, negotiated significant changes to the draft agreement" before signing; agreement upheld); Acton v. Acton, 674 So. 2d 613 (Ala. Ct. App. 1995) (mere fact that wife was emotionally distraught not sufficient to show invalidity); Williams v. Williams, 939 So. 2d 1154, 1157 (Fla. Dist. Ct. App. 2006) (mere fact that "Husband did not want to get divorced and that he had misgivings about the agreement and how it would impact him" not sufficient to show that husband was coerced to sign settlement agreement); Crupi v. Crupi, 784 So. 2d 611, 613–14 (Fla. Dist. Ct. App. 2001) ("three Xanax pills, and anxiety

At the same time, undue influence may be present when one spouse obtains the other's consent to an agreement by deliberately encouraging and strengthening the normal emotional distress that the other is suffering. For instance, in *Elliott v. Elliott*,[153] the husband telephoned the wife repeatedly at work and appeared at her workplace several times each week, acting angry and aggressive. He also called her at home repeatedly in the middle of the night. This behavior strengthened the normal stress of divorce to the point where it interfered with wife's job performance, resulting in unfavorable reviews from her employer. The wife signed the husband's proposed agreement solely to prevent future misconduct by the husband, believing that she would inevitably be terminated by her employer for poor job performance unless she did so. The court found the agreement invalid. The important point in these cases is not the stress itself, but rather the fact that the other spouse deliberately encouraged it for the improper purpose of obtaining a favorable agreement.

Economic Pressure

In some cases, undue influence can result from economic as well as personal pressure. In *Rubin v. Rubin*,[154] the husband deliberately failed to give the wife sufficient funds to support herself and the children. As a result, she had to work several different jobs, and she was tired and depressed when the agreement was negotiated. Even though the wife had independent counsel who actually negotiated changes in the initial draft of the agreement, the court still found the contract invalid.

In the above case, the financial pressure was either created or intensified by the wrongful actions of one of the spouses. Where economic pressure is inherent in the fact situation, and is not made worse by the other spouse's wrongful conduct, the agreement remains valid. Indeed, since many divorcing couples are in economic distress, a contrary rule would strike down a great number of fair settlement agreements.

A good demonstration of the rule is *In re Marriage of Gorman*.[155] In that case, the wife moved to Atlanta after the parties separated. She chose a home and signed a contract to purchase. Like most home buyers, she had to make a substantial down payment

---

and pressure to settle are insufficient proof of coercion necessary to set aside such an agreement"); Adams v. Adams, 848 A.2d 991, 994 (Pa. Super. Ct. 2004) ("the mere fact appellant was faced with stress and anxiety resulting from her divorce proceedings does not establish duress in the legal sense"); Pillow v. Pillow, 13 Va. App. 271, 410 S.E.2d 407 (1991) (mere confusion and emotional weakness do not require a finding of undue influence).

153. 667 So. 2d 116 (Ala. Ct. App. 1995); *see also* Jacks v. Jacks, 232 Conn. 750, 657 A.2d 1107 (1994) (husband emotionally abused wife through period before signing of agreement, and she signed only to escape his threatening and intimidating behavior; agreement invalid).

154. 29 Mass. App. Ct. 689, 564 N.E.2d 602 (1991); *see also* Elliott v. Elliott, 667 So. 2d 116 (Ala. Ct. App. 1995) (husband's repeated harassment of wife resulted in poor job performance, and she signed agreement for fear that her continued poor performance would lead to termination by her employer; agreement invalid).

155. 284 Ill. App. 3d 171, 671 N.E.2d 819 (1996); *see also* Tremont v. Tremont, 35 A.D.3d 1046, 1048, 827 N.Y.S.2d 309, 311 (2006) (husband was under economic pressure to settle case quickly, but his problems "were of his own making, not due to overreaching by plaintiff or her attorney"; agreement upheld); Mahon v. Moorman, 234 A.D.2d 1, 650 N.Y.S.2d 153 (1996) (financial pressure is not equivalent to duress).

at closing. The husband promised to send her the funds she needed to make the down payment, but only if she signed the agreement. The wife, fearful of not closing, signed the agreement, but then sought to set it aside. The court held that the agreement was valid.

There is no doubt that the wife in *Gorman* was under economic pressure. That pressure resulted, however, from her own decision to sign a contract to purchase property without having an assured source of funds to make the down payment. The opinion does not suggest that the husband was responsible to any degree for the wife's decision to sign that contract, and he was certainly not under any duty to send her large sums of money upon demand. Because the financial pressure resulted largely from the wife's own actions, the court correctly upheld the agreement.

Independent Counsel

Undue influence can also occur when one spouse takes advantage of the other's ignorance of relevant legal principles. Most often, this happens when the victimized spouse lacks counsel. For instance, in *Robert O. v. Ecmel A.*,[156] the trial court held that the agreement was invalid for undue influence. The Delaware Supreme Court affirmed:

> The Family Court's findings are supported by more than sufficient evidence, including the statements made during the parties' discussions about the agreement, the wife's ignorance of her legal rights, the similarity between the ultimate agreement and the husband's initial demands, the absence of independent counsel or advice to the wife, the previous affection and trust between the parties, and the wife's fear of losing custody of the twins.[157]

Likewise, in *Tenneboe v. Tenneboe*,[158] the contract called for the husband to pay $700 per week in support. Since his net income was only $812.57 per week, the contract was substantially unfair. Moreover, the husband had not been represented by counsel, and he testified that the wife's counsel had not told him that changed circumstances must exist before spousal support can be modified. The court found that the evidence was sufficient to invalidate the agreement.[159]

Several collateral factors can greatly strengthen an argument for undue influence based upon lack of counsel. Where the agreement is drafted by an attorney spouse who actually gave legal advice to the other party, the case for undue influence borders upon overwhelming. In this circumstance, an attorney-client relationship exists between the spouses, and any significant degree of unfairness will make the contract invalid. For

---

156. 460 A.2d 1321 (Del. 1983), *overruled on other grounds*, Sanders v. Sanders, 570 A.2d 1189 (Del. 1990).

157. *Id.* at 1324.

158. 558 So. 2d 470 (Fla. Dist. Ct. App. 1990).

159. For additional case law finding lack of counsel to be a significant factor in a finding of undue influence, *see* Matos v. Matos, 932 So. 2d 316, 320 (Fla. Dist. Ct. App. 2006) ("'Settlement' agreements entered into between the parties, acting without counsel and without full and fair disclosure of the parties' assets, should be viewed with skepticism"; where husband was physically abusive to wife during marriage and did not fully disclose marital assets, error to enforce agreement).

instance, in *Webb v. Webb*,[160] the husband gave the wife legal advice and specifically urged her not to obtain her own counsel. The court held that it would "carefully scrutinize" agreements signed where one spouse acts as the other's attorney,[161] and it found the agreement invalid. Likewise, in *Williams v. Waldman*,[162] the attorney husband who drafted the agreement failed to inform the wife that his law practice was community property. The court refused to enforce that portion of the agreement that awarded the practice entirely to the husband.

In addition, undue influence is more likely when a spouse who had counsel made affirmative efforts to prevent the other spouse from retaining similar assistance. For instance, in *Lowrey v. Lowrey*,[163] the husband had counsel, but the wife was unrepresented. The husband "told her 'you get you an attorney and we will see you in court. We will destroy you. You will never live in this town again and you will never ever see your children again.'"[164] The wife then signed a seriously unfair agreement. The court held that the agreement was invalid for overreaching.

The argument for undue influence is also stronger where the attacking spouse is unfamiliar with English. In *Tal v. Tal*,[165] discussed previously, the wife was unemployed and not fluent in English. The husband, who earned $171,000 per year and was fluent in English, pressured her into signing an highly unequal agreement. Stressing (among other facts) the language barrier faced by the wife, the court found the agreement invalid.

While lack of counsel is an important factor in determining undue influence, it is not alone sufficient to prove that the contract is invalid.[166] In particular, lack of counsel is significant only when it results from ignorance or overreaching. Where a spouse who understands the importance of counsel deliberately fails to seek legal advice, undue influence has generally been rejected.[167] This conclusion even holds true where the

---

160. 16 Va. App. 486, 431 S.E.2d 55 (1993).

161. 431 S.E.2d at 60; *see also* Kerr v. Kerr, 8 A.D.3d 626, 779 N.Y.S.2d 246 (2004) (where wife alleged the husband, a matrimonial attorney, agreed to represent her and asked her not to retain independent counsel, trial court properly refused to grant summary judgment that agreement was valid, even though agreement stated that both parties were without counsel).

162. 108 Nev. 466, 836 P.2d 614 (1992).

163. 919 So. 2d 1112, 1121 (Miss. Ct. App. 2005).

164. *Id.* at 1121.

165. 158 Misc. 2d 703, 601 N.Y.S.2d 530 (1993).

166. *See In re* Marriage of Baltins, 212 Cal. App. 3d 66, 260 Cal. Rptr. 403 (1989); Tenneboe v. Tenneboe, 558 So. 2d 470 (Fla. Dist. Ct. App. 1990); *In re* Marriage of Brandt, 140 Ill. App. 3d 1019, 489 N.E.2d 902 (1986); Tirrito v. Tirrito, 191 A.D.2d 686, 595 N.Y.S.2d 786 (1993); Zambito v. Zambito, 171 A.D.2d 918, 556 N.Y.S.2d 789 (1991); Kramer v. Kramer, 711 N.W.2d 164, 169 (N.D. 2006) ("merely because parties are not represented by counsel when they sign a written agreement dividing their marital property is not, by itself, sufficient justification for relief").

167. *See* Keyser v. Keyser, 182 Mich. App. 268, 451 N.W.2d 587 (1990); Toughill v. Toughill, 609 N.W.2d 634, 640 (Minn. Ct. App. 2000) ("there is nothing inherently coercive or fraudulent about knowingly choosing to proceed without counsel and, as a result, being somewhat intimidated by being forced to deal directly with another party's attorney"; husband made a voluntary choice to represent himself and negotiated changes to the wife's draft agreement during four hours of negotiation with her counsel); Tremont v. Tremont, 35 A.D.3d 1046, 1048, 827 N.Y.S.2d 309, 311 (2006)

spouse with counsel is an attorney, as long as that spouse did nothing to prevent the other spouse from seeking counsel.[168]

Undue influence is especially unlikely where the unrepresented spouse has been advised to seek independent counsel. The cases are particularly strong where the advice was given in the agreement itself,[169] in a letter or other formal writing,[170] or on the record in open court.[171] Where the unrepresented spouse was advised to seek counsel only orally, the cases still tend to show little sympathy for a spouse who failed to obtain counsel, so long as the represented spouse is able to meet the factual burden of proving that the advice was given.[172]

(husband "made a conscious choice not to seek the assistance of counsel regarding the negotiation of the agreement directly with plaintiff"; agreement upheld); Lazich v. Lazich, 233 A.D.2d 425, 650 N.Y.S.2d 268 (1996) (husband had no counsel, but was law school graduate; lack of counsel not a factor); Mahon v. Moorman, 234 A.D.2d 1, 650 N.Y.S.2d 153 (1996) (showing little sympathy for husband who deliberately chose not to retain counsel); Kalra v. Kalra, 170 A.D.2d 597, 566 N.Y.S.2d 356 (1991) (44-year-old professional engineer deliberately fired one attorney and failed to retain another; contract valid); Gloor v. Gloor, 190 A.D.2d 1007, 594 N.Y.S.2d 471 (1993); Chauhan v. Thakur, 184 A.D.2d 744, 585 N.Y.S.2d 482 (1992) (noting that unrepresented husband, a professional engineer, had made numerous revisions to the agreement during negotiations); Bonem v. Garriott, 159 A.D.2d 206, 552 N.Y.S.2d 16 (1990); Amestoy v. Amestoy, 151 A.D.2d 709, 543 N.Y.S.2d 141 (1989) (experienced businesswoman did not consult attorney until the day on which she signed the agreement); Crothers v. Crothers, 2001 SD 78, 630 N.W.2d 103, 107 (wife had no counsel and claimed that she could not afford one, yet her income was similar to husband's income; trial court properly refused to set stipulation aside); Pillow v. Pillow, 13 Va. App. 271, 410 S.E.2d 407 (1991) (successful insurance agent voluntarily chose not to hire counsel).

Lack of counsel is especially insignificant when the unrepresented spouse drafted the agreement. *See* Autin-Germany v. Germany, 789 So. 2d 608 (La. Ct. App. 2001).

168. *See In re* Marriage of Hamm-Smith, 261 Ill. App. 3d 209, 633 N.E.2d 225 (1994).

169. *See* Croote-Fluno v. Fluno, 289 A.D.2d 669, 671, 734 N.Y.S.2d 298, 300 (2001) ("Tellingly, the separation agreement contained a provision advising each party of his or her right to consult 'independent legal counsel[.]'"); Lavelle v. Lavelle, 187 A.D.2d 912, 590 N.Y.S.2d 557 (1992) (where contract itself stated that husband had made a conscious decision not to seek counsel and that he had not been given any legal advice by wife's counsel, undue influence was not present); Vann v. Vann, 767 N.W.2d 855, 861 (N.D. 2009) (husband lacked counsel, but "signed an accompanying affidavit to the property settlement agreement, stating he had the opportunity to be represented by counsel"; agreement valid).

170. *See In re* Marriage of Umphrey, 218 Cal. App. 3d 647, 267 Cal. Rptr. 218 (1990) (where husband told wife in writing to seek counsel if she did not understand agreement, wife's failure to understand her rights was her own fault; no undue influence); Buffett v. Buffett, 166 A.D.2d 819, 563 N.Y.S.2d 167 (1990) (husband's attorney recommended in writing that wife seek own counsel, and wife was financially able to do so; no undue influence).

171. *See* Bruckstein v. Bruckstein, 271 A.D.2d 389, 390, 705 N.Y.S.2d 391, 392 (2000) (husband "was admonished repeatedly to obtain counsel, and on several occasions during the hearing expressly acknowledged that he waived his right to retain counsel and agreed to the terms of the settlement"; settlement valid).

172. *See* Acton v. Acton, 674 So. 2d 613 (Ala. Ct. App. 1995) (wife admitted that husband had told her to seek independent counsel); Ricca v. Ricca, 57 A.D.3d 868, 869, 870 N.Y.S.2d 419, 420 (2008) (agreement valid even though husband lacked counsel, where mediator "repeatedly urged" husband to retain an attorney); Skotnicki v. Skotnicki, 237 A.D.2d 974, 654 N.Y.S.2d 904 (1997) (educated husband with business experience was told twice to hire counsel, but did not do so;

Where the victim spouse has independent counsel, undue influence is much harder to prove. In order to prevail, the attacking spouse must generally show that the guilty spouse discouraged or otherwise interfered with the right to consult counsel. For example, in *In re Marriage of Baltins*,[173] the husband "actively interfered with [the wife's] obtaining legal assistance and conducted himself in a manner calculated to deprive Wife of representation by counsel. He told wife that he would not discuss anything with a lawyer, but would only deal with her directly."[174] As a result, the wife signed the agreement without consulting her attorney. The court found the agreement invalid.

Likewise, in *In re Marriage of Richardson*,[175] the wife's first lawyer advised her not to sign the agreement. The husband then provided the wife with a new lawyer, who had minimal domestic relations experience. This attorney reviewed the husband's financial disclosure for only 20 minutes, and then allowed the wife to sign the agreement, which gave her only 7.55 percent of the marital property. The court had little difficulty concluding that the husband had interfered with the wife's right to consult counsel.

Less direct methods of interference have also been held sufficient to negate the theoretical presence of counsel. In *Derby v. Derby*,[176] the wife approached the husband in a parking lot with a separation agreement. Although the husband had counsel, he signed the agreement immediately without seeking legal advice. The husband was greatly stressed by the marital breakdown, and the wife encouraged him to believe that signing the agreement would save the marriage. In reality, however, she had been seeing another man and did not have a bona fide intent to reconcile. Her false promise preyed upon the husband's emotional weakness, thus preventing him from realizing the full benefit of independent counsel. The court found the agreement invalid for undue influence.

If counsel was present but was not truly independent, the mere presence of counsel might not prevent a finding of undue influence. For instance, in *Vandenburgh v. Vandenburgh*,[177] the agreement was nominally drafted by a neutral attorney who

---

agreement valid); Nasifoglu v. Nasifoglu, 224 A.D.2d 504, 637 N.Y.S.2d 792 (1996); Sidden v. Mailman, 137 N.C. App. 669, 677, 529 S.E.2d 266, 271–72 (2000) ("Plaintiff [wife] was told by Defendant's attorney she could have an attorney review the Agreement before she signed it"; wife nevertheless "chose to sign the Agreement without the advice of an attorney, even though she had a business attorney and an accountant who regularly represented her in her psychotherapy practice"; no undue influence).

173. 212 Cal. App. 3d 66, 260 Cal. Rptr. 403 (1989). *But see* Sharp v. Sharp, 179 Ariz. 205, 877 P.2d 304 (Ct. App. 1994) (wife failed to consult counsel for several weeks after husband told her she would get a better deal from him by negotiating herself; wife's failure to consult counsel was her own fault, and undue influence was not present).

174. 260 Cal. Rptr. at 414.

175. 237 Ill. App. 3d 1067, 606 N.E.2d 56 (1992).

176. 8 Va. App. 19, 378 S.E.2d 74 (1989). *But see* Gainey v. Gainey, 382 S.C. 414, 427, 675 S.E.2d 792, 799 (Ct. App. 2009) (where wife and her former counsel both testified that wife released former counsel because husband told her to do so, and wife thereafter proceeded without counsel, "this is insufficient evidence that Husband committed any act of deception that prevented Wife from being represented by an attorney").

177. 194 A.D.2d 957, 599 N.Y.S.2d 328 (1993).

favored neither party. The parties immediately reconciled for two weeks after the agreement was signed, but the reconciliation failed and they separated permanently. One day later, the wife became the attorney's secretary. The agreement allowed the wife to buy the marital home, the most substantial asset of the parties, for a minimal sum. Commenting that agreements prepared by one attorney for both parties should be reviewed with heightened scrutiny, the court found the agreement invalid.

New York has a formal presumption that an agreement is invalid for overreaching if one attorney represented both spouses and provided disproportionate assistance to them. "[E]vidence that one attorney ostensibly represented both parties to a settlement agreement raises an 'inference of overreaching on the part of the party who is the prime beneficiary of the assistance of the attorney,' which may be rebutted if it appears that the agreement 'is fair and equitable, or that both parties freely agreed to its terms with a thorough understanding thereof.' "[178]

Nevertheless, a conflict of interest or other obstacle to the independence of counsel will be recognized only where it is serious. Because courts favor negotiated settlements, the strong trend is to permit conflicts of interest that are not substantial.[179] Also, even a serious conflict of interest can be expressly waived in the agreement.[180]

Where the attacking party had counsel and there was no interference with the right of consultation, undue influence has generally been rejected.[181]

Substantive Fairness

Not surprisingly, courts are much more willing to find undue influence where the terms of the agreement are substantively unfair to the disadvantaged spouse. For instance, in *In re Marriage of Baltins*,[182] the court relied substantially upon the fact that the agree-

---

178. Tuccillo v. Tuccillo, 8 A.D.3d 659, 660, 779 N.Y.S.2d 234, 235 (2004) (quoting Bartlett v. Bartlett, 84 A.D.2d 800, 800, 444 N.Y.S.2d 157, 158 (1981).

179. *See* Clooten v. Clooten, 520 N.W.2d 843 (N.D. 1994) (parties reached agreement themselves and wife then hired attorney to draft a formal contract; attorney had previously drafted a will for both parties; conflict was insubstantial, and agreement was valid); *In re* Marriage of Broday, 256 Ill. App. 3d 699, 628 N.E.2d 790 (1993) (where husband's attorney had represented both parties in the past, but wife was told multiple times to obtain independent counsel, no undue influence).

180. *See In re* Marriage of Egedi, 88 Cal. App. 4th 17, 105 Cal. Rptr. 2d 518 (2001) (agreement valid where both spouses used the same attorney, where conflict of interest was expressly disclosed and voluntarily waived); Smith v. Smith, 188 A.D.2d 1004, 591 N.Y.S.2d 662 (1992).

181. *See* Smith v. Smith, 188 A.D.2d 1004, 591 N.Y.S.2d 662 (1992) (presence of competent independent counsel prevented undue influence); Knutson v. Knutson, 639 N.W.2d 495 (N.D. 2002) (affirming trial court opinion finding that wife, who had competent independent counsel, was not a victim of undue influence); Warner v. Warner, 183 W. Va. 90, 394 S.E.2d 74 (1990) (refusing to find undue influence, where parties were separated when agreement was signed and wife had independent counsel; wife did not claim undue influence until over two months after the agreement was signed).

182. 212 Cal. App. 3d 66, 260 Cal. Rptr. 403 (1989); *see also* Tchorzewski v. Tchorzewski, 278 A.D.2d 869, 870, 717 N.Y.S.2d 436, 437 (2000) (contract recited that full disclosure had been made, but husband's pension had not been valued; wife lacked counsel; and division of marital assets was substantially unequal; agreement invalid for overreaching); Peters v. Peters, 150 A.D.2d 763, 542

ment gave the wife only 10–15 percent of community estate and inadequate support for herself and the parties' child.

Indeed, where the parties had a confidential relationship when the contract was signed, some courts will presume that an unfair agreement is the product of undue influence.[183] The case law on confidential relationships is discussed in § **4.03**.

Timing

Where the attacking spouse does not attempt to repudiate the agreement until some time after it is signed, a finding of undue influence is less likely. In particular, see the ratification cases discussed below in § **4.073**. Conversely, where the attacking spouse acts promptly, the court is more likely to find that undue influence existed.[184]

Where the agreement is signed only a short time after the divorce case is filed, undue influence may be more likely. In *Peterson v. Peterson*,[185] the stipulation was signed within 24 hours after service of the divorce complaint upon the wife. In addition, the husband had threatened to kill the wife and children in the recent past, and the wife had no counsel. The trial court set aside the stipulation, and the appellate court affirmed. "As a matter of public policy, a stipulation in a divorce proceeding which occurs this rapidly, with the use of one attorney and under serious threats of harm to one of the parties, should be viewed with great skepticism."[186]

Along similar lines, when the nondrafting spouse signs the agreement only a short time after reading it, one would think that undue influence is somewhat more likely. The point has been made with particular force in the antenuptial agreement cases. *See* § **10.02**. The only case to expressly consider the point in the separation agreement context suggests that lack of time to review was not a major factor, a holding that these authors would question.[187] Lack of time does not alone compel a finding of undue influence, so the decision is correct to some extent, but lack of time is certainly

---

N.Y.S.2d 212 (1989) (where agreement gave husband all of jointly titled marital home, error to deny wife's motion to set aside for undue influence without even holding a hearing).

183. *See, e.g., Baltins*, 212 Cal. App. 3d 66, 260 Cal. Rptr. 403; Robert O. v. Ecmel A., 460 A.2d 1321 (Del. 1983), *overruled on other grounds*, Sanders v. Sanders, 570 A.2d 1189 (Del. 1990); Bell v. Bell, 38 Md. App. 10, 379 A.2d 419, 422 n.2 (1977) (citing the cases); Cardinal v. Cardinal, 275 A.D.2d 756, 757, 713 N.Y.S.2d 370, 371–72 (2000) (error to uphold separation agreement without holding a factual hearing; "[t]he evidence in the record concerning the plaintiff's mental condition at the time the separation agreement was executed, the circumstances under which it was executed, and the terms of the agreement itself, are sufficient to create an inference of overreaching by the defendant which requires further inquiry"). *But cf. In re* Marriage of Kieturakis, 138 Cal. App. 4th 56, 85, 41 Cal. Rptr. 3d 119, 140 (2006) ("the presumption of undue influence cannot be applied to marital settlement agreements reached through mediation").

184. *E.g.*, Tenneboe v. Tenneboe, 538 So. 2d 470 (Fla. Dist. Ct. App. 1990) (prompt repudiation was one factor in attacking spouse's favor).

185. 555 N.W.2d 359 (N.D. 1996).

186. *Id.* at 362.

187. Mormello v. Mormello, 452 Pa. Super. 590, 682 A.2d 824 (1996), *overruled on other grounds*, Stoner v. Stoner, 572 Pa. 665, 819 A.2d 529 (2003).

a relevant factor. The wife in that case was under considerable pressure to sign, had no counsel, and did not even read the agreement, factors that suggest strongly that undue influence was present. (The court did ultimately find the agreement invalid for fraud, but its holding on the undue influence issue remains questionable.)

Length of Negotiations

Some courts have also noted that a finding of undue influence is more likely where the negotiations between the parties lasted for only a brief time. For instance, in *In re Marriage of Perry*,[188] the court found undue influence where the agreement was made after only 15 minutes of negotiations.

The length of negotiations is obviously only one factor, and it is not itself determinative. In *In re Marriage of Steadman*,[189] the court found no undue influence where there were only two hours of negotiations. The wife had counsel, the court noted, and the agreement was the product of arm's-length negotiating.

Undue influence may be somewhat less likely where the agreement took considerable time and effort to negotiate.[190]

Voluntary Agreement Clause

Some agreements contain a specific provision that the agreement was signed voluntarily, without any form of undue influence. Such a provision may be one factor pointing against a finding of undue influence, but it is not conclusive on the question.[191]

Objective Standard

Even if the one spouse was actually deprived of his or her own free will, contracts are generally judged under an objective rather than a subjective standard. Thus, the attacking spouse must show not only that he or she was deprived of free will, but also that the reasonable person would have been deprived of free will. Phrased conversely, this rule requires that the parties take reasonable measures for their own protection against undue influence. Where such measures are not taken, the victim is in a sense responsible for his or her own predicament.

The most common application of this rule occurs when the party attacking the agreement failed to read it. Even if such a party signed the contract in ignorance, the

---

188. 96 Ill. App. 3d 370, 421 N.E.2d 274 (1981).

189. 283 Ill. App. 3d 703, 670 N.E.2d 1146 (1996); *see also* Hestek v. Hestek, 587 N.W.2d 308, 310 (Minn. Ct. App. 1998) (upholding agreement made only two days after filing of action and 18 days before hearing; wife had summarily consented to agreement in open court).

190. *See* Glorvigen v. Glorvigen, 438 N.W.2d 692, 697 (Minn. Ct. App. 1989) (agreement made after one month of "highly detailed and comprehensive" negotiations; no undue influence).

191. *See* Schlottach v. Schlottach, 873 S.W.2d 928 (Mo. Ct. App. 1994); Schoradt v. Rivet, 186 A.D.2d 307, 587 N.Y.S.2d 794 (1992); *but cf. In re* Marriage of Kieturakis, 138 Cal. App. 4th 56, 90, 41 Cal. Rptr. 3d 119, 144 (2006) ("the presumption of undue influence [arising from substantive unfairness] should not attach in this case because the parties acknowledged in the [marital settlement agreement] that no undue influence was exercised").

courts have been extremely reluctant to grant relief.[192] The only case to grant relief in this situation involved specific pressure on the wife not to read the agreement.[193]

Another common application occurs when the attacking spouse claims that the agreement is a product of the inherent pressures of litigating a divorce case. Regardless of the actual subjective effect of these pressures upon a particular spouse, the law expects all spouses to withstand the normal stresses of daily life. "Stress accompanies virtually all marital breakups, and we could not enforce any pretrial agreements if stress alone prevented their enforcement."[194] One court generalized this principle into a flat rule that undue influence cannot result from emotional pressures imposed from a source other than the opposing spouse.[195]

A different result may obtain where the emotional stress was the result of the other party's conduct. In *Rubin v. Rubin*,[196] the husband caused the wife's emotional stress and tired condition by deliberately failing to provide sufficient funds, forcing the wife to work at several different jobs to support herself and the children. The court distinguished an earlier contrary decision on grounds that the stress in that case had been an unavoidable consequence of divorce. Because the stress in the case at hand was caused by the husband, the court found the contract invalid.

A final application of the objective element of undue influence involves oral stipulations made in open court. Courts are generally reluctant to find undue influence in this setting, as the courtroom setting is generally not favorable to the exertion of undue influence by either spouse.[197]

---

192. *See, e.g.*, Mason v. Mason, 873 S.W.2d 631 (Mo. Ct. App. 1994) (ignorance of plain language of contract was not a defense to its validity); J.R.S. v. P.J.S., 155 A.D.2d 323, 547 N.Y.S.2d 294 (1989) (husband, an experienced attorney, did not read contract before signing it; no undue influence), *appeal dismissed*, 75 N.Y.2d 938, 554 N.E.2d 1276, 555 N.Y.S.2d 688 (1990); Vann v. Vann, 767 N.W.2d 855, 862 (N.D. 2009) ("absent any evidence James Vann was precluded from reading the property settlement agreement, he is not excused from his obligation to read a legal document before signing it."); Pillow v. Pillow, 13 Va. App. 271, 410 S.E.2d 407 (1991) (successful insurance agent voluntarily chose not to read agreement thoroughly; no undue influence).

193. *In re* Marriage of Staszak, 223 Ill. App. 3d 335, 584 N.E.2d 926 (1991) (husband pressured wife not to read agreement, and told her she would receive nine months of custody, while agreement gave custody entirely to husband; wife had no counsel; agreement invalid).

194. Bendekgey v. Bendekgey, 154 Vt. 193, 576 A.2d 433 (1990); *see, e.g.*, Flynn v. Flynn, 232 Ill. App. 3d 394, 597 N.E.2d 709 (1992) (contract not invalid merely because wife was anxious when she agreed to it); McMahan v. McMahan, 567 So. 2d 976 (Fla. Dist. Ct. App. 1990); Grindinger v. Grindinger, 29 Mass. App. Ct. 689, 564 N.E.2d 602 (1991); Gaton v. Gaton, 170 A.D.2d 576, 566 N.Y.S.2d 353 (1991) (noting that party claiming undue influence was represented by counsel, who did all of the negotiating); Cantamessa v. Cantamessa, 170 A.D.2d 792, 565 N.Y.S.2d 895 (1991); Maury v. Maury, 2008 WL 2609702 (Ohio Ct. App. 2008); *In re* Marriage of Banks, 887 S.W.2d 160 (Tex. Ct. App. 1994).

195. Sharp v. Sharp, 179 Ariz. 205, 877 P.2d 304 (Ct. App. 1994). *But see infra* notes 198–205 (substantial case law invalidating agreements for undue influence exerted by nonparties).

196. 29 Mass. App. Ct. 689, 564 N.E.2d 602 (1991).

197. *See, e.g.*, Washo v. Washo, 170 A.D.2d 827, 565 N.Y.S.2d 897 (1991) (husband claimed that he agreed to settlement while under the influence of blood pressure medication; husband had consented to agreement under direct questioning by trial judge, who observed nothing unusual about his behavior; agreement valid); *In re* Marriage of Bries, 499 N.W.2d 319 (Iowa Ct. App. 1993)

Undue Influence by Nonparties

Undue influence can be exerted by persons other than the spouses themselves.[198] Where the trial judge placed "substantial pressure" upon the parties to settle the case and the wife repudiated the agreement the day after she signed it, one court found the agreement invalid.[199] In another case, the trial judge stated that he would consider the husband's failure to settle as a factor in setting attorney's fees. When the husband expressed uncertainty whether he wanted to accept the wife's settlement offer, the judge harshly cross-examined the husband on whether he consented to the offer, permitting only yes or no answers on pain of being held in contempt. The appellate court held that trial judges must have patience with troubled and indecisive divorce litigants, and it held that the settlement was invalid.[200]

Settlement pressure from the court is particularly troublesome when it suggests that the case has been prejudged. In *In re Marriage of Hitchcock*,[201] the court told the parties before hearing evidence how it intended to rule. Based upon these comments, the wife settled the case. The appellate court set the agreement aside, noting that the judge had made his comments before hearing evidence.

Courts have likewise held that a settlement agreement is invalid if it results from application of improper pressure by a mediator.[202]

Despite the above cases, the court is allowed to apply some pressure on the parties to settle the case. Where the pressure was not extreme under the circumstances, appellate courts have been reluctant to invalidate the resulting agreement.[203] One court stated in dicta that the court's comments on the law do not generally constitute undue influence,[204] a statement that is consistent with the general rule that parties are not

---

(husband assented to stipulation in open court without any reference to alleged hearing problem; contract valid).

198. *See generally* RESTATEMENT (SECOND) OF CONTRACTS § 177(3) (1981) ("If a party's manifestation of assent is induced by one who is not a party to the transaction, the contract is voidable by the victim unless the other party to the transaction in good faith and without reason to know of the undue influence either gives value or relies materially on the transaction[.]").

199. Burr v. Burr, 148 Vt. 207, 531 A.2d 915, 917 (1987).

200. Peskin v. Peskin, 271 N.J. Super. 261, 638 A.2d 849 (1994). *See also* Loss v. Loss, 608 So. 2d 39 (Fla. Dist. Ct. App. 1992) (judge must use "great caution and circumspection" when getting involved in negotiations between parties).

201. 265 N.W.2d 599 (Iowa 1978).

202. *See* Vitakis-Valchine v. Valchine, 793 So. 2d 1094, 1099 (Fla. Dist. Ct. App. 2001) ("it would be unconscionable for a court to enforce a settlement agreement reached through coercion or any other improper tactics utilized by a court-appointed mediator"). The trial court in Vitakis-Valchine refused to consider a claim of mediator misconduct; the appellate court remanded for a factual hearing.

203. *See, e.g.*, Washo, 170 A.D.2d 827, 565 N.Y.S.2d 897 (judge did not exert undue pressure upon husband to accept agreement); Blejski v. Blejski, 325 S.C. 491, 480 S.E.2d 462 (Ct. App. 1997) (court commented from the bench that unvested pensions were not divisible, a position that was perhaps valid at the time it was made, but that was later rejected by appellate case law; comment did not unfairly cause wife to sign agreement).

204. *Blejski*, 325 S.C. 491, 480 S.E.2d 462.

entitled to rely upon statements of law made by persons other than their own counsel. *See* § **4.044**.

Undue influence can likewise be exerted by a spouse's own attorney. In *In re Marriage of Moran*,[205] the wife's attorney negotiated a settlement without her knowledge. Although she objected to the terms and continually questioned the truth of the husband's financial disclosure, her attorney threatened to quit on the eve of trial unless she signed the agreement. The agreement also gave the attorney a fee that was clearly excessive compared to the work actually done. When the wife consulted the judge about the agreement, he told her it was the best she could do and that she would lose if the case were tried. The court found the agreement invalid for undue influence.

Likewise, in *Summers v. Summers*,[206] the husband offered to settle the case. The wife's attorney told her that she should accept the offer or "she would probably not get a penny and that he was tired of fooling with the case."[207] He also allegedly yelled at her and used profanity. The court held that these allegations, if proven, were sufficient to set the agreement aside.

In both of the above cases, the attorney used threats and pressure to coerce the client into accepting an undesirable settlement. Where the attorney exerts no undue pressure, but merely points out the excessiveness of his client's demands, the resulting agreement is probably valid.[208]

A Texas court held that coercion or undue influence cannot come from a party's own attorney.[209] This holding seems doubtful. There is no reason why an attorney could not improperly coerce a settlement, and the above cases held on the facts that an attorney had done so. On the facts of the Texas case, however, the wife alleged only that her attorney told her that if she refused to accept the husband's settlement offer, the court would tell her to accept it. It is doubtful that this statement rises to the level of undue influence at all; the attorney was essentially telling the wife that the husband's offer was similar to what the court would have ordered if the case did not settle. Given the body of case law holding that a party's own attorney can improperly coerce a settlement, the Texas court would have done better simply to find no undue influence on the facts.

Where undue influence is exerted by a person not connected to the case, one court held that the contract would be invalid only if the influencing party was acting as the other spouse's agent.[210]

---

205. 136 Ill. App. 3d 331, 483 N.E.2d 580 (1985).

206. 186 W. Va. 635, 413 S.E.2d 692 (1991).

207. 413 S.E.2d at 697.

208. *See In re* Marriage of Cierny, 187 Ill. App. 3d 334, 543 N.E.2d 201, 208 (1989) (attorney told husband that his settlement demands were unreasonable and that he would withdraw if the husband continued to be "bullheaded"; no undue influence).

209. *See* Lee v. Lee, 44 S.W.3d 151, 154 (Tex. Ct. App. 2001) ("[t]o invalidate an agreement based on undue influence or duress, the coercion must come from the opposing party to the agreement, not the claimant's attorney").

210. *See* Hill v. Hill, 94 N.C. App. 474, 380 S.E.2d 540 (1989) (parties' son allegedly exerted undue influence on wife, but was not acting as husband's agent, contract was valid).

§ 4.053 Fraud

Fraud is one of the most common defenses raised in separation agreement cases. One decision defined the defense as follows:

> To rescind a contract on the ground of fraud, a party must show by clear and convincing evidence [that] there was a material misrepresentation made that was reasonably believed and detrimentally relied on by the that party. . . . In other words, "if one represents [to a person] what is really false, in such a way to induce a *reasonable* man to believe it, and the representation is meant to be acted on," and that person detrimentally acts on the misrepresentation, there is an action based on fraud.[211]

Thus, an agreement is invalid for fraud if (1) one party made a misrepresentation; (2) the misrepresentation was of a material fact; (3) the misrepresentation was deliberate; (4) the other party detrimentally relied on the misrepresentation; and (5) the reliance was reasonable.

The attacking party must plead fraud specifically in his or her complaint or answer,[212] and prove it by clear and convincing evidence.[213]

Misrepresentation

The first element of fraud is a specific misrepresentation. Where the party who procured the agreement neither misrepresented nor failed to disclose any material fact, the agreement is not invalid for fraud.[214]

The clearest type of misrepresentation is an affirmative statement of an untrue fact. A good example is *Rocca v. Rocca*,[215] where the husband testified that he had no interest in certain tracts of land titled in the name of his father. In fact, the husband had equitable ownership of the land, and his father had agreed to sign the properties over to the husband whenever the husband wanted. In addition, the evidence showed that the agreement had been reached for the specific purpose of depriving the wife of any interest in the properties. A final divorce decree was reopened for fraud on the court.[216]

---

211. Wells v. Wells, 12 Va. App. 31, 401 S.E.2d 891, 892 (1991) (quoting Jefferson Standard Ins. Co. v. Hedrick, 181 Va. 824, 27 S.E.2d 198, 202 (1943)); *see also* Grasse v. Grasse, 254 S.W.3d 174 (Mo. Ct. App. 2008); *In re* Marriage of Turner, 803 S.W.2d 655, 661 (Mo. Ct. App. 1991).

212. Boyle v. Burkich, 245 A.D.2d 609, 665 N.Y.S.2d 104 (1997).

213. Hallas v. Moule, 252 A.D.2d 768, 676 N.Y.S.2d 274 (1998).

214. *E.g.*, Derby v. Derby, 8 Va. App. 19, 378 S.E.2d 74 (1989); *see Grasse*, 254 S.W.3d at 180–181 (rejecting wife's claim that husband told her his business was worth only $210,000; that number appeared on confusing handwritten document, and it appeared to be a statement of the amount invested by husband, not the value of the company; many other numbers also appeared on the same sheet).

215. 760 N.E.2d 677 (Ind. Ct. App. 2002).

216. *See also* Blanchard v. Blanchard, 108 Nev. 908, 839 P.2d 1320 (1992) (husband's financial statement listed Florida property as a marital asset, when it had actually been forfeited for nonpayment of taxes); Fine v. Fine, 12 A.D.3d 399, 786 N.Y.S.2d 57 (2004) (wife's allegation that husband disclosed annual income of $45,000, when his actual annual income was $120,000, stated

In order to serve as the basis for a claim of fraud, a misrepresentation must be untrue when made, and not simply become untrue at a later point in time. This point is particularly important when the misrepresentation is a promise rather than a statement of fact. Where one spouse makes a promise in good faith but then fails to keep it, the representation was true when it was made, and fraud is not present.[217] Conversely, if the promising spouse had no intent to keep the promise at the time it was made, a valid misrepresentation has been made, and the contract should be set aside if the attacking party proves the remaining elements of fraud.[218]

A misrepresentation need not necessarily be made to the opposing party. In states that require the court to approve separation agreements, *see generally* § **4.041**, a misrepresentation made to the court can constitute fraud.[219]

Nondisclosure

In a larger number of fraud cases, one spouse will claim that the other spouse committed fraud by failing to disclose a material fact. As a prerequisite to such a claim, the attacking spouse must first establish that the other spouse knew the undisclosed fact.[220] The defending spouse is not required to disclose a fact of which he or she is unaware.

If the other spouse did know the undisclosed fact, the question then becomes whether the fact was actually disclosed. This question is often a classic issue of fact: The attacking spouse will state that the fact was not disclosed, the defending spouse

---

a sufficient claim of fraud to survive a motion to dismiss); *Wells*, 12 Va. App. 31, 401 S.E.2d 891 (husband stated in deposition that he had received no compensation or benefits from corporation since 1987, when in fact he was entitled to 98 percent of its profits and was the sole signatory of its bank account).

217. *See* Joplin v. Joplin, 88 Ark. App. 190, 195, 196 S.W.3d 496, 498 (2004) ("a broken promise is not fraud," though it may support an action to enforce the agreement); *In re* Marriage of Pfeifer, 862 S.W.2d 926 (Mo. Ct. App. 1993) (husband promised to take care of wife after divorce, and then failed to keep his promise; promise was made in good faith; no fraud); *In re* Marriage of Auble, 125 Or. App. 554, 866 P.2d 1239 (1993) (husband's promise to collect only nominal child support from wife was made in good faith; no fraud).

218. *E.g.*, Young v. Williams, 47 A.D.3d 1084, 850 N.Y.S.2d 262, 265 (2008) ("a misrepresentation may include 'a present, but undisclosed, intent not to perform'") (quoting Van Kleeck v. Hammond, 25 A.D.3d 941, 943, 811 N.Y.S.2d 452 (2006)).

219. *See* Hurst v. Hurst, 2008 WL 2687093 (Ohio Ct. App. 2008) (parties failed to inform court of side agreement that materially altered their overall bargain; agreement invalid for fraud).

220. *See* Empie v. Empie, 46 A.D.3d 1008, 846 N.Y.S.2d 811, 813 (2007) (husband failed to disclose airport authority's interest in purchasing property, but "the record fails to establish that any definite offer was conveyed to plaintiff until after the parties entered into the separation agreement"; independent appraiser testified that the authority's interest in the property, without an actual offer being made, would not have changed his valuation; "nondisclosure of any such potential interest in the commercial property, without more, does not amount to fraud"); Drewry v. Drewry, 8 Va. App. 460, 383 S.E.2d 12 (1989) (parties agreed to value property using real estate tax assessment; after agreement, husband sold property for higher amount; no fraud, because husband did not know at the time that the tax assessment was inaccurate); *see also In re* Marriage of Dimmit, 132 B.R. 617 (Bankr. W.D. Mo. 1991) (husband could not have fraudulently concealed intention to declare bankruptcy, as he had no such intention until after the divorce).

will state that the fact was disclosed, and the court will have to determine whose testimony is more credible.

Information that is disclosed late in the litigation process is still disclosed, so long as the receiving spouse had a reasonable time period to process the information under the circumstances involved.[221]

Objective evidence, when available, is more probative on the question of disclosure than either party's subjective testimony.[222] From the drafter's standpoint, the best way to avoid a claim of nondisclosure is to disclose relevant facts in either the agreement itself or an appendix attached to it. A contractual provision stating that full disclosure was made is also some evidence that all relevant facts were disclosed, although it is not conclusive on the question.[223] Such a provision is a two-edged sword, however, for it also creates a contractual duty of disclosure that might not otherwise have existed.[224]

Where the defending spouse did fail to disclose a material fact, then question is then whether the defending spouse had a duty to disclose it. Such a duty can come from several possible sources.

The Contract Itself. The contract itself may contain a clause stating that the parties have fully disclosed their assets. "Such provisions do not call for a minute examination of syntax. They require the disclosure by one party to the other of all matters which in good conscience ought to be disclosed."[225] If full disclosure is not made, the agreement

---

221. *See In re* Marriage of Briddle, 756 N.W.2d 35, 41 (Iowa 2008) (where husband's corporations produced financial records only after several court orders were entered against them, but wife and her experts did have requested records for two weeks prior to negotiation of agreement, finding no fraud; wife "was in possession of the relevant financial information sufficiently in advance of the mediation conference to engage in meaningful negotiations").

222. *See In re* Marriage of Kieturakis, 138 Cal. App. 4th 56, 41 Cal. Rptr. 3d 119 (2006) (where record contained e-mails and documents showing that husband received substantial ongoing royalty payments, trial court properly rejected wife's claim that royalty payments had not been disclosed).

223. *See* Hallas v. Moule, 252 A.D.2d 768, 676 N.Y.S.2d 274 (1998).

A provision stating each party has provided all information requested by the other is not equivalent to a full disclosure clause. Daughtry v. Daughtry, 128 N.C. App. 737, 497 S.E.2d 105 (1998). The former provision leaves open the possibility that the other spouse might not have requested relevant information. If the information should have been requested, there may well be no fraud because reliance upon silence was unreasonable. *See* note 272 *infra.* If the other spouse was unaware that the information existed, however, or if the failure to inquire was otherwise reasonable, fraud might still exist.

224. *See* Atkins v. Atkins, 534 N.E.2d 760, 763 (Ind. Ct. App. 1989).

225. *Id.*

In *In re* Marriage of St. Sauver, 196 Or. App. 175, 181–82, 100 P.3d 1076, 1081 (2004), the agreement provided that neither party "has unreasonably overstated or understated the value of any asset." The husband disclosed to the wife his retirement account, but told her that she had no interest in it. The court held that statement did not breach the quoted clause, which applied only to misrepresentation of value.

The wife in *St. Sauver* apparently did not seek relief for fraud outside the limits of the disclosure clause. The husband's statement was certainly a misrepresentation, but most courts deny relief for misrepresentations of law, on the theory that divorce litigants should reasonably rely upon their

may be invalid for fraud.[226] Alternatively, the court can find a material breach of the disclosure provision, which is sufficient to rescind the contract.[227] Contractual disclose provisions can be enforced even if the agreement has been incorporated into a judgment.[228]

Clearly Essential Facts. If the contract contains no full disclosure clause, a duty to disclose can still exist in three separate situations. First, there may be some facts that are so material to the parties' underlying bargain that they must always be disclosed. In *In re Marriage of Dimmit*,[229] for example, the court held that the agreement would be a product of a fraud if the husband had failed to disclose an intention to declare bankruptcy after the case was over. Since bankruptcy would destroy the divorce court's property settlement, it was so material that an inherent duty of disclosure existed. On the facts, however, the court held that the husband did not intend to declare bankruptcy until his business failed after the divorce was over.

---

own attorneys for legal advice, and not upon statements made by the opposing party. *See* note 247 *infra*.

226. *See* Etzion v. Etzion, 62 A.D.3d 646, 649, 880 N.Y.S.2d 79, 83 (2009) (where husband represented in agreement that he had "no active deals or pending negotiations relating to the sale or reorganization of Variety," and then sold Variety shortly after the divorce for a price greatly in excess of the value given to it in the agreement, wife's allegation that husband failed to disclose pending negotiations was sufficient to survive a motion to dismiss).

227. *See Atkins*, 534 N.E.2d 760 (failure to disclose impending merger that doubled the value of certain stock was material breach); Lee v. Lee, 93 N.C. App. 584, 378 S.E.2d 554 (1989) (failure to disclose $102,000 debt receivable was material breach).

The material breach argument is especially strong if the disclosure clause itself states that any violation is a sufficient basis for rescission. *See* Reiner v. Reiner, 59 A.D.3d 420, 420–21, 874 N.Y.S.2d 143, 144–45 (2009) (wife submitted appraisals suggesting that husband had undervalued marital real property; agreement provided that "[s]hould any material representation turn out to be substantially and materially false, such party's reliance thereon in error shall be deemed sufficient reason to set aside the financial terms of this Agreement"; wife "set forth a basis to set aside the agreement under the unambiguous terms of the agreement itself").

Without formally finding fraud or material breach, a New York court relied upon a full disclosure provision in finding an agreement invalid for overreaching, where material assets had in fact not been disclosed. *See* Tchorzewski v. Tchorzewski, 278 A.D.2d 869, 870, 717 N.Y.S.2d 436, 437 (2000) (contract recited that full disclosure had been made, but husband's pension had not been valued; wife lacked counsel, and division of marital assets was substantially unequal; agreement invalid for overreaching).

228. *See* White v. White, 274 Ga. 884, 885, 561 S.E.2d 801, 802 (2002) (where "Mr. White had fraudulently hidden assets to prevent their equitable division in the divorce," trial court did not err by applying nondisclosure provisions of agreement; nondisclosure was sufficient fraud to justify setting aside the judgment).

The authors would have argued in *White* that the judgment did not need to be set aside, as the agreement's nondisclosure provisions were just as much incorporated into the judgment as the substantive provisions. To enforce the substantive provisions without also enforcing the nondisclosure provisions would be to enforce only selected parts of the judgment.

229. 132 B.R. 617 (Bankr. W.D. Mo. 1991).

Where bankruptcy does not destroy the equity of the property settlement, there is no inherent duty to disclose an intention to declare bankruptcy after the divorce case is complete.[230]

Discovery Request. Second, a duty to disclose obviously arises from a properly phrased discovery request in the underlying divorce action. In *Barganier v. Barganier,*[231] the wife filed a request for production asking the husband to reveal "all appropriate forms and schedules" regarding the parties' federal income tax liability. The wife also requested a listing of all current debts. The husband failed to reveal that he had taken accelerated depreciation on a particular building, dramatically reducing the tax basis. He then signed an agreement awarding the wife 57 percent of the net proceeds from the sale of the building, failing to inform the wife that because of the low basis, capital gains taxes on the sale would be substantially greater than the profit. When the building sold, before the divorce, the husband failed to disclose the resulting substantial tax liability, in violation of his continuing duty to update his discovery answers. The court held that the husband was required to disclose the low basis of the property and the existence of the tax debt, and it set the agreement aside for fraud.

Likewise, in *Ray v. Ray,*[232] the wife sold her pharmacy shortly before the divorce. The transaction included a sales agreement and a covenant not to compete, each giving the wife a substantial lump sum. The wife disclosed the sales agreement, but "deliberately concealed [the noncompete agreement] in response to discovery requests and during depositions," and deliberately delayed payment under that agreement until after the divorce was over.[233] A final judgment approving the parties' agreement was reopened for extrinsic fraud, and the agreement was set aside.

Where a financial affidavit is required by statute or court rule, there is obviously a legal duty to disclose all information that should appear in the affidavit.[234]

Confidential Relationship. Third, there is a duty to disclose all material facts where the spouses enjoyed a confidential relationship at the time of the nondisclosure.[235] Case law on determining the confidential nature of the parties' relationship is discussed in § **4.03**.

---

230. *See* Price v. Price, 5 So. 3d 1151, 1156 (Miss. Ct. App. 2009) (wife did not commit fraud by failing to disclose her intention to declare bankruptcy after the divorce case, where wife discharged only her own debts, not debts owed jointly with husband, husband "is actually in a better financial position now than he was prior to Jennifer's filing bankruptcy").

231. 669 So. 2d 933, 934 (Ala. Ct. App. 1995).

232. 374 S.C. 79, 647 S.E.2d 237 (2007).

233. *Id.* at 82, 647 S.E.2d at 238–39.

234. *See* Murphy v. Murphy, 212 A.D.2d 583, 622 N.Y.S.2d 755 (1995) (husband failed to reveal assets in court affidavit; reopening incorporated agreement for fraud); *cf.* Buckler v. Buckler, 195 W. Va. 705, 466 S.E.2d 556 (1995) (statutory duty to disclose still exists, even where parties have signed an agreement).

235. *E.g., In re* Marriage of Baltins, 212 Cal. App. 3d 66, 260 Cal. Rptr. 403 (1989); Webb v. Webb, 16 Va. App. 486, 431 S.E.2d 55 (1993).

No Duty to Disclose. Where there is no contractual or statutory duty to disclose, no properly phrased discovery request, and no confidential relationship, the general rule is that there is no duty to disclose.

For example, in *Kornberg v. Kornberg*,[236] the court held that the husband had no duty to disclose his intention not to declare a postdivorce dividend from a certain corporation. The parties' relationship was not confidential, and in any event, various financial documents disclosed to wife revealed that declaration of a dividend was highly unlikely. Likewise, in *McClellan v. McClellan*,[237] the court held that the husband had no duty to disclose existence of his retirement plan. The wife had counsel and took discovery, and she should have learned of the existence of the plan. Indeed, a New York court even went so far as to hold that where the parties' relationship was not confidential, one spouse did not have a duty to disclose that the other spouse's consent to the agreement was influenced by unilateral mistake.[238]

Courts have held with particular clarity that where no confidential relationship is present, neither spouse has a duty to disclose the commission of adultery.[239]

Courts have also held that there is no duty to disclose information that should reasonably be known the other spouse.[240] This result can also be reached by holding that the other spouse knew the truth, and thus could not actually have relied on the nondisclosure, or that the other spouse should have known the truth, and thus could reasonably have relied on the nondisclosure.[241]

In all of the above cases, the court upheld an agreement that could be construed to provide an undue benefit to one party or the other. The underlying rationale is simple:

---

236. 542 N.W.2d 379 (Minn. 1996).

237. 52 Md. App. 525, 451 A.2d 334 (1982).

For additional cases holding that there is no duty to disclose in the absence of the specific fact situations set forth above, *see* Kavner v. Geller, 49 A.D.3d 281, 282, 854 N.Y.S.2d 343, 344 (2008) (where wife "was an intelligent professional separately represented by counsel in the negotiations in this adversarial proceeding," no inherent duty to disclose existed); March v. March, 233 A.D.2d 371, 650 N.Y.S.2d 750 (1996); Daughtry v. Daughtry, 128 N.C. App. 737, 497 S.E.2d 105 (1998); Hill v. Hill, 94 N.C. App. 474, 380 S.E.2d 540 (1989).

238. Vermilyea v. Vermilyea, 224 A.D.2d 759, 636 N.Y.S.2d 953 (1996) (one spouse has no duty to disclose knowledge that other spouse's consent to the agreement is influenced by a unilateral mistake).

239. Winborne v. Winborne, 41 N.C. App. 756, 255 S.E.2d 640, *cert. denied*, 298 N.C. 305, 259 S.E.2d 918 (1979); Bearden v. Bearden, 272 S.C. 378, 252 S.E.2d 128 (1979); Barnes v. Barnes, 231 Va. 39, 340 S.E.2d 803 (1986). *But cf.* Greenland v. Greenland, 29 So. 3d 647, 2009 WL 4730819 (La. Ct. App. 2009) (where wife "made an overt attempt to hide the fact that she was being supported by a third party at the time she was negotiating with [him] for spousal support," husband stated a cause of action to rescind spousal support obligation for fraud, as wife's cohabitation would have been a defense to spousal support). The wife's actions in Greenland appear to have gone beyond mere nondisclosure, and constituted positive misrepresentation.

240. *See* Etzion v. Etzion, 62 A.D.3d 646, 654, 880 N.Y.S.2d 79, 86–87 (2009) (husband "did not have a duty arising out of the marital relationship to volunteer information freely available in the public domain regarding the possibility that the Greenpoint-Williamsburg waterfront might be rezoned for residential development, and that such a rezoning could lead to a possible increase in the market value" of husband's business; possibility of rezoning was public knowledge).

241. See the discussion of actual and reasonable reliance later in this section.

freedom of contract. Freedom of contract means not only the right to reach a bargain the court deems to be fair, but also the right to reach a bargain that the court deems to be unfair, as long as the parties reached that result through procedurally fair, arm's-length bargaining. At one level, this conclusion follows from the rule that the parties can determine the fairness of a separation agreement better than the court. But the point is true even where the agreement is stipulated to be substantively unfair. Freedom to contract means little unless the parties are free to make their own mistakes, and to live with the consequences.

Waiver of Disclosure. If a duty to disclose material facts exists, can it be waived by the agreement? In *March v. March*,[242] the contract contained an express waiver of all disclosure beyond what the parties had actually provided. The court relied in part upon this waiver in finding that the husband had no affirmative duty to disclose to the wife a certain retirement plan. Likewise, in *Luftig v. Luftig*,[243] the court relied upon a similar provision in finding that the husband had no duty to disclose that he intended to work rather than retire after the divorce was over.

Where a statute or rule requires mandatory disclosure from all divorce litigants, the duty to disclose may not be waivable. In California, for example, such a waiver is invalid as against public policy.[244]

Representation of Fact

The second element of fraud is proof that the subject of the misrepresentation or non-disclosure was a material *fact*. Fraud cannot be based upon misrepresentation of non-disclosure of an opinion unless "extraordinary circumstances" are present.[245]

There are two situations in which courts are especially reluctant to find that a misrepresentation was one of fact rather than opinion. First, representations as to the controlling law generally involve opinion, because they are legal conclusions drawn from primary facts (statutes and case law) that are equally available to both parties. For example, in *In re Marriage of Turner*,[246] the husband falsely told the wife that she had no right to any portion of his pension. The parties had been separated for over a year at the time, and the wife had her own independent attorney. The court held that the husband's misstatement was a matter of opinion, and that no fraud was present.[247]

---

242. 233 A.D.2d 371, 650 N.Y.S.2d 750 (1996).

243. 239 A.D.2d 225, 657 N.Y.S.2d 658 (1997); *see also* Berman v. Berman, 217 A.D.2d 531, 629 N.Y.S.2d 82 (1995).

244. *In re* Marriage of Fell, 55 Cal. App. 4th 1058, 64 Cal. Rptr. 522 (1997).

245. *In re* Marriage of Turner, 803 S.W.2d 655, 661 (Mo. Ct. App. 1991).

246. *Id.* at 661.

247. For additional cases specifically holding that a spouse has no duty to disclose an opinion of law regarding retirement benefits, *see* Cucchiaro v. Cucchiaro, 165 Misc. 2d 134, 627 N.Y.S.2d 224 (1995) (wife knew husband had pension, but husband failed to disclose conclusion that pension was marital property; no fraud); Dalton v. Dalton, 164 N.C. App. 584, 596 S.E.2d 331 (2004) (alleged misrepresentation of North Carolina law regarding division of retirement benefits was not a proper basis for fraud); Avriett v. Avriett, 88 N.C. App. 506, 363 S.E.2d 875 (1988), *aff'd mem.*, 322 N.C. 468, 368 S.E.2d 377 (1988) (husband failed to disclose his attorney's opinion on a question of military retirement law; no fraud).

A misrepresentation of law can constitute fraud when extraordinary circumstances are present. The most common such circumstance occurs when one spouse has special knowledge about the law that is not available to the other. For example, where one spouse is an attorney and the other is unrepresented, a deliberate misstatement of law does constitute fraud.[248]

Second, along similar lines, representations of the value of marital assets are often held to be statements of opinion. When both parties have equal access to the underlying financial data, value is a secondary conclusion and not a primary fact. For instance, in *Mitchell v. Mitchell*,[249] the husband misrepresented the value of his pension. The wife had access to all of the plan documents, however, and had a full and fair chance to value the pension herself. The court held that the representation was one of opinion, and that fraud was not present.[250]

For cases holding that other misrepresentations of law were not fraud, *see* Xenitelis v. Xenitelis, 241 A.D.2d 490, 661 N.Y.S.2d 23 (1997) (no duty to disclose fact that equitable distribution laws existed);

248. *See* Elliott v. Elliott, 667 So. 2d 116 (Ala. Ct. App. 1995) (attorney husband told unrepresented wife that court's review of agreement was merely preliminary, when in fact court was conducting a final review; agreement set aside for fraud).

249. 888 S.W.2d 393 (Mo. Ct. App. 1994).

250. *See also* Lentz v. Lentz, 271 Mich. App. 465, 477, 721 N.W.2d 861, 868–69 (2006) (where husband gave wife and her experts full access to records of his real estate development business, and wife paid little attention to the business, trial court properly refused to find fraud; husband "was not required to compel defendant to review the business records or to make specific projections regarding potential profits"); Kojovic v. Goldman, 35 A.D.3d 65, 72, 823 N.Y.S.2d 35, 40 (2006) (where husband disclosed all material facts needed to value minority interest in company, fraud not present merely because wife "now believes her husband privately harbored a more optimistic assessment of the potential value of his minority interest"); Clooten v. Clooten, 520 N.W.2d 843 (N.D. 1994) (where both spouses had equal opportunity to value business, husband did not commit fraud by understating its value); *In re* Marriage of Auble, 125 Or. App. 554, 866 P.2d 1239 (1993) (where wife knew husband had pension, failure to disclose its exact value was not fraud); *In re* Marriage of Curtis, 106 Wash. App. 191, 197, 23 P.3d 13, 17 (2001) ("A party who voluntarily chooses not to value an asset before settlement 'should not be allowed to return to court to do what should have been done prior to entry of the final decree[.]'") (quoting *In re* Marriage of Maddix, 41 Wash. App. 248, 253, 253, 703 P.2d 1062, 1065 (1985)).

In *In re* Marriage of Burkle, 139 Cal. App. 4th 712, 43 Cal. Rptr. 3d 181 (2006), the husband met a duty of disclosure imposed by California law by giving the wife full access to all primary financial documents involving his business. The court rejected the wife's argument that the husband was required to provide some form of specific written summary of the primary documents, or otherwise further disclose facts to which her attorneys and experts had been given full access.

In Grace v. Grace, 253 Mich. App. 357, 367, 655 N.W.2d 595, 601 (2002), the husband represented to wife that $750,000 was half of marital estate, so that entire estate was worth $1.5 million. After divorce, the wife learned that he had previously filled out a mortgage application stating a net worth of $5,145,000, and expert witnesses testified that the marital estate was worth at least $4 million. The court found that fraud was present and awarded the wife substantial damages. One senses from the opinion that the husband was guilty of something more serious than good-faith undervaluation of the marital estate. There is very little discussion, however, of whether the wife could reasonably have retained her own expert and discovered the undervaluation before trial.

Where the parties lack equal access to the primary financial data, representations of value are almost always treated as statements of fact. In this situation, the guilty spouse has concealed not a debatable conclusion, but rather the essential facts needed to draw any form of accurate conclusion at all. For instance, in *In re Marriage of Richardson*,[251] the husband told the wife that his business was worth $10.5 million, when it was actually worth $24 million to $37 million at the time, and $41 million only eight months later. The husband had provided the wife with financial information about the company, but insisted that the wife dismiss her experienced matrimonial attorney and hire an inexperienced young lawyer who reviewed the financial information for only 20 minutes. The court held that the husband had effectively denied the wife equal access to the financial information, and found the agreement invalid for fraud.[252]

Materiality

In addition to proving that the representation was one of fact, the attacking spouse must also show that the fact involved was a material one. A fact is material if its disclosure or correct representation would have made a significant difference in the attacking spouse's decision to sign the agreement. For instance, in *Gaines v. Gaines*,[253] the husband told the wife that he needed his entire military pension for his own support after retirement. He neglected to correct this statement when he accepted a civilian job offer during the divorce proceedings at a salary only slightly less than the salary he had earned in the military. The court held that the wife would not have signed the agreement if she had known about the new position, and found the agreement invalid for fraud.

A fact is not material if the attacking spouse would have signed the agreement even if it had been correctly represented or disclosed. Courts tend to find the fact immaterial in several different types of cases. First, where the fact is entirely irrelevant to the divorce settlement, it is obviously not material. This holding applies most frequently to representations involving marital fault. In *In re Marriage of Dimmit*,[254] for example, the husband failed to disclose the fact that he was having an affair and the fact that he intended to marry his paramour after the divorce. The court held that these facts were not material, as their disclosure would not have caused to the wife to refuse to sign the agreement.[255]

---

251. 237 Ill. App. 3d 1067, 606 N.E.2d 56 (1992).

252. *Id.* For additional cases finding fraud, based upon failure to disclose facts necessary to form a reasonable opinion of value, *see* Billington v. Billington, 27 Conn. App. 466, 606 A.2d 737 (1992) (husband failed to disclose actual written offer to purchase business at price over 50 percent greater than stated in his own financial affidavit); Atkins v. Atkins, 534 N.E.2d 760 (Ind. Ct. App. 1989) (husband failed to disclose impending merger that materially increased the value of the company).

253. 188 A.D.2d 1048, 592 N.Y.S.2d 204 (1992).

254. 132 B.R. 617 (Bankr. W.D. Mo. 1991).

255. *See also* Dayton v. Dayton, 175 A.D.2d 427, 572 N.Y.S.2d 487 (1991) (husband did not tell wife that he regained his job shortly before the divorce; not material, as wife did not assume when signing the agreement that husband would be permanently unemployed; rather, she expected that husband would find new employment shortly).

Second, courts also tend to find that a representation is immaterial when it involves an asset that would have constituted the representing spouse's separate property. For instance, in *Tirrito v. Tirrito*,[256] the husband failed to disclose a personal injury settlement to the wife. The court held that the settlement was not material, as it would have been nondivisible separate property in the divorce case. A similar result is possible in states that do not formally recognize the concept of separate property, if the parties' contributions to the asset were so disproportionate that it would have been awarded entirely to the spouse who failed to disclose it.[257]

A fact is also immaterial when it is small in amount. In *Paul v. Paul*,[258] the husband represented his income at $40,000. After the agreement was signed, the wife moved to set it aside, arguing that his income was actually $41,465. The court rejected the wife's argument. There was no doubt that the husband's income was a material fact, but the amount of the misrepresentation was simply too small to make a difference.[259]

Finally, some courts will hold that misrepresented or nondisclosed fact is immaterial when the disadvantaged party shows no subjective interest in learning the truth.[260] Other courts will find in the same situation that the fact was material, but the disadvantaged party did not actually rely on the misrepresentation or nondisclosure.[261] Either way, fraud is clearly not present.

There is some suggestion in the cases that a misrepresented or undisclosed fact may be less likely to be material if the amount at issue is small, the misrepresenting or non-

---

256. 191 A.D.2d 686, 595 N.Y.S.2d 786 (1993).

257. *See* Gaw v. Sappett, 62 Mass. App. Ct. 405, 816 N.E.2d 1027 (2004) (husband did not disclose to wife his ownership interest in certain real property, but trial court expressly held that wife would have received no portion of husband's interest had the case been litigated, as interest was brought into the marriage and wife had not contributed to its acquisition and preservation; husband believed in good faith, in reliance upon advice of counsel, that he owned no interest in the properties; trial court properly found no fraud).

258. 177 A.D.2d 901, 576 N.Y.S.2d 658 (1991).

259. *See also* Empie v. Empie, 46 A.D.3d 1008, 846 N.Y.S.2d 811, 813 (2007) (husband failed to disclose airport authority's interest in purchasing property, but "the record fails to establish that any definite offer was conveyed to plaintiff until after the parties entered into the separation agreement"; independent appraiser testified that the authority's interest in the property, without an actual offer being made, would not have changed his valuation; "nondisclosure of any such potential interest in the commercial property, without more, does not amount to fraud"); Abrams v. Abrams, 240 A.D.2d 445, 658 N.Y.S.2d 432 (1997) (husband's failure to disclose single payment received from creditor was not material); Nardecchia v. Nardecchia, 155 Ohio App. 3d 40, 45, 798 N.E.2d 1198, 1202 (2003) (where husband disclosed income of $75,088, and his actual income "could have been slightly more than $80,000" due to "to payments for comp time and vacation time that Dean had failed to use," and error was "nonrepetitive and unique to the given year," difference was not large enough to justify a claim for fraud).

260. *See* Sidden v. Mailman, 137 N.C. App. 669, 529 S.E.2d 266 (2000) ("[e]ven if Defendant had made the disclosure of the value of the State Retirement account to Plaintiff, she would not have been aware of such value because she refused to participate in the process of disclosure and refused to look at what Defendant attempted to disclose to her"; existence of account was therefore not a material fact).

261. *See* note 269 *infra*.

disclosing spouse acted in good faith, and the complaining spouse has engaged in other misconduct of equal or greater magnitude.[262]

Intent

If the spouses did not enjoy a confidential relationship, the attacking spouse must show that the misrepresentation or nondisclosure was intentional.[263] This requirement is met if the misrepresentation or nondisclosure was made with the intent that it be relied upon by the injured spouse.[264]

The cases generally do not interpret the intent requirement strictly, and many cases fail to discuss the element at all. In effect, there is almost a presumption that a significant misrepresentation or nondisclosure was intentional. As one court noted, "It is seldom possible to show intent by direct evidence; usually it must be shown by the totality of the circumstances."[265]

In *In re Marriage of Broday*,[266] the husband did not disclose to the wife his profit-sharing plan. The court held that the nondisclosure was not intentional, and thus that there was no fraud. *Broday* cuts against the clear trend to minimize the intent requirement; the court may have been influenced by the fact that the wife deliberately failed to seek counsel, conduct discovery, or otherwise take the most basic steps to protect her interest.

If the spouses had a confidential relationship at the time of the misrepresentation or nondisclosure, "[i]t is irrelevant whether [the guilty party] intentionally or negligently made the representations."[267]

Actual Reliance

After proving intentional misrepresentation or nondisclosure, the attacking spouse must prove that he or she actually relied on the misrepresented or undisclosed information.[268]

---

262. *See Gaw*, 62 Mass. App. Ct. at 413–14, 816 N.E.2d at 1034 (to the extent that husband's financial disclosure was not perfect, errors were not intentional and wife had been held in contempt for deliberate, unjustified refusal to comply with other provisions of agreement; "a Probate Court may, under general principles of equity jurisprudence, deny relief to a party seeking enforcement of any aspect of a separation agreement . . . where that party has herself engaged in inequitable conduct that constitutes an evasion of the spirit of the bargain or that injures or destroys the right of the other party to receive the expected fruits of the agreement"; no fraud).

263. *See id.* (where husband believed in good faith, in reliance upon advice of counsel, that he had no interest in certain real property, his failure to disclose that interest was not fraud).

264. *See generally* Wells v. Wells, 12 Va. App. 31, 401 S.E.2d 891, 892 (1991).

265. *In re* Marriage of Baltins, 212 Cal. App. 3d 66, 260 Cal. Rptr. 403, 415 (1989).

266. 256 Ill. App. 3d 699, 628 N.E.2d 790 (1993); *see also* Romero v. Romero, 959 So. 2d 333, 338 (Fla. Dist. Ct. App. 2007) ("the trial court's finding that the Former Husband failed to disclose his Qtera stock options, which had not vested at the time of dissolution, is not analogous to a finding that the Former Husband submitted a fraudulent financial affidavit"; apparently relying on lack of any evidence that husband had fraudulent intent).

267. *Baltins*, 212 Cal. App. 3d 66, 260 Cal. Rptr. at 417.

268. *See In re* Marriage of Pierce, 206 Or. App. 699, 705, 138 P.3d 889, 892 (2006) ("Husband has the burden of proving that any misrepresentation was material and that the failure to disclose the value of marital assets affected his agreement to sign the stipulated judgment[.]")

Actual reliance is usually not an issue, but it may become significant if the attacking spouse had knowledge of the misrepresentation or nondisclosure. For example, where the husband failed to disclose an asset of which the wife had actual knowledge, a New York court held that fraud was not present.[269]

Also, if the evidence shows that the attacking spouse would have signed the agreement even if he or she had known the misrepresented or undisclosed fact, actual reliance is not present. In *Sargent v. Sargent*,[270] for instance, the wife expressly admitted she did not believe husband's statement that he owned assets worth $2 million, and said she believed his true net worth was $14 million or more. The husband's actual net worth was $17 million. The court held that there was no actual reliance, and therefore no fraud.[271]

In view of the above cases, counsel for the attacking spouse should make certain before claiming fraud that the client will not admit lack of actual reliance. Counsel

---

269. Berman v. Berman, 217 A.D.2d 531, 629 N.Y.S.2d 82 (1995); *see also* Joplin v. Joplin, 88 Ark. App. 190, 195, 196 S.W.3d 496, 498 (2004) (wife claimed that husband fraudulently concealed fact that certain real property had been given to both spouses and not only to him, but "at several points in her testimony, she acknowledged that she knew prior to the divorce that the properties were given to both her and appellant"; no actual reliance and no fraud); Crupi v. Crupi, 784 So. 2d 611, 614 (Fla. Dist. Ct. App. 2001) (where wife "knew about the inaccuracies and inconsistencies in the affidavit of her husband but signed the Mediated Settlement Agreement anyway," trial court correctly refused to find fraud); *In re* Marriage of Gorton & Robbins, 342 Mont. 537, 182 P.3d 746 (2008) (husband's failure to disclose $135,000 appraisal of five-acre property was not fraud, where wife knew that two adjoining properties of two and a half acres had each been advertised at $110,000); Head v. Head, 59 Md. App. 570, 477 A.2d 282 (1984) (where wife knew that husband had failed to disclose true value of assets, she could not have relied on his nondisclosure; no fraud); Lentz v. Lentz, 271 Mich. App. 465, 477, 721 N.W.2d 861, 869 (2006) (husband gave wife and her experts full access to records of his real estate development business, but wife "chose not to take any interest in the businesses, and she declined to have her attorney review the separation agreement"; no fraud); Etzion v. Etzion, 62 A.D.3d 646, 654, 880 N.Y.S.2d 79, 86–87 (2009) (husband "did not have a duty arising out of the marital relationship to volunteer information freely available in the public domain regarding the possibility that the Greenpoint-Williamsburg waterfront might be rezoned for residential development, and that such a rezoning could lead to a possible increase in the market value" of husband's business; possibility of rezoning was public knowledge); Christian v. Christian, 742 N.W.2d 819, 828 (N.D. 2007) (husband had full knowledge of wife's remainder interest in property owned by her mother, but did not remember the interest until after the agreement was signed; "Timothy Christian was in as good a position as Diane Christian to have the remainder interest included and the other property professionally assessed before the settlement agreement was signed"; no fraud); *In re* Marriage of Schell, 191 A.D.2d 570, 594 N.Y.S.2d 807 (1993) (wife signed joint tax return, which listed the husband's major assets; no fraud).

270. 677 A.2d 528 (Me. 1996).

271. *See also Joplin*, 88 Ark. App. at 194–95, 196 S.W.3d at 498 (wife "does not say how the 1998 purchase induced her to enter into the 2002 settlement, nor does she say what she would have done differently had she known the truth"; no fraud); *In re* Marriage of Pfeifer, 862 S.W.2d 926 (Mo. Ct. App. 1993) (wife admitted that she "probably would have" signed the agreement even if the husband had not made misrepresentation; no fraud); *Pierce*, 206 Or. App. at 705, 138 P.3d at 892 ("Husband offered no evidence to the effect that, had he known the precise value of the marital assets, he would not have agreed to the stipulated judgment"; no fraud, even though parties had confidential relationship).

for the defending spouse would be equally well advised to expressly ask the attacking spouse, in deposition if not in trial, whether he or she actually relied on the misrepresentation. An unfavorable response to this question will not hurt, and a favorable answer could change a losing case into a winning one.

Reasonable Reliance

Even if the attacking spouse suffered actual harm from relying on a misrepresentation, it is still necessary that the reliance be reasonable. Under the general law of contracts, reliance is reasonable only where the party attacking the agreement used due diligence to protect his or her interests.[272] Phrased conversely, a party is not allowed to rely upon a representation unless the party takes at least basic steps to ensure that the representation is accurate.

The extent to which this requirement applies to separation agreements is a closely debated issue. In *Billingsly v. Billingsly*,[273] the court held that the requirement does not apply at all, and thus that no showing of due diligence need be made. The court relied heavily upon the fact that all parties to divorce cases are required to file financial affidavits, and upon the strong public policy of full and frank disclosure in divorce cases. In light of this policy, the court held that any substantial misrepresentation or nondisclosure of a material fact should be sufficient to set the agreement aside, even if the attacking spouse took no steps to ensure the accuracy of the representation before relying upon it.

An Indiana court took a similar approach in *Dodd v. Estate of Yanan*.[274] The wife in that case claimed fraud even though she had failed to conduct any discovery at all in the divorce action. The court held that due diligence did require the wife to review any information presented to her, but it did not require her actually to seek information that she did not already have. Because the wife had no information, she had nothing to review, and the court held that she had used due diligence.

Despite these decisions, the majority rule is that spouses in divorce cases are required to take reasonable measures for their own protection. The duty, however, is not a strict one:

> As a general rule, a person has a right to rely on a representation " . . . and need make no further inquiry." . . . While the common law affords reasonable protection against fraud in dealing, it " 'does not go to the romantic length of giving indemnity against the consequences of indolence and folly, or a careless indifference to the ordinary and accessible means of information.'" . . . However, one "must not say or do anything to throw [another] off his guard or to or to divert him from making the inquiries and examination which a prudent man ought to make."[275]

---

272. RESTATEMENT, *supra* note 110, § 172.

273. 220 Conn. 212, 595 A.2d 1377 (1991).

274. 587 N.E.2d 1348 (Ind. Ct. App. 1992).

275. Wells v. Wells, 12 Va. App. 31, 401 S.E.2d 891, 893 (1991) (quoting Cerriglio v. Pettit, 113 Va. 533, 75 S.E. 303, 308 (1912)); Harris v. Dunham, 203 Va. 760, 127 S.E.2d 65, 72 (1962); Horner v. Ahern, 207 Va. 860, 153 S.E.2d 216, 219 (1967).

In most cases, therefore, the representation must only appear plausible in light of "ordinary and accessible sources of information."[276] The exact definition of "ordinary and accessible sources of information" is a question of fact, but most cases find that it encompasses at least the actual fruits of the discovery process. Thus, where the attacking party had his or her own independent counsel and expert witnesses, reliance on the opposing party's statements is generally not reasonable.[277]

In addition, unless a confidential relationship is present, the attacking party must use the discovery process for his or her own self-protection. Thus, where the attacking spouse completely failed to take discovery, the courts have shown little sympathy when marital assets are omitted or undervalued. For example, in *In re Marriage of Broday*,[278] where the wife deliberately declined to seek counsel and completely failed to investigate husband's finances, the court refused to find fraud. The divorce process is adversarial in nature, and the parties should know better than to trust one another blindly.[279]

The same result has been reached where the discovery taken is not reasonable under the circumstances. For instance, in *Green v. Green*,[280] the agreement transferred

---

276. *Wells*, 401 S.E.2d at 893.

277. *See* Maier v. Maier, 221 A.D.2d 193, 633 N.Y.S.2d 165 (1995); Patti v. Patti, 146 A.D.2d 757, 537 N.Y.S.2d 241 (1989); *see also* Tubbs v. Tubbs, 648 So. 2d 817 (Fla. Dist. Ct. App. 1995) (no fraud where wife had counsel and expert witness, and thus had independent knowledge of value of marital estate); Micale v. Micale, 542 So. 2d 415 (Fla. Dist. Ct. App. 1989) (wife had been officer and director of corporation and had extensive knowledge of its financial affairs; no fraud); Shultis v. Reichel Shultis, 1 A.D.3d 876, 878, 768 N.Y.S.2d 38, 40 (2003) ("we see no justifiable basis for his reliance on any alleged misrepresentations inasmuch as the effect of the new term could have been discerned through the exercise of ordinary intelligence").

278. 256 Ill. App. 3d 699, 628 N.E.2d 790 (1993).

279. *See also* McMurry v. McMurry, 957 S.W.2d 731 (Ky. Ct. App. 1997) (where wife took no discovery, claim of fraud rejected); Sargent v. Sargent, 677 A.2d 528 (Me. 1996) (wife rejected her own attorney's strong advice to take discovery; any reliance wife placed on husband's misrepresentation of his own net worth was not reasonable); Kojovic v. Goldman, 35 A.D.3d 65, 72, 823 N.Y.S.2d 35, 40–41 (2006) (wife, a former equity research assistant at Morgan Stanley with a degree in finance, along with her experienced counsel and accountant, could have freely availed themselves of any number of valuation and discovery procedures during the divorce proceeding but declined to do so; no fraud on the facts, even if husband "had additional information that he kept to himself" about the company's value); *In re* Marriage of Shaner, 252 Ill. App. 3d 146, 624 N.E.2d 1217 (1993) (where contract awarded wife $2,453.74 as 50 percent of the equity in the marital home, but record showed that 50 percent of the equity was actually $10,983.69, no fraud was present, as wife had failed to use due diligence to discover the error; remanding to consider defense of mutual mistake); Eihusen v. Eihusen, 272 Neb. 462, 469, 723 N.W.2d 60, 65 (2006) (in the divorce case, "Linda had the same avenues of discovery which she has employed in the present [postjudgment action], but elected not to utilize them to her advantage"; no fraud; "we cannot conclude that Linda exercised the requisite due diligence"); Cosh v. Cosh, 45 A.D.3d 798, 800, 847 N.Y.S.2d 136, 138 (2007) ("[t]he defendant was fully aware of the parties' assets and, contrary to the advice of her counsel, chose to forego an independent appraisal of their real property and the plaintiff's business interest"; no fraud); March v. March, 233 A.D.2d 371, 650 N.Y.S.2d 750 (1996) (where wife had full chance to take discovery, no fraud); Klein v. Klein, 2008 WL 5064848 (Ohio Ct. App. 2008) (where wife knew of husband's annuity and did not seek to value it, trial court did not err in finding no fraud).

280. 327 S.C. 577, 491 S.E.2d 260 (Ct. App. 1997).

a certain building from the husband to the wife. The husband failed to disclose that the building was in poor condition, but the wife had never even asked to inspect the building before signing the agreement. The court held that due diligence required the wife to make at least some effort to inspect the building, and it refused to set the agreement aside.[281]

Green suggests that the parties may have a particular duty to take measures to inspect and value significant assets awarded to them by the agreement. Parties who deliberately decline to examine a package before purchase should not express surprise when the contents turn out to be less than expected.

What if a spouse relies upon material informally provided by the other side, but conducts no formal discovery? In *Shirk v. Shirk*,[282] the court held emphatically that such reliance was reasonable. To rule otherwise would force parties to take formal discovery, the court held, a requirement that would increase the time and cost to litigate divorce cases.

While reliance upon informal discovery may not be unreasonable, formal discovery still offers great advantages. To begin with, the duty of disclosure imposed by a formal discovery request is substantial. There may be a duty to avoid actual lies in informal discovery, but the status of the duty to make positive disclosure is not so clear. Second, formal discovery yields a better record of response and request, a record that makes misrepresentation or nondisclosure easier to prove. Finally, even if reliance on informal discovery is reasonable, reliance on formal discovery is unquestionable. In light of these facts, prudent counsel will always confirm all material facts with discovery requests. With regard to the costs of divorce litigation, the authors' experience is that narrowly drafted requests and responses are within the means of most clients. To the extent that a cost problem does exist, the remedy should be to make formal discovery more affordable, not to substitute informal discovery.

With regard to the content of discovered information, most cases recognize that due diligence requires only a basic inquiry and not extensive analysis.[283] Thus, where there is some valid reason why the misrepresented or concealed fact should not have been uncovered through basic discovery, reasonable reliance is probably present.

There are several fact situations in which courts are particularly likely to find that a fact was not reasonably discoverable. First, courts have been reluctant to require that the parties continuously take discovery throughout the entire divorce process. Thus, where one spouse misrepresents or conceals a fact that arose shortly before divorce,

---

281. *See also* Selke v. Selke, 600 N.E.2d 100 (Ind. 1992) (wife knew husband had pension but did not request any information on its value; no reasonable reliance); Berman v. Berman, 217 A.D.2d 531, 629 N.Y.S.2d 82 (1995) (where wife voluntarily took only limited discovery, no fraud was present).

282. 551 N.W.2d 504 (Minn. Ct. App. 1996). The court's opinion was reversed on appeal on another issue; the reversing opinion did not address the question of informal discovery. Shirk v. Shirk, 561 N.W.2d 519 (Minn. 1997).

283. *E.g.*, *In re* Marriage of Lindjord, 234 Ill. App. 3d 319, 600 N.E.2d 431 (1992) (stressing that due diligence requirement is not rigidly enforced where the other spouse is guilty of unconscionable behavior).

most courts find that the reliance was reasonable. For instance, in one case the husband listed an asset in his financial affidavit at $225,000, failing to disclose that he had in hand a written offer to purchase it for $380,000. Three days after the divorce, the husband sold the asset for $360,000. The court set the agreement aside for fraud.[284] Likewise, where the husband failed to disclose an impending merger, and the merger was not reported in the newspaper until the day on which the agreement was signed, another court held that the wife had reasonably relied on the nondisclosure.[285]

Second, courts do not insist that discovery be employed where the guilty spouse has somehow diverted the innocent spouse from making normal inquiries. For example, in *Wells v. Wells*,[286] the husband made misrepresentations in a deposition taken under oath. Although the wife had reason to suspect the truth of the statements, she did not have actual knowledge that they were false. Because "statements made under oath are commonly accepted" and may "cause even a prudent person to refrain from making further inquiries," the wife had no duty to investigate the statements.[287] The court reversed a lower court holding that the wife's reliance was unreasonable.

Courts are particularly likely to find that one spouse has diverted the other from making normal inquiries where that spouse was encouraged not to seek independent counsel. For instance, in *Cook v. Cook*,[288] the husband told the wife that he would leave the country or go to jail if she hired counsel. The wife did consult an attorney briefly, but she appeared pro se in the divorce action. In addition, the husband's attorney's signed the agreement as counsel of record, but wife's attorney did not. A trial court opinion rejecting the wife's claim of fraud was reversed upon appeal.

Normal inquiries can also be diverted by the general conduct of the opposing party during negotiations. In *Shafmaster v. Shafmaster*,[289] the husband urged the wife to hire an accountant to value the marital estate before she hired a lawyer. In keeping with this promise, the husband voluntarily disclosed a wealth of financial information about his assets. The wife did as the husband suggested, had an accountant value the marital estate, and then sought counsel. Based upon the accountant's report, the parties drafted an agreement, but the husband specifically refused to include a clause requested by the wife providing that the parties had fully disclosed their assets. The wife signed the agreement, and then learned that the husband had failed to disclose certain financial information.

The husband argued that the wife's reliance on the information he voluntarily disclosed was unreasonable, because his failure to sign the disclosure clause should have been a "red flag" to the wife that his disclosure was incomplete. The court disagreed,

---

284. Billington v. Billington, 27 Conn. App. 466, 606 A.2d 737 (1992).

285. Atkins v. Atkins, 534 N.E.2d 760 (Ind. Ct. App. 1989). *See also* Rupley v. Rupley, 776 S.W.2d 849 (Ky. Ct. App. 1989) (wife not chargeable with knowledge of value of business in 1987 merely because she had been officer and director of corporation in 1984).

286. 12 Va. App. 31, 401 S.E.2d 891, 893 (1991).

287. *Id.*

288. 112 Nev. 179, 912 P.2d 264 (1996).

289. 138 N.H. 460, 642 A.2d 1361 (1994).

finding that the negotiations had been conducted in an atmosphere of openness and voluntarily disclosure. In light of this pattern of conduct, the court held that the disclosure clause issue should not necessarily have alerted the wife that the husband's financial information was unreliable. A decision upholding the agreement was reversed, and the agreement was held invalid for fraud.

In some cases, the mere size of the marital estate may limit the duty to inquire. In *Blanchard v. Blanchard*,[290] the husband told the wife that the parties owned land in Florida. After the agreement awarded the land to the wife, she discovered that it had been seized several years ago for nonpayment of taxes. The court noted that the marital estate contained a large number of assets, and that the husband generally kept most of the parties' financial records. Because there was no particular reason for the wife to investigate the Florida real property more than any other asset, the court held that the wife's reliance on the husband's financial statement was reasonable. A trial court decision dismissing the wife's petition to set aside the agreement was therefore reversed.

There is some suggestion that neither party can reasonably rely upon a fact when the agreement itself states otherwise. In *In re Marriage of Goldberg*,[291] the husband agreed to pay alimony for 24 months after the wife's remarriage. He did so in reliance upon the wife's counsel's statement that he was unaware of any intention on the part of the wife to remarry immediately following the divorce. The wife did in fact remarry, but the court refused to set the agreement aside. Because the contract anticipated remarriage, the court held, the husband could not reasonably rely upon counsel's statement.

The court's reasoning does not hold water. The agreement did not anticipate remarriage; on the contrary, if the husband's testimony was credible, the husband was expressly told that the wife would not remarry. The opinion seems to suggest that there could not have been any fraud even if the wife herself had denied any intention to remarry—a result that would encourage the parties to lie to each other when negotiating agreements. Of more concern, however, is the fact that the statement was made by the wife's counsel, who was hardly in any position to know his client's intentions regarding remarriage. The very wording of counsel's statement also suggests that the statement was not based upon complete information. Still another problem is the possibility that the wife's intention to remarry might have changed after the statement was made. Based upon these factors, the husband in *Goldberg* probably did act unreasonably by relying upon counsel's statement. But if the wife herself had told the husband directly that she did not intend to remarry, when in fact she did so intend, the agreement should have been invalid for fraud. To rule otherwise would be to reward the wife for telling a direct lie.

---

290. 108 Nev. 908, 839 P.2d 1320 (1992).

291. 282 Ill. App. 3d 997, 668 N.E.2d 1104 (1996); *see also* Belcourt v. Belcourt, 911 So. 2d 735 (Ala. Civ. App. 2005) (trial court did not err in rejecting husband's claim that he signed the agreement in reliance upon wife's promise to pay him $7,000, where husband read the agreement and no such promise was contained within it).

No-Reliance Clause. Some separation agreements contain a statement that neither party has relied upon any representations made by the other, or even a general statement that neither party committed fraud upon the other. These clauses are one factor indicating that there was no actual reliance and that any actual reliance that did exist was unreasonable.[292] They are not, however, conclusive on the question.[293]

Damages

Finally, an agreement will not be found invalid for fraud unless the fraud inflicted some form of harm upon the attacking spouse. In *Voight v. Voight*,[294] the wife failed to disclose to the husband an IRA and a bank account. She then signed an agreement that contained a clause stating that the parties had fully disclosed their assets. The court conceded that the nondisclosure was wrongful, but found that the IRA was divided equally between the parties under a residuary clause in the agreement. The court then held that the bank account was not divisible property, because it was beneficially owned by a third party. As a result of these findings, the nondisclosure had inflicted no harm on the husband, and the court refused to set the agreement aside.

Likewise, in *Arquiette v. Arquiette*,[295] the husband concealed from the wife the fact that he had selectively cut timber from certain land. The court refused to set the agreement aside for fraud. The husband had used the proceeds from selling the timber to maintain the land itself, the court explained, and the selective cutting had actually increased the value of the property. Because the wife suffered no damages, there had been no fraud.

Civil Action. As an alternative to setting aside the agreement, a spouse who is victimized by fraud may be able to seek relief in an independent civil action. Such an action

---

292. *See* Grubman v. Grubman, 191 A.D.2d 194, 594 N.Y.S.2d 220 (1993); Luftig v. Luftig, 239 A.D.2d 225, 657 N.Y.S.2d 658 (1997).

293. *See* Marjon v. Lane, 995 So. 2d 1086, 1087 (Fla. Dist. Ct. App. 2008) (error not to consider fraud, even though agreement stated that it was not a product of duress; "the clause at issue does not bar the trial court's consideration of whether the Agreement was procured by fraud, duress, or coercion"); *Blanchard*, 108 Nev. 908, 839 P.2d 1320 (finding fraud despite such a clause); Gottlieb v. Such, 293 A.D.2d 267, 267–68, 740 N.Y.S.2d 44, 45 (2002) ("Nor does the agreement purport to exculpate the parties from the consequences of fraudulent misrepresentation. Had such a provision been included in the separation agreement, it would not be enforceable[.]"); Rumore v. Wamstad, 751 So. 2d 452, 456 (La. Ct. App. 2000) ("The provision of the Settlement Agreement acknowledging no fraud in the making of this settlement can not be used to defeat the allegation of fraud because if the allegation of fraud is proven, the Settlement Agreement is void[.]").

294. 645 N.E.2d 623 (Ind. Ct. App. 1994).

295. 198 A.D.2d 858, 604 N.Y.S.2d 427 (1993); *see also* Price v. Price, 5 So. 3d 1151, 1156 (Miss. Ct. App. 2009) (wife did not commit fraud by failing to disclose her intention to declare bankruptcy after the divorce case, where wife discharged only her own debts, not debts owed jointly with husband; husband "is actually in a better financial position now than he was prior to Jennifer's filing bankruptcy").

is always permitted before entry of divorce decree. After entry of a decree, some states hold that the decree is res judicata on the validity of the agreement, and that a civil action for fraud is not permitted. Other states permit a civil action if the facts demonstrate sufficient fraud to reopen a judgment.[296]

§ 4.054 Mistake

Separation agreements may also be attacked on grounds of mistake. To invalidate an agreement on grounds of mistake, the attacking party must show (1) that a mistake was made; (2) that the mistake was mutual, or that a unilateral mistake was induced by the other party's conduct; (3) that the mistake was one of fact; (4) that the attacking party exercised due diligence; and (5) that the mistake was material.

Existence of a Mistake

The first element of mistake is proof that a mistake actually was made. A mistake exists when both parties are in error on some existing fact that is relevant to their underlying bargain. For example, in *In re Marriage of Agustsson*,[297] the agreement called for a lump sum distribution of the husband's pension. The husband believed that each party would pay his or her own taxes, while the wife believed that the husband would pay all of the taxes. Given the substantial size of the tax consequences, the court set the agreement aside on grounds of mistake.

Likewise, in *Gramanz v. Gramanz*,[298] the parties believed that certain leases owned by a community property corporation were essentially worthless. Based upon this belief, they agreed to value the corporation at $300,000. The leases proved to have considerable nuisance value as a encumbrance upon the property involved, however, and a large corporation was willing to pay a substantial sum to remove them. As a result, the husband sold his stock in the company for $6.45 million. The court held that the stipulation as to value was the product of a mutual mistake, and it set the stipulation aside.[299]

---

296. A detailed examination of this law on this subject lies outside the scope of this treatise. For a full discussion, *see generally* Brett R. Turner, *Common-Law Fraud as a Remedy for Asset-Related Misconduct*, 7 DIVORCE LITIG. 205 (1995).

Civil actions sounding in contract may be permitted in some states that do not permit civil actions sounding in tort. *See* Grace v. Grace, 253 Mich. App. 357, 367, 655 N.W.2d 595, 601 (2002) (where agreement does not merge into decree, defrauded party can bring action for damages, so long as action sounds in contract and not tort; where husband fraudulently undervalued marital estate, awarding wife damages equal to difference between amount awarded to wife in agreement and half of properly valued marital estate).

297. 223 Ill. App. 3d 510, 585 N.E.2d 207 (1992).

298. 113 Nev. 1, 930 P.2d 753 (1997).

299. For additional case law finding a mutual mistake, *see* Richard v. Boggs, 162 P.3d 629 (Alaska 2007) (where agreement was based upon mutual false assumption that home could be saved from risk of foreclosure only by awarding it outright to husband, and agreement also failed to dispose of substantial marital property, and neither party had counsel, trial court did not err in reopening judgment and setting aside agreement).

Sometimes a mistake involves the method by which the agreement accomplishes its end. In *Seymour v. Seymour*,[300] the parties believed that the husband could properly transfer half his shares in his family's company to the wife. Neither party was aware that certain stock transfer restrictions gave other family member shareholders a right of first refusal. The trial court set the agreement aside for a mistake of fact, and the appellate court affirmed.

In order to serve as the basis for setting aside an agreement, a mistake must involve a fact that existed at the time the agreement was signed. "[A] contract may not be reformed or rescinded based upon a mutual mistake of fact if the mistake relates to a mistaken belief, judgment, or expectation as to future, rather than past or present, facts, occurrences or events."[301] For example, where both parties believed that the assets awarded to the wife would generate sufficient income to support her in the future without additional alimony, and the belief was ultimately incorrect due to later changes in economic conditions, one court refused to the agreement aside.[302]

Where the parties had no understanding or belief at all on an issue at the time of divorce, that issue cannot be the subject of a mutual mistake.[303]

A mistake is also present when through an error of transcription by the scrivener, the words of the agreement fail to express the bargain actually made by the parties. Courts tend to treat these *clerical error* issues as questions of construction and reformation rather than validity, and they are discussed in more detail in § **5.09**. The discus-

---

300. 960 So. 2d 513, 518 (Miss. Ct. App. 2006); *see also* Banker v. Banker, 56 A.D.3d 1105, 870 N.Y.S.2d 481 (2008) (where restrictive covenant prevented implementation of in-kind division of property set forth in stipulation, stipulation was properly reformed for mutual mistake).

301. Ryan v. Ryan, 220 W. Va. 1, 6, 640 S.E.2d 64, 69 (2006).

302. *See id.*; *see also* Magowan v. Magowan, 73 Conn. App. 733, 812 A.2d 30 (2002) (where trustees of husband's trust were not required to pay certain expenses, their unwillingness to follow parties' request that they pay those expenses after the divorce was not sufficient to show a mutual mistake as to any fact existing at the time of divorce; husband "was aware that he did not have the right to demand invasion of the trust or demand performance from the trustees"); Ludlow v. Ahrens, 812 S.W.2d 245 (Mo. Ct. App. 1991) (IRS audit after signing of separation agreement imposed substantial tax liability; no mutual mistake of present fact, as the parties could not have made a mutual mistake regarding a tax debt that did not exist when the agreement was made); Etzion v. Etzion, 62 A.D.3d 646, 880 N.Y.S.2d 79 (2009) (rezoning of property after divorce was not a sufficient mistake to set aside agreement; mistake must involve fact existing at the time agreement was signed).

If a future event is critical to the parties' resolution of an issue, the prudent drafter should consider making the event an express condition. For example, some agreements make the amount of spousal support expressly dependent upon the amount of the recipient's income. See § **6.031**. In the absence of such a condition, however, a mutual mistake regarding a future fact is not a basis for setting the agreement aside.

303. Brown v. Brown, 226 A.D.2d 1010, 641 N.Y.S.2d 209 (1996) (failure to provide that alimony would terminate on retirement was not a mutual mistake; parties had never considered the issue in negotiating the agreement).

sion in this section focuses upon the situation that results when the underlying bargain itself is a product of mistake.[304]

Apart from the above points, whether a mutual mistake was actually made is generally an issue of fact. Where the mutual mistake was limited to a previous rejected offer, and there was no evidence that the mistake was carried through subsequent negotiations into the final agreement, one court found that no mistake had been made.[305]

Where both parties to the agreement file a joint motion to rescind it on grounds of mutual mistake, the motion should almost always be granted.[306]

Mutual versus Unilateral Mistake

As a general rule, a contract can be set aside for mistake only if the mistake was mutual. "[A] unilateral mistake by a party to a contract, unaccompanied by fraud, imposition, undue influence or other like circumstances of oppression is insufficient to avoid a contract."[307] For example, in *Pillow v. Pillow*,[308] the wife tried to set aside an agreement because she mistakenly believed that the husband's income was $100,000. The court rejected her argument, finding that husband did not believe that his income was $100,000. Thus, the wife's mistake was unilateral and not mutual.[309]

---

304. *But see* Kelley v. Kelley, 953 So. 2d 1139 (Miss. Ct. App. 2007) (contract can be reformed only for mutual clerical mistake in drafting agreement, and not for mutual substantive mistake in deciding consent of terms to be drafted). The parties in Kelley were both unaware of deterioration in their home's foundation that materially decreased its value. The court reversed a trial court decision granting relief, finding that the mistake did not involve the drafting of the agreement.

Kelley is a confusing opinion. The court relied on Ivison v. Ivison, 762 So. 2d 329 (Miss. 2000), which relied on Johnson v. Consol. Am. Life Ins. Co., 244 So. 2d 400 (Miss. 1971), which relied upon a provision presently found at 66 AM. JUR. 2D *Reformation of Instruments* § 17 (Westlaw 2008). That provision states only that a mutual substantive mistake does not permit "relief by way of reformation." *Id.* This makes sense, as there is no way for the court to know what provision the parties would have agreed to (or even if they would have been able to agree at all) had they known the correct facts.

But the general rule is the court can *set aside* an agreement based upon a substantive mutual mistake of fact, if the other requirements of the doctrine set forth in this section are met. *See Seymour*, 960 So. 2d at 518 (setting agreement aside for a substantive mistake of fact as to the existence of certain stock transfer restrictions, which is clearly more than a mere clerical mistake in drafting). Setting the agreement aside does not interfere with the parties' bargain, as that bargain itself assumed the correctness of material fact that is now known to be untrue. In the great majority of the cases cited in this chapter granting relief for a mutual mistake, the mistake was substantive and not a simple error in drafting.

305. Lowry v. Lowry, 99 N.C. App. 246, 393 S.E.2d 141 (1990).

306. *See* Barber v. Barber, 878 So. 2d 449 (Fla. Dist. Ct. App. 2004) (error to deny motion, which was entirely unopposed).

307. *Lowry*, 99 N.C. App. 246, 393 S.E.2d 141; *accord* Richards v. Richards, 78 Conn. App. 734, 829 A.2d 60 (2003); *In re* Marriage of Lorton, 203 Ill. App. 3d 823, 561 N.E.2d 156 (1990).

308. 13 Va. App. 271, 410 S.E.2d 407 (1991).

309. *See also* Kartzmark v. Kartzmark, 709 So. 2d 583 (Fla. Dist. Ct. App. 1998) (error to grant relief for husband's unilateral mistake as to tax consequences of agreement); Kornberg v. Kornberg, 542 N.W.2d 379 (Minn. 1996) (where husband expected that certain corporation would fail to declare a postdivorce dividends, and the fact was apparent from financial documents disclosed

Likewise, in *Ward v. Ward*,[310] a divorcing couple owned two pieces of real estate, a home and a townhouse. Their written property settlement agreement provided that the parties would both properties. The parties would divide equally the proceeds from sale of the townhouse, and the wife would receive 100 percent of the proceeds from sale of the home. The husband moved to reform the agreement, arguing that the parties had actually agreed to divide the equity in the home equally. The wife agreed that an equal division had been discussed, and that she expected such a division to be included in the written contract, which was drafted by the husband's counsel. She testified, however, that she had been aware that the written contract awarded her 100 percent of the equity, and that her intention was to sign an agreement giving her that sum. In other words, she testified that any mistake was made by the husband alone. There was no contrary evidence. The court expressly held that the wife had no duty to inform the husband of his own mistake. In the absence of such a duty, there was no fraud, and the husband's unilateral mistake was not a sufficient basis for setting aside the agreement.

A mutual mistake of fact is particularly likely to justify relief where the court was involved in the negotiations and was actively misled by the mistake. In *Culver v. Culver*,[311] the parties accidentally based the agreement's support provisions on the husband's gross rather than net business income. The trial court set the agreement aside, commenting that it felt a special responsibility to correct the error because the court itself had been instrumental in its commission. The appellate court held that the trial court had properly found the agreement invalid.

At common law, an agreement can be set aside for the unilateral mistake of one party alone, if that mistake was induced by the bad-faith conduct of the opposing party.[312] For example, in *Troiano v. Troiano*,[313] a parcel of real property was acquired by a husband, a wife, and the wife's mother. The intention of the parties was to acquire the property as tenants in common. The husband, however, had the contract and deed drafted so that the parties were joint tenants with right of survivorship. His motive was selfish and fraudulent: He expected that the mother would die first, and he desired to obtain her interest for free. The mother and wife failed to read the documents at closing, and inadvertently agreed to take title as joint tenants. The court held that the

---

to wife, any mistake on wife's part was unilateral); Mitchell v. Mitchell, 888 S.W.2d 393 (Mo. Ct. App. 1994) (refusing to set agreement aside for wife's unilateral mistake on value of marital asset); Harrington v. Harrington, 281 N.J. Super. 39, 656 A.2d 456 (1995) (where husband's business dissolved after contract was signed, and business was basis of the agreement's entire property division provision, error to summarily uphold agreement; remanding for hearing); Freidman v. Freidman, 247 A.D.2d 430, 668 N.Y.S.2d 713 (1998) (refusing to set agreement aside for unilateral mistake in computing marital share of retirement benefits); Gocek v. Gocek, 417 Pa. Super. 406, 612 A.2d 1004 (1992) (wife construed language dividing survivor benefits to divide retirement benefits as well; this fact alone was not sufficient to set the agreement aside, as any mistake would be unilateral).

310. 239 Va. 1, 387 S.E.2d 460 (1990).

311. 651 So. 2d 21 (Ala. Ct. App. 1994).

312. *E.g.*, RESTATEMENT (SECOND) OF CONTRACTS § 153 (1981).

313. 549 So. 2d 1053 (Fla. Dist. Ct. App. 1989).

wife's and mother's unilateral mistake was induced by the husband's bad conduct, and it reformed the documents so that the parties were tenants in common.

The argument for setting aside an agreement based upon unilateral mistake is also strong when the parties have a confidential relationship. *See* § **4.03**. In the context of a confidential relationship, a party with superior knowledge of a material fact, or even superior access to the means of obtaining knowledge of that fact, has a duty to disclose that fact to the other spouse.[314]

Some jurisdictions have liberalized the conditions under which relief can be granted for unilateral mistakes of fact. For instance, in *In re Marriage of Agustsson*,[315] the court held that the agreement would be set aside even if the mistake were unilateral rather than mutual. "[R]escission is a proper remedy for either a unilateral or mutual mistake of fact when the party seeking rescission shows by clear and convincing evidence that (1) the mistake is of a material nature; (2) the mistake is of such consequence that enforcement is unconscionable; (3) the mistake occurred notwithstanding the exercise of due care by the party seeking rescission; and (4) rescission can place the other party in status quo."[316]

Mistake of Fact

In order to justify rescinding the contract, the mistake must be a mistake of fact. Like the fraud cases, *see* § **4.053**, the mistake cases clearly hold that a mistake of law is not sufficient. In *In re Marriage of Lorenz*,[317] the husband agreed to pay child support for parties' emancipated daughter. Some time later, he tried to set the agreement aside, arguing that both parties had mistakenly believed that the daughter was not

---

314. *See* Brewer v. Federici, 93 Cal. App. 4th 1334, 113 Cal. Rptr. 2d 849 (2001) (where husband signed agreement in actual ignorance of value of wife's pension, which wife had listed as "unknown" on financial statement, agreement set aside for mistake; confidential relationship placed upon wife a fiduciary obligation to disclose the value of the pension).

Brewer relied very heavily upon the California notion that all spouses negotiating a separation agreement have a confidential relationship. For the reasons stated in § **4.03**, this rule is not good policy. It ignores the adversarial nature of most relationships between divorcing spouses, and encourages spouses not to take reasonable measures to protect themselves against financial misconduct. The husband in Brewer had every opportunity to value the pension during discovery, and unless the wife interfered with his ability to use the discovery process for his own self-protection, most states would not have much sympathy for the husband's position. Brewer is nevertheless typical of how unilateral mistake claims are viewed in states that insist that spouses necessarily have a confidential relationship while negotiating a separation agreement.

315. 223 Ill. App. 3d 510, 585 N.E.2d 207 (1992).

316. 585 N.E.2d at 214. *See also* Bishop v. Bishop, 60 Ark. App. 164, 961 S.W.2d 770 (1998) (agreement can be set aside for unilateral mistake if mistake renders the agreement unconscionable). *But cf.* Welkener v. Welkener, 71 S.W.3d 364, 366–67 (Tex. Ct. App. 2001) (where wife made unilateral mistake in believing wrongly that agreement awarded her a share of future increases in husband's retirement benefits, but wife did not prove that husband's "monthly retirement payments were likely to increase in the future," insufficient evidence existed that enforcing the contract would be unconscionable).

317. 104 Or. App. 438, 801 P.2d 892 (1990).

emancipated. The court held that the agreement was enforceable. Since the husband knew the daughter's age, his error was essentially a mistake of law, and not a mistake of fact.[318]

A minority of cases hold that an agreement could be rescinded for a mutual mistake of law, citing language to this effect in a leading contract law treatise.[319] But the treatise admits that the traditional rule is otherwise. In the family law setting, the majority of the cases to date have followed the traditional rule, and held that a separation agreement cannot be rescinding for a mutual mistake of law.[320]

It is especially appropriate that relief be denied for mistake of law when the mistake is unilateral. Separation agreements are signed to settle litigation—a pending or highly foreseeable divorce case—and in that context parties should be relying upon their own attorneys for advice on legal issues. Reliance on the other party would be more justified where there is a confidential relationship or one party has superior access to the law, but those are recognized exceptions to the traditional rule at least in the fraud context,[321] and probably in the mistake context as well. Research for this volume did not reveal any case law setting aside any separation agreement on grounds of a mutual mistake of law.

The mistake cases also agree with the fraud cases that a mistake of opinion is not a mistake of fact. The point is again most commonly applied to the value of a marital asset, which is a matter of opinion only. Thus, the mere fact that the parties' opinion as to the value of an asset is ultimately proven to be mistaken does not justify setting aside the agreement.[322] If the rule were otherwise, many agreements would become invalid,

---

318. *See also* Janusz v. Gilliam, 404 Md. 524, 536, 947 A.2d 560, 567 (2008) ("The rule that a mistake of law is not grounds for rescission is founded on the principle that ignorance of the law is no excuse[.]"); *In re* Marriage of Banks, 887 S.W.2d 160 (Tex. Ct. App. 1994) (wife's ignorance of her rights under doctrine of reimbursement was unilateral error of law that was not sufficient to invalidate agreement); Dalton v. Dalton, 164 N.C. App. 584, 596 S.E.2d 331 (2004) (alleged mistake regarding North Carolina law on division of retirement benefits was not sufficient basis for setting agreement aside); Pillow v. Pillow, 13 Va. App. 271, 410 S.E.2d 407 (1991) (refusing to reopen for mutual mistake involving tax law).

319. *See In re* Lemieux, 157 N.H. 370, 373, 949 A.2d 720, 724 (2008) ("Modern contract law does not distinguish between mistakes of fact and mistakes of law, but treats both alike for purposes of equitable relief[.]"); *see also* Meyer v. Meyer, 952 So. 2d 384, 391 (Ala. Civ. App. 2006) (dicta). Both of these cases cite 27 RICHARD A. LORD, WILLISTON ON CONTRACTS § 70:106, at 533 (4th ed. 2003).

320. *E.g., Janusz*, 404 Md. 524, 947 A.2d 560; *Dalton*, 164 N.C. App. 584, 596 S.E.2d 331 (also citing Lord and following the traditional rule).

321. *See* note 248 *supra.*

322. *See* Mitchell v. Mitchell, 888 S.W.2d 393 (Mo. Ct. App. 1994) (mistake as to value was mistake of opinion, and thus not sufficient to reopen the decree); Wourms v. Wourms, 166 Ohio App. 3d 519, 524, 851 N.E.2d 553, 557 (2006) (where parties agreed that condominium was worth $530,000, a "subsequent $615,000 appraisal . . . does not demonstrate that the parties were mistaken in their opinion, especially as an appraisal for purposes of refinancing may not reflect the price on which a willing buyer and a willing seller necessarily would agree"; no indication that parties were unaware of material facts necessary to value the property).

as value is simply not a neutral fact that can objectively be determined. Even the best experts, with complete knowledge of the underlying facts, often have different opinions as to the value of property.

A mutual mistake regarding the underlying facts necessary to determine value,[323] or a mutual error in underlying valuation methodology,[324] can be a sufficient basis for setting aside an agreement.

Due Diligence

A contract generally cannot be set aside for mistake where the mistake results from the negligence of the attacking party.[325]

Due diligence is obviously not present where the attacking party simply failed to read the agreement. For instance, in *Mason v. Mason*,[326] the husband claimed he was unaware that a certain insurance obligation imposed in the agreement was long-term and unmodifiable. This fact was clear from the language of the agreement, however, and the court held that the husband should have been aware of it.

The attacking party is also generally charged with knowledge of reasonable financial disclosure submitted by the other spouse. In *Vermilyea v. Vermilyea*,[327] the contract understated the present value of husband's pension, but the correct value was stated in an evaluator's report, to which wife had full access. The court refused to set the agreement aside.[328]

---

323. *See* Gramanz v. Gramanz, 113 Nev. 1, 930 P.2d 753 (1997) (mutual mistake regarding the nuisance value of certain leases owned by a community property company; after parties valued corporation at $300,000, another corporation bought the company for $6.45 million to have leases removed; setting the agreement aside); *cf.* Barber v. Barber, 878 So. 2d 449 (Fla. Dist. Ct. App. 2004) (error to deny parties' joint motion to rescind agreement based upon mutual mistake of fact, apparently regarding facts upon which an opinion of value was based).

In Krize v. Krize, 145 P.3d 481, 490 (Alaska 2006), the parties agreed to let husband retain two properties in return for a giving a third to the wife. But the wife then learned that the value of the first two properties had increased "dramatically." *Id.* The trial court awarded the wife one of the two properties, and the appellate court affirmed. The properties had not been appraised when agreement was reached, the court explained, and parties did not have a "full understanding" of their value. *Id.* The court seemed to regard the agreement as one made without knowledge of the underlying facts necessary to determine value.

324. *See* Nardecchia v. Nardecchia, 155 Ohio App. 3d 40, 798 N.E.2d 1198 (2003) (setting aside agreement for mutual failure to include employer contributions in valuing parties' retirement accounts; mistake involved valuation methodology and was clearly more than a difference in opinion).

325. *See In re* Marriage of Agustsson, 223 Ill. App. 3d 510, 585 N.E.2d 207 (1992) (recognizing the requirement, but finding it met on the facts).

326. 873 S.W.2d 631 (Mo. Ct. App. 1994).

327. 224 A.D.2d 759, 636 N.Y.S.2d 953 (1996).

328. *See also* Kornberg v. Kornberg, 542 N.W.2d 379 (Minn. 1996) (wife apparently expected that certain corporation would declare a postdivorce dividend, but unlikelihood of this result was apparent from financial documents available to wife at the time; no mistake).

Material Mistake

Finally, in order to justify rescission, the mistake must be a material one.[329] There is not a great deal of case law on this element, but it would seem to be similar to the requirement under the doctrine of fraud that the misrepresented or undisclosed fact be material. As noted above, *see* § **4.053**, the general rule in the fraud cases is that a fact is material if the attacking party would not have signed the agreement if he or she had known the truth.

Where separate mutual mistakes are made in favor of each party, it may be error to assume too quickly that the mistakes are offsetting.[330]

§ 4.06 Substantive Defenses

The most controversial defenses to separation agreements are those that arise not from procedural inequity in the bargaining process, but rather from substantive disparity in the terms of the agreement.

The law on substantive disparity is divided between three competing positions. One group of states holds that an agreement is invalid for unconscionability if its terms suffer from gross substantive disparity.[331] These states review the substantive sufficiency of the agreement, but find unconscionability only where the disparity is extreme. This position is discussed in § **4.061**.

A second group of states likewise reviews substantive disparity, but under a more liberal standard that the first group of states. In these states, an agreement is invalid for substantive disparity not only if it is unconscionable, but also if it is merely unfair.[332]

---

329. *See, e.g., Agustsson*, 223 Ill. App. 3d 510, 585 N.E.2d 207.

330. *See Nardecchia*, 155 Ohio App. 3d 40, 798 N.E.2d 1198 (where parties inadvertently failed to include employer contributions in valuing both parties' retirement accounts, error to hold that same division would have resulted in both parties' benefits being valued correctly; unacceptably speculative to assume that the mistakes were offsetting).

331. *E.g.*, MONT. CODE ANN. § 40-4-201(2) (Westlaw 2008) ("the terms of the separation agreement . . . are binding upon the court unless it finds, after considering the economic circumstances of the parties and any other relevant evidence produced by the parties . . . that the separation agreement is unconscionable"); *In re* Marriage of McNeil, 367 Ill. App. 3d 676, 856 N.E.2d 15 (2006) (error to reject unconscionability defense without holding an evidentiary hearing); Bailey v. Bailey, 231 S.W.3d 793 (Ky. Ct. App. 2007); West v. West, 891 So. 2d 203, 213 (Miss. 2004) (substantive unconscionability and procedural unconscionability are separate and independent bases for attacking agreement); Tremont v. Tremont, 35 A.D.3d 1046, 1048, 827 N.Y.S.2d 309, 311 (2006) ("an agreement is not unconscionable merely because some terms may seem improvident; it must shock the conscience to be set aside"); Crawford v. Crawford, 524 N.W.2d 833, 836 (N.D. 1994) ("Whether a party has agreed to the terms of a stipulation becomes irrelevant in light of the damage enforcement of an unconscionable decree would do to the duty and reputation of courts to do justice.").

332. *E.g.*, Pouech v. Pouech, 180 Vt. 1, 10–11, 904 A.2d 70, 76 (2006) ("the family court erred by refusing to consider wife's maintenance request because of her failure to prove duress, unconscionable advantage, or another basis for overturning a contract. Rather, the court should have given the parties an opportunity to present evidence on the fairness of their stipulation.").

Most of these states also hold that the trial court must approve a separation agreement before it can be deemed valid under the law of contracts. The end result is a considerable amount of court interference with the bargaining process. Courts in these states justify that interference by citing the strong state interest in marriage and divorce, and by claiming that the divorce setting does not lend itself to unregulated private bargaining. The policy behind this position is discussed and critiqued in § **4.04**. The definition of unfairness is discussed in § **4.062**.

A third group of states rejects the premise that substantive disparity alone is ever a sufficient reason for setting aside a separation agreement. In these states, no matter how one-sided an agreement may be, it is not unconscionable unless the substantive disparity is also accompanied by significant bargaining inequity.[333] A good example is *Galloway v. Galloway*,[334] where the agreement awarded the husband 94 percent of the marital estate, but "there was no evidence of overreaching or oppressive behavior by husband."[335] The court held that the agreement was not unconscionable. "[E]very person . . . is entitled to dispose of [his] property, in such manner and upon such terms as he chooses, and whether his bargains are wise, or discreet, or profitable, or unprofitable, or otherwise, are considerations not for courts of justice, but for the party himself to deliberate upon."[336] This passage was quoted from a 1920 decision not involving domestic relations, showing clearly that the court was applying in the divorce setting the exact same rules of contract law it would apply in any other setting. This reasoning is typical of courts following the third position; these courts simply do not agree that the divorce setting is materially different from other settings in which private contracts are negotiated.

To see at a glance the tremendous distinction between the second and third groups of states, contrast the result and reasoning in *Galloway* with the following passage from *Pouech v. Pouech*,[337] in which the Vermont Supreme Court explained why that state's law requires the court to approve all separation agreements as fair and reasonable:

---

333. *See* Crupi v. Crupi, 784 So. 2d 611, 614 (Fla. Dist. Ct. App. 2001) (apparently holding that Florida law permits no substantive review of mediated agreement, over a dissent arguing for fairness review; neither opinion discusses the possibility of review for unconscionability); King v. King, 114 N.C. App. 454, 442 S.E.2d 154 (1994); Galloway v. Galloway, 47 Va. App. 83, 92, 622 S.E.2d 267, 272 (2005) (party claiming unconscionability "must prove both 1) a gross disparity existed in the division of assets and 2) overreaching or oppressive influences"); Shenk v. Shenk, 39 Va. App. 161, 179, 571 S.E.2d 896, 906 (2002) (to overturn agreement for unconscionability, attacking party "must prove both (1) a gross disparity existed in the division of assets and (2) overreaching or oppressive influences created an unfair process"; first element alone is not sufficient).

334. 47 Va. App. 83, 622 S.E.2d 267 (2005). *But cf.* Sims v. Sims, 55 Va. App. 340, 685 S.E.2d 869 (2009) (recognizing a limited exception to Galloway for cases in which gross substantive disparity is accompanied by a high degree of objective financial need, such as where a spouse is likely to become a public charge if the agreement is enforced).

335. *Galloway*, 47 Va. App. at 92, 622 S.E.2d at 272.

336. *Id.* at 93, 622 S.E.2d at 272 (quoting Smyth Bros. v. Beresford, 128 Va. 137, 170, 104 S.E. 371, 382 (1920)).

337. *Pouech*, 180 Vt. at 12, 904 A.2d at 77–78.

Our holding is based on the simple truth that an agreement in anticipation of divorce is not the same as any ordinary contract. Public policy favors parties settling their own disputes in a divorce, but, as noted, the family court has a statutorily authorized role to play in divorce proceedings to assure a fair and equitable dissolution of the state-sanctioned institution of marriage. . . . This is particularly true when one or both parties challenge the fairness of agreements that are often made under trying and emotional circumstances.

Viewed from a nationwide perspective, *Pouech* and *Galloway* are both minority positions. A majority of states follows the first position set forth above, holding that the divorce setting is unique enough that separation agreements can be overturned for substantive disparity alone, if the disparity is extreme enough to make the agreement unconscionable. But these states do not go so far as to allow an agreement to be overturned for mere unfairness, or to require court approval as a condition to validity of the agreement.

Policy Concerns

States clearly differ in the degree of substantive insufficiency they are willing to accept in separation agreements. The split in authority evolves from different views on the strength of the state's interest in marriage and divorce, and the extent to which divorce litigation is a suitable arena from the normal private bargaining process.

The clear majority position, however, is that the divorce setting merits at least some court supervision of the private bargaining process. "[I]n recognition of the intimate nature of the relationship and the ability of a strong and persistent spouse to overwhelm the other spouse, . . . the law has established a measure of protection for parties from their own irresponsible agreements."[338]

For the reasons suggested in § 4.04, the need for protection does not extend so far as to justify a requirement that private agreements be approved by the court before they are binding under the law of contracts. The great majority of all separation agreements are carefully negotiated between capable parties with full opportunity to seek advice of counsel. When a separation agreement is voluntarily and knowingly signed, it is a better resolution of the divorce case than any judge could ever impose. Settlements also benefit the entire public by reducing the need to devote scarce judicial resources to a contested divorce trial. Given the voluntary nature of most separation agreements and their clear policy advantages, separation agreements should be presumed valid, and they should not be overturned simply because the trial judge would have preferred that the parties strike a different bargain.

It is equally wrong, however, to allow no substantive review of separation agreements at all. Courts disfavoring substantive review often claim that they are treating separation agreement just like other contracts. A businessperson is bound by a com-

---

338. Shraberg v. Shraberg, 939 S.W.2d 330, 333 (Ky. 1997).

mercial contract regardless of substantive disparity, these courts reason, so a divorce litigant should be equally bound.

For two distinct reasons, this reasoning does not hold water. First, divorce is simply not a setting similar to a commercial agreement. Commercial agreements are signed between persons who have voluntarily entered into a business relationship. It is fair to assume, and even to insist, that persons who enter into business relationships have a certain amount of experience in the field they are entering, and in the field of contracts generally. Against this background, it is appropriate to require clear proof of invalidity before finding a business contract to be unenforceable.

Divorce cases, however, are different. While some parties are experienced with the process of negotiating agreements, many parties to separation agreements have no commercial experience whatsoever. Independent counsel can compensate to some extent for their client's shortcomings, but many parties to divorce cases are not fully aware of the importance of retaining counsel. In addition, even parties who are experienced in commercial matters will sometimes make irrational decisions in their divorce cases, because divorce is a setting unusually conducive to emotional thinking. Finally, and most importantly, while society insists that persons who voluntarily enter into business relationships have a certain level of expertise, it does not apply the same standards to persons who marry. Marriage is for everyone, not only for those who have the ability to negotiate a fair contract.

Because entry into marriage does not require the same resume as entry into business, it is not reasonable to assume that separation agreements are just like commercial contracts. As a class, parties to divorce cases are less experienced with contracts, and more likely to be thinking emotionally rather than rationally. These obstacles are not high enough to justify a requirement that separation agreements be approved before they are binding, but they are high enough to exert influence upon the law. The standard for a valid separation agreement should be harder to meet than the standard for a valid commercial contract.

Second, even if the law does apply the same contract rules to businesspersons and divorcing spouses, there is still an argument for substantive review of separation agreements. Courts often claim that business contracts are binding regardless of substantive sufficiency. But this is clearly not true. Assume that a businessperson signs an unwise agreement that creates a debt that he is not able to repay. The agreement is completely voluntary; there is no bargaining inequity; the businessperson simply misjudges his own ability to generate future income. This agreement is entirely valid under the law of contracts, but the businessperson still has a very powerful avenue for relief: He can have the debt discharged in bankruptcy. Bankruptcy relief is not a minor or trivial right; on the contrary, the power to provide such relief is expressly granted to Congress in the U.S. Constitution.[339] The policy of giving relief to the "honest but unfortunate debtor" is therefore of constitutional magnitude.

---

339. *See* U.S. Const. art. I, § 8, cl. 4.

For many years, property division obligations, whether court-ordered or contractual, were subject to discharge in bankruptcy.[340] This right of discharge was perennially problematic, as it was persistently abused by dishonest debtors who were actually well able to pay their property division obligations.[341] Congress tried for a time to require that bankruptcy judges differentiate between debtors who could and could not repay their property division debts, and to consider the harm inflicted upon the debtor's spouse if the debt was discharged.[342] But this balancing test was uniquely despised by bankruptcy judges,[343] as it forced them to think and act like family law judges—a task that was probably outside their job description and certainly outside their comfort zone.

As a result, under a landmark 2005 reform of federal bankruptcy law, property division obligations can no longer be discharged in bankruptcy liquidation proceedings.[344] This reform is a great benefit that will significantly improve the enforceability of property division awards against spouses who are actually able to pay them.

But the 2005 bankruptcy reforms were not based upon any belief that the "honest but unfortunate debtor" policy should not apply to domestic relations obligations. Applying that policy in federal bankruptcy court was an epic mistake, because bankruptcy judges are neither inclined nor well suited to review the affordability of domestic relations obligations. But there is nevertheless a powerful argument that the policy should be applied by state court judges, when determining whether private agreements are enforceable in divorce cases.[345]

If state court judges do not consider the affordability of family law obligations, the result is clearly to make family law agreements *more enforceable* than ordinary business contracts. A business contract, no matter how voluntary and valid it may be, is subject to discharge in bankruptcy if it imposes a sufficiently harsh result upon the

---

340. *See generally* Brett R. Turner, *The Vampire Rises: Discharge of Property Division Obligations Under Chapter 13 of the Bankruptcy Code in Post-2005 Litigation*, 19 DIVORCE LITIG. 1 (2007).

341. *See, e.g., In re* Smither, 194 B.R. 102, 112 (Bankr. W.D. Ky. 1996) (noting perennial problem of "high to moderate income debtors discharging property settlements which their former spouses are entitled to and in most cases desperately need").

342. *See* 11 U.S.C. § 523(a)(15) (repealed 2005); *see generally* Turner, *supra* note 340, at 3–5.

343. *See Smither*, 194 B.R. at 106 (balancing test is "a paving stone on the road to the region of Hades reserved for litigation nightmares"); *In re* Butler, 186 B.R. 371, 372 (Bankr. D. Vt. 1995) (balancing test is "a pernicious creature. Using it is equivalent to applying acupuncture without a license").

344. *See* 11 U.S.C. § 523(a)(15) (Westlaw 2008). Discharge is permitted in Chapter 13 liquidation proceedings, *see id.* § 1328(a) (not listing § 523(a)(15) as a provision that applies under Chapter 13). It is not clear whether Congress realized that the modification to § 523(a)(15) would not apply in Chapter 13 cases, but the trend is clearly against allowing federal courts to discharge any domestic relations obligation. A debtor must act in good faith to obtain a Chapter 13 discharge, *see id.* §§ 1307(c), 1325(a)(3), and this requirement should further limit post-2005 Chapter 13 discharges. *See generally* Turner, *supra* note 340, at 6–10.

345. For an alternate version of this argument, made with more detailed reference to bankruptcy law, see Turner, *supra* note 340, at 11–15.

debtor. The effect is to provide a safety net for those who assume commercial obligations. To avoid forcing debtors into perpetual poverty, the law allows them to seek relief from any contract they sign, no matter how voluntary it may be, if they are left unable to pay their obligations.

Parties who sign domestic relations agreements are entitled to the same safety net as those who sign ordinary business agreements. At a minimum, that safety net should provide protection equal to the protection given to commercial contracts by the law of bankruptcy. Thus, even if an agreement is completely voluntary, it should be still invalid for unconscionability if its provisions are so substantively one-sided as to render one spouse effectively bankrupt. The law allows relief from commercial contracts under these circumstances, and it should allow relief from domestic relations contracts as well.

§ 4.061 Unconscionability

As noted in **§ 6.06**, the nationwide case law is divided on the substantive sufficiency requirement for separation agreements. Some states allow only limited substantive review; other states allow substantive review for unconscionability; other states allow substantive review for unfairness. This section focuses upon the second position, which allows the court to set aside a separation agreement if its substantive terms are unconscionable.

General Rule: Gross Substantive Disparity

Courts have used differing language in their attempts to grasp the elusive concept of unconscionability. One court defined the term as follows:

> [U]nconscionability [is] an inequality so strong, gross, and manifest that it must be impossible to state it to one with common sense without producing an exclamation at the inequality of it.[346]

An Illinois court gave a similar definition:

> An unconscionable bargain has been defined as one "which no man in his senses, not under delusion, would make, on the one hand, and which no fair and honest man would accept, on the other."[347]

The varying language of these definitions contains a common theme: the underlying bargain must be unusually one-sided. At the risk of stating the obvious, to determine the nature of the underlying bargain, the court must compare the attacking spouse's

---

346. Peirick v. Peirick, 641 S.W.2d 195, 197 (Mo. Ct. App. 1982); *see also* Crawford v. Crawford, 524 N.W.2d 833, 836 (N.D. 1994) ("so blatantly one-sided and so rankly unfair under the uncovered circumstances that courts should not enforce it"); *In re* Marriage of Smith, 115 S.W.3d 126, 135 (Tex. Ct. App. 2003) ("the term 'unconscionable' describes a contract that is unfair because of its overall one-sidedness or the gross one-sidedness of its terms").

347. *In re* Marriage of Carlson, 101 Ill. App. 3d 924, 428 N.E.2d 1005, 1010 (1981) (quoting Hume v. United States, 132 U.S. 406, 410 (1889)).

benefits under the agreement with what those benefits would be if the agreement had not been signed. The result of this comparison determines whether the bargain is so one-sided that it fails the test of conscionability.

Extent of Disparity

It is important to stress that unconscionability requires considerably more than mere inequality:

> It was neither Judge Hinkel or this Court that entered into a contract agreeing to pay [the amounts at issue]. Appellant did it to himself. If persons of sound mind, with the assistance of counsel, desire to enter into agreement that they later feel are unjust or inequitable, they have created their own problems. People are entitled to enter into contracts that contain the potential for egregious results.[348]

Likewise, an agreement is not unconscionable merely because it is unfair.[349] "The parties alone are competent to say what is reasonable to resolve a lawsuit and what is not. If the parties choose to settle a case without fraud or coercion after adequate opportunity to engage in discovery—from which ample knowledge must be presumed—they should not be heard to assail the relative fairness of the bargain."[350]

Unconscionability is present, however, when the substantive terms of the agreement are grossly disparate from the terms that a court would be likely to order if the

---

348. Baran v. Jaskulski, 114 Md. App. 322, 689 A.2d 1283, 1289 (1997); *see also* Doukas v. Doukas, 47 A.D.3d 753, 754, 849 N.Y.S.2d 656, 657 (2008) ("[j]udicial review is to be exercised sparingly, with a goal of encouraging parties to settle their differences on their own").

349. *See, e.g., In re* Marriage of Rosevear, 65 Cal. App. 4th 673, 76 Cal. Rptr. 2d 691 (1998); Petracca v. Petracca, 706 So. 2d 904 (Fla. Dist. Ct. App. 1998) (distinguishing prior case law applying a fairness test to antenuptial and midnuptial agreements, on grounds that those cases involved confidential relationships, while in most cases the parties to a separation agreement have an adversarial relationship); *In re* Marriage of Bielawski, 328 Ill. App. 3d 243, 764 N.E.2d 1254 (2002); Flynn v. Flynn, 232 Ill. App. 3d 394, 597 N.E.2d 709 (1992); West v. West, 891 So. 2d 203, 213 (Miss. 2004) ("the terms of the property settlement agreement are less than desirable, but we cannot say that no spouse in his or her right mind would agree to what is, at worst, a begrudging but generous offer on Tim's part"); *Peirick,* 641 S.W.2d at 197; Cheruvu v. Cheruvu, 59 A.D.3d 876, 878, 874 N.Y.S.2d 296, 299 (2009) ("While the agreement here appears to contain generous provisions for the wife and children, it is certainly not manifestly unfair[.]"); Tremont v. Tremont, 35 A.D.3d 1046, 1048, 827 N.Y.S.2d 309, 311 (2006) ("an agreement is not unconscionable merely because some terms may seem improvident; it must shock the conscience to be set aside"); Lounsbury v. Lounsbury, 300 A.D.2d 812, 814, 752 N.Y.S.2d 103, 107 (2002) ("although defendant may have 'given more' than he might legally have been compelled to give, considered in its totality, the separation agreement hardly 'shock[s] the conscience'"); King v. King, 114 N.C. App. 454, 442 S.E.2d 154 (1994); Pillow v. Pillow, 13 Va. App. 271, 410 S.E.2d 407 (1991).

350. *Petracca,* 706 So. 2d at 912.

case had been litigated without an agreement. The clearest examples of substantive disparity are cases in which the spouse attacking the agreement receives essentially no benefit from the agreement at all. In this situation, the agreement is often found to be unconscionable.[351]

Where the attacking spouse does receive some benefit, but significantly less benefit than the spouse would receive if the case were litigated without an agreement, the key question is whether gross disparity is present. In most states, the definition of grossly disproportionate is an issue left to the courts. A exception is Louisiana, where an agreement awarding either spouse less than 75 percent of that spouse's 50 percent interest in the community estate is subject to rescission by either spouse.[352]

To gain a feeling for the extent of disparity that renders an agreement unconscionable, it is necessary to review the holdings in specific cases. These is general agreement that the disparity must be extreme. This treatise will generally use the adjective "gross," which conveys a good general sense of the level of disparity needed. Courts have generally found agreements to be unconscionable when the less wealthy spouse receives a grossly insufficient property division award,[353] and when the more wealthy

---

351. *See* Burke v. Sexton, 814 S.W.2d 290 (Ky. Ct. App. 1991) (wife waived all rights and marital estate and received no alimony); *In re* Marriage of Johnson, 339 Ill. App. 3d 237, 243, 790 N.E.2d 91, 96 (2003) (agreement awarded pension to husband, but required him to make monthly property division payments with a present value greater than value of the pension; wife received no maintenance but agreement recited that both parties were fully able to support themselves; "[t]he settlement agreement effectively leaves [husband] in penury"); Brash v. Brash, 407 Mass. 101, 551 N.E.2d 523 (1990) (oral agreement permitting husband to retain all marital assets after 19-year marriage); Gibson v. Gibson, 284 A.D.2d 908, 908, 726 N.Y.S.2d 195, 196 (2001) (wife "received no share of the business that was the sole source of income for both parties and received no share of the parties' net assets of approximately $235,000," leaving her with " no resources and no source of income or other means of support"); Sims v. Sims, 55 Va. App. 340, 685 S.E.2d 869 (2009) (wife with no earning capacity after 38-year marriage received nothing from the marital estate except for her own personal property, and waived spousal support completely).

352. LA. CIV. CODE art. 814.

353. *See In re* Marriage of Salby, 126 P.3d 291 (Colo. Ct. App. 2005) (agreement awarded husband over $1 million in property, $700,000 of which was marital, while awarding the wife only $123,000); *In re* Marriage of Bisque, 31 P.3d 175, 179 (Colo. Ct. App. 2001) (agreement awarded wife "the bulk of the marital estate, including the marital home and an adjacent lot," and trial court found that "husband's 'will was simply overborne by his aggressive, persistent, overbearing spouse'"; agreement set aside as unconscionable); Kuroda v. Kuroda, 87 Haw. 419, 958 P.2d 541 (1998) (wife received all property, half of the husband's future income, and husband was required

spouse is burdened with a grossly excessive property division.[354] Agreements have likewise been held unconscionable when a support award grossly failed to meet the needs of the dependent spouse,[355] and when a support obligation was grossly excessive compared to the means of the supporting spouse.[356]

On the other hand, where there is no gross disparity between the benefits under the agreement and the benefits without the agreement, the agreement is conscionable.

---

to pay all of her attorney's fees); *In re* Marriage of Richardson, 237 Ill. App. 3d 1067, 606 N.E.2d 56 (1992) (wife received only 7.55 percent of marital estate worth over $500,000); Weinstock v. Weinstock, 167 A.D.2d 394, 561 N.Y.S.2d 807 (1990) (wife waived property division rights in $2 million estate, receiving in return only modest alimony; alimony was payable only if wife was employed and was taking at least six credits of college courses); Schneider v. Schneider, 110 Ohio App. 3d 487, 674 N.E.2d 769 (1996) (wife received $25,000 of $224,000 home; husband had made wrongful threat to seek custody if wife did not sign); Derby v. Derby, 8 Va. App. 19, 378 S.E.2d 74 (1989) (wife received 100 percent of the parties' most substantial asset, which was worth $423,000; rest of property was divided equally, but wife preserved her right to future spousal support).

354. *See* Weber v. Weber, 589 N.W.2d 358 (N.D. 1999) (after marriage of only 27 days, agreement deprived husband of his residence and awarded him less property than he brought into the marriage).

355. *See* Elliott v. Elliott, 667 So. 2d 116 (Ala. Ct. App. 1995) (after 14-year marriage, wife received no alimony and only a single encumbered piece of real property, plus her premarital assets); *In re* Marriage of Frey, 258 Ill. App. 3d 442, 630 N.E.2d 466 (1994) (homemaker wife received no alimony after 17-year marriage; property settlement existed, but was not unusually generous); *In re* Marriage of Pond, 676 N.E.2d 401 (Ind. Ct. App. 1997) (where husband earned income of $463,000 and wife's income was about $35,000, clause requiring wife to pay husband's attorney's fees if she attacked validity of agreement was unconscionable; other provisions of agreement were valid); Crawford v. Crawford, 524 N.W.2d 833 (N.D. 1994) (agreement awarded only six months of support to wife, a cancer survivor who earned just $300 per month; husband was a physician earning $130,000 per year; agreement also awarded husband marital home and custody of all four children, and required wife to pay $15 per month in child support).

356. *See* Legree v. Legree, 560 So. 2d 1353 (Fla. Dist. Ct. App. 1990) (husband agreed to pay $300 per week in child support, leaving him only $80 per week for his own support); Shraberg v. Shraberg, 939 S.W.2d 330 (Ky. 1997) (husband agreed to pay $160,000 in spousal and child support, from a total income of $200,000); Dobesh v. Dobesh, 216 Neb. 196, 342 N.W.2d 669 (1984) (agreement setting alimony at $400 per month, where payor-husband's expenses exceeded his income); Santini v. Robinson, 68 A.D.3d 745, 891 N.Y.S.2d 100 (2009) (65-year-old husband gave wife almost half his pension, and promised in addition to pay lifetime alimony with 4 percent annual increase; promissory note for wife's interest in husband's vacation and sick time included 9 percent interest from date of judgment, even though time was not in pay-out status; alimony and interest provisions were unconscionable); Wisniewski v. Cairo, 305 A.D.2d 788, 759 N.Y.S.2d 798 (2003) (child support obligation was nearly three times guideline amount and approximately 65 percent of the husband's net income; husband also received more than half of the marital assets); Tartaglia v. Tartaglia, 260 A.D.2d 628, 689 N.Y.S.2d 180 (1999) (wife received bulk of marital property, leaving husband with income of $7,860 per year from which to purchase life and medical insurance to benefit wife and children).

Agreements have been held conscionable despite considerable disparity in value in both the property division[357] and support awards.[358]

---

357. *See* McMahan v. McMahan, 567 So. 2d 976 (Fla. Dist. Ct. App. 1990) (marital property was divided equally; husband was charged with all the debts, but wife had accepted reduced alimony); *In re* Marriage of Bielawski, 328 Ill. App. 3d 243, 764 N.E.2d 1254 (2002) (wife received 33 percent of the total assets and 60 percent of the nonpension assets, plus $5,000 per month in survivor benefits after husband's death); *In re* Marriage of Gorman, 284 Ill. App. 3d 171, 671 N.E.2d 819, 827 (1996) (employed wife received $137,000 in property, while husband received between $350,000 and $400,000; disparity "does not remotely rise to the level of unconscionability"); *In re* Marriage of Steadman, 283 Ill. App. 3d 703, 670 N.E.2d 1146 (1996) (wife received 16.7 percent to 23.7 percent of the marital estate); *In re* Marriage of Brandt, 140 Ill. App. 3d 1019, 489 N.E.2d 902 (1986) (wife received $75,000 of $315,000 estate); Cameron v. Cameron, 265 S.W.3d 797, 800 (Ky. 2008) (agreement was conscionable, even though husband gave up half of his nonmarital property; wife did not receive maintenance); Keyser v. Keyser, 182 Mich. App. 268, 451 N.W.2d 587 (1990) (wife deliberately told husband she wanted only a pickup truck and certain personal property, and that he could have the rest of the marital estate; dissent would have found agreement unconscionable); Schlottach v. Schlottach, 873 S.W.2d 928 (Mo. Ct. App. 1994) (wife received 60 percent of marital estate; not unconscionable to husband); Logiudice v. Logiudice, 67 A.D.3d 544, 889 N.Y.S.2d 164 (2009) (stipulation awarded husband 60 percent of marital assets after 42-year marriage; husband was retired but wife was still employed; stipulation was not unconscionable); Curtis v. Curtis, 20 A.D.3d 653, 656, 798 N.Y.S.2d 764, 767 (2005) (trial court did not err in finding agreement conscionable without even holding a hearing, even though agreement awarded husband 100 percent of two largest marital assets; wife "has offered nothing beyond conclusory allegations relevant to the value of the equity, if any, in the marital residence or to the value of plaintiff's pension plan"); Middleton v. Middleton, 174 A.D.2d 655, 571 N.Y.S.2d 516 (1991) (wife received $10,000 monetary award and waived her interest in husband's pension; perhaps improvident, but not unconscionable); Lockhart v. Lockhart, 159 A.D.2d 283, 552 N.Y.S.2d 286 (1990) (wife received home, while husband received other real property, his pension, and $10,000 upon sale of the home); Hill v. Hill, 94 N.C. App. 474, 380 S.E.2d 540 (1989) (wife received $68,500 in cash and $1,000 per month for life out of marital estate worth at least $2 million; terms had first been proposed by the wife herself); Vann v. Vann, 767 N.W.2d 855 (N.D. 2009) (agreement awarding husband only 7.5 percent of marital estate was conscionable, where state treated premarital assets as marital property, and husband owned only 12 percent of the parties' total assets on the date of marriage; husband was also substantially underemployed during marriage); Knutson v. Knutson, 639 N.W.2d 495 (N.D. 2002) (wife received over $500,000 from divisible estate worth $2,143,500; no spousal support, but wife expected to earn $40,000 in year following divorce); Allocca v. Allocca, 23 Va. App. 571, 478 S.E.2d 702 (1996) (equal division of property, except that each party waived rights in the other's retirement benefits; husband's benefits were based upon 18 years of employment, while wife's benefits were based on only five to seven years of employment; conscionable despite the resulting disparity in value).

One case specifically rejected a contention that changed circumstances rendered the property division grossly disparate, where the changed circumstances was foreseeable when the agreement was negotiated. *See* McCaughey v. McCaughey, 205 A.D.2d 330, 612 N.Y.S.2d 579 (1994) (wife waived all discovery, and husband received home, pension, and $1.5 million payout from law firm; wife received installment payments, that became onerous to husband after he lost his job; loss of employment was foreseeable, and agreement was not unconscionable to husband).

358. *See In re* Marriage of Christen, 899 P.2d 339 (Colo. Ct. App. 1995) (agreement to set support so that postdivorce net incomes of the parties are equal is not unconscionable on its face); Grubman v. Grubman, 191 A.D.2d 194, 594 N.Y.S.2d 220 (1993) (wife received apartment for life, $350,000 monetary award, and $17,000 per month alimony); Washo v. Washo, 170 A.D.2d 827, 565

The definition of gross disparity can be significantly influenced by the fairness of the procedures under which the agreement was signed. Bargaining inequity, even if not sufficient by itself to render the agreement invalid, tends to reduce the threshold for gross disparity.[359]

Conversely, when a party knowingly signs an unequal agreement to make a fast exit from the marriage, the level of disparity necessary to find the agreement unconscionable can be very high.[360] Some courts also tend to deny relief to a party who knowingly signs an unequal agreement out of feelings of guilt.[361]

N.Y.S.2d 897 (1991) (husband agreed to pay modest alimony to wife who was capable of supporting herself; agreement may have been improvident, but it was not unconscionable); Hardenburgh v. Hardenburgh, 158 A.D.2d 585, 551 N.Y.S.2d 552 (husband agreed to pay wife $3,800 per month in support; his gross monthly income was only $5,400, but wife was in failing health), *appeal dismissed*, 76 N.Y.2d 982, 563 N.Y.S.2d 769 (1990); Kramer v. Kramer, 711 N.W.2d 164 (N.D. 2006) (agreement awarded parties their own personal property and vehicles, while equally dividing home and husband's pension, and required husband to pay $500 per month in permanent spousal support; wife's property award was apparently somewhat larger than husband's; rejecting husband's claim that agreement was unconscionable).

359. *See In re* Marriage of Bisque, 31 P.3d 175, 179 (Colo. App. 2001) (agreement awarded wife "the bulk of the marital estate, including the marital home and an adjacent lot," and trial court found that "husband's 'will was simply overborne by his aggressive, persistent, overbearing spouse'"; agreement set aside as unconscionable); *In re* Marriage of Rolf, 303 Mont. 349, 16 P.3d 345 (2000) (agreement gave wife $10,000 cash award, plus ownership of her small medical billing company; husband had net worth of nearly $1 million but marriage lasted only two years until separation; agreement may have been intended as temporary and may have resulted from coercion of wife; affirming trial court ruling that agreement was unconscionable if intended to be permanent, and increasing wife's property settlement to $80,000); Eberle v. Eberle, 766 N.W.2d 477 (N.D. 2009) (wife received only a vehicle, her personal property, and a small checking account, and waived spousal support, while husband received almost the entire marital estate; wife lacked counsel and husband threatened to seek custody if she did not sign; agreement was substantively and procedurally unconscionable).

360. *See* Pace v. Pace, 24 So. 3d 325, 330 (Miss. Ct. App. 2009) (agreement requiring husband to pay very substantial support was not unconscionable, where husband signed it to obtain quick divorce; "[t]he fact that he 'was in the unfortunate position of having a pregnant girlfriend and a hostile wife' affords Sidney little sympathy") (quoting the trial court)); Lyons v. Lyons, 289 A.D.2d 902, 905, 734 N.Y.S.2d 734, 737 (2001) ("While plaintiff may have been able to negotiate a better agreement had she not been so anxious to quickly end this marriage, given the admitted financial situation of the parties, the terms of the separation agreement cannot be considered manifestly unfair[.]"); Shenk v. Shenk, 39 Va. App. 161, 179, 571 S.E.2d 896, 906 (2002) (husband deserted wife, leaving her with control of business, and later assigned business to her formally; construing assignment to be a form of separation agreement, and finding agreement to be conscionable even though it awarded husband almost no value; business had prospered under wife's sole management); *cf. Santini*, 68 A.D.3d at 749, 891 N.Y.S.2d at 103 (where husband "acknowledged at trial that he was willing to give the defendant everything as long as he retained his pension," unequal property division that left husband his pension was not unconscionable).

361. *See* Dwyer v. Dwyer, 190 Misc. 2d 319, 324, 737 N.Y.S.2d 806, 810 (Sup. Ct. 2001) (husband, "while under stress and experiencing some impairment of judgment, was well aware of the consequences of signing the agreement," and "his motive for signing the agreement was to rid himself of his feelings of guilt"; not unconscionable).

In comparing the benefits received with and without the agreement, the court should look to the total overall benefits and not to the amount recovered on each relevant issue. For instance, division of marital property must be examined together with allocation of marital debts. When a spouse receives more than half of the marital property but must also pay more than half of the marital debts, the combination may well be conscionable.[362]

The same concept applies to support. Where the wife with a smaller earning capacity waived alimony completely, but received a generous $94,000 property settlement, one court found the agreement conscionable.[363] The alimony provisions were probably unconscionable viewed in isolation, but in the context of the entire agreement the overall bargain was not unreasonable. Likewise, courts have upheld agreements that combine a smaller property division award with a substantial award of alimony.[364]

Procedural Unconscionability

Some states refer to extreme bargaining inequity as procedural unconscionability, and treat it as either an independent basis for setting the agreement aside[365] or as a nec-

---

Guilt is a much more debatable issue than desire for a quick divorce, because one of the main purposes of substantive sufficiency review is to protect divorcing parties from their tendency to think emotionally. At its worst, the above line of cases is highly judgmental; the court agrees with the attacking party's feelings of guilt and enforces the agreement as a penalty. Feelings of guilt, where objectively justified, should probably still reduce the threshold for unconscionability, but they should not be a complete bar to substantive review.

362. *See* McMurry v. McMurry, 957 S.W.2d 731 (Ky. Ct. App. 1997) (husband received almost all of the parties' assets, but was burdened with debts exceeding his income); *In re* Dissolution of Marriage of De St. Germain, 977 So. 2d 412, 420 (Miss. Ct. App. 2008) (husband received nearly all of the marital property, but also assumed all marital debt; no inequality of bargaining power; agreement conscionable).

363. Smith v. Smith, 188 A.D.2d 1004, 591 N.Y.S.2d 662 (1992); *see also* Flynn v. Flynn, 232 Ill. App. 3d 394, 597 N.E.2d 709 (1992) (wife waived alimony but received 62 percent of marital estate; agreement not unconscionable); Cameron v. Cameron, 265 S.W.3d 797, 800 (Ky. 2008) (agreement was conscionable, even though husband gave up half of his nonmarital property; wife did not receive maintenance); Sorrentino v. Pearlstein, 55 A.D.3d 901, 867 N.Y.S.2d 113 (2008) (husband accepted liability for all but $15,000 of the parties' substantial tax liability, but was not required to pay maintenance and was liable for only one year of wife's health insurance; agreement was conscionable); Morad v. Morad, 27 A.D.3d 626, 812 N.Y.S.2d 126 (2006) (property division favored wife, but husband paid no maintenance despite significant income disparity, he received the full value of his medical practice, and wife agreed to accept 43 percent of the marital debt); Lounsbury v. Lounsbury, 300 A.D.2d 812, 752 N.Y.S.2d 103 (2002) (agreement awarded marital home to wife and required husband to make future mortgage payments, but husband received his business and all of the parties' race horses, wife received no spousal support and child support was set below the guideline amount; not unconscionable); Akgul v. Akgul, 175 A.D.2d 194, 572 N.Y.S.2d 338 (1991) (wife waived alimony and received no interest in husband's business, but received the entire marital home; agreement valid).

364. *See In re* Marriage of Lindjord, 234 Ill. App. 3d 319, 600 N.E.2d 431 (1992) (after short marriage, wife received only 11 percent of marital property but $28,000 in alimony; not unconscionable).

365. *See* West v. West, 891 So. 2d 203, 213 (Miss. 2004).

essary prerequisite for reviewing the substantive conscionability of the agreement.[366] Procedural unconscionability tends to focus mostly upon whether a spouse's consent was coerced by a pattern of behavior, and it is therefore discussed together with undue influence and overreaching in § **4.052**.

Absolute versus Relative Standard

In some states, the test for unconscionability is at least partly absolute, and not entirely relative. For example, in *Sims v. Sims*,[367] the wife signed a agreement that contained gross substantive disparity. The husband received 100 percent of the marital estate (except for the wife's personal property), and the wife completely waived spousal support. She received only the husband's promise to hold her harmless from future liability on the marital home, which had $200,000 in equity. The wife had only a third-grade education, and suffered from diabetes, rheumatoid arthritis, and frequent mood swings. She had married the husband at age 16, and remained married to him for 38 years. She had essentially no ability to support herself, and would have become a public charge if the agreement were enforced.

The trial court followed prior Virginia case law seeming to hold that substantive disparity is not a sufficient basis for finding an agreement to be unconscionable.[368] The appellate court reversed, finding that the gross substantive disparity, combined with the wife's "pecuniary necessities,"[369] was sufficient proof of unconscionability. The court noted that in prior cases involving gross substantive disparity, the disadvantaged spouse had not been left literally without a means for self-support. The "pecuniary necessities" identified by the court therefore amount to a severe degree of objective financial need.

Under the reasoning of cases like *Sims*, unconscionability is essentially an objective test. If the agreement leaves the disadvantaged spouse with sufficient income or property to meet his or her daily needs at a minimally acceptable standard of living, the agreement is conscionable. This is true even if there is gross disparity between the overall level of benefits awarded to the spouses under the agreement.[370] In other words, an agreement is unconscionable under these cases only if it leaves the disadvantaged spouse without some objective minimum amount of financial resources.

---

366. *See* Vann v. Vann, 767 N.W.2d 855 (N.D. 2009); Eberle v. Eberle, 766 N.W.2d 477 (N.D. 2009).

367. 55 Va. App. 340, 685 S.E.2d 869 (2009).

368. *See* Galloway v. Galloway, 47 Va. App. 83, 92, 622 S.E.2d 267, 272 (2005); Shenk v. Shenk, 39 Va. App. 161, 179, 571 S.E.2d 896, 906 (2002).

369. *Sims*, 55 Va. App. at 351, 685 S.E.2d at 874.

370. *See* Luftig v. Luftig, 239 A.D.2d 225, 657 N.Y.S.2d 658 (1997) (where wife received $797,000 property settlement and $201,000 in spousal support, agreement was not unconscionable); Knutson v. Knutson, 639 N.W.2d 495 (N.D. 2002) (wife received over $500,000 from divisible estate worth $2,143,500; no spousal support, but wife expected to earn $40,000 in year following divorce); Pelfrey v. Pelfrey, 25 Va. App. 239, 487 S.E.2d 281 (1997) (where husband was awarded full ownership of two expanding companies, agreement was conscionable, even though husband assumed substantial support obligations); Pillow v. Pillow, 13 Va. App. 271, 410 S.E.2d 407 (1991) (husband received car, boat, personal property, and an interest in the marital home; agreement conscionable).

Effect of Unconscionability

When courts find an agreement to be unconscionable, they generally strike down the entire agreement.[371] As the Kentucky Supreme Court stated in *Shraberg v. Shraberg*,[372] "Quite plainly, upon a finding of unconscionability, the trial court may fully decide the case as if there had been no agreement."

In some circumstances, however, the court may properly find that only part of an agreement is unconscionable, if that part is fairly severable from the remainder of the contract. In *In re Marriage of Pond*,[373] the contract provided that the wife would pay the husband's attorney's fees if she attacked the agreement. Her income was roughly $35,000, while the husband earned an income of $463,000. The court found the attorney's fees provision unconscionable, even while finding the rest of the agreement valid.

The difference between *Shraberg* and *Pond* involved the severability of the provisions at issue. The wife in *Shraberg* apparently argued that the court should reform the agreement so that it met the minimum requirements of conscionability, requirements that would still tolerate a great deal of inequity in her favor. The support provisions of the agreement were a single bargain, however, a bargain that was tainted by unconscionability. If the court had reformed those provisions, it would have rewritten the parties' bargain. In *Pond*, by contrast, the attorney's fees provision was severable from the remainder of the contract, and it reached a result that was clearly more unfair than the remainder of the agreement. Because the provision was severable, the court was able simply to remove it without affecting the remainder of the parties' bargain.

When a court finds that an unconscionable agreement is not severable, the net effect is to discourage egregiously unfair agreements. The party drafting the agreement knows that if the agreement is too unfair, it will fail the conscionability test, and the court will divide property and set support as if no agreement existed. To avoid this situation, parties proposing unequal agreements will naturally tend to limit the decree of unfairness. If unconscionable agreements could be reformed, by contrast, spouses would have every incentive to propose unfair agreements. Even if the agreement failed the test of conscionability, it could simply be reformed to include the maximum legally permitted degree of inequality. By penalizing parties who draft unconscionable agreements, the rule against reformation discourages egregious unfairness.

§ 4.062 Unfairness

As noted in § **6.06**, the nationwide case law is divided on the substantive sufficiency requirement for separation agreements. Some states allow only limited substantive review; other states allow substantive review for unconscionability; still other states allow substantive review for unfairness.

This section discusses substantive review in the last group of states: those that allow the court to set aside an agreement on the basis that it is unfair. The policy behind this position is closely linked to the policy behind the rule that a separation agreement is

---

371. Shraberg v. Shraberg, 939 S.W.2d 330 (Ky. 1997).
372. *Id.* at 334 (Ky. 1997).
373. 676 N.E.2d 401 (Ind. Ct. App. 1997).

not valid as a contract unless it is first approved by the court, and it is therefore discussed in § **4.04**. Summarized briefly, these states believe that regulation of the private right to contract is justified by the strong state interest in marriage and divorce.

While most states following a fairness standard do so in the context of a court approval requirement, a few states allow fairness review as a contractual defense.[374] The rationale is, again, the strength of the state's interest in fair divorce settlements.

The main focus of this section is on the manner in which the third group of states defines unfairness. The exact language of the unfairness standard varies from state to state. A typical example is the Indiana standard, under the agreement must be free from "unfairness, unreasonableness [or] manifest inequity."[375]

A Massachusetts court listed eight factors that should be considered in evaluating fairness:

> (1) the nature and substance of the objecting party's complaint; (2) the financial and property division provisions of the agreement as a whole; (3) the context in which the negotiations took place; (4) the complexity of the issues involved; (5) the background and knowledge of the parties; (6) the experience and ability of counsel; (7) the need for and availability of experts to assist the parties and counsel; and (8) the mandatory, and if the judge deems it appropriate, the discretionary factors set forth in [the property division statute].[376]

The core concept of all the various different definitions of fairness is that the court should set aside the agreement where either spouse receives significantly less than that spouse would receive in the absence of an agreement. The difference between unfairness and unconscionability is thus a matter of degree. The key to both concepts is the disparity between benefits received with and without the agreement, but the amount of the necessary disparity is different. Where the disparity is gross or overwhelming, the agreement is unconscionable; where the disparity is merely substantial or significant, the agreement is only unfair.

---

374. *E.g.*, ARIZ. REV. STAT. ANN. § 25-317(B) (Westlaw 2008); *In re* Marriage of Egedi, 88 Cal. App. 4th 17, 22, 105 Cal. Rptr. 2d 518, 522 (2001) ("The trial court also had the power to invalidate the [marital settlement agreement] if it was inequitable[.]").

375. Gabriel v. Gabriel, 654 N.E.2d 894, 897 (Ind. Ct. App. 1995).

For additional cases holding that an unfair separation agreement is invalid, *see* Shaver v. Shaver, 611 So. 2d 1094, 1096 (Ala. Ct. App. 1992) (agreement can be set aside if "one-sided and inequitable"); Sharp v. Sharp, 179 Ariz. 205, 877 P.2d 304, 310 (Ct. App. 1994) (agreement must be "fair and equitable"); Prinz v. Prinz, 596 So. 2d 807, 808 (Fla. Dist. Ct. App. 1992) (trial court "may set aside a property settlement agreement in order to do equity and justice between the parties"); Knox v. Remick, 371 Mass. 433, 358 N.E.2d 432, 435 (1976) ("fair and reasonable"); Faherty v. Faherty, 97 N.J. 99, 477 A.2d 1257, 1261 (1984) ("just and equitable"); Funderburk v. Funderburk, 286 S.C. 129, 332 S.E.2d 205 (1985) ("fairness under all the circumstances"); *cf.* Nitkiewicz v. Nitkiewicz, 369 Pa. Super. 504, 535 A.2d 664 (unless the enforcing spouse made full and fair disclosure of his assets, agreement must be fair and reasonable), *allocator denied*, 551 A.2d 216 (Pa. 1989); Gangopadhyay v. Gangopadhyay, 184 W. Va. 695, 403 S.E.2d 712 (1991) (oral agreement must be fair and reasonable).

376. Dominick v. Dominick, 18 Mass. App. Ct. 85, 463 N.E.2d 564, 569, *cert. denied*, 392 Mass. 1103, 465 N.E.2d 262 (1984).

Some states that follow the unfairness standard will claim to follow the unconscionability standard, but then adopt unfairness as the standard for unconscionability. In Colorado, for example, a separation agreement "is subject to review under the conscionability standard, including whether it is fair, just, and reasonable."[377] This sort of statement confuses the law, as is it settled in most other contexts that unconscionability is more extreme than unfairness. The better practice is to adopt the unfairness standard expressly, so that parties and trial judges know the standard by which the validity of divorce settlements should be determined.

An agreement is clearly not unfair merely because the trial judge believes that the party attacking the agreement should have insisted upon different terms.[378] "The family court is not obligated to reject a stipulation merely because the agreement does not divide the marital property or provide maintenance precisely in the manner or the amount that it would have had the agreement not existed."[379] "[B]ecause in many cases a range of possible property divisions likely would be just and proper, a trial court ordinarily should accept a marital settlement agreement that provides for a division of property within that range."[380] Judicial second-guessing of litigation strategy is especially discouraged when both parties have able counsel, and when the case is mediated.[381]

Nevertheless, occasional decisions have allowed trial courts to make decisions that come closer to imposing the court's own view of the case upon the parties.[382] This sort of overly active review is the major institutional weakness of the fairness standard in general and the court approval variant of that standard in particular. When fairness is to any extent debatable, and the party attacking the agreement had full knowledge of the facts and full opportunity to obtain independent counsel, the better practice is to resolve that debate in favor of the agreement. Competently represented parties with full knowledge of the facts should be allowed to litigate the case without undue interference from the court.

The practical definition of unfairness, like the practical definition of unconscionability, is best understood by reviewing the specific facts of the cases. At a minimum, any agreement that is unconscionable is certainly unfair, so the cases cited in **§ 4.061**

---

377. *See In re* Marriage of Bisque, 31 P.3d 175, 179 (Colo. Ct. App. 2001).

378. *See* Voigt v. Voigt, 670 N.E.2d 1271, 1277 (Ind. 1996) ("[T]he power to disapprove a settlement agreement must be exercised with great restraint. A trial judge should not reject a settlement agreement just because she believes she could draft a better one[.]").

379. Pouech v. Pouech, 180 Vt. 1, 12, 904 A.2d 70, 77 (2006); *see also* Burnett v. Burnett, 290 S.C. 28, 347 S.E.2d 908, 910 (Ct. App. 1986) ("when a husband and wife freely and voluntarily enter into an agreement which is procedurally fair, they should be in a better position than any judge to know whether it is substantively fair").

380. *In re* Marriage of Grossman, 338 Or. 99, 107, 106 P.3d 618, 622 (2005).

381. *See* Cloutier v. Cloutier, 814 A.2d 979, 983 (Me. 2003) ("in the normal course, the court should honor an agreement reached by the parties," especially when reached through mediation).

382. *See id.* at 983–84 (trial court properly refused to approve agreement to sell marital home, as "[wife's] ability to pay for alternative housing, in relation to [husband's], was insufficient" in the court's opinion); Gorman v. Gorman, 883 A.2d 732, 737 (R.I. 2005) (trial court properly refused to affirm agreement that "did not represent the 'fifty-fifty' approach that the Family Court had considered to be fair in view of both the length of the marriage and the other equitable considerations").

finding the agreement to be invalid apply under the unfairness standard as well. This is a useful starting point, as the number of states following the unconscionability standard is greater and there is accordingly a larger body of available law.

Cases finding that an agreement fails the fairness test tend to find significant disparity between the amount awarded to the attacking party under the agreement and the amount that spouse would receive if the case were litigated.[383] The disparity is not, however, as great as the disparity in cases finding the agreement to be unconscionable. A moderate amount of disparity is generally not sufficient to show that the agreement is unfair.[384]

The bar for unfairness is probably somewhat lower when the court believes that the agreement is contrary to the best interests of the parties' children. Of course, agreements dealing directly with child custody and child support are always subject to court review,[385] but courts in unfairness states tend to extend that active review even to property division issues, if the interests of children are indirectly involved.[386]

§ 4.063 Applying the Standard

Unfairness versus Unconscionability: Which Test Applies

Most states choose between unfairness and unconscionability as a matter of policy, and apply the chosen test to all separation agreements. In a few states, however, different tests may apply at different times to different issues. In New York, for instance, waivers of alimony must be fair and reasonable when made, and conscionable at the time of divorce. Property division provisions, by contrast, are judged under a pure unconscionability test.[387]

Because antenuptial agreement are signed while the parties still enjoy a confidential relationship, some states judge antenuptial agreements under a stricter standard of

---

383. *See, e.g., In re* Marriage of Thornhill, 200 P.3d 1083 (Colo. Ct. App. 2008) (agreement required husband to pay wife half of marital estate, but in payment spread over 10 years without interest; husband's business was materially undervalued; wife lacked counsel, and while her father helped her negotiate, he was CFO of the business and had a conflict of interest; agreement was not fair and reasonable); Tal v. Tal, 158 Misc. 2d 703, 601 N.Y.S.2d 530 (1993) (wife received $125,000 of net estate worth roughly $350,000 and waived alimony completely; husband's annual income was $171,000, while wife was unemployed 38-year-old who spoke no English); Dewbrew v. Dewbrew, 849 N.E.2d 636, 646 (Ind. Ct. App. 2006) (agreement failed to divide marital home and husband's businesses; because of ambiguity, trial court erred by refusing to set agreement aside).

384. *See, e.g.,* Tubbs v. Tubbs, 648 So. 2d 817 (Fla. Dist. Ct. App. 1995) (wife received 34 percent of the marital property and only seven years of alimony after marriage of unspecified length; agreement was a bad bargain, but it was not so unfair as to justify court in setting it aside); *In re* Marriage of Takusagawa, 38 Kan. App. 2d 401, 166 P.3d 440 (2007) (husband received assets worth $629,000 while wife received assets worth between $670,000 and $1,500,000; agreement was fair to wife, even though husband earned $84,500 and wife earned only $49,000).

385. *See* § **3.07**.

386. *See Cloutier,* 814 A.2d at 983 (trial court properly refused to enforce agreement to sell marital home, where it was in best interests of children to keep them in the same school district, and court believed that wife's ability to pay for alternate housing was "insufficient").

387. *See* Smith v. Smith, 188 A.D.2d 1004, 591 N.Y.S.2d 662 (1992); Zipes v. Zipes, 158 Misc. 2d 368, 599 N.Y.S.2d 941 (1993).

substantive fairness. Where a separation agreement merely restated and reaffirmed the language of an antenuptial agreement, one court held that the antenuptial agreement test should be applied.[388]

Waiver
The right to have a separation agreement reviewed for substantive sufficiency cannot be waived in the agreement.[389]

Time of Application
Different courts evaluate the substantive sufficiency of the agreement at different times. Some courts evaluate sufficiency as of the date on which the agreement was signed.[390] Other courts evaluate sufficiency as of the time the divorce decree is rendered.[391]

Regardless of when the test is applied, the court cannot refer to postdivorce events in determining substantive sufficiency.[392]

Proving Substantive Insufficiency
Regardless of whether the relevant test is unconscionability or unfairness, the essence of the substantive insufficiency issue is a comparison between the rights of the attacking spouse with and without the agreement. Inevitably, therefore, the court must make some attempt to determine how the case would have been decided if no agreement were present. Otherwise, there is simply no way to determine whether the agreement is fair or conscionable. Assume, for instance, that an agreement awards the wife a lump sum property settlement of $10,000 after a 20-year marriage. This sum would probably be fair and reasonable if the divisible estate were worth $20,000, and it would probably be unconscionable if the divisible estate were worth $2 million. In order to tell the difference between these two fact situations, the court must make some determination of how the case would be resolved without the agreement.

A few isolated cases have held to the contrary. For instance, in *In re Marriage of Caras*,[393] the court made the amazing holding that it need not determine the value of the divisible estate in order to determine whether the agreement is unconscionable. If this holding is taken literally, it would completely prevent any form of meaningful

---

388. *In re* Marriage of Lemoine-Hofmann, 827 P.2d 587 (Colo. Ct. App. 1992).

389. Picard v. Picard, 708 So. 2d 1292 (La. Ct. App. 1998).

390. *E.g., In re* Marriage of Smith, 115 S.W.3d 126, 135 (Tex Ct. App. 2003) ("While the value of the property that each party received under the contract now seems quite disproportionate, we do not evaluate whether the contract is unconscionable years later. Rather, we look to the circumstances at the time the parties entered into the contract."); Bendekgey v. Bendekgey, 154 Vt. 193, 576 A.2d 433 (1990) (increase in value of marital home after signing of agreement did not make agreement unfair).

391. *E.g.,* Knox v. Remick, 371 Mass. 433, 358 N.E.2d 432 (1976); *see also* Bailey v. Bailey, 231 S.W.3d 793, 796 (Ky. Ct. App. 2007) ("A separation agreement which was originally determined not to be unconscionable may later be modified if due to a change in circumstances the agreement has become unconscionable[.]").

392. *See In re* Marriage of Hamilton, 254 Mont. 31, 835 P.2d 702 (1992) (postdivorce gifts and inheritances were not relevant to determining fairness of agreement).

393. 263 Mont. 377, 868 P.2d 615 (1994).

unconscionability review, for the court cannot know whether a given award is reasonable unless it has some basic indication of what the attacking party would have received without the agreement.[394] An award that is reasonable in an estate of modest size may be unconscionable when the divisible estate is worth millions of dollars.

While the court must make some independent determination of the equities of the case, it is obviously not desirable that the court should conduct the same sort of inquiry it would undertake in a litigated case. The entire purpose of a private settlement is to avoid such an extensive inquiry. This point was probably the underlying concern of the court in *Caras*, and viewed in the proper light the concern is entirely valid. The court overstated the case, however, by stating that the value of the divisible estate is irrelevant. A more accurate statement is that the trial court must walk a rather fine line: It must value the divisible estate with sufficient accuracy to make a fair determination of substantive sufficiency, but it must avoid relitigating the merits of the entire action.

The practical compromise that has emerged in most states is that the court should take a broad overall look at the parties' financial situation. The court need not classify each and every asset as divisible or nondivisible, and it is certainly not required to insist upon evidence of the parties' finances beyond what is presented by the parties themselves.[395] It must, however, make a rough finding as to the value of the divisible estate and the likely division of that estate if no agreement were present. Without at least a general finding along these lines, it is not possible to make a reasonably accurate determination of whether the agreement is unfair or unconscionable.

The burden of presenting evidence on the likely benefits with the agreement lies upon the attacking spouse. Where the attacking spouse introduced no evidence on this point, one court held that it lacked sufficient evidence to determine whether the agreement was unconscionable.[396]

§ 4.07 Changes in Character

The preceding sections of this chapter set forth the law used to determine the prima facie validity of the agreement. This determination is normally final. In some cases, however, the actions of the parties can make an otherwise valid contract invalid. Likewise, the parties can also make an invalid contract valid. This section discusses the rules of law governing these changes in character.

The various available procedural defenses to the enforcement of separation agreements fall into two classes. The first class is based upon passage of time; the second class is based upon the conduct of the parties.

---

394. *See* Petracca v. Petracca, 706 So. 2d 904, 912 (Fla. Dist. Ct. App. 1998) ("it is undoubtedly true that in deciding the reasonableness of a marital property settlement, the court is really trying the merits of the underlying dispute").

395. *See In re* Marriage of Turner, 803 S.W.2d 655, 661 (Mo. Ct. App. 1991); Secor v. Secor, 790 S.W.2d 500 (Mo. Ct. App. 1990).

396. King v. King, 114 N.C. App. 454, 442 S.E.2d 154 (1994).

§ 4.071 Limitations

The first set of procedural defenses are all based upon the amount of time that elapses between the signing of the agreement and the first attempt to enforce or recognize it. If that time period is sufficiently long, the agreement may be invalid.

In some states, there may be a statute of limitations on separation agreement defenses. New York, for example, requires that all such defenses be raised within a six-year period.[397] Where the attacking spouse has no reason to suspect that the agreement might be invalid, the limitations period is two years from the time when the invalidity should reasonably have been discovered.[398] If a party fails to raise an applicable defense within the proper limitations period, an invalid agreement is thereby rendered valid.

One case held that the statute of limitations may apply only when a claim of invalidity is raised offensively in an action to set the agreement aside, and not when used passively as a defense to enforcement.[399] The lack of similar cases from other states suggests that the general rule may be to the contrary.

The statute of limitations may be tolled during any period in which the presence of grounds to set the agreement aside was fraudulently concealed from the innocent spouse.[400]

§ 4.072 Laches

A spouse who is injured by an unenforceable agreement cannot sit on his or her rights for several years before seeking to overturn the contract. Instead, the disadvantaged spouse has a duty to take prompt action upon discovering the invalidity of the agreement. If prompt action is not taken, the agreement is ratified and becomes enforceable.

The exact definition of "prompt actions" depends upon the facts. Most of the cases finding the requirement to be met involve delays of three years or more.[401]

§ 4.073 Ratification

The second class of procedural defenses is based upon the conduct of the parties. Under the doctrines of ratification and estoppel, an otherwise invalid agreement may become

---

397. *See, e.g.*, N.Y. C.P.L.R. § 213 (1990); Percoco v. Lesnak, 24 A.D.3d 427, 806 N.Y.S.2d 674 (2005); Riley v. Riley, 179 A.D.2d 950, 579 N.Y.S.2d 134 (1992); Emery v. Emery, 166 A.D.2d 787, 563 N.Y.S.2d 526 (1990); Zipes v. Zipes, 158 Misc. 2d 368, 599 N.Y.S.2d 941 (1993) (noting that limitations period runs during the marriage as well as after).

398. *See* DeLuca v. DeLuca, 48 A.D.3d 341, 851 N.Y.S.2d 539 (2008) (action barred on the facts); Gargulio v. Gargulio, 201 A.D.2d 617, 608 N.Y.S.2d 238 (1994) (action is timely if brought within two years after discovery of grounds for invalidity; action barred on the facts); Cucchiaro v. Cucchiaro, 165 Misc. 2d 134, 627 N.Y.S.2d 224 (1995) (wife should have known that husband's pension was marital property more than two years before she filed to set separation aside for failure to disclose that fact, and her action was therefore time-barred).

399. *See* Picard v. Picard, 708 So. 2d 1292 (La. Ct. App. 1998).

400. *E.g.*, Nessler v. Nessler, 387 Ill. App. 3d 1103, 902 N.E.2d 701 (2008).

401. *See* Capone v. Capone, 148 A.D.2d 565, 539 N.Y.S.2d 35 (1989) (wife waited four years before attacking agreement; agreement ratified); Patti v. Patti, 146 A.D.2d 757, 537 N.Y.S.2d 241 (1989) (three years); Lowry v. Lowry, 99 N.C. App. 246, 393 S.E.2d 141 (1990) (three years).

valid if the parties act as if it were enforceable. By contrast, under the doctrines of abandonment and reconciliation, an otherwise valid agreement may become invalid if the parties act as if it were not enforceable.

A party who knows or has reason to know that an agreement is invalid is not permitted to accept benefits under the agreement for a substantial period and then attempt to attack it. Instead, where the attacking party has knowingly accepted benefits under the agreement for a significant period of time, he or she has ratified the agreement and cured any causes of invalidity.

The definition of a significant period of time depends upon the facts. Acceptance of benefits for a period of over two years is almost certain to result in ratification.[402] In addition, there is some authority finding ratification if benefits were accepted for less than two years.[403]

Ratification may not be present when a spouse accepts benefits that he or she would have been entitled to even if the contract were invalid.[404] In other words, acceptance of uncontested benefits does not constitute ratification.

Acceptance of benefits obviously does not constitute ratification where the accepting spouse had no reason to know that the agreement was invalid.[405]

---

402. Taplin v. Taplin, 611 So. 2d 561 (Fla. Dist. Ct. App. 1992) (two years); La Marca v. Kissell, 269 A.D.2d 835, 702 N.Y.S.2d 490 (2000) (three and a half years); Wilson v. Neppell, 253 A.D.2d 493, 677 N.Y.S.2d 144 (1998) (three years); Stacom v. Wunsch, 162 A.D.2d 170, 556 N.Y.S.2d 303 (1990) (wife accepted more than $1.8 million under agreement over five-year period; agreement ratified); Niosi v. Niosi, 226 A.D.2d 510, 641 N.Y.S.2d 93 (1996) (payment of maintenance for six years ratified agreement); In re Marriage of Schell, 191 A.D.2d 570, 594 N.Y.S.2d 807 (1993) (eight years); Gloor v. Gloor, 190 A.D.2d 1007, 594 N.Y.S.2d 471 (1993) (four years); Torsiello v. Torsiello, 188 A.D.2d 523, 591 N.Y.S.2d 472 (1992) (two years); Lavelle v. Lavelle, 187 A.D.2d 912, 590 N.Y.S.2d 557 (1992) (31 months); Johnson v. Johnson, 180 A.D.2d 530, 580 N.Y.S.2d 250 (1992) (six years); Akgul v. Akgul, 175 A.D.2d 194, 572 N.Y.S.2d 338 (1991) (six years); Moore v. Moore, 108 N.C. App. 656, 424 S.E.2d 673 (1993) (two years).

403. See Ricca v. Ricca, 57 A.D.3d 868, 870 N.Y.S.2d 419 (2008) (almost two years); Lyons v. Lyons, 289 A.D.2d 902, 904, 734 N.Y.S.2d 734, 737 (2001) ("by accepting benefits pursuant to the agreement for several months before seeking to amend the complaint, plaintiff is deemed to have ratified the agreement"); Carlson v. Carlson, 255 A.D.2d 873, 680 N.Y.S.2d 362 (1998) (14 months); Skotnicki v. Skotnicki, 237 A.D.2d 974, 654 N.Y.S.2d 904 (1997) (14 months); Reader v. Reader, 236 A.D.2d 829, 653 N.Y.S.2d 768 (1997) (15½ months); Goodwin v. Webb, 357 N.C. 40, 577 S.E.2d 621 (2003) (wife accepted lump sum payment of $160,000 under agreement; summarily approving the dissenting opinion in Goodwin v. Webb, 152 N.C. App. 650, 568 S.E.2d 311 (2002)); Hill v. Hill, 94 N.C. App. 474, 380 S.E.2d 540 (1989) (wife signed amended contract two weeks after original contract; wife alleged that duress by parties' son tainted first agreement, but son was not present at signing of amendment; contract ratified).

404. In re Marriage of Steadman, 283 Ill. App. 3d 703, 670 N.E.2d 1146 (1996); Eberle v. Eberle, 766 N.W.2d 477, 486 (N.D. 2009) (wife "did not receive and accept any advantages and benefits she would not be entitled to if the judgment is reversed because it is inconceivable that she may receive less than she is entitled to under the original judgment"); McBride v. McBride, 797 S.W.2d 689 (Tex. Ct. App. 1990).

405. See Webb v. Webb, 16 Va. App. 486, 431 S.E.2d 55 (1993) (wife accepted benefits before learning of husband's fraud; no ratification).

§ 4.074 Reconciliation

The opposites of the doctrine of ratification are the doctrines of reconciliation and abandonment. Just as the former doctrine can save an otherwise invalid agreement, so can the latter doctrines strike down an otherwise valid agreement.

The Traditional Rule

The law on reconciliation is in a state of transition. A New Jersey court stated the traditional rule as follows:

> [T]he modern view is that the executory provisions of a property settlement agreement are deemed to be abrogated by a subsequent reconciliation of the parties, unless it can be shown by the party seeking to enforce the agreement that the parties intended otherwise, but that the executed provisions of a property settlement agreement are unaffected by the reconciliation. . . . The philosophy underpinning the theory of abrogation is that, since the policy of courts is to encourage and strengthen the bond of marriage, it is the presumed intent of the parties at the time of the reconciliation to resume the marital relationship in all respects and abrogate any prior agreements restricting or inhibiting the rights of one of the spouses, unless they indicate otherwise at the time of the reconciliation.[406]

Thus, under the traditional rule, reconciliation invalidates the executory provisions of the agreement, but the executed provisions remain valid.

Burden of Proof. "The party seeking to avoid an agreement based on a defense of reconciliation has the burden of proving that the reconciliation was genuine."[407]

Defining Reconciliation. "[W]hat constitutes a reconciliation is not susceptible to a simple definition and generally depends upon the facts."[408] At the simplest level, however, reconciliation can be defined as the ending of separation and the resumption of a marital relationship.[409] The most obvious form of reconciliation is the remarriage of the parties.[410] Any substantial resumption of the marital relationship, however, qualifies as a reconciliation.

---

406. Brazina v. Brazina, 233 N.J. Super. 145, 558 A.2d 69, 72 (1989); *see also* Cox v. Cox, 659 So. 2d 1051 (Fla. 1995); Crenshaw v. Crenshaw, 12 Va. App. 1129, 408 S.E.2d 556 (1991).

407. Jacobsen v. Jacobsen, 41 Va. App. 582, 591, 586 S.E.2d 896, 900 (2003).

408. *Brazina*, 233 N.J. Super. 145, 558 A.2d at 71.

409. Yeich v. Yeich, 11 Va. App. 509, 399 S.E.2d 170 (1990).

410. *See* Garland v. Garland, 79 Ark. App. 10, 84 S.W.3d 44 (2002); Ray v. Ohio Nat'l Ins. Co., 537 So. 2d 915 (Ala. 1989); Baird v. Baird, 696 So. 2d 844 (Fla. Dist. Ct. App. 1997); Thomas v. Thomas, 571 So. 2d 499 (Fla. Dist. Ct. App. 1990); Barnedt v. Wilder, 137 Idaho 415, 49 P.3d 1265 (Ct. App. 2002); *In re* Marriage of Allen, 31 Kan. App. 2d 31, 59 P.3d 1030 (2002); Batten v. Batten, 125 N.C. App. 685, 482 S.E.2d 18 (1997); Wolski v. Wolski, 210 Wis. 2d 184, 565 N.W.2d 196 (1997).

A Kentucky court set forth a partial list of factors to be considered in determining whether the parties reconciled:

> We could not possibly enumerate all of the factors which might come into play for a trial court to consider in determining whether reconciliation has occurred. We mention only a few: (1) whether the parties have resumed residing with each other; (2) the nature in which they hold their personal property, including bank accounts; (3) their failure to carry out other executory provisions of the contract; (4) activities of the parties in which normally only married couples participate; (5) whether the parties attended marriage counseling (here, both parties attended, but Lynea stopped going); and (6) other factors of which this Court is not now mindful. A guiding light might be that reconciliation occurs where, from all appearances and for a substantial period of time, it seems purely an oversight that the agreement has not been rescinded or the divorce action dismissed. As mentioned, this process is a very dense and thorny undergrowth of fact-finding through which the trial court must hack out on its way to a conclusion.[411]

Several sample cases show how the definition works in practice. In *Rudansky v. Rudansky*,[412] the parties sold their former residences and commenced living together. They had sexual relations, and filed joint tax returns listing their status as married. Finally, the wife gave up employment and returned to her role as homemaker. The court held that these facts were sufficient to constitute reconciliation.

Conversely, in *Fletcher v. Fletcher*,[413] the parties spent five to six consecutive evenings together. They had family time with their children, and had sex three to four times during the period. The court held that reconciliation would be present if the parties either subjectively intended to resume their marital relationship, or publicly held themselves out as married.[414] There was no holding out, so the issue was whether the parties subjectively intended to resume their former relationship. The court noted that the parties were together for less than a week, and that the wife had retained a separate

---

411. Cameron v. Cameron, 265 S.W.3d 797, 800 (Ky. 2008).

412. 223 A.D.2d 500, 637 N.Y.S.2d 97 (1996); *see also In re* Estate of Britcher, 38 A.D.3d 1223, 1223, 833 N.Y.S.2d 332, 333 (2007) (parties "never divorced and in fact reconciled and resumed their marital relationship" from 1995 until 2004); Mullen v. Mullen, 260 A.D.2d 452, 688 N.Y.S.2d 208 (1999) (seven years of joint residency, including a regular sexual relationship, constituted reconciliation); *In re* Estate of Archibald, 183 N.C. App. 274, 644 S.E.2d 264 (2007) (parties did not divorce, resumed living together, and held themselves out as married).

413. 123 N.C. App. 744, 474 S.E.2d 802 (1996); *see also* Rosner v. Rosner, 66 A.D.3d 983, 888 N.Y.S.2d 121 (2009) (1992 waiver of equitable distribution in prior divorce action was not binding, where action was dismissed and parties continued to live together until at least 2004, filing joint tax returns during that period).

414. *Accord* Schultz v. Schultz, 107 N.C. App. 366, 420 S.E.2d 186 (1992).

residence throughout the period. Based upon these facts, the court found that there had been no reconciliation.

As *Fletcher* suggests, the ending of a separation without a resumption of the marital relationship is not reconciliation. Thus, mere isolated acts of sexual intercourse do not constitute reconciliation.[415] Likewise, a short trial period of living together is not sufficient:

> The primary purpose of the court is . . . to encourage a reconciliation. . . . Spouses frequently need time apart from each other to ponder whether they wish to remain married and to glean greater insight into the character and motivations of the other before they can forgive and forget. Not only does this take time to accomplish but it also often requires a "trial reconciliation" before they can agree to permanently resume the marriage in all its aspects. To encourage a reconciliation and the resumption of the marriage it is important that we not impose legal consequences which could discourage the parties from attempting a reconciliation out of fear that an unsuccessful reconciliation effort could result in adverse legal consequences. For these reasons we believe that the preferable rule is to hold that a reconciliation should not be deemed to have occurred until the parties have successfully completed the exploratory stage of a reconciliation and have agreed upon a true and genuine reconciliation, that is to say, when the parties have resolved their differences and agree to permanently resume their former relationship as husband and wife.[416]

---

415. Brazina v. Brazina, 233 N.J. Super. 145, 558 A.2d 69, 71 (1989); *Fletcher*, 123 N.C. App. 744, 474 S.E.2d 802; Jacobsen v. Jacobsen, 41 Va. App. 582, 591, 586 S.E.2d 896, 900 (2003) ("Resumption of sexual relations is only a factor in establishing a valid reconciliation[.]").

416. *See Brazina*, 233 N.J. Super. 145, 558 A.2d at 71; *In re* Estate of K.J.R., 348 N.J. Super. 618, 624, 792 A.2d 561, 565 (App. Div. 2002) ("At the most, petitioner and decedent merely spoke by long distance telephone, without any physical contact or face-to-face visits" and "made no endeavor to reunite physically" over four-to-five-month period; no reconciliation); Russo v. Russo, 305 A.D.2d 486, 486, 759 N.Y.S.2d 742, 743 (2003) ("the parties lived together briefly after entering into the separation agreement and at a subsequent time, but their conduct demonstrated a mutual acknowledgment that the marriage was dead and that they did not intend to reconcile"); Klein v. Klein, 246 A.D.2d 195, 676 N.Y.S.2d 69 (1998) (mere cohabitation does not alone constitute reconciliation); Lippman v. Lippman, 192 A.D.2d 1060, 596 N.Y.S.2d 241 (1993) (brief period of cohabitation did not invalidate agreement); Camp v. Camp, 75 N.C. App. 498, 331 S.E.2d 163 (1985) (10-day trial period not reconciliation), *cert. denied*, 314 N.C. 663, 335 S.E.2d 493 (1985).

Longer periods of contact less than full cohabitation are likewise unlikely to be treated as a real reconciliation.[417] Even full cohabitation may not be sufficient where the cohabitation lasted less than a year, especially if marital litigation remained pending.[418]

Finally, a reconciliation exists only if both spouses are attempting in good faith to resume the marital relationship. "Good faith embodies honest purpose, and a fundamental expectation of fair and reasonable conduct."[419] If one spouse attempts reconciliation for the purpose of avoiding an undesirable agreement, there is no valid reconciliation and the agreement remains valid.[420]

Executory Provisions. The executory provisions of a separation agreement are those that have not yet been implemented by the parties. The most common types of executory provisions are future spousal and child support.[421] Property division provisions

---

417. *See* Cameron v. Cameron, 265 S.W.3d 797, 800 (Ky. 2008) ("the parties had spent some time together, including two short vacation trips to Mexico and several weekends," but wife "continued to reside with her mother in Mason County and kept her personal property separate from that of Donald," and parties never resumed permanent cohabitation; no reconciliation); Barton v. Barton, 790 So. 2d 169, 175 (Miss. 2001) (despite sporadic cohabitation between separation and husband's death, husband told friends that wife was having an affair and that "he was glad to be getting rid of his wife"; no reconciliation); Thompson v. Thompson, 294 A.D.2d 943, 943, 741 N.Y.S.2d 641, 642 (2002) ("the parties intermittently lived under the same roof between March 1994 and the summer of 1998, but [they] came and went as they pleased, maintained separate bedrooms and never had sexual relations, did not share bank accounts or personal belongings, and filed separate tax returns"; no reconciliation); Zambito v. Zambito, 171 A.D.2d 918, 566 N.Y.S.2d 789 (1991) (while parties were allegedly cohabiting, husband had mail sent to sister's home, kept an answering machine there, and continued to pay child support; no reconciliation).

418. *See* Guriel v. Guriel, 55 A.D.3d 540, 541, 865 N.Y.S.2d 611, 612 (2008) ("The parties' cohabitation for eight months following the execution of the agreement did not raise an issue of fact regarding an intention to reconcile[.]"); *but cf.* Heskett v. Heskett, 245 S.W.3d 222 (Ky. Ct. App. 2008) (18-month resumption of marital relationship beginning in 2003 was sufficient to invalidate prior separation agreement, even though reconciliation did not last much longer than a year).

419. Jacobsen v. Jacobsen, 41 Va. App. 582, 591, 586 S.E.2d 896, 900 (2003).

420. *Id.* at 592, 586 S.E.2d at 900. The husband in Jacobsen told a family friend that he "was only back with wife so he could get the house." He also continued a relationship with a paramour, which included a camping trip and an out-of-state visit. The court held that the husband never had a true intention to reconcile with the wife, so that the agreement remained valid.

421. *See, e.g.*, Yeich v. Yeich, 11 Va. App. 509, 399 S.E.2d 170 (1990) (alimony provision invalidated by reconciliation).

Several states hold that reconciliation automatically abrogates the terms of a separation agreement (*e.g.*, future support), but does not abrogate the terms of a property settlement agreement unless the parties so intend. Garland v. Garland, 79 Ark. App. 10, 84 S.W.3d 44 (2002); Brinkmann v. Brinkmann, 772 N.E.2d 441, 448 (Ind. Ct. App. 2002) ("property settlement agreements are not automatically terminated by the subsequent reconciliation of the parties absent clear proof the parties so agreed or intended"); Vaccarello v. Vaccarello, 563 Pa. 93, 757 A.2d 909 (2000).

can also be executory if the transfer of possession has not yet taken place.[422] A waiver of future inheritance rights is executory.[423]

Executed Provisions. The executed provisions of a separation agreement are those that have already been implemented by the parties. The most common type of executed provision is a property division that has actually been carried out.[424]

Integrated Bargain Agreements. Under the traditional doctrine of reconciliation, executed provisions are normally not invalidated by a reconciliation. There is one situation, however, in which even the executed provisions may be invalid. Parties to divorce cases sometimes sign integrated bargain agreements, in which the spousal support provisions are consideration for the property division. For instance, the wife might agree to accept only 35 percent of the marital estate, relying upon an unusually generous spousal support provision. If only the spousal support provisions of such an agreement were invalidated, serious injustice would result. A North Carolina decision states the rule:

> In such an agreement, the provisions are so interdependent that the execution of one portion of the agreement necessarily requires the execution of the other part. Conversely, if one section of the agreement fails or is declared invalid— for example, if the support provisions of an agreement are terminated because the parties reconcile—other provisions of the agreement negotiated with that support provision in mind, in fairness must also fail.[425]

Whether an integrated bargain exists depends upon whether the parties intended the support provisions to be consideration for the property division. There is a presumption that the agreement is not integrated (that is, it is severable), so that the burden of proof is on the party who claims that an integrated agreement exists.[426]

The integrated bargain issue arises more frequently in the construction context. Construction cases raising the issue are discussed in **§ 6.012**.

---

422. *See* Cox v. Cox, 659 So. 2d 1051 (Fla. 1995) (future installments of wife's share of husband's military retirement benefits were executory).

423. *See In re* Estate of Archibald, 183 N.C. App. 274, 644 S.E.2d 264 (2007).

424. *See* Adcock v. Adcock, 259 Ga. App. 514, 577 S.E.2d 842 (2003); Morrison v. Morrison, 102 N.C. App. 514, 402 S.E.2d 855 (1991).

425. Stegall v. Stegall, 100 N.C. App. 398, 397 S.E.2d 306, 310 (1990), *cert. denied*, 322 N.C. 274, 400 S.E.2d 461 (1991).

Despite the broad statement quoted in the text, a later North Carolina case held that the executed portions of a property division provision in an integrated bargain agreement survive reconciliation. *Morrison*, 102 N.C. App. 514, 402 S.E.2d 855. *Morrison* could obviously cause severe inequity where an unequal property division has already been implemented in consideration for a large support award. A better approach would have been to invalidate the executory provisions and determine the marital estate as if the executed portion did not exist. *See* Garland v. Garland, No. 0751-90-2 (Va. Ct. App. Apr. 2, 1991). To protect third parties, however, the executed portions should still be sufficient to convey legal title.

426. *Morrison*, 102 N.C. App. 514, 402 S.E.2d 855.

Recent Changes: The Intent-Based Standard

As noted above, the traditional common law doctrine of reconciliation is in the midst of a period of change. This change is a result of parallel changes in the public policies that underlie separation agreements.

At common law, the concept of separation was essential to the definition of a separation agreement. Parties who were not separated were not permitted to sign marital agreements, and separation agreements were invalid if the parties did not separate either before or immediately after signing the agreement. *See* § **3.01**. Along similar lines, under the common law, the executory parts of the separation agreement became invalid if the parties ever ended their separation by attempting reconciliation. The basis for this rule was not the intent of the parties, but rather the fundamental public policy that only separated persons could sign separation agreements. When the parties ceased to be separated, their separation agreement violated public policy. Thus, to the extent that the agreement was not yet executed, its provisions became invalid. Because this doctrine was a rule of public policy, it applied regardless of the parties' intent.

In recent years, the public policy underlying marital agreements in general has changed dramatically. Today there is essentially no doubt that marital agreements of all types are consistent with and even favored by public policy, as long as they pass review under the law of substantive validity. In particular, as discussed earlier in this treatise, the law no longer holds that marital agreements signed during the marriage are void for encouraging divorce. On the contrary, such agreements are routinely enforced. *See* § **3.01**.

This change in public policy has disrupted the theoretical basis for the doctrine of reconciliation. Since marital agreements can now be signed by nonseparated parties, it is no longer true that reconciliation destroys the essential foundation for a separation agreement. In other words, it is no longer against public policy for nonseparated persons to sign separation agreements. Since actual separation is no longer an essential element of validity, there is no reason that an interruption in the parties' separation should necessarily make their agreement invalid.

At the same time, however, there are still valid reasons why reconciliation should have an effect upon separation agreements. Where the parties truly reconcile and resume their former relationship as husband and wife, they frequently cease the actual performance of their agreement. Moreover, if the reconciliation lasts for a sufficiently long period of time, subsequent changes in circumstances may make the agreement outdated. In either of these circumstances, the actions of the parties themselves suggest that the agreement is no longer controlling. In other words, the parties have demonstrated an intention to abandon their agreement. As separation has ceased to become an absolute legal requirement for signing a marital agreement, courts have tended to rely less upon public policy and more upon the intention of the parties as a basis for the doctrine of reconciliation.

The change from a rule of policy to a rule of intent is still in process in most jurisdictions. The initial break in the common law rule was a series of decisions holding that the executory portions of the agreement survive reconciliation if the parties so intended. The easiest cases were those in which the agreement itself contained a specific clause stating that the agreement would survive reconciliation.[427] The clear trend in these cases is to enforce these provisions.

A somewhat harder issue is presented when the parties' intent appears not in the agreement itself, but rather in the parties' actions during the period of reconciliation. Nevertheless, the recent decisions all appear willing to look to conduct as well as to the contract. For instance, where the parties do not completely carry out some of the terms of their agreement, that fact is evidence that the entire agreement is voided by the reconciliation.[428] Likewise, if property that was given to one spouse is used interchangeably by both spouses, the parties may have implicitly modified their agreement by abandoning the relevant provision.[429] On the other hand, where the parties continue to follow the agreement during reconciliation, the agreement may be valid even if it has not yet been fully executed.[430]

Most of these decisions relying upon the intent of the parties treated intent as an exception to the executed/executory distinction. A growing number of recent decisions,

---

427. *See, e.g.*, Jennings v. Jennings, 12 Va. App. 1187, 409 S.E.2d 8 (1991); Yeich v. Yeich, 11 Va. App. 509, 399 S.E.2d 170 (1990); *see also Cox*, 659 So. 2d 1051 (stating in dicta that survival provision would be enforceable); Pugsley v. Pugsley, 288 A.D.2d 284, 285, 733 N.Y.S.2d 125, 126–27 (2001) ("[A] provision of the separation agreement itself required that any reconciliation must be reduced to writing. No reason has been offered by the plaintiff which would justify ignoring this specific provision of the parties' agreement[.]"); Zambito v. Zambito, 171 A.D.2d 918, 566 N.Y.S.2d 789 (1991) (no reconciliation; court gave at least some weight to clause in agreement providing that any future reconciliation must be in writing). *But cf.* Slotnick v. Slotnick, 891 So. 2d 1086, 1088 (Fla. Dist. Ct. App. 2004) (provision that agreement will survive reconciliation must be explicit; where agreement did not mention reconciliation or remarriage, the necessary explicit statement was lacking).

428. *See* Garland v. Garland, 79 Ark. App. 10, 84 S.W.3d 44 (2002) (wife's failure to enforce agreement after parties resumed living together was one significant factor convincing court that parties had reconciled); Gerard v. Gerard, 636 So. 2d 849 (Fla. Dist. Ct. App. 1994) (wife gave husband deed to marital home in exchange for lump sum payment; after reconciliation, husband never recorded the deed, and wife used the lump sum payment for general marital expenses; agreement invalid).

A provision stating the agreement survives reconciliation can also be made in a related document, such as a postreconciliation written reaffirmation of the agreement. *See* Katz v. Beckman, 302 A.D.2d 561, 756 N.Y.S.2d 258 (2003) (where wife signed a memorandum reaffirming the agreement shortly before divorce action was filed, she waived her right to argue that agreement was abrogated by prior reconciliation).

429. Stegall v. Stegall, 100 N.C. App. 398, 397 S.E.2d 306, 313–14 (1990), *cert. denied*, 322 N.C. 274, 400 S.E.2d 461 (1991).

430. *See In re* Marriage of Vella, 237 Ill. App. 3d 194, 603 N.E.2d 109 (1992) (parties followed agreement during reconciliation); Kaouris v. Kaouris, 91 Md. App. 223, 603 A.2d 1350 (1992) (where both parties followed agreement during 16-month reconciliation, there was no intent to abandon, and agreement remained valid); *Pugsley*, 288 A.D.2d 284, 733 N.Y.S.2d 125 (husband moved back into marital home but both parties continued to perform obligations under agreement; no intent to reconcile); Lippman v. Lippman, 192 A.D.2d 1060, 596 N.Y.S.2d 241 (1993) (parties maintained separate residences and followed financial terms of agreement during brief period of cohabitation); see also Kuchera v. Kuchera, 983 So. 2d 776, 780 (Fla. Dist. Ct. App. 2008) (where parties "were unwilling even then to reconcile without a court order making a formal declaration that their [separation agreement] is valid," agreement survived reconciliation).

however, do not mention the distinction at all.[431] The logical conclusion is that in these cases, the court viewed the intent of the parties as the only relevant issue.

The common law tendency to treat reconciliation as a rule of public policy has not by any means disappeared entirely. For instance, the Florida Supreme Court's most recent decision on reconciliation emphasizes the traditional rule, overlooking the intent-based analysis of at least one earlier case.[432] Likewise, North Carolina defines reconciliation as either an objective holding out as married persons or a subjective intent to have a marital relationship.[433] This approach mixes both trends. The former definition points toward an objective, policy-based doctrine; the latter definition points toward a subjective, intent-based doctrine. In short, the current state of the law is a mixture of policy-based and intent-based rules, but the trend in the law is generally toward intent and away from policy.

The authors believe that the trend toward an intent-based reconciliation doctrine is sound. There is no longer any reason, as a matter of public policy, why the end of the parties' separation must necessarily mean the end of their separation agreement. It is true in many cases that parties who reconcile will intend to abandon the executory provisions of their agreement, and when this is so, the parties' intention should be respected. Intention to abandon those provisions may even be so common that proof of objective reconciliation should create a presumption of abandonment.[434] But there is no reason to impose upon the parties a rule that will be, in a least some cases, contrary to their intention. Where the parties actually intend to retain the executory portion of their agreement, the arguments in favor of invalidity all reduce down to the old notion that only separated parties can sign marital agreements. That notion, when stated openly and examined critically, has lost its validity. The better rule is therefore to look primarily to the intent of the parties in determining the effect of reconciliation upon a separation agreement.

---

431. *See* Muchesko v. Muchesko, 191 Ariz. 265, 955 P.2d 21 (1997) (effect of reconciliation upon agreement depends on parties' intent); *Gerard*, 636 So. 2d 849 (possibly superseded by Cox v. Cox, 659 So. 3d 1051 (Fla. 1995), as set forth infra note 432); Dring v. Dring, 87 Haw. 369, 956 P.2d 1301 (1998) (reconciliation does not automatically abrogate agreement; remanding for consideration of the parties' intent); *Vella*, 237 Ill. App. 3d 194, 603 N.E.2d 109; *cf. Kaouris*, 91 Md. App. 223, 603 A.2d 1350 (traditional rule applies only where separation is consideration for the agreement; where separation is not consideration, issue is one purely of intent).

Several states hold that reconciliation automatically abrogates the terms of a separation agreement (*e.g.*, future support), but does not abrogate the terms of a property settlement agreement unless the parties so intend. *Garland*, 79 Ark. App. 10, 84 S.W.3d 44; Brinkmann v. Brinkmann, 772 N.E.2d 441, 448 (Ind. Ct. App. 2002) ("property settlement agreements are not automatically terminated by the subsequent reconciliation of the parties absent clear proof the parties so agreed or intended"); Vaccarello v. Vaccarello 563 Pa. 93, 757 A.2d 909 (2000).

432. *Cox*, 659 So. 3d 1051, departing to some extent from *Gerard*, 636 So. 2d 849.

433. Fletcher v. Fletcher, 123 N.C. App. 744, 474 S.E.2d 802 (1996).

434. If such a presumption applies only to the executory provisions of the agreement, it would strongly resemble the common law rule, except that it would be only a presumption and not an absolute rule of law.

Effect on Equitable Distribution. If an executed property division provision survives reconciliation, should the property involved be divided upon divorce? A large majority of cases say yes, on grounds that the provision constitutes an express or implied agreement to classify the asset involved as separate property.[435] Any appreciation in the asset after reconciliation may be marital property, however, if it was caused by the efforts of one or both parties.[436]

Effect of Divorce Decree. The effect of the divorce decree upon the doctrines of reconciliation depends upon how the divorce decree treated the agreement. Where the agreement was merged or incorporated into the decree, the language of the contract acquires the force of a court order. Since the parties cannot revoke or abandon a court order by contract, the general rule is that reconciliation will not invalidate a merged or incorporated agreement.[437]

Conversely, if the decree merely approved the agreement without incorporating or merging its terms, the language of the agreement does not attain the status of a court order. The validity of the agreement under normal contract law does become res judicata, as discussed in the following subsection, but a finding that the agreement is valid does not protect the agreement from subsequent abandonment. Accordingly, the general rule is the reconciliation can invalidate an agreement that was merely approved by the divorce decree.[438]

§ 4.075 Abandonment

As noted in the previous subsection, the modern trend is to define reconciliation as a resumption of the marital relationship made with intention to abandon all or part of an existing agreement. The doctrine of abandonment, however, is much broader than reconciliation alone. If the parties both intend at any time, for any reason, to destroy the binding effect of the agreement, the agreement becomes unenforceable.

The clearest cases of abandonment are those in which both parties expressly state an intention not to follow the agreement.[439] It is necessary, of course, that these statements refer to the entire agreement; abandonment is not present merely because each party breaches or intends to breach a different provision of the contract. A prolonged

---

435. *See, e.g.*, Kaminsky v. Kaminsky, 364 S.E.2d 799 (W. Va. 1987).

436. *See, e.g.*, Brazina v. Brazina, 233 N.J. Super. 145, 558 A.2d 69, 71 (1989).

437. Pietranico v. Pietranico, 224 A.D.2d 673, 639 N.Y.S.2d 62 (1996); Pinsley v. Pinsley, 168 A.D.2d 863, 564 N.Y.S.2d 528 (1990); Wareham *ex rel.* Trout v. Wareham, 716 A.2d 674 (Pa. Super. 1998); *see also* Yeich v. Yeich, 11 Va. App. 509, 399 S.E.2d 170 (1990). *But see* Barnedt v. Wilder, 137 Idaho 415, 49 P.3d 1265 (Ct. App. 2002) (remarriage of parties to each other abrogated agreement that merged into divorce decree); *cf.* Knowles v. Thompson, 697 A.2d 335 (Vt. 1997) (parties abandoned agreement incorporated into temporary order).

438. *See* Crenshaw v. Crenshaw, 12 Va. App. 1129, 408 S.E.2d 556 (1991).

439. *See* Maruri v. Maruri, 582 So. 2d 116 (Fla. Dist. Ct. App. 1991) (where husband breached contract and wife instructed her attorney not to enforce it, contract had been abandoned); *Knowles*, 697 A.2d 335 (where both parties asked court not to follow different portions of agreement, agreement had effectively been abandoned).

failure to enforce the agreement or to present it to the court in a litigated divorce cases can give rise to an inference that the unenforcing spouse intends to abandon it.[440]

Complete abandonment automatically occurs when the parties sign an new agreement that is inconsistent with their prior agreements.[441] Where the new agreement is consistent with previous contracts, however, both documents are probably still valid.[442]

The parties can also agree to abandon specific provisions of their agreement, without abandoning others.[443] Courts are reluctant to find such waivers based upon conduct alone, particularly when the acting spouse did not subjectively intend to abandon any provision of the agreement.[444]

The ability of the parties to abandon all or part of their agreement may be limited if the agreement has been incorporated or merged into a divorce decree. *See* § **6.07.**

---

440. *See* Painter v. Painter, 823 So. 2d 268, 270 (Fla. Dist. Ct. App. 2002) (where both parties failed to comply with agreement and each acquiesced in the other's actions, settlement agreement had been abandoned); Childers v. Childers, No. 2659-98-3 (Va. Ct. App. 1999) (prolonged failure to present agreement to court, combined with conduct of husband in ignoring the agreement for over a year, justified finding of abandonment).

441. *See* Stegall v. Stegall, 100 N.C. App. 398, 397 S.E.2d 306 (1990) (second agreement with integration clause supplanted first agreement), *cert. denied*, 328 N.C. 274, 400 S.E.2d 461 (1991).

442. *See* Scherl v. Scherl, 569 A.D.2d 192, 569 N.Y.S.2d 192 (1991) (after agreeing that wife's support should cease on cohabitation, parties signed modification agreement; agreement modified support without mentioning cohabitation, but stated that any unmodified provisions of first agreement were still valid; cohabitation clause was not abandoned); Smith v. Smith, 794 S.W.2d 823, 828 (Tex. Ct. App. 1990) (agreement styled as "Addendum to Agreement Incident to Divorce" did not supplant earlier agreement). Abandonment does not occur merely because the parties disagree on the meaning of the agreement. Clark v. Clark, 535 A.2d 872 (D.C. 1987).

443. *See* Weathersby v. Weathersby, 693 So. 2d 1348 (Miss. 1997) (wife waived provision giving her the right to choose appraiser to help determine sale price; instead of appointing appraiser, she filed to enforce agreement and offered her own testimony as to value); Laurence v. Rosen, 229 A.D.2d 373, 645 N.Y.S.2d 773 (1996) (wife failed to seek spousal support arrears for the deliberate purpose of encouraging husband to make voluntary payments for college education of children; arrears waived).

444. *See* Ferraro v. Janis, 62 A.D.3d 1059, 880 N.Y.S.2d 201 (2009) (where husband proposed to use proceeds of sale of property to pay his own tax debts, and wife did not objection for more than three years, wife's conduct showed only passive acquiescence and not affirmative waiver; wife was entitled to her share of the proceeds); Peck v. Peck, 232 A.D.2d 540, 649 N.Y.S.2d 22 (1996) (where husband knew that wife often misplaced checks, requested new ones, and waited long periods before cashing them, this behavior did not constitute abandonment; wife did not intend to waive any rights under the agreement); Fox v. Ridinger, 234 A.D.2d 131, 651 N.Y.S.2d 41 (1996) (wife did not file for increased support under escalator clause for 10 years, but raised issue informally with husband on occasion; no waiver); Wehrkamp v. Wehrkamp, 773 N.W.2d 212, 216 (S.D. 2009) (child did not waive right to enforce college tuition provision of parents' separation agreement by delaying for 30 years; "the mere lapse of time does not support a waiver," and delay actually benefitted father, who was better able to afford obligation when he was older).

§ 4.08 Procedural Issues

This section discusses the law on a variety of procedural points that arise when the court determines the validity of a separation agreement.

Pleading

In states that require the court to approve separation agreements, *see* § **4.04**, a party seeking to rely upon a separation must file a pleading asking the court to approve it.

In states that do not require court approval, it is obviously not necessary to seek such approval in a pleading. But a party seeking to avoid the contract is likely to file pleadings requesting relief inconsistent with the agreement, so it will usually be necessary to raise the agreement as a defense. It may also be necessary to file a pleading if one desires the agreement to be incorporated or merged into the order. *See* § **5.01**. Finally, some states positively require that the agreement be filed with the court.[445]

In all states, if an issue involving the agreement is actually litigated without objection, any defect in pleading is likely to be waived.[446]

Under most state rules of civil procedure, when a complaint alleges that an agreement is invalid for fraud, fraud must be pled with specificity.[447] Specificity normally requires an express statement identifying the matter that was misrepresented or not disclosed, stating the truth if there was a misrepresentation, stating the source of any duty to disclose, and alleging the other elements of fraud set forth in § **4.053**.

Choice of Law

The validity of a separation agreement is determined under normal choice of law principles. Where the agreement contains a choice of law provision, the law chosen will be applied unless it has no relationship whatsoever to the transaction.[448] In the absence of a choice of law clause, a majority of states apply the law of the state with the most significant connection to the transaction. This is almost always be the state in which the parties separated and intended to be divorced.[449] A minority of states look directly to the law of the state in which the contract was formed.[450]

---

445. *E.g.*, Va. Code Ann. § 20-109 (Westlaw 2010) ("if a stipulation or contract signed by the party to whom such relief might otherwise be awarded is *filed before entry of a final decree*, no decree or order . . . shall be entered except in accordance with that stipulation or contract") (emphasis added).

446. *See* Hogan v. Hogan, 2008 WL 5205327, at *6 (Ohio Ct. App. 2008) ("[w]hile neither party affirmatively pled mutual mistake," mutual mistake was nevertheless "tried with both parties' consent"; trial court did not err in finding a mutual mistake and setting the agreement aside).

447. *E.g.*, Carter v. Carter, 3 So. 3d 397 (Fla. Dist. Ct. App. 2009).

448. *See* § **5.03**.

449. Church v. McCabe, 25 A.D.3d 454, 455, 808 N.Y.S.2d 204, 205 (2006) (where "separation agreement is in a format recognized under, and governed by, Hong Kong law," applying that law to determine validity of the agreement).

450. *See* § **5.03**.

Guardian Ad Litem

If a spouse who is subject to duress or undue influence refuses to hire counsel, or terminates the employment of existing counsel, can the court appoint a guardian ad litem to protect that spouse's interest? Such a guardian was appointed on the facts in *Buckler v. Buckler*,[451] although the court seemed to question whether this procedure would be proper where the spouse in question was not actually legally incompetent. The question was not directly raised on appeal, however, and the court assumed for purposes of deciding the case that the guardian was properly appointed.[452]

Where a guardian is appointed, whether properly or improperly, the guardian must investigate the facts with reasonable care, and take the same sorts of measures a prudent person would take in determining whether to sign an agreement. In *Buckler*, the guardian viewed his role as providing protection against the possibility that the wife would be subject to improper influence. He made certain that she was not subject to duress or pressure, but did not actively investigate the facts or determine the fairness of the agreement. The court criticized the guardian quite vigorously, and remanded the case for additional financial disclosure.

Failure of Divorce

By definition, a separation agreement is drafted at a time when the parties believe that their marriage will terminate in divorce.[453] When this belief rises to the level of a condition, it may have consequences for the validity of the agreement.

The law on conditions in separation agreement is set forth in § 7.04. Briefly stated, the parties are free to agree that certain provisions or even their entire agreement is subject to one or more conditions. When the conditions are not met, any provisions of the agreement that are inseverable from those conditions become invalid.

When a divorce of the parties is a condition to the validity of an agreement, there are two ways in which the condition might fail. First, the parties might reconcile and decide not to get divorced at all. Because this topic is heavily interwoven with the common law rule that a separation agreement without actual separation is invalid, it is discussed separately in § 4.074. To summarize that discussion, there is a good chance that a true reconciliation abrogates at least the executory provisions of a separation agreement. In some states, this is a rule of public policy that applies regardless of the parties' intentions. In other states, the courts will pay more attention to the actual intention of the parties.

Second, even if the parties continue to desire a divorce, the divorce might fail to take place in the time and manner anticipated. This issue is generally approached under

---

451. 195 W. Va. 705, 466 S.E.2d 556 (1995).

452. *Id. See also* Graham v. Graham, 40 Wash. 2d 64, 240 P.2d 564 (1952) (court can appoint guardian if spouse is incompetent, but cannot appoint guardian to protect competent spouse against his or her own misjudgment; error to appoint guardian for wife without holding hearing and giving her opportunity to argue against appointment).

453. An agreement based upon continuation rather than termination of the marital relationship is a midnuptial agreement, *see* § 1.01, and its validity is determined under the principles discussed in **chapter 16** of this treatise.

the traditional law of conditions. The cases can be categorized according to the reason why divorce failed to occur.

Abatement. When one party dies before a divorce decree has become final, the divorce action immediately abates.[454] The cases are divided as to the effect of such abatement on a prior separation agreement. There is general agreement that the key issue is whether the parties intended to create an agreement that would survive death. A majority of cases finds that such intent exists on the facts;[455] a minority holds that it does not.[456]

In states that require court approval of separation agreements, the death of a party may destroy the court's power to approve the agreement, and therefore render it unenforceable, even if both parties intended that it survive.[457] The result has the potential to work serious injustice, and it is another reason why the authors believe that court approval requirements are not wise policy. *See* § **4.04**.

Lack of Jurisdiction. In one recent case, the parties' divorce failed because the court that rendered it lacked subject matter jurisdiction. The court nevertheless held that the agreement continued to be enforceable, finding that the invalidity of the decree did not effect the validity of the contract.[458] In effect, the court held that divorce by the particular court involved at the particular time expected was not a condition to the enforceability of the agreement.

---

454. *See, e.g.*, Wear v. Mizell, 263 Kan. 175, 946 P.2d 1363 (1997); *In re* Marriage of Alfieri, 203 A.D.2d 562, 611 N.Y.S.2d 226 (1994); State ex rel. Litty v. Leskovyansky, 77 Ohio St. 3d 97, 671 N.E.2d 236 (1996); Socha v. Socha, 183 Wis. 2d 390, 515 N.W.2d 337 (1994); *see generally* BRETT R. TURNER, EQUITABLE DISTRIBUTION OF PROPERTY § 3.3 (3d ed. 2005 & Supp. 2007).

455. *See* Barton v. Barton, 790 So. 2d 169 (Miss. 2001); *In re* Estate of Shatraw, 66 A.D.3d 1293, 1295, 887 N.Y.S.2d 722, 724 (2009) ("the obligation to transfer the real estate was a contractual right created when the parties executed the separation agreement and passed to the wife's estate upon her death"; but spousal support provisions did not survive); Brower v. Brower, 226 A.D.2d 92, 653 N.Y.S.2d 386 (1997) (contract still had effect after death of party; distinguishing Passmore v. King, 186 A.D.2d 241, 588 N.Y.S.2d 344 (1992), because divorce action was pending there, whereas no divorce action had yet been filed in *Brower*); *In re* Pavese, 195 Misc. 2d 1, 12, 752 N.Y.S.2d 198, 207 (Surr. Ct. 2002) (agreement "clearly evidences the parties intent that it be an independent contract to be performed regardless of whether the parties ever actually terminate the marriage"; excellent discussion); Mack v. Estate of Mack, 206 P.3d 98 (Nev. 2009) (agreement remained valid even after husband murdered wife); Brown v. Brown, 90 Ohio App. 3d 781, 630 N.E.2d 763 (1993); Spiegel v. KLRU Endowment Fund, 228 S.W.3d 237 (Tex. Ct. App. 2007) (mediated agreement); Lindsay v. Lindsay, 91 Wash. App. 944, 957 P.2d 818 (1998).

In *In re* Estate of Bullotta, 575 Pa. 587, 838 A.2d 594 (2003), the court rejected an argument that the agreement necessarily fails to survive the death of either party. The court did not seem to contemplate the possibility that the parties might have intended the agreement to be enforceable only if they were actually divorced.

456. *In re* Marriage of Wilson, 245 Kan. 178, 777 P.2d 773 (1989); Passmore v. King, 186 A.D.2d 241, 588 N.Y.S.2d 344 (1992).

457. *See In re* Marriage of Rettke, 696 N.W.2d 846 (Minn. App. Ct. 2005).

458. Lipps v. Loyd, 967 P.2d 558 (Wyo. 1998).

Failure on the Merits. While the great majority of divorce actions end with a divorce being granted, there are still a few cases in which grounds for a fault-based divorce are not established, and a no-fault divorce is either not requested or not available. When the parties are not actually divorced, their agreement may no longer be valid.[459]

There is, however, no reason why the parties could not intend their agreement to be binding regardless of whether the divorce action succeeds or fails. The issue should be determined by the intent of the parties, and not by any absolute rule.

Discovery

Where a spouse states a prima facie case for invalidating a separation agreement, that spouse should normally be allowed to conduct reasonable discovery.

The court may deny discovery if a prima facie case has not been stated.[460]

Discovery should be limited to matters relevant to the validity of the agreement.[461] Additional discovery will probably be needed if the agreement is set aside, but that discovery should normally wait until the court actually rules that the agreement is invalid.[462]

Hearing

When one spouse attacks a separation agreement, the court cannot simply ignore the attack and enforce the agreement. If the attacking spouse fails to allege a sufficient prima facie basis for overturning the agreement, the court must enter an order that explains why the attack fails as a matter of law.[463] The court need not, however, hold a factual hearing.[464]

If the attacking spouse does allege a prima facie basis for overturning the agreement, the court must then hold an evidentiary hearing to determine whether the allegations are supported by the facts. Failure to hold such a hearing, where a prima facie case of invalidity has been alleged, is serious procedural error.[465]

---

459. *See* Tarone v. Tarone, 25 A.D.3d 779, 780, 809 N.Y.S.2d 150, 151 (2006) ("in view of the determination that the plaintiff failed to establish his entitlement to a divorce, the stipulation of settlement should have been vacated").

460. *See* Carter v. Carter, 3 So. 3d 397, 398 (Fla. Dist. Ct. App. 2009).

461. *See* Kramer v. Kramer, 711 N.W.2d 164 (N.D. 2006).

462. *E.g.*, Fakiris v. Fakiris, 177 N.Y.S.2d 540, 575 N.Y.S.2d 924 (1991); *see generally* 1 BRETT R. TURNER, EQUITABLE DISTRIBUTION OF PROPERTY § 4:2 nn.2–7 (3d ed. 2005).

463. *In re* Marriage of McNeil, 367 Ill. App. 3d 676, 856 N.E.2d 15 (2006).

464. *See* Paul v. Paul, 177 A.D.2d 901, 576 N.Y.S.2d 658 (1991).

465. *See* Marjon v. Lane, 995 So. 2d 1086, 1087–88 (Fla. Dist. Ct. App. 2008) ("where a party, such as Mr. Marjon, sufficiently pleads duress, coercion, or fraud in the inducement, he or she is entitled to a hearing on the merits of the motion"); Daughtrey v. Daughtrey, 944 So. 2d 1145, 1148 (Fla. Dist. Ct. App. 2006) (error to find scrivener's error without holding evidentiary hearing; "unsworn representations by counsel about factual matters do not have any evidentiary weight in the absence of a stipulation"); *In re* Marriage of McNeil, 367 Ill. App. 3d 676, 856 N.E.2d 15 (2006); Harrington v. Harrington, 281 N.J. Super. 39, 656 A.2d 456 (App. Div. 1995) (remanding for factual hearing on whether agreement existed to begin with and whether any agreement that did exist was invalid for mutual mistake); Cardinal v. Cardinal, 275 A.D.2d 756, 713 N.Y.S.2d 370 (2000); Manes v. Manes, 215 A.D.2d 455, 626 N.Y.S.2d 471 (1995) (reversing summary judgment

Attorney-Client Privilege

A few decisions have begun to consider the extent to which testimony relevant to the validity of a separation agreement may fall with the attorney-client privilege. These cases arise when a spouse retains an attorney, signs an agreement, and then attempts to set that agreement aside. If the attack is based upon duress, undue influence, or fraud, testimony of the attacking spouse's attorney may be very relevant in determining whether the agreement was truly voluntary.

The first important point in these cases is that the attorney-client privilege applies only to confidential communications between attorney and client.[466] Statements made by the attorney and client are clearly not privileged if they were addressed to or even made in the presence of third persons.[467] Thus, statements made by the attorney to the other spouse, opposing counsel, or a trial judge would normally not be privileged. Statements made in mediation are discussed in **§ 2.08**.

A second important point is that when a spouse claims affirmative relief, he or she often waives the attorney-client privilege regarding matters essential to resolving that claim.[468] For example, if a spouse represented by counsel claims that an agreement is invalid for fraud because of a false representation made to counsel, and there is a facially credible claim that counsel was either not misled or knew the truth from other sources, it would be difficult to litigate the claim fairly without inquiring into matters that are normally privileged. Some claims of duress, undue influence, and lack of capacity to contract might likewise require testimony of the attorney, who may have unique insight into the client's state of mind at the time the agreement was signed.[469] Finally, in disputes involving the authority of the attorney to settle the case, the court

---

upholding agreement, where there was a triable issue of fact on whether the husband had concealed assets); Maury v. Maury, 2008 WL 2609702 (Ohio Ct. App. 2008).

A hearing is required even where the agreement has already been approved by the court, so that it is necessary to reopen a final judgment to obtain relief, so long as a prima facie case for reopening the judgment is pled. *See* Hinson v. Hinson, 985 So. 2d 1120, 1121 (Fla. Dist. Ct. App. 2008) ("the former wife properly pleaded specific allegations of fraud which constituted a 'colorable entitlement to relief' and entitled the former wife to an evidentiary hearing").

466. *See generally* 98 C.J.S. Witnesses § 316 (Westlaw 2008).

467. *Id.* §§ 321, 327. The privilege does not cease to apply, however, merely because agents of the attorney (*e.g.*, an associate, secretary, or law clerk) were present, so long as these persons were providing necessary assistance to the attorney in representing the client. *Id.* § 327.

468. *See In re* Marriage of Bielawski, 328 Ill. App. 3d 243, 764 N.E.2d 1254 (2002) ("there are cases which state that the attorney-client privilege may be waived as to a communication put 'at issue' by a party who is a holder of the privilege").

Bielawski rejected a claim of privilege, as the spouse attacking the agreement had also sued her former attorney for malpractice, and past case law established that such a claim waived the privilege as regards prior communication between attorney and client. Had the client not filed the malpractice action, the court would have had to consider the extent to which the privilege was waived when the client sought to set the agreement aside.

469. Some of these claims might be resolved on grounds that the attorney's observations of the client's state of mind are not a *communication*. But those observations may in many cases be based upon communications—statements made to the attorney, with no third parties present, suggesting that the client was or was not acting voluntarily, or that the client was or was not aware of or relying

must of course inquire into many normally privileged communications regarding the extent of the attorney's authority.[470]

Fraudulent Transfers

A transfer under a separation agreement can be set aside as a fraudulent conveyance if it defrauds a creditor or other third party.[471]

Attorney's Fees

At least one court has held that a party who files a separate action to vacate a separation agreement is not entitled to invoke the normal statute permitting awards of attorney's fees in domestic relations cases.[472]

Appeal

An order setting aside a separation is an interlocutory order that cannot be immediately appealed. Instead, the issue should be raised in an appeal from the final property division.[473]

---

upon misrepresented or concealed facts. Effective cross-examination of the attorney's conclusory observations may require disclose of confidential communications.

470. *See* Gravley v. Gravley, 278 Ga. 897, 898, 608 S.E.2d 225, 226–27 (2005). The attorney in Gravley clearly testified regarding the extent of his authority; there is no mention of any objection based upon privilege.

471. *See* Mejia v. Reed, 31 Cal. 4th 657, 74 P.3d 166, 3 Cal. Rptr. 3d 390 (2003).

472. *See* Fine v. Fine, 26 A.D.3d 406, 407, 810 N.Y.S.2d 211, 212 (2006) ("A plenary action to vacate a stipulation of settlement on the basis of fraud, is not a matrimonial action . . . the Supreme Court erred in awarding the plaintiff an attorney's fee" under the normal domestic relations attorney's fees provision[.]).

473. *See* Memmolo v. Memmolo, 576 A.2d 181 (Del. 1990); Shapiro v. Shapiro, 432 So. 2d 739 (Fla. Dist. Ct. App. 1983); Dexter v. Dexter, 7 Va. App. 36, 371 S.E.2d 816 (1988). An order refusing to set aside a separation agreement can be appealed in most states, as long as the agreement will control the court's ultimate decision in the case. Case v. Case, 73 N.C. App. 76, 325 S.E.2d 661, *cert. denied*, 313 N.C. 597, 330 S.E.2d 606 (1985); Urban v. Urban, 332 Pa. Super. 373, 481 A.2d 662 (1984) (appeal from order striking defendant's answer as untimely filed); Owney v. Owney, 8 Va. App. 255, 379 S.E.2d 745 (1989) (appeal from order construing agreement and ordering payment of temporary support in accordance with its terms); *but see* Tidwell v. Tidwell, 496 So. 2d 91 (Ala. Ct. Civ. App. 1986) (order denying motion to set aside oral agreement not appealable); Simmons v. Simmons, 549 So. 2d 105 (Ala. Ct. Civ. App. 1989) (applying Tidwell without stating whether agreement was oral or written).

Construction of Separation Agreements: Theory | 5

§ 5.01 Separation Agreements and Divorce Decrees

The preceding chapters in this work considered whether a separation agreement was formed, and if so whether it was valid under the law of contracts. Assuming that a valid agreement existed, we move now to consider how that agreement should be construed.

The first step in construing any separation agreement is to determine the relationship between the agreement and the divorce decree. If the parties have already been divorced, their divorce decree may have an important effect upon the nature of the underlying agreement.

§ 5.011 General Rule: Approval

To determine the relationship between the agreement and the divorce decree, we must consider the meaning of three familiar terms: approval, merger, and incorporation. These terms have been as much discussed and as little understood as any three words in the history of law. Nevertheless, the concepts behind the terms are remarkably simple in operation. The confusion displayed by many of the decisions is almost purely a matter of conflicting terminology.

Thus, the first step toward clarifying the law on this subject is to define all three terms clearly. Traditionally, there have been two ways in which a divorce decree can treat a valid separation agreement. First, the decree can simply note the existence of the agreement and hold that it is valid. For purposes of this treatise, we will call this option *approval*.

Second, the court can adopt the terms of the agreement as terms of the decree, and order that the agreement itself have no future independent validity. Because the terms of the agreement are said to merge into the divorce decree, we will call this option *merger*.[1] It can be seen from these definitions that *approval* and *merger* are the exact opposites of each other. *Approved* agreements are contracts but not judgments, while *merged* agreements are judgments but not contracts.

In addition, a number of states recognize a third alternative. Divorce litigants have traditionally been frustrated by the need to elect between treating their agreement as a contract and treating it as a decree, and they have often wished for a combination of the best elements of both choices. States responding to this desire have created a third alternative, which we will call *incorporation*. *Incorporated* agreements are treated as part of the decree, but they also retain independent validity as a contract.[2] There are therefore two coexisting documents, a decree and a contract, both of which must be considered when the agreement is construed.

It is essential to realize that the above definitions are not the definitions used by all of the reported cases. In particular, states that have not recognized the third alternative frequently use "incorporation" as a synonym for *merger*. Nevertheless, once we control for differences in terminology, every state recognizes the same set of possible relationships between a decree and a valid agreement. To emphasize that all three options are terms of art that should be given a clear and uniform meaning, we will place them in *italics* whenever they appear in this treatise.

To determine which of the three options applies in a particular case, we begin with the simplest alternative. When the court divorces parties who have signed a separation agreement, the decree at the very least contains an express or implied finding that the agreement is valid. The general rule, therefore, is that the relationship between the decree and the agreement is that of *approval*.

After noting the general rule, we must then ask if there is sufficient evidence to justify departing from that rule. This process requires that we consider the other two alternatives: *merger* and *incorporation*.

---

1. *E.g.*, Phillips v. Phillips, 93 Idaho 384, 386, 462 P.2d 49, 51 (1969) ("If the agreement is so merged into the decree, the rights and duties of the parties are no longer determined by reference to the agreement or contract of the parties, but rather are determined by and enforced through the judgment and decree of the court[.]"); Grace v. Grace, 253 Mich. App. 357, 364, 655 N.W.2d 595, 600 (2002) ("When a property settlement agreement is incorporated and merged in a divorce judgment, it becomes a disposition by the court[.]") (quoting Marshall v. Marshall, 135 Mich. App. 702, 712–13, 355 N.W.2d 661 (1984)); Emery v. Smith, 361 S.C. 207, 214, 603 S.E.2d 598, 601 (Ct. App. 2004) ("By merging the agreement into the decree, the court transformed it from a contract between the parties into a decree of the court[.]"); Pauling v. Pauling, 837 P.2d 1073, 1077 (Wyo. 1992) ("once merged, the agreement loses its existence as a separately enforceable contract, thus limiting each party to judgment remedies and defenses and foreclosing any contract action").

2. *See* Washington v. Washington, 56 A.D.3d 463, 464, 867 N.Y.S.2d 478, 479 (2008) ("An agreement that is incorporated, but not merged, into a judgment of divorce is a legally-binding independent contract between the parties[.]"); Brink v. Brink, 55 A.D.3d 601, 602, 867 N.Y.S.2d 94, 95 (2008) ("The terms of a separation agreement incorporated but not merged into a judgment of divorce operate as contractual obligations binding on the parties[.]").

§ 5.012 *Exception: Merger*

The distinction between *merger* and *approval* is a simple one: Does the contract continue to exist as an independent document? If the answer is yes, then *merger* has not occurred, and we must proceed to the next alternative. If the answer is that the contract lacks independent validity, however, then *merger* is present.[3]

The simplest evidence of *merger* is an express statement in the divorce decree. Where the decree directly states that the contract shall have no independent validity, *merger* has clearly occurred. Conversely, if the decree directly states that the contract shall still be valid, *merger* has not occurred.[4]

In most cases, however, the divorce decree contains no express statement on the continuing validity of the contract. In this event, the next source to examine is the contract itself. If the contract answers the question and the decree is silent, it is logical to assume that the court intended to follow the option chosen by the parties.[5]

If neither the agreement nor the decree states that the contract will lose independent validity after the signing of the decree, a majority of states hold that *merger* does not occur. As an exception to the general rule, *merger* exists only where there is some supporting evidence in the decree or the agreement.[6]

A minority of states, however, presume that in the absence of contrary evidence, the parties intend *merger*.[7] Decisions adopting this rule have generally been slow to

---

3. *See generally* Johnston v. Johnston, 297 Md. 48, 465 A.2d 436 (1983); Parrish v. Parrish, 30 Mass. App. Ct. 78, 566 N.E.2d 103 (1991); Nicholson v. Combs, 550 Pa. 23, 703 A.2d 407 (1997); Riffenburg v. Riffenburg, 585 A.2d 627 (R.I. 1991).

4. *See, e.g.,* Flynn v. Flynn, 42 Cal. 2d 55, 265 P.2d 865 (1954); Peck v. Peck, 707 A.2d 1163 (Pa. Super. Ct. 1998); Jones v. Jones, 438 Pa. Super. 26, 651 A.2d 157 (1994).

5. For decisions relying on a direct statement that the agreement would survive the decree, *see* LaPrade v. LaPrade, 189 Ariz. 243, 941 P.2d 1268 (1997); Marshick v. Marshick, 24 Ariz. App. 588, 545 P.2d 436 (1976); Moore v. Moore, 389 Mass. 21, 448 N.E.2d 1255 (1983); *Johnston*, 297 Md. 48, 465 A.2d 436; Makarchuk v. Makarchuk, 59 A.D.3d 1094, 1095, 874 N.Y.S.2d 649, 650 (2009) ("It is of no consequence that the decree did not contain a nonmerger clause inasmuch as the parties' intent to incorporate and not merge the agreement in the decree is clear from the language of those instruments[.]"); Treadway v. Smith, 325 S.C. 367, 479 S.E.2d 849 (Ct. App. 1996); Bruni v. Bruni, 924 S.W.2d 366 (Tex. 1996); Rubio v. Rubio, 36 Va. App. 248, 255, 549 S.E.2d 610, 614 (2001).

6. *Parrish*, 30 Mass. App. Ct. 78, 566 N.E.2d 103; Lipschutz v. Lipschutz, 391 Pa. Super. 537, 571 A.2d 1046, *allocatur denied*, 589 A.2d 692 (Pa. 1990).

7. *See LaPrade*, 189 Ariz. 243, 941 P.2d 1268 (merger occurs unless contract provides otherwise); Phillips v. Phillips, 93 Idaho 384, 387, 462 P.2d 49, 52 (Idaho 1969) ("it will be further presumed that the agreement is merged into the decree of divorce"); Pauling v. Pauling, 837 P.2d 1073, 1078 (Wyo. 1992) ("when, in the absence of clear and convincing evidence to the contrary, the parties enter into a settlement agreement in contemplation of divorce and the district court's divorce decree incorporates or adopts by reference that agreement, the agreement is presumed to merge into the decree and will no longer be given effect"); *see also* TEX. FAM. CODE ANN. § 154.124(c) (child support agreement *merges* unless decree states otherwise).

New York holds that oral stipulations *merge* into the judgment until the stipulation provides otherwise. *See* Vest v. Vest, 50 A.D.3d 776, 855 N.Y.S.2d 597 (2008).

An extreme version of the minority rule, favoring merger so strongly as to overcome in at least some situations the contrary intent of the parties, is discussed in **§ 5.014.**

recognize true *incorporation*, which allows the agreement to be enforceable as both a contract and a judgment. *See* § **5.013**. If the court must make an either/or change between *merger* and *approval*, there is good reason to prefer *merger*, as it permits enforcement of the agreement with the generally stronger judgment remedies. *See* § **7.03**. States following the minority rule also tend to hold that contract-based spousal support is modifiable unless the agreement provides otherwise. *See* § **6.032**. A presumption of *merger* is less attractive in states that presume that contractual spousal support is nonmodifiable, as the effect of *merger* is to make spousal support modifiable, so that a *merger* presumption and a nonmodifiability presumption are effective opposites.

The normal principles of issue preclusion apply to the question of merger. Thus, where the court held in a previous action that the agreement was or was not *merged* into the decree, that holding is binding in all future actions in which *merger* is at issue.[8]

Merger and "Merger"

When an agreement or decree is silent on whether the agreement is intended to have independent validity, but states expressly that the agreement shall "merge" into the decree, does the agreement actually *merge* into the decree? The commonsense answer is yes. *Merger* is a term of art, and those who use it should be expected to use it responsibly.

But the commonsense answer is clearly not the law. However clear the meaning of *merger* may be in theory, "merger" has been defined so many ways by so many courts that its practical meaning is often ambiguous. Moreover, parties persist in signing separation agreements that clearly anticipate the continued existence of the agreement after entry of the decree, and then providing that the agreement shall "merge" into the court's judgment.

A few examples demonstrate the extent of the problem. The case used as an example in the first edition of this treatise was *Bercume v. Bercume*.[9] The agreement in that case provided for a permanent waiver of the right to collect alimony. It further provided that the agreement would merge into the divorce decree. Some time after the divorce, the wife sought alimony, arguing that under Massachusetts law, the court can never disclaim its own ability to make a future award of spousal support. The parties can waive this right by contract, but since the agreement merged into the decree there was no contract, and the mere presence of the waiver in the decree had no legal effect.

The wife's argument was a logical and correct application of the theoretical concept of *merger*, and the court essentially recognized the fact. The court was troubled, however, by the fact that the parties obviously intended to waive future awards of alimony. Struggling for a way to reach the instinctively right result, the court ruled that even where the contract merged, the court must still consider the intention of the parties in applying the law of court-ordered alimony. This holding inflicts serious damage upon the law, for it is axiomatic that when an agreement *merges, the agreement literally*

---

8. *See* Ballestrino v. Ballestrino, 400 Pa. Super. 237, 583 A.2d 474 (1990).

9. 428 Mass. 635, 704 N.E.2d 177 (1999).

no longer exists. Thus, the parties did not express their intention to waive alimony in any legally recognizable manner.

The problem, however, as the court recognized, is that this technically correct application of the concept of *merger* was not intended by the parties. In reality, therefore, the agreement contradicted itself. It stated at one point that would *merge* into the decree; it stated at another point that alimony was permanently waived. Both of these provisions cannot be valid. If the parties intended to waive alimony, then they necessarily must not have intended *merger,* for a *merged* waiver of alimony has no effect.

Because the agreement in *Bercume* contradicted itself, it was ambiguous on the crucial question of *merger.* From the face of the agreement, there is good reason to question whether the parties really understood the technical meaning of *merger.* Moreover, the express *merger* provision was very general, while the waiver of alimony provision was very specific. Under the rule that specific provisions control over general ones,[10] there is a strong likelihood that despite their use of the word "merger," the parties did not intend that the agreement *merge* into the decree in the sense that it would lose independent existence. Instead of twisting the concept of *merger* like a pretzel to reach the intuitively correct result, the court should probably have held that the agreement did not *merge* at all.

In the case law decided since publication of the first edition, two cases are particularly good examples of confusion over *merger* and "merger." In *Ottino v. Ottino,*[11] the agreement provided that the parties would contribute to the postmajority college education of their children. This is a perfect permissible contractual provision, *see* § **6.044**, but one that the court in most states cannot order of its own initiative. The agreement was then "merged" into the divorce decree, apparently at the request of the parties.

When the children went to college, the husband refused to pay. He argued that the agreement ceased to exist after it *merged* into the decree, and that without an agreement the court had no jurisdiction to order him to pay college support. This is again a completely correct application of the concept of *merger.* But if the parties had truly intended *merger,* why did they include a postmajority support provision in their agreement? The actions of the parties, if not their underlying intentions, were confused and contradictory.

The *Ottino* court held, again completely correctly, that the specific intention of the parties to pay college support controlled over the general technical meaning of *merger.* But the court's opinion significantly confused the law. The court first noted claimed that the purpose of *merger* is "to prevent the relitigation" of the validity of the agreement.[12] This is demonstrably false; the validity of the agreement is res judicata even if the agreement is only *approved. See* § **4.02**.

Next, the court stated that "settlement agreements are typically merged with divorce decrees in order to bring the court's contempt powers to bear on defiant former spouses."[13] Enforcement by contempt certainly requires that the terms of the agreement

---

10. *See* § **5.06**, note 148.
11. 130 N.M. 168, 21 P.3d 37 (Ct. App. 2000).
12. *Id.* at 173, 21 P.3d at 42.
13. *Id.*

be part of the decree, but the terms of the agreement can become part of the decree even if the agreement is only *incorporated*—treatment that makes the language of the agreement enforceable as *either* a contract *or* a judgment. *See § 5.013.* The distinguishing feature of *merger* is not that the agreement is enforceable by contempt, but rather that it ceases to exist independently as a contract.

The court did not seem to grasp the concept of true *incorporation*, and indeed it stated that "once an agreement between divorcing parties has been adopted and incorporated into the final divorce decree, the underlying agreement is deemed to have merged with the decree."[14] A good part of the problem, therefore, was confusion between *merger* and *incorporation*. If the agreement was *incorporated* into the decree and not *merged*, then it still existed as a contract and the college support provision could be enforced.

Instead of finding *incorporation*, however, *Ottino* found *merger*—and then held that merger is an equitable doctrine that the court can ignore when the ends of justice require.[15] The holding is technically wrong: A rule of law for determining what language does and does not have the force of contract or judgment is necessarily a rule of law, not a rule of equity. But the court saw no other way to enforce the college support provision.[16] While the final result is clearly equitable, the underlying reasoning is an excellent demonstration of why *merger* is such a frustrating subject. The term has a clear legal meaning, but many parties refuse to use it.

A second modern case demonstrating confusion over *merger* and "merger" is the Virginia opinion in *Smith v. Smith.*[17] Some time after the divorce, the wife in *Smith* began cohabiting with a third party. Under a controlling statute, court-ordered spousal support generally terminates if recipient cohabits with another person in a relationship analogous to marriage.[18] The husband agreed that the spousal support effectively was court-ordered,[19] because the agreement merged into the decree. Amazingly, the wife "conceded [that] the agreement merged into the final decree."[20] Given that the agreement *merged*, the husband's position was absolutely correct. A *merged* agreement does not exist after the decree is entered, and it can be modified on the same basis as a court order.

Yet the court held otherwise. Virginia is a conservative southern state with a strong tradition of deferring to private contracts. It provides by statute that spousal support

---

14. *Id.* at 172, 21 P.3d at 41.

15. *Id.* at 173, 21 P.3d at 42.

16. Indeed, if a general *merger* provision prevailed over a specific college support or other provision with only a contractual remedy, then such provisions would be a real trap for parties and their counsel. The only available remedy might suddenly disappear, based upon a vague reference to merger in a boilerplate provision of the agreement located many pages away. The problem with *Ottino* is not that the court reached the wrong destination, but that the court trampled on the concept of *merger* in the process of getting there.

17. 41 Va. App. 742, 589 S.E.2d 439 (2003).

18. *Id.* at 744, 589 S.E.2d at 440.

19. VA. CODE ANN. § 20-109(A) (Westlaw 2011). Support terminates under the statute only if the cohabitation lasts for a period of one year or longer, unless termination would be unconscionable.

20. 41 Va. App. at 744, 589 S.E.2d at 440.

provisions in separation agreements cannot be modified unless the agreement expressly permits modification.[21] Because this statute has no express exception for merged agreements, the court held that even *merged* agreements cannot be modified except as permitted by the agreement itself. This result is clearly inconsistent with the technical concept of *merger*, for a *merged* agreement has no existence as a contract. There was therefore nothing in the facts to which Virginia's statutory contract policy could attach. To the court, however, the concrete policy was more important than the somewhat technical concept of *merger*. By placing the policy on a higher plane than a coherent definition of merger, the court created confusion in Virginia law as to what *merger* means.

Moreover, when one examines the facts of *Smith* carefully, there is considerable reason to suspect that the confusion inflicted on the concept of *merger* was unnecessary. The agreement in *Smith* "affirmed, ratified, and incorporated" the parties' agreement.[22] That phrase does not use "merger" or any other phrase suggesting that the parties intended the agreement to have no independent existence. *Merger* was an issue only because the wife apparently conceded that the agreement *merged*. The basis for this concession is unclear. In addition, the agreement in *Smith* predated the Virginia statute terminating support upon cohabitation, and thus was probably not governed by that statute at all.[23] The court could have resolved the case either by holding that the agreement did not *merge* to begin with, or by holding that the statute could not be applied retroactively. The end result was clearly correct, but the reasoning used to get there inflicts much needless injury upon the meaning of *merger*.

In sum, it is difficult to make reliable statements about "merger," because neither courts nor parties to separation agreements are consistently defining the term in a consistent manner. Clearly, the courts are viewing this entire area of the law as one in which the specific terms of the agreement (*Bercume, Ottino*) and even statutory policy choices (*Smith*) are vastly more important than legal theory. Bluntly put, the cases are consistently defining "merger" in a way that allows enforcement of provisions to which both parties have plainly agreed. As a matter of end result, this flexible approach is clearly justified.

The authors wish, however, that the courts would make a greater effort to reach that end result without inflicting needless damage on the concept of *merger*. Properly understood, *merger* is the situation that results when the parties intend to agree upon language that shall be enforceable *only as a judgment*. Stated differently, the parties are essentially saying to the court, "We want you to decide this case as if it had been litigated and not settled; but here are the terms that we want you to place in the final judgment." Parties sometimes do this because they wish to avoid consequences that the law attaches to a formal agreement, such as limitations on the modifiability of spousal support. This is not a commonly intended result, and that is why an agreement *merges* into the judgment only when there is clear evidence that the parties intended that their divorce settlement be enforceable only as a judgment and not as a contract.

---

21. VA. CODE ANN. § 20-109(C) (Westlaw 2008).
22. 41 Va. App. at 744, 589 S.E.2d at 440.
23. Hering v. Hering, 33 Va. App. 368, 533 S.E.2d 631 (2000).

In cases like *Bercume* and *Ottino*, in which the parties clearly did intend that their divorce settlement be enforceable as a contract, the best approach is to stop assuming that "merger" necessarily means *merger*. It may in some cases; some parties understand that a merged agreement no longer exists as a contract.[24] But when there is any indication that the parties intended to retain their contractual remedies, and especially when they agreed to significant terms that can *only* be enforced as a contract, the agreement clearly was never truly intended to *merge* into the judgment. In other words, courts and parties are so confused about *merger* that the term "merger" may well be inherently ambiguous, so that the true intent of the parties must be determined by extrinsic evidence.[25]

Drafting Concerns

From a drafting viewpoint, prudent counsel will avoid any use of the bare word "merger" without considerably additional explanatory text. The word is so ambiguous, and its meaning is so likely to be controlled by other provisions, that the word alone should not be trusted to mean anything. The safest option is to state in clear and express language whether the parties anticipate enforcement as a contract, as a judgment, or both.[26] Similar language should be placed into the divorce decree if at all possible. This approach may require a bit of additional drafting time, but it could save everyone much trouble in the future.

Note that there is also a degree of risk to using the bare term "incorporation." That risk is discussed in the drafting concerns at the end of § **5.013**.

§ 5.013 Exception: Incorporation

If the court finds that the contract was not *merged* into the decree, it must then consider whether the contract was *incorporated* into the decree.

Incorporation and "Incorporation"

The term "incorporation" is the subject of considerable confusion in a significant number of states. In theory, the term is clear and precise. An *incorporated* agreement constitutes both a judgment and a contract, and it can be enforced with either judgment or contract remedies, at the option of the enforcing spouse.

The problem is that a significant number of states insist that an agreement can be either a contract or a judgment, but not both. When the law does not recognize true

---

24. *See, e.g.,* Turenne v. Turenne, 884 So. 2d 844, 849 (Ala. 2003) (where divorce decree stated that agreement "merged into this Order," finding *merger* on the facts).

25. *See* Parrish v. Parrish, 30 Mass. App. Ct. 78, 566 N.E.2d 103 (1991) (error to find that contract did not survive, based solely upon agreement's use of the term "merger"; remanded for a fuller review of the evidence).

26. The drafter should also be aware that if the agreement states that it is enforceable only as a judgment, but specific terms of the agreement can be enforced only as a contract, there is an *extremely* high degree of risk that court will find those specific terms enforceable contractually, regardless of the merger language. In those few cases where true *merger* is anticipated, therefore, it is essential to review the agreement carefully and make certain that there is an available judgment remedy for all provisions.

incorporation, it must then decide how to respond when the decree or the agreement provided that the contract should be "incorporated" into the decree. The general rule in these states is that "incorporated" can mean either *approved* or *merged*, depending on the totality of the circumstances.[27] For example, in *Soll v. Soll*,[28] the contract provided that the parties would comply with court orders. The husband argued that the decree merely *approved* the agreement, so there was only a contract and no court order to enforce. Given the obvious intent of the agreement that court orders be enforceable as such, however, the court found that the word "incorporation" was intended to mean *merger*.

There are also a number of decisions that state in general terms that an agreement that is "incorporated" into the decree becomes a part of the decree and loses its identity as a contract.[29] These cases essentially hold that "incorporation" means *merger* as a matter of law.

The best approach, however, is to hold that "incorporated" means *incorporated*. For example, in *Johnston v. Johnston*,[30] the court noted that "once incorporated, the contractual provisions becomes part of the decree, modifiable by the court where appropriate and enforceable through contempt proceedings." Nevertheless, "where the parties intend a separation agreement to be incorporated but not merged in the divorce decree, the agreement remains a separate, enforceable contract and is not superseded by the decree."[31] An *incorporated* agreement therefore constitutes both a judgment and a contract.[32]

---

27. *See, e.g.,* Bennett v. Bennett, 250 N.W.2d 47 (Iowa 1977); Greiner v. Greiner, 61 Ohio App. 2d 88, 399 N.E.2d 571 (1979); Taylor v. Taylor, 10 Va. App. 681, 394 S.E.2d 864 (1990).

28. 429 Pa. 312, 632 A.2d 581 (1993).

29. *See* Price v. Price, 705 So. 2d 488 (Ala. Ct. App. 1997); Matsunaga v. Matsunaga, 99 Hawai'i 157, 164, 53 P.3d 296, 303 (Ct. App. 2002) ("[a] property settlement agreement incorporated into a decree of divorce loses its separate existence and becomes part of the decree" (quoting Wallace v. Wallace, 1 Haw. App. 315, 315, 619 P.2d 511, 511 (1980))); Jones v. Jones, 179 Ohio App. 3d 618, 628, 903 N.E.2d 329, 336 (2008) ("a separation agreement loses its contractual nature when it is incorporated into a divorce decree"); Thomas v. Thomas, 76 Ohio App. 3d 482, 602 N.E.2d 385 (1991).

30. 297 Md. 48, 465 A.2d 436, 440 (1983).

31. *Id.* at 441.

32. For other cases recognizing *incorporation* as a distinct alternative to *merger* and *approval*, *see* Flynn v. Flynn, 42 Cal. 2d 55, 265 P.2d 865, 866 (1954) ("[w]hether or not a merger is intended, the agreement may be incorporated into the decree"); Armstrong v. Armstrong, 248 Ark. 835, 454 S.W.2d 660 (1970) (court can incorporate agreement, thus making it enforceable by contempt, without merging it into decree); Rodriguez v. Rodriguez, 818 N.E.2d 993, 995–96 (Ind. Ct. App. 2004) ("The marital settlement agreement, which was incorporated into the dissolution decree by the trial court, is considered to be a contract[.]"); DePaolo v. DePaolo, 104 A.D.2d 631, 480 N.Y.S.2d 10 (1984) (agreement and contract can coexist as valid documents); Nicholson v. Combs, 550 Pa. 23, 703 A.2d 407 (1997); Swartz v. Swartz, 456 Pa. Super. 16, 689 A.2d 302 (1997); *cf.* Riffenburg v. Riffenburg, 585 A.2d 627, 631 (R.I. 1991) ("if the judgment explicitly states that the judgment's treatment of the matter shall have independent validity from the separation agreement, then the judgement shall have such validity").

In Hering v. Hering, 33 Va. App. 368, 372–73, 533 S.E.2d 631, 633 (2000), the court noted that "[o]ur previous decisions and those of the Supreme Court of Virginia draw a distinction among

Incorporation is also recognized by the Uniform Marriage and Divorce Act (UMDA). The UMDA originally stated that the parties must choose between *approval* and *merger*, but a subsequent amendment to the act changed its position. The UMDA now provides:

Terms of agreements set forth in the decree are enforceable by all remedies available for enforcement of a judgment, including contempt, *and are enforceable as contract terms.*[33]

The drafters explained the change:

[T]he original 1970 Act . . . required a choice between "merging" the agreement in the judgment and retaining its character as a contract. Strong representations as to the undesirability of such a choice, in the light of foreign doctrines as to the enforceability of judgments, as compared with contract terms, in this area of the law, made by persons and groups whose expertise entitled them to respect, led the Conference, in 1971, to change its former decision.[34]

In some states that recognize true *incorporation*, the court is not required to grant every request that a separation agreement be *incorporated* into the decree. Rather, the court has discretion on the issue.[35] The normal practice is to grant the request, but court may deny the request if it finds the agreement to be questionable or unfair. Other states have held by statute, however, that the trial court must grant a request to *incorporate* an agreement.[36]

In states where *incorporation* is recognized, it can be either express or by reference. Express *incorporation* is easily determined: To the extent the provisions are the decree are the same as the provisions of the agreement, *incorporation* has occurred.[37] This is true even if the decree does not expressly state that the contract is incorporated.

---

situations where an agreement is affirmed, where it is incorporated into a decree, or where, as here, the agreement is 'affirmed, ratified, incorporated, but not merged' into the final decree." These situations are, in the order discussed by the court, *approval*, *merger*, and true *incorporation*. The court's recognition of the distinction between *merger* and *incorporation* is excellent, but its decision to refer to both *merger* and *incorporation* as variants of "incorporation" materially confuses the law.

33. UMDA § 306, 9A U.L.A. 147, 217 (1987) (emphasis added).

34. UMDA § 306 cmt., 9A U.L.A. at 218.

35. *See, e.g.*, Gravley v. Gravley, 278 Ga. 897, 898, 608 S.E.2d 225, 227 (2005) ("we have left it within the discretion of the trial court whether such agreements should be incorporated, in whole or in part, in the final judgment and decree of divorce"); Doering v. Doering, 54 Va. App. 162, 170, 676 S.E.2d 353, 356 (2009) (trial court did not err in refusing to *incorporate* agreement, where agreement called for more support than the husband could afford to pay, so that parties would be before the court "on a weekly basis" for contempt proceedings if agreement were *incorporated*); Mayers v. Mayers, 15 Va. App. 587, 425 S.E.2d 808 (1993).

36. *See, e.g.*, Mo. Rev. Stat. Ann. § 452.325(4) (1997).

37. *See* Wierwille v. Wierwille, 34 Ohio St. 2d 17, 295 N.E.2d 200 (1971); Webber v. Olsen, 157 Or. App. 585, 971 P.2d 448 (1998); Bruni v. Bruni, 924 S.W.2d 366 (Tex. 1996); 24 Am. Jur. 2d *Divorce & Separation* § 1131 (Westlaw 2008).

The court cannot, of course, *incorporate* an agreement by making an order that differs materially from the agreement's terms.[38]

Incorporation by reference is a harder question. The best evidence is obviously an express statement that the terms of the agreement are included in the decree just as if they had been copied word for word.[39] An express order directing the parties to perform their obligations under the contract is equally good.[40] Where one court referred to the agreement in the decree, noted that a copy was on file with the court, and stated its intention to enforce the agreement if required, it found sufficient evidence of *incorporation*.[41]

Where the decree does not contain dispositive language, the court can again look to the agreement. Absent contrary language in the decree, it is again logical to assume that the court intended to adopt the parties' preference.[42] Intention to *incorporate* the agreement is shown by any language indicating that the language of the agreement shall be included in the order, but the agreement shall not cease to exist as an enforceable contract.[43]

As a special exception to the general rule of *approval*, *incorporation* occurs only if there is some supporting evidence in the decree or the agreement. Thus, where both documents are silent, the agreement is only *approved*.[44]

The court may expressly *incorporate* part and not all of the parties' agreement.[45] Likewise, the court may *incorporate* provision of an agreement even if the court could not include those provisions in an independent order.[46]

---

38. *See* Engineer v. Engineer, 187 S.W.3d 625, 626–27 (Tex. Ct. App. 2006) ("the Family Code does not, as outlined above, authorize a court to modify an agreement (to resolve ambiguities or otherwise) before incorporating it into a decree.").

39. *See, e.g.*, Johnston v. Johnston, 297 Md. 48, 465 A.2d 436, 437 (1983) ("made a part hereof as if fully set forth").

40. *See* Lay v. Lay, 912 S.W.2d 466 (Mo. 1995). *Incorporation* can also exist if the court "otherwise makes clear that [the agreement's] provisions are to be regarded not merely as covenants of the parties but also as court directives." Ruppert v. Fish, 84 Md. App. 665, 581 A.2d 828, 832 (1990).

41. Fishkin v. Fishkin, 201 A.D.2d 202, 615 N.Y.S.2d 899 (1994).

42. *See* LaPrade v. LaPrade, 189 Ariz. 243, 941 P.2d 1268 (1997); *Johnston*, 297 Md. 48, 465 A.2d 436; Makarchuk v. Makarchuk, 59 A.D.3d 1094, 1095, 874 N.Y.S.2d 649, 650 (2009) ("It is of no consequence that the decree did not contain a nonmerger clause inasmuch as the parties' intent to incorporate and not merge the agreement in the decree is clear from the language of those instruments[.]").

43. *Id.* (relying on provision that enforceability of agreement would not depend upon court approval).

44. *See Ruppert*, 84 Md. App. 665, 581 A.2d 828. *Incorporation* obviously cannot occur where neither party has requested it in their pleading. Frisella v. Frisella, 872 S.W.2d 637 (Mo. Ct. App. 1994).

45. *Ruppert*, 84 Md. App. 665, 581 A.2d 828; Owney v. Owney, 8 Va. App. 255, 379 S.E.2d 745 (1989).

46. *See, e.g.*, Albrecht v. Albrecht, 19 Conn. App. 146, 562 A.2d 528 (1989) (postmajority child support); Jackson v. Jackson, 102 N.C. App. 574, 402 S.E.2d 869 (1991) (postmajority child support); *In re* Marriage of Porter, 100 Or. App. 401, 786 P.2d 740 (1990) (alimony in a nominal amount), *cert. denied*, 796 P.2d 1206 (Or. 1990); *see generally* S. GREEN & J. LONG, MARRIAGE AND FAMILY LAW AGREEMENTS § 4.03 (1984 & Supp. 1991).

As noted above, if the court finds that the contract was not *incorporated*, it has decided only that the language of the agreement was not repeated in the decree. An unincorporated agreement still falls under the general rule of *approval*, and it is therefore still valid as a contract.[47]

Where an agreement calls for *incorporation*, but it is not actually incorporated into the judgment, it may be possible to reopen the judgment for mistake. In *Ventura v. Leong*,[48] the parties' agreement provided that it would be "incorporated, but not merged" into the decree. The decree nevertheless failed to *incorporate* the agreement. The trial court refused to permit enforcement by contempt, but the appellate court reversed. "Inasmuch as the agreement clearly evinces the parties' intent both that it be incorporated in the judgment of divorce and that it not merge therein . . . , the mistake in the judgment should be cured so as to conform its terms with the parties' unequivocal intent."[49]

Policy Concerns

There is no reason to force the parties to make an either/or choice between *merger* and *approval*. When this choice is required, parties who desire provisions that are enforceable only by contract (e.g., college support, nonmodifiable spousal support) must settle for *approval*, and thereby lose the right to enforce other provisions that would clearly be enforceable by contempt if the agreement were *merged*. The law should not require agreements to be either fully a contract or fully a judgment; there should be a middle ground.

The best middle ground is to recognize true *incorporation*, allowing the agreement to constitute at the same time both a contract and a judgment. It can then be enforced using either set of remedies, at the option of the enforcing spouse. Provisions that the court cannot order by itself can be enforced with contract remedies, while the more effective judgment remedies can be used to enforce other provisions.

There will obviously be a few situations in which there is conflict between the contract and judgment remedies. For example, a spouse might attempt to enforce spousal support in a contract action after the agreement has been modified in a judgment action. These situations are not very common, and they can be handled with fact-specific rules. For example, when the parties agree to modifiable spousal support, they generally cannot enforce the original agreement in a contract action regarding payments properly modified in a modification action. *See* § **6.032**. To the extent these special rules are a mild burden, the burden is much less than forcing the parties to make an artificial choice between *approval* and *merger*.

---

47. Owney v. Owney, 8 Va. App. 255, 379 S.E.2d 745 (1989).

48. 68 A.D.3d 1318, 1318 N.Y.S.2d 687, 688 (2009).

49. 890 N.Y.S. 2d at 688; *see also* Crain v. Crain, 109 A.D.2d 1094, 487 N.Y.S.2d 221 (1985) (where incorporation clause was omitted from divorce decree by oversight, mistake could be corrected retroactively). *But see* Unger v. Unger, 145 Misc. 2d 633, 547 N.Y.S.2d 529 (Sup. Ct. 1989) (refusing to allow retroactive incorporation).

Drafting Concerns

"Incorporation," like "merger," has been given many meanings by many courts, and it is hazardous to use either term without further explanation. The agreement should certainly recite how the parties desire that it be treated in the decree, but the best option is to state expressly the substance of the desired treatment, and not to rely upon buzzwords. If the parties intend *merger*, the agreement should state that it shall have no independent validity as a contract after entry of the decree, and it should avoid provisions not enforceable by judgment remedies. If the parties intend *approval*, the agreement should state that it shall not constitute a term of the decree and shall not be enforceable with judgment remedies.

The most common situation, of course, is that the parties intend the agreement to be enforceable as either a contract or a judgment, at the option of the enforcing spouse. In states that recognize true incorporation, this result can be reached directly. The agreement should state that it shall be incorporated but not merged into the final judgment, that it shall constitute both a contract and a judgment, and that it can be enforced with either judgment or contract remedies.

The most dangerous situation occurs when the parties desire true *incorporation*, but the state in question has been reluctant to recognize that option. There is a very real risk that a court reviewing the agreement will fail to understand the parties' intent, and will force upon them a choice between *merger* and *approval*. If the parties nevertheless desire to attempt to achieve true *incorporation*, a provision like this one might be attempted:

> The primary intention of the parties is that this agreement be incorporated into a final decree of divorce and be enforceable as a judgment. The parties also intend that the agreement remain enforceable as a contract, at the option of the enforcing spouse, to the extent that such enforcement is consistent with the parties' primary intention that the agreement be enforceable as a judgment. The parties have been informed that such dual enforcement is possible in a significant number of other states.

This provision would then be followed by a representative citation to one or two cases recognizing true *incorporation*.[50] The parties should probably be advised that this language is likely to result in *merger* (because that the parties' primary intention) if the court insists upon an artificial choice between *merger* and *approval*. But the language has at least a fighting chance to convince an uncertain court to recognize true *incorporation*.

§ 5.014 Alternatives to Merger and Incorporation: A Better Way?

Merger, incorporation, and *approval* are not inherently complex subjects. In fact, it is possible to articulate without much difficulty a coherent definition of each term. A *merged* agreement is a judgment but not a contract; an *approved* agreement is a contract but not a judgment; an *incorporated* agreement is both a contract and a judgment.

---

50. *See generally* note 32 *supra*.

Despite these clear theoretical definitions, the case law on *merger* and *incorpora-tion* still tends toward confusion. The problem is not that the definitions are unclear, but rather than so many parties and courts refuse to follow them. If a *merged* agreement does not exist as a contract after the final decree is entered, an agreement that expects to be *merged* should not include provisions that can be enforced only as a contract. Such an agreement is at war with itself; it includes terms that cannot possibly be enforced. Yet many parties persist in signing such agreements, thereby forcing the courts to decide which of two mutually inconsistent intentions was intended to be primary.[51]

The courts have also been reluctant to follow through with the logical consequences of *merger* and *incorporation*. If an *incorporated* agreement is both a contract and judg-ment, it can be enforced using either contract or judgment remedies, at the option of the enforcing spouse. Yet some courts continue to have difficulty seeing how the same doc-ument can be both a contract and a judgment.[52] If a *merged* agreement does not exist as a contract, then *there is literally no agreement left* after the final decree is entered. Yet some courts are reluctant to find that an agreement simply disappeared, and they keep finding ways to bring back a contract after it has *merged* into the judgment.[53]

Because courts and parties are so reluctant to follow the theoretically clear concepts of *merger* and *incorporation*, the applied case law of "merger" and "incorporation" is highly inconsistent. During the late 1970s and early 1980s, this uncertainty reached the point where three states—North Carolina, South Carolina, and West Virginia—tried a different path. This section examines and evaluates the law in these three states.

All three states took similar paths. The first state to act was West Virginia. In a landmark 1978 decision, *In re Hereford's Estate*,[54] the West Virginia Supreme Court criticized the importance of "words of art" in determining the relationship between agreements and divorce decree, and adopt the following standard instead:

> [I]n the absence of a specific provision to the contrary in a property settlement agreement appended to, made a part of, or incorporated by reference into the court order, which provision specifically and unambiguously denies the court jurisdiction in one or more of the regards just discussed, it shall be presumed that regardless of the language used, whether it be "ratified and confirmed," "merged," or any other language of like import, that a periodic payment to which reference is made in a divorce decree is judicially decreed alimony or alimony and child support and is subject to the continuing jurisdiction of the circuit court.

In short, the court assumed that all agreements attached to or incorporated into the divorce decree *merged* into the agreement. This result applied *regardless of the intent of the parties*, unless "a specific provision to the contrary" was placed in the agree-

---

51. Several leading cases involving such agreement are discussed in **§ 5.012**, beginning with the text accompanying note 9.

52. *See* **§ 5.013**.

53. *E.g.*, Smith v. Smith, 41 Va. App. 742, 589 S.E.2d 439 (2003).

54. *In re* Hereford's Estate, 162 W. Va. 477, 487–88, 250 S.E.2d 45, 52 (1978).

ment.[55] Because the new rule applied an artificial presumption to determine the intent of the parties, the court held that it would apply only prospectively.

The next state to act was North Carolina. In the 1983 case of *Walters v. Walters*,[56] the North Carolina Supreme Court held that any agreement that is even *presented* to the court automatically *merges* into the decree. Unlike West Virginia, which at least allows the parties to avoid *merger* by including clear contrary language in the decree, *Walters* did not allow the parties to avoid *merger* by any act short of refusing to present the agreement to the court at all.

Finally, in the later 1983 case of *Moseley v. Mosier*,[57] the South Carolina Supreme Court held that every separation agreement *merges* into the divorce decree unless the agreement expressly provides otherwise. Because the parties can provide otherwise, this approach is closer to the West Virginia rule. In order to provide otherwise, however, *Moseley* requires that the agreement contain *substantive* terms inconsistent with *merger*; a mere express anti-*merger* provision is not enough. For instance, to avoid court modification of spousal support, the agreement must expressly state that spousal support is not modifiable, and not simply state in the abstract that *merger* is not intended.

All three opinions were deliberate attempts by the courts to avoid perceived past confusion on the subject of divorce decrees and separation agreements. *Moseley* opined that "[t]he parties' intent is rarely revealed from the agreement's words of art" on *merger, incorporation*, and *approval*, because "[g]enerally, those terms are used without intending or implying any particular legal consequences."[58] *Walters* expressed a belief that its decision would "clarify an aspect of family law which has suffered through many years of confusion" on the relationship between agreements and decrees. *Hereford* used language of almost utopian aspiration:

> We dream today of inaugurating a system of domestic relations law in this State which is not dependent upon the use of words of art. Any experienced lawyer knows that as often as not so called "words of art" are used without intending or implying any particular legal consequences, only later to have those consequences imposed upon unsuspecting parties by courts. The Court suspects that this is what happened with regard to the so-called words of art used in both the property settlement agreement and the divorce decree in the case before us, as both parties to this appeal rely upon conflicting words of art.[59]

Policy Concerns

The goal of the courts in *Hereford*, *Walters*, and *Moseley* was to eliminate confusion and create simplicity. That goal was successfully achieved; all three states now have a simple rule (North Carolina) or at least a strong and simple presumption (South Caro-

---

55. *Id.*
56. 307 N.C. 381, 298 S.E.2d 338 (1983).
57. 279 S.C. 348, 306 S.E.2d 624 (1983).
58. *Moseley*, 306 S.E.2d at 627.
59. 162 W. Va. at 486, 250 S.E.2d at 51.

lina and West Virginia) for determining whether an agreement *merges* into a divorce decree.

To create the desired simple rule, all three opinions stretched the judicial power to the limit. Particularly troubling is *Walters*, which held that express contractual language rejecting *merger* would not be enforceable. This is a very substantial departure from common law contracts principles, and the court's willingness to act without supporting legislation is an act of significant judicial activism. *Hereford* and *Moseley* were more open to contrary language in the agreement or decree, and they are proportionally less troubling, but the creation of a brand-new *merger* presumption is still an action commonly reserved for the legislature.

Was the activist approach of the courts justified? The answer is yes only if *merger* and *incorporation* case law before all three decisions was so deeply confused as to be in a state of crisis. None of the three opinions cited hard evidence of such confusion; instead, they stated without authority that it existed. *Moseley*, for example, stated that terms such as *merger* "[g]enerally . . . are used without intending or implying and particular legal consequences,"[60] but the court cited no authority to support the statement. *Hereford* likewise asserted without justification that "[a]ny experienced lawyer knows that as often as not so called 'words of art' are used without intending or implying any particular legal consequences." Such sweeping unsupported assertions are more associated with legislative than judicial action.

None of the three courts cited any substantial body of secondary authority identifying a crisis in the law of merger and incorporation. The present authors cannot find such authority, either. On the contrary, there is at least some authority agreeing with the authors that any confusion in existing law was manageable through normal means. For example, a leading North Carolina commentator found that the *Walters* court's description of confusion in prior law was "inartful," while the leading pre-*Walters* opinion was written "with some success and considerable coherence."[61]

Artificial creation of simplicity might be justifiable if there is no less intrusive way of resolving the *merger* issue within reasonable time and cost parameters. But *merger* cases are not drastically harder to resolve than any other cases requiring construction of ambiguous contracts. Many drafters understand the concept of *merger* and *incorporation* and write clear agreements and decrees. This state of affairs may not be fully apparent to appellate judges, who disproportionately see cases in which agreements are unclear. But it is very dangerous to generalize from appealed cases, which are only a

---

60. *Moseley*, 306 S.E.2d at 627. To the extent that the *Moseley* court intended to rely upon its own experience with *merger* cases, the authors note that the appellate courts see only a very small fraction of all divorce cases. There are many divorce cases never seen by the appellate courts, in which terms such as *merger* and *incorporation* are routinely used correctly. Moreover, in the process of writing this treatise, the authors found many appellate cases showing a similarly correct use of terminology.

61. Sally B. Sharp, *Semantics as Jurisprudence: The Elevation of Form Over Substance in the Treatment of Separation Agreements in North Carolina*, 69 N.C. L. Rev. 319, 328, 335 (1991). Sharp also criticized the *Walters* court for encouraging parties not to present the agreements to the court, arguing that agreements not presented to the court were less likely to be fully reviewed for voluntariness and substantive sufficiency.

small fraction of the total cases settled or even tried. This is still another reason why broad sweeping changes are best reserved for legislative action; appellate judges do not see a fair and representative selection of the cases filed in the trial courts. There is a good argument to be made that all three cases drew an inaccurate generalization about *merger* and anti-*merger* provisions, based upon exposure to a very limited selection of cases in which the agreements were unusually unclear.

Cases admittedly do exist in which drafters use terms of art without understanding or intending their meaning. For example, some agreements include both "merger" provisions and substantive provisions that cannot be enforced if the agreement actually *merges*. But there is no evidence that these agreements are creating a problem that requires sweeping judicial or even legislative action. On the contrary, the common law construction process is dealing with these cases successfully, usually by holding that the specific substantive provisions of the agreement are controlling over broad but general terms of art. *See* § **5.012**. As long as the common law construction process continues to work successfully, there is no need for radical reform. This lack of need may explain why no other state since 1983 has followed *Hereford*, *Walters*, or *Moseley*.

In other words, while confusion over *merger* and *incorporation* exists, that confusion does not arise from unclear case law. *Merger* and *incorporation* have clear and precise meanings, and the great majority of court decisions have recognized them. The confusion arises because a minority of drafters persist in using "merger" and "incorporation" loosely, resulting in conflict between the general *merger* and *incorporation* language and the substantive provisions of the decree. The proper remedy for this problem is not radical reform in the case law, but rather patient and ongoing efforts to educate the drafters. Even while such efforts remain pending, however, the problems arising from uninformed use of "merger" and "incorporation" can comfortably be handled by the existing case law on construing separation agreements and divorce decrees.

Drafting Concerns

Specific suggestions on the use of "merger" and "incorporation" are set forth in the discussion of drafting concerns in § **5.012** and § **5.013**. To summarize briefly the essential points made in those sections:

1. Avoid unexplained use of any term of art in this area, including especially "merger" and "incorporation." Instead, state expressly whether the parties wish the agreement to be enforceable only as a judgment (*merger*), only as a contract (*approval*), or either a judgment or a contract as the option of the enforcing spouse (true *incorporation*).

2. If *merger* is intended, state expressly that the agreement shall not exist as a contract after the decree is entered. Then review the agreement very carefully to make certain that it contains no provisions that cannot be enforced as a judgment. Problem areas include college support for children (§ **6.044**) and especially modification of spousal support (§ **6.032**). If an agreement with a *merger* clause includes substantive provisions enforceable only as a contract, the chances are good that the substantive provisions will control over the general *merger* clause.

3. If true *incorporation* is intended, make certain that the law of the state in question recognizes true *incorporation*. In the absence of positive case law allowing an agreement to be both a contract and a judgment at the same time, state expressly that this result is desired. Be prepared for the possibility that a court unable to grasp the concept of true *incorporation* may force a choice between *merger* and *approval*. If possible, state expressly whether the parties' primary intent is to allow enforcement as a judgment or a contract, in the event that the court forces the parties to choose one or the other.

§ 5.02 General Rule: Separation Agreements as Contracts

Separation agreements are normally interpreted by the same principles of law that govern the construction of contracts generally.[62]

Incorporated agreements are usually construed as contracts rather than judgments.[63]

A few cases suggest that the intent of the court might carry weight if an *incorporated* agreement is ambiguous.[64] This is a questionable assertion, as the agreement was made by the parties, not by the court. In states that require court approval of separation agreements, *see generally* § **4.04**, representations made by the parties to the court might be important evidence of the parties' construction of the agreement. But in general, the intent of the court is no more relevant than the intent of any other third party

---

62. *See* Keffer v. Keffer, 852 P.2d 394 (Alaska 1993); Tanner v. Tanner, 57 Cal. App. 4th 419, 67 Cal. Rptr. 2d 204 (1997); Clark v. Clark, 535 A.2d 872 (D.C. 1987); Rimkus v. Rimkus, 199 Ill. App. 3d 903, 557 N.E.2d 638 (1990); Feick v. Thrutchley, 322 Md. 111, 586 A.2d 3 (1991); Hughes v. Hughes, 23 S.W.3d 838 (Mo. Ct. App. 2000); Boyett v. Boyett, 799 S.W.2d 360 (Tex. Ct. App. 1990). *But see* Pacifico v. Pacifico, 190 N.J. 258, 265, 920 A.2d 73, 77 (2007) ("the law grants particular leniency to agreements made in the domestic arena," thus allowing "judges greater discretion when interpreting such agreements") (quoting Guglielmo v. Guglielmo, 253 N.J. Super. 531, 542, 602 A.2d 741, 746 (App. Div. 1992)).

The New Jersey standard is a minority rule; most states do not expressly apply a different standard of construction to marital agreements.

63. *See* Albrecht v. Albrecht, 19 Conn. App. 146, 562 A.2d 528 (1989); *In re* Marriage of Sweders, 296 Ill. App. 3d 919, 695 N.E.2d 526 (1998); Stevens v. Stevens, 11 A.D.3d 791, 791, 783 N.Y.S.2d 683, 684 (2004) ("A matrimonial stipulation of settlement, which is incorporated but not merged into a judgment of divorce, is an independent contract subject to the normal rules of contract interpretation[.]"); Lelux v. Chernick, 119 Ohio App. 36, 694 N.E.2d 471 (1997); Ahern v. Ahern, 15 S.W.3d 73, 81 (Tenn. 2000) ("In the event the MDA is ambiguous, it is the intent of the parties that is relevant, not the intent of the trial judge[.]"); Woolam v. Tussing, 54 S.W.3d 442, 449 (Tex. Ct. App. 2001) ("A marital property agreement is treated as a contract and its meaning is governed by the law of contracts, but not by the law of judgments, even though the agreement is incorporated into a final divorce decree."); Spradley v. Hutchinson, 787 S.W.2d 214 (Tex. Ct. App. 1990); White v. White, 257 Va. 139, 509 S.E.2d 323 (1999).

64. *See Hughes,* 23 S.W.3d at 841 ("When an incorporated portion of a decree is ambiguous, it is quite pertinent to determine what the dissolution court understood and intended when it incorporated the provisions in question[.]").

to the agreement. The construction of the agreement should depend upon the intent of the parties.

Standard of Review

The proper construction of a contract is ordinarily an issue of law. Appellate review is therefore de novo, and the trial court's decision should receive no particular discretion.[65]

If the contract is unclear or incomplete, and the extrinsic evidence is conflicting, the proper balancing of that evidence is a question of fact. The trial court's decision will therefore be affirmed as long as it is supported by at least some evidence.[66]

§ 5.03 Choice of Law and Forum Provisions

Separation agreements are subject to the same choice of law rules that apply to contracts generally. The modern rule is that the court applies the law of the state with the most significant relationship to the transaction.[67] This is frequently the state in which the contract was signed.[68] Still, another state's law could apply where that state had a closer connection with the agreement. A number of states reach this result more directly, following the traditional rule that a contract must be construed under the law of the state in which it was signed.[69]

The parties are free, of course, to specify the controlling law in their agreement. These *choice of law clauses* are enforceable,[70] as long as the state chosen bears some reasonable relationship to the dispute at issue.[71]

---

65. *See, e.g.*, Webster v. Webster, 566 So. 2d 214 (Miss. 1990); Glassberg v. Obando, 791 S.W.2d 486 (Mo. Ct. App. 1990); *see generally* RESTATEMENT (SECOND) OF CONTRACTS § 212(2) & cmt. d (1979).

66. *See, e.g.*, Miller v. Miller, 133 N.H. 587, 578 A.2d 872 (1990); Emery v. Emery, 166 A.D.2d 787, 563 N.Y.S.2d 526 (1990); *see generally* RESTATEMENT (SECOND) OF CONTRACTS § 212(2) & cmt. e (1979).

67. RESTATEMENT (SECOND) OF CONFLICT OF LAWS § 188 (1969).

68. *See* Premo v. Premo, 419 Mass. 1011, 646 N.E.2d 1027 (1995) (construing Maryland agreement under Maryland law).

69. *See generally* 16 AM. JUR. 2D *Conflict of Laws* § 94 (1998).

70. *See* Blitz v. Fla. Dep't of Revenue *ex rel.* Maxwell, 898 So. 2d 121, 125 (Fla. Dist. Ct. App. 2005); Keeton v. Keeton, 807 So. 2d 186 (Fla. Dist. Ct. App. 2002); Torres v. McClain, 140 N.C. App. 238, 535 S.E.2d 623 (2000); *see generally* RESTATEMENT (SECOND) OF CONFLICT OF LAWS, *supra* note 67, § 187.

71. *See Torres*, 140 N.C. App. 238, 535 S.E.2d 623 (parties had reasonable relationship with Illinois, even though agreement was signed on Okinawa; parties were Illinois domiciliaries serving there on military duty).

The most common situation in which a state lacks a reasonable relationship to the dispute involves modification of child support after all interested parties have left the state. *See In re* Marriage of Crosby, 116 Cal. App. 4th 201, 10 Cal. Rptr. 3d 146 (2004) (applying California law despite choice of law provision opting for Idaho law, where the parties and their children had left Idaho); Wagner v. Wagner, 885 So. 2d 488 (Fla. Dist. Ct. App. 2004) (where child and both parties had moved to Florida, modification of child support should be governed by Florida law, despite an express choice of law clause in the agreement opting for law of California).

Since incorporated agreements are generally construed as contracts and not as judgments, *see* § **5.02**, the above rules are fully applicable to *incorporated* agreements.[72] In determining whether the agreement was *merged, incorporated,* or *approved* by the divorce decree, the court looks to the law of the state of divorce, and not the law chosen by the parties.[73]

If foreign law controls, but neither party supplies the court with sufficient material to determine what foreign law provides, the court may assume that foreign law is the same as local law.[74]

A provision choosing the controlling state law must be distinguished from a *choice of forum clause*—a provision choosing the state in which suit to enforce the agreement either may or must be brought.[75] The modern rule is that choice of forum clauses are enforceable, so long as the forum chosen is reasonable.[76]

A choice of forum clause will not be enforced where the chosen forum has declined jurisdiction, so that enforcement would leave the parties with no forum in which to litigate.[77]

§ 5.04 Clear and Complete Agreements: Plain Meaning

Where a separation agreement is clear and complete, the court must give its terms their normal plain meaning.[78] "[W]e accord the words used by the parties their usual, ordinary and accepted meaning unless there is evidence that they intended to employ the language is a special or technical sense."[79] "We will enforce the plain language of the agreement even if an argument can be made that a particular provision of the agreement is not necessarily consistent with one of the parties' interests."[80]

---

72. *Premo,* 419 Mass. 1011, 646 N.E.2d 1027.

73. Peterson v. Peterson, 333 S.C. 538, 510 S.E.2d 426 (1998).

74. *See, e.g.,* Storozynski v. Storozynski, 10 A.D.3d 419, 420, 781 N.Y.S.2d 141, 142 (2004) ("Since the parties neither invoked Polish law nor supplied applicable citations to it . . . , they are presumed to agree that the law of New York controls the interpretation of the agreement[.]").

75. *See In re* Marriage of Walker, 287 Ill. App. 3d 634, 678 N.E.2d 705 (1997) (refusing to construe choice of law provision to control the proper forum for enforcement).

76. *See* Hendry v. Hendry, 339 N.J. Super. 326, 335, 771 A.2d 701, 706 (2001) (enforcing forum selection clause consenting to New Jersey jurisdiction); *see generally* M/S Bremen v. Zapata Offshore Co., 407 U.S. 1 (1972).

77. *See* Pek v. Prots, 409 N.J. Super. 358, 364, 976 A.2d 1145, 1148 (Ch. Div. 2008).

78. Goldberg v. Goldberg, 290 Md. 204, 428 A.2d 469 (1981).

79. Feick v. Thrutchley, 322 Md. 111, 586 A.2d 3, 4 (1991); *see also* McIlmoil v. McIlmoil, 784 So. 2d 557, 561 (Fla. Dist. Ct. App. 2001) ("absent any evidence that the parties intended to endow a special meaning in the terms used in the agreement, the unambiguous language is to be given a realistic interpretation based on the plain, everyday meaning conveyed by the words"); Deel v. Deel 909 N.E.2d 1028, 1033 (Ind. Ct. App. 2009) ("the terms must be read within the four corners of the document and given their plain and ordinary meaning").

80. Asherman v. Asherman, 221 P.3d 302, 305 (Wyo. 2009).

Under the plain meaning rule, the court should interpret each party's promises "by the objective test of what [the] promise would be understood to mean by a reasonable person."[81] The construction of a clear and complete agreement is a question of law, and the appellate court is not required to give any particular deference to the trial court's decision.[82]

Because language is construed objectively and not subjectively, "[t]he fact that both sides ascribe different meanings to the language does not mean the language is ambiguous."[83] Rather, the court must examine the language used and determine whether is has a single clear objective meaning.

In determining the plain meaning of the words used in the contract, courts frequently refer to dictionaries. Courts pay particular attention to *Black's Law Dictionary*, as it provides definitions of terms as used in a legal context.[84] The decisions also make widespread use, however, of common popular dictionaries.[85] Where legal and nonlegal sources yield conflicting definitions of a term, the term has no plain meaning.[86]

When a provision in an agreement relates to a technical subject, the words of that provision must be given their accepted meaning in the relevant technical field. For example, in *Smith v. Smith*,[87] the court held that a detailed provision allocating tax

---

81. *Id.* at 305; *see also In re* Marriage of Simundza, 121 Cal. App. 4th 1513, 1518, 18 Cal. Rptr. 3d 377, 381 (2004) (contract construction is controlled by objective intent; "[t]he parties' undisclosed intent or understanding is irrelevant") (quoting Founding Members of the Newport Beach Country Club v. Newport Beach Country Club, Inc., 109 Cal. App. 4th 944, 955, 956, 135 Cal. Rptr. 2d 505, 514 (2003)); Reno v. Haler, 734 N.E.2d 1095, 1099 (Ind. Ct. App. 2000) (where wife clearly signed informal handwritten agreement providing for "joint custody," not relevant that wife may have defined joint custody different from its objective meaning, or even "contends she does not remember agreeing to joint custody but only to sole custody"; wife was bound by objective language of agreement); Hughes v. Hughes, 23 S.W.3d 838, 840 (Mo. Ct. App. 2000) ("words of the agreement [are given] their plain and ordinary meaning as understood by a reasonable and average person," and not necessarily the meaning that the parties now say they intended); Stevens v. Stevens, 11 A.D.3d 791, 792, 783 N.Y.S.2d 683, 684–85 (2004) ("Defendant's interpretation of the stipulation, which consists of an unexpressed subjective intent, is insufficient to override its plain language[.]").

82. *See, e.g.*, Bergman v. Bergman, 25 Va. App. 204, 487 S.E.2d 264 (1997).

83. Kipp v. Kipp, 844 So. 2d 691, 693 (Fla. Dist. Ct. App. 2003); *see also* Ivison v. Ivison, 762 So. 2d 329, 335 (Miss. 2000).

84. *See, e.g.*, Slorby v. Slorby, 760 N.W.2d 89 (N.D. 2009); Kurtz v. Jackson, 859 S.W.2d 609, 612 n.2 (Tex. Ct. App. 1991).

85. *See, e.g.*, *In re* Marriage of Holderrieth, 181 Ill. App. 3d 199, 536 N.E.2d 946 (1989); Glassberg v. Obando, 791 S.W.2d 486 (Mo. Ct. App. 1990).

86. Wedin v. Wedin, 57 Ark. App. 203, 944 S.W.2d 847 (1997); Kripp v. Kripp, 578 Pa. 82, 92, 849 A.2d 1159, 1164 (2004) ("in common usage, as various dictionaries reflect, the word 'cohabit' has several definitions"; term was therefore ambiguous).

87. 15 Va. App. 371, 423 S.E.2d 851 (1992). *But cf.* Recker v. Recker, 48 Va. App. 188, 192, 629 S.E.2d 191, 193 (2006) ("gross retirement annuity benefits" as used in separation agreement meant common meaning of benefits before any reductions, and not technical meaning under federal civil service regulations allowing limited deductions). The regulatory definition in *Recker* applied primarily to qualified orders directing the federal government to comply with state court orders, and there was no evidence that the parties had considered the regulations in drafting their agreement.

liability must be construed in light the technical usage of terms in federal income tax law. Another common usage of technical language occurs when the agreement refers to concepts from statutory or case law.[88]

Where a term is given one meaning by statute for use in litigated cases, but has several meanings in common usage, the statutory meaning is not the plain meaning. The parties are permitted to define terms in manner different from the manner chosen by the legislature.[89]

§ 5.05 Unclear or Incomplete Agreements: The Parol Evidence Rule

Under the well-known parol evidence rule, when an agreement is clear and complete, the court cannot look to evidence outside the four corners of the agreement (*extrinsic* or *parol evidence*) to determine its proper construction.[90]

The most common type of parol evidence is oral testimony as to the actual intention of the parties in signing the agreement. But the legal definition of parol evidence covers any evidence at all that is outside the four corners of the document. Thus, parol

---

88. *See* Kuper v. Woodward, 684 A.2d 783, 784 (D.C. 1996) (agreement to pay support until child was "emancipated"; defining emancipation with reference to settled legal definition in cases with no agreement); Pate v. Pate, 280 Ga. 796, 797, 631 S.E.2d 103, 104 (2006) (where definition of income in child support provision was unclear, proper to construe agreement to adopt definition of income in relevant child support guidelines); Reno v. Haler, 734 N.E.2d 1095, 1099 (Ind. Ct. App. 2000) (where wife agreed to "joint custody," and term was not further defined, proper to apply meaning of joint custody in litigated cases; "[t]he provisions to which Wife now objects are consistent with Indiana's definition of joint legal custody, to which Wife agreed by signing" the agreement); Baran v. Jaskulski, 114 Md. App. 322, 689 A.2d 1283, 1285 (1997) ("*Crawford* credits" construed with reference to leading Maryland decision that permitted such credits in litigated cases).

89. *See Kripp*, 578 Pa. at 92, 849 A.2d at 1164 ("There is nothing in 23 Pa.C.S. § 3706 or in the Divorce Code to show that the General Assembly intended that the definition of cohabitation set forth in the statute be incorporated into or control private agreements or that the courts are foreclosed from applying the law of contracts to determine the parties' intent on such a matter[.]").

If an agreement is ambiguous, however, and no clear resolution is provided by extrinsic evidence, the court may prefer a construction that reaches the same result as the law would reach without an agreement. *See* § **5.06**, note 162.

90. *See, e.g.*, Kipp v. Kipp, 844 So. 2d 691, 694 (Fla. Dist. Ct. App. 2003) ("[a]s we find no ambiguity in the language, it would be inappropriate for this court to consider parol evidence"); *In re* Marriage of McKeon, 252 Mont. 15, 826 P.2d 537 (1992); Laurence v. Rosen, 229 A.D.2d 373, 645 N.Y.S.2d 773 (1996); Ebert v. Ebert, 320 S.C. 331, 465 S.E.2d 121 (Ct. App. 1995); Kurtz v. Jackson, 859 S.W.2d 609 (Tex. Ct. App. 1991); *see generally* RESTATEMENT (SECOND) OF CONTRACTS §§ 212–213 (1979); *cf. In re* Marriage of Druss, 226 Ill. App. 3d 470, 589 N.E.2d 874, 878 (1992) (mere fact that provision was "totally irrational and illogical" was not a valid reason to admit extrinsic evidence, where language of provision was clear). *But cf.* Marcolongo v. Nicolai, 392 Pa. Super. 208, 572 A.2d 765 (1990) (even though language of agreement was clear and complete, agreement could still contain implied promises).

evidence can take the form of a writing. In *Cavazos v. Cavazos,*[91] for example, the divorce decree expressly incorporated an agreement of the parties taking the form of four written "schedules." The question was whether a fifth, unsigned schedule was part of the parties' bargain. The fifth schedule was inconsistent with the four corners of the other four schedules, which contain a clause stating that they reflected the parties' entire bargain. The court held that the fifth schedule constituted inadmissible parol evidence.

When the agreement is not clear and complete, extrinsic evidence is an important factor to consider in construing the agreement. While the law looks to clarity and completeness before looking at extrinsic evidence, many attorneys and parties look first for extrinsic evidence, and then worry about whether it is admissible. The practical question regarding extrinsic evidence therefore becomes: Under what conditions is it admissible?

The simple answer, as noted above, is that parol evidence cannot be considered where the contract is both clear and complete. Clarity and completeness are two distinct tests, and parol evidence is inadmissible only where both requirements are met. Thus, in order to admit parol evidence, the proponent must show that the agreement is either unclear or incomplete.

The determination of whether an agreement is unclear or incomplete is an issue of law, not an issue of fact. Thus, an appellate court is not required to give any particular deference to the trial court's decision.[92]

§ 5.051 Unclear Agreements

An agreement is unclear when a plain meaning cannot be discerned from the face of the document.[93] Courts sometimes use "ambiguity" as a synonym for "lack of clarity," and speak in terms of an agreement having more than one possible meaning. "An instrument is ambiguous when the language is reasonably susceptible to more than one

---

91. 941 S.W.2d 211, 212 (Tex. Ct. App. 1996).

92. *See, e.g.,* Bergman v. Bergman, 25 Va. App. 204, 487 S.E.2d 264 (1997).

93. *See, e.g.,* Feick v. Thrutchley, 322 Md. 111, 586 A.2d 3 (1991).

For specific sample cases finding an agreement to be unclear, see Heyda v. Heyda, 94 Md. App. 91, 615 A.2d 1218 (1992) (contract awarded wife survivorship benefits, but federal government employees can choose between two different survivorship annuities; remanding to determine which benefits the parties intended to divide); In re Marriage of Mease, 320 Mont. 229, 237, 92 P.3d 1148, 1153 (2004) ("the term 'gross disposable income' is ambiguous because gross income usually means before tax income . . . and disposable income usually means income left after payment of taxes and other deductions"); Moon v. Moon, 140 Or. App. 402, 914 P.2d 1133 (1996) (agreement assigned to husband"residence and real property" located at stated address; provision was ambiguous regarding status of adjacent vacant lot with separate tax number, but no separate mailing address); Phillips v. Phillips, 164 Vt. 600, 664 A.2d 272 (1995) (agreement required husband to provide all insurance benefits existing on January 1, 1991, and January 1, 1992, but different benefits existed on these dates; remanding to determine which benefits the parties intended to require).

In addition, many other cases construing specific unclear terms are summarized in Appendix A.

meaning."[94] But multiple meanings alone is not the test in every case. An agreement that reveals no clear meaning from its face is just as unclear as an agreement that reveals multiple possible meanings. The simplest statement of the question, therefore, is to ask whether a single clear meaning is apparent from the face of the agreement.

"[L]anguage is not rendered ambiguous merely because the parties do not agree on its meaning."[95] Otherwise, the mere existence of a dispute over construction would permit introduction of extrinsic evidence, and the parol evidence rule would be meaningless. An agreement is unclear for purposes of the parol evidence rule only if the court finds, using an *objective* test, that the language does not have one single clear meaning.

In determining whether an agreement is clear, it is important to look at the entire contract. In *Bitz v. Bitz*,[96] the agreement clearly divided a parcel of land by awarding three acres to the husband and five acres to the wife. Unfortunately, the agreement noted that the complete parcel was only "approximately eight acres," and precise measurement revealed that its actual size was 7.98 acres. The husband argued that the agreement was clear and gave him exactly three acres, and he was certainly correct that part of the agreement required that result. But it was equally clear that another part of the agreement awarded the wife exactly five acres, and the parcel was not large enough to enforce both provisions completely. The court therefore held that the agreement was ambiguous, and remanded the case for consideration of extrinsic evidence. Where an agreement contains multiple provisions, each independently clear, reaching results not compatible with one another, the agreement as a whole is ambiguous.

§ 5.052 Incomplete Agreements

An agreement that is clear is not necessarily complete. In *Smith v. Smith*,[97] the agreement stated the parties would file a joint tax return, and that any liability would be allocated between them in the same manner traditionally used by their tax preparer. The method was not expressly stated in the agreement, yet it was clearly essential to implementing the parties' bargain. Because the contract failed to include a provision necessary to its enforcement, it was an incomplete agreement, and the court held that admission of extrinsic evidence was required. The incomplete agreements rule is sometimes known as the partial integration doctrine, because the actual agreement of the parties is only partly integrated into their written contract.[98]

---

94. *In re* Marriage of Holderrieth, 181 Ill. App. 3d 199, 536 N.E.2d 946, 949 (1989); *see also* Baldwin v. Baldwin, 19 Conn. App. 420, 562 A.2d 581 (1989) ("[a] word is ambiguous when it is capable of being interpreted by reasonably well informed persons in either of two or more senses").

95. *Holderrieth*, 181 Ill. App. 3d 202, 536 N.E.2d at 949.

96. 934 So. 2d 507 (Fla. Dist. Ct. App. 2005).

97. 15 Va. App. 371, 423 S.E.2d 851 (1992).

98. *Id.*

For additional cases holding that agreements are incomplete, *see* Badell v. Badell, 122 Idaho 442, 835 P.2d 677 (1992) (agreement that accountant would allocate tax refund between parties after considering stated factors was incomplete, as agreement did not specify weight to be given to factors, and whether the accountant could consider additional factors not stated in the agreement); Soto v. Soto, 936 S.W.2d 338 (Tex. Ct. App. 1996) (agreement provided that husband would retain

An agreement can be complete on some issues and incomplete on others. In *Smith*, for example, the court excluded parol evidence on another issue, holding that the agreement was clear and complete as to that matter. Extrinsic evidence is admissible only on those specific issues on which the agreement is incomplete.

In *Smith*, the contract was incomplete because it failed to specify an essential term. Other agreements are incomplete simply because there were additional terms, negotiated by the parties, which were not set forth in the agreement. There is a general presumption that the agreement sets forth the parties' entire bargain, and the burden of proof is therefore placed upon the party who seeks to add additional unwritten terms. At a minimum, those terms must be consistent with the written language of the agreement.[99]

Where the new term is not inconsistent with the written language, but relates to the same general subject matter, the courts are generally reluctant to permit extrinsic evidence.[100] The rationale of these cases is that if the parties had intended to include this term, they would have included it in their agreement.

Courts are especially reluctant to admit parol evidence of an unstated condition upon an apparently absolute obligation. For example, in *Thomas v. Thomas*,[101] the court held that it was error to admit evidence that husband's apparently absolute obligation to provide insurance was actually conditional upon wife's compliance with certain property division provisions. When a promise is absolute on the face of the agreement, it is generally not possible to qualify that promise with additional unstated terms.[102]

---

ownership of all real property in his possession; extrinsic evidence admissible to determine which specific properties the husband possessed).

99. *See generally* RESTATEMENT (SECOND) OF CONTRACTS § 216 (1979).

100. *See* Greenburg v. Greenburg, 26 Conn. App. 591, 602 A.2d 1056 (1992) (contract to pay for college expenses cannot be supplemented by additional term giving father the right to select which college the child attended); Barelli v. Barelli, 113 Nev. 873, 944 P.2d 246 (1997) (refusing to find prior oral agreement regarding employment of wife after divorce); Hickman v. Hickman, 937 P.2d 85 (Okla. 1997) (refusing to recognize alleged collateral agreement that husband would pay all future tax debts on marital income; agreement was silent on the subject, so that parties were require to share such debts equally); Cavazos v. Cavazos, 941 S.W.2d 211, 212 (Tex. Ct. App. 1996) (where agreement stated on its face that stock in corporation would be awarded to husband, unsigned written document stating that 25 percent of stock would be placed into trust for children was not a term of the agreement). *But cf. In re* Marriage of Steffen, 467 N.W.2d 490 (S.D. 1991) (contract that awarded assets to husband was not inconsistent with wife's claim of an oral agreement that husband would hold certain assets in trust for her benefit); Gray v. Todd, 819 S.W.2d 104 (Tenn. Ct. App. 1991) (parol evidence can be used to show oral agreement that property awarded to one spouse was held in trust for the other; argument failed on the facts).

101. 577 N.E.2d 216 (Ind. 1991).

102. For additional cases refusing to read conditions onto a facially absolute promise, *see* Sassano v. Sassano, 721 So. 2d 444 (Fla. 5th Dist. Ct. App. 1998) (where agreement required two payments of $40,000 for the wife's interest in certain stock options, neither of which depended upon whether and when the options were exercised, court properly excluded evidence that these amount should be reduced by capital gains taxes due on exercise of the options); Stream v. Stream, 614 So. 2d 138 (La. Ct. App. 1993) (facially absolute alimony provision was not conditional upon wife maintaining safe home for parties' children); Hopper v. Hopper, 113 Nev. 1138, 946 P.2d 171 (1997) (parol evidence rule barred contention that absolute custody award to mother was conditioned upon

One particularly common example of an incomplete agreement is a written contract that is executed at the same time as another document. For instance, in *Matlock v. Matlock*,[103] the parties simultaneously executed both a separation agreement and a qualified domestic relations order (QDRO) needed to divide the husband's retirement benefits. The court held that the agreement itself was not a complete statement of the parties' agreement, and it reversed a lower court decision that applied the parol evidence rule to permit consideration of the QDRO in construing the agreement.

Some agreements contain a specific provision stating that the agreement reflects the entire bargain of the parties. Such an provision is powerful evidence that the agreement is complete, and it places a heavy burden upon a spouse who contends otherwise. For example, in *O'Connor v. O'Connor*,[104] the agreement provided on its face that the husband would pay a certain mortgage. The husband alleged that this apparently absolute term was subject to an agreed-upon but unstated condition: that the wife had no intention of moving from her present home in Tennessee. (The wife actually moved to Minnesota shortly after the agreement was signed). The agreement, however, contained an entire-bargain clause. In light of that clause, the court held that the agreement stated the parties' entire bargain, and it refused to hear parol evidence of the parties' actual intent.[105]

Nevertheless, an entire-bargain clause does not demonstrate as a matter of law that the contract is automatically complete. For instance, in *Smith*, the agreement was incomplete because it failed to specify an essential term—the precise method used in previous years by the preparer of the parties' tax returns. The agreement would not have been any more complete merely because it contained an entire-bargain provision. In other words, the fact that an agreement purports to be complete is certainly good evidence of completeness, but it does not foreclose the possibility that important terms may have been omitted.[106]

---

the father receiving additional visitation and the mother obtaining counseling and not living in Hollywood); Kurzon v. Kurzon, 246 A.D.2d 693, 668 N.Y.S.2d 242 (1998) (where contract on its face provided for both child support until college graduation and payment of college tuition, court refused to find implied term that child support would cease when college tuition became payable); Brown v. Brown, 226 A.D.2d 1010, 641 N.Y.S.2d 209 (1996) (refusing to hold that facially absolute alimony provision was intended to terminate upon retirement).

103. 444 Pa. Super. 507, 664 A.2d 551 (1995).

104. 228 A.D.2d 156, 644 N.Y.S.2d 174 (1996).

105. For additional cases enforcing an entire-bargain clause, *see* Dzina v. Dzina, 2009 WL 98444, at *5 (Ohio Ct. App. 2009) ("By virtue of the agreement's integration clause, the prior written indemnification agreement has no force or effect[.]"); Sadur v. Ellison, 553 A.2d 651 (D.C. 1989); *Hickman*, 937 P.2d 85 (in refusing to recognize collateral oral agreement regarding tax liability, court relied significantly upon entire-bargain provision); Hickman v. Hickman, 937 P.2d 75 (Okla. 1997) (parol evidence rule barred evidence of oral representation that omitted tax liability would be assigned to husband; contract had entire-bargain provision); *Cavazos*, 941 S.W.2d at 212 (in finding that unsigned writing was not part of parties' agreement, court relied partly on entire-bargain provision).

106. *See also* Ruggles v. Ruggles, 116 N.M. 52, 860 P.2d 182 (1993) (agreement awarded wife a share of husband's retirement benefits, but failed to specify whether wife's interest would be paid

Where an agreement does not contain an entire-bargain clause, the court is more likely to find that the parties did not intend to rescind prior agreements, especially if they involve materially different subjects.[107]

The parol evidence rule cannot be used, of course, to exclude evidence of an agreement made *after* the signing of the agreement under construction.[108] Such agreements may or may not be enforceable, *see* § **6.07**, but they cannot be excluded as parol evidence.

§ 5.053 *Other Exceptions to the Parol Evidence Rule*

Background Facts. Some authority suggests that parol evidence is admissible to show the general background fact situation against which the parties negotiated their agreement. This type of parol evidence is admitted not to vary the language of the agreement, but rather to assist the court in determining the meaning of the words used.[109]

Validity. The above discussion of parol evidence assumes that the contract is legally valid. Where one spouse claims that the agreement is invalid, the parol evidence rule does not apply. Alternately stated, parol evidence is always admissible to determine the validity, as opposed to the construction, of an agreement.[110] For example, while parol evidence would not generally be admissible in the above example to show that the parties intended to use a different cost-of-living index than the one stated in the agreement, parol evidence could be admitted to show that the scrivener accidentally typed the wrong name into the final agreement, *see* § **5.09**, or that the parties made a mutual mistake in determining the name of the index they wanted to use, *see* § **4.054**.

Compliance. The above discussion also assumes that the question before the court is one of construction. Once the construction of a contract is established, parol evidence is always admissible to show compliance.[111] For example, if the contract requires the husband to pay the wife $40,000, he can always introduce parol evidence to prove that the required payment has been made.

---

through immediate offset or reserved jurisdiction; agreement was ambiguous, despite presence of entire-bargain clause).

107. *See* Perricone v. Perricone, 292 Conn. 187, 197, 972 A.2d 666, 674 (2009) (separation agreement did not rescind earlier confidentiality agreement; "it is highly improbable that the parties intended that, upon the division of the marital property, the confidentiality agreement would be invalid, thereby exposing the plaintiff's business immediately to the harm that the agreement was intended to prevent").

108. *See* Hartley v. Miller, 2009 WL 1110819 (Ohio Ct. App. 2009) (trial court erred by excluding as extrinsic evidence handwritten agreement signed after former written separation agreement).

109. *See In re* Marriage of Sievers, 78 Wash. App. 287, 897 P.2d 388 (1995).

110. *See, e.g.*, Krysa v. Sieber, 113 Ohio App. 3d 572, 681 N.E.2d 949 (1996) (admitting extrinsic evidence of parties' negotiations to show mathematical error in computing amount of payment intended to equalize division of assets); Espenshade v. Espenshade, 729 A.2d 1239, 1241 (Pa. Super. Ct. 1999) (parol evidence admissible to determine whether parties ever intended to be bound by contract, and to determine whether agreement was invalid as a collusive fraud upon one of the parties' creditors).

111. *See generally* 32A C.J.S. *Evidence* § 1229 (Westlaw 2008).

Waiver. A party obviously cannot raise a parol evidence rule objection to evidence that he or she introduced. If a party lodges such an objection and loses, he or she is free to introduce parol evidence as a fallback measure, without waiving the original objection. Preservation of the objection does not require the objecting party to allow the other side's extrinsic evidence to remain uncontested.[112]

§ 5.054 Types of Extrinsic Evidence

The term *extrinsic evidence* is not subject to precise definition. Extrinsic evidence is generally any evidence, apart from the four corners of the written contract itself, that tends to shed light on the terms of the bargain that the parties actually made.

Prior Negotiations. One particularly useful form of extrinsic evidence is the position taken in negotiating the original agreement. For instance, in *Ochs v. Ochs*,[113] the question was whether agreement-based spousal support terminated when the wife started cohabiting with another man. The contract was silent on the question, but the husband had suggested during the original negotiations that support cease upon cohabitation, and the wife had rejected the idea. The court held that the support did not terminate.

Likewise, in *Roddenberry v. Roddenberry*,[114] the question was whether the wife's right to share in the husband's "profit participation income" from the *Star Trek* franchise applied only to the original series, or whether it applied to income from subsequent spin-offs. The court noted that the husband had specifically rejected an earlier draft provision that would give the wife a share of all income directly or indirectly produced from the *Star Trek* concept. This rejection, the court held, showed the husband's intent to limit the wife to a share of the income from the original series, which was the only *Star Trek* product produced during the marriage.[115]

Prior Agreements. Courts also tend to look at prior agreements signed by the parties, on the theory that where no evidence indicates otherwise, the present agreement was intended to continue without changing the provisions of the prior agreement. For instance, in *Jennings v. Jennings*,[116] the husband agreed to pay the wife half of certain royalties. The issue was whether gross or net royalties should be divided. The court noted that in a prior agreement, the husband had promised to "split the proceeds evenly down the middle."[117] The language, the court held, showed an intention to divide the net royalties.[118]

---

112. Thomas v. Thomas, 577 N.E.2d 216 (Ind. 1991).

113. 540 So. 2d 190 (Fla. Dist. Ct. App. 1989).

114. 44 Cal. App. 4th 634, 51 Cal. Rptr. 2d 907, 911 (1996).

115. *See also* Frager v. Frager, 949 S.W.2d 173 (Mo. Ct. App. 1977) (noting that wife had opposed during negotiation any time limit upon the husband's duty to pay her medical expenses, as she had substantial health problems at the time).

116. 12 Va. App. 1187, 409 S.E.2d 8 (1991).

117. 409 S.E.2d at 11.

118. *See also In re* Marriage of McKeon, 252 Mont. 15, 826 P.2d 537 (1992) (maintenance "for life" lasted until wife's death, and did not stop when her social security benefits became payable; relying in part upon similar language in earlier agreement between the parties).

Testimony of the Parties. Another important source of extrinsic evidence is the testimony of the parties and their original attorneys. In *Roddenberry v. Roddenberry*,[119] the attorney who represented the wife testified that the provision at issue was intended to apply only to the extent that the income in question arose from the husband's activities during the marriage, and that it was not intended to give the wife a share of income from future *Star Trek* products traceable to postdivorce efforts. The court relied heavily on this testimony in denying the wife a share of the income from postmarital *Star Trek* products.

Because the testimony of the parties is self-interested, it is likely to be given little weight if contradicted by other evidence.[120] Where the parties' testimony is not contradicted by other evidence, however, and especially on points as to which the parties' testimony is not conflicting, such testimony receives considerable weight.

Course of Performance. Courts also tend to look to the prior performance of the agreement by the parties. The assumption behind this type of evidence is that parties' course of performance reflects their own understanding of how their contract should be construed.[121]

For example, in *In re Marriage of Mease*,[122] the agreement was ambiguous as to whether the husband's support should be a stated percentage of his income before or after taxes. The husband's first payment under the agreement, made before the dispute arose, was 15 percent of his before-tax income. The trial court found the payment to be controlling evidence that the parties intended to pay the obligation on before-tax income, and the appellate court affirmed. "Robert's conduct is the best evidence of his intent, even though it is contrary to his testimony of intent at trial."[123]

Likewise, in *Patterson v. Patterson*,[124] the agreement gave the wife 50 percent of the husband's "net income." This key term was not expressly defined. In the past, however, the husband had paid the wife exactly half of every paycheck he received, and the wife had never objected. In remanding the case for consideration of extrinsic evidence, the court held that this parties' past course of performance was some evidence of their intention.[125]

---

119. Roddenberry v. Roddenberry, 44 Cal. App. 4th 634, 51 Cal. Rptr. 2d 907 (1996).

120. *See* Hughes v. Hughes, 23 S.W.3d 838, 841 n.1 (Mo. Ct. App. 2000) ("The trial court wisely elected not to be guided by the subjective recollection of either of the parties, recognizing that memories are notoriously subject to the coloring effect of self-interest[.]").

121. *See* Patterson v. Taylor, 140 N.C. App. 91, 97, 535 S.E.2d 374, 378 (2000) ("[A] trial court . . . may also consider extrinsic evidence of the conduct of the parties as they carry out the agreement. Indeed, because actions speak louder than words, such evidence may be particularly persuasive[.]").

122. 320 Mont. 229, 92 P.3d 1148 (2004).

123. *Id.* at 238, 92 P.3d at 1154.

124. 72 Ohio. App. 3d 818, 596 N.E.2d 534 (1991); *see also* Eickhoff v. Eickhoff, 263 Ga. 498, 435 S.E.2d 914 (1993) (where agreement awarded wife half of husband's pension, husband argued that wife's interest attached only to net benefits after taxes, but for over two years he had paid her half of the gross benefits; construing agreement to divide gross and not net benefits).

125. *See also* Herzog v. Herzog, 887 A.2d 313 (Pa. Super. Ct. 2005) (where agreement required husband to pay for improvements to wife's home, and wife ordered $2.3 million in improvements

In addition to looking at actual prior performance, courts have also placed weight upon postcontract statements by the parties showing their understanding of the obligations placed upon them. In *Martens v. Dunham*,[126] for instance, the court attached substantial weight to a postagreement letter that stated one party's interpretation of the contract.[127]

Like all extrinsic evidence, past performance is relevant only when the agreement is unclear or incomplete.[128]

Course of Trade. The court can also look at evidence of how the ambiguous term in question has been construed in other contexts. For example, in *In re Marriage of Mease*,[129] where trial court had to construe the phrase "gross disposable income," it relied on material part upon testimony from an expert accountant regarding the common usage of "gross" and "disposable." The trial court's reliance was affirmed on appeal. "[E]vidence of the technical accounting definitions of gross and disposable was admissible to show the parties' intent as those words are to be interpreted as usually understood by professionals in the course of trade usage."[130]

§ 5.055 *Procedures for Considering Extrinsic Evidence*

While the plain meaning of an unambiguous agreement is an issue of law for the court,[131] the weight of extrinsic evidence is a question of fact. Where a contract is found to be ambiguous, therefore, the court must hold a hearing at which the parties can submit evidence on the meaning of the ambiguous language. Failure to hold such a hearing is significant procedural error.[132]

The standard for appellate review of extrinsic evidence is discussed in **§ 5.02**.

---

to $75,000 home, relying in part upon much more reasonable selection of improvements wife discussed with builder before agreement was signed).

126. 571 So. 2d 1190 (Ala. Ct. App. 1990).

127. *See also* Mackey v. Mechetti, 695 So. 2d 472 (Fla. Dist. Ct. App. 1997) (in holding medical insurance obligation to be in the nature of spousal support, court noted that the husband had treated it as such in prior motions); Cramer v. Smith, 572 N.W.2d 445 (S.D. 1997) (looking at postcontract correspondence between parties' counsel).

128. *See* Rubin v. Rubin, 234 A.D.2d 185, 651 N.Y.S.2d 482 (1996) (where agreement required husband to pay cost of wife's insurance coverage, husband was liable for the actual cost of such coverage, even though he had for several years paid only the cost of covering himself under his own employer's policy; past performance could not avoid clear language of contract).

129. 320 Mont. 229, 92 P.3d 1148 (2004).

130. *Id.* at 238, 92 P.3d at 1154.

131. *See* **§ 5.04**, note 82.

132. *See* Page v. Page, 77 Conn. App. 748, 825 A.2d 187 (2003) (error to construe ambiguous provision without holding evidentiary hearing); Bitz v. Bitz, 934 So. 2d 507 (Fla. Dist. Ct. App. 2005) (error not to hold evidentiary hearing); Wagner v. Wagner, 885 So. 2d 488, 493 (Fla. Dist. Ct. App. 2004) ("[b]ecause the parties disagree as to the intent of their agreement in these ambiguous areas, the trial court should have taken evidence regarding that intent"); Pacifico v. Pacifico, 190 N.J. 258, 267, 920 A.2d 73, 78 (2007) (where testimony was conflicting on construction of ambiguous agreement, "the judge had no alternative but to conduct an evidentiary hearing at which the parties' credibility could be assessed and their intentions gleaned").

§ 5.06 Unclear and Incomplete Agreements: Rules of Construction

The most important source when construing an unclear or incomplete agreement is extrinsic evidence on the actual intent of the parties. In addition, however, the courts often look to various common law rules of contract construction. None of these rules is a substitute for evidence on the intention of the parties,[133] but they can be important to the result when the extrinsic evidence does not yield a clear answer.

Construction in Favor of Handwritten Terms

Where other factors are equal, a handwritten provision will prevail over a conflicting typewritten or printed provision.[134] The rationale is that handwritten provision was probably given a greater degrees of serious consideration by the parties and their attorneys than a typed provision.

Construction against the Drafter

An unclear or incomplete agreement is generally construed against the party who drafted it.[135]

When an agreement is vigorously negotiated, the final document sometimes consists of a mixture of language contributed by each party. In this type of agreement, the court will construe each individual provision against the party who drafted it.[136] Where the specific language at issue cannot be attributed to either party, there is at least some authority for construing the agreement against the party who prepared the final draft, on grounds that that party had better control over the language used.[137] There is also

---

133. For cases applying this point to the rule favoring construction against the drafter, *see* note 142 infra.

For cases applying this point to other rules of construction, *see* Kripp v. Kripp, 578 Pa. 82, 93, 849 A.2d 1159, 1165 (2004) ("Appellee's contention that [the ambiguous agreement's] meaning should not be determined through parol evidence of the parties' intent; but should flow from a construction of contractual terms that achieves fairness, is without merit[.]").

134. *See* Russell v. Gill, 715 So. 2d 1114 (Fla. 1st Dist. Ct. App. 1998) (handwritten provision terminating support on remarriage controlled over contrary typed provision).

135. *See, e.g.,* Franklin v. Franklin, 262 Ga. 218, 416 S.E.2d 503 (1992); Deel v. Deel, 909 N.E.2d 1028 (Ind. Ct. App. 2009); Miller v. Miller, 1 So. 3d 815 (La. Ct. App. 2009); Bernal v. Nieto, 123 N.M. 621, 943 P.2d 1338 (Ct. App. 1997); *In re* Marriage of Winningstad, 99 Or. App. 682, 784 P.2d 101 (1989).

Courts are especially likely to a construe an agreement against the drafter when the agreement was drafted by an attorney spouse, and the other spouse lacked independent counsel. Williams v. Waldman, 108 Nev. 466, 836 P.2d 614 (1992).

136. Dube v. Horowitz, 258 A.D.2d 724, 684 N.Y.S.2d 689 (1999) (construing alimony provision against husband, who drafted it, even though the great majority of the contract was drafted by the wife). *But cf.* Behrns v. Behrns, 102 Conn. App. 96, 924 A.2d 883 (2007) (where court found that defendant's attorney drafted ambiguous provision, but record showed that provision had been drafted by plaintiff's counsel and only modified by defendant's counsel, error to construe agreement against defendant).

137. *E.g.,* Galloway Corp. v. S.B. Ballard Constr. Co., 250 Va. 493, 464 S.E.2d 349 (1995).

authority suggesting that a provision of unclear authorship should be construed against the party who benefits from it, on the assumption that the beneficiary was responsible for the favorable language.[138]

In some situations, the identify of the drafter may be so unclear that the doctrine should not be applied:

> [T]he panel oversimplified the matrimonial settlement process by concluding that James' lawyer "drafted" the [property settlement agreement]. To be sure, James' lawyer drafted the first version. However, Ginger's lawyer drafted the second. Thereafter, James' lawyer drafted the third. The fourth and final draft was essentially the third draft with handwritten interlineations that reflected Ginger's changes. That is the way property settlement agreements are developed. Rarely is one party's version accepted without negotiation and input from the other. Thus, no singular "drafter" within the meaning of the doctrine of contra proferentem penned the agreement in this case.[139]

The rule of construction against the drafter is subject to the same limitations as rules of construction generally. Thus, it does not apply where the contract is unambiguous. A clear and complete provision must be given its plain meaning, even where that plain meaning favors the drafter.[140] Where the contract is ambiguous, the court must attempt to determine the intent of the parties from extrinsic evidence. The agreement can be construed against the drafter only when the extrinsic evidence itself is unclear.[141] The actual intent of the parties, where it can be reasonable determined from the evidence, is always more important that the identity of the drafter.

The rule of construction against the drafter can be waived by an express provision in the agreement.[142]

---

138. *E.g.*, VNB Mortg. Co. v. Lone Star Indus., Inc., 215 Va. 366, 209 S.E.2d 909 (1974); Standard Ice Co. v. Lynchburg Diamond Ice Factory, 129 Va. 521, 106 S.E. 390 (1921).

139. Pacifico v. Pacifico, 190 N.J. 258, 268–69, 920 A.2d 73, 79 (2007). *Pacifico* also suggested that where both parties have equal bargaining power and equal control over the language of the agreement, it should not be construed against the drafter.

140. Kincaid v. Kincaid, 117 Ohio App. 3d 148, 690 N.E.2d 47 (1997).

141. *See* Eveland v. Eveland, 156 S.W.3d 366, 369 (Mo. Ct. App. 2004) ("Ambiguities should only be construed against the drafter when other means of construction fail and the intent of the parties cannot be ascertained from other sources[.]"); Miller v. Miller, 1 So. 3d 815, 819 (La. Ct. App. 2009) ("If the intent of the parties cannot be ascertained from the terms of the written contract or parol evidence about that intent, ambiguous contract provisions will be construed against the party who prepared it[.]"); *Pacifico*, 190 N.J. at 268–69, 920 A.2d at 78 (2007) (if "the court is unable to determine the meaning of the term [from extrinsic evidence], contra proferentem may be employed as a doctrine of last resort"); *In re* Marriage of Neal, 181 Or. App. 361, 45 P.3d 1011 (2002) (error to construe agreement against the drafter before considering extrinsic evidence).

142. *See* Young v. Stump, 294 Ga. App. 351, 353–54, 669 S.E.2d 148, 151 (2008) (enforcing express provision providing that "[b]ecause this Settlement Agreement is a joint effort of the parties, it should be construed with fairness as between the parties and not more strictly enforced against one or the other party").

Construction to Give Effect to Every Provision

Courts generally construe unclear or incomplete agreements so that each and every provision of such an agreement has some effect upon the parties' obligations. "No part [of the agreement] should be rejected as surplusage unless absolutely necessary, since it is presumed that the parties inserted each provision deliberately and for a purpose."[143] In other words, courts disfavor a construction that would make one or more provisions of the agreement superfluous.

A good example is *Riggs v. Riggs*.[144] The agreement in that case provided that (1) the husband would pay the wife $255,000 within 12 months; (2) that he would pay 8.5 percent interest on any payments on the $255,000 made after 12 months; and (3) that he would make further payments of $5,000 per month for 72 months. The issue was whether the husband was in breach of the agreement if he did not pay the $255,000 within 12 months. The trial court held no, reasoning that if payment were absolutely required within 12 months, the second provision above would be superfluous. It held instead that the $255,000, like the additional $5,000 payments, had to be paid within 72 months. On appeal, the appellate court reversed, reasoning that the trial court's order made the specific reference to 12 months in the first provision redundant. Requiring payment within 12 months would not make the second clause redundant, the court explained, because it functioned as a sort of liquidated damages provision, stating the consequences that would ensue in the event that the husband breached the first provision.

Another example is *In re Marriage of Bolton*.[145] In that case, the agreement required the husband to make the mortgage payment on the marital home, which the agreement stated as $752.45 per month. The agreement further provided that the wife would be responsible for taxes and insurance upon the home. A problem arose because the stated sum of $752.45 per month included taxes and insurance. Thus, the contract on its face required both parties to pay the same obligation. The court refused to hold that the husband was responsible for all of the taxes and insurance, because that would make the wife's stated obligation superfluous. It further refused to make the wife pay all of the taxes and insurance, however, as that would make the $752.45 figure superfluous. Instead, the court ordered the wife to be responsible for all taxes and insurance beyond those included in the $752.45 figure, a construction that gave effect to both of the competing provisions.

Construction Given by the Parties Themselves

The court should generally construe the contract in the same way it has traditionally been construed and applied by the parties themselves. This principle of construction

---

143. *In re* Marriage of Holderrieth, 181 Ill. App. 3d 199, 536 N.E.2d 946, 949 (1989).

144. 205 A.D.2d 864, 613 N.Y.S.2d 454 (1994).

145. 950 S.W.2d 268 (Mo. Ct. App. 1997); *see also In re* Marriage of Blum, 377 Ill. App. 3d 509, 879 N.E.2d 940, 951 (2007) (where agreement stated that support was "reviewable" after 61 months, rejecting wife's argument that provision anticipated modification for changed circumstances and not de novo review; modification was available by statute even without the review provision, so that wife's argument made review provision superfluous).

is merely a restatement of the rule that the parties' prior course of dealing is relevant extrinsic evidence of their intention, and the cases are discussed in the section above on extrinsic evidence. *See* § **5.054**.

Construction in Favor of Specific Terms

Another rule of construction states that specific terms generally control over general terms.[146] In *Frager v. Frager*,[147] paragraph 12(b) of the agreement stated that the husband would pay the wife's medical expenses until her death or remarriage. Paragraph 12(d) stated that all obligations included in paragraph 12 would terminate upon the wife's death or remarriage, or after a period of 10 years. The issue was whether the 10-year time limitation applied to the medical expenses. The court held that the specific termination provision set forth in paragraph 12(b) controlled over the general termination provision for all of paragraph 12.

Construction in Light of Other Provisions

The particular provision being construed should be considered in light of all of the other provisions set forth in the agreement. In other words, agreements should be construed as a unified whole, and specific provisions should not be judged in isolation from the remainder of the parties' bargain.

For example, in *Keller v. Keller*,[148] the agreement reduced the husband's spousal support obligation by a stated percentage of the wife's "income from all sources." The question was whether capital gains constituted income. The provision in question had no definition of income, but it appeared immediately after a provision requiring the parties to exchange federal income tax returns, and the reduction was made annually as of the date when the exchange was supposed to take place. The court held that in light of the first provision, the term "income" in the second provision was intended to mean income as defined under federal tax law. Thus, capital gains were treated as income under the agreement.[149]

One particular corollary of the other-provisions rule goes by the Latin phrase *expressio unius est exclusio alterius*, "the inclusion of one thing is the exclusion of

---

146. *See In re* Marriage of Crowder, 77 P.3d 858, 861 (Colo. Ct. App. 2003) ("[i]n resolving conflict between terms of an agreement, specific provisions prevail over general provisions"; provision specifically addressing college education prevailed over provision stating that child support generally would terminate upon emancipation).

147. 949 S.W.2d 173 (Mo. Ct. App. 1977).

148. 877 S.W.2d 192, 194 (Mo. Ct. App. 1994).

149. *See also* Mason v. Mason, 873 S.W.2d 631, 634 (Mo. Ct. App. 1994) (where agreement required husband to maintain "a policy of insurance on his wife," husband argued that phrase was too vague to be enforced; court noted that immediately preceding sentence dealt with health insurance, and found the provision enforceable); Purdy v. Purdy, 715 A.2d 473, 474–75 (Pa. Super. Ct. 1998) (contract provided that alimony would terminate after three years if wife "received or shall receive" proceeds from sale of certain property; agreement required husband to provide life insurance until proceeds were "received," and awarded wife 50 percent of husband's pension if proceeds were not "received"; alimony terminated only when wife had actual possession of the proceeds, and not when she had a right to receive proceeds in the future).

others." A good example is *Uram v. Uram*.[150] In that case, the husband agreed to pay "costs of . . . college . . . including the costs of such items as tuition, fees and books." The agreement did not define "costs," but it did include three examples: tuition, fees, and books. By including these examples, the court held, the parties indicated their intention to include within the definition of "costs" only things similar to the three listed expenses. It therefore held that room and board costs—an expense different in nature from the items listed—were not covered by the agreement.[151]

Construction against an Absurd Result

An unclear or incomplete agreement will be construed to avoid an absurd result. In *Del Castillo v. Del Castillo*,[152] the agreement required the father to pay for the child's "education . . . beyond the high school level." The court held that only the costs of undergraduate education were covered. If the agreement included post-undergraduate costs, it could make the father liable for the remainder of the child's life, a result that the court expressly characterized as absurd.[153]

One particular type of absurd result that the courts try especially hard to avoid is a construction that allows one party to impose substantial unexpected adverse consequences upon the other. The New York courts have stated this point as a rule against construing the agreement to leave one party at the mercy of the other.[154]

---

150. 65 Ohio App. 3d 96, 582 N.E.2d 1060, 1061 (1989).

151. *See also* Harrington v. Perry, 103 N.C. App. 376, 406 S.E.2d 1, 3 (1991) (where parties agreed to divide "net recovery after attorney's fees", attorney's fees were the only valid deduction in determining net recovery); Ellis v. Taylor, 316 S.C. 245, 449 S.E.2d 487, 488 (1994) (father agreed to pay college costs over and above child's "scholarship, grant or other assistance"; provision applied only to financial aid in the nature of a gift, so that father had to repay amounts covered by student loans).

152. 420 Pa. Super. 520, 617 A.2d 26, 27 (1992).

153. For additional cases refusing to adopt absurd constructions, *see* Brender v. Brender, 199 A.D.2d 665, 605 N.Y.S.2d 411 (1993) (contract required husband to cover wife under his professional corporation's group health insurance, but husband could not legally do so; refusing to read agreement to require impossible task, and remanding for evidence as to the parties' actual intent); Hughes v. Hughes, 23 S.W.3d 838, 841 (Mo. Ct. App. 2000) (where contract provided that spousal support would cease upon wife's "employment," term was limited to substantial permanent employment that reduced wife's need for support, and did not apply to literally any employment at all); Keller v. Keller, 877 S.W.2d 192 (Mo. Ct. App. 1994) (agreement reduced husband's support obligation by percentage of wife's taxable income; absurd to consider support payments as income for purposes of this provision, as support would become self-reducing); Emery v. Emery, 166 A.D.2d 787, 563 N.Y.S.2d 526 (1990) (husband's promise to pay wife the difference between their retirement incomes would be construed to mean half the difference; literal interpretation would lead to absurd result).

154. *See* Comras v. Comras, 195 A.D.2d 358, 600 N.Y.S.2d 61 (1993) (husband's agreement to assume the wife's interests in certain partnerships required only that he use his best efforts to obtain the consent of the other partners to the transfer, and did not make him absolutely liable if the partners refused to consent); Haskin v. Mendler, 184 A.D.2d 372, 584 N.Y.S.2d 851 (1992) (agreement provided that deed be "recorded at [husband's] expense"; husband must pay not only the formal cost of recording, but also real estate transfer tax; contrary result would let husband impose unreasonable liability upon wife); *see also* Burns v. Burns, 157 P.3d 1037, 1041 (Alaska 2007)

A good example of unexpected adverse consequences is *Herzog v. Herzog*.[155] The agreement in that case required the husband to pay for improvements to a home just acquired by the wife. The husband expected, based upon discussions with the wife and a contractor before the agreement was signed, that the home and improvements together would cost roughly $150,000. The wife then selected improvements costing $2.3 million, and argued that the husband should pay for them. The trial court held otherwise, and the appellate court affirmed. "For wife to suggest that the language of the marriage settlement agreement provides her with absolutely unfettered discretion as to the improvements to the $75,000 modular home, such that she can spend approximately $2.3 million on improvements, including $893,000 worth of fencing and $950,000 worth of landscaping, is nothing short of unreasonable, and frankly, is absurd."[156]

It is extremely important to note that the reasonableness of the result is a factor only where the contract is unclear or incomplete. Where the language of the contract is clear, "it is beyond the province of the court to evaluate the wisdom of the contract terms agreed to by the parties."[157] This is true even where the clear provision at issue reaches an unfair result:

> Likewise, we hold that in domestic cases, in the absence of undue influence, breach of fiduciary duties, etc., at the time of inceptions, persons who, with the assistance of counsel, enter to contract settling rights to property (contracts that may later prove to be disadvantageous to them) will, generally, be left in the condition in which they placed themselves.[158]

The court added in a footnote:

> We are reminded of part of the ballad "Betsy and I Are Out" that reads:
>
> > Draw up the papers, lawyer, *and make 'em good and stout,*
> > For things at home are crossways, and Betsy and I are out.[159]

(five-year minimum duration provision applied to spousal support generally and not only to payments from husband's dental practice income; otherwise husband could terminate support simply by switching careers; "[a]llowing Troy the unilateral power to reduce the support he owed would violate ... the principles of good faith and fair dealing"); Janson v. Janson, 773 A.2d 901, 904 (R.I. 2001) ("when a provision in a settlement agreement is ambiguous, we have held that the practice of this Court is to 'adopt that construction which is most equitable and which will not give to one party an unconscionable advantage over the other'") (quoting Flynn v. Flynn, 615 A.2d 119, 122 (R.I. 1992)).

155. 887 A.2d 313 (Pa. Super. Ct. 2005).

156. *Id.* at 317.

157. *In re* Marriage of Druss, 226 Ill. App. 3d 470, 589 N.E.2d 874, 878 (1992).

158. Baran v. Jaskulski, 114 Md. App. 322, 689 A.2d 1283, 1289 (1997).

159. *Id.* at 1289 n.4 (quoting WILL CARLTON, *Betsy and I Are Out*, in FARM BALLADS (1878) (emphasis added)).

For additional cases holding that the court cannot pass judgment upon the wisdom of the contract, *see* D'Ascanio v. D'Ascanio, 237 Conn. 481, 678 A.2d 469 (1996) (where contract provided that monthly support dropped from $700 to $350 upon wife's cohabitation, court had no equitable power to decide that support would drop only to $600); Kaffenberger v. Kaffenberger, 228 A.D.2d

Construction in Favor of a Reasonable Result

An ambiguous agreement is generally construed in favor of a reasonable result.[160] This rule is essentially the reverse side of the rule against construing an agreement to reach an absurd result.

As one particular application of this rule, ambiguous agreements are sometimes construed to favor the result that would have been reached if the parties had signed no agreement and instead litigated the case.[161] The parties are clearly permitted to reach a difficult result than the law would otherwise impose,[162] but where the language of the agreement is ambiguous, it is probably unlikely that they intended to reach a greatly differing result.

Agreements are more likely to be construed in favor of reasonable results in states that tend to regulate to the private bargaining process in divorce cases more closely, and especially in states that require court approval of separation agreements.

Construction against Forfeiture

Courts generally prefer to construe agreements in a manner that avoids forfeiture. In *Cortez v. Cortez*,[163] the agreement provided that the wife would make mortgage payments on the jointly titled marital home after divorce. If she fell 60 days behind, the husband could take sole title by paying off the mortgage, unless the wife redeemed the property by paying the delinquent amount within 30 days. The wife fell behind, and the husband paid the entire mortgage. The wife then attempted to redeem. Her check to the husband was mailed within the 30-day period, but received after that period ended.

743, 643 N.Y.S.2d 740 (1996); Chamberlin v. Chamberlin, 693 A.2d 970 (Pa. Super. Ct. 1997) (court must enforce support provision as written, even if it believed that provision unreasonable).

160. *See In re* Marriage of Hahn, 324 Ill. App. 3d 44, 47, 754 N.E.2d 461, 463 (2001) ("[w]hen a term is susceptible to two different interpretations, the court must follow the interpretation that establishes a rational and probable agreement"; where agreement required child support until graduation from high school, support terminated when the child received General Education Development (GED) certificate); Janson v. Janson, 773 A.2d 901, 904 (R.I. 2001) ("when a provision in a settlement agreement is ambiguous, we have held that the practice of this Court is to 'adopt that construction which is most equitable and which will not give to one party an unconscionable advantage over the other'") (quoting Flynn v. Flynn, 615 A.2d 119, 122 (R.I. 1992)).

161. *See* Kuper v. Woodward, 684 A.2d 783, 784 (D.C. 1996) (agreement to pay support until child was "emancipated"; defining emancipation with reference to settled legal definition in cases with no agreement); Pate v. Pate, 280 Ga. 796, 797, 631 S.E.2d 103, 104 (2006) (where definition of "income" in child support provision was unclear, proper to construe agreement to adopt definition of income in relevant child support guidelines); Reno v. Haler, 734 N.E.2d 1095, 1099 (Ind. Ct. App. 2000) (where wife agreed to "joint custody," and term was not further defined, proper to apply meaning of joint custody in litigated cases; "[t]he provisions to which Wife now objects are consistent with Indiana's definition of joint legal custody, to which Wife agreed by signing" the agreement); *Janson*, 773 A.2d at 904 (where "agreement and the court's decision were silent with respect to when the wife was entitled to receive either actual or equivalent pension payments, the trial justice should have resolved the ambiguity based upon principles of equitable distribution").

162. *See* § **5.04**, note 89.

163. 145 N.M. 642, 203 P.3d 857 (2009).

The agreement was not clear as to whether payment had to be sent or received within 30 days. To avoid forfeiture of the wife's interest, the court held that the wife's payment was timely.

§ 5.07 Validity of Incomplete Agreements

In some cases, the agreement will fail to make any provision at all on a term that is relevant to the parties' bargain. When the term involved lies near the core of the parties' bargain, the traditional rule was that the agreement was too vague to be enforced. The standard example was a contract for the sale of goods that was silent as to quantity or price.[164]

A good example in the separation agreement context is *Walker v. Walker.*[165] The parties in that case made an oral stipulation to divide certain real property in kind. The stipulation was vague as to the share each spouse would receive, which is obviously an essential term in any stipulation dividing property. The extrinsic evidence showed that the minds of the parties never met on any plan for dividing the property. The trial court nevertheless adopted the husband's proposed construction, but the appellate court reversed. "Where, as here, the parties lack the requisite meeting of the minds when they enter into an oral stipulation, the appropriate relief is rescission of the stipulation."[166]

It is critical to note that the court in *Walker* clearly found that the language of the stipulation was ambiguous. When an agreement has a single plain meaning, that meaning controls even if it was not subjectively intended by one party. The law requires agreement on the *language* of the agreement, not upon its subjective interpretation. *See* § 5.04. Where the language is ambiguous, however, the evidence must show that the minds of the parties met as to all essential terms of the bargain. If the minds of the parties did not meet, the agreement may be too vague to be enforced.

Likewise, in *Miller v. Miller,*[167] the husband agreed "to begin setting funds aside for the minor children to attend post-secondary education." This language was unclear regarding material terms, and no parol evidence was introduced to remedy the lack of clarity. "The record contains no evidence whatsoever from which this court could clarify the intent of the parties as to: when Darrell was to begin setting aside funds; how much he was to set aside; where he was to place or invest the funds; and what percentage of the children's college education was to be borne by Darrell."[168] Because these terms were essential, the court refused to enforce the agreement. "Without any evidence of the parties' intent, in light of the above, we are constrained to set aside [the provision] related to the payment of college expenses for vagueness and ambiguity."[169]

---

164. *See generally* 17A AM. JUR. 2D *Contracts* §§ 190, 195 (Westlaw 2008).
165. 67 A.D.3d 1373, 888 N.Y.S.2d 823 (2009).
166. 888 N.Y.S.2d at 825.
167. 1 So. 3d 815, 816 (La. Ct. App. 2009).
168. *Id.* at 819.
169. *Id.*

It should be stressed one more time that only in rare cases will an agreement be unenforceable for vagueness. When essential terms are stated in objectively clear language, the language is enforceable even if one party claims to have had a different subjective intention, *see* § **5.04**. If essential terms are not stated clearly in the agreement itself, they can be supplied through parol evidence, *see* § **5.05**, or rules of construction, *see* § **5.06**, and sometimes even added by the court (*see* the discussion later in this section). The agreement is unenforceable only when *all* of these sources fail completely to provide a clear meaning for an essential term.[170]

Definition of an Essential Term

As noted above, the traditional rule was that the contract must include provisions addressing all terms that are essential to the parties' bargain. The trend in recent years has been to construe the definition of "essential terms" narrowly. The Uniform Commercial Code, for instance, allows the court to presume that a contract that is silent as to price was intended to require payment of a reasonable price.[171]

This trend is influencing case law on separation agreements. For instance, the modern trend is to enforce agreements that require a parent to pay "reasonable" college costs.[172] This situation is somewhat analogous to a missing price term, and a strong majority of the cases hold that the court can supply the missing term. A small minority of cases refuse to enforce terms of this sort, essentially holding that the term is so essential that the court cannot supply it.

Nonessential Terms: Addition by the Court

When an omitted term is not absolutely central to the parties' bargain, the common law recognizes a series of default rules for supplying a missing term.[173] These rules apply only where the agreement itself does not provide otherwise.

The only default rule applied in the separation agreement cases is the default rule regarding time. Where the agreement provides no time period within which an obligation must be performed, the law presumes that performance is due within a reasonable time.[174]

Default Rules versus Extrinsic Evidence

When the express terms of an agreement are silent on a relevant but nonessential term, should the court look first to extrinsic evidence, or should it look first to the default

---

170. *See In re* Marriage of Thompson, 27 S.W.3d 502, 506 (Mo. Ct. App. 2000) (division of accounts "in kind" could be resolved by the normal construction process, so that agreement was not void for vagueness).

171. UCC § 2-305.

172. *See* § **6.044**, note 657.

173. *See generally* RESTATEMENT (SECOND) OF CONTRACTS § 204 (1981).

174. *See* Cavanagh v. Cavanagh, 33 Mass. App. Ct. 240, 598 N.E.2d 677 (1992); Kendall v. Kendall, 44 A.D.3d 827, 828, 843 N.Y.S.2d 679, 680 (2007) (where agreement did not specify a time period for exercise of husband's option to refinance certain property, option must be exercised within a reasonable time); Ebert v. Ebert, 320 S.C. 331, 465 S.E.2d 121 (Ct. App. 1985).

rules for adding such terms set forth in this subsection? There was some suggestion in older cases that the default rules apply first. The clear modern trend, however, is to look first to extrinsic evidence. In other words, the default rules apply only where neither the agreement itself nor the extrinsic evidence reveals the terms of the parties' bargain.[175]

The *Restatement (Second) of Contracts* suggests that the default rule would apply where it is so well known that the parties must have been aware of it when they signed the agreement. As an example, the *Restatement* cites the case of an undated check. Even if there is an oral agreement not to cash the check for six months, the rule that an undated check can be cashed immediately is so clear and well known that the parties must have included it in their agreement. "[M]ost competent adults have reason to know the rule."[176] Conversely, the *Restatement* also cites the example of a check given to a person to whom the maker owes two separate debts. There is a default rule that a check applies to the debt that matured first, but that rule is not well understood by the general public, and extrinsic evidence of a different intention is therefore admissible.[177]

§ 5.08 Implied Obligation of Good Faith and Fair Dealing

Modern contract law construes every contract to contain an implied promise that the parties will implement its provisions in good faith, and that they will deal fairly with each other within the limits of the contractual language.[178]

"A marital dissolution agreement, like any other contract, contains an implied covenant of good faith and fair dealing both in the performance and in the interpretation of the contract."[179] For example, in *Belkin v. Belkin*,[180] the contract provided that the wife would obtain a mortgage on the marital home, and the husband would assist her in doing so. The wife filed only one mortgage application, which was denied, and refused to seek the husband's assistance. The court held that she had not made a good-faith effort to comply with her obligation, and that she was in breach of the agreement.[181]

---

175. *See generally* RESTATEMENT, *supra* note 174, § 216, cmt. b; 4 SAMUEL WILLISTON, A TREATISE ON THE LAW OF CONTRACTS § 440 (3d ed. 1961).

176. RESTATEMENT, *supra* note 174, § 216, cmt. b, illus. 1.

177. Id., illus. 2.

178. *See generally Id.* § 205 (1979).

179. Long v. McAllister-Long, 221 S.W.3d 1, 9 (Tenn. Ct. App. 2006).

180. 193 A.D.2d 573, 597 N.Y.S.2d 421 (1993).

181. *See also* Marquis v. Marquis, 175 Md. App. 734, 931 A.2d 1164 (2007) (husband breached implied duty of good faith by failing to cooperate with wife in obtaining qualified order awarding wife a stated percentage of military retirement benefits assigned to her in agreement); Larson v. Larson, 37 Mass. App. Ct. 106, 636 N.E.2d 1365 (1994) (where contract set support at percentage of earned income, husband breached implied duty of good faith by taking voluntary early retirement); *Long*, 221 S.W.3d at 9 (husband breached implied duty of good faith by failing to pay certain debts from which he was required to hold wife harmless); Elliott v. Elliott, 149 S.W.3d 77 (Tenn. Ct. App. 2004) (husband breached implied duty of good faith by failing to comply with wife's direction that certain stock options held for her benefit be exercised, and then failing to notify her of his failure).

In *Jacobsen v. Weiss*,[182] the agreement awarded to the husband the net proceeds from the sale of certain property. The wife failed to take all of the available tax deductions, so that the net proceeds were unreasonably small. The court held that in determining net proceeds, the wife would be charged with all tax deductions that she reasonably should have taken.

In adopting the above-discussed rule that an agreement will not be construed to permit one party to impose unreasonable adverse consequences upon the other,[183] some courts have specifically stated that such a construction would violate the implied duty of good faith.[184]

The implied obligation of good faith may apply to third parties as well. For instance, in *Badell v. Badell*,[185] the agreement provided that parties' tax refund would be allocated by their accountant. The court held that the contract required the accountant to act in good faith and not arbitrarily. Thus, the accountant's allocation of the tax refund was subject to judicial review, and it could be overturned if the accountant acted arbitrarily.

The implied obligation of good faith requires only that the parties make normal efforts to complete their agreement. In *State ex rel. LaBarge v. Clifford*,[186] the contract provided that the wife would receive certain payments from the husband when his debts were reduced to a stated level. The court held that the agreement imposed no duty upon the husband to reduce his debts to the stated amounts by any specific time. It noted, however, that there was no evidence that the husband was not acting in good faith. If the husband had been maintaining unusually large cash reserves and intentionally failing to pay off his debts, for the purpose of avoiding liability to the wife, the court might have reached a different result.

Along similar lines, in *Faith v. Faith*,[187] the contract expressly required the husband to use his best efforts to purchase a certain warehouse. If the purchase was not reasonably possible, the parties agreed to renegotiate their agreement. When the seller of the warehouse raised the price to an unreasonably high level, the husband voluntarily abandoned the transaction. The trial court held that because the husband's abandonment was voluntary, he had not used his best efforts to complete the sale. The appellate court reversed, noting that two expert witnesses had agreed without contradiction that the price demanded by the seller was commercially unreasonable. The obligation of

---

182. 260 A.D.2d 308, 689 N.Y.S.2d 75 (1999).

183. *See* § **5.06**, note 155.

184. *See* Burns v. Burns, 157 P.3d 1037, 1041 (Alaska 2007) (five-year minimum duration provision applied to spousal support generally and not only to payments from husband's dental practice income; otherwise husband could terminate support simply by switching careers; "[a]llowing Troy the unilateral power to reduce the support he owed would violate ... the principles of good faith and fair dealing"); Comras v. Comras, 195 A.D.2d 358, 600 N.Y.S.2d 61 (1993); Haskin v. Mendler, 184 A.D.2d 372, 584 N.Y.S.2d 851 (1992); *see* also § **6.031**, note 447 (cases citing implied duty of good faith and fair dealing as basis for holding that law of imputed income applies to definition of income under separation agreements).

185. 122 Idaho 442, 835 P.2d 677 (1992).

186. 979 S.W.2d 206 (Mo. Ct. App. 1998).

187. 709 So. 2d 600 (Fla. 3d Dist. Ct. App. 1998).

best efforts, the court held, did not require the husband to purchase the warehouse at any price. The court concluded that the husband had used his best efforts to buy the warehouse, but that those efforts had simply not been successful.

The implied obligation of good faith and fair dealing may not apply to an agreement that has *merged* into the divorce decree.[188]

§ 5.09 Drafting Errors in the Agreement

When construing the separation agreements, the court can look past typographical or clerical errors made by the drafter. This rule is another application of the general principle that the goal of construction is to determine the intention of the parties. If an inadvertent error of the scrivener causes the agreement to read differently from the true intent of the parties, the language of the agreement is not binding.

Most of the cases involve situations where because of a clerical error, the written agreement does not accurately state the real intention of the parties. In these cases, a strict construction of the agreement would lead to an impossible or absurd result. For example, in *Keffer v. Keffer*,[189] the contract contained an alimony formula that would give wife all of husband's income. The court held that the formula was the result of a drafting error, and it construed the agreement to provide for a different formula.[190]

The court is particularly likely to correct errors in the transcription of the parties' bargain when it finds that the drafting party has deliberately misstated that bargain in an attempt to obtain terms more favorable than those actually agreed upon. For instance, in *In re Marriage of Sievers*,[191] the court held that the party reducing a prior agreement to a formal writing has a duty of good faith to record the terms of the bargain accurately. The court then awarded attorney's fees as a sanction against a party who had breached that duty.

---

188. *See In re* Marriage of Corona, 172 Cal. App. 4th 1205, 1221, 92 Cal. Rptr. 3d 17, 30 (2009) ("we find no basis to imply a covenant of good faith and fair dealing—and corresponding duty— into the terms of the parties' merged judgment").

189. 852 P.2d 394 (Alaska 1993).

190. For additional cases correcting a drafting mistake, *see* Newell v. Hinton, 556 So. 2d 1037 (Miss. 1990) (parties agreed that wife would receive "1984" Mustang, but that car had been traded in for 1985 Mustang shortly before the agreement was signed; parties had obviously intended to award wife the new car); Ventura v. Leong, 68 A.D.3d 1318, 890 N.Y.S.2d 687, 689 (2009) (where separation agreement stated that it would not merge into judgment, and judgment incorporated agreement without expressing that it did not merge, reforming judgment to include nonmerger language; "the mistake in the judgment should be cured so as to conform its terms with the parties' unequivocal intent"); Emery v. Emery, 166 A.D.2d 787, 563 N.Y.S.2d 526 (1990) (husband's promise to pay wife the difference between their retirement incomes would be construed to mean half the difference; literal interpretation would lead to absurd result); Johnson v. Johnson, 379 N.W.2d 215 (Minn. Ct. App. 1985) (due to typographical error, support ceased on death or remarriage of "respondent" payor; reforming agreement so that support terminated on death of payee); Krysa v. Sieber, 113 Ohio App. 3d 572, 681 N.E.2d 949 (1996) (correcting mathematical error in computing amount of payment intended to equalize division of assets).

191. 78 Wash. App. 287, 897 P.2d 388 (1995).

When an alleged error is substantive rather than clerical, the error cannot be corrected as a matter of construction. Thus, the court generally cannot add a new term that was not present in a facially complete agreement.[192] It may be possible, however, to reform or even overturn the agreement under the law of substantive mistake. *See* **§ 4.054**.

---

192. *See In re* Marriage of Thomason, 802 P.2d 1189 (Colo. App. 1990) (husband agreed to pay wife $87,500 from his retirement fund, but contract was silent on tax consequences; trial court erred by requiring husband to hold wife harmless from any taxes incurred on the transfer); Brown v. Brown, 226 A.D.2d 1010, 641 N.Y.S.2d 209 (1996) (where agreement provided for termination only upon death, remarriage, or cohabitation, support did not terminate upon the additional condition of husband's retirement).

Construction of Separation Agreements: Application **6**

§ 6.01 Classifying the Provisions

The first step in determining the practical construction of any specific term is to determine whether that term is in the nature of property division, spousal support, or child support. Often, the applicable rules of construction will be different, depending upon which type of term is involved.

The first and most important piece of evidence on the nature of any term is that label given to that term by the agreement itself. As we shall see, however, that label is never automatically controlling. The nature of the term is determined by its contents, and the courts sometimes find that the contents of a term are different from its label.

§ 6.011 *Spousal Support versus Property Division*

The distinction between spousal support and property division is clear in theory, but it is sometimes unclear in practice. The conceptual difference is easily stated: Spousal support is intended to provide continuing financial assistance to maintain a certain standard of living after the divorce, while property division is intended to award the receiving spouse a certain specific share of property acquired before the divorce.

The major practical problem in distinguishing spousal support from property division is federal and state income tax law, which provides different tax consequences for the two types of payments.[1] For this reason, parties frequently mislabel payments in order to obtain more favorable tax

---

1. *See generally* 34 AM. JUR. 2D *Federal Taxation* ¶¶ 19,350–19,407 (Westlaw 2008).

treatment. Since labels attached for tax purposes are not controlling under the law of domestic relations, the court must look beneath the surface of the agreement to determine the true purpose of the payments.

Courts considering whether payments constitute property division or spousal support frequently consider parol evidence. "[T]he term 'alimony,' especially when used in separation agreements, may be described as latently ambiguous."[2]

In determining the true nature of periodic payments, courts look at a wide variety of factors.

Language of the Agreement. As noted above, a state divorce court is not bound by the manner in which the parties chose to label the payments.[3] That label is, however, one factor that the court can consider in determining the true purpose of the payments.[4] Labeling for general purposes is probably more important than labeling for tax or bankruptcy purposes, as there is a greater tendency to mislabel payments for these specific areas.[5]

Tax Treatment. The manner in which the parties have traditionally treated the payments on their income tax returns is likewise one relevant factor to be considered, but it is not in any sense dispositive of the question.[6]

---

2. D'Huy v. D'Huy, 390 Pa. Super. 509, 568 A.2d 1289, 1294, *allocatur denied*, 581 A.2d 572 (Pa. 1990) (quoting Kohn v. Kohn, 242 Pa. Super. 435, 364 A.2d 350 (1976)); Puckett *ex rel.* Puckett v. Puckett, 41 Wash. App. 78, 702 P.2d 477, 480 (1985) ("there is no magic in the use of terms such as alimony, maintenance or property award"), *overruled in part on other grounds*, Porter v. Porter, 107 Wash. 2d 43, 726 P.2d 459 (1986); *see also* Hayes v. Hayes, 100 N.C. App. 138, 394 S.E.2d 675 (1990) (where contract ambiguous, error to decide the question without holding a hearing and considering extrinsic evidence).

3. *See, e.g.*, Skvarch v. Skvarch, 876 P.2d 1110 (Alaska 1994) (payments were labeled as "rehabilitative alimony," but property division term stated the parties' interests in postsupport terms; obligation was property division); King v. King, 276 Mont. 500, 917 A.2d 434 (1996) (where wife received no interest in husband's business, payments that were labeled as maintenance were actually in the nature of property division); Holcomb v. Holcomb, 132 N.C. App. 744, 513 S.E.2d 807 (1999). *But see* Crosby v. Lebert, 285 Ga. 297, 676 S.E.2d 192 (2009) (where obligation to make car payments was labeled as alimony, summarily finding that obligation was alimony; no analysis of other factors.

4. *See* Ebert v. Ebert, 320 S.C. 331, 465 S.E.2d 121 (Ct. App. 1985) (relying in part upon clause in agreement stating that payments were not alimony for tax purposes).

5. *See* Braswell v. Braswell, 881 So. 2d 1193 (Fla. Dist. Ct. App. 2004) ($42 million payable at a rate of $6 million per year was property division; payments did not terminate upon death or remarriage, and were labeled as property division in general, although labeled as support for purposes of bankruptcy).

6. *E.g.*, Langley v. Johnson, 27 Va. App. 365, 499 S.E.2d 15 (1998).

Fairness of the Property Division. Where the payments labeled as property division do not fairly divide the available property, the court is more likely to find that payments labeled as support were actually intended as division of property. For instance, in *D'Huy v. D'Huy*,[7] the parties had three major marital assets. The agreement gave one of the assets to the children, and the husband received the other two in exchange for a lump sum payment. The payment was only a small portion of the worth of the assets. In addition, the husband agreed to make regular monthly payments to the wife for a period of 10 years. Because the payments were in a specific determinable amount and the lump sum payment was so small, the court held that the periodic payments were actually part of the property division.[8]

On the other hand, if the payments labeled as property division reach a fair division of the available property, or reach a division that favors the support recipient, payments labeled as support are more likely to actually constitute support. For example, in *Berry v. Berry*,[9] the wife received almost all of the marital estate plus periodic payments "for her support and maintenance" equal to half of husband's retirement pay. Because the division of marital property was already so favorable to the wife, the court held that the periodic payments were not consideration for property settlement.

Time of Termination. Payments that cease upon death or remarriage are generally treated as spousal support, even if they are labeled as property division. Property division rights are absolute, and the presence of these conditions, which are traditionally applied to spousal support awards, is good evidence that the payments are in the nature

---

7. 390 Pa. Super. 509, 568 A.2d 1289 (1990).

8. *See also* McIntyre v. McIntyre, 824 So. 2d 206 (Fla. Dist. Ct. App. 2002) ($3,500 per month for an indefinite duration, terminable upon wife's death or remarriage, was nevertheless property division; obligation was labeled as such in agreement, alimony was expressly waived, and division of other assets greatly favored husband); Brinkmann v. Brinkmann, 772 N.E.2d 441, 446 (Ind. Ct. App. 2002) ($277,240 in weekly installments over 10 years and one month was property division; noting that property division would not comply with statutory equal division presumption of payments were alimony); Chroniger v. Chroniger, 914 So. 2d 311, 315 (Miss. Ct. App. 2005) (36 monthly payments in fixed amounts were nonmodifiable lump sum alimony; payments were consideration for property division); *King*, 276 Mont. 500, 917 A.2d 434 (where wife received no interest in husband's business, payments that were labeled as maintenance were actually in the nature of property division); *Ebert*, 320 S.C. 331, 465 S.E.2d 121 (agreement stated that wife was receiving 35 percent of marital estate, and her share was almost exactly 35 percent if transfer of home was treated as property division; transfer was not spousal support).

9. 550 So. 2d 1125, 1126 (Fla. Dist. Ct. App. 1989), *cert. denied*, 563 So. 2d 631 (1990).

of support.[10] One court even went so far as to suggest that payments that terminate upon death or remarriage cannot as a matter of law be treated as property division.[11]

Payments that expressly do not terminate upon death or remarriage are more likely to be treated a property division.[12]

If payments terminate when the recipient becomes eligible to receive other benefits, such as social security or retirement benefits, that fact is some evidence that the payments are spousal support.[13]

Modifiable Payments. Payments that are subject to modification are generally spousal support, as property division payments are not subject to subsequent modification.[14]

---

10. *See* Howard v. Janowski, 226 A.D.2d 1087, 641 N.Y.S.2d 940 (1996); Petty v. Petty, 548 So. 2d 793 (Fla. Dist. Ct. App. 1989) (payments were alimony, where they ceased upon remarriage and were in separate section from property division provisions); *Langley*, 27 Va. App. 365, 499 S.E.2d 15 (fact that payments terminated upon death was some evidence that they were in the nature of spousal support); *cf.* Deel v. Deel, 909 N.E.2d 1028 (Ind. Ct. App. 2009) (absence of provision continuing payments after recipient's death was some evidence that payments were spousal support). *But see McIntyre*, 824 So. 2d 206 ($3,500 per month for an indefinite duration, terminable upon wife's death or remarriage, was nevertheless property division; obligation was labeled as such in agreement, alimony was expressly waived, and division of other assets greatly favored husband).

McIntyre is distinctly outside the general consensus that indefinite payments, terminating on the recipient's death or remarriage, are spousal support. In light of the unequal division of other assets, the court would have done better to hold that the case involved a integrated bargain, in which property division and alimony were reciprocal consideration for one another. *See* § **6.012**.

11. Kizziah v. Kizziah, 651 N.E.2d 297 (Ind. Ct. App. 1995).

12. *See* Braswell v. Braswell, 881 So. 2d 1193 (Fla. Dist. Ct. App. 2004) ($42 million payable at a rate of $6 million per year was property division; payments did not terminate upon death or remarriage, and were labeled as property division in general, although labeled as support for purposes of bankruptcy); *Brinkmann*, 772 N.E.2d at 446 ($277,240 in weekly installments over 10 years and one month, with 5 percent interest, surviving the recipient's death or remarriage; "it is apparent from the settlement agreement language that this is a property settlement," even though payments were labeled as alimony).

13. *See Deel*, 909 N.E.2d 1028 (where "[t]he termination of payments at age sixty-five coincides with Wife becoming eligible for Social Security and Medicare," payments were spousal support).

14. *See* Joyce v. Joyce, 563 So. 2d 1126 (Fla. Dist. Ct. App. 1990) (payments were alimony, where property division provisions were in separate provision of agreement, there was no evidence that the payments were additional consideration for the property, and the payments were expressly modifiable under certain circumstances); *In re* Marriage of Miller, 207 Or. App. 198, 140 P.3d 1172 (2006) (monthly obligation was labeled as spousal support, did not bear interest, and was modifiable if husband's income dropped; wife was in need of support to transition into the job market; obligation constituted spousal support).

Likewise, a self-modifying obligation is more likely to be spousal support. *Langley*, 27 Va. App. 365, 499 S.E.2d 15 (presence of consumer price index escalator provision was some evidence that obligation constituted spousal support).

Payments of Variable Amount. Along similar lines, where the payments vary in amount depending upon the financial conditions of the parties, they are more likely to be spousal support.[15]

Payments of a Definite Amount. When the payments are in a definite amount, they are more likely to be property division,[16] especially if interest accrues on any unpaid balance.[17] When they are in an indefinite amount, they are more likely to be spousal support.

Interest. Installment payments on a property division obligation should ideally require payment of interest from the date of divorce forward, as property division obligations are generally due at the time of divorce.[18] The absence of an interest provision is therefore one factor suggesting that the payments are spousal support.[19]

Section of the Agreement. Courts will sometimes attach particular importance to the section of the agreement in which the obligation appears. For instance, in *Myers v. Myers*,[20] the husband agreed to pay "maintenance," but the provision was located in the property division paragraph and could at the husband's option be paid directly out of his military retirement pay. A separate paragraph established another obligation that was labeled as alimony. The court had little trouble finding that the "maintenance"

---

15. *See In re* Estate of Shatraw, 66 A.D.3d 1293, 1294, 887 N.Y.S.2d 722, 723–24 (2009) (agreement awarded husband's pension to wife "in lieu of maintenance," and expressly provided that if "the pension benefit is not provided to the wife, then she reserves the right to seek alimony/maintenance"; agreement also allowed husband to retain $500 per month from pension under certain circumstances; because "the amount the husband was required to pay the wife under this provision of the agreement was dependent upon his existing financial situation, . . . the purpose of the pension payments was to provide the wife with a form of maintenance").

16. *See Braswell*, 881 So. 2d 1193 ($42 million payable at a rate of $6 million per year was property division; payments did not terminate upon death or remarriage, and were labeled as property division in general, although labeled as support for purposes of bankruptcy); *In re* Marriage of Dundas, 355 Ill. App. 3d 423, 427, 823 N.E.2d 239, 243 (2005) (husband's promise to pay wife's car loan was property division and not maintenance, where payments ceased when loan ended, and agreement expressly waived maintenance for both parties); D'Huy v. D'Huy, 390 Pa. Super. 509, 568 A.2d 1289 (1990).

17. *Brinkmann*, 772 N.E.2d at 446 ($277,240 in weekly installments over 10 years and one month, with 5 percent interest, surviving the recipient's death or remarriage; "it is apparent from the settlement agreement language that this is a property settlement," even though payments were labeled as alimony).

Postjudgment interest on *past due* payments has the same character as the payments themselves. Thus, interest on property division payments is property division, and interest on spousal support payments is spousal support. *Braswell*, 881 So. 2d 1193.

18. *See generally* BRETT R. TURNER, EQUITABLE DISTRIBUTION OF PROPERTY § 9:10 (3d ed. 2005).

19. *See* Deel v. Deel, 909 N.E.2d 1028 (Ind. Ct. App. 2009) .

20. 560 N.E.2d 39, 40 (Ind. 1990).

payments were property division.[21] Conversely, in *Jacobson v. Jacobson*,[22] the payments were also called "maintenance," but the property division provisions were located in a separate section elsewhere in the agreement. The court held that the payments were clearly spousal support.[23]

Along similar lines, where spousal support is expressly waived in the agreement, periodic payments are more likely to be treated as property division.[24]

Maintenance of Property. Payments to maintain property pending sale are generally treated as property division.[25]

Periodic monetary payments to support a spouse pending sale would seem to be support. One court reached a contrary result where extrinsic evidence suggested that the payments were compensation for interest that would have been earned on a monetary award if sale had not been delayed.[26]

Bankruptcy Cases. The above discussion is based only upon cases considering whether an obligation is property division or spousal support under state domestic relations law. This issue also arises under bankruptcy law, as the controlling rules for discharge of property division obligations are very different from the controlling rules for discharge of spousal support obligations.[27] Because the federal cases clearly apply federal common law, they are not precedential authority in state domestic relations law

---

21. *See also* Stockbridge v. Reeves, 640 So. 2d 947 (Ala. Ct. App. 1994) (provision requiring payment from retirement benefits, located in section with the heading "Property Settlement," was in the nature of property division).

22. 177 Wis. 2d 539, 502 N.W.2d 869 (Ct. App. 1993).

23. *See also* Cortese v. Cortese, 341 Mont. 287, 289, 176 P.3d 1064, 1066 (2008) (where "the property distribution and maintenance provisions are in separate sections of the agreement," and "the separation agreement's provisions concerning its tax consequences reiterate that only the provisions in the maintenance section . . . constitute maintenance," payments set forth in maintenance section were spousal support).

24. *See* Stacy v. Stacy, 53 Va. App. 38, 669 S.E.2d 348 (2008) (where agreement expressly waived all spousal support, trial court erred by holding that obligation to make mortgage payment was spousal support, even though agreement stated that provision was in the nature of spousal support for bankruptcy purposes).

25. *See* Ebert v. Ebert, 320 S.C. 331, 465 S.E.2d 121 (Ct. App. 1985).

26. *Id.* (noting also that the agreement stated that the payments were not alimony for tax purposes).

27. To summarize the controlling rules briefly, spousal support obligations are never dischargeable. 11 U.S.C. § 523 (a)(5) (Westlaw 2011). Property division obligations to a spouse are not dischargeable in chapter 11 cases, *id.* § 523(a)(15), but are dischargeable under chapter 13 cases. *Id.* § 1328(a)(2) (including § 523(a)(5), but not § 523(a)(15), in the list of exemptions to discharge under Chapter 13); *see generally* Turner, *supra* note 18, § 9:22; Brett R. Turner, *The Vampire Rises: Discharge of Property Division Obligations under Chapter 13 of the Bankruptcy Code in Post-2005 Litigation*, 19 Divorce Litig. 1 (January 2007).

cases.[28] They are, however, a very close analogy. The bankruptcy cases lie outside the scope of this volume, but they have been well summarized in other sources.[29]

A provision stating that an obligation is in the nature of spousal support for bankruptcy purposes may not necessarily mean that the provision constitutes spousal support under state law.[30]

Lump Sum Spousal Support

The distinction between spousal support and property division substantially overlaps the distinction between lump sum and periodic alimony. Where the court analyzes the issue as a choice between periodic alimony for support or lump sum alimony for the purpose of dividing property, it is essentially deciding the same alimony versus property division issue addressed above.

There may be cases, however, in which the parties agree to lump sum payments for purposes of support. Such payments are usually treated similarly to property division, in that they are not modifiable and do not terminate on remarriage.[31]

The fundamental distinction between periodic and lump sum alimony normally depends upon the certainty of the amount. If the amount of the payments is uncertain, the obligation is clearly periodic in nature. For example, in *Miller v. Hawkins*,[32] the agreement called for support until child reached age 23 or graduated from college. Because it was impossible to determine with certainty when the child would graduate, the total amount payable could not be computed in advance. The court held that the obligation was periodic and not lump sum support, so that it terminated upon remarriage.

Likewise, an express clause permitting modification by the court normally indicates a periodic award.[33] Modification is permitted only if the award is periodic in nature.

Lump sum and periodic alimony can be especially hard to distinguish when the lump sum is payable in installments. One recent decision rejected a proposed rule that all contingent or conditional obligations are periodic alimony, and instead held that the proper characterization depends on the intent of the parties. Where the contract labeled

---

28. "Because whether an obligation is maintenance or part of the parties' property settlement is a question of state law, separate from and unaffected by whether the payments constituted a dischargeable debt under federal bankruptcy law, we do not find the cases to which respondent cites controlling here, as no bankruptcy proceeding is involved." *In re* Marriage of Dundas, 355 Ill. App. 3d 423, 427, 823 N.E.2d 239, 243 (2005).

29. *See generally* Amy G. Gore, *Property and Support Obligations in Bankruptcy Cases*, 5 DIVORCE LITIG. 22 (1993); Annotation, *Debts for Alimony, Maintenance and Support as Exceptions to Bankruptcy Discharge*, 69 A.L.R. FED. 403 (1984 & Supp. 1999).

30. *See Stacy*, 53 Va. App. 38, 669 S.E.2d 348 (where agreement expressly waived all spousal support, trial court erred by holding that obligation to make mortgage payment was spousal support, even though agreement stated that provision was in the nature of spousal support for bankruptcy purposes).

31. *E.g.*, Mallery-Sayre v. Mallery, 6 Va. App. 471, 370 S.E.2d 113 (1988).

32. 14 Va. App. 192, 415 S.E.2d 861 (1992).

33. *Id.*

the payments "alimony in gross" and stated the amount as a total sum payable in a specific number of installments, the payments were held to be lump sum alimony.[34]

Where the amount is certain and the agreement is silent on modification, but the obligation is stated as a periodic amount rather than a lump sum, the trend is to find the obligation periodic.[35] Where the obligation is stated as a single amount, the cases tend to find the obligation to be lump sum support.[36] The method of statement is only a general guideline, however, and it is not controlling in every instance.[37]

Mississippi has a formal presumption that alimony is periodic unless the agreement clearly provides that it is lump sum.[38]

§ 6.012 Integrated Bargain Agreements

The above analysis of property division and spousal support payments assumes that the two types of payments are independent from each other. In at least some cases, however, the spousal support provisions and the property division provisions will be consideration for each other. For example, the wife might agree to reduced alimony in exchange for a larger share of the divisible estate. When the property division and spousal support provisions are interrelated in this manner, the contract is said to be an integrated bargain agreement.

The burden of proving that the contract is an integrated bargain agreement lies upon the proponent.[39] What must be proven is simply the fact that the property division and the spousal support provisions were consideration for each other—that is, that the parties intended to strike one inseverable bargain on both issues, rather than striking an independent settlement of each one. In most situations, if the property division and support provisions are each similar to what the court would have ordered without the

---

34. Turner v. Turner, 180 Mich. App. 170, 446 N.W.2d 608 (1989).

35. *See* Shepherd v. Collins, 283 Ga. 124, 125, 657 S.E.2d 197, 198–99 (2008) (obligation to make exactly 180 payments in varying but stated monthly amounts, not terminable upon remarriage, but terminable upon death, was periodic alimony); *In re* Marriage of Harris, 284 Ill. App. 3d 389, 672 N.E.2d 393, 394 (1996) ($606 per month in "transitional maintenance" for 10-year period was periodic support).

36. *See* John v. John, 893 S.W.2d 373 (Ky. Ct. App. 1995) (agreement to pay $1,320,000 over 10 years was lump sum support); McDonald v. McDonald, 683 So. 2d 929, 931 (Miss. 1996) (agreement to pay $660,000 in "lump sum alimony" in monthly installments was lump sum obligation even though it ceased upon husband's death).

37. *See, e.g.*, Pinka v. Pinka, 206 Mich. App. 101, 520 N.W.2d 371 (1994) (contract required alimony until death or remarriage or passage of four years; "[t]hereafter alimony . . . shall be forever barred"; obligation was lump sum support, even though stated in periodic terms).

38. *See* West v. West, 891 So. 2d 203, 212–13 (Miss. 2004) ("Unless it is clear from the record what sort of alimony award is given, we must construe the alimony as being periodic and not lump sum"; obligation that appeared to be periodic, but that was referred to as lump sum in court order approving agreement, was periodic).

39. *See, e.g.*, Gignilliat v. Gignilliat, 723 So. 2d 90 (Ala. Ct. App. 1998); Keeler v. Keeler, 958 P.2d 599 (Idaho Ct. App. 1998) (evidence of integration must be clear and convincing, and apparent from the face of the agreement); Holcomb v. Holcomb, 132 N.C. App. 744, 513 S.E.2d 807 (1999); Williams v. Williams, 120 N.C. App. 707, 463 S.E.2d 815, *aff'd mem.*, 343 N.C. 299, 469 S.E.2d 553 (1995).

agreement, the two provisions are probably independent of each other. The common feature of most integrated bargains is therefore that the parties set the level of support either artificially high or artificially low, as consideration for an offsetting difference of roughly equal value in the opposite direction in the property division provisions.

A provision stating expressly that the agreement does or does not contain an integrated bargain is significant evidence that an integrated bargain is or is not present. Such a provision may not be controlling, however, if it conflicts with other provisions of the agreement.[40]

The presence of a provision stating that the contract is the parties' entire bargain is irrelevant to whether the agreement states an integrated bargain.[41] The mere fact that property division and support awards are made at the same time is likewise not sufficient to show an integrated bargain.[42]

As explained below, *see* §§ **6.032, 6.034**, payments in integrated bargain agreements are treated like property division payments: They are not modifiable, and they do not terminate on remarriage.[43]

There is obviously a considerable overlap between integrated bargains and disguised property settlements. In the authors' opinion, however, both concepts are useful. The concept of disguised property settlement focuses upon the fact situation where, most often for tax purposes, a lump sum monetary award intended to equalize the property division is stated in the form of alimony. Where a disguised property settlement is involved, one expects to find at least some evidence that property division was intended: perhaps a lump sum amount payable in installments, or a nonmodifiability clause, or at least extrinsic evidence suggesting that the purpose of the award was to divide property. In some cases, however, the parties truly do exchange increased or decreased traditional spousal support payments for a smaller or larger property division

---

40. *See* Holmes v. Holmes, 17 So. 3d 666, 673 (Ala. Ct. App. 2009) (where agreement provided that it was an integrated bargain, but also provided that spousal support would be modifiable, provisions were conflicting; remanding for consideration of parol evidence).

41. *Holcomb*, 132 N.C. App. 744, 513 S.E.2d 807. *But cf.* Beasley v. Beasley, 707 So. 2d 1107 (Ala. Ct. App. 1997) (where contract contained both a no-modification clause and an entire bargain clause, plain language revealed integrated bargain).

The no-modification clause in *Beasley* was a mere general provision against unwritten modification, a provision that some courts have held does not apply to the court. *See* § **6.032**, note 278. Assuming that the provision did apply to the court, it was alone a sufficient basis for finding an integrated bargain.

To the extent that *Beasley* relied upon the presence of an entire bargain clause, its holding is illogical. As *Holcomb* noted, the fact that an agreement recites the parties' entire bargain says nothing about whether that bargain is integrated or severable. Future decisions should therefore avoid construing *Holcomb* to provide that the presence of an entire bargain clause is alone sufficient evidence of an integrated bargain.

42. *Gignilliat*, 723 So. 2d 90.

43. *See generally* DuValle v. DuValle, 348 So. 2d 1067 (Ala. Civ. App. 1977); O'Hara v. O'Hara, 564 So. 2d 1230 (Fla. Dist. Ct. App. 1990); Lemons v. Lemons, 112 N.C. App. 110, 434 S.E.2d 638 (1993); Hayes v. Hayes, 100 N.C. App. 138, 394 S.E.2d 675 (1990); *see generally* Annotation, *Modification of Agreement-Based Divorce Decree—Alimony*, 61 A.L.R.3D 520 §§ 19–23 (1975 & Westlaw Supp. 2008).

award.[44] When the parties agree to exchange greater support for less property, or less support for greater property, the fact of that exchange must have consequences upon modification and termination. To modify or terminate the support award in these circumstances is to alter the terms of the underlying bargain in a manner that the law should not permit.

The risk of relying only upon the disguised property settlement concept, while ignoring the integrated bargain concept, is that the law will place too much importance upon whether the payments have at least some of the attributes of property division. Even where those attributes are entirely absent, however, payments that were intended as reciprocal consideration for the property division should be treated as property division. The concept of an integrated bargain focuses directly upon whether the parties *intended* the property division and support provisions to be reciprocal. The concept of a disguised property settlement, by contrast, tends to focus on whether the payments have at least some of the common characteristics of a lump sum property division award. Because each concept focuses upon a different key fact, the concepts are ultimately complementary and not confusing.

§ 6.013 Spousal Support versus Child Support

The distinction between child support and spousal support can also be difficult to draw. The fundamental difference between the two payments is again simply stated: Spousal support is for the benefit of the receiving spouse, while child support is for the benefit of the children.

Some courts have approached this issue simplistically, holding that the label given to the payments controls. For example, in *Harris v. Harris*,[45] the court held under the parol evidence rule that "alimony" payment constitute spousal and not child support.[46] Most states, however, are willing to consider the possibility that the label might not be controlling, especially when payments that are labeled in one manner are subject to contingencies associated with the other.

For instance, in *Terry v. Terry*,[47] the contract required certain payments "for support of minor children." The payments continued until a specific date, however, and ended before that time only if the wife remarried, the children were emancipated, *and* they completed their "formal education." Because of the specific termination date and the express mention of remarriage, the court held that the payments were spousal support.

---

44. *See, e.g.*, Lucas v. Elliott, 3 Cal. App. 4th 888, 4 Cal. Rptr. 2d 746, 747 (1992) ("Relying on all provisions of the agreement, including in part, the division of property," agreement called for spousal support; support was the product of integrated bargain); Keffer v. Keffer, 852 P.2d 394 (Alaska 1993) (wife waived her interest in retirement benefits in exchange for additional alimony).

45. 553 So. 2d 129 (Ala. Civ. App. 1989).

46. *See also* DeBoer v. DeBoer, 669 N.E.2d 415 (Ind. Ct. App. 1996) (payments labeled as "alimony" can be property division or spousal support, but not child support); Shapiro v. Shapiro, 346 Md. 648, 697 A.2d 1342 (1997) (incorporation of agreement requiring payment of "alimony" was res judicata that payments were not child support).

47. 28 Ark. App. 169, 771 S.W.2d 321, 321 (1989).

Similarly, in *Petty v. Petty*,[48] the agreement provided that the wife would receive periodic payments. The payments were denominated as "permanent alimony," but the contract expressly stated that the wife would use the payments to support children as well as herself. On the other hands, the payments ceased upon remarriage, and were in a separate section from provisions dealing with children. The payments were again held to be spousal support.[49]

Unified Support

Distinguishing spousal support from child support is most difficult when the contract calls for unified support: a single lump sum periodic payment to support both spouse and children. In this instance, the court must first look to any evidence that the parties intended a specific part of the lump sum to be for a particular purpose.[50] For instance, in *Lieberman v. Lieberman*,[51] the husband agreed to pay the wife $2,600 per month for three years; $2,400 per month for the following three years; and $1,800 per month thereafter. The payments were reduced by $900 per month upon the death, custody change, emancipation, or remarriage of each of the parties' two children. In light of the overall schedule, the court had little difficulty concluding that the first $1,800 per month was child support, and that all additional payments were spousal support.[52]

Where there is no indication that the parties intended any specific allocation of the payments, the court may or may not be able to allocate the payments itself. In *Carey v. Carey*,[53] where no allocation was evident from the face of the contract, the court held that no allocation could be made and treated the entire amount as nonmodifiable spousal support. Conversely, in *Nooner v. Nooner*,[54] the court held without discussion that

---

48. 548 So. 2d 793 (Fla. Dist. Ct. App. 1989).

49. *See also* Rockefeller v. Rockefeller, 225 Ark. 145, 980 S.W.2d 255 (1998) (payments were treated as alimony for tax purposes, and their amount remained unchanged after a change in custody of the minor children; payments were alimony and not child support); Bondy v. Levy, 121 Idaho 993, 829 P.2d 1342 (1992) (agreement expressly stated that payments were made under I.R.C. § 71, which provides that spousal support is deductible for tax purposes, but amount dropped if husband retained custody of children for a significant period; agreement was ambiguous on whether payments were partly child support; remanding for extrinsic evidence).

50. *See* Wagner v. Wagner, 885 So. 2d 488 (Fla. Dist. Ct. App. 2004) ("the trial court must resolve . . . what portions of the family support payment the parties intended to allocate to spousal and child support, respectively"); Huhn v. Stuckmann, 321 Wis. 2d 169, 176, 772 N.W.2d 744, 748 (Ct. App. 2009) (issue is not whether payments are "primarily" spousal or child support; remanding with instructions to consider possibility that the obligation had both spousal support and child support components).

51. 81 Md. App. 575, 568 A.2d 1157 (1990).

52. *See also* Beard v. Beard, 12 Kan. App. 2d 540, 750 P.2d 1059 (1988) (contract reduced unified support by 25 percent upon emancipation of each of two children, and by 50 percent upon wife's remarriage; dicta that unified sum was half alimony and half child support); O'Hara v. O'Hara, 564 So. 2d 1230 (Fla. Dist. Ct. App. 1990) (payments were spousal support, where they were classified as alimony for tax purposes, and neither party had introduced much evidence on the children's needs when seeking to modification); Carter v. Carter, 215 Va. 475, 211 S.E.2d 253 (1975) (trial court properly allocated unified sum evenly among wife and two children).

53. 9 Kan. App. 2d 779, 689 P.2d 917 (1984).

54. 278 Ark. 360, 645 S.W.2d 671 (1983).

unified support could always be allocated by the court. The court presumably intended to permit allocation even if the actual intention of the parties could not be determined.

§ 6.014 Property Division versus Child Support

Property division and child support awards are unlikely to be confused in most cases. One exception is provisions for exclusive use of the marital home, which are usually an incident of child support where minor children are involved.[55] The same rule sometimes applies when one spouse is ordered to make mortgage payments on the home.[56] Where a term that appears to be property division is actually in the nature of child support, the term is subject to the court's modification power. *See generally* **§ 6.042**.

Provisions regarding the income tax exemption for dependent child are also usually child support rather than property division.[57]

§ 6.02 Property Division Provisions

The most important substantive portion of most separation agreements is the provision or provisions that divide the parties' property. In many cases, the property division will be the most substantial part of the agreement in absolute dollar terms. Even where the support provisions do transfer more dollars, their full effect is not felt until the future, so that the property division has more immediate financial significance. Also, the property division provisions are normally drafted first, as the parties cannot determine their support needs until they know how their property will be divided.

§ 6.021 Assets Divided by the Agreement

The parties are generally free to transfer in a separation agreement ownership of any asset they own. Because the agreement is enforced under the law of contracts and not the law of property division, the agreement may divide assets that could not be divided by the court if the agreement did not exist. *See* **§ 3.04**. Likewise, the court may enforce a property division contract between the parties even where the court would lack jurisdiction to apply the relevant property division statute.[58]

---

55. *See, e.g.*, Kuscik v. Kuscik, 154 A.D.2d 655, 546 N.Y.S.2d 659 (1989) (provision requiring husband to pay certain expenses on wife's home was child support; obligation therefore stopped upon emancipation, even though agreement stated no termination condition); *see generally* 24 Am. Jur. 2d *Divorce & Separation* § 1010 (Westlaw 2008).

56. *See* Keesee v. Keesee, 48 Ark. App. 113, 891 S.W.2d 70 (1995) (provision requiring home payments until youngest child turned 18 was child support; agreement required only minimal direct child support); Swartz v. Swartz, 456 Pa. Super. 16, 689 A.2d 302 (1997) (treating mortgage obligation as child support). *But cf.* Kraisinger v. Kraisinger, 928 A.2d 333 (Pa. Super. Ct. 2007) (husband's obligation to purchase farm for wife and make future mortgage payments was property division, not child support; obligation labeled as property division, and "the length of the payments is not in any way related to the age of the children or any other milestone in the children's lives"; wife had power to sell farm at any time and use proceeds for her own benefit).

57. *See, e.g.*, Freeman v. Freeman, 29 Ark. App. 137, 778 S.W.2d 222 (1989).

58. Grider v. Grider, 62 Ark. App. 99, 968 S.W.2d 653 (1998) (legal separation action).

No particular formal words are required in order to transfer an asset to a party. Any language indicating transfer of ownership is generally sufficient to indicate the parties' intent. Language that appears suggestive rather than mandatory, however, may not be sufficient.[59]

Fixed Amount versus Percentage

When an asset is divided in kind, the agreement is sometimes unclear as to whether each spouse's share is a fixed amount or a percentage. Where a percentage is intended, the agreement is sometimes ambiguous as to when the percentage is to be measured. This issue is closely related to the amount of a monetary award made for the purpose of dividing a specific asset, and the cases are therefore discussed in § **6.025**.

Retirement Benefits

Retirement benefits are among the most common types of property owned by divorcing parties, and there is a substantial body of law construing separation agreement dividing such benefits.

Provisions dividing "retirement benefits" are generally applied to any benefit that is awarded as a return of prior contributions, even if the employer gives the benefits another name. For instance, agreements that divide military retirement benefits apply to all postretirement benefits received from the military, even if those benefits are labeled as "retainer pay" rather than "retired pay."[60] A provision dividing "retirement funds of any description" applied to a 401(k) plan labeled by the employer as a "Savings and Investment Plan."[61] An agreement dividing "post-retirement benefit increases" gave the wife a share of enhanced retirement benefits due to early retirement, although it did not apply to entirely new early retirement benefits created by the employer after the divorce.[62]

---

59. *See* Despathy v. Despathy, 149 N.C. App. 660, 662, 562 S.E.2d 289, 291 (2002) (agreement provided that 1967 Buick "should be distributed to Wife," while 1970 Buick "should be distributed to Husband"; language was only a suggestion for the court and was not mandatory).

60. *See* Feick v. Thrutchley, 322 Md. 111, 586 A.2d 3 (1991); *In re* Marriage of Lawson, 409 N.W.2d 181 (Iowa 1987).

61. Holloman v. Holloman, 691 So. 2d 897, 898 (Miss. 1996); *see also* Dougherty v. Dougherty, 109 Conn. App. 33, 42–43, 950 A.2d 592, 598–99 (2008) (husband's "defined benefit retirement plan" included both his "annuity savings account and a monthly pension paid for life"; noting that husband's financial affidavits "were misleading as to the nature and value of the plaintiff's deferred compensation benefits"); Johnson v. Johnson, 37 S.W.3d 892, 896 (Tenn. 2001) ("'All military retirement benefits' . . . comprehensively references all amounts to which the retiree would ordinarily be entitled as a result of retirement from the military[.]"); Hale v. Hale, 42 Va. App. 27, 32, 590 S.E.2d 66, 68 (2003) ("[w]e interpret the word 'plan' to encompass the sum of all individual plans husband's employer provided, including both the UNICare and the 401(k) plans"). *But see* Dreiss v. Dreiss, 258 A.D.2d 499, 684 N.Y.S.2d 627, 628 (1999) (agreement dividing "certain pension plans" and "net pension benefits" did not apply to savings and investment account).

62. Olivo v. Olivo, 82 N.Y.2d 202, 624 N.E.2d 151, 604 N.Y.S.2d 23 (1993); *see also* Royalty v. Royalty, 264 S.W.3d 679, 685 (Mo. Ct. App. 2008) (stated percentage division of "the pension and retirement plan" applied to subsidized early retirement benefits).

The same rule applies to voluntary separation incentives and special separation benefits, special military benefits given to service members who retire voluntarily before their normal retirement benefits vest. These benefits are treated as benefits acquired in exchange for normal benefits, and thus within the scope of a provision dividing "retirement benefits."[63]

One court even went so far as to hold that life insurance can constitute a retirement account. In *Rushton v. Lott*,[64] the agreement awarded the husband his "retirement accounts." The wife testified that she believe the life insurance at issue to be similar to an IRA, and she introduced some evidence that both parties had treated the insurance as an IRA in negotiating the agreement. The court upheld a trial court decision accepting the wife's position. This case reaches to the very limits of what can be called a retirement benefit. A court could easily have held that the plain meaning of the term "retirement account" simply does not include life insurance, and that contrary extrinsic evidence was inadmissible under the parol evidence rule. *See* §§ **5.04–5.05**.

Broad provisions referring to property in general may or may not apply to retirement benefits. In *McCarroll v. McCarroll*,[65] the issue was whether a reference to "all movable property" included retirement benefits. The court held that the phrase in question was ambiguous. Based upon extrinsic evidence, it held that retirement benefits did fall within the scope of the provision.

Disability Benefits. Where the agreement divides retirement benefits, and the owning spouse receives disability benefits, the disability benefits are still divisible to the extent that they are consideration for loss of marital retirement benefits or a return of prior marital contributions.[66] To the extent that the benefits reflect insurance-type compensa-

---

63. Kelson v. Kelson, 675 So. 2d 1370 (Fla. 1996); *see also* Boedeker v. Larson, 44 Va. App. 508, 605 S.E.2d 764 (2004) (where agreement divided husband's military retirement benefits, and husband later received career status bonus under 37 U.S.C.A. § 322 that materially reduced his military retirement, bonus was divisible under the agreement).

64. 330 S.C. 418, 499 S.E.2d 222, 223 (Ct. App. 1998).

65. 680 So. 2d 681, 685 (La. Ct. App. 1996), *aff'd & rev'd on other grounds*, 701 So. 2d 1280 (La. 1997).

66. Evans v. Evans, 820 A.2d 394, 397 (Del. Fam. Ct. 2001) ("disability retirement benefits, received as a result of an injury occurring after the parties' divorce, are properly considered retirement benefits pursuant to a settlement agreement between the parties") (applying Maryland law); *In re* Marriage of Schurtz, 382 Ill. App. 3d 1123, 1125, 891 N.E.2d 415, 417–18 (2008) (where agreement divided retirement benefits, and husband received disability benefits in lieu of retirement benefits, trial court properly construed agreement to divide disability benefits); Davis v. Davis, 286 Ill. App. 3d 1065, 678 N.E.2d 68 (1997); Fultz v. Shaffer, 111 Md. App. 278, 681 A.2d 568 (1996); Dexter v. Dexter, 105 Md. App. 678, 661 A.2d 171 (1995); Lebac v. Lebac, 109 Md. App. 396, 675 A.2d 131 (1996).

A large body of case law applies this doctrine to require a military service member to compensate a former spouse for loss of retirement benefits upon election of military disability benefits. Those cases are discussed in § **3.04**.

tion for lost future wages, however, they are outside the scope of an agreement dividing retirement benefits.[67]

A provision dividing a "pension" is somewhat broader, and may be construed to divide disability benefits, especially if they were part of the pension at the time when the agreement was signed.[68]

Case law addressing federal limits on the division of military and veteran's disability benefits is discussed in § **3.04**.

Survivor Benefits. The cases are split on whether an agreement dividing "retirement benefits" also divides survivor benefits. One line of cases holds no.[69] These cases generally stress the fact that survivor benefits are not divided between the parties, but rather are awarded only to the owning spouse's surviving spouse. A promise to divide benefits accruing during the owning spouse's lifetime is different from a promise to divide benefits payable only after the other spouse's death.

When survivor benefits are not deemed divided by language that divides retirement benefits, the owning spouse is then free to elect survivor benefits for a future spouse. The cost of those benefits is likely to further reduce the first spouse's share of the retirement benefits.[70] *It is therefore essential, when drafting language dividing retirement benefits, to account expressly for survivor benefits.* Otherwise, the result upon retirement may be very different from what the former spouses expect.

---

67. *Davis*, 286 Ill. App. 3d 1065, 678 N.E.2d 68; Cioffi v. Cioffi, 885 A.2d 45, 50 (Pa. Super. Ct. 2005) (disability benefit due before retirement age).

68. *See* Rosenberger v. Rosenberger, 63 A.D.3d 898, 900, 882 N.Y.S.2d 426, 429 (2009) (where stipulation was entered after husband applied for disability benefits, provision awarding wife a portion of husband's pension included disability benefits; "the stipulation of settlement nevertheless provided for a division of his pension without reference to whether the pension was based on accident disability or referable to ordinary service retirement").

69. *See* Black v. N.Y. State & Local Emps.' Ret. Sys., 30 A.D.3d 920, 818 N.Y.S.2d 640 (2006); Van Buren v. Van Buren, 252 A.D.2d 952, 675 N.Y.S.2d 739 (1998); Keith v. Keith, 241 A.D.2d 820, 661 N.Y.S.2d 74 (1997) (provision awarding wife specific stated sum from retirement benefits did not divide survivor benefits; agreement had separate life insurance provision); DeGaust v. DeGaust, 237 A.D.2d 862, 655 N.Y.S.2d 670 (1997) (survivor benefits not divided); *In re* Marriage of Hayes, 228 Or. App. 555, 208 P.3d 1046 (2009); Kadlecek v. Kadlecek, 93 S.W.3d 903, 907 (Tex. Ct. App. 2002) ("the language in the divorce decree's clause awarding Marilyn a portion of any retirement pay that Edward receives was insufficient to award her the right to a survivor annuity").

The argument in favor of this position is stronger with regard to preretirement death benefits, which are not purchased with a reduction in normal retirement benefits and therefore have a weaker connection with the benefit already divided. *See* Kazel v. Kazel, 3 N.Y.3d 331, 819 N.E.2d 1036, 786 N.Y.S.2d 420 (2004); McCoy v. Feinman, 99 N.Y.2d 295, 785 N.E.2d 714, 755 N.Y.S.2d 693 (2002).

70. *See* Lemesis v. Lemesis, 38 A.D.3d 1331, 1332, 834 N.Y.S.2d 597, 598 (2007) (where agreement divided retirement benefits without mentioning surviving benefits, and husband subsequently elected survivor benefits for his second wife, first wife was entitled only to her percentage share of benefits payable to husband after deduction for second wife's survivor benefits).

Another line of cases holds that an agreement dividing "retirement benefits" does divide survivor benefits.[71] These cases generally stress that regardless of their difference in form, retirement benefits and survivor benefits come from the same ultimate source: the contributions made to the pension plan by the owning spouse and the employer during a period of employment. Indeed, postretirement survivor benefits must generally be purchased by accepting reduced retirement benefits. Since survivor benefits and retirement benefits come from the same source, and election of the former reduces the latter, there is reason to hold that the two assets are fundamentally similar.

Where the agreement does divide survivor benefits, it divides all such benefits, even if the agreement is mistaken as to the precise name of the benefit program.[72] Time limits upon the obligation to provide survivor benefits, however, are generally enforced.[73]

Certain types of federal retirement and survivor benefits are awarded to the non-owning spouse directly, without need for any state court order. These benefits can be waived, but only by specific language. Where the agreement contained only a general waiver of property rights "hereinafter acquired," one court held that the language was not sufficiently specific to waive a foreign service spouse annuity.[74]

When one spouse designates the other as beneficiary of ERISA-regulated survivor benefits or life insurance, waiver of beneficiary rights is controlled by federal and not state law.[75] Federal common law will nevertheless enforce such a waiver "so long as it is specific, knowing, and voluntary."[76]

Benefits after Death. ERISA does not allow a qualified domestic relations order (QDRO) to provide that an alternate payee's right to receive retirement benefits is transferable to an heir if the alternate payee dies before the owning spouse.[77] Where the plan at issue is not governed by ERISA, provision allowing transfer of an alternate payee's rights by inheritance are generally permitted.[78]

---

71. Zito v. Zito, 969 P.2d 1144 (Alaska 1998); *In re* Marriage of Wahl, 945 P.2d 1229 (Alaska 1997).

72. Fox v. Office of Pers. Mgmt., 100 F.3d 141 (Fed. Cir. 1996) (agreement awarding wife part of husband's military survivor benefits was sufficient to award wife part of his civil service survivor benefits; husband waived military benefits to receive enhanced civil service benefits after agreement was signed).

73. *See* Janofsky v. Janofsky, 232 A.D.2d 457, 648 N.Y.S.2d 164 (1996) (provision giving wife death benefit if husband died before retirement did not require benefit when husband died after retirement).

74. *See* Nicholson v. Nicholson, 21 Va. App. 231, 463 S.E.2d 334, 337 (1995).

75. Egelhoff v. Egelhoff, 532 U.S. 141 (2001).

76. Keen v. Weaver, 121 S.W.3d 721, 727 (Tex. 2003).

77. *See* BRETT R. TURNER, EQUITABLE DISTRIBUTION OF PROPERTY § 6:19, at 97 n.6 (3d ed. 2005 & Supp. 2007). The rationale is that a testamentary transfer is made under the law of estates, so that it cannot be part of a qualified *domestic relations* order.

78. *See* Plachy v. Plachy, 282 Ga. 614, 652 S.E.2d 555 (2007) (involving federal civil service retirement, which expressly allows transfer of an alternate payee's rights); Divich v. Divich, 2003 SD 73, 665 N.W.2d 109 (2003) (state retirement benefits).

Marital Share. When the court divides retirement benefits, it normally divides only that portion of the benefits that was acquired during the marriage.[79] If a separation agreement calls for a stated percentage division of the benefits, without limiting the percentage to those benefits that were acquired during the marriage, the nonowner's percentage attaches to the entire pension.[80]

Some states limit the types of postdivorce benefit increases to which the nonowning spouse's percentage interest attaches.[81] These limits do not apply where the parties have contracted otherwise.[82]

Where the agreement states a method for determining the marital share of the pension, that method will be respected by the court.[83]

Division. Retirement benefits can be divided by either of two distinct methods. Under the immediate offset method, the nonowning spouse's share is awarded at the time of divorce in a single lump sum payment of cash or other property. Under the deferred distribution method, the nonowning spouse receives a stated percentage of each future payment made to the owning spouse.[84] Even in a state where the courts prefer one of

---

79. *See generally* TURNER, *supra* note 76, § 6:25; *cf.* Underwood v. Underwood, 282 Ga. 643, 651 S.E.2d 736 (2007) (rejecting husband's astounding argument that contractual provisions making percentage divisions of retirement benefits are inherently too vague for enforcement).

80. *See In re* Marriage of Wahl, 945 P.2d 1229 (Alaska 1997); *In re* Marriage of Woodford, 254 Mont. 501, 839 P.2d 574 (1992); Hoshor v. Hoshor, 254 Neb. 743, 580 N.W.2d 516 (1998); Steffenson v. Olsen, 360 S.C. 318, 322, 600 S.E.2d 129, 131 (Ct. App. 2004) ("Had the parties intended to limit the award to those benefits accrued during the marriage, they could have so provided[.]"); Hodge v. Hodge, 197 P.3d 511, 514 (Okla. Civ. App. 2008) ("the consent decree clearly awards Wife 50% of Husband's military retirement, not limited to the extent the retirement funds were acquired during coverture"); Contreras v. Contreras, 974 S.W.2d 155 (Tex. Ct. App. 1998); Callahan v. Callahan, 184 Vt. 602, 958 A.2d 673 (2008); *see also* Russell v. Russell, 922 So. 2d 1097 (Fla. Dist. Ct. App. 2006) (wife's interest included cost of living increases and interest during husband's postretirement participation in deferred retirement option plan program); Kincaid v. Kincaid, 117 Ohio App. 3d 148, 690 N.E.2d 47, 48 (1997) (provision awarding wife 25 percent of the "ultimate value" of the husband's retirement benefits included additional benefits acquired after the divorce upon the husband's early retirement); *cf.* Hullett v. Towers, Perrin, Forster & Crosby, Inc., 38 F.3d 107 (3d Cir. 1994) (error to grant summary judgment that provision applied only to retirement benefit accrued during the marriage; remanding for consideration of extrinsic evidence); Boyett v. Boyett, 254 Neb. 743, 580 N.W.2d 516 (1998) (where wife's share attached to pension and not marital share of pension, any mistake was unilateral by husband, and therefore not a proper basis for reformation).

81. TURNER, *supra* note 76, § 6:26.

82. *See* Matlock v. Matlock, 444 Pa. Super. 507, 664 A.2d 551 (1995); Hurley v. Hurley, 960 S.W.2d 287, 288 (Tex. Ct. App. 1997) (where agreement awarded wife half of marital share "if, as and when received," wife was entitled to half of postdivorce increases); Pate v. Pate, 874 S.W.2d 186, 188 (Tex. Ct. App. 1994) (agreement stated that wife's percentage would be multiplied by benefit "at retirement"; error to limit wife's percentage to benefits that accrued before divorce).

83. *See* Hargrave v. Hargrave, 728 So. 2d 366, 366 (Fla. 4th Dist. Ct. App. 1999) (agreement to award the wife half of the husband's retirement benefits "accruing during the marriage and income thereon" applied to marital contributions, plus interest, and did not apply to interest earned on premarital balance).

84. *See generally* TURNER, *supra* note 76, §§ 6:31–6:32.

these two methods over the other, the parties are free to choose either method in a separation agreement.[85] Where an agreement does not clearly choose between these two division methods, the contract is ambiguous and the court must look to extrinsic evidence.[86]

In many cases, retirement benefits are divided by deferred distribution, with the nonowner receiving a certain percentage of each future payment made to the owner. In these cases the court must consider not only whether the benefits are to be divided, but also the time at which the nonowner's percentage is applied. Where the agreement called for division "when said pension is in pay status," one court held that the percentage was applied at the time of receipt, so that the nonowner's percentage attached to postdivorce benefit increases.[87] Another court held that similar language required division on the date of the husband's actual retirement, even though the husband retired early.[88] Where the agreement awarded to the husband all "benefits accruing to husband subsequent to the date of signing," and the husband was able to retire earlier because he worked additional years after the marriage, another court held that the benefits received by reason of earlier retirement did not accrue after the date of signing.[89]

If the agreement is silent as to the time at which a percentage-based deferred distribution is applied, the percentage is generally applied to each individual payment at the time it is made, so that the spouses share the effect of postdivorce passive gains and losses.[90]

One court suggested that when the agreement is ambiguous as to the time at which deferred distribution payments start, it is preferable that the payments start as of the time when the owning spouse is eligible to retire, so that the owning spouse does not have complete control over when the nonowning spouse starts to receive benefits.[91]

Note that the date on which the marriage ends for purposes of computing the marital share is not necessarily the date as of which the parties' interests are distributed.[92]

---

85. Ruggles v. Ruggles, 116 N.M. 52, 860 P.2d 182 (1993).

86. *Id.*

87. *Matlock*, 444 Pa. Super. at 514, 664 A.2d at 552.

88. Weiner v. Weiner, 253 A.D.2d 428, 676 N.Y.S.2d 640, 642 (1998) (where wife's share of husband's retirement benefits were to start "at the time of his retirement," and husband retired at age 58, error to hold that wife's benefits would begin at age 62).

89. *In re* Marriage of Frain, 258 Ill. App. 3d 475, 630 N.E.2d 523, 523 (1994); *see also* Hullett v. Towers, Perrin, Forster & Crosby, Inc., 38 F.3d 107 (3d Cir. 1994) (error to grant summary judgment that benefits due upon retirement became payable only when husband actually retired, as opposed to when retirement benefits became fully payable; remanding for consideration of extrinsic evidence).

90. *See* Beike v. Beike, 805 N.E.2d 1265, 1269 (Ind. Ct. App. 2004) (wife was awarded 36 percent of husband's pension, which then dropped in value when employer went bankrupt; parties shared loss in value, despite provision stating that wife would have no interest in benefit accruals attributable to postdivorce employment; provision applied only to new benefits, not to passive changes in the value of existing benefits).

91. *See* Garcia v. Garcia, 147 N.M. 905, 227 P.2d 621 (Ct. App. 2009), *cert. granted.*

92. *See* Smith v. Smith, 59 A.D.3d 905, 906–07, 874 N.Y.S.2d 300, 302 (2009) (where agreement awarded wife a portion of the husband's retirement benefits through January 1, 1998, that date

Gains and Losses. Many provisions dividing retirement benefits are implemented some time after the agreement is signed. It is therefore necessary to determine whether the division includes gains and losses in the benefits between the signing and implementation.

When the agreement awards a specific lump sum, that exact sum is normally awarded, regardless of gains or losses.[93] When a percentage is awarded, and a date is specified, the specified date obviously controls. If no date is stated, there is a general preference for applying the percentage as of the date of implementation, as least as regards passive growth (as opposed to new contributions) after the date of signing.[94]

Enforcement. Federal law prevents state courts from enforcing an agreement to divide retirement benefits *against the plan administrator* unless the obligations are stated by the court in a QDRO.[95] While QDROs most often take the form of a separate document, the agreement itself can constitute a QDRO, if it meets the technical requirements[96] and is *incorporated* or *merged* into the divorce decree.[97]

It is important to understand that a QDRO is not a substantive order in its own right, but rather a device for enforcement of a pension division made previously by agreement or litigated decree.[98] Like any other enforcement device, QDROs can be added or modified as needed after the divorce is over, so long as the court is only enforcing and not substantively modifying its prior division of the pension. Thus, where an agreement divides retirement benefits and no QDRO is entered at the time of divorce, a QDRO can be entered freely at a later date,[99] so long as the division made in the QDRO is consistent with the original agreement.[100] If a QDRO is originally entered, but it departs

---

should not be used to determine wife's interest, where agreement expressly stated that wife's share would be determined as of January 1, 2000).

93. *See* Romer v. Romer, 44 So. 3d 514 at 522 (Ala. Ct. App. 2009) (where agreement awarded wife $600,000 from husband's retirement account, wife received only that amount; "by setting forth a sum certain that was to be paid to the wife, the parties implicitly determined that the husband alone would bear the risk of any decrease in the value of his account or benefit from any increase in the value of his account").

94. *See* Lewis v. Lewis, 53 Va. App. 528, 540, 673 S.E.2d 888, 894 (2009) (where agreement specified a percentage but stated no date, wife received passive growth on her share through date of actual distribution).

95. *See generally* TURNER, *supra* note 76, §§ 6:18–6:19.

96. *See* 29 U.S.C. § 1056(d) (Supp. 1999). For a general discussion of the elements of a QDRO, see TURNER, *supra* note 76, § 6.19.

97. *See* Ross v. Ross, 308 N.J. Super. 132, 705 A.2d 784 (1998).

98. *See generally* TURNER, *supra* note 76, § 6:20.

99. Zito v. Zito, 969 P.2d 1144 (Alaska 1998); *see also* Marquis v. Marquis, 175 Md. App. 734, 931 A.2d 1164 (2007) (husband breached implied duty of good faith by failing to cooperate with wife in obtaining qualified order awarding wife a stated percentage of military retirement benefits assigned to her in agreement).

100. *See* Meissner v. Schnettgoecke, 211 S.W.3d 157, 161 (Mo. Ct. App. 2007) (where agreement awarded wife $20,000 from wife's pension plan, error to grant QDRO awarding wife $20,000 from husband's 401(K) plan; result was impermissible modification of the agreement).

materially from the language of the agreement, the QDRO can be freely modified at any future point to restore compliance with the agreement.[101]

Where no QDRO is issued, federal law does not prevent enforcement of an agreement to divide retirement benefits against the pension-owning spouse individually.[102]

As a matter of state law, an agreement to divide retirement benefits by QDRO does not prevent their division by other means, if a QDRO is not available.[103] As a corollary of this rule, retirement benefits due after signing of an agreement but before formal implementation of a QDRO are subject to division by other means, such as direct payments between the parties.[104]

Residuary Clauses

Some agreements contain a residuary clause providing that all assets not divided in the agreement will be awarded to one spouse or the other. These clauses award the named spouse ownership of all omitted assets.[105] A residuary clause can also divide undivided assets in specific stated percentages between the parties.[106]

Indemnity Provisions

Some agreements contain a provision in which the parties promise to take no steps that would deprive the other spouse of an asset awarded to that spouse under the agreement. These provisions are particularly common in agreements dividing retirement benefits, as there are many ways in which the owner of such benefits can make elections that

---

101. *See* Self v. Self, 907 So. 2d 546, 549 (Fla. Dist. Ct. App. 2005) (where agreement divided retirement benefits as property division, but QDRO provided that wife's benefit ceased upon death or remarriage, proper to amend QDRO to remove that provision, which did not appear in the original agreement).

102. Eickhoff v. Eickhoff, 263 Ga. 498, 435 S.E.2d 914 (1993).

In Gruber v. Gruber, 261 Neb. 914, 626 N.W.2d 582 (2001), the parties signed an agreement that anticipated division of the husband's state pension by qualified order. The parties then learned that state law did not recognize such a qualified order, and the husband argued that the pension could not be divided. The court held otherwise, finding that the pension award could be enforced by direct payments between the parties.

103. *See* Patricia A.M. v. Eugene W.M., 24 Misc. 3d 1012, 1014, 885 N.Y.S.2d 178, 181 (Sup. Ct. 2009) ("Nothing in the stipulation limited [the wife's] entitlement to that property so that it could only be collected pursuant to a QDRO. The QDRO was merely a way to facilitate distribution of her share[.]").

104. Cifaldi v. Cifaldi, 118 Conn. App. 325, 333, 983 A.2d 293, 299 (2009) (wife was entitled to benefits due after signing of agreement but before plan administrator approved a QDRO; "the plaintiff's property interest in portions of the defendant's pension benefits was not predicated on the processing of paperwork").

105. *See* Waller v. Morgan, 656 So. 2d 835 (Ala. Ct. App. 1995); Buys v. Buys, 924 S.W.2d 369 (Tex. 1996); Tharp v. Tharp, 772 S.W.2d 467, 468 (Tex. Ct. App. 1989) (agreement awarded "remainder of the marital estate" to husband; wife could not thereafter partition husband's community property pension, which was not mentioned in agreement).

106. *See* Osial v. Cook, 803 A.2d 209, 214 (Pa. Super. Ct. 2002) (58 percent/42 percent ratio).

would reduce or eliminate the value of the other spouse's interest. These provisions have been enforced by the courts.[107]

Where the agreement contains no express indemnity provision, many courts are willing to imply one, finding that the agreement is breached if either party takes voluntary action to reduce the benefits promised to the other.[108]

The most common application of express and implied indemnity provisions involves military retirement and disability benefits. These provisions are part of the ongoing debate over division of military retirement and disability benefits, and they are therefore discussed in § **3.04**.

§ 6.022 Assets Not Divided by the Agreement

There is no requirement that a separation agreement must divide each and every asset owned by the parties.[109] When the agreement does not expressly divide a particular asset, and the agreement was intended as a complete division of all marital property, the courts generally hold that assets not expressly divided were awarded to the owning spouse.[110]

If the agreement was not intended as a comprehensive settlement of all property interests, then the agreement does not prevent the court from dividing assets not expressly allocated by contract.[111] Whether the court has jurisdiction to divide omitted assets is discussed below.[112]

If an asset was omitted because the owning spouse failed to disclose its existence, it may also be possible to overturn the agreement on grounds of fraud. *See* § **4.053**.

---

107. *See* Lejeune v. Lejeune, 625 So. 2d 213 (La. Ct. App. 1993) (husband lost retirement benefits by returning to work part-time; ordering husband to pay wife her interest in the benefits, even if he was not actually receiving them).

108. *See* Stanley v. Stanley, 956 A.2d 1, 2 (Del. 2008) (where husband's voluntary election of social security disability benefits caused significant reduction in his private pension, trial court properly ordered husband to compensate wife for harm done).

109. *In re* Marriage of Goldin, 923 P.2d 376 (Colo. App. 1996).

110. *See* Parr v. Parr, 773 S.W.2d 135 (Mo. Ct. App. 1989) (contract awarded to husband all assets not expressly awarded to wife; provision barred wife from later obtaining part of husband's retirement pay); Patzer v. Patzer, 792 P.2d 1101 (Mont. 1990) (contract that was "full and final settlement" prevented wife from thereafter obtaining part of husband's retirement benefits, even those benefits were not expressly mentioned in the agreement); *In re* Marriage of Wise, 46 Ohio App. 3d 82, 545 N.E.2d 1314, 1317 (1988) (where agreement was intended to divide all property, but husband's pension was omitted through wife's own "inexcusable neglect and carelessness," wife was not entitled to any part of pension).

111. *See* Hartley v. Hartley, 205 P.3d 342, 351 (Alaska 2009) (where agreement did not address cost of survivor benefit, but divorce was not yet final, trial court did not err in allocating cost; "[i]f there is no agreement as to the division of a particular piece of property, the superior court has discretion to divide that property equitably"); Kammerer v. Kammerer, 278 A.D.2d 282, 283, 717 N.Y.S.2d 322, 323 (2000) ("The defendant did not waive her right to share in the plaintiff's pension to the extent that it constituted marital property, . . . since the parties' separation agreement did not mention or refer to the plaintiff's pension[.]"); Clanin v. Clanin, 918 S.W.2d 673 (Tex. Ct. App. 1996).

112. *See infra* note 112 and accompanying text.

Sometimes an agreement will mention an asset only by awarding part of that asset to one spouse. These partial awards are generally construed to provide implicitly that the unmentioned part of the asset is awarded to the other spouse.[113]

Waiver of Rights

Separation agreements frequently contain a clause stating that except as provided in the agreement, each party waives all rights in property owned by the other. The effect of these provisions depends upon the type of property division system followed in the state at issue.

In community property states, community assets that are not expressly divided by the divorce decree are owned by the parties as tenants in common.[114] Thus, when a separation agreement waives rights in property owned by the other spouse, it effectively requires that all assets not otherwise divided by the agreement be divided equally between the parties. Community property governs ownership during the marriage, and an undivided community asset is therefore owned in equal shares by both spouses.[115]

In equitable distribution states, marital property exists only for the limited purpose of allocating assets between the parties in a litigated divorce case.[116] In these states, an undivided marital asset is owned not by both parties together, but rather by the party or parties who own legal title to the asset. Thus, the effect of a property division waiver is to require that undivided assets be divided according to legal title.[117] Likewise, unallocated debts must be divided according to legal title.[118] Some decisions allow the agree-

---

113. *See In re* Marriage of Simundza, 121 Cal. App. 4th 1513, 18 Cal. Rptr. 3d 377 (2004) (provision awarding wife $200 per month from husband's pension implicitly awarded husband the remaining amount); Doyle v. Sullivan, 149 Misc. 2d 910, 566 N.Y.S.2d 997 (1991) (stipulation that wife would receive 50 percent of husband's pension was implied waiver of her right to receive more than 50 percent).

114. *See, e.g.*, Soto v. Soto, 936 S.W.2d 338 (Tex. Ct. App. 1996).

115. *See* Garcia v. Meyer, 122 N.M. 57, 920 P.2d 522 (1996) (agreement divided vested options but was silent on unvested options, and waived each spouse's right in property owned by the other; community share of unvested options could be divided between parties).

116. *See generally* TURNER, *supra* note 76, §§ 2:5, 2:7, 9:28.

117. *See* D'Errico v. D'Errico, 281 Ga. 508, 509, 640 S.E.2d 30, 31 (2007) (wife had no interest in home owned by husband alone; "The separation agreement neither diminishes Husband's ownership rights nor grants any such rights to Wife"); Wolshire v. Wolshire, 905 N.E.2d 1051, 1057 (Ind. Ct. App. 2009) (trial court erred by dividing military retirement benefits omitted from separation agreement); Hannigan v. Hannigan, 50 A.D.3d 957, 857 N.Y.S.2d 201 (2008) (error to divide retirement benefits omitted from stipulation of settlement); March v. March, 233 A.D.2d 371, 650 N.Y.S.2d 750 (1996) (noting that wife had counsel and should have discovered omitted retirement benefits); *Hickman*, 937 P.2d 85.

A few states have enacted statutes that permit the court to divide omitted property even after the divorce decree is final. *See* Wright v. Michaud, 959 A.2d 753, 755 (Me. 2008); *see generally* BRETT R. TURNER, EQUITABLE DISTRIBUTION OF PROPERTY § 9:28 (3d ed. 2005).

118. Hickman v. Hickman, 937 P.2d 85 (Okla. 1997) (debt imposed after the marriage as a result of IRS audit was shared equally by both parties; debt arose from year in which parties filed joint tax return).

ment to reserve the court's power to divide specific assets at a later time,[119] but this result requires specific language in the agreement; it is not the general rule.

A waiver of rights prevents division even if a subsequent retroactive change in the law adds materially to the divisible estate.[120]

A waiver of property division rights does not automatically waive the right to partition jointly titled property.[121] Note, however, that such a waiver is generally implied from an exclusive use provision. *See* § **6.027.**

A waiver of property division rights does not prevent the court from looking to the assets involved as a source for spousal support.[122]

After-Acquired Property

One issue involving the scope of the agreement that arises with particular frequency is the division of property acquired after the agreement is signed. If the agreement contains an express waiver of rights in property "hereafter acquired," or words of similar effect, then rights to after-acquired property are waived.

Where the agreement contains no such provision, the issue is closer. In *Eberhardt v. Eberhardt*,[123] the wife waived her rights to all real property to which the husband owned legal title. Ten months after the agreement was signed, the parties purchased real property together. The court held that the agreement was ambiguous regarding after-acquired property, and remanded for admission of extrinsic evidence.

When the agreement is unclear, the courts are generally reluctant to hold that the parties intended to divide after-acquired property. For example, in *Roddenberry v. Roddenberry*,[124] the court held that the wife's right to share in husband's "profit participation income" from the *Star Trek* franchise did not apply to new *Star Trek* products produced by the husband after the marriage. Likewise, an agreement dividing "post-retirement benefit increases" applied only to increases in existing retirement benefits,

---

119. *See* Brenenstuhl v. Brenenstuhl, 169 N.C. App. 433, 436, 610 S.E.2d 301, 303 (2005) ("[i]ssues of retirement will be addressed at a future date," as used in incorporated agreement, was sufficient to reserve court's jurisdiction to divide military retirement pay at a later date, even after entry of divorce decree); Gilmore v. Garner, 157 N.C. App. 664, 668, 580 S.E.2d 15, 18 (2003) (under agreement, wife "agrees not to make any demand on Husband at the present time," but "each [party] may draw Railroad Retirement benefits in accordance with law when they are eligible to so draw"; trial court properly construed language as a contractual promise to pay wife a share of the pension equal to her rights under state equitable distribution law, even though wife did not invoke that right until long after the divorce).

120. Himes v. Himes, 12 Va. App. 966, 407 S.E.2d 694 (1991) (retroactive invalidation of U.S. Supreme Court decision preventing division of military retirement benefits).

121. Diggs v. Diggs, 116 N.C. App. 95, 446 S.E.2d 873 (1994); *see also* Newborn v. Clay, 263 Ga. 622, 436 S.E.2d 654, 655 (1983) (waiver of property in "possession" of other spouse did not waive rights in jointly titled real property, merely because the other spouse physically resided there when agreement was signed).

122. Kinne v. Kinne, 599 So. 2d 191 (Fla. Dist. Ct. App. 1992) (retirement benefits); Bauer v. Votta, 104 Md. App. 565, 657 A.2d 358 (1995) (retirement benefits); Dugas v. Dugas, 332 So. 2d 501 (La. Ct. App. 1976).

123. 203 A.D.2d 946, 611 N.Y.S.2d 402 (1994).

124. 44 Cal. App. 4th 634, 51 Cal. Rptr. 2d 907, 911 (1996).

and did not apply to entirely new early retirement benefits created by the employer after the divorce.[125]

Special rules may apply to property that is acquired as a result of owning other property. For example, in *Mason v. Mason*,[126] the agreement awarded the husband 16,066 shares of stock. After the agreement was signed, the stock split one for two. The court held that the husband was entitled to the additional shares attributable to his stock award. In other words, the court construed the agreement to award the husband 16,066 shares as of the date the agreement was signed, including the benefit of any future stock split. Other courts have applied similar reasoning to dividends and other earnings generated by specific assets.[127]

§ 6.023 Transfer of Title

Assets Conveyed. In construing provisions transferring title to specific assets, courts use common sense in determining the precise assets involved. In *Moon v. Moon*,[128] the agreement assigned to the husband the "residence and real property" located at a stated address. The court held that this provision applied not only to the home located at the address, but also to an adjacent vacant lot. The lot had a separate tax number, but no separate mailing address. The agreement contained a provision stating that neither party had any asset not listed in agreement, a provision that would be contradicted by the facts unless the parties intended to treat the residence and the lot as a single entity.

Estate Conveyed. When a separation agreement transfers title to property, the normal assumption is that the estate conveyed is full ownership. The parties are free, however, to convey lesser interests. For instance, in *In re Will of Ault*,[129] the agreement gave wife possession of two paintings during her lifetime, and provided that upon husband's death he would bequeath them to his descendants. The wife died first, and the court held that the husband was entitled to return of the paintings. Thus, the court construed the agreement to give the wife only a life estate in the paintings.

Likewise, a promise to convey normally includes the entire interest of the conveying spouse. In *Milligan v. Neibuhr*,[130] the parties owned two adjacent lots, one of which had an easement of passage over the other. The agreement awarded the wife "any and all interest" possessed by the husband in the lot that was subject to the easement.[131] The court held that the agreement not only gave the wife fee simple ownership of the lot, but also destroyed the easement.

---

125. Olivo v. Olivo, 82 N.Y.2d 202, 624 N.E.2d 151, 604 N.Y.S.2d 23 (1993).

126. 180 Vt. 98, 904 A.2d 1164 (2006).

127. *See* Ader v. Ader, 22 A.D.3d 289, 290, 803 N.Y.S.2d 10, 11 (2005) ("The agreement plainly and unambiguously provides that defendant is entitled to all accretions and earnings on the shares to which she is entitled under the agreement and makes no distinction between dividend earnings and earnings adjustment units[.]").

128. 140 Or. App. 402, 914 P.2d 1133 (1996).

129. 207 A.D.2d 312, 615 N.Y.S.2d 681 (1994).

130. 990 S.W.2d 823 (Tex. Ct. App. 1999).

131. *Id.* at 825.

An order can convey to one spouse equitable ownership of assets titled in the name of the other. This is a common option with regard to stock options, which often cannot be transferred directly to the nonowning spouse. A present value award is theoretically possible, but stock options are extremely difficult to value if the company is not publicly traded. The agreement can therefore order the employee spouse to hold certain options for the other spouse's benefit, and to exercise those options upon written request, paying the proceeds to the other spouse.[132]

Transfer Restrictions. A provision requiring conveyance of specific assets is not enforceable if the owning spouse is not permitted by law to transfer the asset.[133]

Implementation. Provisions that give ownership of an asset of a particular spouse implicitly require the other spouse to take reasonable steps to implement the provision.[134]

Such provisions do not, however, make the transferred spouse strictly liable if third parties interfere with the transfer. In *Comras v. Comras*,[135] the husband promised to assume the wife's interest in certain partnerships. The partnerships were able to demand additional cash contributions from the partners, and the wife wished to be removed from the obligations to make them. The partnership agreements provided, however, that the partners must approve any transfer of a partnership interest. The wife argued that the husband was strictly liable if the partners refused to consent, but the court disagreed, finding that the husband was obligated only to use his best efforts to obtain the consent of the other partners.

Documents. Many separation agreements contain provisions requiring the parties to execute all documents necessary to implement their property division. These provisions are generally enforceable.[136]

Provisions requiring execution of documents may not apply where signing the document would inflict unanticipated harm upon the signing spouse. In *Banks v. Banks*,[137] the wife promised to "cooperate" with the husband in filing future tax returns for years covered by the marriage. The husband asked the wife to reduce his tax liability by signing a joint return. The wife refused to sign, on the basis by that signing she would

---

132. *See* Elliott v. Elliott, 149 S.W.3d 77, 87 (Tenn. Ct. App. 2004) (sanctioning the husband for failing to follow such a provision).

133. *See* Seymour v. Seymour, 960 So. 2d 513 (Miss. Ct. App. 2006) (husband's stipulation to transfer stock to wife was unenforceable, where it violates enforceable transfer restrictions properly placed upon the stock under the law of corporations); Sangiorgio v. Sangiorgio, 173 Misc. 2d 625, 662 N.Y.S.2d 220 (Sup. Ct. 1997) (provision giving nonveterinarian wife 51 percent of stock in veterinary practice was void as against public policy).

134. *See* Marcolongo v. Nicolai, 392 Pa. Super. 208, 572 A.2d 765, 766 (1990) (statement that each party "shall be entitled to full and individual ownership" of certain assets constituted an implied promise by the other party to convey those assets), *allocatur denied*, 593 A.2d 420 (1990).

135. 195 A.D.2d 358, 600 N.Y.S.2d 61 (1993).

136. *See* Lyon v. Lyon, 209 A.D.2d 592, 619 N.Y.S.2d 300 (1994) (requiring execution of documents granting easements and approving plat so that land could be developed).

137. 648 So. 2d 1116, 1117 (Miss. 1994).

make herself liable for any deficiencies arising from the husband's treatment of his own income. The trial court ordered her to sign, making a separate order directing the husband to hold the wife harmless from all future liability. The appellate court reversed, noting that the wife had experienced great difficulty obtaining the husband's compliance with other provisions of the agreement. In light of these difficulties, the court did not place great faith in the hold-harmless provision, and it found that the risks of signing were greater than the benefits.

§ 6.024 Debts

In addition to dividing the parties' assets, most separation agreements also allocate the parties' liabilities. Since allocation of debt is not required, courts generally enforce these provisions only to the extent of their language. Where a debt falls within the language of such a provision, however, the courts are skeptical of attempts to avoid liability.[138]

When a party agrees to assume a particular liability, he or she is normally responsible for that entire liability, regardless of how and when it becomes payable. For instance, in *Mowers v. Mowers*,[139] the contract made the husband responsible for paying a mortgage. The husband failed to pay, and under the terms of an acceleration clause in the mortgage, the entire principal became due. The court held that the husband was responsible for paying the entire balance.[140]

If a debt assigned to one spouse is paid off by the other, the spouse who paid off the debt can seek reimbursement from the assigned payor. For example, if the court orders one spouse to make mortgage payments on the home, and the other spouse sells the home and repays the mortgage, the first spouse remains liable for the principal balance of the mortgage on the date of repayment.[141]

---

138. *See* Curtis v. Curtis, 680 So. 2d 1327, 1328 (La. Ct. App. 1996) (provision allocating "farming indebtedness" to husband included income tax liability arising from farming operations); Thomas v. Thomas, 206 A.D.2d 909, 614 N.Y.S.2d 839 (1994) (agreement the wife would bear "present debt" of store did not apply to tax deficiency; deficiency did not exist when agreement was signed; parties' agreement to split any tax deficiency resulting from an audit applied, even though no formal audit was conducted).

139. 229 A.D.2d 941, 645 N.Y.S.2d 232 (1996).

140. *See also* Daley v. Carlton, 19 So. 3d 781 (Miss. Ct. App. 2009) (where agreement required husband to pay mortgage as alimony, and mortgage had large balloon payment due in the future, husband was responsible for entire mortgage; noting that agreement required husband to obtain sufficient life insurance to cover entire amount due on mortgage).

141. Jones v. Jones, 722 So. 2d 768 (Ala. Ct. App. 1998) (husband promised to make payments on wife's car; car was wrecked and lien paid off by insurance; husband liable for the amount of the payoff); Riley v. Riley, 61 Ark. App. 74, 964 S.W.2d 400 (1998); Mount v. Mount, 624 So. 2d 1001 (Miss. 1993); Guntert v. Daniels, 240 A.D.2d 789, 658 N.Y.S.2d 521 (1997) (car payments). Butterworth v. Butterworth, 226 A.D.2d 899, 640 N.Y.S.2d 366 (1996); *see also* Ferrara v. Ferrara, 42 A.D.3d 426, 839 N.Y.S.2d 789 (2007) (where husband prepaid mortgage, he was still responsible for taxes and insurance until date when mortgage would have ended if not repaid). *But see* White v. White, 257 Va. 139, 509 S.E.2d 323 (1999) (where wife sold property and paid mortgage from proceeds, husband's obligation to pay mortgage terminated).

Like assets, debts can be divided not only by express provisions listing individual debts awarded to each party, but also by residuary provisions awarding all unallocated debts to a specific party.[142] These provisions apply to all debts, even those not known to the parties at the time the agreement was signed.[143]

Omitted debts are generally treated in the same manner as omitted assets.[144] Thus, where the agreement makes no mention of a given debt, liability for that debt is determined under substantive principles of debtor-creditor law, and not under the law of domestic relations. A debt imposed by an Internal Revenue Service audit of a joint tax return, for example, is generally owed jointly by both spouses.[145]

Refinancing. When a debt titled in the name of both parties is awarded to one party alone, must that party make reasonable efforts to remove the other party from the obligation? At least one court has found such obligation.[146] Another court, however, has refused to do so.[147]

The latter position seems more logical, as refinancing a debt is a substantially different obligation than merely paying it. Many creditors may refuse to remove the other spouse's name from the debt, and a hold-harmless obligation should avoid any financial prejudice. If an obligation to refinance is implied, it should definitely require only reasonable efforts, as the decision whether to permit refinancing is ultimately that of the creditor. The nonowning spouse's name can certainly be removed from a secured debt if the asset is sold, but sale under the pressure of a divorce case might not result in fair market value, and it is quite a stretch to imply an obligation to sell from a provision that merely allocates a joint debt. The better position is that mere allocation of a joint debt does not create an obligation to sell or refinance.

Hold-Harmless Provisions. Instead of directly providing that a given party will pay a given debt, some agreements provide that one party must hold the other harmless from any liability on the debt. Some courts hold that a hold-harmless provision does not require payment to the creditor; rather, liability exists only if the enforcing spouse has actually paid off the debt and seeks repayment.[148] Other courts hold that a hold-harmless provision does require actual payment.[149] It seems pointless to require the enforcing debt actually pay the debt before seeking relief, especially where the debt is already overdue, and the latter position is therefore better reasoned. Still, unless the drafter is confident that the state in question will not follow the former position, the

---

142. *E.g.*, Money v. Money, 297 S.W.3d 69 (Ky. Ct. App. 2009).

143. *Id.*

144. *See* § **6.022**, note 76.

145. Hickman v. Hickman, 937 P.2d 75 (Okla. 1997).

146. Phillips v. Delks, 880 N.E.2d 713 (Ind. Ct. App. 2008).

147. Bailey v. Mann, 895 N.E.2d 1215, 1218 (Ind. 2008) ("The Property Settlement Agreement requires the wife to make payments on the lease, but does not require her to refinance or remove the husband's name from the lease[.]").

148. *See In re* Reiff, 166 B.R. 694 (Bankr. W.D. Mo. 1994); Jernigan v. Jernigan, 623 So. 2d 630 (Fla. Dist. Ct. App. 1993).

149. *See* Long v. McAllister-Long, 221 S.W.3d 1 (Tenn. Ct. App. 2006).

better practice when dividing a debt is to order the responsible spouse to pay it, and not simply to hold the other harmless.

A hold-harmless provision does not require the responsible spouse to remove the other spouse's name from a joint debt, especially if removal would require refinancing on unfavorable terms or sale of the property.[150]

A hold-harmless provision is not violated when the spouse responsible for the debt lists it as an expense for purposes of spousal support.[151]

At least one court has refused to require the beneficiary of a hold-harmless clause to mitigate damages.[152]

Wrongful Debts. Agreements sometime provide that liability for wrongfully incurred debts that surface after the date of the agreement will be allocated to the incurring spouse. These provisions most commonly apply when the IRS assesses a tax deficiency after the agreement is signed, for one or more tax years that occurred during the marriage. The courts generally construe these provisions in favor of the innocent spouse, especially when the wrongful conduct is flagrant.[153]

§ 6.025 Monetary Awards

While most agreements allocate the assets of the marriage between the parties, the final allocation of assets is often different from the desired equitable division of the marital estate. This disparity occurs because allocation of tangible property is influenced by concerns other than equitable division of value. A professional practice, for instance, must be awarded to the professional spouse, while the marital home is usually awarded to the spouse who receives custody of the children. In addition, while the property rights of most spouses are generally equal, equal division of individual assets would leave the parties as joint owners—a recipe for future litigation. To avoid this problem, most agreements award entire assets to one spouse or the other. It is a rare case, however, where the desired allocation of entire assets works out to an equal or near-equal division.

To resolve the disparity between final physical possession of the assets and the equitable property rights of the parties, most agreements require one spouse to make a direct monetary payment to the other. Such an award need not be definite in amount.[154]

---

150. *See* Eaton v. Grau, 368 N.J. Super. 215, 223–24, 845 A.2d 707, 712 (2004) (hold-harmless provision required husband to pay mortgage, but did not require him to remove wife's name from it by sale or refinancing; "we do not read the obligation to further require defendant to take preventative or preemptive steps to avoid actual loss to plaintiff"); Barnes v. Barnes, 28 So. 3d 300 (Ala. Civ. App. 2009) (following *Eaton*).

151. McKee v. McKee, 52 Va. App. 482,, 664 S.E.2d 505 (2008).

152. *See* Citibank (S.D.) NA v. Berg, 2009 WL 653037 (Ohio Ct. App. 2009) (where wife breached hold-harmless clause by incurring additional debt on joint credit card, husband was not required to mitigate damages by cancelling card after he first learned of wife's use, particularly since wife had expressly requested that husband not cancel the card).

153. *See* Gillman v. O'Connell, 176 A.D.2d 305, 574 N.E.2d 573 (1991) (tax debt allocated to wife, whose questionable deductions were to blame for the liability).

154. *See* Sutton v. Sutton, 28 Ark. App. 165, 771 S.W.2d 791 (1989) (contract could properly award wife property division payments of $500 per month until death or remarriage).

When a monetary award cannot be paid in a single lump sum from available liquid assets, one common option is to require the payor to assume a mortgage and use the proceeds to pay the award. Agreements to obtain a mortgage are generally construed to require the payor spouse to make a good-faith effort to obtain the required financing.[155]

Percentage Award. While many monetary awards are stated as a specific amount of dollars, some lump sum awards are stated as a percentage of the value of the asset. Most states will find a percentage award only where a percentage is stated in the agreement. If the agreement states only a lump sum, the amount of the award is exactly that amount.[156] If the agreement is unclear, the cases tend to hold that any agreement that mentions a percentage constitutes a percentage award, even if a lump sum is also mentioned.[157]

The key issue in applying a percentage award is determining the date upon which the percentage is applied. The first resource in resolving this issue is the language of the agreement.[158] Where the agreement is silent, the courts tend to measure the percent-

---

155. *See* Belkin v. Belkin, 193 A.D.2d 573, 597 N.Y.S.2d 421 (1993) (payor who filed only one mortgage application and failed to seek the payee's assistance in the manner required by the contract did not make a good-faith effort).

156. *See* Duran v. Duran, 2003 SD 15, 657 N.W.2d 692 (2003) (agreement awarded wife $38,000 from husband's stock plans to pay certain stated debts; wife's award was exactly $38,000, regardless of subsequent increases or decreases in value of stock plans).

157. Rogers v. Rogers, 919 So. 2d 184, 186 (Miss. Ct. App. 2005) ("one-half (½) of Robert Earl Rogers, Jr. 401K in the approximate sum of $69,000"; wife received half of plan, including future gains and losses). The authors find it significant that the agreement in *Rogers* referred to $69,000 as an "approximate sum," thus suggesting that the intent to make a percentage award was primary.

158. *See* Rivero v. Rivero, 963 So. 2d 934, 936 (Fla. Dist. Ct. App. 2007) (where agreement awarded the wife "½ of the *present* value of the Husband's profit sharing plan," wife was not entitled to any portion of future appreciation in plan balance) (emphasis added); Reiff v. Reiff, 40 A.D.3d 346, 346, 836 N.Y.S.2d 119, 120 (2007) ("By dividing the value of the account as of a date certain, the agreement protected plaintiff in case Shell shares subsequently declined in price. Plaintiff may not have the agreement rewritten simply because the price of Shell shares has increased[.]"); Musci v. Musci, 2006 WL 3208558, at *9–10 (Ohio Ct. App. 2006) ("Immediately upon the execution of this agreement, husband shall assign by appropriate order twenty-five percent (25%) of the account balance" to the wife; because transfer was required immediately, wife's interest was 25 percent of balance on date of agreement); Baker v. Baker, 38 Va. App. 384, 388, 564 S.E.2d 164, 166 (2002) (agreement "is unambiguous in providing an allotment to the wife of one-half of the profit sharing plan 'valued as of the date of [the] agreement'"; error to award wife subsequent gains and losses).

Where the agreement states that both spouses will receive specific percentages of an asset as of a certain date, and the value of the asset later drops, it is not possible to award both spouses the exact amount stated in the plain language of the agreement. Necessarily, therefore, the agreement as a whole is ambiguous, and the result depends upon parol evidence. *See* Jardine v. Jardine, 918 So. 2d 127, 136 (Ala. Civ. App. 2005).

Where a monetary award from the value of a retirement plan could not be paid until a QDRO was drafted, entered, and accepted by the plan, one court looked past language similar to the above cases. *See* Shorter v. Shorter, 851 N.E.2d 378, 386 (Ind. Ct. App. 2006) (agreement awarded wife "one-half of the value in the husband's 401(k) and one-half of the value in the husband's pension plan as of this date," trial court erred in denying wife gains and losses through date on which QDRO became effective).

age as of the date of actual transfer, so that the parties share passive gains and losses between the date of the agreement and the date of distribution.[159]

Similar rules of construction apply when fungible assets are divided in kind.[160]

Deferred Award. Another option where liquid funds are not immediately available is to defer the award over a period of years.

Where a deferred award permits several alternative payment options, the payor may choose which one to comply with. For instance, in *Brown v. Brown*,[161] the agreement required the husband to pay "$12,000 annually or $3,000 quarterly." The court reversed a lower court decision requiring quarterly payments, holding that the husband had the right to pay the amount due in an annual sum.

Since the present value of a deferred award is less than the present value of an immediate award, it is essential for the protection of the recipient spouse that a deferred award include interest at a commercially reasonable rate. Traditionally, however, many courts have looked with disfavor upon interest provisions. As a result, the cases generally hold that interest is payable only where the agreement so provides.[162]

Asset-Specific Deferred Award. A deferred award will sometimes be tied to the recipient's interest in a specific asset. The most common example is a provision deferring payment of one spouse's interest in the marital home during a period of exclusive use. This type of award is due when the exclusive use ends. For case law on determining that point in time, see **§ 6.027**.

Where an asset-specific deferred award is stated as a specific sum, the specific sum is the amount due before any income tax payable by either the payor[163] or the recipient.[164]

In most cases, a deferred award becomes payable upon sale of the asset. For this purpose, a sale occurs when the owner transfers the property, receiving in return some

---

159. *See* Taylor v. Taylor, 258 Wis. 2d 290, 297, 653 N.W.2d 524, 528 (Ct. App. 2002) ("in agreeing to accept a percentage share of a variable asset, Susan agreed to assume a proportionate share of any subsequent gains or losses until such time as she liquidates the asset"); *cf.* Page v. Page, 77 Conn. App. 748, 749, 825 A.2d 187, 188 (2003) ("[t]he Husband shall immediately transfer to the Wife by way of a Qualified Domestic Relations Order or nontaxable rollover a one-half interest" in this pension plan; language was ambiguous, and trial court erred by denying the wife gains and losses without holding an evidentiary hearing).

160. *E.g., Reiff*, 40 A.D.3d at 346, 836 N.Y.S.2d at 120 (2007); *Taylor*, 258 Wis. 2d 290, 653 N.W.2d 524.

161. 255 A.D.2d 209, 680 N.Y.S.2d 15, 15 (1998).

162. *See* Osborn v. Osborn, 159 Vt. 95, 614 A.2d 390, 392 (1992) (agreement gave husband choice to pay either $200,000 within 45 days, or $200,000 at a rate of $400 per month starting in 18 months; refusing to allow interest on the second alternative, even though this reading made the first alternative superfluous, as no reasonable payor would ever elect it).

163. *See* Sassano v. Sassano, 721 So. 2d 444 (Fla. 5th Dist. Ct. App. 1998) (where agreement required two payments of $40,000 for the wife's interest in certain stock options, neither of which depended upon whether and when the options were exercised, court properly excluded evidence that these amount should be reduced by capital gains taxes due on exercise of the options).

164. Kilbride v. Kilbride, 234 A.D.2d 780, 650 N.Y.S.2d 889 (1996).

valuable consideration. Sale does not occur if the owner merely changes the form in which the asset is held, without giving up ownership or obtaining consideration.[165]

If the deferred award is not due upon sale, or if a change in ownership does not qualify as a sale, an asset-specific deferred award may attach to any new property that is traceable to the asset to which the award attaches.[166] It does not give the payee any right to help manage the property[167] or to share in future changes in value.[168] If the award is not asset-specific, it does not attach to replacement assets.[169]

Time of Payment. The time for performance of a monetary award is not an absolute rigid requirement, unless the contract states that time is of the essence.[170]

Security. The wise drafter will secure a monetary award, particularly one due over time, with a contractual lien upon some or all of the payor's assets. In the absence of such a lien, there is a very real risk that the monetary award will be discharged in bankruptcy.[171]

In drafting security provisions, it may be important to observe the requirements imposed by general debtor-creditor law. In *Gioia v. Gioia*,[172] the parties agreed that the husband would pay a deferred monetary award of $55,000 in exchange for the wife's interest in the home. To secure the payment, the agreement provided that the husband would prepare a deed conveying his entire interest to the wife. The wife could then simply record that deed if the husband defaulted, thus avoiding the expense and difficulty of formal foreclosure proceedings. Unfortunately, New York law imposed limits on the ability of creditors to avoid the mandatory legal protections of foreclosure proceedings. The court held that those limits had been violated, that the contractual security arrangement was in substance a mortgage, and that the wife could not record the deed without filing foreclosure proceedings. In short, separation agreements are still subject to any relevant statutes providing debtors with general protection from their creditors, and agreements must be drafted with this point in mind.

---

165. *See* Reynolds v. Reynolds, 627 So. 2d 452 (Mo. Ct. App. 1993) (corporation spun off part of its operations into new corporation; spin-off was not a sale).

166. *See id.* (where wife had right to receive 10 percent of proceeds upon sale of certain stock, her right attached to stock in new corporation, created when original corporation spun off part of its business into a new entity).

167. *See* Ward v. Ward, 705 So. 2d 498 (Ala. Ct. App. 1997) (wife's right to receive half of profit of husband's farm did not require husband to consult her regarding which tax deductions he would take).

168. Kartzmark v. Kartzmark, 709 So. 2d 583 (Fla. 4th Dist. Ct. App. 1998).

169. *See* Morse v. Morse, 60 Ark. App. 215, 961 S.W.2d 777 (1998) (wife's general monetary award was not attached to home, so that when home burned and husband collected insurance proceeds, wife had no specific interest in receiving any portion of the payment).

170. Brown v. Brown, 90 Ohio App. 781, 630 N.E.2d 763 (1993).

171. *See generally* TURNER, *supra* note 76, § 9:22.

172. 234 A.D.2d 588, 652 N.Y.S.2d 63 (1996).

Additional Security. Where there is reason to suspect that a contractual monetary award might not be paid, the trial court may have jurisdiction to require the payor spouse to post security.[173]

§ 6.026 Sale of Marital Assets

While most agreements award sole ownership of each asset to one party, sometimes an agreement will leave the parties as joint owners of an asset. This approach is extremely troublesome if the parties are expected to cooperate to manage the assets, and few agreements anticipate a lengthy period of joint control over commonly held property.

If the parties desire joint ownership without cooperation, one feasible alternative is to sell the asset immediately upon divorce. Each party then receives his or her fair share of the proceeds. Agreements to sell property are common in divorce cases, and the courts enforce them as written.[174]

Sale. Where the agreement requires division of proceeds upon sale, courts tend to hold that any method for withdrawing equity will trigger the stated division. Stated differently, a "sale" is any transaction that withdraws value from the property. For example, in *Knutson v. Knutson*,[175] the agreement awarded the wife half of the proceeds from sale of the home. The husband then refinanced the property, obtaining a lump sum amount in exchange for a larger debt. The court held that the transaction was essentially a sale, so that the wife was entitled to half of the lump sum amount.

Seller. Sale provisions typically either permit one party to make the sale, or appoint a neutral person to complete this task. Who completes the sale is not a major issue, and if the other party sells the asset in good faith for a fair price, there has been substantial compliance with the sale provision.[176]

Price. One difficult issue with any agreement to sell is determining a fair price. Price is easily determined when there is an ongoing public market. Where the market is limited, however, the final sale price depends greatly upon the initial offering price, a subject upon which parties frequently disagree.

Disagreements upon price can be avoided by providing that the price will be set by one or more appraisers. These provisions tend to avoid disputes, and are construed as written.[177]

---

173. Comras v. Comras, 195 A.D.2d 358, 600 N.Y.S.2d 61 (1993) (husband had threatened bankruptcy; proper to require security).

174. *See* Troy Sav. Bank v. Calacone, 209 A.D.2d 777, 617 N.Y.S.2d 995 (1994) (parties agreed to split proceeds of sale, and bank then foreclosed upon the property, leaving a surplus over the mortgage balance; surplus held to be proceeds of sale).

175. 973 P.2d 596 (Alaska 1999).

176. Peretta v. Peretta, 203 A.D.2d 668, 610 N.Y.S.2d 374 (1994).

177. *See* Andrews v. Andrews, 229 A.D.2d 366, 644 N.Y.S.2d 781 (1996) (where contract required each party to appoint an appraiser, and those appraisers to select a third if they disagreed, court erred by appointing its own appraiser; appointment was inconsistent with the contract).

A provision requiring the parties to agree upon any modification to a stated price is probably not a good idea, as one spouse can prolong the sale by refusing to agree.[178]

An agreement to list a property for sale at a stated price does not prevent sale for a lower price if the list price proves to be too high. A listing price represent an initial offer price, and offers no guarantee against sale for a lesser amount if the initial offer price proves to be too high.[179] Sale for a higher amount than the stated price is probably technically a breach, but it is hard to see how the breach could realistically inflict harm.[180]

Unless the agreement clearly states otherwise, sale provisions require sale at arm's length and for fair market value.[181]

Timing. Courts disfavor provisions that give one party unfettered discretion as to when (if ever) the sale will take place. In *Cavanagh v. Cavanagh*,[182] the agreement stated that the husband would purchase the wife's interest in the marital home for $397,000. Three payments of $100,000 were due within the following year, and the remaining $97,000 was due "upon the sale."[183] The husband argued that he was under no obligation to sell the property, and could refuse to do so indefinitely if he wanted, thus delaying the wife's $97,000 payment. The court disagreed, finding that the agreement was silent as to time of performance, and applying the general rule that where no time is specified, performance is required within a reasonable time. It therefore ordered the husband to pay the wife $97,000 within six months.

Likewise, in *Ebert v. Ebert*,[184] the agreement required sale of the marital home, with the husband paying the wife $4,000 per month until sale and assuming responsibility for certain expenses. The agreement was silent as to the time within which the home would be sold. The court held that in the absence of a time provision, it would require performance within a reasonable time. The case was remanded to the trial court to determine a precise period for sale.

Sale provisions will sometimes tie the time requirement to approval of the transaction by a governmental body. These provisions are construed where possible to provide a reasonable opportunity for obtaining the approval required.[185]

---

178. *See* Proctor v. Proctor, 122 Ohio App. 3d 356, 701 N.E.2d 36 (1997) (agreement required sale of home for $300,000, or for a lesser sum if parties agreed to it; home could not be sold for $300,000, and wife refused to agree to a lesser price; trial court improperly modified agreement by reducing the sale price). The court did note that the husband could buy the home from the wife by paying her her share of the $300,000.

179. Paul v. Paul, 252 A.D.2d 869, 675 N.Y.S.2d 713 (1998).

180. *See* Phillips v. Delks, 880 N.E.2d 713 (Ind. Ct. App. 2008) (sale for higher price was not error, as sale did not harm complaining spouse).

181. *See* Kinberg v. Kinberg, 59 A.D.3d 236, 874 N.Y.S.2d 400 (2009) (sale of apartment in Israel to parties' daughter for $53,000, when value of apartment was $160,000, was not at arm's length).

182. 33 Mass. App. Ct. 240, 598 N.E.2d 677 (1992).

183. 598 N.E.2d at 678.

184. 320 S.C. 331, 465 S.E.2d 121 (Ct. App. 1985).

185. *See* Blake v. Blake, 229 A.D.2d 509, 645 N.Y.S.2d 851 (1996) (parties agreed to sell property if subdivision approval was not "obtained within one year"; time period ran from submission

When the agreement states a specific time period within which sale must take place, the limit is not absolute. The time for performance is not mandatory unless the agreement states that time is of the essence.[186]

Maximum flexibility in time of sale is generally in the best interests of both parties. It is an unfortunate fact of life that buyers are often unwilling to pay a high price when they suspect that the seller is under time pressure to complete the transaction. Thus, short and inflexible sale periods often result in sale at a reduced price.[187] A better option is to provide for sale in a reasonably timely manner, with flexibility to adjust the price in response to market conditions, and with clear provisions governing maintenance of the property during the sale period. This option tolerates some delay in sale, but the delay may in many cases result in a better price. If there is concern over potential misconduct by one spouse during the sale period, a provision requiring the use of "best efforts" to complete the sale might provide appropriate protection, while retaining sufficient flexibility to obtain the best possible sale price.[188]

Delayed Sale. A provision requiring sale after a specific period of time, with the sale proceeds to be divided in a specified manner, is not too vague to be enforced.[189]

Where sale is delayed, provisions should be made for the use and maintenance of the assets during the delay period. Unless the parties agree otherwise, the right to use and duty to maintain presumably would fall upon the spouse who holds legal title to the asset.[190]

Where the dependent spouse expects to live off of income generated by the sale proceeds, it may also be a good idea to provide support payments until the sale is complete. Where the sale was not completed within a reasonable time, one court held that such support payments could be terminated by the court.[191]

---

of request for approval and not from signing of agreement).

186. Mayers v. Mayers, 15 Va. App. 587, 425 S.E.2d 808 (1993).

187. For example, in Faith v. Faith, 709 So. 2d 600 (Fla. 3d Dist. Ct. App. 1998), the parties agreed that their entire agreement would be contingent upon the husband's purchase of a certain warehouse. After the agreement was signed, the seller increased his asking price substantially. The court did not state the reason for the increase, but the increase seems like a logical act a seller might take if he knew or suspected that the buyer was under pressure to complete the transaction. The husband refused to buy at the higher price, and the court held that the price increase made the transaction commercially unreasonable, so that the husband's refusal was justified. *Faith* is not precisely a sale case, but it shows how transactions incident to divorce can backfire when the parties are acting under time pressure.

188. *See id.* (contract required husband to use his best efforts to complete a certain business deal).

189. Sheppard v. Sheppard, 229 Ga. App. 494, 494 S.E.2d 240 (1997).

190. *See* Wolshire v. Wolshire, 905 N.E.2d 1051 (Ind. Ct. App. 2009) (where parties agreed that husband would receive 17.5 percent of the proceeds of delayed sale of marital home, and agreement was silent on expenses, error to order husband to pay 17.5 percent of taxes, insurance, and maintenance between divorce and date of sale).

191. *See* Ray v. Ray, 707 So. 2d 358 (Fla. 2d Dist. Ct. App. 1998). The court did note that termination could not be retroactive to a date before the date of filing of the motion to terminate.

Net Proceeds. When the parties agree to sell property, they often divide only the net proceeds, after subtraction of various expenses of the sale. The existing case law construes these provisions literally.[192] In *Osborn v. Osborn*,[193] the parties agreed to divide the "sale proceeds less commissions paid to any broker or Trustee reasonably necessary to procure a buyer." The property at issue was real property in Portugal, and under Portuguese law, all real property owned by nonresidents had to be titled in the name of a resident trustee. The trustee holding the property demanded a fee in order to permit sale, and without this trustee's consent, sale was impossible. The court held that the fee was not a "commission" paid "to procure a buyer," and refused to subtract the fee in determining net proceeds. If the fee was a bona fide expense of sale, then a more result-oriented court could have held that it was within the spirit of the parties' intent. The court may have suspected that the fee was not bona fide, but it did not expressly so state in its opinion.[194]

Conversely, in *Jacobsen v. Weiss*,[195] the definition of net proceeds permitted deduction of taxes. The wife deliberately refused to take all available tax deductions, thereby decreasing the net proceeds available to be divided. The court charged the wife with all deductions she reasonably could have taken, finding that any other construction of the agreement would lead to an absurd result.

When the property sold is encumbered by a lien, net proceeds are determined using the amount of the lien as sale. The date of the agreement or the date of divorce should not be used unless the agreement expressly so requires.[196]

At least one court has awarded the occupying spouse credit for postdivorce improvements to the property before dividing the net proceeds.[197] This result is far from obvious,[198] so where improvements are expected, their value should probably be excluded from the definition of net proceeds.

In drafting a provision dividing net proceeds, the wise drafter will always consider the possibility that the asset may sell for a loss. Where the agreement does not expressly consider that possibility, an agreement dividing net proceeds will probably be read to require a similar division of any net liability.[199] If the asset sells for no net pro-

---

192. *See* Schwartz v. Greico, 901 So. 2d 297, 300 (Fla. Dist. Ct. App. 2005) (agreement provided that "the husband shall pay to the wife one-sixth of the net proceeds of the sale"; obligation was one-sixth of total proceeds, not one-sixth of proceeds from husband's 50 percent interest in property).

193. 159 Vt. 95, 614 A.2d 390, 392 (1992).

194. *See also* Brown v. Keating, 182 A.D.2d 552, 582 N.Y.S.2d 422, 422 (1992) (in determining "net proceeds" from sale of marital residence, closing costs must be subtracted).

195. 260 A.D.2d 308, 689 N.Y.S.2d 75 (1999).

196. Knutson v. Knutson, 973 P.2d 596 (Alaska 1999).

197. *Id.*

198. *See* Field v. Kaliszewski, 250 A.D.2d 728, 673 N.Y.S.2d 195 (1998) (where agreement was silent on payment of home-related expenses during period of exclusive use before sale, credit for payment of those expenses was not available).

199. *See* Fuchs v. Fuchs, 236 A.D.2d 585, 653 N.Y.S.2d 948 (1997) (where wife exercised option to purchase home for half of appraised value minus mortgage balance, and mortgage balance exceeded appraised value, husband was responsible for half of deficit).

ceeds at all, neither spouse is entitled to receive anything, even if positive value existed when the agreement was signed.[200]

When a sale provision applies to a business, the court may face difficult issues in determining how much actual consideration is attributable to the sale itself. The basic problem is that business sales are frequently accompanied by noncompetition or future employment agreements, and that for tax-related as well as divorce-related reasons, the parties have a strong incentive to treat part of the actual sale consideration as consideration for the related agreement. The litigated cases hold strongly in this situation that the court has power to look beneath the surface of all of the sale documents to determine the true, actual consideration for sale of the business.[201] The agreement cases appear to be taking the same position.[202]

A provision entitling a party to receive proceeds from sale of property does not entitle that party to an ownership interest in the property, especially where the sale requirement is conditional.[203]

Enforcement. Where one party refuses to cooperate with an agreement to sell property, the court may appoint a commissioner to conduct the sale.[204]

Sale to a Party: Options and Similar Arrangements
In some cases one party wants possession of an asset while the other party wants the asset to be sold. The logical course of action is this situation is for the first party to purchase the second party's interest.

Such a purchase is only possible, however, if the first party has sufficient funds or can obtain sufficient financing. Moreover, the second party will sometimes want the additional security of knowing that the asset was sold for fair value on the open market, rather than for an agreed-upon price that might be incorrect. When financial resources may be lacking or a market sale is needed to test value, some agreements will give the first party an option to purchase the asset if certain conditions are met. These option provisions are clearly enforceable.[205]

---

200. Gipp v. Gipp, 37 A.D.3d 406, 829 N.Y.S.2d 630 (2007) (where parties agreed to split equally proceeds from sale of golf course, and golf course was foreclosed upon by creditor, rejecting one spouse's argument for a lump sum award equal to half the value of the course at the time of the agreement).

201. *See, e.g.,* Hoeft v. Hoeft, 74 Ohio App. 3d 809, 600 N.E.2d 746 (1991) (formal breakdown of consideration, $60,000 for sale and $225,000 for covenant not to compete, was absurd on its face; remanding with instructions to determine how much of the stated consideration for the covenant was actually consideration for the sale); *see generally* TURNER, *supra* note 76, § 5:23, at 363–67.

202. *See* Zesiger v. Zesiger, 14 F. Supp. 2d 314 (S.D.N.Y. 1998) (noting that tax treatment is relevant in determining the actual sale consideration, but is not dispositive).

203. *See* Judge v. Judge, 14 So. 3d 162, 166 (Ala. Civ. App. 2009) (where agreement stated that parties' son would receive proceeds if home was sold, and home was never sold, son received nothing; trial court erred by awarding son fee simple ownership of home).

204. Mayers v. Mayers, 15 Va. App. 587, 425 S.E.2d 808 (1993).

205. *See* Palermo v. Palermo, 34 A.D.3d 548, 824 N.Y.S.2d 654 (2006) (where agreement gave husband option to purchase home, error to order sale on the open market).

One particularly common limitation on option provisions is time. When an option must be exercised within a specific time period, the courts have construed the requirement literally, refusing to allow purchase if the option is exercised even a few days late.[206]

Where a letter exercising an option was mailed during the time period, but not received until afterward, one court held that the date of mailing controlled.[207] The option itself was ambiguous, parol evidence provided no clear answer, and using the date of mailing allowed the court to avoid a forfeiture.

Price. Where an option is delayed until a future date (often the emancipation of the youngest child), and the agreement does not clearly require otherwise, an option provision will be construed to refer to the price at the time when the option is exercised, and not when the agreement was originally signed.[208]

Replacement. One rather uncommon alternative to sale of an asset is to allocate the asset to one party, but to require that party to acquire for the other party a similar asset of equal value. This type of provision occasionally governs division of the marital home in agreements between wealthier parties. Because these provisions are unusual, the general trend is to construe them strictly.[209]

§ 6.027 *Exclusive Use*

Another option for implementing joint ownership without joint control is to give one spouse the exclusive right to possession of the asset for some period of time before sale. The most common example of such an arrangement involves the marital home, which is often awarded to the custodial parent during the minority of the children, and then sold or otherwise divided between the spouses. Short periods of exclusive use are also awarded to cover the time in which a home or other substantial asset is on the market awaiting sale.

An exclusive use provision should carefully state that it involves only use and not actual ownership. In *Williams v. Williams*,[210] the agreement provided that the wife could live in the home, but that it "goes back" to the husband if the wife moved to another location. The court held that the intention was to give the husband only physical

---

206. *See* Kendall v. Kendall, 44 A.D.3d 827, 843 N.Y.S.2d 679 (2007) (agreement gave wife option to purchase asset by paying $220,000 to the wife by stated date; where wife failed to make the payment by the stated date, option was lost, even though agreement did not state that time was of the essence); Bresnan v. Bresnan, 156 A.D.2d 532, 548 N.Y.S.2d 803, 804 (1989) (where husband was "a few days" late in exercising option to purchase marital home, option had expired and wife could not be forced to convey her interest).

207. Cortez v. Cortez, 145 N.M. 642, 648, 203 P.3d 857, 863 (2009).

208. *See* Pacifico v. Pacifico, 190 N.J. 258, 269, 920 A.2d 73, 79 (2007) ("where the sale of a marital asset is to abide a future event, for example the coming of age of a child, and no alternative is provided, current market value as of the time of the triggering event is presumed").

209. *See, e.g.*, Lang v. Lang, 551 So. 2d 547 (Fla. Dist. Ct. App. 1987) (enforcing plain language of contract that stated that husband "shall" buy or build wife a new home).

210. Williams v. Williams, 202·W. Va. 41, 501 S.E.2d 477, 478 (1998).

possession, and not beneficial ownership. The language of the agreement was unclear, however, and it clearly created a risk that the wife would lose her share of the home's value.

When exclusive use is awarded, the agreement should include provisions for maintaining the asset during the period of use. These provisions are generally construed to preserve the value of the asset for use and division at a later time.[211]

If provisions regarding maintenance are not carefully drafted, they may conflict with one another. In *In re Marriage of Bolton*,[212] the agreement required the husband to pay the mortgage payment for a home occupied by the wife. The agreement stated the amount of the monthly mortgage payment as $752.45. The agreement further provided that the wife would be responsible for taxes and insurance upon the home. Unfortunately, like most mortgage payments, the $752.45 figure included taxes and insurance. Thus, the contract on its face required both parties to pay the same obligation. The court ultimately ordered the wife to be responsible for all taxes and insurance beyond those included in the $752.45 figure, a construction that gave effect to both of the competing provisions. The lesson to be learned is that when drafting a promise to pay a mortgage, counsel should make certain to learn what expenses the payment covers.

When one spouse has exclusive use of a jointly owned asset, that spouse may have a fiduciary duty to manage the property with the other spouse's interest in mind. For instance, in *Marshall v. Grauberger*,[213] the husband agreed to hold certain stock for five years and then give it to the wife. If he sold the stock before the five years ended, he was to give the wife the proceeds. During the five-year period, the husband sold his own stock in the same corporation at a substantial profit, but he did not sell the wife's stock, which then declined substantially in value. The court found that he had breached his fiduciary duty to protect the wife's interest.[214]

A promise to give one spouse exclusive use of a jointly titled asset operates to waive the right to partition that asset during the exclusive use period.[215]

Termination. The termination of exclusive use is often a subject for dispute between the parties. Unlimited exclusive use of real property is an invalid restriction on alienation of land, and where the contract states no limit, one court implied that the use

---

211. *See* Mancini v. Mancini, 216 A.D.2d 535, 628 N.Y.S.2d 803 (1995) (husband's obligation to pay mortgage on marital residence until sale did not terminate upon wife's remarriage).

212. 950 S.W.2d 268 (Mo. Ct. App. 1997).

213. 796 P.2d 34 (Colo. App. 1991).

214. *See also* Cravero v. Holleger, 566 A.2d 8 (Del. Ch. 1989) (agreement gave husband exclusive use of trailer park, and required him to pay wife her interest if he sold it or died owning it; while agreement did not create a trust, husband did have implied duty of good faith in executing contract); Long v. Long, 196 Wis. 2d 691, 539 N.W.2d 462, 466 n.3 (Ct. App. 1995) (stipulation that wife could "use" certain bank accounts permitted her to withdraw funds from them, but did not prevent court from holding her accountable on a dissipation theory for any funds spent for a wrongful purpose).

215. *See, e.g.*, Diggs v. Diggs, 116 N.C. App. 95, 446 S.E.2d 873 (1994).

lasted only for a reasonable duration.[216] Where the wife had had exclusive use of the marital home for 11 years, four of which were after the emancipation of the youngest child, the court found that a reasonable period had expired. Conversely, another court held that a reasonable period lasts until the death of the party to whom indefinite exclusive use is given.[217]

If the agreement does state a time limit, the provision is valid even if the period of exclusive use is long.[218]

Exclusive use generally does not terminate upon the remarriage of the occupying spouse.[219] If it is intended as a form of child support, it might terminate when the youngest child reaches majority.[220] In either situation, of course, the parties are free to provide otherwise in the agreement.

The above discussion assumes that the agreement actually awards exclusive use to one spouse. Where the agreement definitely requires sale, but fails to state a period during which the sale must take place, the trend is to require sale within a short period. *See* § **6.026**. Where the agreement does not absolutely require sale, but only requires division of the proceeds in a stated manner if and when sale should occur, then under the principles set forth above, the courts will generally not require that sale take place at any specific time.

§ 6.028 Modification and Termination

As a general rule, of course, property division orders cannot be modified after they have become final.[221] This rule applies with equal force to property division provisions in separation agreements.[222]

---

216. Sherman v. Sherman, 168 A.D.2d 550, 563 N.Y.S.2d 424 (1990); *but see* Keevan v. Keevan, 796 So. 2d 379 (Ala. Ct. App. 2001) (unlimited exclusive use was enforceable); Miller v. Miller, 133 N.H. 587, 578 A.2d 872 (1990) (enforcing contract that gave wife exclusive use of the marital home until she decided to sell it).

217. *Diggs*, 116 N.C. App. 95, 446 S.E.2d 873.

218. *See* Sklarin v. Sklarin, 204 A.D.2d 428, 612 N.Y.S.2d 64 (1994) (provision giving wife exclusive use until death or remarriage was valid; provision not limited to a reasonable time).

219. Strickland v. Strickland, 589 So. 2d 1033 (Fla. Dist. Ct. App. 1991).

220. Grizzell v. Grizzell, 583 So. 2d 1349 (Ala. Ct. App. 1991). If intended as property division, exclusive use does not terminate upon the death of the nonoccupying spouse. Fecteau v. Se. Bank, 585 So. 2d 1005 (Fla. Dist. Ct. App. 1991) (provision could not be spousal support, as parties expressly reaffirmed it after wife's remarriage).

221. *See generally* TURNER, *supra* note 76, § 9.24.

222. *See* Ray v. Ray, 707 So. 2d 358 (Fla. 2d Dist. Ct. App. 1998); Proctor v. Proctor, 122 Ohio App. 3d 356, 701 N.E.2d 36 (1997) (agreement required sale of home for $300,000, or for a lesser sum if parties agreed to it; home could not be sold for $300,000, and wife refused to agree to a lesser price; trial court improperly modified agreement by reducing the sale price); *In re* Marriage of Thomason, 802 P.2d 1189 (Colo. App. 1990) (error to add entirely new provision not present in original agreement); Agerskov v. Gabriel, 596 So. 2d 1172 (Fla. Dist. Ct. App. 1992) (error to order husband to pay rent for use of marital home); Kuhnke v. Kuhnke, 556 So. 2d 1121 (Fla. Dist. Ct. App. 1991) (court had no power to modify contractual provisions for sale of marital home); *In re* Marriage of Franks, 275 Mont. 66, 909 P.2d 712 (1996) (court cannot modify property settlement agreement that is not unconscionable); Castiglione v. Castiglione, 259 A.D.2d 582, 686 N.Y.S.2d

Nevertheless, if the contract itself anticipates modification, the court will follow its terms. A good example is *Greer v. Greer*,[223] in which the parties were divorced while federal law prohibited state courts from dividing military retirement pay.[224] The wife received no part of that pay, but the parties expressly agreed that the wife could get a share of it in the future if Congress changed the law. Congress did so in 1983,[225] and the wife sued to enforce the contract. The court distinguished the general rule and enforced the modification provision.[226]

Some states also allow the parties to modify their property division by subsequent agreement. Modification may be permitted even where the contract has been *approved* or *incorporated* into the decree.[227]

Remarriage. As a corollary of the general rule that property division obligations are not modifiable, such obligations do not terminate upon the recipient's spouse's remarriage.[228]

The parties can provide for property division payments to terminate on remarriage if they do so expressly.[229] One common situation in which a remarriage provision tends to appear involves exclusive use of the marital home, which often terminates when the resident spouse remarries. This type of provision is triggered by the mere

---

486 (1999) (where stipulation divided pension equally, error to reduce alimony by amount of pension benefits awarded; reduction effectively modified the property division).

In Stepp v. Stepp, 955 P.2d 72 (Okla. 1998), the court held that when the husband discharged in bankruptcy his half of a joint debt, making the wife liable for the entire amount, the court could modify the decree to order the husband to pay the same debt as nondischargeable spousal support. *Stepp* is the only case nationwide to permit a substantive modification of a property division agreement, and it is probably limited to the specific fact situation in which bankruptcy threatens to destroy fundamental elements of the parties' bargain.

223. 807 P.2d 791 (Okla. 1991).

224. *See generally* TURNER, *supra* note 76, § 6:3.

225. *See id.*

226. *See also In re* Whitman, 81 Ohio St. 3d 239, 690 N.E.2d 535 (1998) (court can modify property division where original agreement so permits); Wright v. Wright, 2008 WL 4885677, at *4 (Ohio Ct. App. 2008) ("after a separation agreement has been incorporated into a decree of dissolution, the parties to a separation agreement may modify its terms by subsequent acts or agreements so long as it is supported by consideration"; particularly since agreement itself expressly reserved parties' right to modify it in the future).

227. *See* IND. CODE ANN. § 31-15-2-17(c) (Westlaw 2010) ("The disposition of property settled by an agreement described in subsection (a) and incorporated and merged into the decree is not subject to subsequent modification by the court, except as the agreement prescribes or the parties subsequently consent[.]"); Humber v. Bjornson, 8 So. 3d 995, 1002 (Ala. Ct. App. 2008); Brown v. Brown, 796 S.W.2d 5 (Ky. 1990); *see generally* § 6.07.

228. *See* Surratt v. Surratt, 85 Ark. App. 267, 148 S.W.3d 761 (2004); Mancini v. Mancini, 216 A.D.2d 535, 628 N.Y.S.2d 803 (1995) (husband's obligation to pay mortgage on marital residence until sale did not terminate upon wife's remarriage).

229. *See* Kuhl v. United Airlines, Inc., 237 A.D.2d 577, 655 N.Y.S.2d 619 (1997) (agreement that terminated wife's rights in husband's retirement benefits upon her remarriage did not violate public policy).

act of remarriage, even if the resident spouse divorces before the court actually orders termination.[230]

Death. Property division obligations generally do not terminate upon the death of either party after entry of the divorce decree.[231] The effect of death before entry of a divorce decree is discussed in § **4.08**.

While death does not terminate property division rights, death does in some cases change the nature of the asset being divided. The most common example is retirement benefits, which stop upon the death of the employee spouse, and are replaced with survivor benefits. The death of the alternate payee under a QDRO is discussed in § **6.021**.

Disguised Support. Modification could be permitted, of course, if an obligation that is labeled as property division is actually spousal or child support. *See* § **6.01**.

Clarification. In all states, of course, the court is permitted to clarify an ambiguous property settlement without violating the rule against modification.[232]

Enforcement. As long as a court does not change the substantive rights of the parties, the court is free to adopt any enforcement device permitted by the law of contracts.[233] Enforcement is not modification, even if the precise enforcement measure used is not expressly permitted by the agreement.

§ 6.03 Spousal Support Provisions

§ 6.031 Construction in General

Waiver

Provisions in separation agreements that waive spousal support are generally enforced as written. *See* § **6.061**. These provisions prevent future awards of support not only under principles of waiver, but also under the independent rule that a court that makes no support award at the time of divorce and that does not reserve jurisdiction over the issue loses jurisdiction to make a support award at a later date.[234]

---

230. Kaye v. Kaye, 203 A.D.2d 689, 610 N.Y.S.2d 632 (1994).

231. *E.g.*, Malicoate v. Standard Life & Accident Ins. Co., 999 P.2d 1103 (Okla. Civ. App. 2000); Divich v. Divich, 2003 SD 73, 665 N.W.2d 109 (2003).

232. *See, e.g., Ex parte* Bonds, 581 So. 2d 484 (Ala. 1991); Aarvig v. Aarvig, 248 N.J. Super. 181, 590 A.2d 704 (Ch. Div. 1991).

233. *See, e.g.*, Horchover v. Field, 964 P.2d 1278 (Alaska 1998) (trial court properly ordered an accounting to determine whether husband had complied with the agreement; order was not improper substantive modification). For a general discussion of the distinction between modification and enforcement in litigated case, see TURNER, *supra* note 76 §§ 6:20, 9:25.

234. *See generally* 27B C.J.S. *Divorce* § 593 (Westlaw 2008).

Some states hold that a waiver of spousal support is enforceable only if it is expressly stated.[235]

In *Goppert v. Goppert*,[236] the court suggested that the husband might be estopped from relying upon an alimony waiver if his bad-faith conduct created the wife's financial need. The court did not mention any express reservation of jurisdiction and it did not explain how a theory of estoppel could give the court subject-matter jurisdiction to make an award of alimony after the divorce decree was final.

Amount of Support

Most support clauses require set support at a specific amount. The parties are free, however, to establish a formula or schedule of differing amounts to be paid at different times. Such a schedule is enforceable even if the court itself lacks the power to award variable support where no agreement exists.[237] When the amount due under a variable support provision rises or falls, the change takes effect immediately, without the need for a court order modifying the obligation.[238]

While most escalator provisions are a straight function of income, some escalator provisions combine a fixed award with an additional variable amount, or even make two distinct variable amounts.[239] An escalator clause obviously prevents either spouse from arguing that a mere change in income is an unforeseen changed circumstance for purposes of modification, since the original agreement foresaw the possibility that income would change.[240]

Some courts have approved the use of language that is even less specific than a formula or schedule. For instance, a Colorado court enforced an agreement to provide "whatever may be necessary" for support of children,[241] while a New York court approved an agreement to "increase . . . support only in an amount correlated to any

---

235. *See* Jones v. Jones, 162 N.C. App. 134, 137, 590 S.E.2d 308, 310 (2004) ("Because such waivers must be express, general releases are insufficient to waive a spouse's right to alimony"; oral out-of-court statements not sufficient); Napier v. Napier, 135 N.C. App. 364, 520 S.E.2d 312 (1999) (general release not sufficient, where it did not expressly mention spousal support).

236. 642 So. 2d 589 (Fla. Dist. Ct. App. 1994).

237. *See* West v. West, 891 So. 2d 203 (Miss. 2004) (escalation clause in spousal support provision was not illegal); *In re* Marriage of Mease, 320 Mont. 229, 92 P.3d 1148 (2004); Curtis v. Curtis, 151 A.D.2d 945, 543 N.Y.S.2d 220 (1989); *In re* Marriage of Perez, 60 Wash. App. 319, 803 P.2d 825 (1991) (enforcing agreement that required support in amount computed by applying present financial facts to prior child support guidelines); *see generally* Annotation, *Escalation Clause in Divorce Decree*, 19 A.L.R.4TH 830 (1983).

238. *See* Muir v. Muir, 925 So. 2d 356 (Fla. Dist. Ct. App. 2006); Tapp v. Tapp, 887 So. 2d 442 (Fla. Dist. Ct. App. 2004).

Of course, if a variable support provision is modifiable, *see* § **6.032**, either party is free to ask the court to modify the provision for changed circumstances, either before or after a self-executing adjustment. *Tapp*, 887 So. 2d 442.

239. *See* Laurence v. Rosen, 229 A.D.2d 373, 645 N.Y.S.2d 773 (1996) (50 percent of gross income plus 15 percent of gross income between $32,000 and $50,000).

240. Cunningham v. Cunningham, 345 N.C. 430, 480 S.E.2d 403 (1997).

241. *In re* Marriage of Meisner, 807 P.2d 1205, 1208 (Colo. App. 1990).

increase in income."[242] Conversely, where the contract provided merely that one spouse would "always take care of" the other, one court found the provision too vague for enforcement.[243]

Where the payor spouse breaches an escalator clause that is based upon facts within the payor's control (e.g., adjusted gross income as set forth on a federal tax return), the payee may obtain arrears at the higher amount retroactive to the date when support should have been increased.[244]

Fluctuations in amount under an escalator clause do not result from any change in the language of the agreement. They are therefore not modification, as that term is used in a specific statute, case, or provision of the agreement preventing modification.[245]

Income. Increasing or decreasing support provisions often depends upon the level of the parties' net or gross income. As a result, there is a substantial body of authority defining these terms.

It is important to note that concepts such as income and net income are used in different ways in different agreements. Thus, the definitions of these terms depend upon the facts, and particularly upon a full consideration of the language of the agreement (and extrinsic evidence if the agreement is unclear or incomplete). Phrased differently, there is no one single mandatory definition of gross or net income for all agreements that leave these terms undefined.[246] In particular, a court is not required to follow the tax law definition of gross income.[247]

Despite this uncertainty, it is generally true that courts lean toward broadness in defining such terms as "income" or "wages."[248] These terms normally include retirement

---

242. *See* Lahaie v. Lahaie, 222 A.D.2d 869, 635 N.Y.S.2d 108, 109 (1995).

243. Yedvarb v. Yedvarb, 237 A.D.2d 433, 655 N.Y.S.2d 84, 84 (1997).

244. Van Alfen v. Van Alfen, 909 P.2d 1075 (Alaska 1996); Rolnick v. Rolnick, 290 N.J. Super. 35, 674 A.2d 1006 (App. Div. 1996).

245. McLaughlin v. McLaughlin, 178 Ohio App. 3d 419, 898 N.E.2d 79 (2008).

246. Patterson v. Patterson, 72 Ohio. App. 3d 818, 596 N.E.2d 534 (1991).

247. *See* Weiss v. Weiss, 289 A.D.2d 498, 498, 735 N.Y.S.2d 582, 583 (2001) ("We reject the appellant's contention that in determining whether he was entitled to enter a judgment for overpayment of spousal support the Family Court should have applied the broad definition of income contained in Internal Revenue Code § 61 to the parties' stipulation[.]").

248. *See* Dowd v. Dowd, 96 Conn. App. 75, 82, 899 A.2d 76, 82 (2006) (where agreement based support upon "gross annual earned income," rejecting husband's argument that certain distributions from corporation were return on investment, and finding them to be earned income); Medvey v. Medvey, 83 Conn. App. 567, 850 A.2d 1092 (2004) (husband's income included amounts earned by husband for work for prior employer, even though husband directed former employer to transfer those amounts to his new employer; husband had substantial interest in new employer's profits); D'Avignon v. D'Avignon, 945 So. 2d 401, 409 (Miss. Ct. App. 2006) (refusing to construe "net earnings" to include only military retirement pay, and not other sources of income); Pezzullo v. Palmisano, 261 A.D.2d 173, 689 N.Y.S.2d 500 (1999) (trial court did not err in accepting income listed on financial statement husband filed with loan application, even though husband testified that he inflated his financial condition in order to obtain the loan); *see generally* Annotation, *Separation Agreement—Alimony—"Income,"* 79 A.L.R.2D 609 (1961).

benefits,[249] capital gains,[250] and income tax refunds.[251] Where the obligation was based upon the payor's "gross disposable income," one court held after considering extrinsic evidence that gross income was intended.[252] Where net income is used, the agreement may allow or disallow specific individual deductions.[253]

Where the agreement calls for an automatic change upon the occurrence of an event or condition, at least one court has held that support reverts back to its prior amount if the event or condition ceases to exist.[254]

If a court adopts a given construction of gross or net income in one construction action, that definition is binding in future actions between the same parties.[255]

Where an escalator provision was based upon earned income, one court held that the husband breached his implied duty to execute the agreement in good faith by taking voluntary early retirement, thereby eliminating his earned income.[256] This case suggests that normal imputed income principles may apply when defining the term "income" in an agreement.[257] The parties are free, of course, to apply imputed income principles by express agreement.[258]

Escalator clauses based upon "salary" are narrower than those based upon income, and would appear to exclude unearned investment income. It is a close issue, how-

---

249. Dube v. Horowitz, 258 A.D.2d 724, 684 N.Y.S.2d 689 (1999); Keene v. Keene, 175 A.D.2d 666, 572 N.Y.S.2d 592, 593 (1991).

250. Keller v. Keller, 877 S.W.2d 192, 194 (Mo. Ct. App. 1994).

251. Donato v. Lucarelli, 109 A.D.2d 741, 486 N.Y.S.2d 58 (1985).

252. *In re* Marriage of Mease, 320 Mont. 229, 237, 92 P.3d 1148, 1153 (2004).

253. *See* Krane v. Krane, 99 Conn. App. 429, 430, 913 A.2d 1143, 1144 (2007) (enforcing agreement providing that if husband was employed by subchapter S corporation, "he shall not be entitled to deductions for business expenses as made by the corporation").

254. *See* Kim v. Kim, 173 Vt. 525, 526, 790 A.2d 381, 383 (2001) (where maintenance automatically decreased upon husband's retirement, and husband returned to the work force after retiring, alimony returned to higher amount; "[i]t would violate the intent of the agreement if defendant could escape the higher alimony amount by simply announcing his retirement and then returning to work").

255. Lee v. Lee, 189 A.D.2d 952, 592 N.Y.S.2d 495 (1993); *but cf. In re* Marriage of Pihaly, 258 Ill. App. 3d 851, 627 N.E.2d 1297 (1994) (prior order that reduced support but made no express holding on the definition of net income had no precedential value).

256. Larson v. Larson, 37 Mass. App. Ct. 106, 636 N.E.2d 1365 (1994); *see also* Stamerro v. Stamerro, 889 A.2d 1251 (Pa. Super. Ct. 2005) (applying imputed income principles in determining husband's income under agreement; likewise relying upon the implied duty of good faith and fair dealing).

257. *See also* Hecker v. Hecker, 568 N.W.2d 705 (Minn. 1997) (imputation of income to wife who made essentially no effort to improve her earning capacity is especially appropriate where parties agreed that purpose of spousal support was rehabilitative); *see generally* Laura W. Morgan, Child Support Guidelines: Interpretation and Application § 2.04 (2008); Laura W. Morgan, *Imputed Income: 1995 Comprehensive Update*, 7 Divorce Litig. 29 (1995); Laura W. Morgan, *Counting What's Not There: Recent Case Law on Imputing Income in Spousal and Child Support Cases*, 4 Divorce Litig. 197 (1992).

258. *See* Wertheim v. Wertheim, 711 So. 2d 183 (Fla. 4th Dist. Ct. App. 1998) (husband promised to use "best efforts" to maximize his income until age 50; where husband sold practice, but sale did not reduce his income, there was no breach of agreement).

ever, whether "salary" includes irregular compensation, such as bonuses.[259] Given these problems, the prudent option is probably to base escalator provisions on income rather than salary.

Narrow escalator clauses that are not subject to modification can lead to injustice. For example, in *Eckert v. Eckert*,[260] the agreement based support upon a specific definition of income. It then prohibited modification of the amount of alimony. The result left the husband free to deliberately structure his compensation to avoid the agreement's definition of income. The Connecticut Supreme Court held that he was permitted to do this, and refused to grant relief to the wife. When an escalator clause is based upon a narrow definition of income, the agreement should probably permit modification, or take other steps to prevent this sort of financial manipulation.[261]

Duration

The parties are free to provide by contract the date upon which support will cease. When the plain language of the contract suggests permanent support, the courts will implement that language.[262] Likewise, the courts will respect language awarding support for a shorter time period. *See* § **6.036**.

When the duration of support is unclear, courts try to avoid construing the language in a way that permits either party to exert unilateral control over the duration.[263]

§ 6.032 Modification

The modifiability of spousal support is among the more complex separation agreement construction issues. Instead of applying a simple legal test, the court must ask a series of difficult subsidiary questions. The ultimate answer is frequently unclear until several of these questions have been fully considered.

To begin with, the court must use the rules discussed in § **6.01** above to determine whether the contract requires true periodic spousal support payments. If the provision

---

259. *See* Isham v. Isham, 292 Conn. 170, 184, 972 A.2d 228, 237 (2009) (error to hold that "salary" unambiguously excluded bonuses; remanding for consideration of parol evidence).

260. 285 Conn. 687, 941 A.2d 301 (2008) .

261. The authors would argue that a deliberate reduction in income as defined by the agreement would be a breach of the husband's implied duty of good faith and fair dealing. *Cf.* §§ **3.04, 6.021** (substantial case law holding that agreement is breached when divisible retirement benefits are waived in favor of nondivisible disability benefits). This argument was not presented in *Eckert*, but nothing in *Eckert* suggests that the court would have been receptive to it.

262. *In re* Marriage of McKeon, 252 Mont. 15, 826 P.2d 537 (1992) (as a matter of law, maintenance "for life" lasted until wife's death, and did not stop when her social security benefits became payable; contrary evidence barred by parol evidence rule).

263. Burns v. Burns, 157 P.3d 1037, 1041 (Alaska 2007) (five-year minimum duration provision applied to spousal support generally and not only to payments from husband's dental practice income; otherwise husband could terminate support simply by switching careers; "Allowing Troy the unilateral power to reduce the support he owed would violate ... the principles of good faith and fair dealing"); Slorby v. Slorby, 760 N.W.2d 89, 93 (N.D. 2009) (where support ended when wife became "eligible" for social security, condition was met when wife met the requirements for applying for social security; no requirement that wife actually apply, as application was solely within her control).

is a disguised division of property, it is clearly not modifiable.[264] Likewise, contractual lump sum spousal support is ordinarily not subject to modification.[265] Conversely, if the provision is disguised child support, it probably is modifiable. *See* § **6.013**.

If true spousal support payments are involved, the court must next consider whether the payments are part of an integrated bargain agreement. *See generally* § **6.012**. If an integrated bargain has been made, the payments are not modifiable.[266]

Assuming that the payments involve true spousal support that are not part of an integrated bargain, the court must next determine the relationship between the agreement and the decree. The law on this subject is discussed further in § **5.012**. In some states, the court can always modify an agreement that has been *merged* into the divorce decree. This is true even where the agreement itself specifically prevents modification, since a merged agreement is invalid as a contract, and the court cannot disclaim its own power to modify spousal support.[267] In other states, the court cannot modify a *merged* support provision.[268]

If the agreement was *approved* or *incorporated*, the court finally reaches the core issue: whether the power to modify spousal support for changed circumstances extends to the support provisions of a separation agreement. On this question there is a deep and serious split of authority. The decisions can be broken down into three distinct approaches.

Modifiability Favored

One group of states holds that the court always has power to modify support for changed circumstances, *unless the agreement itself provides otherwise.*[269] A few states

---

264. *See* Myers v. Myers, 560 N.E.2d 39 (Ind. 1990); *cf.* Rodgers v. Rodgers, 561 So. 2d 1357, 1357 (Fla. Dist. Ct. App. 1990) ("[i]f a party to a dissolution agreement wishes monthly support payments to be construed as alimony, and therefore modifiable in the future, it is prudent that such intent be expressed in the agreement").

265. *See, e.g.*, Brunner v. Ormsby, 10 So. 3d 18, 24 (Ala. Ct. App. 2008); Bonfiglio v. Pring, 202 Mich. App. 61, 507 N.W.2d 759 (1993); Mallery-Sayre v. Mallery, 6 Va. App. 471, 370 S.E.2d 113 (1988).

266. Keffer v. Keffer, 852 P.2d 394 (Alaska 1993); O'Hara v. O'Hara, 564 So. 2d 1230 (Fla. Dist. Ct. App. 1990); Hughes v. Hughes, 553 So. 2d 197 (Fla. Dist. Ct. App. 1989); Keeler v. Keeler, 958 P.2d 599 (Idaho Ct. App. 1998); *but cf. In re* Marriage of Jones, 222 Cal. App. 3d 505, 271 Cal. Rptr. 761 (1990) (noting that modification statute was passed for the express purpose of avoiding difficult question of whether spousal support provisions were part of an integrated agreement).

267. *See, e.g.*, Appels-Meehan v. Appels, 167 Ariz. 182, 805 P.2d 415 (Ct. App. 1991); Kennedy v. Kennedy, 53 Ark. App. 22, 918 S.W.2d 197 (1996); Hamel v. Hamel, 539 A.2d 195 (D.C. 1988); McFadden v. McFadden, 386 Pa. Super. 506, 563 A.2d 180 (1989).

268. *See* Rockwell v. Rockwell, 681 A.2d 1017 (Del. 1996); Bowman v. Bowman, 567 N.E.2d 828 (Ind. Ct. App. 1991) (enforcing no modification clause, even though contract merged into decree); Horsey v. Horsey, 329 Md. 392, 620 A.2d 305 (1993); Smith v. Smith, 41 Va. App. 742, 589 S.E.2d 439 (2003).

269. *See, e.g.*, MD. CODE ANN. FAM. LAW, § 8-103(b) (1996); KY. REV. STAT. § 403.180(6) (1984); *In re* Marriage of Burke, 39 P.3d 1226 (Colo. App. 2001); Emmel v. Emmel, 671 So. 2d 282 (Fla. Dist. Ct. App. 1996); Harmon v. Harmon, 629 So. 2d 1011 (Fla. Dist. Ct. App. 1993); Ashworth v. Busby, 272 Ga. 228, 526 S.E.2d 570 (2000); Varn v. Varn, 242 Ga. 309, 248 S.E.2d 667 (1978); *In re* Marriage of Brent, 263 Ill. App. 3d 916, 635 N.E.2d 1382 (1994); Bowman v. Bowman, 567 N.E.2d

take this rule to an extreme by holding that the parties cannot agree to make true periodic spousal support nonmodifiable.[270]

Whether the agreement provides otherwise is a question of construction. Since modifiability is favored, these states generally require that any provision forbidding modification be expressly and clearly stated.[271] An express clause stating that support shall not be modifiable is usually sufficient.[272] Such a provision can be made by negative implication.[273] A general statement that the *agreement* shall not be modified may be sufficient if the agreement is otherwise silent, but it will not control over another provision anticipating modification of support specifically.[274] There is no requirement that a waiver of modification must appear in the same paragraph as the support provision.[275]

---

828 (Ind. Ct. App. 1991); Wheeler v. Wheeler, 154 S.W.3d 291, 295 (Ky. Ct. App. 2004); Staple v. Staple, 241 Mich. App. 562, 616 N.W.2d 219 (2000); Boden v. Boden, 229 S.W.3d 169, 173 (Mo. Ct. App. 2007); Toni v. Toni, 636 N.W.2d 396 (N.D. 2001) (following *Staple*); In re Marriage of Miller, 207 Or. App. 198, 140 P.3d 1172 (2006); Banker v. Banker, 196 W. Va. 535, 474 S.E.2d 465 (1996); Blackhurst v. Blackhurst, 186 W. Va. 619, 413 S.E.2d 676 (1991).

270. *See* McDonald v. McDonald, 683 So. 2d 929 (Miss. 1996) (although lump sum support is nonmodifiable); Hayes v. Hayes, 100 N.C. App. 138, 394 S.E.2d 675 (1990) (agreement cannot prevent court from modifying true spousal support).

271. *Burke*, 39 P.3d 1226; *Varn*, 242 at 309, 311, 248 S.E.2d at 669 ("very clear waiver language which refers to the right of modification"); Vargas v. Vargas, 654 So. 2d 963 (Fla. Dist. Ct. App. 1995); *Brent*, 263 Ill. App. 3d 916, 635 N.E.2d 1382. *But cf. Ashworth*, 272 Ga. 228, 526 S.E.2d 570 (if right to modify is waived expressly, agreement need not go further and recite that the right waived is statutory).

272. *See* Sadur v. Ellison, 553 A.2d 651 (D.C. 1989); O'Hara v. O'Hara, 564 So. 2d 1230 (Fla. Dist. Ct. App. 1990); Cannon v. Cannon, 270 Ga. 640, 514 S.E.2d 204 (1999); Geraghty v. Geraghty, 259 Ga. 525, 385 S.E.2d 85 (1989); Paffrath v. Paffrath, 977 S.W.2d 283, 285 ("it is the intention of the parties that said maintenance shall be non-modifiable"; no modification; rejecting argument that parties' intention was different from the actual effect of their agreement); *Boden*, 229 S.W.3d at 173 ("[t]hese provisions of maintenance are non-modifiable"); Fincklin v. Fincklin, 240 N.J. Super. 204, 572 A.2d 1199 (Ch. Div. 1990); In re Marriage of McInnis, 199 Or. App. 223, 240, 110 P.3d 639, 648 (2005) (while parties cannot deprive the court of its power to modify support, "the parties' waiver of the right to seek modification of spousal support is valid and enforceable"); Croom v. Croom, 305 S.C. 158, 406 S.E.2d 381 (1991); Nichols v. Nichols, 162 Wis. 2d 96, 469 N.W.2d 619 (1991); Lipps v. Loyd, 967 P.2d 558 (Wyo. 1998); *see also Harmon*, 629 So. 2d 1011 (general waiver of right to collect additional alimony waived right to subsequent modification).

273. *See* Paynton v. Paynton, 914 S.W.2d 63 (Mo. Ct. App. 1996) ("Only the provisions with regard to child custody and child support shall be subject to modification"; spousal support not modifiable).

274. *See* Smith-Cooper v. Cooper, 344 S.C. 289, 295–96, 543 S.E.2d 271, 274–75 (Ct. App. 2001) (agreement provided that "this agreement shall not be modifiable by any court without the consent of both parties," but also "clearly and unambiguously envisions that Husband's alimony obligation will be reduced as Wife receives social security disability benefits or becomes employed," and husband told court when agreement was approved that he would pay spousal support only until wife received disability or returned to work; error to hold that obligation could not be reduced as wife became self-sufficient).

275. *In re* Marriage of Schweitzer, 289 Ill. App. 3d 425, 682 N.E.2d 759 (1997) (enforcing waiver stated in separate paragraph).

Where an express no-modification clause is enforceable, modification is not permitted, either directly[276] or indirectly,[277] without the consent of both parties. If a nonmodifiable support provision is modified once by agreement of the parties, future modifications without the consent of the parties still violate the nonmodification provision.[278]

If the clause prevents only modification by the parties, however, it may not prevent modification by the court.[279] Also, the clause might not be enforceable if it would make one spouse a public charge.[280]

Where the clause in question does not clearly prevent modification, states following this rule are likely to find that modification is still permitted. For example, a clause that sets forth a specific schedule of amounts or that requires payments of a specific duration does not generally imply nonmodifiability.[281] A general statement that support was "fixed until [the wife] remarries" was held not sufficiently clear, as "fixed" might simply mean established until a change in circumstances occurs.[282] A general statement that the support is "contractual" is not sufficient to prevent modification, as contractual support can sometimes be modified.[283] A provision limiting modification by the par-

---

276. *See* Michaelson v. Michaelson, 359 Ill. App. 3d 706, 715, 834 N.E.2d 539, 546 (2005) ("Robert cannot sidestep the express language of the contract, which clearly provides for an in gross maintenance award that is nonmodifiable[.]"); Richardson v. Richardson, 218 S.W.3d 426 (Mo. 2007) (rejecting argument that nonmodification provision should not be enforceable if unconscionable at the time modification is sought); Maxwell v. Maxwell, 375 S.C. 182, 187, 650 S.E.2d 680, 683 (Ct. App. 2007) (nonmodifiable support provision overrides statutory bar to awarding alimony to adulterous spouse; wife's postagreement adultery not grounds to terminate support).

277. *See In re* Marriage of Waldren, 217 Ariz. 173, 171 P.3d 1214 (2007) (where enforceable nonmodification provision exists, provision cannot be avoided by using court rule permitting reopening of judgments for equitable reasons); Edens v. Edens, 137 N.M. 207, 109 P.3d 295 (Ct. App. 2005) (trial court properly refused to reopen nonmodifiable alimony for general equitable reasons).

278. *See* Thomas v. Thomas, 171 S.W.3d 130 (Mo. Ct. App. 2005). In theory, a modification with consent of the parties could rescind the nonmodification provision, but the rescinding provision would have to be express. If the modification agreement is silent as to future modification, but the original agreement prohibited modification by the court, the original nonmodification provision remains effective.

279. *See* Parker v. Parker, 543 So. 2d 1298 (Fla. Dist. Ct. App. 1989) (contract prevented modification except if written and signed by parties; clause did not apply to court); Filipov v. Filipov, 717 So. 2d 1082 (Fla. 4th Dist. Ct. App. 1998); Vargas v. Vargas, 654 So. 2d 963 (Fla. Dist. Ct. App. 1995); Brenizer v. Brenizer, 257 Ga. 427, 360 S.E.2d 250 (1987); Young v. Beckman, 147 S.W.3d 899 (Mo. Ct. App. 2004). *But see In re* Marriage of Pearson, 965 P.2d 268 (Mont. 1998) (general provision against modification applies to spousal support, even though spousal support not mentioned).

280. Pinsley v. Pinsley, 168 A.D.2d 863, 564 N.Y.S.2d 528 (1990); James H. v. Angel H.H., 179 Misc. 2d 561, 685 N.Y.S.2d 590 (Fam. Ct. 1999); *but see* Nichols v. Nichols, 162 Wis. 2d 96, 469 N.W.2d 619 (1991) (contrary dicta).

281. *See In re* Marriage of Ousterman, 46 Cal. App. 4th 1090, 54 Cal. Rptr. 2d 403 (1996) (provision preventing modification before stated date implicitly allowed modification as to payments due after that date, even though agreement on its face stated that payment would stop on that date; court had jurisdiction to extend payments); *In re* Marriage of Jones, 222 Cal. App. 3d 505, 271 Cal. Rptr. 761 (1990); *see also* Aldinger v. Aldinger, 813 P.2d 836, 838 (Colo. App. 1991) (court could modify agreement-based alimony awarded for 24 months "or until further order of this court").

282. Kizziah v. Kizziah, 651 N.E.2d 297 (Ind. Ct. App. 1995).

283. Beeler v. Beeler, 820 S.W.2d 657 (Mo. Ct. App. 1991).

ties themselves does not limit modification by the court.[284] A general blanket release of all claims against the other spouse also does not prevent modification.[285] Even if one party expressly rejected modifiability during negotiations, support is still modifiable if agreement is silent on the subject.[286]

Where the divorce decree states whether agreement-based support is modifiable or nonmodifiable, that statement may be binding in a future modification action.[287]

Limited Modifiability Favored

A second group of states follows the same rule as to modifiability. When the agreement is silent, however, these states apply a higher standard than the normal changed-circumstances test to determine whether support should actually be modified.

The simplest statement of the higher standard comes from *DeCristofaro v. DeCristofaro*,[288] where the court observed that modification of agreement-based support requires "something more than a 'material change of circumstances.'" This test was met where the husband's financial situation deteriorated and the wife breached the agreement by failing to pay child support.[289] The test was not met where the wife was employable and had $100,000 equity in her home.[290]

New York allows modification only in cases where "extreme hardship" is present.[291] This standard requires "proof that [the party seeking modification] is actually unable to support herself and is in actual danger of becoming a public charge."[292] Where the husband remarried and the wife's earnings increased, one court held that extreme hardship was not present.[293] A mere change in child custody is also not "extreme hardship."[294] Conversely, where the husband lost his employment and his pension was worth $10,000 less than previously projected, so that the support payments exceeded one-third of his income, one court held that the husband had properly pled undue hardship.[295] The

---

284. Sutherland v. Sutherland, 107 Conn. App. 1, 944 A.2d 395 (2008).

285. Fukuzaki v. Superior Court, 120 Cal. App. 3d 454, 174 Cal. Rptr. 536 (1981); Vargas v. Vargas, 654 So. 2d 963 (Fla. Dist. Ct. App. 1995); Carter v. Carter, 318 N.J. Super. 34, 722 A.2d 977 (1999).

286. Beck v. Kaplan, 566 N.W.2d 723 (Minn. 1997).

287. *See* Czapla v. Czapla, 94 S.W.3d 426 (Mo. Ct. App. 2003).

288. 24 Mass. App. Ct. 231, 508 N.E.2d 104, 108 (1987); *see also* Coppinger v. Coppinger, 57 Mass. App. Ct. 709, 785 N.E.2d 1251 (2003).

289. Cournoyer v. Cournoyer, 40 Mass. App. Ct. 302, 663 N.E.2d 863 (1996).

290. Hayes v. Lichtenberg, 442 Mass. 1005, 663 N.E.2d 566 (1996).

291. Harkavy v. Harkavy, 167 A.D.2d 510, 562 N.Y.S.2d 182, 183 (1990).

292. Fetherston v. Fetherston, 172 A.D.2d 831, 569 N.Y.S.2d 752, 754 (1991).

293. Dworetsky v. Dworetsky, 152 A.D.2d 895, 544 N.Y.S.2d 242 (1989).

294. *Id.*; *see also* McKeown v. Woessner, 249 A.D.2d 396, 671 N.Y.S.2d 134 (1998) (voluntary early retirement, accompanied by attractive retirement incentive, was not undue hardship).

295. Hawley v. Hawley, 247 A.D.2d 806, 669 N.Y.S.2d 406 (1998). *See also* Miller v. Miller, 18 A.D.3d 629, 630, 796 N.Y.S.2d 97, 99 (2005) (error to find no extreme hardship without a hearing, where husband alleged a "50% reduction in his earning capacity due to economic conditions and increased expenses incurred as a consequence of having one of the parties' two children, their son, reside with him while still being obligated to pay the plaintiff child support for that child");

"extreme hardship" rule can be waived for purposes of review in the state supreme court,[296] but apparently not for purposes of review in family court.[297]

In Florida, a spouse seeking modification of agreement-based support bears "an exceptionally heavy burden."[298] This test was not met where the wife claimed she did not realize the size of her expenses until after the divorce,[299] but it was met where the wife failed in a good-faith attempt to start a horse-breeding business.[300]

In Maine, the standard is "changed circumstances beyond a mere showing that there has been a substantial change in the parties' respective economic circumstance[s]."[301] The mere fact the wife won $4 million in the state lottery, payable over 20 years, was not sufficient reason to justify a reduction in the husband's support obligation under this test.[302]

In Alabama, "an alimony arrangement based on an agreement of the parties should be modified only for clear and sufficient reasons and only after a thorough investigation."[303] Where the wife became disabled and lost essentially all her assets, while the husband had increased income and lived with his new wife in a $239,000 home, one court held that this standard had been met.[304]

These higher standards can be waived by specific language in the agreement.[305] Where the language is not express, however, the courts are reluctant to imply waiver.[306]

Robinson v. Robinson, 176 Misc. 2d 952, 674 N.Y.S.2d 921 (Sup. Ct. 1998) (husband was on full medical disability, with social security as his only income; extreme hardship present).

296. *See* Glass v. Glass, 16 A.D.3d 120, 120–21, 791 N.Y.S.2d 15, 16 (2005) ("where a judgment of divorce incorporates by reference, but does not merge with, a stipulation of settlement between the parties . . . the parties to such agreement may contractually provide for a support modification on a lesser standard than legally required").

297. *See* Smith v. Smith, 44 A.D.3d 1081, 1082, 842 N.Y.S.2d 617, 619 (2007) (parties cannot confer upon family court the power to modify agreement-based spousal support; court lacks jurisdiction "to modify a support agreement merely because the parties to the agreement have deemed it so"), *aff'd sub nom.* Johna M.S. v. Russell E.S., 10 N.Y. 364, 889 N.E.2d 471, 859 N.Y.S.2d 594, (2008).

298. Andrews v. Andrews, 409 So. 2d 1135 (Fla. Dist. Ct. App. 1982).

299. *Id.*

300. Gardner v. Edelstein, 561 So. 2d 327 (Fla. Dist. Ct. App. 1990).

For additional case law establishing a higher standard for modifying agreement-based support, see Swift v. Swift, 566 A.2d 1045 (D.C. 1989) (unmerged support provision can be modified only for unforeseen changed circumstances). *But see* Blackburn v. Michael, 515 S.E.2d 780 (Va. Ct. App. 1999) (expressly reversing a trial court decision adopting a higher standard for modifying agreement-based spousal support).

301. Day v. Day, 717 A.2d 914, 916 (Me. 1998).

302. *Id.*

303. Glover v. Glover, 730 So. 2d 218, 20 (Ala. Ct. App. 1998).

304. *Id.*

305. Streit v. Streit, 237 A.D.2d 662, 653 N.Y.S.2d 986 (1997). *But see* Robinson v. Robinson, 176 Misc. 2d 952, 674 N.Y.S.2d 921 (Sup. Ct. 1998) (undue hardship is standard for modifying judgment, and it applies even where contract states a higher standard; suggesting that contract claim might exist if contractual standard was not met).

306. *See Streit*, 653 N.Y.S.2d at 987 (provision permitting modification "upon a showing of changed circumstances" did not waive the higher standard).

Modifiability Disfavored

Finally, a third group of states flatly holds that the court has no power to modify the spousal support provisions of an *unmerged* separation agreement.[307] In these states, the support obligation is not modifiable unless the agreement itself expressly so permits.

The parties are free, of course, to state in their agreement that support will be modifiable. In this event, the court will treat the support as if it were court-ordered.[308] If the provision is not express, these states are normally reluctant to find a modifiable obligation.[309]

Of course, even in the absence of a modifiability clause, these states will enforce a modification agreement consented to by both parties.[310]

It is worth stressing again that the statutes dealing with modification apply only to a limited class of cases: those involving true spousal support that is not part of an integrated bargain agreement and that was not merged into the divorce decree. As discussed above, where any of these conditions are not met, the modifiability of the provision depends upon principles of law other than the modification statute.

---

307. *See* Kennedy v. Kennedy, 53 Ark. App. 22, 918 S.W.2d 197 (1996); Nooner v. Nooner, 278 Ark. 360, 645 S.W.2d 671 (1983); Harry M.P. v. Nina M.P., 437 A.2d 158 (Del. 1981); *In re* Marriage of Ehinger, 34 Kan. App. 2d 583, 121 P.3d 467 (2005); *In re* Marriage of Jones, 22 Kan. App. 2d 753, 921 P.2d 839 (1996); Carey v. Carey, 9 Kan. App. 2d 779, 689 P.2d 917 (1984); Wagner v. Wagner, 535 So. 2d 1269 (La. Ct. App. 1998); Stream v. Stream, 614 So. 2d 138 (La. Ct. App. 1993); Thomas v. Thomas, 159 Ohio App. 3d 761, 825 N.E.2d 626 (2004); Peck v. Peck, 707 A.2d 1163 (Pa. Super. Ct. 1998); Nassa v. Nassa, 399 Pa. Super. 58, 581 A.2d 674 (1990); Borden v. Borden, 649 A.2d 1028 (R.I. 2994); Riffenburg v. Riffenburg, 585 A.2d 627 (R.I. 1991); Pendleton v. Pendleton, 22 Va. App. 503, 471 S.E.2d 783 (1996); *see generally* Annotation, *Modification of Agreement-Based Divorce Decree—Alimony*, 61 A.L.R.3D 520 § 8 (1975 & Supp. 1991).

In Indiana, a spousal support provision cannot be modified where the court could not make the same support order in the absence of a contract. Voight v. Voight, 670 N.E.2d 1271 (Ind. 1996). *Voight* did not reach the question of whether support can be modified if the court could make the same order in the absence of a contract.

308. *See In re* Marriage of Hedrick, 21 Kan. App. 2d 962, 911 P.2d 192 (1996) (agreement expressly stated that support could be modified for a material change in circumstances; reducing support after wife's income increased upon her graduation from law school); Bauer v. Votta, 104 Md. App. 565, 657 A.2d 358, 359 (1995) (obligation to pay "true modifiable alimony" was modifiable by the court); *cf.* Doering v. Doering, 54 Va. App. 162, 172, 676 S.E.2d 353, 358 (2009) (where agreement expressly allowed modification, no requirement that court incorporate agreement into decree before modifying spousal support).

309. *See Pendleton*, 22 Va. App. 503, 471 S.E.2d 783 (provision that contract would be construed and governed by Virginia law did not require court to apply law on modifying court-ordered support; provision was merely a choice of law clause); *but cf.* Stout v. Stout, 719 So. 2d 727 (La. Ct. App. 1997) (where agreement required permanent alimony in decreasing amounts, and was silent on modification, error to find not modifiable; remanding for consideration of extrinsic evidence).

310. *E.g.*, *Thomas*, 159 Ohio App. 3d at 765, 825 N.E.2d at 629 ("Although the trial court does not have jurisdiction to grant Soltis's unilateral motion to terminate spousal support, the trial court would have jurisdiction to terminate spousal support if the parties made a joint request in writing[.]").

Combination of Rules

Some states apply different rules to the modifiability of spousal support, depending upon how the agreement was treated in the divorce decree. Where the agreement was *incorporated*, support is generally modifiable; where the agreement was only *approved*, support is not modifiable.[311] In either instance, of course, the parties are free to provide otherwise by express provision.

Many of these holdings come from states that do not recognize true *incorporation*, holding instead that any agreement that is "incorporated" merges into the decree. *Merged* support obligations, of course, can be modified in a large number of states.[312]

Contracts Limiting Modification

The contract may limit modification without preventing it altogether.[313] For example, the parties may agree to permit modification only if the wife's earnings rise above a certain level,[314] or to prohibit modification based upon certain events.[315]

In states that favor modifiability of agreement-based spousal support, partial limitations upon modification will be enforced only where their language is clear. For instance, in *Aronson v. Aronson*,[316] the contract provided that the wife's earnings would not be a changed circumstance for purposes of modification. The court indicated that the clause was enforceable, but that did not prevent the trial court from holding that the wife's inheritance was a sufficient changed circumstance to permit modification.[317]

A Connecticut case held that where support is expressly based upon gross income, and is expressly agreed to be modifiable, earning capacity cannot be used as the basis for modification.[318] The result is highly questionable. Earning capacity is always a

---

311. *See, e.g.*, Beeler v. Beeler, 820 S.W.2d 657 (Mo. Ct. App. 1991); *Ex parte* Owens, 668 So. 2d 545 (Ala. 1995) (incorporated spousal support can be modified; seeming to suggest contrary rule for unincorporated support).

312. *See supra* note 266.

313. *See* Shapiro v. Shapiro, 346 Md. 648, 697 A.2d 1342 (1997) (error to hold that contract must either be completely modifiable or not modifiable at all); *cf.* Tremaine v. Tremaine, 235 Conn. 45, 663 A.2d 387 (1995) (clause allowing court to award support, which could not exceed seven years and which would cease upon death or remarriage, did not allow court to award lump sum support).

314. *See In re* Marriage of Mateja, 183 Ill. App. 3d 759, 540 N.E.2d 406 (1989) (enforcing clause preventing any modification unless the wife's earnings were above $13,000).

315. *See* Driscoll v. Driscoll, 568 N.W.2d 771 (S.D. 1997) (agreement can provide that certain events shall not be changed circumstances); Aronson v. Aronson, 245 N.J. Super. 354, 585 A.2d 956 (App. Div. 1991) (agreement that wife's increasing earnings would not be changed circumstances).

316. 245 N.J. Super. 354, 585 A.2d 956 (App. Div. 1991).

317. *See also* Grachek v. Grachek, 750 N.W.2d 328, 331 (Minn. Ct. App. 2008) (language waiving right to modification generally did not waive right to invoke specific state statute allowing for cost-of-living increases in alimony awards, where cost-of-living increases were not expressly mentioned, and appendix to agreement expressly contemplated such increases); *In re* Marriage of Brent, 263 Ill. App. 3d 916, 635 N.E.2d 1382, 1383 (1994) (support would decrease by 50 percent of wife's additional net income, "except, maintenance shall be reduced only if" wife worked "at least ten hours per week"; 10-hour limit applies only to modification based upon wife's increased income, and does not limit modification based upon husband's decreased ability to pay).

318. Danehy v. Danehy, 118 Conn. App. 29, 982 A.2d 273 (2009).

factor in modifying alimony obligations generally, as obligors can otherwise easily manipulate their actual earnings to reduce support. Nothing in the agreement expressly waived the court's power to consider earning capacity. Moreover, even if modification depended upon the contract alone, the implied duty of good faith and fair dealing, *see* **§ 5.08**, would prevent a party from unreasonably decreasing his or her own income, and would therefore require at least some consideration of earning capacity. Future cases should hold that consideration of earning capacity is barred only by very clear language in the agreement.

Contracts Encouraging Modification

Most modification cases involve contracts that attempt to limit the court's power to modify support. Some contracts, however, attempt to encourage modification by providing for review at certain specific times even if the normal changed circumstances test is not met. A substantial body of case law enforces these provisions, permitting modification without proof of a material change in circumstances.[319]

An agreement requiring review of support after a specific period permits the court to terminate support entirely if the recipient has no remaining need.[320] Conversely, the court may refuse to make any modification at all if need remains, even though circumstances have changed.[321]

Related to a contractual review provision is a provision awarding no support, but expressly reserving jurisdiction to make an award for a limited or even unlimited

---

319. *See, e.g.*, Taylor v. Taylor, 117 Conn. App. 229, 978 A.2d 538 (2009) (enforcing agreement requiring reconsideration of alimony after the husband reached age 65 or wife's father died); Cushman v. Cushman, 93 Conn. App. 186, 888 A.2d 156 (2006) (enforcing clause requiring de novo review of support award after four years); Weber v. Weber, 268 N.J. Super. 64, 632 A.2d 857 (1993) (review de novo after 73 months); Blum v. Koster, 235 Ill. 2d 21, 35–36, 919 N.E.2d 333, 342 (2009) (where agreement required review after 61 months, "Steven did not have the burden of proving a substantial change in circumstances"); *In re* Marriage of Golden, 358 Ill. App. 3d 464, 831 N.E.2d 1177 (2005); *In re* Marriage of Wilson, 225 Ill. App. 3d 115, 589 N.E.2d 614, 615 (1992) (support modifiable if federal income tax law changed to "affect" 73-month minimum duration for deducting alimony payments in excess of $10,000 per year; decrease in statutory period to 37 months was sufficient, even though it had no direct adverse financial impact upon husband); Fabre v. Fabre, 2008 WL 4767047 (Ohio Ct. App. 2008) (review after 12 months); McDonnal v. McDonnal, 293 Or. 772, 652 P.2d 1247 (1982).

New York does not permit de novo review in the family court. *See* Smith v. Smith, 44 A.D.3d 1081, 1082, 842 N.Y.S.2d 617, 619 (2007) (parties cannot confer upon family court the power to modify agreement-based spousal support under any standard other than the statutory one; court lacks jurisdiction "to modify a support agreement merely because the parties to the agreement have deemed it so"), *aff'd sub nom*, Johna M.S. v. Russell E.S., 10 N.Y. 3d 364, 889 N.E.2d 471, 859 N.Y.S.2d 594, 2008 WL 1860165 (2008). But de novo review may be permitted in the state supreme court. *See* Glass v. Glass, 16 A.D.3d 120, 120–21, 791 N.Y.S.2d 15, 16 (2005) ("where a judgment of divorce incorporates by reference, but does not merge with, a stipulation of settlement between the parties . . . the parties to such agreement may contractually provide for a support modification on a lesser standard than legally required").

320. Consorti v. Consorti, 175 A.D.2d 940, 572 N.Y.S.2d 815 (1991).

321. *See* Walsh v. Walsh, 207 A.D.2d 394, 615 N.Y.S.2d 717 (1994) (payor's income dropped but he received $100,000 inheritance; no modification).

period of time in the future. These provisions also are generally enforced.[322] A general reservation of the court's power to award support in the future does not remove the normal requirement that the petitioning party meet the changed circumstances test.[323]

Contracts Requiring Modification

A small number of contracts even go so far as to require modification in certain circumstances. Where the amount of the modification is specified in advance, the agreement is simply one to provide variable support; the cases on this point are considered in § **6.031**.

A contract will occasionally provide that the support must be modified by the court when certain events occur, without stating the amount of the modification. These provisions are disfavored and construed strictly, but they will be enforced when their terms are met.[324]

Waiver

The parties are free to waive any contractual limitations they may have placed upon the court's power to modify support. The fact that such limitations were waived regarding one modification, however, does not necessarily waive the limitations regarding future modifications.[325]

Limited Power to Modify

A few states place statutory limits on the court's power to order spousal support. These provisions do not limit the enforceability of agreements to provide support where the limitations are not met, *see* § **3.05**, but they may prevent the court from modifying such support.[326]

Changed Circumstances

Where contractual spousal support is modifiable, and there is no automatic higher standard for modifying contractual support, and no other standard for modification is stated in the agreement, the general rule is that modification can be granted only where a material change in circumstances has occurred.[327]

The general rule is that the change in circumstances must be one that the parties did not anticipate in drafting the agreement. For instance, in *Beck v. Kaplan*,[328] the

---

322. *See* Davis v. Davis, 372 S.C. 64, 641 S.E.2d 446 (Ct. App. 2006) (where divorce decree reserved jurisdiction to award alimony for period of five years, trial court did not err by making an alimony award within the five-year period).

323. Buckley v. Buckley, 43 Mass. App. Ct. 716, 679 N.E.2d 596 (1997).

324. *See* Phelps v. Phelps, 225 A.D.2d 768, 640 N.Y.S.2d 148, 149 (1996) (agreement provided that decrease in husband's income below $300,000 "shall entitle him to a reduction" in support; where husband's income dropped below the indicated level, error to deny reduction).

325. Little v. Little, 441 Pa. Super. 185, 657 A.2d 12 (1995).

326. *See* Cox v. Cox, 833 N.E.2d 1077 (Ind. Ct. App. 2005).

327. *See, e.g.*, Beck v. Kaplan, 566 N.W.2d 723 (Minn. 1997).

328. *Id.*; *see also* Buettner v. Buettner, 183 S.W.3d 354 (Tenn. Ct. App. 2005) (deferring to trial court's factual finding that parties anticipated possibility that wife would return to full-time

evidence showed that the parties had considered and rejected a provision varying the amount of support along with the cost of living. This rejection showed, the court held, that the parties had considered the effect of inflation in drafting the agreement. Thus, mere inflation was not a sufficient change in circumstances to permit modification. Conversely, in *Bogan v. Bogan*,[329] the evidence showed that the parties did not contemplate the husband's retirement in setting the amount of spousal support. The husband's retirement was therefore a changed circumstance for purposes of modification.

Unmodifiable Spousal Support: Drafting Concerns

In the great majority of states, the parties can choose in their separation agreement whether they wish spousal support to be modifiable. The manner of making this choice varies—some states require an express statement of unmodifiability, while others merely require the absence of a statement permitting modifiability—but there is general agreement that the parties can create either modifiable or unmodifiable spousal support.

From the standpoint of the drafter, how should this choice be made? The authors suggest that it must be made with a clear eye toward the consequences of each choice. The advantage of unmodifiable support is that the client is spared the difficulty of defending a future modification action and the potential inconvenience of an unfavorable modification. The disadvantage of unmodifiable support is that the client is stuck, in good times and bad, with the exact same spousal support obligation set forth in the agreement. To choose between modifiable and unmodifiable support, the parties must balance these effects against each other.

In considering the relative advantages of modifiable and unmodifiable support, the authors suggest paying attention to two specific points. First, while an adverse modification of spousal support can be an inconvenience, all such modifications are made by a neutral judge who has heard evidence and whose decision can be appealed. There are, no doubt, some modification decisions that are unfair to one party or the other, but the great majority of all modification decisions result from a good-faith attempt by a neutral judge to be fair to both parties. In a sense, the harm caused by any modification is "filtered through" the equitable discretion of a court. If the agreement prohibits modification, by contrast, the result is unfiltered; modification is absolutely forbidden, regardless of the degree to which this result is or is not equitable. In the authors' assembled experience researching family law issues, rarely does the law of domestic relations reach a harsher result than when it enforces an unmodifiable spousal support provision in the face of facts normally justifying modification. This harshness is fully justified, for the parties must live with the consequences of their own joint decision on the modifiability question. But in most cases, modification is an inconvenience, while lack of modification can inflict real harm. In most cases, it is better to permit a potential

---

employment after divorce); *see also In re* Marriage of Fletcher, 214 Or. App. 585, 167 P.3d 984 (2007) (allowing parol evidence as to purpose of spousal support provision, so that court could determine whether parties intended emancipation of the children to be a basis for modification or termination).

329. 60 S.W.3d 721 (Tenn. 2001).

adverse modification (if a trial court finds modification equitable) than to prohibit any modification at all (regardless of whether modification is or is not equitable).

Second, it is important to give consideration to the costs and benefits of modifiable support on the facts of the case at hand. Most divorcing parties have an earning capacity, and the great majority are actually employed. When payors determine the affordability of alimony, they traditionally look at the difference between their earning ability and their personal needs. When payees determine the need for alimony, they traditionally look at the difference between their monthly expenditures and their earning ability. In both cases, earning ability is a vital component of the calculation. When parties agree to nonmodifiable spousal support, they are essentially gambling that their earning ability will remain forever at or above its present level, so that the burden of paying support or the need to receive it will not increase beyond present levels.

In the long run, however, every employed person will ultimately leave employment. Those who are fortunate will retire normally, with thanks for a long period of successful service; those who are less fortunate will leave early, as a result of economic conditions (downsizing) or even medical disability. Barring an early death, it is absolutely foreseeable that every support payor and every support recipient will ultimately suffer a serious drop in earned income. Thus, from the standpoint of an employed person, an agreement setting a flat amount of unmodifiable spousal support is therefore often an unwise gamble. There is a substantial risk that the payor will lose employment early and be unable to afford the award. Likewise, the payee may lose employment early and need more funds for support than the unmodifiable agreement permits. In both situations, as noted above, the trial court will not have any equitable discretion to address any hardship.

The subject of modification can also be approached, using a similar analysis, from the viewpoint of expenses. Every unmodifiable support provision is based upon the assumption, by both the payor and the payee, that expenses will remain at or near their current levels. As people get older, however, their expenses tend to go up. This is true not only because standards of living rise, but also because older persons have additional medical expenses. In a managed care environment, it is obviously naive to assume that insurance will cover all of the added expenses. If unmodifiable support is a gamble that expenses will not significantly increase, then the gamble seems like a losing proposition for the great majority of divorcing parties.

There are, of course, situations where unmodifiable support is a better gamble. A wealthy obligor or obligee may have sufficient assets to generate a reasonable stream of income, regardless of employment. An older homemaker, with no current earning capacity at all, cannot be harmed by early loss of employment (although early increased medical expenses would still be possible). Those whose financial situations are more stable, and less dependent upon continued employment, are harmed less by unmodifiable support.

The great majority of persons, however, are dependent for their financial welfare upon continued employment and upon continued reasonable health. Where these dependencies exist, an unmodifiable support provision is uncomfortably close to Russian roulette. The client might benefit by avoiding the inconvenience of an adverse modification; some clients will certainly win the gamble and avoid problems. If income drops or expenses increase in an unforeseen manner, however, the result can be drastically harsh, and there will be little or no chance of a judicial remedy. Most persons purchase insurance on the theory that a modest cost today is better than taking the chance of a calamitous loss tomorrow. For exactly the same reasons, unmodifiable spousal support is not in the best interests of a great majority of divorce clients.

§ 6.033 Termination upon Remarriage

In addition to providing that support will cease at a time certain, agreements often provide that it will cease upon the occurrence of certain events. The most common of these events is the remarriage of the recipient spouse.

The process for determining whether agreement-based spousal support terminates on remarriage is similar to the test for determining modifiability in general. Initially, the court must verify that the payments are true spousal support. Property division obligations are not subject to modification and do not terminate upon remarriage.[330] Next, the court must determine whether the payments are part of an integrated bargain agreement. Payment under such an agreement also do not terminate upon remarriage.[331] Then, the court must check to see whether the agreement was *merged* into the decree. If the agreement was *merged*, it loses its independent existence, and it cannot prevent the court from exercising its statutory power to terminate support upon remarriage.[332]

If the payments are true spousal support that was not part of an integrated bargain and that did not merge into the divorce decree, the court must then consider whether the support was periodic. Where the parties agree to provide lump sum spousal support, that support does not terminate upon remarriage.[333]

Finally, if the agreement calls for true periodic spousal support that is not part of an integrated bargain and that did not merge into the divorce decree, the court reaches

---

330. *See* Stockbridge v. Reeves, 640 So. 2d 947 (Ala. Ct. App. 1994); Gieseler v. Gieseler, 787 S.W.2d 810 (Mo. Ct. App. 1990) (even though payments were labeled as "maintenance"); Cortese v. Cortese, 341 Mont. 287, 289, 176 P.3d 1064, 1065 (2008) ("remarriage of the party receiving maintenance terminates the maintenance obligation, unless maintenance payments are intended as part of the property division"); *In re* Marriage of Hahn, 263 Mont. 315, 868 P.2d 599 (1994) (payments labeled inconsistently as both property division and support); D'Huy v. D'Huy, 390 Pa. Super. 509, 568 A.2d 1289, 1294 (1990); Ebert v. Ebert, 320 S.C. 331, 465 S.E.2d 121 (Ct. App. 1985); Bittorf v. Bittorf, 390 S.E.2d 793 (W. Va. 1989); Spencer v. Spencer, 140 Wis. 2d 447, 410 N.W.2d 629 (Ct. App. 1987).

331. Hayes v. Hayes, 100 N.C. App. 138, 394 S.E.2d 675 (1990) (integrated bargain payments do not terminate on remarriage); *but see* Reeves v. Reeves, 890 S.W.2d 369 (Mo. Ct. App. 1994) (summarily dismissing argument that support was an integrated bargain; court did not seem to understand the argument, which was apparently not based upon extensive citation).

332. *See* Shipley v. Shipley, 305 Ark. 257, 807 S.W.2d 915 (1991) (where agreement merged into decree, payments terminated upon remarriage).

333. *See* Chroniger v. Chroniger, 914 So. 2d 311 (Miss. Ct. App. 2005) (even though lump sum was payable in 36 monthly installments); Ebert v. Ebert, 320 S.C. 331, 465 S.E.2d 121 (Ct. App. 1985); Mallery-Sayre v. Mallery, 6 Va. App. 471, 370 S.E.2d 113 (1988).

the merits of a pure substantive question: Does agreement-based spousal support terminate upon remarriage? The cases break down into three distinct categories. The most common rule is that remarriage does terminate support unless the agreement expressly provides otherwise.[334] A minority of states treat the question as a matter of pure intent, and do not seem to require an express provision.[335] Finally, a very small minority of states holds that support terminates only if there is an express provision in the contract that so provides.[336]

In applying the majority rule, the courts are usually reluctant to extend support past remarriage unless the agreement is clear and explicit. A specific provision mentioning remarriage will of course prevent termination.[337] Remarriage is mentioned not only if

---

334. *See, e.g.,* Palmer v. Palmer, 217 Ariz. 67, 170 P.3d 676 (Ct. App. 2007) (nonmodifiable support until date certain stopped upon remarriage; no provision expressly stating that support would not continue beyond remarriage); Crosby v. Tomlinson, 263 Ga. 522, 436 S.E.2d 8 (1993); Daopoulos v. Daopoulos, 257 Ga. 71, 354 S.E.2d 828 (1987); *In re* Marriage of Bowers, 23 Kan. App. 2d 641, 933 P.2d 176 (1997); Messer v. Messer, 134 S.W.3d 570, 572 (Ky. 2004) (collecting the cases; "the intent to require maintenance to continue after the death of either party or the remarriage of the obligee will not be implied but must be expressly stated"); Cates v. Cates, 819 S.W.2d 731 (Mo. 1991) (limited retroactive application); Chiles v. Chiles, 778 P.2d 938 (Okla. Civ. App. 1989); Langley v. Johnson, 27 Va. App. 365, 499 S.E.2d 15 (1998) (where agreement was silent, support terminated upon remarriage); Miller v. Hawkins, 14 Va. App. 192, 415 S.E.2d 861 (1992); Evans v. Evans, 219 W. Va. 736, 639 S.E.2d 828 (2006); *see generally* Annotation, *Modification of Agreement-Based Divorce Decree—Alimony,* 61 A.L.R.3D 520 § 11 (1975 & Supp. 1991).

Evans requires trial courts in future cases, when approving or incorporating separation agreements, to state expressly whether spousal support survives remarriage and death. It will be interesting to see whether this requirement materially reduces the number of cases in which the intention of the parties on these issues is unclear.

335. *E.g.,* Artman v. Hoy, 370 Ark. 131, 257 S.W.3d 864, 2007 WL 1560439 (2007); Williams v. Williams, 276 Conn. 491, 886 A.2d 817 (2005) (where agreement expressly stated that support "may be modifiable" upon remarriage, support did not automatically terminate; rather, remarriage was a potential basis for downward modification, which under Connecticut law required proof of changed financial needs); Telma v. Telma, 474 N.W.2d 322 (Minn. 1991); Hancher v. Hancher, 31 A.D.3d 1152, 1153, 818 N.Y.S.2d 384, 386 (2006) ("Where, however, the parties' separation agreement expressly *or impliedly* provides that spousal support is to continue after the payee's remarriage, such obligation will be enforced[.]") (emphasis added).

336. *See* Terteling v. Payne, 131 Idaho 389, 957 P.2d 1387 (1998) (remarriage terminates support only if it constitutes a change in financial circumstances; where wife and new husband had premarital agreement that limited wife's financial rights, no change in circumstances was present); McMahon v. McMahon, 417 Pa. Super. 592, 612 A.2d 1360 (1992) (split decision holding that support stops upon remarriage only if contract so provides; strong dissent argued for the general rule nationwide).

337. *See Daopoulos,* 257 Ga. 71, 354 S.E.2d 828 (express mention of remarriage is necessary if support is to continue); Fredeen v. Fredeen, 154 A.D.2d 908, 546 N.Y.S.2d 60 (1989) (alimony lasted until a specific date, and would continue after that date if wife was still unmarried; before the specific date, alimony survived remarriage).

it is included in the agreement itself, but also if it is mentioned in related documents.[338] An express no-modification clause[339] or even a statement in a future agreement[340] may be sufficient as well.

Under the majority rule, a provision requiring support for a certain specific duration will usually not be read to contain an implied term continuing support past remarriage.[341] Under the pure intent test, a different result is possible.[342] A clause listing one or more express termination conditions other than remarriage will not generally be

338. *See* Rintelman v. Rintelman, 118 Wis. 2d 587, 348 N.W.2d 498 (1984) (stipulation provided for lifetime support; after stipulation was read into record, court asked husband if support extended past remarriage, and husband answered yes; support did not terminate); Gayler v. Gayler, 20 Va. App. 83, 455 S.E.2d 278 (1995) (agreement terminated support upon death or remarriage, and addendum then provided that support terminate "only" upon death; combined effect of both documents showed intent that remarriage not terminate support).

339. *See In re* Marriage of Sherman, 162 Cal. App. 3d 1132, 208 Cal. Rptr. 832 (1984); Jung v. Jung, 171 A.D.2d 993, 567 N.Y.S.2d 934, 935 (1991) ("unconditional" payments). *But see Palmer*, 217 Ariz. 67, 170 P.3d 676 (nonmodifiable support until date certain stopped upon remarriage; no provision expressly stating that support would continue beyond remarriage).

340. *See* Ryan v. Ryan, 78 P.3d 961 (Okla. Civ. App. 2003) (to the extent obligation to pay mortgage on home was intended as alimony, obligation terminated upon remarriage; but remanding for further evidence on alleged second agreement regarding payment of mortgage after remarriage).

341. *See Palmer*, 217 Ariz. 67, 170 P.3d 676 (nonmodifiable support until date certain stopped upon remarriage); Messer v. Messer, 134 S.W.3d 570, 572 (Ky. 2004); Gunderson v. Gunderson, 408 N.W.2d 852 (Minn. 1987); Miller v. Miller, 784 S.W.2d 891 (Mo. Ct. App. 1990) (although noting that extrinsic evidence is admissible on the question); Kingery v. Kingery, 211 Neb. 795, 320 N.W.2d 441 (1982); *In re* Marriage of Williams, 115 Wash. 2d 202, 796 P.2d 421 (1990); Jacobson v. Jacobson, 177 Wis. 2d 539, 502 N.W.2d 869 (Ct. App. 1993); Miller v. Hawkins, 14 Va. App. 192, 415 S.E.2d 861 (1992).

342. *See* Artman v. Hoy, 370 Ark. 131, 257 S.W.3d 864, 2007 WL 1560439 (2007) (weekly alimony payments for 10 years did not terminate upon remarriage); Telma v. Telma, 474 N.W.2d 322 (Minn. 1991) (spousal support until the earlier of five years or an increase in the wife's adjust gross income over $30,000; support did not terminate upon remarriage); Glenn v. Snider, 852 S.W.2d 847 (Mo. 1993); Hancher v. Hancher, 31 A.D.3d 1152, 1153, 818 N.Y.S.2d 384, 386 (2006) ("a separation agreement providing that spousal support is to be paid for life or for some other fixed duration manifests the parties' intent that the support obligation is to continue despite the payee's remarriage"); Carroll v. Carroll, 236 A.D.2d 353, 653 N.Y.S.2d 643 (1997) (alimony for seven and three-fourths years survived remarriage); Sacks v. Sacks, 168 A.D.2d 733, 563 N.Y.S.2d 884 (1990) (alimony for specific duration does not cease on remarriage).

Artman seems to reject Smith v. Smith, 41 Ark. App. 29, 848 S.W.2d 428 (1993), which adopted the majority rule that the agreement must expressly mention remarriage, and held that alimony payable for a definite term of years did not survive remarriage.

read to exclude remarriage as an additional grounds for termination.[343] A mere reference to "permanent" support also does not prevent termination.[344]

Cases considering whether cohabitation-type relationships constitute "remarriage" are discussed in the following section.

Where support automatically terminates upon remarriage, and the receiving spouse conceals the fact of remarriage from the paying spouse, the receiving spouse must repay all support payments made after remarriage.[345]

§ 6.034 *Termination upon Cohabitation*

Whether agreement-based support ceases on cohabitation depends upon the language of the agreement. The court must initially make the same set of preliminary inquiries it makes in modification and remarriage cases. Thus, if the payments are property division[346] or child support, or if they are part of an integrated bargain agreement, they do not terminate. *See generally* **§ 6.032.**

If the agreement *merges* into the decree, the effect of cohabitation should technically be determined under the same principles that govern spousal support awards made without an agreement.[347] At least one court has refused to apply those principles,

---

343. *See, e.g.*, Maddick v. DeShon, 296 S.W.3d 519, 521 (Mo. Ct. App. 2009) (support "shall only terminate upon the death of Respondent or September 30, 2011"; support survived remarriage); *In re* Marriage of Rufener, 52 Wash. App. 788, 764 P.2d 655 (1986); *but see* Deangelis v. Deangelis, 285 A.D.2d 593, 594, 727 N.Y.S.2d 481, 482 (2001) ("A separation agreement which specifies, in detail, the conditions or events that will trigger the termination of a party's obligation to pay maintenance to his or her former spouse, and fails to include the ex-spouse's remarriage as such a triggering event, will generally be construed as an implicit agreement to continue maintenance even after remarriage[.]"); Chiles v. Chiles, 778 P.2d 938, 939 (Okla. Civ. App. 1989) (support terminated "only upon [the wife's] death"; obligation survived wife's remarriage).

The strictest application of the express statement requirement nationwide is Hardesty v. Hardesty, 40 Va. App. 663, 665, 581 S.E.2d 213, 215 (2003), where the agreement stated "This support cannot be terminated for any reason." The court held 6–5 that remarriage was not expressly mentioned, so the support ceased upon remarriage.

344. Edwards v. Benefield, 260 Ga. 238, 392 S.E.2d 1 (1990); *In re* Marriage of Jensen, 212 Ill. App. 3d 60, 570 N.E.2d 881 (1991).

345. *See* Smith v. Lockwood, 907 S.W.2d 306 (Mo. Ct. App. 1995).

346. *See In re* Marriage of Dundas, 355 Ill. App. 3d 423, 823 N.E.2d 239 (2005) (payments that were in the nature of property division did not terminate upon cohabitation; rejecting argument that payments were spousal support); Stacy v. Stacy, 53 Va. App. 38, 669 S.E.2d 348 (2008) (mortgage obligation was property division, and therefore did not terminate upon cohabitation).

347. *See* Oakley v. Oakley, 165 N.C. App. 859, 599 S.E.2d 925 (2004) (where state law provided that all agreements presented to the court merged into the decree, court analyzed agreement-based cohabitation provision under state cohabitation statute, without even acknowledging the possibility that agreement might state a different standard).

For general treatment of the effect of cohabitation upon award made in litigated cases, *see generally* Wendy S. Ricketts, *The Relevance of Premarital and Postmarital Cohabitation in Awarding Spousal Support*, 7 Divorce Litig. 150 (1995).

however, finding that the public policy of enforcing contracts controlled over the technical doctrine of *merger*.[348]

If none of the above conditions is met, the question depends upon the intention of the parties. Where the agreement is silent, the general rule is that support does not terminate upon cohabitation.[349]

For similar reasons, there is uniform agreement that mere cohabitation does not fall within the scope of a provision terminating support upon "remarriage." The most extreme case is *Buchan v. Buchan*,[350] where the wife refused to remarry for religious reasons and had a priest bless her new relationship. The court held that the contract required a legal and not a social or religious remarriage, and it refused to terminate support.[351]

Support presumably would terminate upon cohabitation if the cohabitation is sufficient to constitute a common law marriage, the state in which the parties live recognizes such marriages, and support terminates upon remarriage.[352]

Cohabitation Statutes

The general rule applies even where the state in question has a statute providing that court-ordered support does cease upon cohabitation. Several obligors have attempted to argue that cohabitation statutes are public policy, and that they apply unless there is a clear contrary statement in the agreement. As noted above, this argument has been accepted in the context of remarriage. The courts have generally held, however, that the public policy behind the cohabitation statute is not as strong, and that it does not apply to agreement-based support. For example, in *In re Marriage of Giles*,[353] the husband agreed to pay alimony until the wife's death or remarriage. The relevant statute provided that cohabitation terminated support unless the parties agreed otherwise in writing. Nevertheless, the court found that by stating only two specific termination conditions, the parties implicitly agreed to exclude any additional conditions. Thus, the

---

348. Smith v. Smith, 41 Va. App. 742, 589 S.E.2d 439 (2003). *Smith* is discussed at some length in § **5.012**.

349. *See* Ochs v. Ochs, 540 So. 2d 190 (Fla. Dist. Ct. App. 1989) (where contract was silent and wife had previously rejected a proposed support clause listing cohabitation as a termination condition, support did not cease upon cohabitation); Croom v. Croom, 305 S.C. 158, 406 S.E.2d 381 (1991) (where agreement did not list cohabitation as grounds for termination, support continued even if wife cohabited solely in order to avoid termination upon remarriage, even though agreement merged into divorce decree); *see generally* Annotation, *Agreement-Based Alimony—Effect of Cohabitation*, 47 A.L.R.4TH 38 (1986 & Westlaw Supp. 2008).

350. 550 So. 2d 556 (Fla. Dist. Ct. App. 1989).

351. *See also* Rockefeller v. Rockefeller, 335 Ark. 145, 980 S.W.2d 255 (1998) (de facto marriage is not sufficient); Bondy v. Levy, 121 Idaho 993, 829 P.2d 1342 (1992); Rivers v. Rivers, 35 A.D.3d 426, 826 N.Y.S.2d 347 (2006) (maintenance payments "shall continue until the death or remarriage of the plaintiff, but in no event shall they continue beyond July 10, 1997"; payments did not cease upon cohabitation); Lopata v. Lopata, 196 A.D.2d 741, 602 N.Y.S.2d 46 (1993).

352. *See* Cathcart v. Cathcart, 307 S.C. 322, 414 S.E.2d 811 (Ct. App. 1992) (recognizing the point, but finding the requirements for a common law marriage not met on the facts).

353. 197 Ill. App. 3d 421, 554 N.E.2d 714 (1990).

payments did not terminate upon cohabitation.[354] In other words, while in most states an express statement is needed to continue support past remarriage, an express statement is not needed to continue support past cohabitation.

Cohabitation statutes should not be applied to contracts drafted before the statutes were enacted, at a time when cohabitation per se did not terminate support. Had the parties known the statute was coming, they might well have drafted their agreement differently. In addition, at least one state has held that retroactive application would unconstitutionally impair the contract.[355]

Express Cohabitation Provisions

While the courts will not infer from a silent agreement that support terminates upon cohabitation, the parties are free to provide for such termination by express provision.

Where a contractual cohabitation clause conflicts with a state cohabitation statute, the contract generally controls.[356] The parties are permitted to agree to a cohabitation standard different from the one provided by law for use in litigated cases.

Pure Cohabitation Clauses. A review of the cases reveals several different types of cohabitation provisions. The most common type of provision is a pure cohabitation clause, providing that support ceases if the recipient "cohabits" with another person. At a minimum, cohabitation requires that the recipient share a common residence or set of residences with his or her paramour.[357] The relationship must be substantially

---

354. *See also* Carlos v. Lane, 275 Ga. 674, 676, 571 S.E.2d 736, 738 (2002) (where agreement waived rights under specific statute, which covered both modification for changed circumstances and termination for cohabitation, alimony did not terminate upon cohabitation; dissent would have required a more specific reference to the cohabitation portion of the statute); *In re* Marriage of Tucker, 148 Ill. App. 3d 1097, 500 N.E.2d 578 (1986) (alimony stopped upon death, remarriage, or the completion of 121 payments; support did not cease upon cohabitation); Woodings v. Woodings, 411 Pa. Super. 406, 601 A.2d 854 (1992) (cohabitation statute does not apply to agreements).

355. *See* Rubio v. Rubio, 36 Va. App. 248, 549 S.E.2d 610 (2001); Hering v. Hering, 33 Va. App. 368, 533 S.E.2d 631 (2000).

356. *See* Graev v. Graev, 46 A.D.3d 445, 450, 848 N.Y.S.2d 627, 632 (2007) ("the parties to a divorce can, by agreement, alter the terms of" New York's cohabitation statute); O'Hara v. O'Hara, 45 Va. App. 788, 613 S.E.2d 859 (2005) (where contractual cohabitation provision required proof by a preponderance of the evidence, and cohabitation statute required proof by clear and convincing evidence, error to apply statutory standard).

357. *See* Olstein v. Olstein, 309 A.D.3d 697, 699, 766 N.Y.S.2d 189, 191 (2003) (wife's son's wife testified that wife resided full-time with her paramour and referred to his residence as "our home"); *cf.* Parnes v. Parnes, 41 A.D.3d 934, 937, 837 N.Y.S.2d 777, 779 (2007) (issue is whether wife and her fiancé cohabited in the same home, "regardless of whose home or residence that may be").

For cases finding no common residence on the facts, see Cook v. Cook, 798 S.W.2d 955, 957 (Ky. 1990) ("Obviously, the parties intended cohabitation to mean 'living in the same house[.]'"); Ciardullo v. Ciardullo, 27 A.D.3d 735, 736, 815 N.Y.S.2d 599, 600 (2006) ("the respondent's boyfriend maintained a separate residence in the one-bedroom apartment he rented from the respondent and the two did not share household expenses or function as an economic unit"; trial court properly found no cohabitation); Pellegrin v. Pellegrin, 31 Va. App. 753, 525 S.E.2d 611 (2000) (where wife and paramour had close romantic relationship, but did not share a common residence

permanent, and not occasional or irregular,[358] but the couple need not spend literally every night together.[359] The relationship must be romantic;[360] a spouse does not cohabit, as that term is commonly used in separation agreements, by living with a friend or housemate.[361] There is no requirement that the recipient cohabit with a person of the opposite sex; a gay or lesbian relationship can terminate support if the other elements of cohabitation are present.[362]

In determining whether the relationship resembles remarriage, most courts will look to the entire factual situation, including but not limited to the financial relationship between the cohabiting parties.[363]

---

or assume the normal duties and obligations of marriage, and no financial dependency existed, trial court did not err by failing to find cohabitation).

358. *Cook*, 798 S.W.2d 955 (where the wife's paramour had his own separate residence, there was no cohabitation); Allen v. Allen, 966 S.W.2d 658, 660 (Tex. Ct. App. 1998) (error to instruct jury that cohabitation "can include an irregular, limited or partial living together for the purpose of having sexual relations").

359. *See* Adamson v. Adamson, 958 S.W.2d 598 (Mo. Ct. App. 1998) (wife and paramour spent substantial time apart because paramour's job required significant travel, but spent all of their available time together; they also bought a joint home, declaring it their principal residence for tax purposes; cohabitation); Barr v. Barr, 922 S.W.2d 419 (Mo. Ct. App. 1996) (wife and paramour spent 10–12 nights per month together; paramour was traveling for remainder of each month; cohabitation); Honeycutt v. Honeycutt, 152 S.W.3d 556, 565 (Tenn. Ct. App. 2003) (wife and paramour resided together for 41 days in late 1999, 206 days in 2000, and 206 days in 2000 (through September), and took trips together to "to New England, Europe, Disney World, Atlanta, Lake Tahoe, and North Carolina"; finding cohabitation); Penrod v. Penrod, 29 Va. App. 96, 510 S.E.2d 244 (1999) (wife spent three to four nights per week together at paramour's home, kept clothing and other personal property there, and took vacation with paramour; sexual relationship was present; finding cohabitation).

360. *See* Tricoles v. Tricoles, 202 A.D.2d 574, 609 N.Y.S.2d 261 (1994) (cohabitation proven by common residence, shared bedroom, and contribution to joint expenses over period of more than six months); Thomas v. Thomas, 76 Ohio App. 3d 482, 487, 602 N.E.2d 385, 388 (1991) (wife and man had sexual relationship allegedly in exchange for wife's part-time secretarial service, but when wife "moved from a smaller to a larger portion of the home . . . [,] there was no indication that she increased the services performed for [the man] commensurately"; cohabitation proven).

361. *See* Clark v. Clark, 33 A.D.3d 836, 838, 827 N.Y.S.2d 159, 161 (2006) (wife and children rented an apartment in the home of another family with at least one male member; trial court properly dismissed without a hearing husband's argument that wife was cohabiting); Austin v. Austin, 170 Ohio App. 3d 132, 135, 866 N.E.2d 74, 76 (2007) (wife and her business partner lived in home with wife's mother and another employee of the business, each having their own bedroom; husband admitted that previous sexual relationship between wife and business partner had ended; error to find cohabitation "akin to a marriage"); Dickerson v. Dickerson, 87 Ohio App. 3d 848, 623 N.E.2d 237 (1993) (wife's daughter and daughter's boyfriend moved in with wife; wife was not cohabiting with daughter's boyfriend within meaning of agreement).

362. *See* Kripp v. Kripp, 578 Pa. 82, 849 A.2d 1159 (2004) (reversing a contrary intermediate appellate court decision); Stroud v. Stroud, 49 Va. App. 359, 641 S.E.2d 142 (2007).

363. *See* Robinson v. Robinson, 788 So. 2d 1092, 1095 (Fla. Dist. Ct. App. 2001) (trial court erred by holding that cohabitation, as used in separate agreement, required proof that "the Wife was financially impacted" by her relationship with paramour); *Barr*, 922 S.W.2d 419 (sharing of expenses not required); Graev v. Graev, 11 N.Y.3d 262, 898 N.E.2d 909, 916, 869 N.Y.S.2d 866 (2008) (economic interdependence not essential to cohabitation); *Honeycutt*, 152 S.W.3d at 564

A minority of decisions construe the general term "cohabitation" to require proof of economic dependency.[364] These courts are adding to the term "cohabitation" an element that is not within its plain meaning. This construction is particularly questionable when the support at issue is subject to general modification, for cohabitation with economic dependency is a generally accepted basis for modification.[365] If "cohabitation" requires economic dependency in an agreement to pay modifiable support, then the cohabitation clause has become meaningless.

Still another minority of decision construes the general term "cohabitation" to require only proof of joint residency.[366]

One decision held that where the state in question has a statute terminating court-ordered support upon cohabitation, the agreement should be construed to define cohabitation in the same way as the statute, absent positive evidence of a different intent.[367] Other decisions have rejected this approach, noting that a cohabitation provision that merely restates the terms of a controlling statute would be superfluous.[368]

There is also authority holding that the word "cohabitation" has no clear meaning, so that the court must look to parol evidence.[369]

Marital Cohabitation Clauses. Another type of cohabitation clause can be called a marital cohabitation provision. This type of provision expressly specifies some additional element over and above mere "cohabitation" that must be met before support terminates.

The most common type of marital cohabitation provision requires that the cohabitation be analogous to remarriage. This language requires not only permanent cohabitation, but also the assumption of mutual duties similar to those present in a real marriage. These duties need not be exclusively financial, and support can terminate

---

("'cohabit' and 'cohabitation' . . . as applied and utilized in common usage, do not require or necessarily include the receipt of financial assistance from or by a cohabitor"); *In re* Marriage of Winningstad, 99 Or. App. 682, 784 P.2d 101 (1989).

364. *See also Thomas*, 76 Ohio App. 3d 482, 602 N.E.2d 385 ("cohabitation (defined as wife residing with an unrelated male)" required some degree of economic support).

365. *See generally* Ricketts, *supra* note 346.

366. *See* Auer v. Scott, 494 N.W.2d 54 (Minn. Ct. App. 1992) ("cohabit" construed to require only joint residence; statute already terminated support if economic dependency were present, so construing agreement to require such dependency would make the cohabitation provision superfluous).

367. Sitarek v. Sitarek, 179 A.D.2d 1064, 579 N.Y.S.2d 522 (1992).

368. *Auer*, 494 N.W.2d 54 (if statutory standard applied, contractual provision would be superfluous); Smith v. Smith, 233 A.D.2d 830, 650 N.Y.S.2d 842 (1996); Pesa v. Pesa, 230 A.D.2d 837, 646 N.Y.S.2d 558 (1996) (cohabitation provision can define cohabitation differently than cohabitation statute); Tricoles v. Tricoles, 202 A.D.2d 574, 609 N.Y.S.2d 261 (1994) (contract showed intent to use a less strict definition than the one provided by statute); Kripp v. Kripp, 578 Pa. 82, 92, 849 A.2d 1159, 1164 (2004) ("There is nothing in [the statute] to show that the General Assembly intended that the definition of cohabitation set forth in the statute be incorporated into or control private agreements[.]").

369. *See* Graev v. Graev, 11 N.Y.3d 262, 898 N.E.2d 909, 916, 869 N.Y.S.2d 866 (2008) (word "cohabitation" used by itself is inherently ambiguous; remanding for consideration of parol evidence).

where there is no economic dependency, so long as there is assumption of nonmonetary duties of a marital nature.[370]

Residency Clauses. The least strict type of cohabitation clause is a residency provision, stating in simple terms that support terminates if the recipient "resides" with a unrelated person of the opposite sex. In *Gordon v. Gordon*,[371] the court construed such a provision to contain an implicit requirement that there be some similarity to remarriage. Conversely, in *Bergman v. Bergman*,[372] the court held quite emphatically that a provision terminating support if the wife "resides with" another man did not require any romantic relationship or similarity to remarriage. The *Gordon* court was probably to some extent imposing its policy beliefs upon the parties. This practice is not entirely uncommon regarding cohabitation provisions, however, as some courts have expressed concern that pure residency clauses might violate public policy.[373]

---

370. Frey v. Frey, 14 Va. App. 270, 416 S.E.2d 40 (1992); *see also* Barr v. Barr, 922 S.W.2d 419 (Mo. Ct. App. 1996) (a relationship can resemble remarriage even if the parties do not expressly hold themselves out as married).

For case law considering whether this standard was met, see Schweider v. Schweider, 243 Va. 245, 415 S.E.2d 135 (1992) (wife and man lived together, shared expenses, and had sexual relationship; standard met); In re Marriage of Leming, 227 Ill. App. 3d 154, 590 N.E.2d 1027 (1992) (agreement terminated support if wife "cohabits with another person on a resident, continuing, conjugal basis"; where the wife was actually engaged to another man, but there was no financial dependency, support did not terminate); Austin v. Austin, 170 Ohio App. 3d 132, 135, 866 N.E.2d 74, 76 (Ohio Ct. App. 2007) (wife and her business partner lived in home with wife's mother and another employee of the business, each having their own bedroom; husband admitted that previous sexual relationship between wife and business partner had ended; error to find cohabitation "akin to a marriage"); Wallenhurst v. Wallenhurst, 116 Ohio App. 3d 823, 689 N.E.2d 586 (1996) (relation was not akin to remarriage, as there was no economic dependency); Stroud v. Stroud, 49 Va. App. 359, 378, 641 S.E.2d 142, 151 (2007) (same-sex relationship can be "analogous to remarriage" even though Virginia public policy absolutely forbids same sex marriages).

There is also a substantial volume of case law applying this standard in the context of state cohabitation statutes, an area of law outside the scope of this volume. *See generally* Ricketts, *supra* note 346.

371. 342 Md. 294, 675 A.2d 540 (1996) ("resides with any unrelated man without benefit of marriage" held to require a relationship similar to marriage, and not mere joint residence).

372. 25 Va. App. 204, 487 S.E.2d 264 (1997).

373. For the reasons discussed in § 3.05, the author believes that these concerns are unfounded. Residency and pure cohabitation provisions are most often used not to control the postmarital sexual behavior of one spouse, but rather to avoid the well-recognized practical difficulty of proving that a relationship involves financial dependency or is analogous to remarriage. Where such a provision is a true product of voluntary consent, there is no reason why it should not be enforced in the manner intended by the parties. Thus, the authors lean toward the position taken in *Bergman*.

A pure residency provision is unusual, however, and the courts would probably do well to find such a provision only where the language of the contract is clear. In most cases, the parties understand that a cohabitation provision is aimed at relationships that are essentially romantic in nature, and not at situations where persons with no romantic relationship merely live together in the same home. While there is no reason why the parties must necessarily have such an understanding, it is not unreasonable to insist that the parties state such an unusual understanding in clear terms.

For cases applying residency provisions, see *Bergman* (where man had no property at former wife's home, had no key to premises, and spent no time there when wife was away, man and wife were not residing together).

Duration of Cohabitation. Where the agreement is silent, there is no minimum time over which the parties must cohabit before support ceases. In theory, a single night of cohabitation will terminate support. The fact situation rarely arises in practice, however, as courts tend to view a certain degree of permanence as part of the definition of cohabitation. Thus, while a single night of cohabitation is technically sufficient, a one-night stand is probably not cohabitation to begin with.

Some express cohabitation provisions do require that the cohabitation last for a stated time period before support will terminate. When applying these provisions, the time period is terminated only by a complete breakdown of the relationship. A mere night or two spent apart, for the specific purpose of evading the time requirement, does not terminate cohabitation for purposes of the time period.[374] Where the provision did not state that the time period had to be consecutive, one court held that it was met where the total period of cohabitation exceeded the stated time, regardless of any interim breaks in cohabitation.[375]

Other Limitations. Where the agreement terminates spousal support upon cohabitation with an unrelated person, cohabitation with a relative is not a terminating event.[376]

Enforcement of a cohabitation provision does not violate a state statutory or constitutional provision against recognizing legal status similar to marriage. "[T]he fact that two individuals are cohabitating does not, in and of itself, confer a legal status tantamount to marriage."[377]

Cohabitation as a Change in Circumstances

The above discussion focuses upon cohabitation as a per se basis for terminating support in a manner similar to the effect of remarriage. Where support does not automatically terminate upon cohabitation, it is still possible that cohabitation might be a sufficient change in financial circumstances to permit discretionary modification or even termination.

For example, in *In re Marriage of Alvin*,[378] the contract expressly provided that alimony would stop upon death or remarriage. Because there was an implied intent to exclude cohabitation from this list of conditions, the trial court erred by treating cohabitation as automatic grounds for termination. The provision was not sufficiently specific, however, to prevent the court from exercising its normal power to modify support for changed circumstances. The court therefore made a separate determination of whether there existed sufficient changed circumstances to modify the award. Since changed circumstances did not exist, the court ultimately held that the support did not terminate.

---

374. *See* Penrod v. Penrod, 29 Va. App. 96, 510 S.E.2d 244 (1999); *see also supra* note 358 (case law holding that cohabitation continues despite occasional nights spent apart from one another).

375. *Barr*, 922 S.W.2d 419.

376. *See* Tarafa v. Takach, 934 So. 2d 524 (Fla. Dist. Ct. App. 2005) (where agreement allowed termination only for cohabitation with "unrelated" male, support did not terminate when wife resided with her cousin).

377. Fitz v. Fitz, 2009 WL 3155124, at *2 (Ohio Ct. App. 2009).

378. 184 Ill. App. 3d 644, 540 N.E.2d 919 (1989).

Where the normal changed circumstances test applies, the court may be able to terminate agreement-based support even where the agreement contains a cohabitation provision that does not apply on the facts. The rationale is that most cohabitation provisions state only the circumstances under which support *will* terminate; they do not state the conditions under which it will not terminate. Stated differently, the termination conditions set forth in a cohabitation provision are not exclusive. If the spousal support at issue is subject to modification under the law of the state involved, *see §* **6.032**, the mere presence of a cohabitation provision does not prevent modification for changed circumstances. The above-cited cases reason that a spouse who is receiving funds from a third party has a reduced need for support, regardless of whether those funds come from employment, gift, or cohabitation.[379] *If an agreement permits modification of support for general changed circumstances*, there is no reason why this line of cases would not permit reduction or termination based upon cohabitation-related financial changes, even if those changes fall outside the language of an express (but not exclusive) cohabitation provision.

Where the court has no power to modify agreement-based spousal support, the above theory obviously does not apply.[380]

To establish cohabitation as a change in circumstances under a modification standard, it is usually necessary to show that the cohabitation had an economic effect upon the financial resources or needs of the recipient spouse.[381]

Procedure

The burden of proving cohabitation is on the spouse who claims it, and the standard of proof is a preponderance of the evidence.[382]

Where the agreement requires proof of common law marriage, the courts generally apply the common law definition of that term, which requires a present agreement to be married and at least some acts of holding out as husband and wife.[383]

If a motion to modify or terminate states a prima facie case of cohabitation, it is error to dismiss the motion without holding a factual hearing.[384]

Where a contract expressly provides for automatic termination of support upon cohabitation, termination occurs without the need for court action. Thus, termination

---

379. *See, e.g.,* Ianitelli v. Ianitelli, 199 Mich. App. 641, 502 N.W.2d 691 (1993); Gayet v. Gayet, 92 N.J. 149, 456 A.2d 102 (1983); McVay v. McVay, 189 W. Va. 197, 429 S.E.2d 239 (1993); *see generally* Brett R. Turner, *Redefining Alimony in a Time of Transition: Recent Case Law Applying the Changed Circumstances Standard,* 6 Divorce Litig. 241, 257–59 (1994).

380. *See* Woodings v. Woodings, 411 Pa. Super. 406, 601 A.2d 854 (1992) (clause preventing judicial modification also prevented judicial termination upon cohabitation).

381. *See also* Wheeler v. Wheeler, 154 S.W.3d 291 (Ky. Ct. App. 2004) (error to modify support downward based upon cohabitation as a change in circumstances; "the trial court must examine Monette's relationship with Mihalek to determine whether the nature of that relationship is such that it constitutes a new 'financial resource' for her").

382. *See* Olstein v. Olstein, 309 A.D.2d 697, 766 N.Y.S.2d 189 (2003); O'Hara v. O'Hara, 45 Va. App. 788, 613 S.E.2d 859 (2005).

383. *See* Enck v. Enck, 187 A.D.2d 897, 591 N.Y.S.2d 79 (1992) (applying this test even though New York abolished common law marriage by statute).

384. Smith v. Smith, 233 A.D.2d 830, 650 N.Y.S.2d 842 (1996).

is retroactive to the date upon which cohabitation began.[385] If the contract does not expressly provide for automatic termination, support stops only upon issuance of an order by the court.[386]

If the rationale is changed economic circumstances arising from cohabitation, and not cohabitation as a per se terminating condition, termination might operate only from the date that a motion to modify was filed.

Where support terminates due to cohabitation, it cannot be reinstated after cohabitation stops.[387]

Drafting Concerns

A surprising number of separation agreements continue to provide that spousal support ceases if the female recipient cohabits with an unrelated adult male. This language is unfortunate in two different respects. First, it may not terminate support if the wife enters into a same-sex relationship, an event that is not uncommon in modern society. Second, it does not terminate support if the wife cohabits with any person to whom she is related, no matter how distant the relationship may be.[388]

A better option is to provide that support ceases if the recipient cohabits with another person in a relationship analogous to remarriage. The "analogous to remarriage" requirement avoids terminating support if the wife merely lives with a friend or housemate with whom she has no romantic relationship. It is flexible enough, however, to accommodate many different types of long-term relationships. It is also construed by a substantial body of case law, which may reduce the chance of future litigation to construe the term.[389]

§ 6.035 Termination upon Death

The test for termination of alimony upon the death of the payor is similar to the tests for modification because of changed circumstances or remarriage. The first step is to classify the payments. *See generally* § 6.031. If the payments are property division[390] or are part of an integrated bargain,[391] they do not cease upon death.

---

385. Draper v. Draper, 40 Conn. App. 570, 672 A.2d 522 (1996); Quillen v. Quillen, 265 Ga. 779, 462 S.E.2d 750 (1995); *cf.* Brown v. Brown, 269 Ga. 724, 506 S.E.2d 108 (1998) (automatic termination provision would be enforceable, but no such provision was present on the facts).

386. *Id.*; Stroud v. Stroud, 54 Va. App. 231, 238, 677 S.E.2d 629, 632 (2009) ("Termination of wife's spousal support, if she allegedly cohabits with another in a relationship analogous to marriage, is not self-executing[.]").

387. Weathersby v. Weathersby, 693 So. 2d 1348 (Miss. 1997); Bergman v. Bergman, 25 Va. App. 204, 487 S.E.2d 264 (1997).

388. *See supra* note 375.

389. *See supra* note 369.

390. *See* McIntyre v. McIntyre, 824 So. 2d 206 (Fla. Dist. Ct. App. 2002); Fecteau v. Se. Bank, 585 So. 2d 1005 (Fla. Dist. Ct. App. 1991); Malicoate v. Standard Life & Accident Ins. Co., 999 P.2d 1103 (Okla. Civ. App. 2000); *In re* Estate of Weller, 179 W. Va. 804, 374 S.E.2d 712 (1988).

391. Lucas v. Elliott, 3 Cal. App. 4th 888, 4 Cal. Rptr. 2d 746 (1992).

True spousal support payments ordinarily cease upon the death of the payor.[392] If the parties agree to the contrary, however, their agreement will be enforced. Most states will recognize a contrary intention only where it appears clearly from the face of the document or from clear extrinsic evidence.[393]

Where the agreement requires maintenance of life insurance for the purpose of securing spousal support, the beneficiary's right to collect postdeath support is reduced by his or her share of the insurance proceeds.[394]

§ 6.036 *Other Grounds for Termination*

In addition to the traditional grounds of remarriage, cohabitation, and death, separation agreements may state additional bases for termination of spousal support. These termination conditions are generally construed in light of the parties' overall intent.

One common type of provision terminates support after the wife has completed a period of education or job training. For instance, in *Somogye v. Somogye*,[395] the husband agreed to pay support until the wife completed a course in learning how to be a court stenographer. The wife then dropped out of the course before completing it. Because the wife herself made completion of the condition impossible, the court held that she had no right to complain it was not met. Accordingly, the husband's support obligation terminated.[396]

A related issue arose in *Hughes v. Hughes*,[397] where the agreement stated that the wife's spousal support would terminate upon "[t]he employment of [the wife]." The court refused to construe the language literally:

---

392. *See In re* Estate of Shatraw, 66 A.D.3d 1293, 887 N.Y.S.2d 722 (2009); Perry v. Estate of Perry, 323 S.C. 232, 473 S.E.2d 860 (1986) (agreement can extend support past death, though it did not do so on the facts); *see generally* Annotation, *Alimony—Death of Obligor*, 79 A.L.R.4TH 10 (1990 & Supp. 1991).

393. *See Lucas*, 3 Cal. App. 4th 888, 4 Cal. Rptr. 2d 746 (presence of provision requiring life insurance on husband's life showed that parties intended support to continue after husband's death); Findley v. Findley, 280 Ga. 454, 454, 629 S.E.2d 222, 224 (2006) ("a clear expression of intent to extend payments beyond the obligor's death"); *In re* Estate of Mackie, 261 S.W.3d 728, 731 (Mo. Ct. App. 2008) (promise to pay support "during her lifetime" did not extend support past death of husband; language was not sufficiently express); *In re* Riconda, 90 N.Y.2d 733, 688 N.E.2d 248, 665 N.Y.S.2d 392 (1997) (provision must be express, or extrinsic evidence must clearly show an intention that liability extend past death); *Malicoate*, 999 P.2d 1103 (where agreement was silent, spousal support terminated upon payor's death); Britton v. Britton, 400 Pa. Super. 43, 582 A.2d 1335 (1990). *But see* Cardwell v. Sicola-Cardwell, 978 S.W.2d 722 (Tex. Ct. App. 1998) (support for defined duration or until wife's death did not terminate upon husband's death; obligation was not spousal support, but rather an obligation to pay money, and it was governed only by the law of contracts).

394. Gray v. Estate of Gray, 993 S.W.2d 59 (Tenn. Ct. App. 1998).

395. 167 A.D.2d 873, 562 N.Y.S.2d 989 (1990).

396. *See also In re* Marriage of Iberti, 55 Cal. App. 4th 1435, 64 Cal. Rptr. 2d 766 (1997) (husband agreed to pay spousal support while wife was in college; wife dropped out because of her mother's mental illness; support terminated); Little v. Little, 441 Pa. Super. 185, 657 A.2d 12 (1995) (agreement to pay support while wife was a full-time student; support terminated when wife spent 28 days in center for treatment of alcohol abuse).

397. 23 S.W.3d 838 (Mo. Ct. App. 2000).

Taken in its broadest sense, the word "employment" is extremely broad—so broad as to lead to some rather absurd applications in this context. Did the parties mean that babysitting, or trips to the farmer's market to sell garden produce, or engagement in a temporary, part-time endeavor, would terminate maintenance? That is certainly not clear, especially in the context of a negotiated thirty-eight month non-modifiable spousal maintenance provision[.][398]

The court therefore held that term "employment" was ambiguous. Turning then to parol evidence, the court concluded that the term "was a reference to full-time employment, or at least substantial regular employment which would take the place of the maintenance."[399]

Another common type of provision terminates support when the payee receives a lump sum property division award, often from delayed sale of a marital asset. Since the purpose of this sort of provision is to support the payee until the lump sum is received, courts are reluctant to apply these provisions until the payee has actual possession of the lump sum.[400] A different result is possible, however, where termination is based upon sale, and completion of the sale is unreasonably delayed.[401]

Once support has completely terminated, it generally cannot be reinstated.[402]

§ 6.04 Child Support Provisions

The law on separation agreements and child support is materially different from the law of separation agreements and spousal support. With respect to spousal support, the only persons affected by the agreement are the parties themselves, and they are free to reach whatever arrangements they desire. With respect to child support, however, the court has a duty to uphold the rights of the children, whose rights cannot be prejudiced by an agreement between the parties.

§ 6.041 Initial Awards

The parties' separation agreement does not control the court's initial child support award. It is, however, one factor to be considered when the court sets the award. *See* § 3.07.

In addition to agreeing upon monetary child support, the parties can also agree that one parent or the other will pay specific expenses, such as summer camp or pri-

---

398. *Id.* at 841.

399. *Id.*

400. *See* Purdy v. Purdy, 715 A.2d 473, 474 (Pa. Super. Ct. 1998) (support terminated when wife "received or shall receive" funds from sale of property; support ends only when wife actually receives the funds).

401. *See* Ray v. Ray, 707 So. 2d 358 (Fla. 2d Dist. Ct. App. 1998) (support stopped when home sold or refinanced; where sale or refinance did not occur in timely fashion, court had authority to select a reasonable termination date, but could not select date before filing of motion to terminate).

402. *See* Lee v. Lee, 945 So. 2d 317 (La Ct. App. 2006) (trial court properly dismissed wife's request for additional alimony, file after termination date of time-limited award).

vate school tuition.[403] Such an obligation does not directly reduce traditional child support, but it is a deviation factor when the court should consider in setting the support amount.[404]

The private school tuition cases are generally resolved by analogy to the college tuition cases, which are discussed in **§ 6.044**. Since private school obligations almost always coexist with traditional child support, the court must be careful not to require the obligor to pay the same expenses twice.[405] A promise to consult the other parent before the costs are incurred requires mere consultation; it does not give the other parent veto power over the expenses.[406] Provisions establishing minimum academic performance requirements are generally enforced.[407] If the child fails to graduate on time, but remains enrolled in school, support does not terminate.[408]

A provision requiring a parent to pay private school tuition under certain conditions does not necessarily mean that payment will not be required if the conditions are not met. The parties cannot by contract prevent the court from ordering private school tuition when the child's best interests so require.[409]

An agreement to pay private school tuition is not necessarily an agreement that the children shall attend private school indefinitely. If the agreement does not expressly consent to attendance at a specific private school, the obligor is free to argue that the best interests of the children require a different private school or even public school.[410] An argument for changing school probably gets stronger as more time passes after the signing of the agreement. For example, an agreement to pay for private elementary

---

403. *See* Love v. Love, 959 P.2d 523 (Nev. 1998) (promise to pay "educational expenses" included private school tuition).

404. Laura W. Morgan, Child Support Guidelines: Interpretation and Application § 4.01 n.9 (2008).

405. *See* Karafiol v. Karafiol, 259 A.D.2d 522, 686 N.Y.S.2d 461 (1999) (where room and board costs at private school were implicitly included in child support provision, school expenses provision construed not to include room and board costs).

406. Pezzullo v. Palmisano, 261 A.D.2d 173, 689 N.Y.S.2d 500 (1999).

407. *See* Afkari-Ahmadi v. Fotovat-Ahmadi, 294 Conn. 384, 985 A.2d 319 (2009). The provision at issue in *Afkari-Ahmadi* established minimum academic standards for remaining in public school, allowing private school if performance dropped below the standard.

408. *See* Bullard v. Swafford, 279 Ga. 577, 619 S.E.2d 665 (2005) (where husband agreed to pay child support while child was in secondary school, and child failed to graduate because of child's excessive absences from class; support did not terminate; child was still enrolled in secondary school, and cost of absences should not include loss of child support).

409. *See* Wen v. Wen, 304 A.D.2d 897, 757 N.Y.S.2d 355 (2003) (agreement required father to pay 80 percent of private school tuition if father consented on a yearly basis to child attending private school; father consented and child "excelled academically and socially for three years," but father refused to consent for a fourth year; trial court nevertheless properly ordered father to pay).

410. *See* Cheruvu v. Cheruvu, 61 A.D.3d 1171, 1174, 878 N.Y.S.2d 208, 211 (2009) (where agreement required husband to pay "all primary and secondary school education expenses limited to tuition for and on behalf of the parties' two children," "the parties failed to include in the stipulation any indication that they anticipated that the children would continue to attend Albany Academy—or any other private school—in future school years").

school might not necessarily obligate a parent to pay for private high school, if there is no evidence that attending a private high school would be in the child's best interests.

§ 6.042 Modification

The role of agreements in modifying child support is similar to the role of agreements in making initial awards. Thus, contract-based child support is always subject to modification by the court.[411] Where the parties agree upon a modification of support, their agreement is not automatically binding.[412] The court should consider the agreement, however, as one relevant factor in setting the proper modified amount of support.[413]

Increases in Amount. Just as the contract does not prevent the court from making a higher initial support award, so does it not prevent the court from making a higher modification award. In other words, the contract cannot prevent the court from increasing child support beyond the stated level. *See* § **3.07.**

Decreases in Amount. Whether the court can decrease child support beneath the stated level is a harder question. Some states hold that a payor can always agree to pay additional child support, so that contractual support cannot be reduced.[414] A rule that the court can increase but not decrease child support does not violate equal protection.[415] Other states hold that if the court has the power to increase support, it must likewise have the power to decrease support.[416]

---

411. *See* Burkley v. Burkley, 911 So. 2d 262 (Fla. Dist. Ct. App. 2005); Kesser v. Kesser, 201 S.W.3d 636 (Tenn. 2006); *see also* Huhn v. Stuckmann, 321 Wis. 2d 169, 179, 772 N.W.2d 744, 749 (Ct. App. 2009) (parties cannot agree to limit modification of child support component of family support).

412. *In re* Marriage of Ingraham, 259 Ill. App. 3d 685, 631 N.E.2d 386 (1994) (automatic escalation clause in child support agreement was not enforceable).

413. *See* § **3.07**; *cf.* Bucholt v. Bucholt, 152 Vt. 238, 566 A.2d 409 (1991) (enforcing stipulation that either party's entry into graduate school would be a sufficient changed circumstance to allow modification of child support; stressing that agreement only triggered court's power to set an appropriate amount of support).

414. Nicholson v. Combs, 550 Pa. 23, 703 A.2d 407 (1997) (for pre-1988 agreements); *see generally* Annotation, *Modification of Agreement-Based Child Support*, 61 A.L.R.3D 657 (1975).

An agreement permitting the wife to set off child support arrearages against property division payments due to the husband is not an implied provision against reduction in child support. Freundlich v. Freundlich, 260 A.D.2d 576, 688 N.Y.S.2d 626 (1999).

415. *Id.*

416. *See* Flannery v. Flannery, 950 P.2d 126 (Alaska 1997); Aga v. Aga, 941 P.2d 1260 (Alaska 1997) (provision that child support would not be reduced below stated amount was unenforceable); *In re* Marriage of Alter, 171 Cal. App. 4th 718, 89 Cal. Rptr. 3d 849 (2009) ("the court always has the power to modify a child support order, upward or downward, regardless of the parents' agreement to the contrary"); *Nicholson*, 550 Pa. 23, 703 A.2d 407 (for post-1988 agreements).

Credits. Where a specific statute provides for credits against child support payments, that statute applies to contractual support, unless the parties have expressly agreed otherwise.[417]

Higher Standard. Some states specifically apply a higher standard to modification of agreement-based child support. Divorce settlements generally result in better settlements at a smaller cost to the parties and the courts, and these advantages do not disappear merely because child support is involved. For this reason, these states are reluctant to modify agreement-based support. A District of Columbia court explained:

> The [higher] standard affords little freedom to the court to change support provisions because it assumes that the parties voluntarily agreed to abide by the specific terms of a separation agreement. It is also based on the premise that at the time of the separation agreement the best interests of the child were a "paramount consideration." . . . Accordingly, the [higher] standard does not diminish the court's responsibility . . . to assure that adequate child support is provided.[418]

A Maryland court stated the same point more simply:

> [The higher standard] simply gives credence to what we think is the soundly based proposition that, while parents, like all humans, often make mistakes, they will not act in a manner detrimental to their children.[419]

The precise language of the higher standard varies from state to state. In the District of Columbia, the parent seeking modification must show "(1) a change in circumstances which was unforeseen at the time the agreement was entered and (2) that the change is both substantial and material to the welfare and best interests of the children."[420] In Massachusetts, the standard is "something more than a material change in circumstances, namely the existence of special equitable considerations which make relief appropriate."[421] In Maryland, the agreement "ordinarily should be given effect; the court should presume, in other words, at least in the absence of compelling evidence to the contrary, that the decision or resolution reached agreeably by the parents is in the best interest of their child."[422] In Montana, agreement-based support can be modified only if changed circumstances render the agreement unconscionable.[423]

---

417. *See In re* Marriage of Briscoe, 134 Wash. 2d 344, 949 P.2d 1388 (1998) (credit for social security benefits received by child).

418. Albus v. Albus, 503 A.2d 1229, 1231 (D.C. 1986).

419. Ruppert v. Fish, 84 Md. App. 665, 581 A.2d 828, 833 (1990).

420. Cooper v. Cooper, 472 A.2d 878, 880 (D.C. 1984).

421. Ames v. Perry, 406 Mass. 236, 547 N.E.2d 309, 312 (1989).

422. *Ruppert*, 84 Md. App. 675, 581 A.2d at 833.

423. *In re* Marriage of Pearson, 291 Mont. 101, 965 P.2d 268 (Mont. 1998).

In Florida, a parent seeking to reduce child support beneath the contractual level must meet a "heavier burden."[424] This burden was not met where the payor assumed custody of the child, but the payor's obligation was offset to some extent by that payee's new child support obligation.[425]

In New York, when the purpose of modification is to further the rights of the parents, there must be "a showing that the agreement was not fair and equitable when entered into, or that an unanticipated and unreasonable change is circumstances has occurred resulting in a concomitant need."[426] This test applies even where the support obligation is based upon an oral stipulation, rather than a formal written contract.[427]

The *Merl* court held that the higher New York standard was not met by the wife's decision to change the children's surname to that of her second husband.[428] Where the only change in circumstances is inflation and increased needs resulting from the child getting older, the New York cases hold that the higher standard is not met.[429] An increase in the payor's income may also not be alone sufficient.[430] Some of the cases even refuse to modify for genuine unexpected changes in circumstances.[431] Conversely, when the purpose of the modification is to uphold the child's right to adequate support, the court can act as if the agreement did not exist.[432]

The higher standard applies only where the separation agreement was *approved* or *incorporated* into the decree. Where the agreement was *merged*, it no longer exists as a contract and the normal changed circumstances test applies.[433]

The cases applying a higher standard generally do so regardless of whether the agreement seeks to increase or decrease the amount of support. Pennsylvania has held

---

424. Tietig v. Boggs, 602 So. 2d 1250, 1252 (Fla. 1992). *See also In re* Marriage of Falat, 201 Ill. App. 3d 320, 559 N.E.2d 33, 37 (1990) (noting that "[s]ettlement agreements as they relate to child support are looked upon favorably by Illinois courts," but setting no specific higher standard).

425. Allison v. Allison, 719 So. 2d 386 (Fla. Dist. Ct. App. 1998).

426. Merl v. Merl, 67 N.Y.2d 359, 493 N.E.2d 936, 502 N.Y.S.2d 713 (1986).

427. Bouille v. Bouille, 192 A.D.2d 802, 596 N.Y.S.2d 524 (1993).

428. *Cf.* Schelter v. Schelter, 159 A.D.2d 995, 552 N.Y.S.2d 477 (1990) (under higher standard, where husband alleged total disability resulting from a work-related injury, error to deny modification without holding a hearing).

429. *See* Jaeger v. Jaeger, 260 A.D.2d 351, 687 N.Y.S.2d 689 (1999); Kaffenberger v. Kaffenberger, 228 A.D.2d 743, 643 N.Y.S.2d 740 (1996); Bouille v. Bouille, 192 A.D.2d 802, 596 N.Y.S.2d 524 (1993); Belkin v. Belkin, 193 A.D.2d 573, 597 N.Y.S.2d 421 (1993).

430. *See* DeCarlo v. DeCarlo, 250 A.D.2d 848, 673 N.Y.S.2d 709 (1998).

431. *See also* Sherman v. Sherman, 28 A.D.3d 738, 814 N.Y.S.2d 244 (2006) (refusing to increase support, even though father's income increased, the child was diagnosed with ADHD, and the child moved to a more expensive home; persuasive dissent would have allowed an increase); Cefola v. Cefola, 231 A.D.2d 600, 647 N.Y.S.2d 800 (1996) (husband's involuntary early retirement due to employer's downsizing not sufficient).

432. *See* Montagnino v. Montagnino, 163 A.D.2d 598, 559 N.Y.S.2d 37 (1990) (where agreement was silent on college expenses, court could exercise its normal authority to order sharing of such expenses); Sujko v. Sujko, 160 A.D.2d 1184, 555 N.Y.S.2d 195 (1990) (where support did not commence under agreement until the following year, proper to award temporary support until that time).

433. Hamel v. Hamel, 539 A.2d 195 (D.C. 1988).

that while contractual child support may be increased, it cannot be reduced below the contractual level.[434] Florida likewise holds that a heavier burden applies only to those who seek to decrease court-ordered child support.[435]

Regardless of which standard applies, if the court properly elects to award more support than required by the agreement, the court must determine whether the rest of the agreement is severable from the child support provisions. Any provisions that are not severable share the fate of the child support provisions.[436] Severability is a question of fact, and it is error to grant summary judgment where the contract is ambiguous.[437]

Of course, if the court awards more support than required by a separation agreement, the disadvantaged spouse cannot recover the difference in a breach of contract action.[438]

Lower Standard. Can the parties agree by contract to permit modification of child support without proof of a material change in circumstances? The general rule is yes, at least so long as the provision does not violate the child's best interests.[439]

The parties can also agree to child support provisions that vary automatically with the parties' incomes. One common such provision is one requiring that support be recalculated periodically under the child support guidelines.[440]

Where an agreement permits proportional reduction of child support as each child is emancipated, the agreement is enforceable with regard to past payments.[441] But since child support is not reduced proportionally upon emancipation under child

---

434. Jones v. Jones, 438 Pa. Super. 26, 651 A.2d 157 (1994). The contract in *Jones* was silent on modification; the court would presumably have reached a different result if the contract expressly called for modifiable support.

435. Tietig v. Boggs, 602 So. 2d 1250 (Fla. 1992); *see also* Thompson v. Thompson, 189 W. Va. 278, 430 S.E.2d 336 (1993) (child support provision in contract implicitly waived statute permitting court to adjust child support if amount awarded varied more than 15 percent from guideline amount; husband's income had dropped, so that guideline amount was more than 15 percent too high).

436. *See* Zerr v. Zerr, 7 Neb. App. 285, 586 N.W.2d 465, 468 (1998) (where agreement expressly provided that it was null and void unless approved by the court, disapproval of the child support clause invalidated the entire agreement); White v. Bowers, 101 N.C. App. 646, 400 S.E.2d 760 (1991); Spagnolo v. Spagnolo, 20 Va. App. 736, 460 S.E.2d 616 (1995) (contract established support below guidelines in exchange for father's agreement to pay college expenses; court could increase support, but if it did so the college expenses provision was invalid, as the two provisions were dependent).

437. *White*, 101 N.C. App. 546, 400 S.E.2d 760.

438. Maki v. Straub, 167 A.D.2d 589, 563 N.Y.S.2d 218 (1990). *But see* Sparacio v. Sparacio, 248 A.D.2d 705, 670 N.Y.S.2d 558 (1998) (awarding contract damages based upon agreement level of spousal and child support, even though judgment had been modified to lesser amount); Nicholson v. Combs, 550 Pa. 23, 703 A.2d 407 (1997) (contract action might be available to recover difference if court reduces child support beneath agreement level).

439. *See* Giacalone v. Giacalone, 876 S.W.2d 616 (Ky. Ct. App. 1994); Aldredge v. Aldredge, 477 So. 2d 73 (La. 1985).

440. *See* Ramon v. Ramon, 49 A.D.3d 843, 855 N.Y.S.2d 184 (2008).

441. Kosnac v. Kosnac, 60 A.D.3d 636, 637, 875 N.Y.S.2d 504, 506 (2009).

support guidelines,[442] there should be a strong case for modifying any such provision prospectively.

Credits. The parties can agree to provide the payor with certain credits against his or her child support obligation.[443] Such an agreement is invalid if inconsistent with the child's interests, as for example if the child never received the real benefit of the credits at issue.

§ 6.043 Postmajority Child Support

In drafting the child support provisions of a separation agreement, the parties are not bound by the same limitations that apply to court-ordered support. In particular, the parties are free to extend child support past emancipation and past the death of the payor. Contracts exercising this freedom are quite common, and there is a substantial body of case law on both postmajority and postdeath support.

Liability

Postmajority child support provisions are one of the most common types of child support clauses found in separation agreements. While a growing number of states allow the court to award at least college expenses without an agreement, many states still hold that the court's power to award support on its own initiative terminates at the age of majority.[444]

In all states, however, the courts will enforce agreements to pay support for older children.[445] The most common type of postmajority support clause, as discussed in **§ 6.044**, is an agreement to pay college expenses. The parties can also contractually obligate themselves to pay normal child support past the age of majority.[446] These types of provisions are particularly common with regard to adult disabled children.[447]

---

442. *See generally* MORGAN, *supra* note 403, § 2.02.

443. Wilderman v. Wilderman, 25 Va. App. 500, 489 S.E.2d 701 (1997) (agreement to give the father credit for certain nonconforming payments was not objectionable on policy grounds, but was invalid under contract law for lack of consideration).

444. *See generally* Cutshaw v. Cutshaw, 220 Va. 638, 261 S.E.2d 52 (1979).

445. *See, e.g.,* Winset v. Fine, 565 So. 2d 794 (Fla. Dist. Ct. App. 1990); Dolce v. Dolce, 383 N.J. Super. 11, 16, 890 A.2d 361, 364 (App. Div. 2006) ("neither law nor public policy intervenes to prohibit the voluntary undertaking by a parent to support a child beyond the presumptive age of emancipation"); Ottino v. Ottino, 130 N.M. 168, 21 P.3d 37 (Ct. App. 2000); Jackson v. Jackson, 360 N.C. 56, 620 S.E.2d 862 (2005), *adopting* Jackson v. Jackson, 169 N.C. App. 46, 54, 610 S.E.2d 731, 737 (2005) (Hunter, J., dissenting) (provision requiring the husband to pay $900 per month even after first child was emancipated did not violate public policy; husband could agree to pay more support than law requires); *Cutshaw,* 220 Va. 638, 261 S.E.2d 52.

446. *See, e.g.,* Sartin v. Sartin, 678 So. 2d 1181 (Ala. Ct. App. 1996).

447. O'Connor v. O'Connor, 71 Ohio App. 3d 541, 594 N.E.2d 1081 (1991) (where an agreement required the father to provide "all of [the child's] support," proper to quantify the obligation by applying the state's child support guidelines).

An agreement to pay postmajority support does not imply an equal obligation to pay premajority support.[448]

Emancipation. The normal termination date for child support is the age of emancipation. In some cases, however, the parties may vary this date by contract.

The most common situation presenting this issue occurs when the legislature changes the statutory age of emancipation. In this situation, if the contract is silent or provides only for termination upon emancipation (or for support during minority), it will be construed to adopt the legal definition of these terms, including any subsequent changes by the legislature. Thus, if the age of emancipation subsequently is reduced, the child support obligation terminates earlier.[449]

Where the agreement refers to a specific age of termination, and the age of majority is subsequently reduced, the cases generally hold that the parties' intention was to continue support until the stated age, regardless of subsequent changes in the law. For example, where the contract called for support until the children reached age 21 or were "otherwise emancipated," a Virginia court held that support continued until age 21.[450]

When the age of majority increases, the increase normally applies to all private agreements.[451] To the extent that a specific earlier termination date was provided by contract, the termination date is contrary to the child's best interests and therefore not controlling. The parties likewise cannot agree in other contexts to a definition of emancipation that is looser than the definition required by law.[452]

A contractual provision defining the age of emancipation, without tying the provision to support by either parent in particular, might be read to require postmajority support by the other parent in the event of a custody change.[453]

---

448. *See In re* Marriage of Bolton, 950 S.W.2d 268 (Mo. Ct. App. 1997) (husband's promise to pay for son's car repairs while son was in college did not require him to pay for car repairs while son was in high school).

449. *See* Shoaf v. Shoaf, 282 N.C. 287, 192 S.E.2d 299 (1972); Meredith v. Meredith, 216 Va. 636, 222 S.E.2d 511, 511 (1976) (support "until such child shall reach his majority"); Mack v. Mack, 217 Va. 534, 229 S.E.2d 895, 896 (1976) (agreement to support "minor children").

450. Paul v. Paul, 214 Va. 651, 203 S.E.2d 123, 124 (1974); *see also* Perkins v. Perkins, 120 N.C. App. 638, 463 S.E.2d 552 (1995) (support until child "otherwise becomes emancipated . . . or attains the age of twenty-two"; support did not stop at age 18, the statutory age of majority). *But see In re* Marriage of Robb, 934 P.2d 927 (Colo. App. 1997) (support until child reached age 21 or was "emancipated by law"; support stopped when age of majority reduced to 19; effect was to make the specific reference to age 21 superfluous).

451. *See* Gore v. Gore, 169 Ariz. 593, 821 P.2d 254 (Ct. App. 1991); Bornemann v. Bornemann, 175 Md. App. 716, 931 A.2d 1154 (2007). Both *Gore* and *Bornemann* involved statutory provisions allowing child support to continue until the child's graduation from high school, even if that date is after age 18.

452. *See* Thomas B. v. Lydia D., 69 A.D.3d 24, 886 N.Y.S.2d 22, 28 (2009) (agreement providing that child would be emancipated upon obtaining full-time employment, where legal definition of emancipation was materially different; "[e]conomic independence from the child's parents is not established by merely working a standard, full-time work week").

453. *See In re* Marriage of Sweders, 296 Ill. App. 3d 919, 695 N.E.2d 526 (1998).

Even where the statutory age of majority remains unchanged, contractual provisions setting forth the date of termination for child support are not binding on the court.[454] On the contrary, the court retains its power to order support until the proper termination date provided by state law, where the best interests of the child so require.

Merger. Where an agreement *merges* into the divorce decree, so that the contract loses all independent existence, does the court's inability to enforce postmajority support as a term of the decree make such support unenforceable? In *Noble v. Fisher*,[455] the court held that *merged* postmajority support provisions cannot be enforced by the wife. It did hold, however, that such provisions can still be enforced by the child as a third-party beneficiary of the agreement.

If the result reached in *Noble* is correct, then the agreement came close to contradicting itself. It placed a major liability upon the husband, but then made it unenforceable by the only other party to sign the agreement. Such a result seems sufficiently unusual that it should be reached only where clearly required by the plain language of the agreement. At a minimum, one would think that the mere presence of a postmajority support provision would be a strong reason to suspect that the parties intended their agreement to be only *approved* or *incorporated* into the agreement, and that they positively rejected *merger*. One court even refused outright to apply the doctrine of *merger* to a postmajority support obligation, holding that it would effective frustrate the intent of the parties.[456]

Modification. Where the court has no common law authority to award postmajority support, the court lacks power to modify the postmajority support provision of an agreement.[457]

Where the court does have common law authority to award postmajority support, modification is of course permitted.[458]

---

454. *See* Patetta v. Patetta, 358 N.J. Super. 90, 817 A.2d 327 (App. Div. 2003) (where child "was living at home and dependent on his parents for his basic needs and proper support while attending college on a full-time basis," child was not emancipated and child support did not cease, despite contractual provision stating that support terminated at age 18).

455. 126 Idaho 885, 894 P.2d 118 (1995).

456. *See* Ottino v. Ottino, 130 N.M. 168, 21 P.3d 37 (Ct. App. 2000).

457. *See* Van Camp v. Van Camp, 333 Ark. 320, 969 S.W.2d 184 (1998); Albrecht v. Albrecht, 19 Conn. App. 146, 562 A.2d 528 (1989); Reininger v. Reininger, 49 Conn. Supp. 238, 871 A.2d 422 (2005); Norris v. Norris, 473 A.2d 380 (D.C. 1984); Jones v. Jones, 244 Ga. 32, 257 S.E.2d 537 (1979); Morrison v. Morrison, 14 Kan. App. 2d 56, 781 P.2d 745 (1989); Hogan v. Hogan, 534 So. 2d 478 (La. Ct. App. 1988), *modified on other grounds*, 549 So. 2d 267 (La. 1989); Rohrbacher v. Rohrbacher, 83 Ohio App. 3d 569, 615 N.E.2d 338 (1992) (modification not permitted after child reached majority; suggesting a different result if petition had been filed during minority); *In re* White, 299 S.C. 406, 385 S.E.2d 211 (Ct. App. 1989); Cutshaw v. Cutshaw, 220 Va. 638, 261 S.E.2d 52 (1979). *See also* § **6.044**, note 536 (specific cases holding that college tuition provisions are not subject to modification). *But see* Ogle v. Ogle, 769 N.E.2d 644, 649–50 (Ind. Ct. App. 2002) (suggesting that express contractual provision permitting modification by the court might be enforceable).

458. *See In re* Marriage of Falat, 201 Ill. App. 3d 320, 559 N.E.2d 33 (1990).

§ 6.044 College Expenses

The most common type of postmajority support provision is an agreement to pay college expenses. College expenses provisions are universally held to be enforceable, even in states where the court itself lacks jurisdiction to order such support without an agreement.[459] In states where the court can order postmajority support, a college expenses provision can still be enforced under the law of contracts, as opposed to the law of child support judgments.[460]

College Expenses and Periodic Child Support

It is important to draw a clear distinction between an agreement to pay postmajority child support and an agreement to pay specific expenses of college. In *Sartin v. Sartin*,[461] the agreement provided that the father "shall continue to support the child" so long as he was in college and certain other conditions were met. The trial court enforced the agreement by making an award of college expenses. The appellate court quite properly reversed, holding that the father had agreed only to extend his normal child support payments past the normal age of termination.

Along similar lines, where an agreement requires payment of both periodic support past age 18 and college tuition, it is error to offset either payment against the other; the payor has two separate, independent obligations.[462] Where period support terminates at a certain age, such termination does not imply termination of the obligation to pay college tuition.[463] Where college tuition is being paid, such payment does not imply

---

459. It is rare to find a court considering this issue directly, for only a few obligors have attempted to argue that courts cannot enforce college support provisions. For cases directly rejecting such an agreement, see Geiringer v. Mowery, 433 Pa. Super. 44, 639 A.2d 1202 (1994); Goss v. Timblin, 424 Pa. Super. 216, 622 A.2d 347 (1993). Powerful indirect support for the majority position can be found in the large number of cases cited in this section that actually enforce a college support provision on the facts.

A consent judgment requiring payment of college costs functions as a contract. Burtch v. Burtch, 972 S.W.2d 882 (Tex. Ct. App. 1998).

460. McDuffie v. McDuffie, 313 S.C. 397, 438 S.E.2d 239 (1993); Treadway v. Smith, 325 S.C. 367, 479 S.E.2d 849 (Ct. App. 1996).

461. 678 So. 2d 1181 (Ala. Ct. App. 1996).

462. *See* Pittman v. Pittman, 84 Ark. App. 293, 139 S.W.3d 134 (2003); *In re* Marriage of Mulry, 314 Ill. App. 3d 756, 732 N.E.2d 667 (2000); Colucci v. Colucci, 54 A.D.3d 710, 712–13, 864 N.Y.S.2d 67, 69 (2008) (where "the provision in the stipulation requiring the father to pay 100% of the children's college education expenses is set forth in a section of the stipulation separate from the section containing his obligation to pay child support," father was required to pay both obligations); Kurzan v. Kurzan, 246 A.D.2d 693, 668 N.Y.S.2d 242 (1998); Werner v. Werner, 176 Misc. 2d 299, 671 N.Y.S.2d 626 (Sup. Ct. 1998); *cf.* Bender v. Bender, 715 A.2d 1199 (Pa. Super. Ct. 1998) (agreement required father to pay reasonable college costs and to establish a general trust for the welfare of the children; two separate obligations existed, so that trust funds could not be used to meet father's college costs obligation).

463. *See In re* Marriage of Crowder, 77 P.3d 858 (Colo. App. 2003); McIlmoil v. McIlmoil, 784 So. 2d 557, 562 (Fla. Dist. Ct. App. 2001); Schiano v. Hirsch, 22 A.D.3d 502, 503, 803 N.Y.S.2d 643, 644 (2005) ("no reasonable construction of the agreement would result in a conclusion that this obligation terminated on the child's 18th birthday").

termination of a separate obligation to pay periodic support past the normal age of majority.[464]

The presence of a periodic support obligation can sometimes influence the construction of the college costs provision. In particular, there is potential for overlap between periodic payments and college room and board expenses. Where the agreement gives the court sufficient flexibility, the decisions made reasonable attempts to avoid making the payor meet the same expenses twice.[465]

Vagueness

Since the costs of college are difficult to anticipate in advance, college support agreements could rarely be enforced if the courts insisted upon a specific listing of the costs and amounts covered. In recognition of this fact, the courts have enforced these agreements even where their language was very broad. For example, agreements to pay "reasonable" college costs are routinely enforced by the courts.[466]

Where the order provides only that the payor has a "moral obligation" to provide college support, there is no legal obligation.[467]

If the agreement is so broad as to reflect only an agreement to agree, it is not enforceable. For instance, where the agreement stated only that the parties would agree

---

464. *See* Ogle v. Ogle, 769 N.E.2d 644 (Ind. Ct. App. 2002).

465. *See id.* at 649–50 ("Jerry may have been entitled to a partial or full abatement of his non-educational child support obligation for the time Stephanie was at college had he petitioned the court for a modification"; periodic payment obligation was modifiable on the facts); Karafiol v. Karafiol, 259 A.D.2d 522, 686 N.Y.S.2d 461 (1999) (where room and board costs at private school were implicitly included in child support provision, school expenses provision construed not to include room and board costs).

For similar reasons, the college support obligation might constitute a valid reason to reduce the guideline amount of child support. *See* P. St. J. v. P.J.T., 175 Misc. 2d 417, 669 N.Y.S.2d 150 (Fam. Ct. 1997) (where one of three children was away at college, and father was paying college costs, proper to credit one-third of college costs to child support obligation).

466. For specific cases enforcing an agreement to pay "reasonable" costs, see Yarbrough v. Motley, 579 So. 2d 684 (Ala. Civ. App. 1991) ("reasonable" expenses); Harvey v. Daddona, 29 Conn. App. 369, 615 A.2d 177, 178 (1992) ("reasonable costs"); Ellis v. Taylor, 316 S.C. 245, 449 S.E.2d 487, 488 (1994) ("reasonable expenses").

For cases enforcing other vague language, see *In re* Pierce, 95 B.R. 154 (N.D. Cal. 1988) ("educational expenses"); Stevens v. Stevens, 798 S.W.2d 136, 137 (Ky. 1990) (contract declared father's "intention" to pay college expenses in an amount to be agreed upon by father and child); Smith v. Smith, 159 A.D.2d 929, 553 N.Y.S.2d 243, 244 (1990) ("all sums necessary or desirable" for support of child included college expenses); Stefani v. Stefani, 166 A.D.2d 577, 560 N.Y.S.2d 862 (1990) (father required to pay expenses only if "financially able"). *But see* Rosen v. Rosen, 105 N.C. App. 326, 413 S.E.2d 6, 8 (1992) (maverick decision holding that expenses "reasonably incurred in the obtaining of an undergraduate college degree" was too vague to be enforced); *cf.* Glassberg v. Obando, 791 S.W.2d 486 (Mo. Ct. App. 1990) (contract requiring payment of unspecified expenses was too broad, but remedy was a court order specifying the expenses; contract was not unenforceable).

467. Madson v. Madson, 636 So. 2d 759, 760 (Fla. Dist. Ct. App. 1994).

upon a proper amount for support while child was in college, a South Carolina court found that there was no real obligation.[468]

Specific Language

Since college expenses and other postmajority child support cannot be awarded by the court in a majority of states, most courts impose such an obligation by contract only where there is supporting language in the contract.[469]

Where the contract does contain supporting language, however, the courts have tended to construe that language to require contribution.[470] It is probably safe to say that most courts recognize the practical need for children to have a college education, and that they generally tend to construe agreements to contain meaningful college support provisions, so long as the agreement contains a reasonable minimum amount of supporting language.

Formalities. A college support provision does not normally require any specific unusual formalities of signing.[471]

Definition of a "College"

Many children choose to attend a traditional four-year college, but some children choose to attend less traditional educational programs. The general trend is to construe the word "college" broadly to include any educational program beyond high school.[472]

---

468. Ellis v. Taylor, 316 S.C. 245, 449 S.E.2d 487, 488 (1994); *see also* Kappus v. Kappus, 208 A.D.2d 538, 616 N.Y.S.2d 790 (1994) (agreement to agree on living allowance for child at college was not enforceable).

469. *See Id.* (agreement to agree on living allowance for child at college could not be enforced); Chesler v. Bronstein, 176 Misc. 2d 237, 672 N.Y.S.2d 82 (1997) (general promise to pay school tuition was intended to refer to private school, and not college; child was two years old when agreement signed).

470. *See Stevens,* 798 S.W.2d at 137 (agreement stating father's "intention" to pay college expenses, in an amount to be agreed upon by father and child, created an enforceable obligation); Mottley v. Mottley, 729 So. 2d 1289, 1289 (Miss. 1999) (promise to pay "educational expenses" applied to college, even though college was not specifically mentioned; over a strong dissent); Nash v. Yablon-Nash, 61 A.D.3d 832, 833, 878 N.Y.S.2d 382, 384 (2009) ("educational and related expenses" included costs of college); Nicholson v. Nicholson, 378 S.C. 523, 527, 663 S.E.2d 74, 76 (Ct. App. 2008) (promise to pay for "educational needs" includes costs of college); *cf.* Hoefers v. Jones, 288 N.J. Super. 590, 672 A.2d 1299 (Ch. Div. 1994), *aff'd per curiam,* 288 N.J. Super. 478, 672 A.2d 1177 (App. Div. 1995) (father agreed to pay private school tuition if "both parties agree," provided that "the issue must be discussed between the parties on an annual basis"; agreement stated an enforceable obligation).

471. *But cf.* Lowe v. Lowe, 47 Conn. App. 354, 704 A.2d 236 (1977) (under specific statute, college support agreement must be in writing).

472. *See* Fritch v. Fritch, 224 Ill. App. 3d 29, 586 N.E.2d 427 (1991) (Art Institute of Chicago); Goss v. Timblin, 424 Pa. Super. 216, 622 A.2d 347, 348 (1993) ("college education" includes three-year program at the Art Institute of Pittsburgh); *In re* Marriage of Oldham, 222 Ill. App. 3d 744, 584 N.E.2d 385 (1991) (DeVry Institute of Technology, offering four-year programs in electronics, computer, and business fields; some traditional liberal arts courses offered and required); *In re*

Some courts are reluctant to include in the definition of "college" an institution that is essentially a trade school.[473] The courts focus upon the type of school, however, and not the type of program. Thus, a program that might not be covered at a trade school probably would be covered in a traditional undergraduate setting, if reasonably necessary for obtaining an undergraduate degree.[474]

Where the agreement terminates college support upon emancipation, and the child attends a military academy, the mere fact that the child is technically paid for service in the military does not constitute emancipation within the meaning of the agreement.[475] In other words, military academies are treated as colleges, and not as traditional military service, for purposes of child support. There is no constitutional obstacle to enforcing an agreement requiring parents to pay tuition at a religious college or private school.[476]

The courts are reluctant to require parents to contribute to the graduate school expenses of their children. Thus, graduate school expenses are generally payable only where the contract expressly so provides.[477]

Choice of Institution

Approval Requirement. Some agreements give the payor the right to approve the child's choice of school. Courts disfavor these provisions, as the power to disapprove the school can easily be used in bad faith to avoid liability altogether. Thus, an absolute right of approval will be granted only where the contractual language is clear.

Marriage of Dieter, 271 Ill. App. 3d 181, 648 N.E.2d 304 (1995) (separately billed flight school cost for aviation science major at state university).

473. *See* Hall v. Day, 273 Ga. 838, 840, 546 S.E.2d 469, 471 (2001) ("Day is not obligated to pay for an education at a trade school, as the decree's plain terms obligate him to pay only for a 'university education.'"); *In re* Marriage of Holderrieth, 181 Ill. App. 3d 199, 536 N.E.2d 946, 947 (1989) (contract to pay the expenses of "college and professional education" did not cover the expenses of a trade school at which the child was studying automobile mechanics); *In re* Marriage of Leming, 227 Ill. App. 3d 154, 590 N.E.2d 1027 (1992) (term did not include Sparks Business College, which provided short-term training in becoming a court reporter, or the International Air Academy, which offered a three-month course in working in the airline industry); Cathcart v. Cathcart, 307 S.C. 322, 414 S.E.2d 811 (Ct. App. 1992) (agreement to pay for "four (4) year undergraduate college education" did not apply to program of less than four years at Midlands Technical College).

474. *See Dieter*, 271 Ill. App. 3d 181, 648 N.E.2d 304 (father must pay flight school costs for aviation major at state university, even though flight lessons at a trade school might not be covered).

475. Howard v. Howard, 80 Ohio App. 3d 832, 610 N.E.2d 1152 (1992) (Coast Guard academy).

476. Hoefers v. Jones, 288 N.J. Super. 590, 672 A.2d 1299 (Ch. Div. 1994), *aff'd per curiam*, 288 N.J. Super. 478, 672 A.2d 1177 (App. Div. 1995).

477. *See* Del Castillo v. Del Castillo, 420 Pa. Super. 520, 617 A.2d 26, 27 (1992) (agreement to pay for the child's "education . . . beyond the high school level" included only college; dissent would have included graduate school); *but see* Allyn v. Allyn, 163 A.D.2d 665, 558 N.Y.S.2d 983, 984 (1990) ("education beyond the high school level" includes both college and medical school).

For example, a mere provision giving the payor the right to "participate" in choosing the school does not give an absolute right of approval.[478] Likewise, where the contract requires payment of reasonable expenses, the payor cannot unilaterally deem the child's choice of school unreasonable.[479]

Where the contract appears to grant a right of approval, the court may avoid the provision to some extent by imposing a requirement of good faith. For instance, in *Tapp v. Tapp*,[480] where the agreement required the husband to pay expenses "at a college or university of the Husband's approval," the court held that the husband was required to act in good faith. On the facts, the contract spoke in terms of a "four year" program, but the husband refused to approve any institution other than a two-year community college. The court held that this refusal was not made in good faith.[481]

A parent can approve a child's choice of school through conduct as well as words. In *Hartle v. Cobane*,[482] the father had a right of approval, but he did not either expressly approve or disapprove the child's choice of school. Instead, he drove the child to campus and helped her move into a dormitory. The court held that these actions showed implied approval of the school, approval that the husband could not subsequently withdraw.[483]

---

478. Tiffany v. Tiffany, 1 Va. App. 11, 332 S.E.2d 796 (1985); *see also* Wineburgh v. Wineburgh, 816 A.2d 1105, 1109 (Pa. Super. Ct. 2002) (provision stating that husband would "have a say" in choice of college did not require child and mother to consult father; error to hold that failure to consult was a complete defense to any payment obligation); Giacalone v. Giacalone, 876 S.W.2d 616 (Ky. Ct. App. 1994) (husband's right to "participate" in deciding whether child attended parochial high school did not give absolute right of approval).

The agreement in *Wineburgh* also expressly provided that the husband "will have the right to approve or disapprove a particular college but will exercise that right in a reasonable fashion." If the agreement required literally no consultation with the father, it is hard to see how the father's right to "approve or disapprove a particular college" had any practical weight at all. But there was no suggestion in the case that the father disapproved the choice of school, or reasonably could have disapproved it; he may simply have been using the failure to consult as a handy excuse for avoiding the obligation.

479. Bender v. Bender, 715 A.2d 1199 (Pa. Super. Ct. 1998). Case law discussing the criteria courts apply in determining whether the choice of institution was reasonable is discussed at note 489 *infra*.

480. 105 Ohio App. 3d 159, 663 N.E.2d 944, 945 (1995).

481. *See also* Harris v. Woodrum, 3 Va. App. 428, 350 S.E.2d 667, 668 (1986) (recognizing express requirement in agreement that father's approval not be unreasonably withheld).

482. 228 A.D.2d 756, 643 N.Y.S.2d 726 (1996).

483. *See also* Heinlein v. Kuzemka, 49 A.D.3d 996, 998, 854 N.Y.S.2d 560, 562 (2008) (where agreement required mother and child to consult with father regarding choice of college, but father refused to accept even registered mail from mother, knew of child's choice of college, and failed to object, consulting requirement was met; "the father cannot avoid his contractual obligations by ignoring the mother's written communications and remaining silent in the face of his admitted knowledge that his son was attending RPI"); Regan v. Regan, 254 A.D.2d 402, 678 N.Y.S.2d 673 (1998) (father who paid for one semester of college, plus several summer courses, implicitly consented to the child's choice of college).

When an approval requirement is clearly present, and approval was clearly denied, the courts will enforce the requirement.[484] Enforcement is especially likely where the child failed even to inform the parent as to the choice of college, as information is a necessary prerequisite to approval.[485]

Silent Agreement. Where the contract is silent on choice of school, the cases are divided. One line of cases holds that the payor must pay the expenses at the college that the child actually attends, regardless of the amount of those expenses.[486] If the payor had desired to limit the obligation to a particular set of schools or to a reasonable cost, such a limitation should have been written into the agreement.

Another line of cases holds that a silent agreement will be construed to contain an implied requirement that the choice of school be reasonable.[487]

A reasonableness requirement can of course be expressly added, either by providing directly that the choice of college must be reasonable or by allowing the payor to approve the child's choice of school, with a requirement that approval not be unreasonably withheld.[488]

---

484. *See* Hartle v. Cobane, 228 A.D.2d 756, 643 N.Y.S.2d 726 (1996) (father not required to pay expenses for summer school, as he had clearly and expressly refused to approve them); Cooper v. Farrell, 170 A.D.2d 571, 566 N.Y.S.2d 347 (1991) (where father had right to make final selection of school, he could not be forced to contribute toward private school he had not chosen); Jones v. Jones, 19 Va. App. 265, 450 S.E.2d 762, 762 (1994) ("Both parents shall agree on the college of attendance[.]"); Harris v. Woodrum, 3 Va. App. 428, 350 S.E.2d 667, 668 (1986) ("subject to the approval of the particular school").

Cases considering provisions limiting the payor's liability to costs at a certain school are discussed at note 512 *infra*. Case law considering provisions limiting the payor's liability to costs at a certain school is discussed at note 512 *infra*. These provisions do not limit the child's choice of school, but rather the amount of the payor's liability.

485. *See* Cricenti v. Cricenti, 60 A.D.3d 1052, 1053, 877 N.Y.S.2d 349, 350 (2009) (where agreement required mother to approve daughter's choice of college, and daughter never even told mother which college she was attending, approval requirement was not met and no liability for college costs existed; "[t]he mother could neither approve of the petitioner's choice of college nor unreasonably withhold such approval in the absence of any awareness of the petitioner's choice").

486. *See* Amie v. Conrey, 801 So. 2d 841 (Ala. Civ. App. 2001) (where agreement required equal division of college expenses without limitation as to school or amount, trial court erred by limiting the amount of future expenses covered); Greenburg v. Greenburg, 26 Conn. App. 591, 602 A.2d 1056 (1992); Hall v. Day, 273 Ga. 838, 840, 546 S.E.2d 469, 471 (2001) ("The decree's plain language does not, however, condition Day's obligation to pay educational expenses upon his daughter's attendance at a university located in Georgia, nor does it limit the amount Day must pay to the amount of tuition at a Georgia university[.]"); Mack v. Mack, 148 A.D.2d 984, 539 N.Y.S.2d 219 (1989).

487. *See* Jack v. Jack, 139 Ohio App. 3d 814, 745 N.E.2d 1101 (2000); Del Castillo v. Del Castillo, 420 Pa. Super. 520, 617 A.2d 26, 27 (1992); Pylant v. Spivey, 174 S.W.3d 143 (Tenn. Ct. App. 2003).

488. *E.g.*, Balk v. Rosoff, 280 A.D.2d 568, 720 N.Y.S.2d 559 (2001).

Reasonable Choice. Where a reasonableness requirement exists, courts have tended to require clear evidence before finding conduct to be unreasonable.[489] When the child selects an unreasonable school, the choice is not a full defense to the obligation, but the payor is only required to pay the amount that would have been due had the child attended a reasonable school.[490]

Reasonableness can be a harder issue when the child is talented. A good example is *Pharoah v. Lapes*,[491] where an unusually brilliant child received a full scholarship at Georgia Tech, but chose to attend the Massachusetts Institute of Technology (MIT) without a scholarship. The majority held that reasonable college expenses included part of the tuition at MIT, as the child had unusual ability and deserved to attend the better school. A dissenting opinion would have held that in light of the full scholarship, tuition at MIT was unreasonable.[492]

Duration of Payment

If the agreement simply requires payment of college expenses, there is no express time limit on the payor's liability.[493] In theory, if the child took one course per year for two decades, nothing would prevent liability. In the real world, most institutions insist that undergraduate education be completed at a reasonable pace, so the issue tends not to arise in the reported cases. Graduate school tends to take longer, but as noted above, only rarely will the courts construe an agreement to require payment of graduate school expenses.

When the agreement contains an express time limit, that limit will be respected. Two types of limits appear in the cases. First, some agreements state the limit in terms of years. These agreements are so obviously enforceable that no one has never contended to the contrary.

Second, some agreements state the limit in terms of age of the children. An agreement to pay the expenses of minor children, for instance, would not include expenses

---

489. *See* Balk v. Rosoff, 280 A.D.2d 568, 720 N.Y.S.2d 559 (2001) (where two schools had "similar status," and child's choice cost three times as much as father's choice, father's refusal to approve child's choice of school was reasonable). *Jack*, 139 Ohio App. 3d 814, 745 N.E.2d 1101 (2000); *Pylant*, 174 S.W.3d 143.

490. *See* Balk, 280 A.D.2d 568, 720 N.Y.S.2d 559 (2001); *Jack*, 139 Ohio App. 3d 814, 745 N.E.2d 1101 (2000); *Pylant*, 174 S.W.3d 143.

491. 391 Pa. Super. 585, 571 A.2d 1070 (1990).

492. *See also* Mack v. Mack, 148 A.D.2d 984, 539 N.Y.S.2d 219 (1989) (choice of school was one factor in determining reasonable college expenses); Bender v. Bender, 715 A.2d 1199 (Pa. Super. Ct. 1998) (where child made comparisons of cost at different schools, and received partial scholarship at school of choice, child's decision was reasonable).

493. *See* Wehrkamp v. Wehrkamp, 773 N.W.2d 212, 216 (S.D. 2009) (where agreement contained no time limit on enforcement of father's obligation to pay college tuition, agreement was enforced 30 years after it was written, when child was married and had two children of her own).

after the age of majority.[494] This type of agreement obviously is seen only in those few states where the age of majority is higher than 18. Where the agreement stated only that the father would pay the college expenses of the "children," a New York court held that the term was ambiguous, and remanded for consideration of extrinsic evidence.[495] Another court held that an agreement to pay the expenses of "children" did not permit termination of support at age 21.[496]

Expenses Covered

"[T]he strictest interpretation of college education necessities may work to destroy the original provision's effectiveness."[497] Where the agreement refers only to reasonable college expenses, it covers both tuition payments and other educational costs, such as textbooks.[498] Tuition includes any fee charged by the college as a requirement for attending classes, regardless of the precise label.[499] In addition, the agreement includes the room and board costs if the child resides away from home.[500] If the child resides at home with the nonpaying spouse, the obligor must pay any extra costs incurred by that spouse due to the child's residence.[501] It is error, however, to charge the obligor with hypothetical room and board cost for student residing at the school.[502]

Expenses incurred for activities other than traditional study should be included if they result in credit toward graduation. For example, a New York court applied this rule to the costs of advanced placement tests that yielded college credit, and to the costs of a semester abroad.[503]

---

494. *See supra* note 448.

495. Cortese v. Redmond, 199 A.D.2d 785, 605 N.Y.S.2d 506, 507 (1993).

496. *In re* Marriage of Wisdom, 833 P.2d 884, 886 (Colo. App. 1992).

497. Meek v. Warren, 726 So. 2d 1292, 1294 (Miss. Ct. App. 1998).

498. Kiev v. Kiev, 454 N.W.2d 544 (S.D. 1990); *see also Meek*, 726 So. 2d 1292.

499. *See* Baker v. Baker, 68 Ohio App. 3d 402, 588 N.E.2d 944, 946 (1990) (payor was responsible for both "general fee" and "undergraduate fee"); *Meek*, 726 So. 2d at 1294 ("lab fee").

500. Reynolds v. Diamond, 605 So. 2d 525 (Fla. Dist. Ct. App. 1992); *Meek*, 726 So. 2d 1292; Shea v. McFadden, 227 A.D.2d 543, 642 N.Y.S.2d 963 (1996); Allyn v. Allyn, 163 A.D.2d 665, 558 N.Y.S.2d 983 (1990); Wiegand v. Wiegand, 349 Pa. 517, 37 A.2d 492 (1944) (unless payor is of limited means); *Kiev*, 454 N.W.2d 544; Douglas v. Hammett, 28 Va. App. 517, 507 S.E.2d 98, 102 (1998) ("A student could not attend college in a vacuum[.]"); *but cf.* Uram v. Uram, 65 Ohio App. 3d 96, 582 N.E.2d 1060, 1061 (1989) ("costs of . . . college . . . including the costs of such items as tuition, fees and books" did not include room and board).

501. Legg v. Legg, 44 Conn. App. 303, 688 A.2d 1354 (1997); Goss v. Timblin, 424 Pa. Super. 216, 622 A.2d 347 (1993).

502. *Goss*, 622 A.2d 347.

503. Kappus v. Kappus, 208 A.D.2d 538, 616 N.Y.S.2d 790 (1994).

The expenses of attending college do not include transportation costs,[504] clothing,[505] a living allowance,[506] medical expenses,[507] or the costs of voluntary extracurricular activities.[508]

Amount Covered

Where the agreement is silent as to amount, one line of cases requires payment of all costs actually incurred, and not merely reasonable costs.[509] Under these cases, the payor has no implied right to be consulted on the amount of cost incurred.[510]

---

504. *See Meek*, 726 So. 2d at 1294 ("educational expenses" do not include "transportation, clothing and other such needs upon which her enrollment in college has no bearing"); McDuffie v. McDuffie, 313 S.C. 397, 438 S.E.2d 239, 240 (1993) ("college expenses"; "Father was not liable for transportation and incidental expenses or spending money").

Conversely, in Nicholson v. Nicholson, 378 S.C. 523, 536–37, 663 S.E.2d 74, 81 (Ct. App. 2008), where the father agreed to meet "educational needs" of the children, the court held that the obligation included "transportation expenses enabling Kyle to attend classes." *Nicholson* raises the possibility that the obligation to pay transportation expenses might be included when the college campus is so spread out that students must drive to class, but not included when the college campus is compact enough that most students walk to class. Also, even where the campus is compact, costs of transportation from home to college would seem to be reasonably necessary.

505. *See Meek*, 726 So. 2d at 1294 ("educational expenses" do not include "transportation, clothing and other such needs upon which her enrollment in college has no bearing"); *Kier*, 454 N.W.2d at 547 ("all of the regular costs in [Tracy's] obtaining a college education" did not include clothing).

In Douglas v. Hammett, 28 Va. App. 517, 507 S.E.2d 98, 100, 102 (1998), the court held that a provision to pay "expenses for college education" required payment of clothing costs, on the theory that "one does have to be clothed for class." The court seemed to suggest that these costs should normally be paid with the child's income, but the child in *Douglas* was unable to work because of limitations imposed upon recipients of full basketball scholarships. *Douglas* is obviously an unusual situation; the father received a substantial benefit from the scholarship, and since inability to work part-time is a condition of such scholarships, requiring the father to pay clothing expenses was entirely reasonable. In most cases, clothing costs are a much closer question.

506. *See* Rogers v. Rogers, 83 Ark. App. 206, 212, 121 S.W.3d 510, 513–14 (2003) ("the trial court erred in ordering Gregory to pay to Breanne $300 per month for what Gregory has characterized as 'spending money'"); *McDuffie*, 313 S.C. 397, 438 S.E.2d at 240 ("college expenses"; "Father was not liable for transportation and incidental expenses or spending money").

507. Taplin v. Taplin, 611 So. 2d 561 (Fla. Dist. Ct. App. 1992).

508. Kaltwasser v. Kearns, 235 A.D.2d 738, 653 N.Y.S.2d 147 (1997) (child's extracurricular soccer expenses were not covered under agreement to pay private school tuition).

509. *See* Simpkins v. Simpkins, 595 So. 2d 493, 494 (Ala. Ct. App. 1991) ("pay for the college education"; father liable for tuition at expensive private university); Hall v. Day, 273 Ga. 838, 840, 546 S.E.2d 469, 471 (2001) ("The decree's plain language does not, however, condition Day's obligation to pay educational expenses upon his daughter's attendance at a university located in Georgia, nor does it limit the amount Day must pay to the amount of tuition at a Georgia university[.]"); Hartley-Selvey v. Hartley, 261 Ga. 700, 410 S.E.2d 118, 119 (1991) ("any and all college expenses"); Forstner v. Forstner, 68 Ohio App. 3d 367, 588 N.E.2d 285 (1990).

510. Fritch v. Fritch, 224 Ill. App. 3d 29, 586 N.E.2d 427 (1991).

A second line of cases will construe a silent agreement to contain an implicit limit based upon the payor's ability to pay.[511] This position has been growing in popularity recently, perhaps as a result of the increasing cost of college tuition.

Some agreements limit the payor's liability to college costs at a defined school, often a local state university. These provisions are generally enforced as an attempt to limit the payor's liability to an affordable level.[512] If the agreement does not expressly refer to the in-state tuition cost, and the child attends a local university after moving out of state, the payor's liability cannot be limited to the in-state amount.[513]

Other Sources of Payment

Some agreements require that college expenses be paid first from certain sources, such as an educational trust or 529 plan. When a spouse seeks contribution to college costs under this type of agreement, the spouse must show first that the primary sources stated in the agreement have been exhausted.[514]

Academic Performance

Where the contract is silent on the child's course load or academic performance, the court should not imply a condition that the child maintain some minimum level of grades or credit hours.[515]

---

511. *See Forstner*, 68 Ohio App. 3d 367, 588 N.E.2d 285 (agreement contained such a provision, but its terms were met, as father was a multimillionaire); Carlton v. Carlton, 670 So. 2d 1129, 1130 (Fla. Dist. Ct. App. 1996) (assuming without explanation that agreement to "share equally in all education expenses" required payment of only reasonable costs).

In addition, some states tend to require that the child's choice of college be reasonable. *See supra* note 487. In most of these decisions, the cost of attending the school is a major factor in determining whether the child's choice is reasonable. In practice, therefore, the reasonableness of the college and the reasonable of the cost tend to be considered together.

512. *See* Morris v. Morris, 251 A.D.2d 637, 676 N.Y.S.2d 202 (1998) (enforcing provision limiting father's liability to costs at State of New York University System).

513. *In re* White, 299 S.C. 406, 385 S.E.2d 211 (Ct. App. 1989).

514. *See* Washington v. Washington, 56 A.D.3d 463, 464, 867 N.Y.S.2d 478, 479 (2008) (where parties agreed that college costs would be paid first from certain trust, and party seeking enforcement "failed to produce any evidence as to the proceeds or balance of the trust," error to award college costs).

515. *See* Bingemann v. Bingemann, 551 So. 2d 1228 (Fla. Dist. Ct. App. 1988) (error to imply condition that child must take 15 credit hours per semester and maintain a 2.0 grade point average), *review denied*, 560 So. 2d 232 (Fla. 1990).

A Missouri statute provides that to receive college support, children must enroll in at least 12 credit hours, and provide each parent with a full transcript. In Shands v. Shands, 237 S.W.3d 597 (Mo. Ct. App. 2007), the court held that compliance with this statute is required even where the obligation to pay college tuition is based upon an agreement, unless the agreement expressly states otherwise.

The authors respectfully submit that *Shands* improperly added language to the agreement. The obligation at issue in that case did not come from statute; it came from the agreement. Courts hold in many other contexts that agreement-based rights are not subject to conditions placed on similar statutory rights. *E.g.*, Kripp v. Kripp, 578 Pa. 82, 849 A.2d 1159 (2004) (definition of cohabitation in state statute, for purposes of terminating spousal support, does not necessarily apply to private agreements). *Shands* should have held that the statutory requirement did not apply.

Express provisions requiring a minimum standard of academic performance are generally enforceable.[516] Provisions requiring maintenance of a stated grade-point average are construed to refer to the child's total average over his or her entire period of college attendance, and not to each semester individually.[517]

Provisions requiring the child to be a full-time student are also generally enforceable.[518] Where the child was forced to work for a semester because of the payor's wrongful failure to meet a college support obligation, one court understandably refused to permit the payor to invoke such a provision.[519]

Financial Ability of the Payor

If the agreement requires payment of expenses without making reference to the payor's financial ability, the payor's financial ability is irrelevant to the obligation.[520]

Some college expense clauses contain an express provision requiring the payor to contribute toward the expenses only if the payor's financial condition so permits at the time when the child actually attends college. Where the agreement does not include a specific test, the court will make its own objective determination of ability to pay.[521] Where the agreement stated quite expressly that the father would be the sole judge of his own ability to pay, one court held there was effectively no enforceable obligation.[522]

Where the agreement speaks in terms of good faith or reasonable costs, the court will look to its own objective definition of these terms, and not to the obligor's own subjective definition.[523] The cases are split on whether ability to pay can be considered as one factor in determining reasonable costs.[524]

---

516. *See* Burtch v. Burtch, 972 S.W.2d 882, 887 (Tex. Ct. App. 1998) (provision requiring the child be "in good standing" at university was not too vague to be enforced).

517. *See id.* (where agreement required child to maintain a C average, provision would be satisfied if child's cumulative average was C or better, even if child's average for one particular semester was a D).

518. *See* § **6.036** (cases enforcing similar provisions in defined duration spousal support provisions).

519. *Burtch*, 972 S.W.2d 882.

520. Ellis v. Taylor, 316 S.C. 245, 449 S.E.2d 487 (1994).

521. *See, e.g.*, Stefani v. Stefani, 166 A.D.2d 577, 560 N.Y.S.2d 862, 863 (1990) (father required to pay if "financially able"; father had net annual income of $23,500; father had ability to pay total of $21,500 in expenses spread over six years, but payment of interest on this amount would be unduly burdensome); Kappus v. Kappus, 208 A.D.2d 538, 616 N.Y.S.2d 790 (1994); Whelan v. Frisbee, 29 Mass. App. Ct. 76, 557 N.E.2d 55, 57 (1990) (mother promised to contribute "in good faith" toward her children's college expenses; where mother had borrowed $100,000 to invest in questionable business, mother should have made a contribution under the agreement); Regan v. Regan, 254 A.D.2d 402, 678 N.Y.S.2d 673, 674 (1998) (promise to pay college costs "if . . . his financial circumstances permit"; finding this test met on the facts); Goss v. Timblin, 424 Pa. Super. 216, 622 A.2d 347, 348 (1993) (parties promised to "assist the children to obtain a college education to the best of their ability"; finding that husband had ability to contribute).

522. Charles v. Leavitt, 264 Ga. 160, 442 S.E.2d 241 (1994).

523. Harvey v. Daddona, 29 Conn. App. 369, 615 A.2d 177, 178 (1992) ("reasonable costs" did not mean only those costs that the father deemed reasonable).

524. *Compare* Carlton v. Carlton, 670 So. 2d 1129 (Fla. Dist. Ct. App. 1996) (relevant), *with* Ellis v. Taylor, 316 S.C. 245, 449 S.E.2d 487 (1994) (not relevant).

Courts are generally reluctant to construe financial ability provisions to place automatic limits upon support, preferring instead to evaluate the payor's entire financial condition. For example, where college support was "based upon" the husband earning an annual income of $55,000, the court held that the agreement set the baseline for modification under the changed circumstances test, but that it did not absolutely require reduction in a father's obligation if income dropped below the stated level.[525]

The payor cannot avoid paying college expenses under a financial ability provision if his or her financial problems are self-inflicted for the bad-faith purpose of reducing support. In other words, in determining ability to pay, the court can follow normal imputation of income principles. If the payor did not act in bad faith, however, self-inflicted financial ability can be considered.[526]

Along similar lines, where the payor completely refuses to provide any information on his or her income and assets, the court may assume that the amount of costs involved is reasonable.[527]

If the agreement requires payment of expenses without mentioning need, lack of need is not a defense to the obligation.[528]

Contributions of the Child

Where the agreement is silent on the child's contributions, the obligor must pay the entire cost of college. Neither the child or the other parent is under any duty to make his or her own contributions.[529] But specific provisions requiring contribution by the child are generally enforced.[530]

Courts are reluctant to hold that the expenses of one child must be paid with the college expense funds of another.[531]

---

525. *See In re* Marriage of Sawyer, 264 Ill. App. 3d 839, 637 N.E.2d 559 (1994) (college support).

526. *See id.* (payor imprisoned for tax evasion; inability to pay was a factor).

527. Bender v. Bender, 715 A.2d 1199 (Pa. Super. Ct. 1998).

528. Frank v. Frank, 402 Pa. Super. 458, 587 A.2d 340 (1991).

529. Fritch v. Fritch, 224 Ill. App. 3d 29, 586 N.E.2d 427 (1991); Riley v. Riley, 29 A.D.3d 1146, 814 N.Y.S.2d 793 (2006) (where husband and wife agreed to share cost of college education "upon their financial means and ability to pay," and parties had ability to pay, error to require child to contribute 17 percent of the cost); *Ellis*, 316 S.C. 245, 449 S.E.2d 487; McDuffie v. McDuffie, 313 S.C. 397, 438 S.E.2d 239 (1993).

530. *See* Troha v. Troha, 105 Ohio App. 3d 327, 663 N.E.2d 1319 (1995) (agreement to pay college expenses with existing college funds of children could not be enforced directly, as children were not parties to the contract; but depletion of college funds construed as a condition to father's liability for further sums). *Cf.* Douglas v. Hammett, 28 Va. App. 517, 507 S.E.2d 98, 100, 102 (1998) (to the extent that child had duty to work, that duty did not apply on the facts, where child received a full basketball scholarship but one condition of such a scholarship was that the child not work).

531. *See Troha*, 663 N.E.2d at 1324 (requirement that children's funds be used for "their college education" required that each child's funds be used for that child, and not that both children's funds be used for the first child alone).

Financial Aid. The liability of the payor for expenses already covered by financial aid is determined first and foremost by the language of the agreement.[532] Where the agreement is silent, the payor is generally not required to pay college expenses covered by a scholarship earned by the child.[533] The cases are divided as to costs covered by student loans[534] and other forms of financial aid.[535]

Modification

Like postmajority child support generally,[536] a contractual obligation to pay college tuition is not subject to modification for changed circumstances.[537]

---

532. *See* Morris v. Morris, 251 A.D.2d 637, 676 N.Y.S.2d 202 (1998) (enforcing provision making father liable only for costs beyond loans and grants); Hartle v. Cobane, 228 A.D.2d 756, 643 N.Y.S.2d 726 (1996) (agreement provided that parties would encourage the child to obtain financial aid; father was liable only for costs above amount of student loans); *cf. Ellis*, 316 S.C. at 247, 449 S.E.2d at 488 (father agreed to pay costs above "scholarship, grant or other assistance"; father had to pay costs reflected by student loans).

533. *E.g., Douglas*, 28 Va. App. 517, 507 S.E.2d 98 (father not liable for expenses covered by child's full basketball scholarship).

534. *See Fritch*, 224 Ill. App. 3d 29, 586 N.E.2d 427 (payor must cover costs paid by student loans). *But see* Histen v. Histen, 98 Conn. App. 729, 911 A.2d 348 (2006) ("the court properly construed the term 'actual costs' in the parties' agreement to not include a deduction for the portion of educational expenses that constituted student loans").

535. *See* Frank v. Frank, 402 Pa. Super. 458, 587 A.2d 340 (1991) (costs paid in part by funds from wife's family trust; husband not entitled to be reimbursed for paying the same expenses). *But see* Regan v. Regan, 254 A.D.2d 402, 678 N.Y.S.2d 673 (1998) (father was not liable to the extent costs were paid with a gift from child's grandfather).

536. *See* § **6.043**, note 455.

537. *See* Miner v. Miner, 48 Conn. App. 409, 709 A.2d 605 (1998).

The law in Florida is unclear. In State *ex rel.* Dodge v. Dodge, 647 So. 2d 170 (Fla. Dist. Ct. App. 1994), the appellate court held that the trial court erred by issuing a sua sponte order that the parties' college support agreement would no longer be enforceable. The rationale was that this relief had not been requested, however, and the decision can be read to suggest that the order would have proper if requested. *See also* Bingemann v. Bingemann, 551 So. 2d 1228 (Fla. Dist. Ct. App. 1988) (modifying postmajority support without expressly discussing whether the court had power to do so). A much better result was reached in Farnsworth v. Farnsworth, 657 So. 2d 1273 (Fla. Dist. Ct. App. 1995), which held that a college support obligation is a contractual provision and not a child support obligation. Since the court's power to modify extends only to child support and not to contractual provisions, *Farnsworth* points toward the general nationwide rule that postmajority support cannot be modified.

In Moss v. Nedas, 289 N.J. Super. 352, 674 A.2d 174 (1996), the agreement required the father to pay all college expenses. The court viewed the agreement as a child support contract, and modified it without heed to the parties' intent, limiting liability to reasonable costs and requiring the mother to consult with the father on the specific school attended. The result was a gross and fundamental breach of the rule that the parties can always agree to pay *more* child support than the law requires. The court also quite blandly rewrote the parties' contract for them, a practice that thousands of court decisions have disapproved. *See* § **5.04**. Even where the court does have authority to modify postmajority support, it should not modify such support downward unless the contract itself anticipates such modification.

Standing to Enforce

The child has standing as a third-party beneficiary to enforce a college support provision.[538]

One court held under very limited circumstances that the nonobligor spouse cannot file an action for damages against the obligor spouse, and that this remedy lies exclusively with the child.[539] The court admitted that a reimbursement theory had not been pled,[540] and this admission severely limits the value of the holding. The court also expressly held that the nonobligor spouse has standing to bring an action for specific performance. The strong general rule in other states is that a parent always has standing to enforce a provision for the child's benefit. *See* § **7.05**. The court would have done better if it had simply followed the majority rule.

§ 6.045 Postdeath Child Support

The parties may also agree to extend child support past the death of the payor. Since this is an exception to the general rule that the payor's death terminates child support, postdeath support is available only where the agreement clearly provides for it.[541]

Obviously, the standard for postdeath support is met where the contract expressly states that death shall not terminate child support. Less specific language may also suffice. For instance, where the contract stated that support would continue until the child graduated from college or reached age 23, one court found that it did not terminate upon the payor's death.[542] In addition to relying on language of the agreement, the court also stressed the fact that the contract required the husband to maintain insurance on his own life. The presence of such insurance, the court said, was a factor in favor of postdeath support.[543]

---

538. *In re* Marriage of Smith, 21 Cal. App. 4th 100, 26 Cal. Rptr. 2d 133 (1991); Noble v. Fisher, 126 Idaho 885, 894 P.2d 118 (1995).

539. *In re* Smith, 21 Cal. App. 4th 100, 26 Cal. Rptr. 2d 133 (1991).

540. *See* 26 Cal. Rptr. 2d at 138 n.7.

541. *E.g.*, Malicoate v. Standard Life & Accident Ins. Co., 999 P.2d 1103, 1114 (Okla. Civ. App. 2000); Wendell v. Sovran Bank, 780 S.W.2d 372 (Tenn. Ct. App. 1989); *but see* Kiken v. Kiken, 149 N.J. 441, 694 A.2d 557 (1997) (child support, including contractual obligation to pay college expenses, survives the payor's death unless the agreement states otherwise).

542. *Wendell*, 780 S.W.2d 372; *see also In re* Marriage of Oldham, 222 Ill. App. 3d 744, 584 N.E.2d 385 (1991) (agreement to pay college expenses survived death of father).

543. *But see* Hornsby v. Anderson, 567 So. 2d 1047 (Fla. Dist. Ct. App. 1990) (similar life insurance is evidence *against* postdeath support).

§ 6.05 Attorney's Fees Provisions

§ 6.051 Statutory Fees Awards

In most states, a specific statute permits the court to award attorney's fees in domestic relations cases. The court must normally consider a variety of factors, including most importantly the parties' respective abilities to pay.[544]

When an action under a separation agreement is brought as a motion in the divorce case, these provisions generally apply.[545] In some states, however, the statutes may not apply in actions to construe a separation agreement. This is particularly true where the enforcing spouse brings a common law contract action, rather than filing a motion in the divorce case.[546]

A few cases construing separation agreements have made attorney's fees awards under other provisions.[547]

§ 6.052 Contractual Waivers

There is some basis for arguing that the court may disregard a contractual waiver of the right to receive a statutory attorney's fees award. The rationale is essentially that the award is an incident of the duty to support the other spouse during the marriage, a duty that generally cannot be waived by contract. *See* § **3.06**. Regardless of whether the court has the power to disregard such a waiver, however, a majority of cases refuse

---

544. *See generally* Brett R. Turner, *Compensating the Family Law Lawyer: Final Attorney's Fees Awards in Domestic Relations Cases*, 8 Divorce Litig. 201 (1996).

545. *See* Amie v. Conrey, 801 So. 2d 841 (Ala. Civ. App. 2001) (on motion to enforce college support provision of agreement, where wife had limited resources and language of college support provision was unambiguously in wife's favor, trial court erred by not awarding the wife attorney's fees); Issler v. Issler, 50 Conn. App. 58, 716 A.2d 938 (1998) (making a statutory fees award); *see also* Day v. Day, 717 A.2d 914 (Me. 1998) (statute applies; awarding no fee on the facts).

546. *See* Lebac v. Lebac, 109 Md. App. 396, 675 A.2d 131 (1996).

547. *See* Murphy v. Murphy, 694 A.2d 932 (Me. 1997) (where husband refused to comply with obligation to hold certain assets in trust for children, awarding attorney's fees under provision permitting such an award where a fiduciary duty was breached).

to do so.[548] Contractual waivers are usually disregarded only where their language is unclear[549] or the provision is otherwise substantially unfair.

One exception is waivers of the right to collect an attorney's fees award in an action involving custody or child support.[550] Applying such waivers would discourage parents from taking actions required by the best interests of the children.

§ 6.053 Mandatory Attorney's Fees Provisions

A growing number of agreement contain a specific provision requiring payment of attorney's fees by a spouse who breaches the contract. These provisions differ from traditional statutory attorney's fees provisions in that they absolutely require an award, rather than leaving the question to the trial court's discretion.

Since courts generally have no inherent power to award attorney's fees, contractual provisions requiring such payment are strictly construed. If any requirement set forth in the provision is not met, fees cannot be awarded.[551]

Nevertheless, mandatory attorney's fees provisions will be enforced where their terms are clearly met. Such provisions are growing in popularity, and a growing number of cases hold that contractual attorney's fees provisions are enforceable.[552] When an

---

548. *See In re* Marriage of Dechant, 867 P.2d 193 (Colo. App. 1993) (waiver can be found invalid if unconscionable, but is otherwise valid); Johnson v. Johnson, 663 So. 2d 663 (Fla. Dist. Ct. App. 1995) (summarily holding that stipulation against attorney's fees was enforceable); Berns v. Halberstam, 46 A.D.3d 808, 848 N.Y.S.2d 323 (2007) (contractual waiver of right to attorney's fees in original agreement prevented award of fees in modification action); Millard v. Millard, 246 A.D.2d 349, 667 N.Y.S.2d 714 (1998) (enforcing waiver); Carpenter v. Carpenter, 19 Va. App. 147, 449 S.E.2d 502 (1994) (upholding stipulation against attorney's fees; seeming to recognize that enforcing stipulation could be an abuse of discretion, but giving the possibility only summary consideration).

One case finds an implied waiver. *See* Rutledge v. Rutledge, 45 Va. App. 56, 608 S.E.2d 504 (2005) (where agreement awarded attorney's fees in two specific instances, neither of which covered modification action, right to attorney's fees was implicitly waived).

549. *See* Sasnett v. Sasnett, 683 So. 2d 177 (Fla. Dist. Ct. App. 1996) (agreement to "utilize" certain funds for attorney's fees and living expenses did not waive wife's right to collect additional sums after the funds in question were exhausted); Jorgenson v. Ratajczak, 592 N.W.2d 527, 530 (N.D. 1999) (stipulation that each party would pay fees "incurred herein" did not bar award for fees incurred on later appeal).

550. Sanchez v. Sanchez, 647 So. 2d 1046 (Fla. Dist. Ct. App. 1994); Bernstein v. Bernstein, 498 So. 2d 1270 (Fla. Dist. Ct. App. 1986).

551. *See* Dallin v. Dallin, 225 A.D.2d 728, 640 N.Y.S.2d 196 (1996) (refusing fees because wife failed to send written notice of breach to husband by certified mail, as agreement required, even though husband obviously had actual knowledge of his own breach).

552. *See* Rose v. Rose, 615 So. 2d 203 (Fla. Dist. Ct. App. 1993); Pond v. Pond, 700 N.E.2d 1130 (Ind. 1998); Curtis v. Curtis, 680 So. 2d 1327 (La. Ct. App. 1996); Lay v. Lay, 912 S.W.2d 466 (Mo. 1995) (dicta); *In re* Marriage of Gibson, 77 S.W.3d 641, 644 (Mo. Ct. App. 2002) ("If a legitimate claim is made for attorney's fees under a provision of a separation agreement, the trial court must comply with that agreement[.]"); Sieratzki v. Sieratzki, 8 A.D.3d 552, 779 N.Y.S.2d 507 (2004); Haydock v. Haydock, 254 A.D.2d 577, 679 N.Y.S.2d 165 (1998); Gillman v. O'Connell, 176 A.D.2d 305, 574 N.Y.S.2d 573 (1991) (awarding attorney's fees against wife, whose wrongful claim of questionable tax deductions triggered an IRS audit); Bromhal v. Scott, 341 N.C. 702, 462 S.E.2d

attorney's fee provision clearly requires payment of fees, the court has no discretion to refuse to make a fee award.[553]

Types of Actions

Many mandatory fees provisions apply only in "actions" involving the agreement. Under this type of provision, neither party can collect attorney's fees if the issue is settled through out-of-court negotiations, without any action or motion being filed.[554]

A provision dealing with attorney's fees in an action to "enforce" the contract applies in a action to construe the contract.[555] A provision applying to an "action . . . under the terms of this Agreement" permitted a fees award in an action to modify contract-based child support.[556] Conversely, a provision permitting recovery of fees "associated with this dissolution" did not permit recovery of fees incurred in a postjudgment support modification action.[557]

An attorney's fees provision that specifically mentions bankruptcy permits a fees award when one spouse unsuccessfully attempts to discharge the obligation.[558]

---

219 (1995) (rejecting argument that attorney's fees provisions violate public policy; distinguishing contrary case law involving contracts outside of the domestic relations context); Herrera v. Herrera, 126 N.M. 705, 974 P.2d 675 (Ct. App. 1999); Sanford v. Sanford, 19 Va. App. 241, 450 S.E.2d 185 (1994).

553. *E.g.* Avellone v. Avellone, 973 So. 2d 1171 (Fla. Dist. Ct. App. 2007) (error to hold that wife should pay part of fee because she was able to do so; agreement required fees award regardless of wife's ability to pay); Ulbrich v. Coolidge, 935 So. 2d 607 (Fla. Dist. Ct. App. 2006); Mott v. Mott, 800 So. 2d 331, 333 (Fla. Dist. Ct. App. 2001) ("when the agreement provides for fees to be awarded to the prevailing party, the trial court is without discretion to decline to enforce that provision"); Coe v. Abdo, 790 So. 2d 1276, 1279 (Fla. Dist. Ct. App. 2001) ("the court has no discretion to refuse to award attorney's fees and costs where required by the contract"); Hutchinson v. Hutchinson, 687 So. 2d 912 (Fla. Dist. Ct. App. 1997); *Pond*, 700 N.E.2d 1130; Leiderman v. Leiderman, 50 A.D.3d 644, 857 N.Y.S.2d 162 (2008); Clark v. Clark, 33 A.D.3d 836, 827 N.Y.S.2d 159 (2006); Zeitlin v. Zeitlin, 250 A.D.2d 607, 672 N.Y.S.2d 379 (1998). *But see* Remington v. Remington, 711 So. 2d 212 (Fla. 4th Dist. Ct. App. 1998) (court can refuse to enforce fees provision when fees resulted from misuse of the judicial system).

554. Valant v. Valant, 437 Pa. Super. 635, 650 A.2d 1087 (1994) (fees provision applied only "should either party have to pursue remedies through the court"; where issue was settled without any court filing, provision did not apply).

555. Badell v. Badell, 122 Idaho 442, 835 P.2d 677 (1992). It likewise applies to fees incurred on a motion to set the agreement aside as invalid. *In re* Marriage of Caras, 263 Mont. 377, 868 P.2d 615 (1994).

556. Noble v. Fisher, 126 Idaho 885, 894 P.2d 118 (1995).

557. Tanner v. Tanner, 57 Cal. App. 4th 419, 67 Cal. Rptr. 2d 204, 207 (1997).

558. *In re* Davidson, 947 F.2d 1294 (5th Cir. 1991).

There is some authority suggesting that the bankruptcy court always has discretion to deny fees, even in the face of a mandatory provision. *In re* Florez, 191 B.R. 112 (Bankr. N.D. Ill. 1995). *Florez* conflicts with *Davidson* and with the common law of contracts, and it should not be followed in future decisions. Where a spouse voluntarily agrees to a mandatory fees provision that covers bankruptcy, and where the fees relate specifically to a nondischargeable obligation, the courts should enforce the contract as written.

When an agreement requires payment of attorney's fees only for contract-related actions, and only part of a given action is contract-related, the court must make a partial fees award to cover the time spent on covered issues.[559]

Florida holds that a mandatory fees provision does not permit recovery for time spent litigating the question of attorney's fees.[560]

To recover fees under a contractual provision, the requesting spouse must seek those fees in the action in which they were incurred. The spouse cannot in a later action request payment of fees incurred in prior litigation.[561]

Eligible Parties

Prevailing Party. Many agreements allow a mandatory fees award only to the "prevailing party." These provisions do not apply to fees sought in actions where the requesting spouse did not prevail. For instance, in *Haskin v. Mendler*,[562] the agreement permitted recovery of attorney's fees by the prevailing party in an enforcement action. The wife filed a such an action, but she did so in the wrong court, and the action was dismissed for lack of jurisdiction. She then filed again in the correct court, and prevailed. The court held that she could not collect attorney's fees for the first action, as she was not the prevailing party.[563]

Where the case involves only a single issue, determining the prevailing party is not overly difficult.[564] If a party received the relief sought, but on a different theory, that party is still the prevailing party for purposes of a fees provision.[565]

A case can have a prevailing party even if it was settled by agreement, if one party settled on substantially the terms proposed by the other.[566] Thus, a spouse with a losing position cannot escape a prevailing party fees award merely by conceding defeat on the eve of trial.

When multiple issues are presented, the prevailing party is the party who seems most successful after an overall review of the issues, the parties' positions, and the final results.[567] If all of the relevant issues have not yet been finally resolved, any resolution

---

559. Griffith v. Griffith, 941 So. 2d 1285 (Fla. Dist. Ct. App. 2006) (error to award attorney's fees for litigating attorney's fees; such fees not recoverable unless expressly permitted by agreement); Pohlman v. Pohlman, 703 So. 2d 1121 (Fla. Dist. Ct. App. 1997).

560. White v. Gordon, 258 A.D.2d 519, 685 N.Y.S.2d 256 (1999).

561. Lay v. Lay, 912 S.W.2d 466 (Mo. 1995).

562. 184 A.D.2d 372, 584 N.Y.S.2d 851 (1992).

563. *See also* Spano v. Spano, 698 So. 2d 324 (Fla. Dist. Ct. App. 1997).

564. For general case law awarding prevailing party fees, see Davids v. Davids, 718 So. 2d 1263 (Fla. 2d Dist. Ct. App. 1998); *In re* Marriage of Pearson, 291 Mont. 101, 965 P.2d 268 (1998); Brod v. Brod, 48 A.D.3d 499, 852 N.Y.S.2d 272 (2008) .

565. Holmes v. Holmes, 125 Idaho 784, 874 P.2d 595 (Ct. App. 1994).

566. Millard v. Millard, 246 A.D.2d 349, 667 N.Y.S.2d 714 (1998).

567. *See* Mott v. Mott, 800 So. 2d 331, 333 (Fla. Dist. Ct. App. 2001) (wife was prevailing party even though husband obtained order terminating his alimony obligation; "[t]he modification obtained by Mr. Mott was not due to any noncompliance on the part of Ms. Mott, but the substantial judgment obtained by Ms. Mott was specifically due to Mr. Mott's noncompliance with the terms of the agreement"); Noble v. Fisher, 126 Idaho 885, 894 P.2d 118 (1995) (wife was overall prevailing party); *Holmes*, 125 Idaho 784, 874 P.2d 595 (remanding for an overall review of the

of which party prevailed is premature.[568] If the court is left with the feeling that neither party was overall more successful than the other, there may not be any prevailing party.[569]

A prevailing party fees provision can be applied against a spouse who unsuccessfully attacks the validity of the agreement.[570]

Defaulting Party. Some agreements require attorney's fees to be paid only in favor of the "defaulting party."[571] This language is narrower than a general reference to the prevailing party, as the defending spouse must be found to be in breach of the agreement before liability will exist.[572] If the defending spouse does not breach the agreement, but merely loses an action to determine the proper construction, there is no liability.[573]

---

results); Pruitt v. Pruitt, 293 S.W.3d 537, 547 (Tenn. Ct. App. 2008) (where "Wife prevailed on most of the issues concerning Husband's breach of the [agreement]," trial court properly awarded prevailing party fees).

568. *See In re* Marriage of Simas, 139 Or. App. 86, 910 P.2d 1159 (1996) (husband prevailed on one issue, but another issue was pending before arbitrator).

569. *See In re* Marriage of Hahn, 263 Mont. 315, 868 P.2d 599 (1994).

570. *See* Clark v. Clark, 33 A.D.3d 836, 827 N.Y.S.2d 159 (2006).

The agreement in *Clark* provided that "in the event one party unsuccessfully sought to invalidate any of the terms of the agreement, that party would reimburse the other for his or her reasonable attorney's fees." The husband filed a motion to terminate spousal support for cohabitation, and the trial court rejected the motion, finding that the wife and children were merely renting an apartment from another family. The appellate court held that the trial court erred by failing to award fees. But the husband was not arguing that any portion of the agreement was invalid. On the contrary, he was seeking to enforce the provision that support would terminate if the wife cohabited with an unrelated adult male. *See* Ferrara v. Ferrara, 42 A.D.3d 426, 839 N.Y.S.2d 789 (2007) (where agreement required fees award in favor of spouse who unsuccessfully attacked agreement, error to award fees against spouse who filed declaratory judgment action to construe agreement).

The end result was not unreasonable, as the husband in *Clark* was making a notably weak argument, and it may have been proper to order him to pay the wife's attorney's fees on that basis. But future cases should refrain from applying mandatory fees provisions relating to attacks on the validity of the agreement when a spouse is merely seeking to enforce an express terminating condition.

571. For case law awarding defaulting-party fees, *see generally* Thomas B. v. Lydia D., 69 A.D. 3d 24, 886 N.Y.S.2d 22 (2009).

Provisions that award attorney's fees against a party who breaches the agreement will be treated as defaulting-party fee provisions, even if that exact term is not used. *See* Stroud v. Stroud, 54 Va. App. 231, 239, 677 S.E.2d 629, 633 (2009) (provision requiring an award of attorney's for "fail[ing] to abide by the terms of this Agreement" was not materially different from a provision requiring an award of fees against a defaulting party).

572. Zeitlin v. Zeitlin, 250 A.D.2d 607, 672 N.Y.S.2d 379 (1998) (error to deny defaulting-party fee award against husband, who breached provision against intoxication in the presence of the children).

573. Belfer v. Merling, 322 N.J. Super. 124, 730 A.2d 434 (Ct. App. 1999); *Ferrara*, 42 A.D.3d 426, 839 N.Y.S.2d 789 (where agreement required fees award in favor of spouse who was "forced to seek aid of counsel in enforcing any rights pursuant to this stipulation," error to award fees against spouse who filed declaratory judgment action to construe agreement); Brown v. Brown, 112 N.C. App. 619, 436 S.E.2d 402 (1992); Stroud v. Stroud, 54 Va. App. at 239, 677 S.E.2d at 633

Likewise, there may be no breaching party in an action to determine the validity of the agreement,[574] or in an action for modification.[575]

An agreement can use the prevailing-party standard for fees on some issue, and the defaulting-party standard for fees on other issues.[576]

Where the defending party breached the agreement, defaulting-party attorney's fees are mandatory even if an enforcement action is settled before trial.[577] Of course, the fact that the case was not tried would seem relevant in determining the amount of attorney's fees reasonably incurred.

To avoid last-second compliance before a technical finding of default, one clever agreement stated that a party who complied only after filing of a legal action would be deemed in default.[578]

Other Issues

Conditions. Where a mandatory attorney's fees provision is subject to conditions, and the conditions are not met, there is no right to recover fees.[579]

Amount. Where the agreement calls for payment of "reasonable" attorney's fees, the definition of reasonableness is determined by the court, using an objective standard.[580] It is error to award "reasonable" attorney's fees without holding a factual hearing on reasonableness.[581]

(2009) (wife did not breach agreement by arguing that husband's spousal support obligation survived cohabitation, even though court eventually concluded that obligation terminated; trial court properly refused to award attorney's fees).

574. *See* Arnsperger v. Arnsperger, 973 So. 2d 681, 682 (Fla. Dist. Ct. App. 2008) ("the wife's motion to enforce the agreement did not allege any default, and the trial court's order determines only the validity of the marital settlement agreement"; trial court properly refused to award attorney's fees); Gottlieb v. Such, 293 A.D.2d 267, 267–68, 740 N.Y.S.2d 44, 45 (2002) ("Defendant's commencement of the fraud action is not a default under the terms of the agreement, and the provision entitling the prevailing party to an award of 'counsel fees in event of default' is not implicated[.]").

575. Krueger v. Krueger, 689 So. 2d 1277 (Fla. Dist. Ct. App. 1997).

576. Millard v. Millard, 246 A.D.2d 349, 667 N.Y.S.2d 714 (1998).

577. *See* Leiderman v. Leiderman, 50 A.D.3d 644, 857 N.Y.S.2d 162 (2008) (where "former wife was successful in obtaining a settlement by which most, if not all, of the terms of the stipulation she alleged the former husband defaulted on, were enforced," error to deny defaulting-party fees).

578. White v. Gordon, 258 A.D.2d 519, 685 N.Y.S.2d 256 (1999).

579. *See* DaLoia v. Burt, 306 A.D.2d 239, 241, 761 N.Y.S.2d 91, 92 (2003) (where mandatory fees provision required that breaching spouse be given notice and 15-day period to cure, and notice provision was not complied with, trial court properly refused to award attorney's fees).

580. Gillman v. O'Connell, 176 A.D.2d 305, 574 N.E.2d 573 (1991).

For cases finding fees at least partly unreasonable, see Griffith v. Griffith, 941 So. 2d 1285 (Fla. Dist. Ct. App. 2006) (error to award attorney's fees for litigating attorney's fees; such fees not recoverable unless expressly permitted by agreement); McMullen v. Kutz, 925 A.2d 832 (Pa. Super. Ct.) (trial court properly concluded that only $1,200 of wife's $3,000 in legal fees was reasonable), *review granted*, 934 A.2d 1162 (Pa. 2007).

581. *In re* Marriage of Doyle, 280 Mont. 429, 929 P.2d 886 (1996).

Some courts hold that a general promise to pay attorney's fees will always be construed to require payment of only reasonable fees.[582] The line of reasoning should be applied cautiously, for there is a risk that the reasonableness limitation could be used to avoid the certainty of a mandatory fees provision, and thereby reduce its deterrent value. When a spouse acts unreasonably in breaching a separation agreement, that spouse is not in any position to second-guess the attorney's fees incurred by the innocent spouse in obtaining a remedy. The reasonableness limitation should be applied only in clear cases, when the fees at issue are plainly unreasonable.

Standing to Enforce. Where a contract provision calls for payment of attorney's fees directly to an attorney, the attorney has standing as a third-party beneficiary to seek enforcement of the provisions.[583]

Relationship to Statutory Fees Award. A contractual attorney's fees provision supplants a statutory attorney's provision to the extent that the two are inconsistent.[584] If the provisions are consistent, however, the statutory provision is not supplanted.[585]

Appellate Fees. Where a contractual attorney's fees provision applies, fees are mandatory not only in the trial court, but also on appeal.[586]

§ 6.06 Other Provisions

§ 6.061 General Releases

Many separation agreements contain a broad general release clause that purports to waive all other causes of action between the parties. These releases are generally interpreted broadly by the courts, and they bar a wide variety of future claims.

Property Division. A general release prevents division of any asset not specifically mentioned in the agreement.[587]

---

582. Rauch v. McCall, 134 Md. App. 624, 761 A.2d 76 (2000); *McMullen*, 925 A.2d 832.

583. *See In re* Marriage of Green, 143 Cal. App. 4th 1312, 49 Cal. Rptr. 3d 908 (2006); Rae F. Gill, P.C. v. DiGiovanni, 34 Mass. App. Ct. 498, 612 N.E.2d 1205 (1993).

584. McMann v. McMann, 942 S.W.2d 94 (Tex. Ct. App. 1997) (where husband received fees under contract, wife could not receive fees under statute).

585. Jordan v. Burgbacher, 180 Ariz. 221, 883 P.2d 458 (1994).

586. *See, e.g.*, Pruitt v. Pruitt, 293 S.W.3d 537 (Tenn. Ct. App. 2008) (affirming trial court's fees award, and making an additional award of appellate attorney's fees).

587. *See, e.g.*, Woolley v. Woolley, 637 So. 2d 74 (Fla. Dist. Ct. App. 1994); Brignac v. Brignac, 698 So. 2d 953 (La. Ct. App. 1997) (promise to bring no future litigation resulting from marriage waived wife's rights in omitted retirement benefits); Pacheco v. Quintana, 105 N.M. 139, 730 P.2d 1 (Ct. App. 1986); Ramsperger v. Ramsperger, 120 A.D.2d 940, 502 N.Y.S.2d 858 (1986); *In re* Wise, 46 Ohio App. 3d 82, 545 N.E.2d 1314 (1988).

In community property states, the effect of a general release is to leave the parties as joint owners of any community asset not expressly divided in the agreement. In equitable distribution states, the effect of a general release is to divide according to legal title all assets not expressly divided otherwise in the agreement.[588]

Support. A general release bars a claim for future alimony.[589] It also bars any action to collect arrearages in temporary support.[590]

Prior Marriages. A general release waives claims arising from prior marriages between the same parties, as well as the present one.[591]

Tax Issues. A general release does not bar either party from seeking innocent spouse relief from a debt owed to the IRS.[592]

Marital Torts. A general release bars all causes of action for torts committed during the marriage.[593] It does not, however, bar claims for torts committed after the signing of the agreement.[594]

---

588. *See generally* § **6.022**, note 112.

589. *See, e.g.,* Swift v. Swift, 566 A.2d 1045 (D.C. 1989) (release waives alimony); *cf.* Skinner v. Skinner, 579 So. 2d 358 (Fla. Dist. Ct. App. 1991) (release bars wife's action to be reimbursed for paying prior medical bill, even though court had issued interlocutory order requiring husband to pay it; order had merged into final decree, which was silent on the subject). *But see* Napier v. Napier, 135 N.C. App. 364, 520 S.E.2d 312 (1999) (general release does not waive alimony, in face of specific statute requiring that any waiver of alimony be express); *see also supra* note 284 (case law holding that general release does not bar subsequent modification of alimony).

590. *See In re* Marriage of Mease, 320 Mont. 229, 92 P.3d 1148 (2004).

591. *See* Barnett v. Platz, 261 Ga. App. 51, 581 S.E.2d 682 (2003) (general release in separation agreement incident to 1997 divorce waived claims arising from earlier marriage and divorce).

592. *See* Avellan v. Avellan, 951 So. 2d 80, 83 (Fla. Dist. Ct. App. 2007) (general release did not prevent the wife from arguing to IRS that she was an innocent spouse with regard to certain joint tax obligations; separation agreement did not address tax liabilities, and prior understanding existed that liabilities were due to husband's unilateral conduct).

The authors would also suggest that innocent spouse relief is an administrative remedy requested from the IRS, and not a claim against the other spouse within the meaning of a general release.

593. *See* Overburg v. Lusby, 921 F.2d 90 (6th Cir. 1990); Coleman v. Coleman, 566 So. 2d 482 (Ala. 1990); Gramer v. Gramer, 207 Mich. App. 123, 523 N.W.2d 861 (1994) (malicious prosecution action for false abuse claim during pendency of divorce case); Henry v. Henry, 534 N.W.2d 844 (S.D. 1995) (assault and battery claim for spousal abuse).

594. *Id.*; *cf.* Feltmeier v. Feltmeier, 207 Ill. 2d 263, 798 N.E.2d 75 (2003) (wife's suit for intentional infliction of emotional distress based upon pattern of spousal abuse was not within general release, where cause of action accrued on date of last tortious act, which was after date of the agreement, even though some of the tortious acts occurred before the date of the agreement).

Contract Claims. One court held that a general release did not bar contract claims that arose from a specific contract between husband and wife, signed independently of their marital relationship.[595]

Guardian of Children. A general release does not bar a spouse from making a claim as guardian for the parties' children, if the claim is otherwise proper under the law. Stated differently, a general release bars only claims made by a spouse in his or her own right, and not claims made on behalf of the children.[596]

Insurance and Survivorship Rights. General releases do not waive the right to collect life insurance or other survivor benefits as named beneficiary of the other spouse. That right is a free gift from the other spouse rather than a legally enforceable claim.[597] Moreover, even if a claim did exist, it would be a claim against the benefit provider and not against the other spouse.[598] For similar reasons, a blanket release does not prevent the releasing party from inheriting under the other party's will.[599]

---

595. *See* Sweeney v. Sweeney, 405 N.J. Super. 586, 966 A.2d 54 (App. Div. 2009) (general release did not bar wife from bringing claim against husband, a professional investor, for his mismanagement of certain funds owned by wife and entrusted to husband's care during marriage; claim arose out of investment contract and not out of marital relationship).

596. *See In re* Estate of Zenkus, 346 Ill. App. 3d 741, 805 N.E.2d 1257 (2004) (general release did not bar wife from seeking letters of administration of the husband's estate as guardian for minor child; release applied only to claims that the wife raised in her own right).

597. *See* Maccabees Mut. Life Ins. Co. v. Morton, 941 F.2d 1181 (11th Cir. 1991) (IRA and life insurance); Jordan v. Burgbacher, 180 Ariz. 221, 883 P.2d 458 (1994) (CDs); Estate of Bowden v. Aldridge, 595 A.2d 396 (D.C. 1991) (beneficiary of IRA); Smith v. Smith, 919 So. 2d 525 (Fla. Dist. Ct. App. 2005) (IRA, retirement plan, and life insurance); Kruse v. Todd, 260 Ga. 63, 389 S.E.2d 488 (1990) (life insurance); *In re* Marriage of Velasquez, 295 Ill. App. 3d 350, 692 N.E.2d 841 (1998) (life insurance; holding over a strong dissent that the right to receive benefits from a land trust had been waived); Deida v. Murphy, 271 Ill. App. 3d 296, 647 N.E.2d 1109 (1995) (CDs and bank accounts); *In re* Estate of Bruce, 265 Mont. 431, 877 P.2d 999 (1994) (IRA); Storozynski v. Storozynski, 10 A.D.3d 419, 781 N.Y.S.2d 141 (2004) (life insurance and IRA); Auten v. Snipes, 370 S.C. 664, 671, 636 S.E.2d 644, 647 (Ct. App. 2006) ("the agreement had only general release language and did not specifically require Parrish and Snipes to waive their expectancy interests in each other's retirement accounts"); Estate of Revis v. Revis, 326 S.C. 470, 484 S.E.2d 112 (Ct. App. 1987); Estate of Anello v. McQueen, 953 P.2d 1143 (Utah 1998) (beneficiary of IRA); *cf.* Cincinnati Life Ins. Co. v. Palmer, 32 Kan. App. 2d 1060, 94 P.3d 729 (2004) (to avoid difficult factual issues in determining intent of parties, Kansas finds waiver of rights as insurance beneficiary only where divorce decree expressly so provides). *But see* Strong v. Omaha Constr. Indus. Pension Plan, 270 Neb. 1, 701 N.W.2d 320 (2005) (general release waived survivorship rights); Stribling v. Stribling, 369 S.C. 400, 407, 632 S.E.2d 291 (Ct. App. 2006) (general release does not automatically waive survivorship rights in IRA, but can if the court finds that the parties so intended; such intent existed on the facts).

598. *Kruse*, 260 Ga. 63, 389 S.E.2d 488.

599. Blunt v. Lentz, 241 Va. 547, 404 S.E.2d 62 (1991).

The above holdings apply only where the release is stated in general terms. A release that specifically waives insurance or survivorship rights will always be enforceable.[600] A general release of rights in a named retirement plan or IRA that does not expressly mention survivor benefits is sufficient in some states,[601] as is a broader waiver of rights in retirement generally.[602] But other states require a specific reference to rights as beneficiary, and hold that a waiver of ownership rights is not sufficient, even if the policy or plan is specifically named in the agreement.[603]

State law does not apply to waivers of survivor benefits or insurance regulated by ERISA, which ordinarily requires that a specific waiver be signed by the beneficiary

---

600. *Bowden*, 595 A.2d 396 (beneficiary of IRA); Lelux v. Chernick, 119 Ohio App. 3d 36, 694 N.E.2d 471 (1997) (life insurance; rejecting dissent's position that waiver must not only refer to life insurance, but also expressly waive rights as beneficiary); *Deida*, 271 Ill. App. 3d 296, 647 N.E.2d 1109 (CDs and bank accounts); Steiner v. Bank One Ind., 805 N.E.2d 421 (Ind. Ct. App. 2004); MacInnes v. MacInnes, 260 Mich. App. 280, 677 N.W.2d 889 (2004); *In re* Estate of Sbarra, 17 A.D.3d 975, 977, 794 N.Y.S.2d 479, 481 (2005) (retirement benefits); *cf. In re* Brown, 229 B.R. 669, 671 (Bankr. E.D. Va. 1998) (general release of rights against husband's "heirs" waived wife's right to inherit from parties' children; property being inherited was within scope of separation agreement); *see generally* 4 LEE R. RUSS & THOMAS F. SEGALLA, COUCH ON INSURANCE §§ 64:22–64:23 (3d ed. 1997 & Supp. 1999).

601. Von Haden v. Supervised Estate of Von Haden, 699 N.E.2d 301 (Ind. Ct. App. 1998) (where contract awarded wife only 50 percent of husband's 401(K) plan, wife could recover only 50 percent of the plan balance upon death); Valentin v. N.Y. City Police Pension Fund, 16 A.D.3d 145, 792 N.Y.S.2d 22 (2005) (marriage lasted less than a year, and husband died only 18 days after agreement was executed); Estate of Anello v. McQueen, 953 P.2d 1143, 1145 (Utah 1998) (provision "relinquishe[d] all claim" to an IRA, and awarded it to one spouse "free and clear of any claim or interest" of the other).

602. *See* Estate of Altobelli v. IBM, 77 F.3d 78 (4th Cir. 1996); Mohamed v. Kerr, 53 F.3d 911 (8th Cir. 1995); Young v. Stump, 294 Ga. App. 351, 353, 669 S.E.2d 148, 150 (2008); Strong v. Omaha Constr. Indus. Pension Plan, 270 Neb. 1, 701 N.W.2d 320 (2005); Roth v. Roth, 413 Pa. Super. 88, 604 A.2d 1033 (1992) (broad waiver of all rights to retirement benefits prevented wife from recovering survivor benefits); *cf.* Nat'l Auto Dealers & Assocs. Ret. Trust v. Arbeitman, 89 F.3d 496, 498 (8th Cir. 1996) (waiver of pension rights "arising out of the marital relationship" not sufficient to waive survivor benefits; wife's rights arose from beneficiary designation); Trueblood v. Roberts, 15 Neb. App. 579, 732 N.W.2d 368 (2007) (provision that each spouse would "retain" their own insurance policies was not sufficient to waive rights as beneficiary; no general waiver in agreement); Spiegel v. KLRU Endowment Fund, 228 S.W.3d 237 (Tex. Ct. App. 2007) (provision awarding retirement plan to one spouse as separate property expressly waives beneficiary rights; noting that other districts in Texas require specific reference to rights as beneficiary).

603. *See In re* Estate of Bruce, 265 Mont. 431, 877 P.2d 999 (1994); Cellers v. Adami, 216 P.3d 1134, 1143 (Wyo. 2009) ("the language in the property settlement agreement or divorce decree must reveal a specific and explicit waiver or relinquishment of the named beneficiary's expectancy interest"; no such waiver was present and wife was permitted to claim survivor benefits from husband's investment account, even though she had waived all ownership rights to account itself); *cf.* East v. PaineWebber, Inc., 131 Md. App. 302, 312, 748 A.2d 1082, 1087 (2000) (waiver of rights "as a spouse" applied only to rights arising from the status of a spouse, and not to rights arising from a beneficiary designation; and waiver of rights against spouse's estate did not apply to survivor benefits, which did not pass through the estate).

and submitted to the plan.[604] But at least some courts have held that other types of waivers may be enforceable under federal common law.[605]

Some states provide by law that entry of a divorce decree revokes prior beneficiary designations in favor of the other spouse.[606] These states clearly do not apply to benefits regulated by ERISA, which are governed by federal common law and not by a specific state's statutes.[607]

Where the agreement waived only the right to receive an "inheritance," one court held that the parties intended to waive the right to take as beneficiary of a trust.[608]

Note that the federal decisions are split on whether federal law permits a waiver of survivor benefits in a separation agreement.[609]

Specific Exceptions. The parties may limit a general release with specific exceptions. For instance, where the parties added to a typewritten general release a handwritten provision reserving the wife's rights in the husband's pension, the court held that the release did not prevent the wife from later obtaining part of husband's retirement pay.[610] Likewise, a release waiving claims arising out of the marriage may not bar claims that did not so arise.[611]

§ 6.062 *Religious Divorces*

Separation agreements will sometimes require one spouse to cooperate with the other in obtaining a formal religious divorce or annulment. The most common fact situation involves a *get*, a religious decree of divorce required by Orthodox Judaism.

The courts have generally enforced these provisions, rejecting constitutional claims based upon the First Amendment.[612] The theory has been that participating in a religious divorce does not require any act of religious faith; it requires only that the spouse in question appear before a religious tribunal and answer questions truthfully.

---

604. *E.g.*, Hayes v. Hayes, 994 So. 2d 246 (Miss. Ct. App. 2008) (separation agreement that did not meet requirements for a QDRO could not waive wife's right to survivor benefits); *Sbarra*, 17 A.D.3d at 977, 794 N.Y.S.2d at 481.

605. *See MacInnes*, 260 Mich. App. 280, 677 N.W.2d 889; Strong v. Omaha Const. Indus. Pension Plan, 270 Neb. 1, 701 N.W.2d 320 (2005).

606. *E.g.*, *In re* Estate of Lamparella, 210 Ariz. 246, 109 P.3d 959 (2005).

607. *See* Egelhoff v. Egelhoff, 532 U.S. 141 (2001); Keen v. Weaver, 121 S.W.3d 721, 727 (Tex. 2003).

608. Flynn v. Flynn, 615 A.2d 119, 120 (R.I. 1992).

609. *See* Estate of Altobelli v. IBM, 77 F.3d 78 (4th Cir. 1996) (reviewing the cases).

610. *See, e.g.*, Parshall v. Parshall, 385 Pa. Super. 142, 560 A.2d 207 (1989).

611. *See* Davis v. Davis, 112 Conn. App. 56, 64, 962 A.2d 140, 146 (2009) (where release applied only to claims arising "by reason of the marriage," release did not bar wife's claim for negligent infliction of emotional distress based upon husband's conduct in negotiating separation agreement; claim did not arise from the marriage).

612. *See, e.g.*, Scholl v. Scholl, 621 A.2d 808 (Del. Fam. Ct. 1992); *In re* Marriage of Goldman, 196 Ill. App. 3d 785, 554 N.E.2d 1016 (1990); Minkin v. Minkin, 180 N.J. Super. 260, 434 A.2d 665 (Ch. Div. 1981); Avitzur v. Avitzur, 58 N.Y.2d 108, 446 N.E.2d 136, 459 N.Y.S.2d 572 (1983), *cert. denied*, 464 U.S. 817 (1983); *see generally* Marcia L. Retchin, *To Get a "Get": Enforcement of Contracts Requiring Spouses to Secure or Accept Religious Divorces*, 6 Divorce Litig. 28 (1994).

Enforcement of a contract to obtain a religious divorce therefore does not coerce the defendant to adopt any particular religious belief.

The courts' willingness to enforce this type of contract is commendable. Where participation in a religious divorce requires only truthful testimony or execution of documents, and not any act of religious faith, First Amendment concerns are less important. Moreover, in every case to meet this fact pattern, the defendant spouse agreed at one point to procure the religious divorce. The issue is, by definition, the enforceability of a contract to obtain a religious divorce. If the defendant spouse changed positions in bad faith, he or she is not being asked to perform any *genuinely* objectionable religious act. Finally, the simple fact is that in almost every case to raise the issue, the defendant's First Amendment argument was an attempt to force the other spouse to consent to a favorable financial settlement.[613] The First Amendment requires that courts respect the religious beliefs of all faiths, but it does not shield defendants who use religion as a tool of coercion. Where the defendant's objection to the religious divorce is not motivated by any genuine religious belief, which has been the fact in the great majority of the cases to date, the defendant is in no position to assert rights under the First Amendment.

§ 6.063 *Exchange of Future Financial Documents*

Separation agreements sometimes require that the parties exchange income tax returns or other similar financial documents. The purpose of these provisions is to assist the parties in determining whether modification is required, or in enforcing the provisions of an income-based escalating support provision.

Because document exchanges aid in enforcement of the agreement, provisions requiring such exchanges are construed liberally. For instance, in *Shoretz v. Shoretz*,[614] the agreement required the husband to provide the wife with a copy of "his IRS return." The husband remarried, and filed jointly with his second wife. To protect the second wife's privacy interest, the husband submitted to the wife a hypothetical return that included only his income. The trial court reviewed the actual return in camera, found that the hypothetical return was accurate, and found no breach. The appellate court reversed, holding that the husband had to provide the wife with his actual tax return, regardless of whether he filed jointly or individually. A dissenting justice argued in light of the in camera review that there was substantial compliance, but compliance in the year in which the case arose did not mean compliance for all time. Under the dissent's approach, either the trial court would have to review the husband's return in camera every year, an unreasonable burden upon the court, or the wife would have no

---

613. *See, e.g.*, Burns v. Burns, 223 N.J. Super. 219, 538 A.2d 438 (Ch. Div. 1987) (husband stated that he would agree to get only if wife placed $25,000 into irrevocable trust for parties' daughter). Some defendants have even used the religious divorce issue to coerce agreement on issues involving the welfare of children. *See, e.g.*, *Goldman*, 196 Ill. App. 3d 785, 554 N.E.2d 1016 (husband refused to consent to get unless wife agreed to give him joint custody of children). To permit this type of extortion is not merely to tolerate, but indeed to provide positive assistance to, a party whose legal position is unconscionable.

614. 186 A.D.2d 370, 588 N.Y.S.2d 274, 274 (1992).

way to make certain that the husband's disclosure of income was accurate. The majority holding reached a much more practical result.

When a party breaches such a provision, the court may award support retroactively, based upon the documents that should have been disclosed.[615] Where a spouse destroys the records with apparent attempt to hide their contents, the spouse could also be held in contempt of court.[616] Where the support recipient refuses to produce records, the recipient loses the right to collect income-based support for the years in which records were not produced.[617] The recipient does not, however, waive the support obligation entirely, so that support is payable in future years if the proper records are provided.[618]

Courts disfavor provisions that impose unreasonably harsh sanctions for nondisclosure of documents. In *Dziarnowski v. Dziarnowski*,[619] the agreement provided on its face that the wife forfeited her entire right to receive support if she failed to provide the husband with a copy of her W-2 statement. The agreement was silent as to time, and the court applied the general rule that time is not of the essence unless the agreement states otherwise, holding that a one-month delay in compliance did not deprive the wife of all future support. The court also held that by making one support payment after the wife's W-2 was late, the husband waived his right to enforce the forfeiture provision. The court was stretching somewhat, particularly on the waiver issue, but in view of the harshness of the penalty provision, the result is easily justified. A more modest penalty provision might have provided that the husband's support obligation was suspended for the months in which the wife's financial documents were overdue.[620] Had the agreement contained such a provision, the court might have been more disposed to give the husband a remedy.

§ 6.064 Medical Expenses

A large number of agreements now require one spouse to pay all or a portion of the medical expenses of the other spouse or the children. These provisions are generally favored, and are construed to implement the intention of the parties.[621] The term "medical expenses" is not too vague to be enforced.[622]

An unconditional agreement to pay medical expenses requires payment of all expenses, even those covered by insurance.[623] The result would presumably be different

---

615. Rolnick v. Rolnick, 290 N.J. Super. 35, 674 A.2d 1006 (App. Div. 1996).

616. *Id.*

617. *Reinhardt*, 204 A.D.2d 1028, 613 N.E.2d 89.

618. *Id.*

619. 14 Va. App. 758, 418 S.E.2d 724 (1992).

620. *See* Reinhardt v. Reinhardt, 204 A.D.2d 1028, 613 N.E.2d 89 (1994).

621. *See* Franklin v. Franklin, 262 Ga. 218, 416 S.E.2d 503 (1992) (nursing home costs were medical expenses to the extent that they covered services charged and supplies required by health care providers; room and board portion of nursing home costs not covered; remanding to allocate total cost between these categories).

622. Lay v. Lay, 912 S.W.2d 466 (Mo. 1995).

623. *See* Stracker v. Stracker, 94 Ohio App. 3d 261, 640 N.E.2d 611 (1994) (expenses covered by wife's new husband's health insurance); *cf.* Franklin v. Franklin, 262 Ga. 218, 416 S.E.2d 503

if the payor purchased the insurance; in this event, purchase of insurance is essentially an act of substantial compliance with the agreement.

Where the agreement requires that medical expenses be paid directly to the provider, and the obligor fails to pay, the innocent spouse can use contempt or other remedies to force the obligor to pay the provider directly.[624] Alternatively, the innocent spouse can pay the provider and then seek reimbursement from the obligor.[625] If the innocent spouse does not pay the expenses directly, however, there is no basis for seeking an award from the obligor.[626]

Some medical expenses provisions require payment only of reasonable expenses. Where such a requirement is not express, some courts have held that it is necessarily implied.[627] An expense is not reasonable if it is for treatment not generally recognized by the medical community.[628]

Many medical expenses provisions require payment of all or part of those expenses not covered by insurance. Under this sort of provision, the payor is not required to pay any expenses covered by any form of insurance, including forms other than health insurance.[629] If the expenses arise from tortious conduct, and a settlement or verdict is recovered from the tortfeasor, the payor is not required to pay medical expenses that were or should have been paid from the recovery.[630]

Some medical expenses provisions require that the payor be consulted before major expenses are incurred. At least one court has held that such a provision is an absolute precondition upon liability, so that if the payor is not consulted, the expenses need not be paid.[631] A dissenting opinion argued convincingly that the expenses would have been incurred regardless of whether the payor had been consulted or not, so that the only real harm inflicted by lack of consultation was the loss of the opportunity to find equivalent treatment at a lesser cost. The majority opinion reached a harsh result; the dissent stated the better position.

Modification

Can an agreement to pay medical expenses be modified for changed circumstances? If the agreement is in the nature of spousal support, and contractual spousal support is subject to modification in the jurisdiction involved, *see generally* **§ 6.032**, the obliga-

---

(1992) (agreement to pay medical expenses not covered by Medicare applied to all expenses, even those Medicare completely refused to cover).

624. *See* Johnson v. Johnson, 848 So. 2d 1272 (Fla. Dist. Ct. App. 2003).

625. *See* Rogers v. Rogers, 83 Ark. App. 206, 121 S.W.3d 510 (2003).

626. *See id.*

627. *See In re* Marriage of Turrell, 335 Ill. App. 3d 297, 781 N.E.2d 430 (2002).

628. *See id.* (unconventional treatment for Lyme disease).

629. *See Rogers*, 83 Ark. App. 206, 121 S.W.3d 510 (where child was injured in automobile accident, father not required to pay expenses that could have been covered by vehicle insurance).

630. *See id.* (child was injured while still a minor, but recovered $75,000 settlement after emancipation, and used proceeds for her own enjoyment; error to order father to pay $4,235.65 in medical expenses).

631. Page v. Baylard, 281 Ga. 586, 642 S.E.2d 14 (2007).

tion is modifiable.[632] Conversely, if the obligation is in the nature of property division, it is not modifiable.[633]

In the specific context of insurance obligations, the logic of the property/support dichotomy eludes the authors. An obligation to maintain medical insurance allocates liability for a future debt, a debt that will not be incurred until long after the marriage is over. Accordingly, it is difficult to see how such an obligation could be in the nature of property division. The obligation could perhaps be *consideration* for the property division, and therefore immune from modification under the normal rules that apply to integrated bargain agreements. *See* § **6.012**. To reach this result, however, the court would have to find evidence of a specific property-for-insurance tradeoff, evidence that none of the above cases expressly found.

Moreover, in most states the parties are permitted to agree to make spousal support obligations either modifiable or nonmodifiable. *See generally* § **6.032**. Thus, the fact that an insurance obligation is in the nature of spousal support does not necessarily make it modifiable.

The real issue in all of the insurance modification cases is whether the parties intended to create a modifiable obligation. The case law would be clearer if the courts addressed this issue directly, rather than engaging in metaphysical debates about the "nature" of insurance obligations.

An agreement to pay medical expenses of "children" ceases to apply when the children reach majority.[634]

§ 6.065 Insurance

As an alternative or supplement to requiring payment of medical expenses, many agreements now require one spouse to maintain health insurance coverage on the other spouse or on the children. In addition, agreements sometimes require one spouse to maintain life insurance coverage, ordinarily as security against the chance that support obligations will be ended by an early death.

The waiver of beneficiary rights in existing life insurance or survivor benefits, kept in force voluntarily by the owner and not required by court order, is discussed in § **6.061**.

Benefits Covered. A provision applying generally to "death benefits" includes life insurance as well as survivor benefits under retirement plans.[635]

---

632. *See* Mackey v. Mechetti, 695 So. 2d 472 (Fla. Dist. Ct. App. 1997); Lundell v. Lundell, 629 So. 2d 1013 (Fla. Dist. Ct. App. 1993); Metz v. Metz, 217 W. Va. 468, 471, 618 S.E.2d 477, 480 (2005) (where agreement required husband to pay for wife's medical insurance, and wife became uninsurable, modifying agreement to require husband to pay wife an amount equal to the former premium, to be used directly toward wife's medical expenses).

633. *See Lundell*, 629 So. 2d 1013; McBride v. McBride, 637 So. 2d 938 (Fla. Dist. Ct. App. 1994).

634. Rohrbacher v. Rohrbacher, 83 Ohio App. 3d 569, 615 N.E.2d 338, 339 (1992).

635. *See In re* Estate of Trevino, 381 Ill. App. 3d 553, 554, 886 N.E.2d 531 (2008) (where agreement required husband to name children as beneficiaries of "any and all retirement plan[s], pension plans, and death benefits," provision applied to life insurance, which is a form of death benefit).

Policies Covered. Where the agreement requires maintenance of a specific policy, it applies not only to the policy stated,[636] but also to any policy acquired to replace the listed policy.[637] A policy that predates the agreement, however, cannot be treated as a replacement for a policy required by the agreement.[638] A provision requiring that life insurance be provided for a specific beneficiary is generally sufficient to meet the requirements of statute providing that divorce revokes a prior beneficiary designation unless the decree expressly provides otherwise.[639]

Amount of Coverage. When the agreement requires continuation of a specific level of health insurance benefits, the benefits are essentially the difference between the coverage and the deductible. Thus, if a new policy provides the same coverage with a greater deductible, the benefits are less and the agreement has been breached.[640]

Some life insurance agreements require coverage equal to a certain level of benefits or a certain cash surrender value. These agreements do not limit the owner's ability to borrow against the policy, encumber it, sell it, or take other actions, so long as the required benefits or value continues to be present.[641]

---

636. *See* Fetner v. Fetner, 293 A.D.2d 645, 741 N.Y.S.2d 256 (2002) (husband was required to keep in force three specific policies).

In Fernandez v. Fernandez, 278 A.D.2d 882, 718 N.Y.S.2d 509 (2000), the husband failed to maintain the original policy, but he acquired for the wife's benefit another policy with identical coverage. The appellate court affirmed a trial court decision refusing to hold the husband in contempt, finding expressly that the wife was not injured, but it nevertheless held that the husband had breached the agreement and ordered him to pay the wife's attorney's fees, both at trial and on appeal.

In Allton v. Hintzsche, 373 Ill. App. 3d 708, 711, 870 N.E.2d 436, 439 (2007), where the agreement required that the husband "maintain a life insurance policy . . . in an amount of not less than $50,000.00 per child," the court held that the provision was ambiguous as to whether the husband was required to keep in force his present policy or obtain a new one. The case was remanded for consideration of parol evidence. A better construction would have been that the husband was required to keep in force some policy in that amount, but that the choice of policy was entirely up to him.

637. Kruse v. Todd, 260 Ga. 63, 389 S.E.2d 488 (1990); *In re* Goodfriend, 151 A.D.2d 669, 542 N.Y.S.2d 379 (1989).

Whether a policy was intended as a replacement policy is a question of fact. *See* Foster v. Hurley, 444 Mass. 157, 826 N.E.2d 719 (2005) (new policy acquired after divorce, naming second wife as beneficiary, was not intended as a replacement policy; husband continued to own previous policy and named wife as beneficiary, although amount was not sufficient to meet husband's obligation under agreement).

638. Lebovitz v. Campbell, 216 A.D.2d 768, 628 N.Y.S.2d 839 (1995).

639. Lincoln Nat'l Life Ins. Co. v. Johnson, 38 F. Supp. 2d 440 (E.D. Va. 1999).

640. Phillips v. Phillips, 164 Vt. 600, 664 A.2d 272 (1995).

641. Champagne v. Champagne, 43 Conn. App. 844, 685 A.2d 1153 (1996).

When the agreement requires that a party maintain life insurance, without listing a specific amount, that party is required to maintain in force the same amount of insurance that existed when the agreement was signed. The agreement is breached if the obligor adds additional beneficiaries, so that the amount of proceeds due to the existing beneficiaries is smaller than it was when the agreement was signed.[642] The agreement provision does not apply to any additional insurance coverage purchased by the obligor on the same policy after divorce, but it does apply to natural increases (e.g., investment or inflation) in the amount of coverage provided at the time of divorce.[643]

Where insurance is intended as security for alimony, and alimony is limited in duration, it may be possible to argue that the recipient is not permitted to collect more than the present value of the amount of alimony remaining at the time of the obligor's death.[644]

Period of Coverage. Where life insurance is provided to secure a spousal support obligation, and the support obligation terminates before the insured spouse's death, the insurance obligation terminates also.[645] Where life insurance secures permanent spousal support, the obligation normally lasts for the obligor's lifetime.[646] Where life insurance is provided as security for child support, the insurance terminates when the child support obligation ends.[647] Otherwise, the obligation lasts for the obligor's lifetime.[648]

---

642. Bernal v. Nieto, 123 N.M. 621, 943 P.2d 1338 (Ct. App. 1997).

643. *In re* Estate of Downey, 293 Ill. App. 3d 234, 687 N.E.2d 339 (1997).

644. *See In re* Estate of Hodges, 807 So. 2d 438 (Miss. 2002).

645. Indeed, termination may be required on the grounds that the beneficiary now lacks an insurance interest in the insured's life. *See* Browning v. Browning, 366 S.C. 255, 266, 621 S.E.2d 389, 394 (Ct. App. 2005) ("once [alimony] ended, Wife no longer had an insurable interest nor, can we discern from the record, a pecuniary interest").

646. *See* Dohn v. Dohn, 276 Ga. 826, 584 S.E.2d 250 (2003) (noting that even if alimony was intended to secure only obligations payable during husband's lifetime, and not to support wife after husband's death, wife still had an interest in securing any arrearage not paid by the husband during his lifetime).

647. Krupnick v. Ray, 61 F.3d 662 (8th Cir. 1995).

648. *See In re* Estate of Belcher, 299 Ga. App. 432, 435, 682 S.E.2d 581, 584 (2009) (where agreement required husband to keep life insurance in force "until either party dies," husband was required in keep insurance in force even after he left state employment); Miller v. Partridge, 734 N.E.2d 1061, 1065 (Ind. Ct. App. 2000) (where agreement required father to keep insurance for child in effect "at all times," provision was not limited to security for child support, and obligation extended past child's emancipation); Martin v. Ealy, 859 So. 2d 1034, 1038 (Miss. Ct. App. 2003); Wilkins v. Lorenz, 2009 WL 74001, *4 (Ohio Ct. App. 2009); Jones v. Harrison, 250 Va. 64, 458 S.E.2d 766 (1995) (rejecting an argument that obligation ceased when children were emancipated, as agreement clearly anticipated that life insurance trust would still exist when the youngest child reached age 25). *Miller* suggested that the court will not look beyond the four corners of the agreement to determine whether the agreement was intended as security for support.

When determining whether the obligation is security for spousal or child support, the court ordinarily looks only to the face of the agreement.[649] When support is intended as security for support, therefore, this fact should be stated expressly.

An order to provide health insurance can last indefinitely.[650]

Remedy. When a life insurance provision is enforced during the obligor's lifetime, the proper remedy is to order the obligor to obtain replacement coverage in the proper amount.[651]

Often, of course, the lack of insurance will not be discovered until after the obligor's death. If the obligor has no insurance at all, the face amount of coverage required can be recovered directly from the obligor's estate.[652] The same rule applies to breach

---

649. "As property settlement agreements are contractual in nature, it is important that parties understand the necessity of clearly identifying the intent of such provisions. Courts will not speculate as to intent and will not look beyond the four corners of the document." *Miller*, 734 N.E.2d at 1065. "Given the lack of an express statement in the judgment that the purpose of the life insurance clause was to secure child support payments or other clear indication of such a purpose, such as linking the amount of insurance that must be maintained to the amount of future support owed, there is no basis for finding such a purpose." *In re* Estate of Lobaina, 267 Mich. App. 415, 422, 705 N.W.2d 34, 39 (2005); *see also In re* Marriage of Osborne, 327 Ill. App. 3d 249, 763 N.E.2d 855 (2002) (where agreement required husband to name wife as beneficiary of life insurance, and agreement was silent as to purpose, obligation was not intended as security for child support); *In re* Marriage of Rolfes, 187 S.W.3d 355 (Mo. Ct. App. 2006) (where husband argued that life insurance obligation was security for support, but agreement was silent on the issue, husband's attempt to terminate support was improper attempt to modify final judgment).

The above cases approach the issue from the viewpoint of the intent of the parties. But that is not the only concern, for the law of insurance generally requires that life insurance beneficiaries have an insurable interest in the insured's life. *E.g., Browning*, 366 S.C. at 266, 621 S.E.2d at 394. *Browning* suggests that if the beneficiary lacks an insurable interest, the obligation to provide insurance must end, regardless of the intent of the parties. The need for an insurable interest was not mentioned in any of the above cases.

650. *See* Winter v. Winter, 167 S.W.3d 239 (Mo. Ct. App. 2005) (where husband was insurable only through wife's employment, agreement that wife would keep husband on her health insurance was enforceable indefinitely; husband was paying premium to wife in advance, so wife was not in any way prejudiced).

651. Fetner v. Fetner, 293 A.D.2d 645, 741 N.Y.S.2d 256 (2002) (where policies lapsed during husband's lifetime, proper to order him to obtain new coverage in same total amount); *cf.* Haydock v. Haydock, 254 A.D.2d 577, 679 N.Y.S.2d 165 (1998) (where husband made wrongful but irrevocable election of survivor benefits under state retirement system, proper to order husband to use his best efforts to obtain passage of a one-person bill permitting his designation to be changed).

Some courts refuse to find breach of the agreement during the obligor's lifetime, as he could always change the beneficiary back to the correct person before dying. *See, e.g.,* Fultz v. Shaffer, 111 Md. App. 278, 681 A.2d 568 (1996).

652. Gray v. Higgins, 205 Ga. App. 52, 421 S.E.2d 341 (1992); Kiltz v. Kiltz, 708 N.E.2d 600 (Ind. Ct. App. 1999); *cf.* Foster v. Hurley, 444 Mass. 157, 826 N.E.2d 719 (2005) (where agreement expressly allowed recovery from obligor's estate if insurance provision was breached, refusing to treat such recovery as the exclusive remedy; other remedies could be used as well).

In Fetner v. Fetner, 293 A.D.2d 645, 741 N.Y.S.2d 256 (2002), the court reversed a lower court decision ordering the husband *during his lifetime* to pay the wife the face amount of the policies if

of an obligation to provide survivor benefits.[653] If the obligor maintains insurance, but names another beneficiary, that beneficiary holds the proceeds in constructive trust for the proper beneficiary.[654] This is true even where the named beneficiary is innocent of any wrongdoing.[655]

If the obligor names an improper beneficiary while the obligation to maintain life insurance remains in effect, but does not die until after the obligation has terminated, there is no substantial breach and the named beneficiary is entitled to the proceeds.[656]

Modification. A provision requiring maintenance of health insurance is very similar to a provision requiring payment of medical expenses. The modification of both types of provisions is therefore discussed in § **6.064.**

Where life insurance is intended as security for alimony or child support, and the amount of insurance required is materially greater than the amount of the remaining obligation, the provision may be subject to modification.[657] Where life insurance is intended as property division, or as a simple contractual promise, the obligation is not modifiable.[658]

---

replacement coverage could not be obtained. The stated reasoning was that the obligation was outside the scope of the agreement, but a judgment for the face amount of policy is clearly a valid remedy against the obligor's estate. A better rationale is that the wife was entitled to receive the face amount of life insurance only upon the husband's death. Since the husband was still alive, *present* payment of the face amount was premature, and would represent a significant windfall to the wife.

653. *Fultz,* 111 Md. App. 278, 681 A.2d 568.

654. *See, e.g.,* Principal Mut. Life Ins. Co. v. Karney, 5 F. Supp. 2d 720 (E.D. Mo. 1998); Kruse v. Todd, 260 Ga. 63, 389 S.E.2d 488 (1990); Flanigan v. Munson, 175 N.J. 597, 818 A.2d 1275 (2003); Jones v. Harrison, 250 Va. 64, 458 S.E.2d 766 (1995); *see generally* 4 LEE R. RUSS & THOMAS F. SEGALLA, COUCH ON INSURANCE § 64:29 (3d ed. 1997 & Supp. 1999); Annotation, *Life Insurance—Divorced Spouse,* 31 A.L.R.4TH 59 (1984). Federal law may prevent imposition of a constructive trust upon survivor benefits. *See* Silva v. Silva, 333 S.C. 387, 509 S.E.2d 483 (Ct. App. 1998); King v. King, 225 Ga. App. 298, 483 S.E.2d 379 (1997).

655. *Id.*

656. *See* Rodriguez v. Rodriguez, 818 N.E.2d 993 (Ind. Ct. App. 2004) (where husband improperly changed beneficiary of insurance from child to wife when child was age 22, but obligation expired at age 23, and husband did not die until child was age 25, wife was entitled to proceeds; obligation had expired by the time of husband's death).

657. *See* Liss v. Liss, 937 So. 2d 760 (Fla. Dist. Ct. App. 2006) (where $1 million in life insurance was intended to secure alimony and child support, alimony had ended, and remaining child support obligation had a present value of $31,000, husband stated a valid claim to modify downward the amount of insurance required; error to dismiss claim without a hearing); Thomas v. Thomas, 577 N.E.2d 216 (Ind. 1991) (requirement to maintain insurance until wife's remarriage was security for spousal support, and therefore subject to modification).

658. Martin v. Ealy, 859 So. 2d 1034, 1038 (Miss. Ct. App. 2003); Batka v. Batka, 171 S.W.3d 757, 763 (Mo. Ct. App. 2005) ("the plain language of the parties' agreement unambiguously demonstrates that they intended Husband's obligation to provide Wife health insurance to be a division of property," and therefore not modifiable).

Death. A provision requiring maintenance of medical insurance terminates upon the recipient's death.[659]

Where the agreement requires maintenance of life insurance for the purpose of securing spousal support, the beneficiary's right to collect postdeath support[660] is reduced by his or her share of the insurance proceeds.[661]

§ 6.066 Custody

Agreements between the parents never bind the court in determining which parent receives custody of the children. A custody agreement is, however, one important factor that the court will consider. *See* § **3.07**. The great majority of all custody agreements are routinely followed when the court makes its final custody award.

Can the parties agree to permit modification of custody at a specific point in the future based upon best interests alone, without any proof of changed circumstances? In *Studenroth v. Phillips*,[662] the court held yes, finding no absolute rule that the changed circumstances test cannot be waived. The court recognized that such a waiver would be unenforceable where it violated the child's interests. It found, however, that the custodial arrangement anticipated by the agreement was an untried form of joint custody, and that the parties desired to facilitate court review to determine whether this new arrangement was working. On these facts, the court held that the waiver of changed circumstances was consistent with the child's interests, and it therefore held that the waiver was enforceable.

One line of decisions holds that agreements to raise or educate a child in a particular religion are unenforceable on First Amendment grounds.[663] An alternate line of decisions holds that such agreements are enforceable to the extent that they are not inconsistent with the children's best interests.[664]

Relocation. One particular subissue upon which custody agreements are particularly important is relocation of the custodial parent. Courts generally apply a balancing test

---

659. *In re* Marriage of Benjamin, 26 Cal. App. 4th 423, 31 Cal. Rptr. 2d 313 (1994).

660. *See generally* § **6.035**.

661. Gray v. Estate of Gray, 993 S.W.2d 59 (Tenn. Ct. App. 1998).

662. 230 A.D.2d 247, 657 N.Y.S.2d 257 (1992).

663. *See, e.g.,* Zummo v. Zummo, 394 Pa. Super. 30, 574 A.2d 1130 (1990); Wolfert v. Wolfert, 42 Colo. App. 433, 598 P.2d 524 (1979); Cooper v. Louque, 551 So. 2d 732 (La. Ct. App. 1989); *see generally* Laura W. Morgan, *The Court's Role in a Child's Religious Upbringing,* 5 Divorce Litig. 11 (1993). This is the majority position, but except for the three cases cited here, all of the decisions taking this position were rendered in 1960 or before. A slight majority of states addressing this issue since 1960 have held that agreements to raise or educate a child in a particular religion can be enforced without violating the First Amendment.

664. *See* Barax v. Barax, 246 A.D.2d 382, 667 N.Y.S.2d 733 (1998) (rejecting argument that provision controls unless it poses serious threat of harm to welfare of children); Perlstein v. Perlstein, 87 A.D.2d 246, 451 N.Y.S.2d 117 (1980); Johns v. Johns, 53 Ark. App. 90, 918 S.W.2d 728 (1996) (oral agreement); Butler v. Butler, 132 So. 2d 437 (Fla. Dist. Ct. App. 1961); Wagshal v. Wagshal, 249 Md. 143, 238 A.2d 903 (1968); Sina v. Sina, 402 N.W.2d 573 (Minn. Ct. App. 1987); MacLagan v. Klein, 123 N.C. App. 557, 473 S.E.2d 778 (1996).

to determine whether a custodial parent who seeks to leave the area can retain custody of the children. One of the most important factors in this balancing test is any agreement of the parties. If the parties agree to permit relocation, relocation is generally permitted.[665] If the agreement restricts relocation, the cases are divided. Some courts have followed the agreement; other courts refused to follow the agreement.[666] Agreement provisions regarding custody are universally regarded as one among many factors relevant to the court's resolution of this issue, *see* § 3.07, and to the extent that the latter line of cases did not consider the agreement as one factor against relocation, the results reached are questionable. No agreement of the parties can ever be binding on any relocation issue, however, and to the extent that the latter line of cases found the agreement contrary to the best interests of the children, the results reached were entirely correct.

Agreements regarding relocation are generally given a commonsense construction. For instance, where the agreement permitted relocation within 60 miles of the Empire State Building, the court held that relocation to a residence within 60 air miles was permitted, even though residence was 77 miles away by road.[667]

§ 6.067 *Arbitration*

Arbitration provisions in separation agreements are generally treated as enforceable by the courts.[668]

Where the provision involves an issue over which the court has ultimate authority, such as custody or child support, the presence of an arbitration clause does not remove that power. In other words, an arbitration award is no more binding upon the court than a full agreement setting forth the same terms.[669] The court will enforce the award only if it finds that the award is consistent with the best interests of the children.

---

665. *See, e.g.,* Smith v. Finger, 187 A.D.2d 711, 590 N.Y.S.2d 301 (1992); *see generally* David M. Cotter, *Oh, the Places You'll (Possibly) Go!: Recent Case Law on Relocation of the Custodial Parent,* 16 DIVORCE LITIG. 152 (2004); Nadine R. Roddy, *Stabilizing Families in a Mobile Society: Recent Case Law on Relocation of the Custodial Parent,* 8 DIVORCE LITIG. 141, 147, 152 (1996).

666. For cases following a provision preventing relocation, see Cohn v. Cohn, 658 So. 2d 479 (Ala. Civ. App. 1994); Warlick v. Warlick, 661 So. 2d 706 (La. Ct. App. 1995); *see also In re* Marriage of Findlay, 296 Ill. App. 3d 656, 695 N.E.2d 548 (1998) (contract can limit relocation, but provision is unenforceable if contrary to children's best interests). For cases refusing to follow such a provision, see *In re* Marriage of Arvin, 689 N.E.2d 1270 (Ind. Ct. App. 1997); *In re* Marriage of Witzenburg, 489 N.W.2d 34 (Iowa Ct. App. 1992); Hill v. Robbins, 859 S.W.2d 355 (Tenn. Ct. App. 1993). *See generally* Cotter, *supra* note 665; Roddy, *supra* note 665, at 152–53.

667. Potier v. Potier, 198 A.D.2d 180, 604 N.Y.S.2d 77 (1993).

668. *See* Masters v. Masters, 201 Conn. 50, 513 N.E.2d 104 (1986); Hughes v. Hughes, 851 P.2d 1007 (Idaho Ct. App. 1993); Reynolds v. Whitman, 40 Mass. App. Ct. 315, 663 N.E.2d 867 (1996); Flaherty v. Flaherty, 97 N.J. 99, 477 A.2d 1257 (1984); Carpenter v. Banker, 291 A.D.2d 283, 738 N.Y.S.2d 44 (2002); Giahn v. Giahn, 290 A.D.2d 483, 736 N.Y.S.2d 394 (2002) (even though arbitrator was a beth din, a Jewish religious court); Crutchley v. Crutchley, 306 N.C. 518, 293 S.E.2d 793 (1982); Kelm v. Kelm, 73 Ohio App. 3d 395, 597 N.E.2d 535 (1992); Bandas v. Bandas, 16 Va. App. 427, 431 S.E.2d 55 (1993).

669. *See* Kinter v. Nichols, 722 A.2d 1274 (Me. 1999) (provision to arbitrate disputes regarding child was enforceable); Hampton v. Hampton, 261 A.D.2d 262, 689 N.Y.S.2d 186 (1999) (arbitration clause applied to child support; court could vacate award if it was contrary to best interests of chil-

Arbitration awards on issues not involving children are also subject to review by the court. Where the state in question requires that the trial court approve all separation agreements before they become binding, the court must apply the same standard to reviewing an arbitration award.[670] If the agreement provides rules for the arbitrator to follow or factors for the arbitrator to consider, the court can reverse the award if the arbitrator arbitrarily refused to follow the terms of the agreement.[671] Where the agreement provides no standard for the arbitrator and does not expressly permit court review, the arbitrator's award must be confirmed unless the result is arbitrary, unconscionable, or against public policy.[672] Unless the agreement provides otherwise, the arbitrator is not bound to follow the substantive property division or support law of the state involved.[673]

A judgment confirming an arbitration award can be reopened under normal rules of state law governing reopening of judgments.[674] It is particularly important that such

---

dren, but child support must be included in issues submitted to arbitrator); Weinstock v. Weinstock, 240 A.D.2d 658, 659 N.Y.S.2d 80 (1997).

New York holds that custody and visitation issues cannot be arbitrated. Glauber v. Glauber, 192 A.D.2d 94, 600 N.Y.S.2d 740 (1993); Lipsius v. Lipsius, 250 A.D.2d 820, 673 N.Y.S.2d 458 (1998); Cohen v. Cohen, 195 A.D.2d 586, 600 N.Y.S.2d 996 (1993).

670. *See* Page v. Page, 281 Ga. 155, 156, 635 S.E.2d 762, 764 (2006) ("Even if a settlement agreement is reached with the assistance of an arbitrator and made part of an arbitrator's award, a trial court still must properly review the award prior to its incorporation into a final decree of divorce[.]"); *Reynolds*, 40 Mass. App. Ct. 315, 663 N.E.2d 867; Franke v. Franke, 268 Wis. 2d 360, 674 N.W.2d 832 (2004) (court approval requirement that applies to separation agreements also applies to arbitration awards; but "courts must give greater deference to an arbiter's award . . . than they would to other types of agreements between parties").

A very interesting dissenting opinion in *Franke* argues that the concept of binding arbitration requires that the court not have broad discretion to approve or disapprove the result reach by the arbitrator. The authors agree, but the authors also disfavor court approval requirements. *See* § 4.04.

The *Franke* dissent objects to a court approval requirement for arbitration awards, but expressed no concern over court approval requirements for agreements generally. The distinction may lie in the majority's statement that arbitration is special because the arbitrator considers not only the desires of the parties, but also "a sense of the public policy underlying divorce law." 268 Wis. at 389, 674 N.W.2d at 846. But this is just another version of the notion that some superior authority, whether a judge or arbitrator, can create a better settlement than the parties themselves. The authors respectfully submit that "a sense of the public policy underlying divorce law" is not necessary for creation of a fair divorce settlement, and that there should be no court approval requirement for *either* arbitration awards or separation agreements generally. Nevertheless, the arbitration award in *Franke* was properly reopened for a very different reason, fraudulent concealment of marital property. That aspect of *Franke* is discussed at note 675 *infra*.

671. Badell v. Badell, 122 Idaho 442, 835 P.2d 677 (1992) (parties agreed that accountant would allocate tax return after considering certain factors; accountant's allocation reversed as arbitrary).

672. Flaherty v. Flaherty, 97 N.J. 99, 477 A.2d 1257 (1984); *Bandas*, 16 Va. App. 427, 431 S.E.2d 55 (rejecting an attack upon the award).

673. *Crutchley*, 306 N.C. 518, 293 S.E.2d 793.

674. *Franke*, 268 Wis. 2d 360, 674 N.W.2d 832 (reopening for fraud).

review be available in cases of fraud,[675] as the arbitration setting is less conducive to full financial disclosure than contested court proceedings.[676]

Some arbitration provisions are limited in scope. For instance, where the parties agreed to submit to arbitration any "dispute" under their agreement, and one party simply refused to pay without raising any real construction issue, one court held that there was no dispute to be arbitrated.[677] The agreement could therefore be directly enforced by the court. Likewise, a provision for arbitration if certain stated conditions were met did not permit arbitration based upon a general change the parties' circumstances.[678]

The parties are free, of course, to waive an arbitration provision by joint agreement.[679] If the parties waive the provision, the court cannot itself assume the powers conferred upon the arbitrator. Thus, where an agreement gives the arbitrator power to modify support, and the parties waive arbitration, the agreement cannot be modified by the court.[680]

Where the agreement permitted mediation at a specific point in time if either party was not satisfied with the implementation of a particular provision, and the parties had informally negotiated their own solution in an attempt to correct problems, one court held that both parties were estopped to insist upon strict compliance with the time limit.[681]

Where the agreement permits enforcement by arbitration or other available remedies, the choice of remedy is left to the plaintiff. The defendant cannot force arbitration

---

675. An excellent example is *Franke*, where the husband failed to reveal to the arbitrator a material change in the value of his business, and had been uncooperative in financial disclosure generally. The court found sufficient basis to reopen a judgment confirming the arbitration award. A dissent would have upheld the award, on the basis that the court's power to review arbitration awards is limited.

The authors confess to criticizing the majority for requiring court approval of arbitration awards. On that point, the approach taken by the dissent is better policy. *See supra* note 670. But on the specific facts of *Franke*, the husband committed fraud in the arbitration. Fraud is a sufficient reason to reopen a final court judgment, and a decision made by an arbitrator should not be more final that a decision made by a judge. It is important to encourage alternative methods of dispute resolution, but not at the expense of tolerating outright fraud by the parties. Failure to disclose marital property should be a sufficient basis for reopening any judgment, arbitration award, mediation award, or separation agreement. *See* § **4.053**.

676. *See also* Addesa v. Addesa, 392 N.J. Super. 58, 75, 919 A.2d 885, 895 (App. Div. 2007) (noting that full financial disclosure is also less likely in mediation).

677. Weinstock v. Weinstock, 240 A.D.2d 658, 659 N.Y.S.2d 80 (1997).

678. Ferney v. Ferney, 251 A.D.2d 101, 674 N.Y.S.2d 35 (1998).

679. Horsey v. Horsey, 329 Md. 392, 620 A.2d 305 (1993).

680. *Id.*; *cf.* Andrews v. Andrews, 229 A.D.2d 366, 644 N.Y.S.2d 781 (1996) (where contract required each party to appoint an appraiser, and those appraisers to select a third if they disagreed, court erred by appointing its own appraiser; appointment was inconsistent with the contract).

681. Gaston v. Gaston, 954 P.2d 572 (Alaska 1998).

unless the contract clearly makes arbitration the *exclusive* remedy.[682] Where the agreement makes arbitration the primary remedy, the agreement will be enforced.[683]

A third-party beneficiary cannot compel arbitration unless the arbitration clause clearly applies to third-party disputes.[684]

§ 6.068 Confidentiality Provisions

As noted elsewhere in this treatise, *see* § **3.08**, there is no inherent policy objection to provisions in which the parties promise not to disclose details of their marriage or its breakup to third persons or to the media. Such provisions are breached, however, only where a preponderance of the evidence shows that the defendant spouse has disclosed information. The mere fact that confidential information has appeared in the media is not sufficient to show a breach, as the information may have been disclosed by other persons, or the media may have learned of it through its own activities and sources.[685] The penalty provision of a confidentiality provision must also be reasonable in amount.[686]

§ 6.069 Antiharassment Provisions

Where the relationship between the parties is acrimonious, separation agreements will sometimes include an express provision stating neither party will harass or annoy the other after the divorce. To avoid flooding the courts with minor litigation, these provisions are generally construed to provide a remedy only for serious misconduct:

> For molestation to be actionable it must be substantial, committed in bad faith and not caused by the other's fault . . . and must be such as is calculated seriously to annoy a person of average sensitivity.[687]

Where the defendant spouse's conduct is sufficiently serious to meet the above standard, the provision can be enforced with an award of money damages.[688] In addition, if the provision is *incorporated* or *merged* into the decree, it can be enforced by

---

682. Rae F. Gill, P.C. v. DiGiovanni, 34 Mass. App. Ct. 498, 612 N.E.2d 1205 (1993).

683. *See* Hampton v. Hampton, 261 A.D.2d 362, 689 N.Y.S.2d 186 (1999) (court could vacate arbitrator's child support award if it was contrary to best interests of children, but child support must be submitted to arbitrator before court review was available); Kinter v. Nichols, 722 A.2d 1274 (Me. 1999) (provision for mediation before filing not satisfied by mediation after filing).

684. *Gill*, 34 Mass. App. Ct. 498, 612 N.E.2d 1205.

685. Anonymous v. Anonymous, 233 A.D.2d 162, 649 N.Y.S.2d 665 (1996).

686. *See id.* at 667 (Ellerin, J., concurring) (suggesting that a liquidated-damages provision of $500,000 per violation may well be unenforceable).

687. Reybold v. Reybold, 45 A.D.2d 263, 357 N.Y.S.2d 231, 235 (1974) (citations omitted).

688. *See* Verdier v. Verdier, 133 Cal. App. 2d 325, 284 P.2d 94, 100 (1955) (awarding $500 damages for unspecified breach of antiharassment provision); Reis v. Hoots, 131 N.C. App. 721, 509 S.E.2d 198 (1998) (awarding $30,000 damages against husband, who intercepted wife's mail, filed frivolous actions against her, and caused issuance of warrant for her arrest over period of seven years); Voshell v. Voshell, 68 N.C. App. 733, 315 S.E.2d 763, 766 (1984) (awarding nominal damages against wife who made harassing telephone calls to husband and sent him harassing letters; noting that husband could have recovered actual damages if he had proven them).

contempt.[689] A violation of an antiharassment provision is normally not a sufficiently material breach to permit rescission of the entire agreement, or constitute a defense to compliance with property division or support obligations.[690]

§ 6.07 Modification by the Parties

Whether or not the court can modify a separation agreement is mostly an issue of contract construction. The issue is therefore considered in the discussion of specific provisions earlier in this chapter.

An entirely separate question is presented, however, when the parties themselves seek to modify the agreement. Since separation agreements are ordinarily controlled by normal contract law, the parties are free to modify their own agreement whenever they desire.

Merger and Incorporation

The parties obviously cannot modify an agreement that was *merged* into the divorce decree, since the agreement no longer exists as a valid document.[691] A *merged*

---

689. No reported case has yet enforced an antiharassment clause in an agreement by contempt, but the courts have used this remedy to enforce antiharassment provisions in divorce decrees. *See* Rutledge v. State, 151 Ga. App. 615, 260 S.E.2d 743, 744 (1979) (husband's harassing and threatening calls to wife and her mother warranted contempt citation); Siggelkow v. State, 731 P.2d 57, 62 (Alaska 1987) (husband's threatening telephone calls to wife, together with his name-calling and obscene gestures directed toward her in public, were punishable as criminal contempt); Lowe v. Lowe, 561 So. 2d 240, 242 (Ala. Civ. App. 1990) (husband's harassing telephone calls to wife constituted contempt); *see also* Kalupa v. Kalupa, 527 So. 2d 1313, 1317 (Ala. Civ. App. 1988) (husband's violation of restraining order entered during pendency of divorce proceedings by shouting and cursing at wife in public punishable as criminal contempt); Leonetti v. Reihl, 154 A.D.2d 675, 546 N.Y.S.2d 879, 880 (1989) (divorced husband's violation of protection and nonharassment order by appearing at wife's home and creating disturbance punishable as contempt); State v. Stahl, 416 N.W.2d 269, 270 (S.D. 1987) (divorced husband's violation of protection and nonharassment order punishable as contempt). *But cf. In re* Coppock, 277 S.W.3d 417, 418 (Tex. 2009) ("the divorce decree does not contain sufficient language to advise the parties that refraining from or engaging in the described conduct is mandatory"; reversing a finding of contempt).

For an excellent review of the law on enforcement of antiharassment provisions generally, see Nadine E. Roddy, *Enforcement of No-Molestation Clauses in Separation Agreements*, 4 DIVORCE LITIG. 55 (1992).

690. *E.g.*, Davies v. Davies, 46 A.D.3d 356, 848 N.Y.S.2d 54 (2007); Long v. Long, 160 N.C. App. 664, 670, 588 S.E.2d 1, 4 (2003) ("the 'no interference' provision of the separation agreement is independent from any other provision of the agreement"). *But see* Weiner v. Weiner, 56 A.D.3d 293, 294, 869 N.Y.S.2d 391, 392 (2008) (defendant husband's unspecified "egregious behavior toward plaintiff has operated to impose a forfeiture of defendant's rights under the parties' settlement stipulation"; recognizing that the general rule is contrary).

691. *See* LaPrade v. LaPrade, 189 Ariz. 243, 941 P.2d 1268 (1997); *In re* Marriage of Becker, 798 P.2d 124 (Mont. 1990) (attempted modification of *merged* contract was invalid attempt to circumvent the divorce decree); Tietjens v. Tietjens, 744 N.E.2d 1064, 1066 (Ind. Ct. App. 2001) ("[T]he settlement agreement was merged and incorporated into the dissolution decree. Until superseded, a party is required to obey a court order[.]"); Miles v. Miles, 355 S.C. 511, 519, 586 S.E.2d

agreement can be modified only under the normal rules governing the reopening of judgments,[692] or perhaps upon entry of a court order to which both parties consent.[693]

If the agreement was *incorporated*, the parties can still modify it. Some courts hold that such a modification does not constitute a parallel modification of the decree, so that the original language continues to control for purposes of judgment remedies.[694] Other states hold that a contractual modification of an *incorporated* agreement modifies both the agreement and the judgment.[695]

The same principles generally applies in reverse when the court attempts to modify the judgment part of an *incorporated* agreement. The modified language controls for purposes of judgment remedies, but either party may still seek to enforce the original language in contract.[696]

136, 140 (Ct. App. 2003) (where agreement *merged* into judgment, party seeking to enforce contractual modification "is trying to modify a written court order by oral agreement of the parties"). *But see* IND. CODE ANN. § 31-15-2-17(c) (Westlaw 2010) ("The disposition of property settled by an agreement described in subsection (a) and incorporated and merged into the decree is not subject to subsequent modification by the court, except as the agreement prescribes or the parties subsequently consent[.]").

In Price v. Price, 705 So. 2d 488 (Ala. Ct. App. 1997), the court held that an incorporated judgment no longer exists as a contract, and therefore cannot be modified. For the reasons set forth in § **5.013**, the court's inability to grasp the concept of true *incorporation* and its consequent undue expansion of the concept of *merger* are unfortunate. If the court's conclusion that the agreement no longer existed is accepted, however, the result reached is correct.

692. *Becker*, 798 P.2d 124.

693. *See Tietjens*, 744 N.E.2d at 1066 (*merged* agreement could be modified if agreement of parties to do so was entered as a court order); Thomas v. Thomas, 159 Ohio App. 3d 761, 765, 825 N.E.2d 626, 629 (2004) ("Although the trial court does not have jurisdiction to grant Soltis's unilateral motion to terminate spousal support, the trial court would have jurisdiction to terminate spousal support if the parties made a joint request in writing[.]").

694. *See* Nicholson v. Combs, 550 Pa. 23, 703 A.2d 407 (1997); *see generally* S. GREEN & J. LONG, MARRIAGE AND FAMILY LAW AGREEMENTS § 4.07 (1984 & Supp. 1991).

695. *See* IND. CODE ANN. § 31-15-2-17(c) (Westlaw 2010) ("The disposition of property settled by an agreement described in subsection (a) and incorporated and merged into the decree is not subject to subsequent modification by the court, except as the agreement prescribes or the parties subsequently consent[.]"); Martin v. Martin, 659 So. 2d 676 (Ala. Ct. App. 1995) (husband waived right to receive $7,500 from sale of marital home by quitclaiming his interest to wife after the divorce); Morris v. Horn, 219 P.3d 198, 204 (Alaska 2009); Brown v. Brown, 796 S.W.2d 5 (Ky. 1990) (parties can modify property settlement agreement without reopening divorce decree); Sparer v. Sparer, 227 A.D.2d 613, 643 N.Y.S.2d 617 (1996) (parties modified incorporated contract by agreeing that wife would take substantially all assets and husband would pay no alimony; enforcing the modification); Wright v. Wright, 2008 WL 4885677, at *4 (Ohio Ct. App. 2008) ("after a separation agreement has been incorporated into a decree of dissolution, the parties to a separation agreement may modify its terms by subsequent acts or agreements so long as it is supported by consideration"; particularly since agreement itself expressly reserved parties' right to modify it in the future); *cf.* Knowles v. Thompson, 697 A.2d 335 (Vt. 1997) (where agreement was incorporated into temporary order, court recognized mutual abandonment of it without suggesting that it had the status of a permanent judgment).

696. DeCristofaro v. DeCristofaro, 24 Mass. App. Ct. 231, 508 N.E.2d 104, 109 (1987) ("[e]ven where [the court] properly refuses specific performance and order support . . . different from that

Modification by the parties of incorporated child support provisions are particularly likely to be found unenforceable.[697]

Approval

Where the original decree only *approved* the agreement, or where no decree has yet been issued, there is no legal obstacle to future modification by the parties. Courts are willing to recognize such modification where the parties have clearly agreed to it.[698] The modification must, of course, be supported by consideration.[699] A contract cannot be modified in a way detrimental to the rights of third-party beneficiaries unless those third parties agree to the change.[700] If the party seeking modification does not present a clear case, the courts are reluctant to find an agreement modified, particular by words or conduct alone.[701]

When a modification agreement replaces an old provision with a new one, any terms of the old provision not expressly included in the new provision become unenforceable. For instance, in *Zembenski v. DeMatteo*,[702] the first agreement contained a child support escalator provision. A modified agreement replaced the child support clause, and included no escalator. The court held that the escalator clause had been removed from the agreement.

Provisions Preventing Modification

Many agreements contain a specific provision that purports to limit certain types of future modification. Some provisions require that future modifications be written. Other provisions require that future modifications be both written and signed by both parties. Still other provisions require that the future modifications be accomplished

---

called for in the agreement, the party aggrieved by that order has a claim for breach of contract"), *cert. denied*, 400 Mass. 1103, 511 N.E.2d 620 (1987); Kellman v. Kellman, 162 A.D.2d 958, 559 N.Y.S.2d 49 (1990).

697. *E.g.*, Dorr v. Dorr, 797 So. 2d 1008, 1013 (Miss. Ct. App. 2001) ("court-ordered obligations for the support of the minor children of divorcing parents may not be modified by the obligor and obligee extrajudicially").

698. *See* LaPrade v. LaPrade, 189 Ariz. 243, 941 P.2d 1268 (1997) (recognizing contractual modification of spousal support); Cox v. Cox, 707 A.2d 1297 (D.C. 1998) (parties can modify child support provision of unincorporated agreement); O'Malley v. Baruch, 239 A.D.2d 477, 658 N.Y.S.2d 364 (1997) (recognizing executed oral modification of separation agreement); McGee v. McGee, 168 Ohio App. 3d 512, 860 N.E.2d 1054 (Ohio Ct. App. 2006) ("while the trial court cannot modify its property division, the parties themselves are free to modify the division by agreement"); Bidwell v. Baker, 193 Or. App. 657, 662, 91 P.3d 793, 796 (2004) ("After the entry of a dissolution judgment, and even pending appeal, the parties are free to negotiate and agree to a modification or settlement of the property division between themselves[.]"); *but cf.* Barnes v. Barnes, 772 S.W.2d 636 (Ky. Ct. App. 1989) (conduct similar to *Klein* held not to be an implicit modification).

699. Bondy v. Levy, 119 Idaho 961, 812 P.2d 268 (1991).

700. Wareham *ex rel.* Trout v. Wareham, 716 A.2d 674 (Pa. Super. Ct. 1998).

701. *See* Sally v. Sally *ex rel.* Magee, 225 A.D.2d 816, 638 N.Y.S.2d 832 (1996) (where first agreement required husband to provide health insurance indefinitely, and second agreement provided that he would provide three years of COBRA coverage, second contract supplemented and did not modify first contract).

702. 261 A.D.2d 471, 690 N.Y.S.2d 123 (1999).

with the same level of formality as the agreement itself, thus requiring such formalities as notarization or witnessing if those formalities were originally present.

In the great majority of states, *none of these provisions are enforceable.* The common law rule is that when the parties agree to modify their agreement, they implicitly agree to modify any provision that would make that modification impossible.[703] Thus, if the agreement requires that future modifications be in writing, and the parties both agree orally upon a modification, they have both implicitly waived the clause preventing oral modification. Under the common law rule, the parties to a contract can never waive their right to modify the agreement in the future.

A minority of states have rejected the common law rule. These states will enforce clauses limiting the future modifiability of the agreement.[704] Also, in states where the original agreement had to be in writing, future modifications may have to be in writing as well.[705]

Drafting Concerns. The authors of this volume are surprised by how many separation agreements contain no-modification provisions. Since these provisions are unenforceable in the great majority of states, their presence serves no useful purpose. They can, in fact, do great harm, for one or both parties may take action in reliance upon their supposed validity. In states where no-modification provisions are clearly unenforceable, these provisions have no place in well-drafted separation agreements.

The authors would further question whether no-modification clauses are a wise idea even in states where they are enforceable. Many drafters insert no-modification clauses into their agreements as a matter of course, apparently in the belief that future modifications of the agreement are hardly ever in the client's interest. The authors would question this belief. Many divorced persons, at one point or another in their postdivorce relationship, find it desirable to modify their separation agreement. These modifications are sometimes made under pressure, and the parties lack the time and energy to

---

703. Only two recent cases specifically apply the common law rule to separation agreements. Filipov v. Filipov, 717 So. 2d 1082 (Fla. 4th Dist. Ct. App. 1998) (where agreement required that all modifications be signed by both parties, enforcing modification signed only by one party); Clark v. Clark, 535 A.2d 872 (D.C. 1987) (enforcing oral modification, despite clause in contract requiring that modification be in writing); *cf.* Sutherland v. Sutherland, 107 Conn. App. 1, 944 A.2d 395 (2008) (provision limiting modification by the parties did not limit modification of support by the court).

There are, however, literally hundreds of cases applying the rule to other types of contracts. *See generally* 17A C.J.S. *Contracts* § 414 (Westlaw 2008). Since no court has ever articulated a reason why the law governing no-modification clauses should be different for separation agreements than for other types of contracts, it is highly likely that the common law rule is in effect in the great majority of jurisdictions.

704. *See* Albrecht v. Albrecht, 19 Conn. App. 146, 562 A.2d 528 (1989), *cert. denied*, 212 Conn. 813, 565 A.2d 534 (1989) (noting that clause preventing future oral modifications is enforceable in Connecticut); Wetherby v. Wetherby, 50 A.D.3d 1226, 854 N.Y.S.2d 813 (2008); Gower v. Gower, 240 A.D.2d 632, 659 N.Y.S.2d 297 (1997) (enforcing clause against oral modification; noting that oral modification can be shown by conduct that is unequivocally referable to the alleged modification, but finding this test not met on the facts).

705. *See* Cook v. Cook, 725 So. 2d 205 (Miss. 1998).

state their modification in a formal writing. Where the no-modification clause requires more formality than mere writing (e.g., notarization), compliance is even harder. Formalities are easier if counsel are consulted, but counsel will charge for their time, and the parties may find the expense unnecessary.

In short, many agreements will ultimately be modified, and in many cases there are powerful practical reasons why modification is likely to be informal. In states where no-modification clauses are enforceable, the practical result of such a provision may well be to strike down a modification that both parties believed and intended to be valid. Fear of this result is essentially the policy reason underlying the common law rule. By routinely including no-modification clauses in separation agreements, drafting attorneys are disregarding the common law's age-old wisdom that the benefits of enforcing informal modifications are greater than the detriments.

If a no-modification clause is to be included, it should at a minimum be discussed with the client. If the effect of the agreement is to strike down otherwise valid modification agreements, the client is surely entitled to be specifically notified of the fact. Moreover, counsel might also consider asking whether the client desires to limit modifiability. If the client is not specifically consulted on the inclusion of such a potentially harmful provision, the client might have a cause of action against the attorney in the event that a modification desired by the client runs afoul of the no-modification clause. Including a no-modification clause as a routine, "boilerplate" provision of every agreement could be a very dangerous practice.

Those who routinely include no-modification clauses might be influenced to some extent by a desire to avoid false claims of oral or informal modification made by the other party.[706] This fear is to some extent overblown. As noted above, courts are

---

706. A strong argument for inclusion of no-modification clauses is made on this basis in 2 Stephen W. Schlissel, Elena Karbatos & Ronald F. Pepplein, Separation Agreements and Marital Contracts 212 (2d ed. 1997). "[I]t is recommended that the agreement at least provide that any modification must be reduced to a single writing and signed by both parties; the problem of a court having to examine a series of written exchanges between the parties to determine the provisions of the modification can be avoided." *Id.* "This will [also] avoiding problems such as waiver of any provision by the failure to insist on strict compliance, oral modification, modification by conduct . . . modification by reference to several writings and the like." *Id.*

To the extent that the above statement recommends inclusion of no-modification clauses as a matter of course in every agreement, the present authors disagree. To begin with, the provision recommended above is unenforceable in a majority of states (although enforceable in New York, where the authors of the above volume practice). Drafters should avoiding including an unenforceable provision in any contract. Moreover, the above passage assumes that any future informal modification would contain unfavorable terms. If a future informal modification were to contain beneficial terms, then a no-modification clause would be a major problem for the client, who might in turn be a problem for the drafting attorney. Thus, before including a provision limiting modification, counsel should at least consider whether the damage done by preventing a future favorable modification is more than damage done by avoiding a future unfavorable modification. To the extent that waiver is a problem, a more limited provision against implied waiver can address that issue without preventing future modifications actually desired by the client. Unless there is clear reason to believe that any future modification would be adverse rather than beneficial, modification is not a problem to be feared and avoided, but rather an event that should be left to the will of the parties themselves.

reluctant to find casual modifications to a written agreement. In the majority of states that do not enforce no-modification clauses, there is no large body of case law considering oral modification issues. Where clear evidence of mutual agreement to the modification is lacking, the courts generally do not find a valid agreement to modify. Note also that the common law of contracts has required for centuries that all modifications be supported by consideration on both sides of the bargain. These rules of law are sufficient to defeat most false claims of oral modification.

To the extent that there remains some danger of fraudulent oral modification claims, that danger must be weighed against the chance that the no-modification provision will strike down an agreement that benefits the client. The authors believe that in most cases, the burden of requiring substantial formalities for each and every attempt to modify a separation agreement is substantial, and that to impose such formalities is to create a real trap for the unwary. On the whole, better results are reached when the agreement does not restrict future modification in any material way.

Merger and Incorporation of Modification Agreements

If the parties agreed to modify a separation agreement, can the modification contract itself be *incorporated* into the decree? Where the original contract was only *approved*, one would think that the modification cannot rise to a higher level. To *incorporate* or *merge* the modification agreement would effectively give similar treatment to the original contract, in violation of the rule that *incorporation* or *merger* cannot be accomplished after the divorce. *See generally* § **5.01**.

The question never arises if the original agreement *merged* into the decree, for, as noted above, in that event there is no contract left to modify. *See* § **5.012**. Where the agreement was *incorporated*, one decision suggests that incorporation of an agreement modifying a property division provision would violate the rule against modifying a final property division judgment.[707] Conversely, a fair number of cases enforce contractual modifications of *incorporated* agreements, without suggesting that such modifications are improper. If the modification is valid under the law of contracts, it is necessarily a product of both parties' consent. The parties are clearly allowed to contract around other substantive rules of property division and spousal support law, and it is hard to see why they should not be permitted to agree upon an otherwise invalid substantive modification. The better practice is therefore to permit *incorporation* of modifications as well as original agreements.

Agreements to Agree

An original separation agreement may provide for modification by agreement of the parties at some future time. At common law, an agreement to sign a contract in the future was too indefinite to be enforced.[708] The separation agreement cases, however, tend to construe the common law rule rather liberally. For instance, in *Bruce*

---

707. Frisella v. Frisella, 872 S.W.2d 637 (Mo. Ct. App. 1994).

708. 17A Am. Jur. 2d *Contracts* § 39 (Westlaw 2008); *see* Silverman v. Silverman, 249 A.D.2d 378, 671 N.Y.S.2d 145 (1998) (agreement to renegotiate spousal support one year after wife's remarriage was an unenforceable agreement to agree).

v. Bruce,[709] the parties agreed to negotiate in good faith to modify the agreement if there was a material change in circumstances. The court rejected an argument that this clause was an unenforceable agreement to agree.[710]

Although an agreement to negotiate may impose a duty to negotiate in good faith, it clearly does not require anything more. In *Rimkus v. Rimkus*,[711] for example, the parties agreed to negotiate an increase in child support if the husband's income became more regular. The court held that this clause did not require the husband actually to begin making support payment when condition in the clause was met.

Abandonment

As a special form of modification, the parties can agree to abandon all or part of their agreement. *See generally* § **4.075**.

Separation Agreements and Antenuptial Agreements

In a growing number of cases, the parties have signed both an antenuptial agreement and a separation agreement. The most common practice is to draft the separation agreement as a comprehensive document that formally revokes the antenuptial agreement and sets forth the complete agreement of the parties regarding all future issues. When this sort of agreement is signed, the antenuptial agreement is superseded.[712]

Where the antenuptial agreement is not formally revoked, it survives the making of a separation agreement. Where a conflict between the agreements exists, the separation agreement is more recent and would therefore probably be controlling.

---

709. 801 S.W.2d 102 (Tenn. Ct. App. 1990).

710. *See also* Bondy v. Levy, 119 Idaho 961, 812 P.2d 268 (1991) (promise to renegotiate agreement if tax law changed was not unenforceable; enforcement was improper on the facts, however, as husband had failed to make formal request for renegotiation); Stevens v. Stevens, 798 S.W.2d 136, 137 (Ky. 1990) (contract required father to pay college expenses in an amount to be agreed upon by father and child; held not an unenforceable agreement to agree).

711. 199 Ill. App. 3d 903, 557 N.E.2d 638 (1990).

712. *E.g.*, Chappelow v. Savastano, 195 Misc. 2d 346, 758 N.Y.S.2d 782 (Sup. Ct. 2003).

Enforcement of Separation Agreements 7

§ 7.01 General Rules

Separation agreements can be enforced by either contract or judgment remedies. The contract remedies apply if the agreement was *approved*; the judgment remedies apply if the agreement was *merged*.

In jurisdictions recognizing the concept of true *incorporation*, the injured spouse has a choice of using either contract or judgment remedies.[1] The choice may be different for each breach, and a spouse who has used one type of remedy in response to a prior breach may use the other type in response to a subsequent breach.[2] Indeed, the enforcing spouse may even plead both remedies in the alternative.[3] The ability to enforce the contract as a judgment without destroying the contract as an independently valid document is the single strongest advance of true *incorporation* over *merger* and *approval*.

---

1. *See, e.g.*, Nicholson v. Combs, 550 Pa. 23, 703 A.2d 407 (1997); Swartz v. Swartz, 456 Pa. Super. 16, 689 A.2d 302 (1997); Irwin v. Irwin, 47 Va. App. 287, 293 n.4, 623 S.E.2d 438, 441 n.4 (2005) ("A property settlement agreement that is incorporated into a final decree is enforceable either under contract law or through the court's contempt power[.]").

2. Larson v. Larson, 30 Mass. App. Ct. 418, 569 N.E.2d 406 (1991); *Nicholson*, 550 Pa. 23, 703 A.2d 407; Lipschutz v. Lipschutz, 391 Pa. Super. 537, 571 A.2d 1046 (1990).

3. Bondy v. Levy, 119 Idaho 961, 812 P.2d 268 (1991).

§ 7.02 Contract Law Remedies

Contract law remedies are available only to enforce *approved* or *incorporated* agreements. If the agreement has *merged* into the divorce decree and lost independent validity, it must be enforced as a judgment and not as a contract.[4]

§ 7.021 Remedies within the Contract

Separation agreements sometimes contain specific provisions that become effective if one spouse breaches other provisions of the agreement. These provisions are generally enforceable. The most common example is a provision that the losing party will pay the prevailing party's attorney's fees.[5]

Where the remedy under the agreement itself is so large as to give the innocent spouse an unjust windfall, the provision is unenforceable. For instance, in *Cooper v. Smith*,[6] the court strongly suggested that the agreement's penalty provision was unenforceable. That provision provided that if the husband fell behind on alimony by more than four months, he would sell the wife 35 percent of the assets of a certain trust for only $100. In *Cooper*, however, the agreement had been *approved* by the divorce decree, and could be collaterally attacked only if it was void. Because the penalty provision was only erroneous, and not void, the court ultimately enforced the provision as written.

A party who is himself guilty of a major breach may not be permitted to rely upon the agreement's own enforcement provisions.[7]

Contractual Liens. One frequent type of enforcement provision is an agreement to secure certain obligations with a lien on the obligor's property. If a lien is placed on real property, the lien is effective only if it has been properly recorded.[8] The parties can also agree to the appointment of a receiver to perform certain acts in the event of breach.[9]

Where the agreement provides that a spouse may secure an obligation with a contractual lien, that spouse is not required to create the lien, and may instead choose other available remedies.[10]

---

4. *See, e.g.*, Halpern v. Rabb, 75 Mass. App. Ct. 331, 338–39, 914 N.E.2d 110, 116 (2009) (wife "could not have maintained a [contract] action for breach of the separation agreement's child support provisions because those provisions merged into the judgments"); Powers v. Powers, 103 N.C. App. 697, 407 S.E.2d 269 (1991) (court cannot order specific performance where contract *merged* into decree); Webber v. Olsen, 330 Or. 189, 998 P.2d 666 (2000).

5. *See, e.g.*, Lang v. Lang, 551 So. 2d 547 (Fla. Dist. Ct. App. 1989) (provision that losing party would pay prevailing party's attorney's fees in any subsequent action on the agreement). Attorney's fees provisions are discussed in detail in **§ 6.05**.

6. 70 Haw. 449, 776 P.2d 1178 (1989).

7. *See* Marcolongo v. Nicolai, 392 Pa. Super. 208, 572 A.2d 765 (1990), *allocatur denied*, 589 Pa. 692, 593 A.2d 420 (1990).

8. *See* Vickroy v. Vickroy, 44 Ohio App. 3d 210, 542 N.E.2d 700 (1988).

9. *See* Young v. Young, 765 S.W.2d 440 (Tex. Ct. App. 1988) (enforcing provision that receiver would divide personal property if parties were unable to agree on a division).

10. Pipitone v. Pipitone, 23 So. 3d 131 (Fla. Dist. Ct. App. 2009).

Acceleration. Another common type of contractual enforcement provision is an acceleration clause, stating that an entire deferred award will become due if the obligor defaults. These provisions are generally enforceable.[11]

In *Scotto v. Scotto*,[12] the court suggested that an acceleration provision might not be enforceable if the breach were trivial or the result of a good-faith error. The court essentially reasoned that an acceleration clause in this situation would be an unreasonable penalty provision, like an unreasonable liquidated damages clause. On the facts, however, *Scotto* found that the breach was substantial and not the result of a good-faith error.

Anticipatory Breach. Where one party states a clear intention not to follow any term of an agreement, that statement constitutes an *anticipatory breach*. Upon such a breach, the innocent spouse may recover the present value of all obligations due under the agreement, including future support payments.[13]

Liquidated Damages. The contract may contain a promise by one party to pay specific sums upon breach of certain promises. These clauses are known as liquidated damages provisions, and they are enforceable only if the amount of damages stated is reasonable in relation to the actual damage suffered by the enforcing spouse.[14]

§ 7.022 Damages

In addition to the agreement's own provisions, the injured spouse can rely on the three traditional contract law remedies: damages, specific performance, and rescission.

The traditional method for enforcing support and monetary award provisions is a money judgment for damages. The amount of damages for breach of a property division obligation is normally the value of the property at issue.[15] The amount of damages

---

11. *See* Scotto v. Scotto, 234 A.D.2d 442, 651 N.E.2d 170 (1996); *cf.* Mowers v. Mowers, 229 A.D.2d 941, 645 N.Y.S.2d 232 (1996) (where husband was responsible for mortgage, and mortgage contained an acceleration provision, husband was liable for entire mortgage balance upon default).

12. 234 A.D.2d 442, 651 N.E.2d 170 (1996).

13. Jenkins v. Jenkins, 991 S.W.2d 440 (Tex. Ct. App. 1999). *But see* Haelterman v. Haelterman, 846 So. 2d 1229 (Fla. Dist. Ct. App. 2003) (anticipatory breach does not apply to contract where only remaining duty is payment of money).

If the present value of future support payments is recovered and paid, the obligor is not liable for future periodic support. *See* Bazzle v. Bazzle, 37 Va. App. 737, 561 S.E.2d 50 (2002).

14. *See* Anonymous v. Anonymous, 233 A.D.2d 162, 649 N.Y.S.2d 665, 667 (1996) (Ellerin, J., concurring) (suggesting that liquidated damages provision requiring payment of $500,000 for each breach of confidentiality provision was unenforceable). *But see* Dougan v. Dougan, 114 Conn. App. 379, 385, 970 A.2d 131, 136 (2009), *cert. granted*, 292 Conn. 920, 974 A.2d 721 (2009) (provision requiring a defaulting party to pay interest from the date of the agreement forward, not from the date of the breach forward, is not an unreasonable penalty).

15. *See* Cordova v. Cordova, 63 A.D.3d 982, 987, 883 N.Y.S.2d 237, 241 (2009) (where agreement required husband to convey property to wife, and husband instead conveyed property to his sisters, trial court properly entered money judgment against husband in an amount equal to the equity value of the property); Elliott v. Elliott, 149 S.W.3d 77 (Tenn. Ct. App. 2004) (division of stock options, where employer did not allow transfer of options; where husband failed to exercise options owned equitably by wife upon wife's request, awarding damages equal to the amount wife would have realized if her options had been properly exercised).

for breach of a support obligation is normally the amount of unpaid support.[16] The award cannot be reduced if the payee's damages are reduced after the fact by benefits from a collateral source.[17] The court can award damages for violation of the spousal support provisions of a separation agreement even if the injured spouse failed to request court-ordered support in the underlying divorce case.[18] To determine how much of an obligation has actually been paid, the court has the power to order one or both parties to make an accounting.[19]

Interest. When the court awards damages for failing to pay a monetary sum, it can also award interest from the date of breach.[20]

Substantial Compliance. When the agreement requires that funds be transferred to a spouse, and the funds are not paid directly but are used for the spouse's ultimate benefit, the use of the funds may be substantial compliance with the agreement.[21]

§ 7.023 Specific Performance

As courts of equity, divorce courts always have the power to grant specific enforcement of separation agreements.[22] The remedy at law must be insufficient, but this requirement is generally treated liberally in domestic cases. For instance, one court held that the remedy at law is always insufficient with regard to the property division portions of the agreement.[23]

The court can clearly order specific performance of the past-due provisions of an agreement to provide periodic payments.[24] Specific enforcement of future payments,

---

16. *See* Sparacio v. Sparacio, 248 A.D.2d 705, 670 N.Y.S.2d 558 (1998) (spousal and child support).

For cases making awards of money damages for breaches of other provisions, *see* Reis v. Hoots, 131 N.C. App. 721, 509 S.E.2d 198 (1998) (antiharassment provision).

17. *See* Gray v. Pashkow, 168 A.D.2d 849, 564 N.Y.S.2d 520 (1990) (in computing damages for husband's failure to pay medical expenses, improper to subtract tax benefit wife may have received for paying the expenses herself).

18. Long v. Long, 102 N.C. App. 18, 401 S.E.2d 401 (1991).

19. *See* Ward v. Ward, 705 So. 2d 498 (Ala. Ct. App. 1997); Horchover v. Field, 964 P.2d 1278 (Alaska 1998).

20. *See, e.g.,* Mowers v. Mowers, 229 A.D.2d 941, 645 N.Y.S.2d 232 (1996) (husband failed to pay mortgage as required by agreement; awarding interest on unmade payments).

21. *See* Willette v. Willette, 53 A.D.3d 753, 861 N.Y.S.2d 204 (2008) (where husband withdrew marital funds from 401(k) plan and used them to reduce line of credit balance on marital home, wife in effect received the full benefit of the withdrawal, and was not entitled to receive half of the amount withdrawn; such a payment would give her the benefit of the funds twice).

22. *E.g.,* Clay v. Faison, 583 A.2d 1388 (D.C. 1990); Condellone v. Condellone, 129 N.C. App. 675, 501 S.E.2d 690 (1998).

23. *Clay,* 583 A.2d 1388; *but see* Allyn v. Allyn, 163 A.D.2d 665, 558 N.Y.S.2d 983 (1990) (where promise to pay college expenses could be adequately enforced by award of damages, error to award specific performance).

24. Eickhoff v. Eickhoff, 263 Ga. 498, 435 S.E.2d 914 (1993) (retirement benefits).

however, might violate a constitutional provision preventing imprisonment for debt.[25] The effect of this rule is to greatly limit the practical effectiveness of specific performance, for there is no way that the injured party can ensure future performance. The limit can be avoided, however, by having the court *incorporate* or *merge* the agreement into the decree; in that event, future payments can be enforced by contempt. *See* **§ 7.031**.

Specific performance usually takes the form of a court order to perform the contract in question.[26] Where a contract to maintain a spouse or child as beneficiary of life insurance is breached and the insured spouse has already died, the designated beneficiary holds the proceeds in constructive trust for the spouse or child.[27]

As a contract remedy, specific performance may not be available where the language of the contract is only a judgment and not a contract—that is, where the agreement *merged* into the decree.[28]

§ 7.024 Rescission

When one party to a contract breaches one or more of its terms, instead of suing for damages or seeking specific performance, the innocent party may elect to rescind the contract. A rescinded contract ceases to exist; none of its provisions is enforceable.[29]

Rescission is not permitted for every breach of an agreement, for fear that minor violations would result in loss of large and important agreements. Instead, the common law permits rescission only for a breach that is material.[30] There is no simple rule for defining a material breach, but the provision involved must be central to the entire bargain of the parties.[31]

The decisions have generally been reluctant to find that minor breaches were sufficiently material to justify invalidation of the entire contract. For instance, courts have held

---

25. *Id. But see Condellone*, 129 N.C. App. 675, 501 S.E.2d 690 (1998) (court can order specific performance of future payments).

26. *Allyn*, 163 A.D.2d 665, 558 N.Y.S.2d 983.

27. *See* **§ 6.065**.

28. *Condellone*, 129 N.C. App. 675, 501 S.E.2d 690. In states that do not recognized true *incorporation*, an "incorporated" agreement is either *merged* or merely *approved*, depending on the intent of the parties. *See* **§ 5.013**. If the court determines that an "incorporated" agreement really *merged* into the decree, the rule cited in this footnote may prevent specific performance.

29. *See* Restatement (Second) of Contracts § 237 (1981) (absence of material breach is a condition on all duties of future performance under an agreement).

30. *See id.*; *In re* Marriage of Smith, 115 S.W.3d 126 (Tex. Ct. App. 2003).

31. *See* Jones v. Jones, 232 A.D.2d 313, 648 N.Y.S.2d 585 (1996) (where wife cashed in and spent bonds in which husband had an interest, material breach justifies rescission of the agreement); Carter v. Carter, 18 Va. App. 787, 447 S.E.2d 522 (1994) (husband discharged property division in bankruptcy; agreement contained specific provision permitting rescission upon material breach).

The court is especially likely to find that a breach is material when it arises from a deliberate attempt by one party to defraud another. *See* Lopez v. Taylor, 195 S.W.3d 627 (Tenn. Ct. App. 2005) (where husband agreed to pay college expenses of child, and wife and child fraudulently submitted excessive claims, husband was relieved of all further obligation to pay college expenses).

that a material breach did not exist when the obligor failed to maintain life insurance,[32] failed to pay a mortgage,[33] or performed an obligation after the stated due date.[34]

Courts will sometimes find that a material breach permits rescission only of that part of the agreement that is inseverable from the part breached. Stated conversely, a material breach may not permit rescission of provisions that are severable from the provision breached.[35]

An immaterial breach can of course be enforced by other contract remedies, such as a claim for damages.

When a party obtains damages for breach, any claim for rescission based upon the same breach is lost.[36]

§ 7.025 Contract Law Defenses

All of the above contract law remedies are subject to normal contract law defenses. The effect of these defenses is altered in some cases if the separation agreement has already been approved by the divorce decree.

Invalidity. Where a separation agreement has been *approved*, *incorporated*, or *merged* into a divorce decree, the divorce decree makes an implied finding that the agreement is valid. Accordingly, the divorce decree prevents either spouse from subsequently rais-

---

32. Brees v. Cramer, 322 Md. 214, 586 A.2d 1284 (1991); *In re* Marriage of Smith, 115 S.W.3d 126 (Tex. Ct. App. 2003) (breach of promise to provide life insurance was not sufficiently material breach to permit rescission of the property division portion of the agreement).

33. Butterworth v. Butterworth, 226 A.D.2d 899, 640 N.Y.S.2d 366 (1996) (husband's failure to pay mortgage did not excuse wife's failure to make installment payments on monetary award).

34. *See* Thomas v. Fusilier, 966 So. 2d 1001 (Fla. Dist. Ct. App. 2007) (wife's 12-day delay in leaving marital home was not a material breach such that husband would be excused from paying $250,000 monetary award); Brown v. Brown, 90 Ohio App. 781, 630 N.E.2d 763 (1993) (husband paid monetary award after due date stated in agreement; breach was not material, as contract did not state that time was of the essence).

For additional cases holding that a breach was not material, *see* Zambito v. Zambito, 171 A.D.2d 918, 566 N.Y.S.2d 789 (1991) (breach of visitation provisions was not material); Fletcher v. Fletcher, 123 N.C. App. 744, 474 S.E.2d 802 (1996) (no material breach; husband did not contact wife before son's dental surgery, failed to cancel certain credit cards, and failed to pay wife her full interest in his pension); Allocca v. Allocca, 23 Va. App. 571, 478 S.E.2d 702 (1996) (husband discharged liability on joint note in bankruptcy, but contract did not expressly assign liability to either party; breach, if any, was not material); *see also* § 6.069 (breach of nonharassment provision is generally not material).

35. *See* RESTATEMENT (SECOND) OF CONTRACTS § 237 & cmt. e (1981); *Lopez*, 195 S.W.3d 627 (material breach of college tuition provision allowed rescission of that provision, but apparently did not render entire agreement invalid).

36. *See* Sullivan v. Sullivan, 976 So. 2d 329, 335 (La. Ct. App. 2008) (once wife obtained a contempt order against husband for failing to make payments under agreement, any claim for rescission merged into the contempt order and was lost).

ing such defenses as fraud or unconscionability.[37] It may still be possible, of course, to reopen the divorce decree under the same rules of law that control reopening of judgments generally. *See* § **4.02**.

Impossibility. The mere fact that the payor spouse lacks sufficient funds to meet an obligation imposed by the agreement does not trigger the common law defense of impossibility.[38]

While the defense of impossibility has not often been argued in actions to enforce separation agreements, courts are generally reluctant to construe an agreement to require a party to perform impossible tasks. In other words, rather than apply the impossibility defense, courts tend to construe the contract so that the defense does not apply.[39]

Waiver. The parties are free to waive compliance with specific provisions of their agreement. Waiver is tantamount to complete or partial abandonment of the agreement, and the cases are discussed in § **4.075**.

Mutual Breach. Parties who have breached separation agreements sometimes attempt to excuse their action by claiming that the other party breached the agreement first. A breach by one party does not automatically justify the other party in refusing to perform.[40] Performance is not required, however, if the provision breached by the other party was a condition, or if the other party committed a material breach of the agreement.

Since an unfulfilled condition is a defense to decree-based as well as contract-based remedies, the law on this subject is discussed in § **7.04**. Material breach is discussed in § **7.024**.

Unclean Hands. Misconduct that is collateral to the agreement does not prevent either spouse from enforcing it.[41]

Slayer Statute. One decision holds that separation agreements are subject to "slayer statutes," provisions that state that a person who murders another cannot recover benefits from the death of the victim. In *In re Marriage of Braun*,[42] the father promised to pay medical and college expenses for his child. The child then murdered the father. The court held that regardless of the language of the agreement, no provision for the child's benefit could be enforced against the father's estate. Provisions for the benefit of the mother, of course, could still be enforced.

---

37. *See* § **4.02**.

38. Barnett v. Barnett, 26 Conn. App. 355, 600 A.2d 1055 (1992).

39. *See* § **5.06**, notes 153–160; *see also* § **5.08**.

40. *E.g.*, Brees v. Cramer, 322 Md. 214, 586 A.2d 1284 (1991).

41. *See* Hilgendorf v. Hilgendorf, 241 A.D.2d 481, 660 N.Y.S.2d 150 (1997) (collateral tax fraud).

42. 222 Ill. App. 3d 178, 583 N.E.2d 633 (1991).

Statute of Limitations. Actions to enforce separation agreements are subject to the normal statute of limitations on actions to enforce contracts generally. Where the contract is signed under seal, the limitations period may be longer.[43] Where the contract is *merged* or *incorporated*, the judgment statute of limitations may apply.[44]

The statute normally starts running upon breach, and not upon the execution of the agreement.[45] Where the injured party could not reasonably have discovered the breach until a later point in time, the statute may not start until the later date.[46]

Where the defendant agreed to make periodic payments, each payment is generally treated as a separate claim, so that only those payments older than the limitations period are time-barred.[47] The payor can direct which precise arrears he intends to pay off with any given payment, and can specifically direct that his payment not be applied to arrears that are time-barred.[48] If the payor fails to provide directions along with the payment, the presumption is that the payments apply to the oldest arrears, even if those arrears are no longer enforceable.[49]

Where the obligor refuses to comply with a provision requiring maintenance of life insurance, a cause of action to recover the proceeds directly from the obligor's estate does not accrue for limitations purposes until the obligor dies.[50]

Laches. The defense of laches prevents enforcement of a contract when the enforcing spouse had delayed unreasonably in enforcing his or her rights, and the delay has inflicted prejudice upon the defendant.[51]

---

43. Treadway v. Smith, 325 S.C. 367, 479 S.E.2d 849 (Ct. App. 1996).

44. Werner v. Werner, 176 Misc. 2d 299, 671 N.Y.S.2d 626 (Sup. Ct. 1998) (*incorporated* agreement governed by 20-year judgment statute, not six-year contract statute); Hershey v. Hershey, 467 N.W.2d 484 (S.D. 1991) (also noting that the judgment statute usually applies to child support provisions).

45. Rosenthal v. Rosenthal, 172 A.D.2d 298, 568 N.Y.S.2d 603 (1991).

46. *See* Bemis v. Estate of Bemis, 967 P.2d 437 (Nev. 1998) (father promised to place funds in trust for children; where parents did not disclose agreement to children, statute did not start to run against children until they should reasonably have had knowledge of their rights; rejecting trial court holding that all children have a duty to investigate the terms of their parents' divorce upon reaching the age of majority).

47. *See* Riley v. Riley, 61 Ark. App. 74, 964 S.W.2d 400 (1998) (agreement to pay mortgage); Crispo v. Crispo, 909 A.2d 308 (Pa. Super. Ct. 2006) (deferred monetary award); *see generally* 24A AM. JUR. 2D *Divorce & Separation* § 870 (1998).

48. *Werner,* 176 Misc. 2d 299, 671 N.Y.S.2d 626.

49. *Id.*

50. Gray v. Higgins, 205 Ga. App. 52, 421 S.E.2d 341 (1992).

51. *See generally* 24A AM. JUR. 2D *Divorce & Separation* § 871 (1998).

While laches is valid defense on the law, the cases are reluctant to apply it on the facts. If the period of delay is reasonable[52] or the prejudice is not extensive,[53] courts are quick to find the defense inapplicable. In addition, some courts are reluctant to bar a cause of action for laches when the relevant limitations period has not expired.[54]

Waiver. The parties are free to waive the terms of a separation agreement that exists only as a contract.

§ 7.03 Decree Remedies

Decree remedies are available only to enforce *merged* or *incorporated* agreements.[55] If the agreement has only been *approved* by the divorce decree, it does not have the status of a judgment, and decree remedies are not available.[56]

---

52. *See* Coscina v. Coscina, 24 Conn. App. 190, 587 A.2d 159 (1991) (delay was not unreasonable where caused by the plaintiff's mental illness); Emery v. Smith, 361 S.C. 207, 219, 603 S.E.2d 598, 604 (Ct. App. 2004) (where husband failed to inform wife of his retirement, wife did not delay unreasonably in seeking a portion of his retirement benefits); Allison v. Hagan, 211 S.W.3d 255 (Tenn. Ct. App. 2006) (wife did not delay unreasonably in selling home, where husband rejected at least one "seemingly reasonable" offer to purchase the property).

Delay in filing a formal action to enforce a contract is almost always reasonable where the enforcing party was attempting to obtain compliance through informal means. *See* McKiever v. McKiever, 305 Ark. 321, 808 S.W.2d 328 (1991) (husband could not rely on wife's delay in enforcing agreement, where husband had failed to cooperate with wife's previous informal attempts to obtain compliance); Bonds v. Bonds, 455 Pa. Super. 610, 689 A.2d 275 (1997) (two-and-one-half-year delay in enforcement not laches; wife informally demanded that husband follow agreement). To rule otherwise would be to penalize the enforcing spouse for attempting to resolve the dispute out of court.

53. *See* Kanaan v. Kanaan, 163 Vt. 402, 659 A.2d 128 (1995) (wife's failure to enforce agreement for slightly less than one year did not give husband a successful laches defense; husband had suffered no prejudice from the delay).

54. *Gray*, 205 Ga. App. 52, 421 S.E.2d 341; Treadway v. Smith, 325 S.C. 367, 479 S.E.2d 849 (Ct. App. 1996).

55. *E.g.*, Shoup v. Shoup, 31 Va. App. 621, 525 S.E.2d 61 (2000).

56. *See generally* 2 HOMER CLARK, THE LAW OF DOMESTIC RELATIONS IN THE UNITED STATES § 19.12 (2d ed. 1987).

Pennsylvania allows decree remedies to be used even if the agreement was neither merged nor incorporated. "A party to an agreement regarding matters within the jurisdiction of the court under this part, whether or not the agreement has been merged or incorporated into the decree, may utilize a remedy or sanction set forth in this part to enforce the agreement to the same extent as though the agreement had been an order of the court except as provided to the contrary in the agreement." 23 PA. CONS. STAT. ANN. § 3105(a) (Westlaw 2010); Annechino v. Joire, 946 A.2d 121 (Pa. Super. Ct. 2008).

§ 7.031 Contempt

The most effective method for enforcing a separation agreement is the court's contempt power. Like all decree remedies, however, contempt is available only where the agreement has been *incorporated* or *merged* into the divorce decree.[57]

When *merger* or true *incorporation* is present, the court may enforce the spousal and child support provisions of the agreement by contempt.[58] The court may even use contempt to enforce provisions of the agreement that the court could not itself order without agreement of the parties.[59]

Most states also allow the use of contempt to enforce the property division provisions.[60] A small minority of states, however, refuse to permit the use of contempt for this purpose.[61]

Contempt can be used only to enforce express duties placed upon the parties by the agreement; it cannot be used to enforce implied duties.[62] Where the terms of the agreement are ambiguous, the ambiguity has not yet been resolved by the court, and the defendant spouse's interpretation of the ambiguous term is not unreasonable, the defendant generally cannot be held in contempt for following his or her construction of the agreement.[63]

---

57. *See* Caccaro v. Caccaro, 388 Pa. Super. 459, 565 A.2d 1199 (1989); *see generally* CLARK, *supra* note 56, § 19.12.

In jurisdictions that do not recognize true *incorporation*, the term "incorporated" is ambiguous, and the court must determine whether it really means *merger* or *approval*. *See* **§ 5.013**. If the court decides that the contract was only *approved*, it does not exist as a judgment, and it cannot be enforced by contempt. *See* Attilli v. Attilli, 722 A.2d 268 (R.I. 1998); Peterson v. Peterson, 333 S.C. 538, 510 S.E.2d 426 (1998).

58. *See Ex parte* Manakides, 564 So. 2d 983 (Ala. Civ. App. 1990) (alimony in gross); Hine v. Hine, 558 So. 2d 496 (Fla. Dist. Ct. App. 1990); *In re* Marriage of Schrader, 462 N.W.2d 705 (Iowa Ct. App. 1990). *But see In re* Green, 221 S.W.3d 645 (Tex. 2007) (alimony can never be enforced by contempt; a unique result of Texas's longstanding hostility toward alimony).

In Johnston v. Johnston, 297 Md. 48, 465 A.2d 436, 440 (1983), the highest court of Maryland held that an incorporated agreement is enforceable by contempt. A lower court unaccountably held to the contrary in Mendelson v. Mendelson, 65 Md. App. 486, 541 A.2d 1331 (1988). *Mendelson* was then overturned by MD. CODE ANN., FAM. LAW § 8-105 (1996). *See* Shapiro v. Shapiro, 346 Md. 648, 697 A.2d 1342 (1997); JOHN F. FADER & RICHARD J. GILBERT, MARYLAND FAMILY LAW § 13-8(c) (2d ed. 1995).

59. *See, e.g.,* Powers v. Powers, 103 N.C. App. 697, 407 S.E.2d 269 (1991) (postmajority child support); *but see* Gaster v. Gaster, 703 A.2d 513 (Pa. Super. Ct. 1997) (college support provision cannot be enforced by contempt).

60. *See* Brown v. Brown, 305 Ark. 493, 809 S.W.2d 808 (1991) (monetary sum due under property settlement provision); Millner v. Millner, 260 Ga. 465, 397 S.E.2d 289 (1990) (interest on property settlement payments); *In re* Marriage of Wiley, 199 Ill. App. 3d 223, 556 N.E.2d 788 (1990) (portion of husband's retirement benefits), *cert. denied,* 133 Ill. 2d 551, 561 N.E.2d 710 (1990).

61. *Hine,* 558 So. 2d 496; Broyles v. Broyles, 573 So. 2d 357 (Fla. Dist. Ct. App. 1990), *cert. denied,* 584 So. 2d 997 (Fla. 1991); Merritt v. Merritt, 693 N.E.2d 1320 (Ind. Ct. App. 1998).

62. Wilson v. Collins, 27 Va. App. 411, 499 S.E.2d 560 (1998).

63. Issler v. Issler, 50 Conn. App. 58, 716 A.2d 938 (1998) (stating the rule, but finding on the facts that the agreement was not ambiguous, and affirming a finding of contempt).

Defenses. When the agreement is *merged* or *incorporated*, the defendant may raise only those defenses normally available in an action to enforce a judgment.[64] Normally, therefore, contract law defenses do not apply. In one case where the agreement was *incorporated*, one court allowed contract law defenses to be considered in assessing damages.[65]

Contempt cannot be used as a remedy when the defendant is unable to comply with the obligation at issue.[66] The burden of showing inability to pay, however, is normally on the defendant.[67]

Courts are reluctant to find a party in contempt for noncompliance with an agreement when the defendant has substantially performed his obligations by other means. For instance, in *Henderson v. Henderson*,[68] the husband agreed to provide the wife with copies of his tax returns. The court upheld a lower court's refusal to hold the husband in contempt for violating this provision, because he had provided the wife with information on his earnings by another method.[69]

§ 7.032 Execution

Another remedy for enforcing a court-ordered obligation is direct execution on the judgment.[70] Execution is available only where the judgment is stated as a sum certain. Where the sum is not expressly stated in the agreement, the enforcing party must obtain a specific money judgment before execution is appropriate.[71]

Execution is generally subject to a series of statutory exemptions, created for the general purpose of protecting debtors against creditors. One court held that the state's homestead exemption did not apply against a spouse, who is a fellow family member rather than the sort of creditor the legislature had in mind in creating the exemption.[72]

§ 7.04 Conditional Obligations

The parties are free to agree that certain promises in their agreement shall be enforceable only if certain other promises have already been performed. When two promises

64. *See* Doherty v. Doherty, 9 Va. App. 97, 383 S.E.2d 759 (1989).

65. Spradley v. Hutchinson, 787 S.W.2d 214 (Tex. Ct. App. 1990) (where both parties breached the agreement, court properly offset their damages and awarded a judgment for the difference).

66. Afkari-Ahmadi v. Fotovat-Ahmadi, 294 Conn. 384, 985 A.2d 319 (2009).

67. *Id.*

68. 288 S.C. 190, 379 S.E.2d 125 (1989).

69. *See also* Fernandez v. Fernandez, 278 A.D.2d 882, 718 N.Y.S.2d 509 (2000) (trial court properly refused to hold husband in contempt for failing to maintain life insurance policy stated in decree, where he provided another with identical coverage, and original insurer was willing to reinstate original policy); Long v. Long, 160 N.C. App. 664, 671, 588 S.E.2d 1, 5 (2003) ("While the deviation in method of payment might have been inconvenient, the deviation did not substantially defeat the purpose of the agreement nor was it a substantial failure to perform[.]").

70. *See generally* 33 C.J.S. *Executions* (Westlaw 2008).

71. *See* Shelley v. Shelley, 212 Ga. App. 651, 442 S.E.2d 847 (1994) (enforcing party could not execute directly on obligation to half of mortgage and repairs on home).

72. Myers v. Lehrer, 671 So. 2d 864 (Fla. Dist. Ct. App. 1996).

have this relationship to each other, the first promise is called a *condition* to the performance of the second. Since conditions can be present in both contracts and judgments, the rules of law discussed here apply regardless of whether the agreement was *merged*, *incorporated*, or merely *approved* by the judgment.

Whether a promise is conditional is a question of fact. For instance, in *Nisbet v. Nisbet*,[73] the husband stopped making support payments required by the agreement. When the wife sued to enforce the agreement, the husband claimed that she had breached the visitation provisions of the agreement, which were conditions to his support obligation. The trial court granted summary judgment against the husband, but the appellate court reversed. The case was remanded for a factual hearing on the husband's allegations.[74]

Conversely, in *Daily v. Daily*,[75] the agreement stated that the wife might lose her eyesight, and then awarded her $1 per month in modifiable spousal support. The husband argued that loss of eyesight was a condition to modification. The court disagreed, noting that the agreement did not use conditional language. Loss of eyesight was only an example of a changed circumstance, the court held, and it was not a limitation upon the provision permitting modification.[76]

As with any factual issue, the cases on conditional obligations reach varying results. If the clear language of the agreement creates a condition, the court will enforce it.[77] One possible exception is child support, which may not be subject to conditions.[78]

---

73. 102 N.C. App. 232, 402 S.E.2d 151 (1991).

74. *See also* Goppert v. Goppert, 642 So. 2d 589 (Fla. Dist. Ct. App. 1994) (remanding with instructions to consider whether wife's waiver of alimony was conditional upon husband's agreement to pay certain tax liabilities).

75. 912 S.W.2d 110 (Mo. Ct. App. 1995).

76. *See also In re* Spirtos, 56 F.3d 1007 (9th Cir. 1995) (wife's agreement to assume 50 percent liability for substantial debt was not conditioned upon husband's performance of other provisions; suggesting a specific reluctance to find conditions in third-party action brought by creditor); Douglas v. Douglas, 616 So. 2d 574 (Fla. Dist. Ct. App. 1993) (husband's obligation to pay mortgage on marital home not conditional upon wife's promise not to reside there with an unrelated adult male).

77. Page v. Baylard, 281 Ga. 586, 642 S.E.2d 14 (2007) (wife's promise to consult husband before incurring major medical expenses was absolute condition upon his liability for such expenses; where wife failed to consult husband, husband was not required to pay expenses); Mallard v. Mallard, 28 A.D.3d 955, 956, 814 N.Y.S.2d 758, 759 (2006) ("as long as [respondent] shall have any obligation respecting alimony hereunder, [petitioner] shall immediately advise him in writing of any change in her own residence . . . in the absence of which written notice [respondent] shall not be o[b]ligated hereunder for alimony"; when wife moved without notifying husband of new address, husband properly ceased alimony payments); First Union Nat'l Bank v. Naylor, 102 N.C. App. 719, 404 S.E.2d 161 (1991) (husband agreed to hold wife harmless from certain debts "[u]pon the said note . . . being paid in full" by wife; husband's promise was clearly subject to a condition).

78. *See Nisbet*, 102 N.C. App. 232, 402 S.E.2d 151 (for policy reasons, adopting a per se rule against conditions on child support obligations).

Provisions involving children may, however, be conditions to other obligations.[79] In addition, transfers to children over and above support requirements can be subject to conditions.[80]

Agreements can provide that some provisions are subject to conditions, while other provisions are unconditional, even if the two types of provisions are otherwise very similar.[81]

Sometimes a condition will contain more than one part. For instance, in *Van Alfen v. Van Alfen*,[82] the agreement provided for an increase in child support when the husband graduated from college and obtained employment. The husband obtained employment while he was still enrolled in school, and the trial court increased support, reasoning that the husband could otherwise avoid the increase by remaining a student forever. The appellate court quite properly reversed, holding that under the clear language of the agreement, support increased only when both parts of the condition were met. If the husband was actually frustrating the spirit of the agreement by unduly delaying his education, the proper remedy was not to ignore the plain language of the contract, but rather to enforce the husband's implied obligation to execute the contract in good faith. On the facts, however, there was no evidence that the husband was acting in bad faith.

If a condition is breached, the conditioned obligation never becomes effective. Where the husband committed an anticipatory breach of the conditioned obligation and the meeting of the condition was only a matter of time, however, one court refused to enforce the condition.[83]

The above cases generally consider whether individual provisions within the agreement are subject to conditions. In some situations, the entire agreement may be subject to a condition. For example, in *Faith v. Faith*,[84] the agreement provided that the husband

---

79. *See* Carlino v. Carlino, 171 A.D.2d 774, 567 N.Y.S.2d 533 (1991) (husband's support obligation was conditioned upon wife's promise not to relocate more than 50 miles away with children).

80. *See* Van Alfen v. Van Alfen, 909 P.2d 1075 (Alaska 1996) (recognizing conditional increase in child support); *In re* Marriage of Druss, 226 Ill. App. 3d 470, 589 N.E.2d 874, 877 (1992) (agreement provided that if wife remarried, the child would become the sole beneficiary of certain insurance, "and in addition thereto" that the child would receive 50 percent of the husband's retirement benefits; wife's remarriage was a condition to child's entitlement to retirement benefits).

81. *See* Auerbach v. Auerbach, 113 Conn. App. 318, 966 A.2d 292 (2009) (enforcing provision that required submission of an accountant's affidavit before seeking modification of support for one basis, but not for seeking modification of support on other bases).

82. 909 P.2d 1075 (Alaska 1996).

83. First Union Nat'l Bank v. Naylor, 102 N.C. App. 719, 404 S.E.2d 161, 162 (1991) (husband agreed to hold wife harmless from certain debts "[u]pon the said note . . . being paid in full" by wife; husband's promise was clearly subject to a condition); *see also* Cavanagh v. Cavanagh, 33 Mass. App. Ct. 240, 598 N.E.2d 677 (1992) (husband promised to pay wife $97,000 upon sale of home, which court held must take place within reasonable time; husband committed anticipatory breach by stating he had no intention to sell the home within the foreseeable future; ordering payment of the $97,000 within six months).

84. 709 So. 2d 600 (Fla. 3d Dist. Ct. App. 1998).

would use his best efforts to purchase a certain warehouse. The parties agreed that if the transaction did occur, their agreement would be renegotiated. The seller then increased the price sharply, to the point where two experts agreed that the transaction was commercially unreasonable. The court held that the husband's best efforts had failed to accomplish a reasonable sale of the warehouse. Since such a sale was a condition upon the entire agreement, the agreement lost all effect.

The entire agreement may also be subject to an implied condition that the divorce expected by the parties actually occurs. When the divorce fails to occur because of a reconciliation, there is a good chance that at least the executory portions of the agreement become invalid. *See* § **4.074**. Where the divorce fails to occur because of death or lack of jurisdiction, the cases are divided. *See* § **4.08**.

§ 7.05 Procedural Questions

A number of special procedural concerns are relevant when one spouse seeks to enforce a separation agreement.

Family Courts

In states with separate family courts, the family court may lack jurisdiction to enforce a separation agreement with contract remedies.[85] Where the agreement is incorporated, however, the family court may be able to apply at least decree-based remedies.[86]

Divorce versus Contract Actions

In some states, contract law remedies might be available only in a separate independent action to enforce the contract. In these states, where the agreement is not *merged* or *incorporated* into the decree, a mere motion in the divorce case would not be a sufficient basis for invoking contract remedies.[87]

Jurisdiction

The court cannot enforce a separation agreement if it lacks personal jurisdiction over the defendant spouse.[88]

---

85. *See* Zamjohn v. Zamjohn, 158 A.D.2d 895, 551 N.Y.S.2d 689 (1990); *cf.* Felicia B. v. Charles B., 178 Misc. 2d 138, 678 N.Y.S.2d 231 (Fam. Ct. 1998) (family court cannot offset damages for violation of property division contract against decree-based child support arrears); Clay v. Faison, 583 A.2d 1388 (D.C. 1990) (family division of trial court is a court of general and not limited jurisdiction, and thus can apply contract remedies).

86. *See* Reinhardt v. Reinhardt, 204 A.D.2d 1028, 613 N.E.2d 89 (1994).

87. *See, e.g.*, Morrow v. Morrow, 103 N.C. App. 787, 407 S.E.2d 286 (1991).

88. *See* Birdsall v. Melita, 260 A.D.2d 809, 688 N.Y.S.2d 283 (1999); O'Bryan v. McDonald, 952 P.2d 636 (Wyo. 1998).

Standing

Standing to enforce the agreement is generally limited to those who benefit from it. Nevertheless, a parent is always permitted to enforce a provision that benefits only the parties' children.[89] Likewise, an adult child always has standing to enforce a college support provision.[90] An attorney has standing to enforce a contractual attorney's fees provision.[91] Either party's trustee in bankruptcy has standing to enforce any obligation of the other, where the amount paid would fall into the debtor's spouse's bankruptcy estate.[92] Finally, some courts have held that creditors have standing to enforce joint promises to repay a debt.[93]

Limitations

Actions to enforce *incorporated* and *merged* agreement as a judgment are subject to the statute of limitations for enforcing judgments.[94] Actions to enforced *approved* agreement, or to enforce *incorporated* agreements as contract, are subject to the statute of limitations for enforcing contracts.

Provisions that require periodic payments are generally construed as a series of individual obligations. Thus, individual payments that are overdue by more than the proper limitations period are time-barred.[95] But the entire obligation is not time-barred merely because the obligation to make periodic payments is itself older than the limitations period.

---

89. *See* Winset v. Fine, 565 So. 2d 794 (Fla. Dist. Ct. App. 1990); Stevens v. Stevens, 798 S.W.2d 136 (Ky. 1990); McCaw v. McCaw, 12 Va. App. 264, 403 S.E.2d 8 (1991); *but see In re* Lazar, 59 Ohio St. 3d 201, 572 N.E.2d 66 (1991) (mother's child support ceased at "majority" as required by contract, despite statute extending duty to support until child graduated from high school; if support was due under the statute, the child and not the mother was the proper plaintiff).

90. *See* § **6.044**, note 537.
An adult child does not, however, have standing to enforce support due during minority. *See, e.g.*, Chen v. Chen, 586 Pa. 297, 893 A.2d 87 (2006).

91. *See* § **6.053**, note 582.

92. Jenkins v. Jenkins, 991 S.W.2d 440 (Tex. Ct. App. 1999).

93. *See* Northen v. Tobin, 262 Ga. App. 339, 344, 585 S.E.2d 681, 686 (2003) (creditor had standing to enforce agreement to pay lien from proceeds of sale of asset); Starrett v. Commercial Bank of Ga., 226 Ga. App. 598, 486 S.E.2d 923 (1997); Pomerantz v. Pomerantz, 236 A.D.2d 596, 654 N.Y.S.2d 36 (1997). *But see* Costanza v. Costanza, 346 So. 2d 1133 (Ala. 1977).

94. *See* Wehrkamp v. Wehrkamp, 773 N.W.2d 212 (S.D. 2009).

95. *E.g.*, Makarchuk v. Makarchuk, 59 A.D.3d 1094, 1095, 874 N.Y.S.2d 649, 650 (2009) ("Plaintiff is seeking to enforce a continuing obligation under a contract, and she therefore may seek damages for those breaches that have occurred within the six years prior to the commencement of the action[.]"); Patricia A.M. v. Eugene W.M., 24 Misc. 3d 1012, 885 N.Y.S.2d 178 (Sup. Ct. 2009) (wife's share of husband's retirement benefits).

Declaratory Judgment Action

In addition to traditional actions for breach or contempt, separation agreements may also be construed by motions to clarify judgments or in actions for a declaratory judgment.[96]

Hearing. When an action to enforce a separation agreement requires resolution of contested material issues of fact, the court cannot resolve those issues without holding a hearing, at which the parties can introduce evidence in support of their positions.[97]

Res Judicata

If a court adopts a given construction of the agreement in one construction action, that construction is binding in future actions between the same parties.[98]

Waiver

See § **4.075**.

Accord and Satisfaction

A party who cashes a check given in full satisfaction of all outstanding obligations may waive the right to collect future sums. Cashing the check constitutes acceptance of an offer, written on the check or in an accompanying letter, to forgive all other amounts owed.

Where the check contains no such language, a party who cashes it does not waive any claims for additional amounts due.[99]

---

96. Coscina v. Coscina, 24 Conn. App. 190, 587 A.2d 159 (1991).
97. *See* Fackelman v. Fackelman, 50 A.D.3d 732, 856 N.Y.S.2d 162 (2008).
98. Lee v. Lee, 189 A.D.2d 952, 592 N.Y.S.2d 495 (1993).
99. Robinson v. Robinson, 961 S.W.2d 292 (Tex. Ct. App. 1997).

Antenuptial Agreements: An Overview | 8

§ 8.01 A Brief History of Antenuptial Agreements

What we today in the United States call an antenuptial agreement or contract (or prenuptial or premarital agreement or contract or marriage settlement; the terms are synonymous) has its origins in 16th-century England.[1]

---

1. Leah Guggenheimer, *A Modest Proposal: The Feminomics of Drafting Premarital Agreements*, 17 WOMEN'S RTS. L. REP. 147 (1996) (citing Judith Younger, *Perspectives on Antenuptial Agreements*, 40 RUTGERS L. REV. 1059, 1060 (1988)); C.M.A. McCauliff, *The Medieval Origin of the Doctrine of Estates in Land: Substantive Property Law, Family Considerations, and the Interests of Women*, 66 TUL. L. REV. 919, 923–29 (1992); LAWRENCE STONE, THE FAMILY, SEX, AND MARRIAGE IN ENGLAND 1500–1800, at 30 (1977).

This is not to suggest, however, that non-English-common law countries do not recognize and enforce antenuptial agreements. *See, e.g.*, H.R. HAHLO, LAW OF HUSBAND AND WIFE 261 (5th ed. 1985) (tracing history of antenuptial contracts in South Africa to the law of Netherlands in 1599); Brown, *A Comparison of Enforcement of Antenuptial Contracts in the United States, Great Britain, France & Quebec*, 6 B.C. INT'L & COMP. L. REV. 475 (Spring 1983) (discussing enforceability of antenuptial contracts in France and Quebec). Jews have utilized marriage contracts called ketubahs for over 2,000 years. *See* Michelle Greenberg-Korbin, *Civil Enforceability of Religious Prenuptial Agreements*, 32 COLUM. J.L. & SOC. PROBS. 359 (1999).

Moreover, the modern antenuptial agreement discussed herein has marked similarities with the Germanic and Anglo-Saxon purchase marriage, where the husband exchanged valuable and promises to provide for his wife after death. SAMUEL GREEN & JOHN V. LONG, MARRIAGE AND FAMILY LAW AGREEMENTS § 2.05, at 109 (1984) (citing 2 W. HOLDSWORTH, HISTORY OF ENGLISH LAW 88–89 (1924) and Whittaker, *Antenuptial Contracts Which Bar Dower*, 9 CENT. L.J. 222 (1879)).

Prior to the enactment of the Statute of Uses,[2] there was no method by which a woman could by her own act bar her right to dower in her husband's lands. The wife's right of dower, therefore, was a restriction on the free alienation of land.[3]

In order to avoid this restriction, prior to marriage the land was conveyed to what was called "uses." Blackstone described the conveyance thus:

> the property or possession of the soil being vested in one man, and the use and profits thereof in another;—Now, though a husband had the use of the lands in absolute fee-simple, yet the wife was not entitled to any dower therein, he not being seised thereof; wherefore it became usual, on marriage, to settle by express deed some special estate to the use of the husband and his wife for their joint lives, in joint-tenancy, or jointure.[4]

Thus, prior to the Statute of Uses, jointures were provisions for the husband and wife for life, for the wife during marriage, and for the wife if she survived the husband, allowing the husband and wife complete use of the land, but also allowing free alienation of the land. Jointures were not attempts to bar the right of dower, because no claim of dower was recognized where the husband had only a beneficial interest in the land, that is, was not seised of the land. Moreover, jointures were not viewed as a method to bar dower, because the husband often settled the land on the wife at the time of the marriage.

After the enactment of the Statute of Uses, however, every person who had a beneficial interest in land was also seised and possessed of the soil itself. Thus, the specifications of the jointure, that is, the antenuptial agreement to create the jointure, could bar dower. Moreover, courts in equity began to enforce these jointures as marriage settlements barring the right of dower, and courts at law began enforcing agreements between husband and wife as purely contracts.

The use of antenuptial agreements grew dramatically after the passage of the statute of frauds.[5] By the mid-17th century, they were important enough to be included in the original Statute of Frauds.[6] By 1700, they were common enough to be the subject of jokes in English popular theater.[7]

One of the earliest cases to come before the courts upon the question of the validity of an antenuptial agreement was *Drury v. Drury*,[8] and its appeal, *Drury v. Buckinghamshire*,[9] decided in 1762. In that case, the wife argued that since she was a minor at the time she signed an antenuptial agreement relinquishing her right of dower

---

2. 27 Hen. VIII, c. 10 (1535).

3. *See* Comment, *Antenuptial Contracts*, 41 MICH. L. REV. 1133 (1943).

4. 2 BLACKSTONE, COMMENTARIES *136 (1756) (*quoted in* Ronken, *Antenuptial Contracts: Their Origin and Nature*, 24 YALE L.J. 65, 65 (1914–15)).

5. Judith T. Younger, *Perspectives on Antenuptial Agreements*, 40 RUTGERS L. REV. 1059, 1060 (1988).

6. 29 Car. II, c. 3 (1677).

7. Younger, *supra* note 5, at 1060.

8. 2 Eden, 39.

9. 2 Eden, 61.

in consideration for certain provisions, the agreement was unenforceable. The House of Lords ultimately stated that the agreement was a bar to dower, and fully enforced the agreement in equity.[10] Thus, as the law developed in England, antenuptial agreements were upheld on three separate grounds: as coming strictly within the Statute of Uses; as not strictly conforming to the statute, but considered beneficial to the wife and thus enforced in equity; and as resting upon the express agreement of the parties as a valid contract.

In the United States, the law developed somewhat differently. Rather than recognizing jointure in equity and law, legislation enacted statutes specifically providing for the recognition of jointures and antenuptial agreements.[11] These statues were modeled after the section of the Statute of Uses that provided: "then in every such case, every woman married having such jointure . . . shall not claim nor have title to any dower in the residue."[12]

Instead of testing the validity of the agreement under the statute, however, courts in the United States merely looked to the provisions of the agreement to see if they were fair and reasonable. If so, the agreement was upheld. For example, in the early case of *Reiger v. Schaible*,[13] the Supreme Court of Nebraska held that an antenuptial agreement will be upheld and deemed sufficient so long as it is equitable and fair in its terms, and so long as it was entered into in good faith. Thus, in the United States, so long as the jointure conformed to the requirements of the statute, it constituted a legal bar to dower. Moreover, if the jointure did not conform, it could still be enforced under equitable principles. In such a case, the court would look to see if the agreement was fair and reasonable.

Because antenuptial contracts could bar dower, antenuptial contracts came to be used for reasons other than acting as a protection for the intended wife. The antenuptial contract came to be used as a protection for the intended husband, his heirs, and his children of a prior wife, and to protect the property from the intended wife herself. Indeed, antenuptial contracts came to be used in any way that parties could vary, create, or relinquish rights and interest in property that each spouse would otherwise have by virtue of the marriage.[14]

Up until 1972, the parties most often used the antenuptial agreement to waive certain rights on the death of the spouse, for example, the right to a homestead allowance, the right of election as a surviving spouse, or the right to a property or family allowance.[15] Parties also frequently used antenuptial agreements to arrange for security for

---

10. *See also* Dyke v. Randell, 13 Eng. L. & E. Rep. 411, 2 De Gex, M & G 209, decided in 1852, upholding the agreement between the parties not in equity, but in law, finding the agreement fully enforceable according to contract principles.

11. *See* 3 C. VERNIER, AMERICAN FAMILY LAW §§ 196, 197 (1935) (collection of statutes authorizing antenuptial agreements barring dower).

12. Comment, *supra* note 3, at 1134.

13. 81 Neb. 33, 115 N.W. 560, 566 (1908).

14. *See* § **8.03** and cases cited therein for this proposition.

15. *See* Homer C. Clark, *Antenuptial Contracts*, 50 COLO. L. REV. 141, 155 (1979); Gamble, *The Antenuptial Contract*, 26 U. MIAMI L. REV. 692, 698 (1972).

children of a previous marriage, to provide life insurance, and to circumvent community property or equitable distribution laws by reclassifying certain named property. Parties were not able, however, to enter into an antenuptial contract that contemplated the divorce or separation of the parties. Such an agreement, the courts held, was contrary to public policy.[16] As the Alaska Supreme Court noted in *Brooks v. Brooks*,[17]

> The traditional common law view was that prenuptial agreements in contemplation of divorce . . . were inconsistent with the sanctity of marriage and the state's interest in preserving marriage and maintaining the financial security of divorced persons. Courts uniformly viewed these agreements as inherently conducive to divorce and as allowing a husband to circumvent his legal duty to support his wife.

In 1970, in the landmark case of *Posner v. Posner*,[18] the Supreme Court of Florida held that antenuptial contracts that contemplate divorce or separation are not invalid per se. Rather, the court will uphold such a contract after review of the contract for fairness in its terms and its execution. Other states followed suit, so that today, antenuptial agreements that contemplate divorce or separation are not invalid per se.[19] In fact, courts now view antenuptial contracts as a means of encouraging marriage.[20]

---

16. Younger, *supra* note 5, at 1069. *See also* 24 AM. JUR. 2D *Divorce and Separation* § 19 (1999) (historical discussion concerning the validity of premarital agreements anticipating divorce or separation); Annotation, *Modern Status of Views as to Validity of Premarital Agreements Contemplating Divorce or Separation*, 53 A.L.R. 4TH 22 (1987).

17. 733 P.2d 1044, 1048 (Alaska 1987).

18. 257 So. 2d 530 (Fla.), *mandate conformed to* 260 So. 2d 536 (Fla. 1972).

19. *See, e.g.*, Reynolds v. Reynolds, 376 So. 2d 732 (Ala. Ct. App. 1979); *Brooks*, 733 P.2d 1044; Spector v. Spector, 531 P.2d 176 (Ariz. Ct. App. 1975); Dingledine v. Dingledine, 523 S.W.2d 189 (Ark. 1975); *In re* Marriage of Franks, 542 P.2d 845 (Colo. 1975); Parniawski v. Parniawski, 359 A.2d 719 (Conn. Super. 1976); Burtoff v. Burtoff, 418 A.2d 1085 (D.C. App. 1980); Scherer v. Scherer, 292 S.E.2d 662 (Ga. 1982); Rossiter v. Rossiter, 666 P.2d 617 (Haw. Ct. App. 1983); Volid v. Volid, 286 N.E.2d 42 (Ill. Ct. App. 1972); *In re* Marriage of Boren, 475 N.E.2d 690 (Ind. 1985); *In re* Marriage of Sell, 451 N.W.2d 28 (Iowa Ct. App. 1989); Ranney v. Ranney, 548 P.2d 734 (Kan. 1976); Holliday v. Holliday, 358 So. 2d 618 (La. 1978); Frey v. Frey, 471 A.2d 705 (Md. 1984); Skelton v. Skelton, 490 A.2d 1204 (Me. 1984); Osborne v. Osborne, 428 N.E.2d 810 (Mass. 1981); Rinveldt v. Rinveldt, 475 N.W.2d 478 (Mich. Ct. App. 1991); Englund v. Englund, 175 N.W.2d 461 (Minn. 1970); Ferry v. Ferry, 586 S.W.2d 782 (Mo. Ct. App. 1979); *In re* Marriage of Keepers, 691 P.2d 810 (Mont. 1984); Buettner v. Buettner, 505 P.2d 600 (Nev. 1973); Marschall v. Marschall, 477 A.2d 833 (N.J. Super. App. Div. 1984); Propp v. Propp, 493 N.Y.S.2d 147 (App. Div. 1985); Motley v. Motley, 120 S.E.2d 422 (N.C. 1961); Gross v. Gross, 464 N.E.2d 500 (Ohio 1984); Freeman v. Freeman, 565 P.2d 365 (Okla. 1977); Unander v. Unander, 506 P.2d 719 (Or. 1973); Laub v. Laub, 505 A.2d 290 (Pa. Super. 1986); Connolly v. Connolly, 270 N.W.2d 44 (S.D. 1978); Duncan v. Duncan, 652 S.W.2d 913 (Tenn. Ct. App. 1983); Huff v. Huff, 554 S.W.2d 841 (Tex. Civ. App. 1977); Huck v. Huck, 734 P.2d 417 (Utah 1986); Padova v. Padova, 183 A.2d 227 (Vt. 1962); Capps v. Capps, 219 S.E.2d 901 (Va. 1975); *In re* Marriage of Matson, 705 P.2d 817 (Wash. Ct. App. 1985); Gant v. Gant, 329 S.E.2d 106 (W. Va. 1985); Hengel v. Hengel, 365 N.W.2d 16 (Wis. Ct. App. 1985).

20. James Herbie DiFonzo, *Customized Marriage*, 75 IND. L.J. 875, 937 (2000).

By way of example, in the case of *In re Marriage of Dawley*,[21] California adopted the modern view that antenuptial agreements contemplating divorce or separation are valid. In that case, the court disapproved of the holding in *In re Marriage of Higgason*,[22] which stated that premarital agreements were invalid unless the parties contemplated a marriage lasting until death. Instead, the *Dawley* court held that premarital agreements contemplating divorce are not invalid per se. Rather, each agreement should be reviewed individually to determine if its terms promoted marital breakdown. Building on *Dawley*, the court in *In re Marriage of Grinius*[23] held that the antenuptial agreement of the parties, which reclassified marital property as separate, was valid and enforceable. The agreement did not foster divorce.

Thus, today antenuptial agreements are valid and enforceable in every state, so long as they are, at a minimum, not violative of public policy[24] and voluntarily entered into.[25] Further, at a minimum, they must be either entered into with full and fair financial disclosure,[26] or substantively not unfair or unconscionable.[27] As to these last two elements, full disclosure and substantive sufficiency, while the Uniform Premarital Agreement Act states that the party attacking the agreement must show both unconscionability *and* lack of disclosure (or fraud/duress, see below), in some states only one of these elements need be met to find the agreement unenforceable.[28]

§ 8.02 The Uniform Premarital Agreement Act

The modern view that antenuptial agreements are generally enforceable has been codified in the Uniform Premarital Agreements Act (UPAA),[29] promulgated by the National Conference of Commissioners on Uniform State Laws (now the Uniform Law Commission) in 1983.[30] As of April 2011, 25 states and the District of Columbia

---

21. 551 P.2d 323 (Cal. 1976).
22. 516 P.2d 289 (Cal. 1973).
23. 212 Cal. Rptr. 803 (Ct. App. 1985).
24. *See* **chapter 9**.
25. *See* **chapter 10**.
26. *See* **chapter 11**.
27. *See* **chapter 12**.
28. *See* **§ 8.02** and note 39, *infra. See generally* Amberlynn Curry, Comment, *The Uniform Premarital Agreement Act and Its Variations Throughout the States*, 23 J. Am. Acad. Matrim. L. 355 (2010).
29. Unif. Premarital Agreements Act, 9B ULA (Master Edition) 369 (1987), *available at* http://www.nccusl.org/Act.aspx?title=Premarital%20Agreement%20Act.
For commentary on the UPAA, see Laura P. Graham, *The Uniform Premarital Agreement Act and Modern Social Policy: The Enforceability of Premarital Agreements Regulating the Ongoing Marriage*, 28 Wake Forest L. Rev. 1037 (1993); Barbara Ann Atwood, *Ten Years Later: Lingering Concerns About the Uniform Premarital Agreement Act*, 19 J. Legis. 127 (1993); Gail Frommer Brod, *Premarital Agreements and Gender Justice*, 6 Yale J.L. & Feminism 229 (1994).
30. The UPAA is effective upon its enactment, and will not be given retroactive effect. Hrudka v. Hrudka, 919 P.2d 179 (Ariz. Ct. App. 1995); Sogg v. Nev. State Bank, 832 P.2d 781 (Nev. 1992).

have approved and adopted the UPAA.[31] Moreover, many states have adopted laws that explicitly recognize and regulate the formation of antenuptial agreements much like the UPAA.[32]

Section 1 of the UPAA makes it explicit that the UPAA applies only to antenuptial agreements, and not to cohabitation, midnuptial, or separation agreements. The commissioners stated in the Prefatory Note that the UPAA was intentionally "limited in scope."[33] Nonetheless, in states that have adopted the UPAA, the courts have applied the principles of the UPAA to midnuptial agreements as well.[34]

Although the UPAA is to be "limited in scope," section 1 of the UPAA expands the definition of "property" to include income and earnings. By employing this broad definition, the commissioners wanted to avoid limiting the UPAA to traditional property rights and apply it to property as cases have defined it in divorce actions.[35]

In section 2, the UPAA dispenses with all formalities of execution[36] except a signed writing by the parties.[37] No consideration is necessary, except the marriage itself.[38] The California courts have consistently interpreted this provision as a statute

---

31. Arizona (1991), Ariz. Rev. Stat. §§ 25-201 *et seq.*; Arkansas (1987), Ark. Code Ann. §§ 9-11-401 *et seq.*; California (1986), Cal. Fam. Code §§ 1600 *et seq.*; Connecticut (1995), Conn. Gen. Stat. §§ 46b-36a *et seq.*; Delaware (1996), Del. Code Ann. tit. 13, §§ 321 *et seq.*; District of Columbia (1996), D.C. Code Ann. §§ 30-141 *et seq.*; Hawaii (1987), Haw. Rev. Stat. §§ 572D-1 *et seq.*; Idaho (1995), Idaho Code §§ 32-921 *et seq.*; Illinois (1990), 750 Ill. Comp. Stat. Ann. 10/1 *et seq.*; Indiana (1997), Ind. Code Ann. §§ 31-11-3 *et seq.*; Iowa (1992), Iowa Code Ann. §§ 596.1 *et seq.*; Kansas (1988), Kan. Stat. Ann. §§ 23-801 *et seq.*; Maine (1987), Me. Rev. Stat. Ann. tit. 19A, §§ 601 *et seq.*; Montana (1987), Mont. Code Ann. §§ 40-2-601 *et seq.*; Nebraska (1994), Neb. Rev. Stat. §§ 42-1001 *et seq.*; Nevada (1989), Nev. Rev. Stat. §§ 123A. 010 *et seq.*; New Jersey (1989), N.J. Stat. Ann. §§ 37:2-31 *et seq.*; New Mexico (1995), N.M. Stat. Ann. §§ 40-4A-1 *et seq.*; North Carolina (1987), N.C. Gen. Stat. §§ 52B-1 *et seq.*; North Dakota (1985), N.D. Cent. Code §§ 14-03.1-01 *et seq.*; Oregon (1988), Or. Rev. Stat. §§ 108.700 *et seq.*; Rhode Island (1987), R.I. Gen. Laws §§ 15-17-1; South Dakota (1989), S.D. Codified Laws §§ 25-2-16 *et seq.*; Texas (1997), Tex. Fam. Code Ann. §§ 4.001 *et seq.*; Utah (1994), Utah Code Ann. §§ 30-8-1 *et seq.*; Virginia (1985), Va. Code Ann. §§ 20-147 *et seq.* The UPAA was also introduced in West Virginia in 2011, HB 2290.

32. The Colorado Marital Agreement Act, Colo. Rev. Stat. Ann. § 14-2-3, also shows the influence of the UPAA. *See also* Tenn. Code Ann. § 36-3-501 (1991).

33. UPAA, Prefatory Note (1983).

34. *E.g.*, Epp v. Epp, 905 P.2d 54 (Haw. Ct. App. 1995); *In re* Marriage of Richardson, 606 N.E.2d 56 (Ill. Ct. App. 1992); Flansburg v. Flansburg, 581 N.E.2d 430 (Ind. Ct. App. 1991); *In re* Estate of Loughmiller, 629 P.2d 156 (Kan. 1981); Prevatte v. Prevatte, 411 S.E.2d 386 (N.C. Ct. App. 1991); *In re* Estate of Gab, 364 N.W.2d 924 (S.D. 1985); *In re* Estate of Beasley, 883 P.2d 1343 (Utah 1994).

35. *See* O'Brien v. O'Brien, 489 N.E.2d 712 (N.Y. 1985) (defining property to include increased earning capacity).

36. *See* § **9.04**.

37. Atassi v. Atassi, 451 S.E.2d 371 (N.C. Ct. App.), *review denied*, 456 S.E.2d 310 (N.C. 1995) (agreement must be signed by parties; wife could not authorize her father to sign for her).

38. The marriage itself is considered the utmost and highest of consideration. Barnhill v. Barnhill, 386 So. 2d 749 (Ala. Civ. App. 1980); Estate of Gillian v. Estate of Gillian, 406 N.E.2d 981 (Ind. Ct. App. 1980); Friedlander v. Friedlander, 494 P.2d 208 (Wash. 1972).

of frauds provision, holding that partial performance may render even an oral agreement enforceable.[39] The traditional defenses based on lack of capacity, however, are expressly preserved.[40]

Section 3 of the UPAA states that the parties are free to contract with any aspect of the rights that arise by operation of marriage, including property rights at divorce, death, or any other contingency,[41] and the modification or elimination of spousal support.[42] The parties are also free to choose the applicable law to govern the construction of the agreement.[43] By allowing the parties to waive spousal support as well as property rights, the UPAA resolved a split on this issue, and clearly favors enforcement of the waiver of all rights.[44] The only limitation is that the parties may not waive child support.[45]

Although the parties may contract to any rights that arise by operation of marriage, section 3 makes it clear that the parties may not contract as to a matter that is "in violation of public policy."[46] What is in violation of public policy is a matter of some debate. The official comment states that the parties are permitted to agree as to choice of abode, the freedom to pursue career opportunities, and the upbringing of children.[47] Nonetheless, in one case, a court held that the parties were not permitted to agree that the wife's sons from a previous marriage could not live with the couple,[48] and several cases have held that the parties are not permitted to agree by prenuptial agreement in what religion to raise the children in the event of a divorce.[49]

Section 4 states that the agreement becomes effective upon marriage,[50] and section 8 states that the marriage tolls the running of the statute of limitations.[51]

---

39. Hall v. Hall, 271 Cal. Rptr. 773 (Ct. App. 1990).

40. UPAA § 2 cmt.

41. UPAA § 3(a)(1–8).

42. UPAA § 3(a)(4).

43. UPAA § 3(a)(7). *See* Julia Halloran McLaughlin, *Premarital Agreements and Choice of Law: "One, Two, Three, Baby, You and Me,"* 72 Mo. L. Rev. 793 (2007).

44. UPAA § 3 cmt. *See, e.g.*, Barnhill v. Barnhill, 386 So. 2d 749 (Ala. Civ. App. 1980); Newman v. Newman, 653 P.2d 728 (Colo. 1982); Parniawski v. Parniawski, 359 A.2d 719 (Conn. Supp. 1976); Gross v. Gross, 464 N.E.2d 500 (Ohio 1984); Hudson v. Hudson, 350 P.2d 596 (Okla. 1960); Unander v. Unander, 506 P.2d 719 (Or. 1973).

45. UPAA § 3(b).

46. UPAA § 3(a)(8).

47. *See* Graham, *supra* note 29.

48. Mengal v. Mengal, 103 N.Y.S. 2d 992 (N.Y. Fam. Ct. 1951).

49. Ramon v. Ramon, 34 N.Y.S. 100 (N.Y. Fam. Ct. 1942); Avitzur v. Avitzur, 459 N.Y.S. 2d 572 (N.Y. Fam. Ct. 1983).

50. UPAA § 4.

51. UPAA § 8. *See In re* Crawford, 730 P.2d 675 (Wash. 1986). *Contra* Freiman v. Freiman, 680 N.Y.S. 2d 797 (N.Y. Sup. Ct. 1998) (six-year statute of limitations for fraud applied, because wife could have discovered fraud during marriage).

Section 6 is "the key operative section of the Act."[52] The party seeking to avoid enforcement of the agreement carries the burden of proof[53] to show that the agreement either (1) was reached involuntarily, that is, was the result of fraud, duress, or undue influence,[54] or (2) was unconscionable when executed *and* resulted from lack of disclosure.[55] The "unconscionability" test is drawn from section 306 of the Uniform Marriage and Divorce Act. By this provision, the UPAA clearly favors enforceability: An agreement is enforceable even if it was unconscionable when executed, so long as the moving party received a fair and reasonable disclosure or waived disclosure or reasonably could have had an adequate knowledge of the relevant information.[56] Indeed, in at least one state, the stakes were raised even higher: The attacking party must show the agreement was the result of involuntariness *and* lack of disclosure *and* was unconscionable.[57] On the other hand, in many states that have not adopted the UPAA, and in case law of states prior to their adoption of the UPAA, the agreement must be both substantively sufficient *and* be the result of adequate disclosure.[58] The only exception is to spousal support: If the agreement leaves one spouse eligible for public assistance, then the court may require the other spouse to provide support sufficient to avoid eligibility.[59]

Section 6 of the UPAA has been strongly criticized for adopting the standard that in order for the agreement to be unenforceable, it must be both unconscionable *and* there must have been nondisclosure by one of the parties.[60]

---

52. UPAA, Prefatory Note.

53. UPAA § 6(a). *See* Chiles v. Chiles, 779 S.W.2d 127 (Tex. Ct. App. 1989).

54. UPAA § 6(a)(1).

55. UPAA § 6(A)(2).

56. For cases holding that antenuptial agreement is valid if either the party has knowledge of other party's assets *or* the agreement is not unconscionable, see Barnhill v. Barnhill, 386 So. 2d 749 (Ala. Civ. App. 1980), *cert. denied*, 386 So. 2d 752 (1980); Del Vecchio v. Del Vecchio, 143 So. 2d 17 (Fla. 1962); Magoon v. Magoon, 780 P.2d 80 (Haw. 1989); Hunsberger v. Hunsberger, 653 N.E.2d 118 (Ind. Ct. App. 1995); Taylor v. Taylor, 832 P.2d 429 (Okla. Ct. App. 1991); Penhallow v. Penhallow, 649 A.2d 1016 (R.I. 1994); Schutterle v. Schutterle, 260 N.W.2d 341 (S.D. 1997); Batleman v. Rubin, 98 S.E.2d 519 (Va. 1957); *In re* Matson, 703 P.2d 668 (1986).

In Pennsylvania, the courts favor enforceability to the highest degree. An antenuptial agreement is enforceable regardless of its provisions, so long as there was accurate disclosure. Simeone v. Simeone, 581 A.2d 162 (Pa. 1990). The rule was stated in verse in Busch v. Busch, 732 A.2d 1274 (Pa. Super. 1999).

57. Penhallow v. Penhallow, 649 A.2d 1016 (R.I. 1994).

58. Lee v. Lee, 816 S.W.2d 625 (Ark. 1991); Burtoff v. Burtoff, 418 A.2d 1085 (D.C. 1980); Scherer v. Scherer, 292 S.E.2d 662 (Ga. 1982); *In re* Marriage of Van Broklin, 468 N.W.2d 40 (Iowa Ct. App. 1991); Edwardson v. Edwardson, 798 S.W.2d 941 (Ky. 1990); Rinvelt v. Rinvelt, 475 N.W.2d 478 (1991); DeLorean v. DeLorean, 511 A.2d 1257 (N.J. Ch. Div. 1986); Howell v. Landry, 386 S.E.2d 610 (N.C. Ct. App. 1989); Gross v. Gross, 464 N.E.2d 500 (Ohio 1984); Button v. Button, 388 N.W.2d 546 (1986).

59. UPAA § 6(b).

60. *See* Atwood, *supra* note 29, at 146.

In section 7, the UPAA provides that the court may enforce the antenuptial agreement even if the marriage is void if the marriage was of significant duration.[61]

An extremely interesting case interpreting the provisions of the UPAA is the California case of *In re Marriage of Bonds*.[62] In this case, Barry Bonds and his wife Sun met in Montreal in August 1987. In November 1987, Sun moved to Phoenix to live with Barry. Shortly thereafter, Barry proposed and the couple set their wedding date for February 7, 1988. In December 1987, Barry made it clear to Sun that they would have to sign an antenuptial agreement. Sun agreed.

The couple had airline reservations for February 5, 1988, to fly to Las Vegas to be married on February 6. On the morning of February 5, just prior to their scheduled departure, Barry and Sun met in Barry's attorney's office. Barry's attorneys presented Barry and Sun the agreement they had prepared. Neither had seen the agreement before. Barry's attorneys told Sun she may want to consult independent counsel. According to Barry, Sun declined consulting independent counsel, stating she didn't want or need a lawyer, since she had no assets.

The agreement referred to a schedule of the parties' property and assets, but there was no such schedule attached. The agreement also contained a provision regarding child support that was clearly unenforceable. The agreement further contained a provision whereby both parties waived community property. Perhaps most interesting, the antenuptial agreement contained a choice of law clause that read, "This Agreement shall be subject to and governed by the laws of the state set forth as the effective place of this Agreement." The "effective place" was never defined.

Barry's attorneys read the agreement aloud line by line to Sun, and explained each provision. Sun's first language is Swedish, but she indicated she understood the agreement.

At trial, the court determined that since the agreement was executed in Arizona, then Arizona law should apply: that was the place the agreement became effective. The court also held that under Arizona law, the agreement was valid.

The California Court of Appeals reversed. The court first held that California law applied because the "key" to the UPAA was section 5, the enforcement section. Since the agreement was to be enforced in California, that law had to apply as to the circumstances surrounding the execution of the agreement as well.

The court next held that the agreement was not enforceable, because Sun did not have the opportunity to consult independent legal counsel. Sun's lack of legal counsel triggered "strict scrutiny" of the agreement and an examination of the "totality of the circumstances" surrounding the execution of the agreement.

What makes this opinion so interesting is that the choice of law portion of the opinion completely misapplies the *Restatement*'s principle concerning choice of law and that the court completely abandons the UPAA's test of enforceability under section 5 in favor of a "totality of the circumstances" test when there is lack of independent counsel.

---

61. UPAA § 7.
62. 83 Cal. Rptr. 2d 783 (Cal. Ct. App. 1999).

In 2010, the Uniform Law Commission began the task of revising the UPAA. The main purpose of the project is to create consistent standards as to waivers of rights on divorce and waivers of rights on the other spouse's death. The revised UPAA will also make the act applicable to both premarital and postmarital agreements.

The Commission has agreed to get rid of the pro-enforcement standard of the UPAA that requires both unconscionability and a failure to disclose. There is an alternative section for states that wish to adopt a standard of fairness at the time of enforcement.

§ 8.03 Trends in the Use of Antenuptial Agreements

As noted in § **8.01**, an antenuptial agreement is a legal contract by which parties entering into marriage attempt to settle the interests of each party in the property of the other during the course of the marriage and upon its termination by death or other means.[63] While such agreements were once disdained, courts have now come to favor them: "There is a strong public policy favoring individuals ordering and deciding their own interests through contractual arrangements including prenuptial agreements."[64]

There is much evidence that antenuptial agreements are favored not only by courts but by persons entering into a marriage as well. In 1996, 5 percent of all couples marrying entered into antenuptial agreements, compared to 1 percent 20 years ago.[65] One commentator in 1994 put the use of antenuptial agreements at 20 percent in second marriages.[66] At least two commentators have estimated that their use tripled between 1978 and 1988.[67]

The increase in the incidence of antenuptial agreements may be due primarily to two factors. The first is the increasing rate of divorce and remarriage. Currently, over 40 percent of marriages involve a second or higher-order marriage for one or both parties, and an estimated 60 percent of those marriages will end in divorce.[68] Older

---

63. *E.g.*, Irvine v. Irvine, 685 N.E.2d 67 (Ind. Ct. App. 1997).

64. Estate of Gillilan v. Estate of Gillilan, 406 N.E.2d 981 (Ind. Ct. App. 1980); *See also In re Marriage of Greiff*, 680 N.Y.S. 2d 894 (App. Div. 1998); Perkinson v. Perkinson, 802 S.W.2d 600 (Tenn. 1990). For an excellent discussion of how societal attitudes toward marriage have influenced attitudes toward antenuptial agreements, see Brian Bix, *Bargaining in the Shadow of Love*, 40 WM. & MARY L. REV. 145 (1998–99).

65. Gary Belsky, *Living by the Rules*, MONEY, May 1996, at 100. David E. Rovella, writing in *New York Law Journal*, Sept. 2, 1999, stated that while there are no statistics for the number of couples that sign antenuptial agreements, "family lawyers agree that there has been a surge in their use by new couples."

66. Amy Sigler, Comment, *Elgar v. Probate Appeal: The Probate Court's Implied Powers to Construe and Enforce Prenuptial Agreements*, 9 CONN. PROB. L.J. 145, 145 (1994).

67. BEVERLY PEKALA, DON'T SETTLE FOR LESS: A WOMAN'S GUIDE TO GETTING A FAIR DIVORCE AND CUSTODY SETTLEMENT 8 (1994); Pam Slater, *Prelude to Partnership*, SACRAMENTO BEE, June 13, 1996, at C1.

68. U.S. DEP'T OF COMMERCE, MARRIAGE, DIVORCE, AND REMARRIAGE IN THE 1990s 5 (1992).

couples tend to plan more carefully and realistically for their futures,[69] and they tend to want to protect their assets for their children.[70]

The second reason is the general rise in personal wealth for the upper and middle-class. Young professionals who have stock options, 401(k)s, and other assets in the booming economy and technology market are attuned to protecting those assets through planning.[71]

It is this rise in the use of antenuptial agreements that makes it imperative for a family law attorney to know how to attack, defend, and construe antenuptial agreements.

§ 8.04 Antenuptial Contracts as Contracts

§ 8.041 *Formation of the Contract: Marriage as Consideration*

Antenuptial contracts are, first and foremost, contracts. Thus, the rules of contract formation apply to antenuptial contracts: There must be offer and acceptance, and there must be consideration.[72]

---

69. Mark Hansen, *Split-Up Insurance*, 85 A.B.A. J. 30 (Nov. 1999); David E. Rovella, *Pre-Nups No Longer Just for the Wealthy*, NAT'L L.J., Sept. 6, 1999, at A1; Albert B. Crenshaw, *To Love, Honor and Protect Your Assets: Older Couples Embrace Prenuptial Agreements*, WASH. POST, Apr. 27, 1993, at 12–13 (Health Section); Mary Sue Donohue, *Seventy and Getting Married? You Might Need a Prenup*, HEALTHNEWSDIGEST.COM, Mar. 31, 2011, http://healthnewsdigest.com/news/ Seniors_320/Seventy_and_Getting_Married_You_Might_Need_a_Prenup.shtml.

70. Wilson v. Moore, 929 S.W.2d 367 (Tenn. Ct. App. 1996) (antenuptial agreements enhance the opportunities for middle-aged persons to remarry by protecting their separate assets for the children of previous marriages); Pajak v. Pajak, 385 S.E.2d 384, 388 (W. Va. 1989). *See* IRA MARK ELLMAN ET AL., FAMILY LAW 801 (3d ed. 1998) (listing financial protection of children from a prior marriage as the usual explanation for premarital agreements); Sarah Ann Smith, *The Unique Agreements: Premarital and Marital Agreements, Their Impact Upon Estate Planning and Proposed Solutions to Problems Arising on Death*, 28 IDAHO L. REV. 833 (1991); Stephen W. Schlissel & Jennifer Rosenkrantz, *Prenuptial Agreements for the Golden Years*, FAM. ADVOC., Winter 2002, at 28.

Press accounts of high-profile divorces may also contribute to the increased popularity of antenuptial agreements. *See* Maura Dolan, *State High Court Rulings Bolster Prenuptial Pacts*, L.A. TIMES, Aug. 22, 2000, at A1 (discussing the California Supreme Court's upholding of an agreement between San Francisco Giants baseball player Barry Bonds and his ex-wife); William C. Symonds, *Divorce, Executive Style*, BUS. WK., Aug. 3, 1998, at 56 (discussing the growing size of judicial awards to ex-wives of corporate chief executives in the absence of antenuptial agreements).

71. Richard Bartke, *Marital Sharing—Why Not Do It By Contract?* 67 GEO. L.J. 1131, 1147–51 (1979) (discussing use of premarital agreements by the wealthy and the sophisticated); Marjorie Schultz, *Contractual Ordering of Marriage: A New Model for State Policy*, 70 U. CAL. L. REV. 270, 285 (antenuptial agreements used by wealthy); Jill Smolowe, *What Price Love? Read Carefully*, TIME, Oct. 15, 1990, at 94–95 (claiming that premarital agreements are "increasingly in vogue among the middle and upwardly mobile classes").

72. UNIF. PREMARITAL AGREEMENT ACT (UPAA) § 2.

Consideration should not be confused with the adequacy of the provisions of the agreement. The marriage itself is the consideration. Indeed, some cases have held that marriage is the "highest" consideration.[73]

Because the marriage itself is consideration, if the marriage does not take place, the agreement is of no force and effect.[74] There is some disagreement, however, as to whether the agreement governs in the event the marriage is annulled.[75]

§ 8.042 Capacity to Contract

Just as parties to an ordinary contract must have capacity to contract, the parties to an antenuptial agreement must have the capacity to contract. The UPAA makes this clear in its comment to section 2. Thus, if a party does not have the requisite capacity, the contract may be set aside on those grounds.[76]

---

73. Magniac v. Thomson, 32 U.S. 348, 1833 WL 4198, at *1 (1833) ("Marriage, in contemplation of the law, is not only a valuable consideration to support such a settlement, but is a consideration of the highest value, and from motives of the soundest policy, is upheld with a strong resolution[.]"); Robinson v. Robinson, 64 So. 3d 1067, 2010 WL 5030120 (Ala. Civ. App. 2010); Akileh v. Elchahal, 666 So. 2d 246, 248 (Fla. Dist. Ct. App. 1996); Prell v. Silverstein, 162 P.3d 2 (Haw. Ct. App. 2007); In re Estate of Parker, 525 N.E.2d 1149 (Ill. Ct. App. 1988); Eule v. Eule, 320 N.E.2d 506 (Ill. Ct. App. 1974); Estate of Gillilan v. Estate of Gillilan, 406 N.E.2d 981 (Ind. Ct. App. 1980); In re Estate of Martin, 938 A.2d 812 (Me. 2008); Watson v. Watson, 497 A.2d 794 (Md. 1984); Rudrick v. Thull, 177 N.E. 513 (Ohio Ct. App. 1931); Bratton v. Bratton, 136 S.W. 3d 595 (Tenn. 2004); Friedlander v. Friedlander, 494 P.2d 208 (Wash. 1972).

A closely related concept is that mutual promises and waivers, no matter how one-sided, are also sufficient consideration. Brown v. Brown, 26 So. 3d 1210 (Ala. Civ. App. 2007); Pulley v. Short, 261 S.W. 3d 701 (Mo. Ct. App. W.D. 2008); In re Estate of Reinsmidt, 897 S.W.2d 73 (Mo. Ct. App. E.D. 1995); Lebeck v. Lebeck, 881 P.2d 727 (N.M. Ct. App. 1994); Colello v. Colello, 780 N.Y.S.2d 450 (N.Y. App. Div. 4 Dep't 2004); In re Estate of Hartman, 582 A.2d 648 (Pa. Super. 1990).

74. UPAA § 4; Reitmeier v. Kalinoski, 631 F. Supp. 565 (D.N.J. 1986); Hurt v. Hurt, 433 S.E.2d 493 (Va. Ct. App. 1993).

75. See Lang v. Reetz-Lang, 488 N.E.2d 929 (Ohio Ct. App. 1985) (where parties to marriage entered into antenuptial agreement transferring husband's sole ownership of his home to tenancy by entireties in husband and wife, and marriage was subsequently annulled for nonconsummation due to fault on part of wife, there was no consideration for marriage or for transfer of property, and agreement was unenforceable). Compare In re Lieberman, 167 N.Y.S. 2d 158 (N.Y. App. Div. 1957), and In re Saffer's Estate, 241 N.Y.S. 2d 681 (Surr. Ct. 1963), aff'd without opinion, 248 N.Y.S. 2d 279 (N.Y. App. Div. 1964), with In re Estate of Simms, 296 N.Y.S. 2d 222 (N.Y. App. Div. 1968).

76. Dexter v. Hall, 82 U.S. 9 (1873) ("The fundamental idea of a contract is that it requires the assent of two minds. But a lunatic or a person non compos mentis has nothing which the law recognizes as a mind, and it would seem, therefore, upon principle, that he cannot make a contract which may have any efficacy as such."). See, e.g., Nanini v. Nanini, 802 P.2d 438 (Ariz. Ct. App. 1990); Estate of Roberts, 388 So. 2d 216 (Fla. 1980); In re Estate of Cobb, 91 P.3d 1254 (Kan. App. 2004); Jackson v. Jackson, 626 S.W.2d 630 (Ky. 1981); Wilkes v. Estate of Wilkes, 305 Mont. 335, 27 P.3d 433 (2001); In re Will of Goldberg, 153 Misc. 2d 560, 582 N.Y.S.2d 617 (Surr. Ct. 1992); Adams v. Adams, 414 Pa. Super. 634, 607 A.2d 1116 (1992); Sanders v. Sanders, 2010 WL 4056196 (Tex. App.—Ft. Worth, Oct. 14, 2010) (wife did not have mental capacity to enter contract, and thus, common law defense of lack of capacity would be sustained).

§ 8.043 Oral Agreements and the Statute of Frauds

While the UPAA requires antenuptial agreement to be in writing,[77] at common law, oral antenuptial agreements are enforceable[78] if they are not in conflict with the applicable statute of frauds.[79] Most states now require the agreement to be in writing.[80]

Part performance will take an agreement out of the statute of frauds.[81] Marriage alone, however, is not considered part performance.[82]

§ 8.044 The Written Agreement

Just like other contracts, more than one writing may constitute the antenuptial contract.[83] Further, a writing subsequent to the marriage but referencing an oral premarital agreement will constitute a sufficient memorandum to satisfy the writing requirement.[84]

§ 8.045 Formalities of Execution

As noted in **§ 8.02**, the UPAA does not require any formalities of execution. Most states have also held that the failure to adhere to the formal requirements of execution will not render the agreement unenforceable.[85]

---

77. Even though the UPAA requires agreements to be in writing, California has held that this requirement is in the nature of a statute of frauds provision, and an oral agreement that has been partly performed is enforceable. Hall v. Hall, 271 Cal. Rptr. 773 (Ct. App. 1990).

78. *E.g.*, *In re* Estate of Cummins, 280 P.2d 128 (Cal. Ct. App. 1955); Lee v. Cent. Nat'l Bank & Trust Co., 308 N.E.2d 605 (Ill. 1974); Marcoux v. Marcoux, 507 N.Y.S. 2d 458 (N.Y. App. Div. 1986). *See generally* Annotation, *Admissibility of Evidence to Establish Oral Antenuptial Agreement*, 81 A.L.R.3D 453 (1977). *But see* Daniels v. Daniels, 663 N.Y.S.2d 141 (N.Y. App. Div. 1997) (oral antenuptial agreements not enforceable).

79. *E.g.*, CAL. CIV. CODE § 5311; COLO. REV. STAT. § 14-2-303; N.D. CENT. CODE § 14-03.1-02; VA. CODE ANN. § 20-149.

80. *E.g.*, *In re* Marriage of Jelinek, 613 N.E.2d 1284 (Ill. App. Ct. 1993) (there can be no oral premarital agreement under the statute of frauds).

81. *E.g.*, Marriage of Lemoine-Hofmann, 827 P.2d 587 (Colo. App. 1992) (each promised to finance the other's education, and one party already had).

82. *E.g.*, O'Shea v. O'Shea, 221 So. 2d 223 (Fla. Dist. Ct. App. 1969); Rossiter v. Rossiter, 666 P.2d 617 (Haw. Ct. App. 1983).

83. Rupert v. Rupert, 637 N.Y.S. 2d 537 (N.Y. App. Div. 1997) (two documents written after execution of first agreement, prior to marriage, and that referred to original agreement, constituted agreement along with original agreement).

84. Ayoob v. Ayoob, 168 P.2d 462 (Cal. Ct. App. 1946); *In re* Estate of Weber, 167 N.E.2d 98 (Ohio 1960); Papaioannou v. Britz, 139 N.Y.S.2d 658 (N.Y. App. Div. 1955). *But see* McMinimee v. McMinimee, 30 N.W.2d 106 (Iowa 1947); Smith v. Farrington, 29 A.2d 163 (Me. 1942); Peterson v. Peterson, 226 N.W. 641 (S.D. 1929).

85. *E.g.*, Tyre v. Lewis, 276 A.2d 747 (Del. Ch. 1971) (widow could not repudiate antenuptial agreement on grounds that one of two witnesses failed to subscribe name as witness); Succession of Haydel, 529 So. 2d 856 (La. Ct. App. 1988) (widow would not repudiate antenuptial agreement on ground that one witness to agreement was not present when decedent signed); Pollack-Halvarson v. McGuire, 576 N.W.2d 451 (Minn. Ct. App. 1998) (agreement not invalid in light of fact that one who signed as notary was not commissioned, when she held herself out as notary and affixed notarial seal).

Some states, however, are quite specific in their requirements, such as notarization, witnessing, acknowledgment, recording, or execution a certain number of days before marriage,[86] and the failure to adhere to the formalities of execution can render the agreement unenforceable.[87]

---

86. *E.g.*, Cal. Civ. Code § 5202; Del. Code Ann. tit. 13, §§ 301, 302; Idaho Code §§ 32-917, 32-918; La. Civ. Code Ann. art. 2331; Mass. Ann. Laws ch. 209, § 26; Minn. Stat. § 519.11; Mo. Ann. Stat. §§ 451.220, 451.230; Mont. Code Ann. § 40-2-312; N.M. Stat. Ann. § 40-2-4; N.Y. Dom. Rel. Law § 236(B)(3); S.C. Code Ann. § 20-5-50.

87. Smith v. Smith, 694 N.Y.S.2d 194 (N.Y. App. Div. 1999) (statutory requirement that agreement be duly acknowledged with will strictly construed). *Cf.* Arzin v. Covello, 669 N.Y.S.2d 189 (N.Y. Sup. Ct. 1998) (unacknowledged agreement is enforceable if the parties subsequently acknowledge the agreement in compliance with statutory requirements). *See generally* Annotation, *Noncompliance with Statutory Requirements Concerning Form of Execution or Acknowledgment as Affecting Validity or Enforceability of Written Antenuptial Agreement*, 16 A.L.R.3d 370 (1967).

Public Policy 9

§ 9.01 Encouraging Divorce, Denying Divorce

As noted in § **8.01**, the traditional view was that antenuptial agreements could control property division upon death, but any attempt to specify the consequences of divorce was void as against public policy. There has been considerable movement away from this view since the leading case of *Posner v. Posner*.[1] Every recent decision to consider the question has held that antenuptial agreements are not invalid merely because they attempt to specify the consequences of divorce.[2] Indeed, as noted in the previous chapter, many states consider antenuptial agreements as a means of encouraging stable marriages.[3]

Nonetheless, certain antenuptial agreements may be void as against public policy. One reason an antenuptial agreement may violate public policy is by encouraging divorce.[4] The most obvious example of this is

---

1. 233 So. 2d 381 (Fla. 1970).

2. *E.g.*, Brooks v. Brooks, 733 P.2d 1044 (Alaska 1987); Newman v. Newman, 653 P.2d 728 (Colo. 1982); Burtoff v. Burtoff, 418 A.2d 1085 (D.C. 1980); Scherer v. Scherer, 292 S.E.2d 662 (Ga. 1982); *In re* Bowen, 475 N.E.2d 690 (Ind. 1985); *In re* Adams, 729 P.2d 1151 (Kan. 1986); Edwardson v. Edwardson, 798 S.W.2d 941 (Ky. 1990); Frey v. Frey, 471 A.2d 705 (Md. 1984); Rinvelt v. Rinvelt, 475 N.W.2d 478 (Mich. Ct. App. 1991); Gross v. Gross, 464 N.E.2d 500 (Ohio 1984); Gant v. Gant, 329 S.E.2d 106 (W. Va. 1985).

3. Irvine v. Irvine, 685 N.E.2d 67 (Ind. Ct. App. 1997) (antenuptial agreements are favored by the law as promoting domestic happiness and adjusting property questions that otherwise would often be a source of fruitful litigation); Brody v. Brody, 862 N.Y.S.2d 738 (N.Y. Sup. Ct. 2008). *See* § **8.01**.

4. "A promise that tends unreasonably to encourage divorce or separation is unenforceable on grounds of public policy." RESTATEMENT (SECOND) OF CONTRACTS § 190(2) (1981).

where the contract requires one party to pay the other party money or property upon divorce that is unreasonably large and not contingent upon future circumstances. The effect of such an agreement, the courts have held, is to encourage divorce.[5] On the other hand, there is no prohibition against the parties agreeing that one spouse would be entitled to a larger share of the marital estate in the event of marital misconduct by one of the parties.[6]

Escalator clauses and sunset provisions have come under attack as promotive of divorce. Under an escalator clause, the longer the parties are married, the greater the monetary settlement awarded to the disadvantaged spouse. Such a clause might encourage a party to act decisively in favor of divorce before the escalator clause kicked in.[7] At least one court has so held.[8] Similarly, under a sunset provision, the terms of the antenuptial agreement expire after the parties have been married for a certain number of years. Again, this might cause a party to act in favor of divorce before the sunset provision kicked in. Although there is no case law directly on point concerning sunset provisions, it is certainly possible to argue that if a party filed for divorce before a sunset provision became effective, the agreement acted as an incentive for divorce.

---

5. *In re* Dajani, 251 Cal. Rptr. 871 (Cal. App. 1988) (contract requiring monetary payment to wife upon death or divorce was void, where payment was oversized in comparison to marital estate); *In re* Noghrey, 215 Cal. Rptr. 153 (Cal. App. 1985) (contract to give wife certain specific assets upon divorce was invalid where assets were large in comparison to marital estate); Gartrell v. Gartrell, 908 N.E.2d 1019 (Ohio App. 2009) (antenuptial agreement that entitled wife to half of the marital residence was void as against public policy; agreement promoted or encouraged divorce or profiteering by divorce by entitling wife to a significant monetary sum for a marriage of very short duration); Neilson v. Neilson, 780 P.2d 1264 (Utah Ct. App. 1989) (promise in a prenuptial agreement that if parties were divorced in action initiated by husband, wife was entitled to one half of husband's stock ownership, was unenforceable on public policy grounds because it unreasonably tended to encourage divorce by providing wife with profit incentive to induce husband to seek dissolution); Dexter v. Dexter, 371 S.E.2d 816 (Va. Ct. App. 1988) (clause requiring husband to pay wife $1,000 per month beginning on date of separation, and payments large in comparison to marital estate; court stated in dicta that clause was unenforceable). *See also* Coggins v. Coggins, 601 So. 2d 109 (Ala. Civ. App. 1992) (antenuptial agreement cannot act to penalize divorce by granting one party disproportionate share of marital estate on divorce).

California appears to be pulling away from *Dajani* and *Noghrey*. *See In re* Marriage of Bellio, 129 Cal. Rptr. 2d 556 (Cal. Ct. App. 4th Dist. 2003) (prenuptial agreement between wife and multimillionaire husband containing $100,000 payment provision upon dissolution did not threaten the marriage relationship, but made it economically feasible for wife to enter into the marriage, where wife's monthly spousal support of $933 from a previous marriage terminated upon her remarriage, and at time of remarriage, her net worth was $60,000, and she earned $12 per hour).

6. Stradther v. Stradther, 526 So. 2d 598 (Ala. Civ. App. 1988) (contract awarded wife certain specific assets in the event husband drank excessively or committed acts of cruelty during the marriage; husband had a previous history of marital misconduct); MacFarlane v. Rich, 567 A.2d 585 (N.H. 1989) (parties agreed that their entire antenuptial agreement would be invalid if husband left wife for another woman).

7. This was precisely the situation in the case of Donald Trump and Marla Maples.

8. Davis v. Davis, 1996 WL 456335 (Conn. Super. Ct. July 29, 1996) (finding agreement unenforceable as it gave husband incentive to divorce because his wife would receive $25,000 for each year the couple lived together).

Closely related to the principle that an antenuptial contract cannot promote divorce is the principle that an antenuptial contract cannot preclude a party from seeking a divorce if grounds for divorce exist. At least one case has held that an agreement restricting the right to sue for divorce violated public policy.[9] On the other hand, in a New Jersey case,[10] the parties agreed that the wife would not seek termination of the marriage for any reason other than 18 months' continuous separation. After the husband vacated the marital home, the wife filed for divorce on the grounds of extreme cruelty. The court enforced the agreement by dismissing the wife's complaint for divorce upon a motion to dismiss by the husband.

The New Jersey case can be reconciled with other case law, whereby the courts have upheld agreements that only a religious court can authorize the divorce for religious reasons.[11]

§ 9.02 The Religious Antenuptial Agreement

Sometimes the parties will enter into a religious antenuptial agreement, either in the United States or in another country, and then seek to enforce that agreement in the United States.[12] There is generally no prohibition against enforcing such an agreement so long as the agreement does not offend the public policy of the forum state.[13]

---

9. Towles v. Towles, 182 S.E.2d 53 (S.C. 1971) (agreement cannot restrict right granted by the state).

10. Massar v. Massar, 652 A.2d 219 (N.J. Super. App. Div. 1995).

11. Avitzur v. Avitzur, 446 N.E.2d 136 (N.Y. 1983) (upholding agreement of Jewish couple to recognize authority of beth din regarding divorce). See § **9.02**.

12. *See also In re* Marriage of Goldman, 554 N.E.2d 1016 (Ill. App. Ct. 1st at Dist. 1990) (ketubah signed by parties to Orthodox Jewish marriage ceremony was intended to be contract rather than poetry or art in connection with ceremony; although parties did not consult attorney prior to signing ketubah, husband and wife went to Jewish bookstore and specifically requested Orthodox Jewish ketubah and it was wife's understanding from talking to husband and reading certain materials supplied by husband that signing the ketubah meant that the status and validity of the marriage would be governed by Orthodox Jewish law); Minkin v. Minkin, 434 A.2d 665 (N.J. Super. Ct. Ch. Div. 1981) (enforcement of ketubah does not violate public policy); Hurwitz v. Hurwitz, 215 N.Y.S. 184 (N.Y. App. Div. 2d Dep't 1926) (antenuptial agreement providing that on husband's death wife shall be entitled to possession of their residence during her widowhood and that rights and privileges granted by Jewish laws may be enforced by wife so far as such laws are not contrary to forum's law). *Cf. In re* Marriage of Victor, 866 P.2d 899 (Ariz. Ct. App. 1993) (ketubah is not a premarital agreement and cannot form the basis for ordering the husband to provide the wife with a *get* (Jewish divorce decree)).

13. *Compare* Aghili v. Saadatnejaki, 958 S.W.2d 784 (Tenn. Ct. App. 1997) (an Islamic antenuptial agreement is a postponed dowry that protects the woman in event of divorce and is enforceable, as it does not offend public policy), *with* Chaudhary v. Ali, No. 0956-94-4 (Va. Ct. App. Jan. 31, 1995) (unreported) (holding that the *nikah nama* signed by the parties prior to their marriage in Pakistan was unenforceable under the law of Virginia as delineated in *Batelman v. Rubin*, 199 Va. 156, 98 S.E.2d 519 (1957)). *See generally* Michelle Greenberg-Kobrin, *Civil Enforceability of Religious Prenuptial Agreements*, 32 COLUM. J.L. & SOC. PROBS. 359 (1999).

For example, in *Chaudry v. Chaudry*,[14] the parties were married in 1958 in Pakistan. At the time of the marriage, the parties entered into a marriage contract, referred to by the court as a *nakahname*. The court stated:

> It is clear from the proofs that the antenuptial agreement provided that the wife, at any time during of after the marriage, on demand could obtain from her husband 15,000 rupees, about $1,500. Although such agreement could have provided that she have additional rights in her husband's property, this one contained no such provision. Under Pakistan law she was not entitled to alimony or support upon a divorce.[15]

The court concluded:

> Additionally, we have concluded that the wife is not entitled to equitable distribution by reason of the antenuptial agreement, which was negotiated on her behalf by her parents. It could have lawfully provided for giving her an interest in her husband's property, but it contained no such provision. It limited her rights to some $1,500 or 15,000 rupees. There is no proof that the agreement was not fair and reasonable at the time it was made. . . .
>
> We see no reason of public policy that would justify refusing to interpret and enforce the agreement in accordance with the law of Pakistan, where it was freely negotiated and the marriage took place.[16]

In *Aziz v. Aziz*,[17] the parties entered into a *mahr*, an Islamic antenuptial agreement, that required the payment of $5,032, with $32 advanced and $5,000 deferred until divorce. The New York court held that the contract conformed to New York's contract requirements and "its secular terms are enforceable as a contractual obligation, notwithstanding that it was entered into as part of a religious ceremony."[18]

---

14. 159 N.J. Super. 566, 388 A.2d 1000 (App. Div. 1978).

15. 388 A.2d at 1004.

16. *Id.* at 1006.

17. 127 Misc. 2d 1013, 488 N.Y.S.2d 123 (Sup. Ct. 1985).

18. 488 N.Y.S.2d at 124. *Accord* Akileh v. Elchahal, 666 So. 2d 246 (Fla. 2d Dist. Ct. App. 1996); Odatalla v. Odatalla, 810 A.2d 93 (N.J. Super. Ch. Div. 2002) (wife was entitled to $10,000 dower in dissolution proceeding as balance of mahr agreement, which was contained within Islamic marriage license at time of marriage ceremony; even though husband argued agreement was too vague to comply with contract law since term "postponed," which referred to balance of funds due under agreement, did not sufficiently define when $10,000 dower was due to his wife, wife offered testimonial evidence that "postponed" portion of agreement was similar to promissory demand note, and thus was payable when she demanded, and all of essential elements of contract were present); *In re* Marriage of Obaidi & Qayoum, 226 P.3d 787 (Wash. Ct. App. 3d Div. 2010) (wife was entitled to the $20,000 mahr, which was a prenuptial agreement based on Islamic law that provided an immediate and long-term dowry to the wife). *Cf.* Zawahiri v. Alwattar, 2008 WL 2698679 (Ohio Ct. App. 10th Dist. 2008) (husband's agreement to provision of parties' Islamic marriage contract, requiring him to pay wife a mahr, or dowry, of $25,000 if parties divorced, was a result of overreaching or coercion, and thus provision was not an enforceable prenuptial agreement; provision was not discussed until two hours before wedding ceremony was scheduled to begin, husband agreed to provision because he was embarrassed, and husband had no opportunity to consult with

Chaudry and *Aziz* should be contrasted with *In re Marriage of Dajani*.[19] In that case, the parties were married in Jordan in 1982. The marriage contract called for a dowry of 3,000 Jordanian dinars, plus an additional 2,000 dinars in cash or household furniture, in the event the marriage was dissolved by divorce or death. The court held that the marriage contract was void because it encouraged divorce: The wife profited and received support only if the marriage was dissolved.

While there is nothing to prevent a court from enforcing a religious agreement entered into in another country or an agreement that conforms to the parties' religious beliefs, parties to antenuptial agreements in the United States should avoid specifying in what religion their children should be raised. Most courts have held that such agreements are unenforceable.[20]

§ 9.03 Conduct during the Marriage

It has been generally held that antenuptial agreements attempting to set the terms of behavior during the marriage are not enforceable,[21] with the courts citing "the well-established rule that it is improper for courts to intervene in a married couple's daily

---

an attorney before agreeing to provision); Ahmed v. Ahmed, 261 S.W.3d 190 (Tex. Ct. App. 2008) (Islamic parties' mahr agreement, whereby husband contracted to give wife $50,000 either at the time of the marriage or deferred in the event of a divorce, was not enforceable as a premarital agreement; premarital agreement was an agreement between prospective spouses made in contemplation of marriage, and, because the parties participated in a valid civil wedding ceremony six months before signing the mahr agreement, they were already spouses, not "prospective spouses," and their agreement could not have been made "in contemplation of marriage.").

19. 204 Cal. App. 3d 1387, 251 Cal. Rptr. 871 (1988).

20. *See* § **9.072**. *See generally* Alexandra Selfridge, *Challenges for Negotiating and Drafting an Antenuptial Agreement for the Religious Upbringing of Future Children*, 16 J. CONTEMP. LEGAL ISSUES 91 (2007); Karel Rocha, *Should Religious Upbringing Antenuptial Agreements Be Legally Enforceable?* 11 J. CONTEMP. LEGAL ISSUES 145 (1999); Jocelyn E. Strauber, *A Deal Is a Deal: Antenuptial Agreements Regarding the Religious Upbringing of Children Should Be Enforceable*, 47 DUKE L.J. 971 (1998).

21. Graham v. Graham, 33 F. Supp. 936 (E.D. Mich. 1940); *In re* Marriage of Higgason, 516 P.2d 289 (Cal. 1973) (concerning medical care); Ball v. Ball, 36 So. 2d 172 (Fla. 1948) (provision concerning punishment and education of children); Isaacs v. Isaacs, 99 N.W. 268 (Neb. 1904) (specifying where parties would live); Favrot v. Barnes, 332 So. 2d 873 (La. Ct. App. 1976) (agreement limiting sexual intercourse to once a week); Koch v. Koch, 232 A.2d 157 (N.J. Super. App. Div. 1967) (provision that husband's mother could live with the couple); Mengal v. Mengal, 103 N.Y.S.2d 992 (N.Y. Fam. Ct. 1951) (children of wife's previous marriage were not to live with couple). *See generally* Laura P. Graham, *The Uniform Premarital Agreement Act and Modern Social Policy: The Enforceability of Premarital Agreements Regulating the Ongoing Marriage*, 28 WAKE FOREST L. REV. 1037, 1060 (1993) (court would be ill-equipped to specifically enforce a provision allocating housework between the spouses, or to measure the value of such work in awarding damages for a spouse's failure to perform).

domestic affairs."[22] Nonetheless, couples have been known to draft detailed agreements concerning the parties' conduct during the marriage. In one agreement that received national attention, Rex and Teresa LeGalley specified how much money they would spend on personal expenses per week ($70), what kind of gas they would buy (Chevron), and how often they would engage in "healthy sex" (three to five times per week).[23]

Notwithstanding the judicial unwillingness to wade through the minutiae of chore-sharing, toilet-cleaning, and dog walking, the Uniform Premarital Agreement Act (UPAA) defines a much broader scope for what may be included in a prenuptial agreement, asserting that parties to an agreement may contract with respect to "any" matter, "including their personal rights and obligations, not in violation of public policy or a statute imposing a criminal penalty."[24] The ALI (American Law Institute) Principles are similarly permissive in terms of scope.[25]

§ 9.04 Spousal Support

§ 9.041 Support Pendente Lite and Attorney's Fees

Because, as noted above, the parties cannot set the terms of the marriage, an agreement cannot control the sharing of expenses during the marriage, since this would negate one spouse's statutory duty to support the other.[26] Because spouses cannot contract away the obligation of support during the marriage, some courts have held that parties cannot contract away the right to pendente lite support and attorney's fees, as those

---

22. Judith T. Younger, *Perspectives on Antenuptial Agreements: An Update*, 8 J. Am. Acad. Matrim. Law. 1, 8 (1992).

One commentator opined that "courts simply do not want to enforce agreements that provide that a treasured snowball collection may be kept in the freezer; that one party must walk the dog, or that a husband has the option to sue for divorce if his wife gains more than fifteen pounds." Allison A. Marston, *Planning for Love: The Politics of Prenuptial Agreements*, 49 Stan. L. Rev. 887, 900 (1997), referring to actual agreements reported in Judith Rehak, *Prenuptial Accords: Walking Down the Aisle and Reading Fine Print*, Int'l Herald Trib., Feb. 25, 1995, at 14.

23. Gary Belsky, *Living by the Rules*, Money, May 1996, at 100.

A list of one man's somewhat bizarre prenuptial agreement provisions can be found at *Sicko "Marriage Contract" One for the Ages*, Smoking Gun, Feb. 17, 2006, http://www.thesmokinggun.com/documents/bizarre/sicko-marriage-contract-one-ages.

24. UPAA § 3(a)(8).

25. Am. Law Inst., Principles of the Law of Family Dissolution: Analysis and Recommendation § 7.03(1) (2002).

26. Borelli v. Brusseau, 16 Cal. Rptr. 2d 16 (Cal. Ct. App. 1993) (spouses cannot delegate the duty of support to a third party); *In re* Mathiasen, 268 Cal. Rptr. 895 (Cal. Ct. App. 1990); Lacks v. Lacks, 189 N.E.2d 487 (N.Y. 1963) (holding that contract to pay a spouse during the marriage is void).

items constitute support during the marriage.[27] Other cases have held that a waiver of temporary spousal support is fully enforceable.[28]

§ 9.042 Permanent Support

Forty-three jurisdictions have abandoned the common law restrictions on premarital waivers of spousal support. In 22 jurisdictions, premarital waivers of spousal support are authorized by statutes that adopt all or substantially all of the provisions of the

---

27. *Borelli*, 16 Cal. Rptr. 2d 16; *Mathiasen*, 268 Cal. Rptr. 2d 895; Scharer v. Scharer, 2001 WL 984728, 30 Conn. L. Rptr. 127 (Conn. Super. July 26, 2001); Lord v. Lord, 993 So. 2d 562 (Fla. Dist. Ct. App. 4th Dist. 2008) (provision of antenuptial agreement that required each party to pay his or her own attorney's fees and costs violated policy against waiver of predissolution support and, thus, was unenforceable); Aguilar v. Montero, 992 So. 2d 872 (Fla. Dist. Ct. App. 3d Dist. 2008) (prenuptial agreement could not waive husband's continuing obligation of support while dissolution proceedings were pending); Lashkajani v. Lashkajani, 855 So. 2d 87 (Fla. Dist. Ct. App. 2d Dist. 2003); Fernandez v. Fernandez, 710 So. 2d 223 (Fla. Dist. Ct. App. 1998); Blanton v. Blanton, 654 So. 2d 1240 (Fla. Dist. Ct. App. 1995); Rosenbaum-Golden v. Golden, 884 N.E.2d 1272 (Ill. App. Ct. 1st Dist. 2008) (provision whereby parties waived their rights to attorney's fees did not constitute a waiver of interim attorney's fees); Eule v. Eule, 24 Ill. App. 3d 83, 320 N.E.2d 506 (1974); Suiter v. Suiter, 138 Idaho 662, 67 P.3d 1274 (2003) (agreement did not relieve wife of her duty to support, despite agreement's provision purporting to relinquish husband's rights in wife's property and earnings; the agreement did not contract away their mutual duties of support); Barber v. Barber, 38 So. 3d 1046 (La. Ct. App. 1st Cir. 2010); Hall v. Hall, 4 So. 3d 254 (La. Ct. App. 5th Cir. 2009) (waiver of interim spousal support in the matrimonial agreement executed by husband and wife prior to the parties' marriage was invalid as against public policy); Loftice v. Loftice, 985 So. 2d 204 (La. Ct. App. 2008) (prenuptial agreements in which a spouse waives his or her right to alimony pendente lite in the event of separation are null and void as against public policy); Holliday v. Holliday, 358 So. 2d 618 (La. Ct. App. 1978); Solomon v. Solomon, 224 A.D.2d 331, 637 N.Y.S.2d 728 (1996) (by waiving spousal support, wife did not waive pendente lite relief, including temporary maintenance, counsel fees, and the right to an injunction to preserve marital assets); Dimick v. Dimick, 112 Nev. 56, 915 P.2d 254 (1996) (antenuptial agreement, providing that husband was to pay wife $200 per month for support, did not bar court award of alimony pendente lite); Motley v. Motley, 255 N.C. 190, 120 S.E.2d 422 (1961); Boyer v. Boyer, 925 P.2d 82 (Okla. Ct. App. 1996) (antenuptial agreement cannot change duty of support during marriage); Walker v. Walker, 765 N.W.2d 747 (S.D. 2009) (public policy precluded the waiver of attorney's fees associated with an alimony award); *In re* Marriage of Burke, 980 P.2d 265 (Wash. Ct. App. 1999). *See also* IOWA CODE ANN. § 596.5 (right of spouse cannot be adversely affected by antenuptial agreement).

28. Beal v. Beal, 88 P.3d 104 (Alaska 2004); Darr v. Darr, 950 S.W.2d 867 (Mo. App. 1997); Rubin v. Rubin, 690 N.Y.S.2d 742 (N.Y. App. Div. 2d Dep't 1999); Kelm v. Kelm, 68 Ohio St. 3d 26, 623 N.E.2d 39 (1993); Musko v. Musko, 697 A.2d 255 (Pa. 1997).

UPAA.[29] An Indiana statute that is similar to the UPAA also allows such a waiver,[30] and a New York statute also allows such waivers.[31]

In 19 jurisdictions, the right to enforce a premarital waiver of spousal support exists pursuant to judicial decision.[32]

New Mexico and South Dakota enacted the UPAA without section 3(a)(4), and thus do not allow parties to waive spousal support.[33] Iowa adopted the UPAA, but added a specific provision prohibiting contracting as to alimony.[34]

In all states, including those that have adopted the UPAA, a waiver of alimony will not be enforced if to do so would render the spouse in need of support a public charge.[35]

§ 9.05 Property Division/Estate Rights

Generally, there is no public policy objection to waiver of rights in marital or community property or rights in the other spouse's estate.[36] In particular, a waiver of rights in

---

29. Ariz. Rev. Stat. § 25-203; Ark. Code Ann. § 9-11-403; Cal. Fam. Code § 1612(c); Conn. Gen. Stat. Ann. § 46b-36d; Del. Code Ann. tit. 13, § 323; D.C. Code Ann. § 30-143; Haw. Rev. Stat. § 572 D-3; Idaho Code § 32-923; 750 Ill. Comp. Stat. 10/4; Kan. Stat. Ann. § 23-804; Me. Rev. Stat. Ann. tit. 19-A, § 604; Mont. Code Ann. § 40-2-605; Neb. Rev. Stat. § 42-1004; Nev. Rev. Stat. § 123A.050; N.J. Stat. Ann. § 37:2-34; N.C. Gen. Stat. § 52B-4; N.D. Cent. Code § 14-03.1-03; Or. Rev. Stat. § 108.710; R.I. Gen. Laws § 15-17-3; Tex. Fam. Code Ann. § 4.003; Utah Code Ann. § 30-8-4; Va. Code Ann. § 20-150.

30. Ind. Code § 31-11-3-5.

31. N.Y. Dom. Rel. Law § 236, pt. B, 3.

32. *Ex parte* Walters, 580 So. 2d 1352, 1354 (Ala. 1991); Brooks v. Brooks, 733 P.2d 1044, 1050–51 (Alaska 1987); Newman v. Newman, 653 P.2d 728, 731–34 (Colo. 1982); Snedaker v. Snedaker, 660 So. 2d 1070, 1072 (Fla. Dist. Ct. App. 1995); Scherer v. Scherer, 249 Ga. 635, 640–41 (1982); Edwardson v. Edwardson, 798 S.W.2d 941, 946 (Ky. 1990); McAlpine v. McAlpine, 679 So. 2d 85, 93 (La. 1986); Austin v. Austin, 839 N.E.2d 837 (Mass. 2005) (antenuptial agreements that waive alimony are not per se against public policy and may be specifically enforced); Vakil v. Vakil, 879 N.E.2d 79 (Mass. 2008) (antenuptial agreement providing that wife would not be "eligible" to receive an award of alimony if she chose to contest husband's request for a divorce was not per se unenforceable on public policy grounds); Frey v. Frey, 471 A.2d 705 (Md. 1984); Hill v. Hill, 356 N.W.2d 49, 55 (Minn. Ct. App. 1984); Gould v. Rafaeli, 822 S.W.2d 494, 497 (Mo. Ct. App. 1991); MacFarlane v. Rich, 567 A.2d 585, 588 (N.H. 1989); Gross v. Gross, 105, 464 N.E.2d 500, 506 (Ohio 1984); Hudson v. Hudson, 350 P.2d 596 (Okla. 1960); Simeone v. Simeone, 525 Pa. 392, 581 A.2d 162 (1990); Hardee v. Hardee, 558 S.E.2d 264 (S.C. 2001); Gilley v. Gilley, 327 S.C. 8, 488 S.E.2d 310, 312 (1997); Cary v. Cary, 937 S.W.2d 777 (Tenn. 1996); Gant v. Gant, 174 W. Va. 740, 329 S.E.2d 106, 112 (1985); Hengel v. Hengel, 122 Wis. 2d 737, 365 N.W.2d 16 (1985).

33. *E.g.*, Rivera v. Rivera, 149 N.M. 66, 243 S.W.3d 1148 (Ct. App. 2010); Sanford v. Sanford, 694 N.W.2d 283 (S.D. 2005).

34. Iowa Code § 596.5(2). *E.g.*, *In re* Marriage of Van Brocklin, 468 N.W.2d 40 (Iowa Ct. App. 1991).

35. Warren v. Warren, 523 N.E.2d 680 (Ill. App. Ct. 1988); *In re* Purcell, 783 P.2d 1038 (Or. 1989).

36. *Hill*, 356 N.W.2d 49; *In re* Estate of Kopecky, 574 N.W.2d 549 (Neb. Ct. App. 1998) (there is nothing to prevent a waiver of the right of election, survivor's rights in homestead, family allow-

a community property state does not violate constitutional provisions relating to community property.[37]

In a small minority of states, the property division clause in an antenuptial agreement is only one factor in the court's final property division on divorce.[38] This rule substantially impairs the intended purpose of most antenuptial agreements, and most states have refused to follow it.[39]

§ 9.06 ERISA Rights

As family law practitioners are painfully aware, the Employee Retirement Income Security Act of 1974 (ERISA) contains an antiassignment clause that prevents pension owners from transferring their pension rights to another person.[40] The only way for a domestic relations court to assign pension benefits is by a qualified domestic relations order (QDRO).[41] Federal law preemption of state law on ERISA rights is clear. What is not so clear is whether private parties can waive any and all ERISA rights by an antenuptial agreement.

First, the law is relatively clear that an antenuptial waiver of *survivor* benefits under an ERISA-qualified plan is ineffective. The surviving spouse's entitlement to an annuity cannot be waived unless the spouse consents to the designation of an alternative beneficiary in writing and the consent acknowledges the effect of the waiver and is witnessed by a notary public or plan representative.[42] No other document will do. Thus, an antenuptial agreement that is not signed by a spouse, and is generally not

---

ance); Kinkle v. Kinkle, 699 N.E.2d 41 (Ohio 1998) (there is no public policy preventing the parties from cutting off one another entirely from any participation in the estate of the other). *Cf.* McKee-Johnson v. Johnson, 444 N.W.2d 259 (Minn. 1989) (waiver possible, but burden of proof shifts to party enforcing agreement if marital property is divided).

37. Fanning v. Fanning, 828 S.W.2d 135 (Tex. Ct. App. 1992) (antenuptial agreements, authorized by amendment to constitution, do not impermissibly impair right to community property). *See also* Dokmanovic v. Schwartz, 880 S.W.2d 272 (Tex. Ct. App. 1994) (antenuptial agreement does not violate Texas constitution by recharacterizing property).

38. Busekist v. Busekist, 398 N.W.2d 722 (Neb. 1987).

39. *See, e.g.,* Hubbard v. Bentley, 17 So. 3d 652 (Ala. Civ. App. 2008) (parties' intent that their agreement would be "considered" by the court created a binding antenuptial agreement that would take immediate effect and would govern the parties' subsequent legal relationship upon the filing of a divorce action).

40. 29 U.S.C. § 1056(d)(3)(A).

41. *Id. See* Roth v. Roth, 506 N.W.2d 900 (Mich. Ct. App. 1993) (containing general historical review of state court authority to divide ERISA-regulated retirement benefits).

42. 29 U.S.C. § 1055(c)(1), (2).

witnessed by a notary public or plan representative, is ineffective to waive survivor benefits.[43]

One decision departs from this rule. In *In re Estate of Hopkins*,[44] the husband and wife executed an antenuptial agreement in 1982 whereby the wife waived any and all rights she had in the husband's ERISA-qualified pension, including survivor rights. The husband then died, and the wife sought her survivor benefits, claiming her waiver was ineffectual because it did not conform to 29 U.S.C. § 1055. The court disagreed, and held that "the specific waiver requirements" of ERISA need not be complied with in order for the waiver to be effective.[45]

Second, the law is not clear whether the parties can waive, by an antenuptial agreement, other ERISA pension rights. For example, in *In re Marriage of Rahn*,[46] the parties executed an antenuptial agreement whereby they agreed that "all of the property now owned or hereafter acquired by husband will remain his sole and separate property throughout the marriage. Wife shall not claim or acquire any interest in any of his property if it increases in value during the marriage, jointly held property being excepted."[47] The wife contended that the trial court erred when it determined that she waived her spousal rights to her husband's ERISA-qualified pension plan. The husband contended that the federal statutes and regulations address the waiver of survivor benefits only, and are silent as to other type of pension benefits under an ERISA-qualified plan. Thus, the husband argued, the wife was free to waive her rights in the husband's pension other than survivor benefits, and the antenuptial agreement was a valid waiver of those rights. The Colorado Court of Appeals upheld the waiver of rights other than survivor benefits, reasoning that ERISA provides the explicit requirements for a spouse's waiver of rights to the "qualified joint and survivor annuity" and the "qualified pre-retirement survivor annuity" in a qualified ERISA plan. Regulations interpreting ERISA's statutory authority specifically state, "An agreement entered into prior to marriage does not satisfy the applicable requirements, even if the agreement is executed within the applicable election period."[48]

Thus, a waiver of a right to survivor benefits in an ERISA-qualified plan in an antenuptial agreement is ineffective and the surviving spouse is entitled to the survivor

---

43. *See* Hagwood v. Newton, 282 F.3d 285 (4th Cir. 2002); Hurwitz v. Sher, 982 F.2d 778 (2d Cir. 1992); Howard v. Branham & Baker Coal Co., 968 F.2d 1214 (6th Cir. 1992); Pedro Enters. v. Perdue, 998 F.2d 491 (7th Cir. 1993); Nat'l Auto. Dealers v. Arbeitman, 89 F.3d 496 (8th Cir. 1996); Nellis v. Boeing Co., 1992 WL 122773 (D. Kan. 1992); Callahan v. Hutsell, Callahan & Buchino, P.S.C., 813 F. Supp. 541 (W.D. Ky. 1992); Zinn v. Donaldson Co., 799 F. Supp. 69 (D. Minn. 1992).

44. 574 N.E.2d 230 (Ill. App. Ct. 1991).

45. *Id.* at 231; *see also* Fox Valley & Vicinity Constr. Workers Pension Fund v. Brown, 897 F.2d 275 (7th Cir. 1990); Critchell v. Critchell, No. 98-FM-1304, 26 Fam. L. Rep. (BNA) 1184 (D.C. Feb. 10, 2000); Savage-Keough v. Keough, 373 N.J. Super. 198, 861 A.2d 131 (App. Div. 2004); Moor-Jankowski v. Moor-Jankowski, 222 A.D.2d 422, 634 N.Y.S.2d 728 (1995).

46. 914 P.2d 463 (Colo. Ct. App. 1995).

47. *Id.* at 464.

48. *Id.*

benefits even if others are named as survivor beneficiaries with the plan administrator. ERISA does not, however, preempt the states from enacting dissolution of marriage laws with respect to the waiver of other interests in an ERISA-qualified retirement plan, despite the antialienation provisions of ERISA. A valid waiver can be enforced through a QDRO, that is, a qualified domestic relations order from the court directing the administrator of the plan to distribute the benefits according to the allocation of rights pursuant to the antenuptial agreement.

Other courts have agreed that ERISA's preemption extends only to survivor benefits and not to other ERISA benefits. Thus, a party is free to waive ERISA benefits other than survivor benefits by an antenuptial agreement.[49]

A New Jersey case, *Hawxhurst v. Hawxhurst*,[50] found that the wife had not waived her rights in her husband's pension, and this case should be contrasted with *Rahn*. In *Hawxhurst*, the husband entered into a prenuptial agreement with his wife. Prior to his divorce, the husband accepted an early retirement package from his employer, which included a lump sum distribution of his ERISA-qualified pension plan. The husband rolled the plan funds into an Independent Retirement Account in his name. Upon his divorce, the husband argued the terms of the prenuptial agreement were preempted by the spendthrift provision of ERISA. After a thorough discussion of the applicable ERISA provisions and the purpose of Congress in enacting ERISA, the court concluded that "established authority in analogous situations supports the conclusion that once distributed, the ERISA anti-alienation provision does not shelter this asset." The court found that once the funds were distributed, "the parties could confer rights in the fund created by distribution as they saw fit. . . . Once distributed, an asset was created which not only became subject to the terms of the pre-nuptial agreement but also was beyond the anti-alienation protections of ERISA." The prevailing view is that ERISA does not protect pension funds after the beneficiary receives the funds.

In contrast to *Rahn* and *Hawxhurst*, some courts have held that an antenuptial agreement cannot waive *any* rights under an ERISA-qualified plan. For example, in *Richards v. Richards*,[51] the parties executed an antenuptial agreement in which each party waived rights in the past and future earnings of the other. The wife specifically

---

49. Critchell v. Critchell, 26 Fam. L. Rep. (BNA) 1184 (D.C. Feb. 10, 2000); *Fox Valley*, 897 F.2d 275; *Moor-Jankowski*, 222 A. D. 2nd 422, 634 N.Y.S.2d 728.

50. 723 A.2d 58 (N.J. Super. 1998).

51. 640 N.Y.S.2d 709 (N.Y. Sup. Ct. 1995), *aff'd*, 648 N.Y.S.2d 589 (N.Y. App. Div. 1996). *See also* Edmonds v. Edmonds, 710 N.Y.S.2d 765 (N.Y. Sup. Ct. 2000). *See generally* K. Vetrano, *Spousal Waiver of Pension Rights, Premaritally and Upon Divorce*, 13 FAIR$HARE 10 (Sept. 1993). *Cf.* Heineman v. Bright, 140 Md. App. 658, 782 A.2d 365 (2001) (widow's waiver in premarital agreement of interest in husband's 401(a) pension plan was binding on her, even though tax law provided that waivers of a surviving spouse's benefit must be made after the participant's death); Strong v. Dubin, 75 A.D.3d 66, 901 N.Y.S.2d 214 (1st Dep't 2010) (for purposes of equitable distribution, a waiver of any interest in a pension as marital property by an otherwise valid prenuptial agreement is not prohibited by the Employee Retirement Income Security Act (ERISA), as amended by the Retirement Equity Act (REA).

waived any claim to the husband's present or future pension, both in equitable distribution and as a survivor. Without distinguishing between survivor rights and other types of rights, the court held that "Federal law precludes giving effect to a prenuptial waiver of spousal rights under ERISA."[52]

These cases obviously provide ammunition to both those wishing to set aside a waiver of ERISA rights and those wishing to enforce a waiver of ERISA rights.

§ 9.07 Welfare of Children

§ 9.071 Child Support and Custody

Like all private contracts, antenuptial agreements generally cannot affect the rights of the parties' children. Thus, public policy clearly prevents the court from enforcing a waiver of child support, custody, or visitation.[53] Rather, the appropriate amount of child support and the proper custodial environment is a matter for the court to decide.

Antenuptial agreements also occasionally attempt to specify each party's parental duties with respect to the other party's children from a prior relationship. One court noted in dicta that such clauses are too vague to be enforced.[54]

§ 9.072 Child's Religious Upbringing

Most courts that have addressed the issue have held that to enforce a religious upbringing agreement would effectively force the court to choose between religions and violate its constitutionally mandated neutrality under *Lemon v. Kurtzman*,[55] and would force the court to violate the constitutional rights of custodial parents in choosing the upbringing of their children, an upbringing that is subject to change upon the parent's authority.

The leading case on this issue, *Zummo v. Zummo*,[56] best summarized these constitutional concerns. The court first noted that excessive entanglement by the court would arise, because the court would be called upon to determine matters of religious orthodoxy in order to enforce the agreement. Both the subject matter and the ambiguities of the order make excessive entanglement in religious matters inevitable if the order is to be enforced. The court then continued and iterated the heart of the holding:

---

52. *Richards*, 648 N.Y.S.2d at 589.

53. Kilgrow v. Kilgrow, 107 So. 2d 885 (Ala. 1958); Edwardson v. Edwardson, 798 S.W.2d 941 (Ky. 1990); Huck v. Huck, 734 P.2d 417 (Utah 1986); *In re* Marriage of Fox, 795 P.2d 1170 (Wash. Ct. App. 1990). *See also In re* Marriage of Burke, 980 P.2d 265 (Wash. Ct. App. 1999) (clause prohibiting parties from recovering, in dissolution action, attorney's fees incurred in litigating parenting issues was void as against public policy).

54. *In re* Garrity/Bishton, 226 Cal. Rptr. 485, 489 (Cal. Ct. App. 1986).

55. 403 U.S. 602 (1971).

56. 394 Pa. Super. 30, 574 A.2d 1130 (1990).

Finally, there is a broader and more fundamental entanglement problem with enforcement of such agreements. Enforcement plainly encroaches upon the fundamental right of individuals to question, to doubt, and to change their religious convictions, and to expose their changed beliefs.

The constitutional freedom to question, to doubt, and to change one's convictions, protected by the Free Exercise and Establishment Clauses, is important for very pragmatic reasons. For most people religious development is a lifelong dynamic process even when they continue to adhere to the same religion, denomination, or sect. It is also generally conceded that the transmission and inculcation of religious beliefs in children is both active and passive, is shared by both parents, and is affected by a wide variety of external factors. Importantly, it is also generally acknowledged that it would be difficult, if not impossible, for an interreligious couple engaged to be married and to project themselves into the future so as to enable them to know how they will feel about religion, if and when their children are born, and as the children grow; and that it would be still more difficult for such a couple to attempt to project themselves into the scenario of a potential divorce after children were born, in order to accurately anticipate the circumstances under which religious upbringing agreements would be enforced if such agreements were given legal effect. Consequently, while religious upbringing agreements may serve an important and beneficial purpose by promoting careful consideration of potential difficulties prior to marriage, and also may carry moral weight and religious sanction, parties entering into such agreements generally will not be able to anticipate the fundamental changes in circumstances between their prenuptial optimism, their struggles for accommodation, and their ultimate post-divorce disillusionment. Consequently, a hopeful and perhaps naive prenuptial assurance of a future commitment to an agreed (usually vague) course of religious instruction for then as yet unborn children in the event of divorce (an often unconsidered possibility), must remain as legally unenforceable in civil courts as the wedding vows the parties even more solemnly exchanged.

The First Amendment specifically preserves the essential religious freedom for individuals to grow, to shape, and to amend this important aspect of their lives, and the lives of their children. Religious freedom was recognized by our founding fathers to be inalienable. It remains so today. Thus, while we agree that a parent's religious freedom may yield to other compelling interests, we conclude that it may not be bargained away.[57]

---

57. 574 A.2d 1130, 1147–48 (1990).

Thus, according to the *Zummo* court, a parent cannot bargain away the right to change his or her religious views and to inculcate his or her child with those views. Other courts have taken the same view.[58]

§ 9.08 Arbitration

There is no public policy objection to arbitration clauses in antenuptial agreements.[59]

§ 9.09 Effect of Invalidity

If part of an antenuptial agreement is unenforceable for public policy reasons, the entire contract is not necessarily invalid. The court may still enforce any clauses that are consistent with public policy and severable from the invalid portion.[60] Of course, the parties may also include such a severability clause.

---

58. *Kilgrow*, 107 So. 2d 885; *In re* Marriage of Weiss, 49 Cal. Rptr. 2d 339 (Cal. Ct. App. 1996); Wolfert v. Wolfert, 598 P.2d 524 (Colo. App. 1979); Sotnick v. Sotnick, 650 So. 2d 157 (Fla. Dist. Ct. App. 1995); Stevenot v. Stevenot, 520 N.Y.S.2d 197 (N.Y. App. Div. 1987) (an oral agreement entered into prior to and during marriage is not binding); MacLagen v. Klein, 473 S.E.2d 778 (N.C. Ct. App. 1996). *See also In re* Marriage of Neuchterlien, 587 N.E.2d 21 (Ill. App. Ct. 1992) (prior to marriage, parties orally agreed to raise any future children as Lutherans). Kendall v. Kendall, 687 N.E.2d 1228 (Mass. 1997) (noting that the majority of courts adhere to the view that predivorce agreements regarding religious upbringing of children are unconstitutionally unenforceable). For an opposing view, see Strauber, *supra* note 20.

59. DeLorean v. DeLorean, 511 A.2d 1257 (N.J. Ch. Div. 1986); Kelm v. Kelm, 623 N.E.2d 39 (Ohio 1993); Bandas v. Bandas, 430 S.E.2d 706 (Va. Ct. App. 1993).

60. Howell v. Landry, 386 S.E.2d 610 (N.C. Ct. App. 1989); Rogers v. Yourshaw, 448 S.E.2d 884 (Va. Ct. App. 1994). *But see* Brennan v. Brennan, 955 S.W.2d 779 (Mo. Ct. App. 1997) (court may not selectively enforce part of agreement and reject part of agreement; agreement must stand as whole or fail as whole).

Procedural Fairness: Voluntariness of Execution 10

§ 10.01 The Confidential Relationship

The law protects parties to an antenuptial agreement more than it protects parties to other types of contracts. There are solid reasons for this special protection. When two parties sign a business contract, each party's primary goal is to make as much money as possible from the transaction. Because each party knows that profit is the primary goal, the parties can take adequate precautions to protect their interests. Since it is obviously in the public interest to encourage businesspeople to protect their own welfare, the law interferes in the parties' relations only when one party deliberately intimidates or deceives the other.

When two parties are engaged to be married, however, neither party reasonably expects that profit is the other's primary motive. Instead, each expects the other will act so as to maximize their mutual benefit. In cases where mutual profit is not the motive, there is immense potential for one party to obtain an unjust windfall at the expense of the other. In other words, people will sign a contract with an intended spouse that they would not think of signing in any transaction based purely on self-interest.[1]

Unless we want to encourage engaged persons to think in terms of self-interest, a goal that may be neither socially useful nor realistically feasible, the law encourages engaged persons to behave in a manner

---

1. *See* Sumpter v. Kosinski, 419 N.W.2d 463, 471 (Mich. 1988) ("when affairs of the heart are involved, legal guidance no matter how appropriate is often not heeded").

morally superior to that of the marketplace.[2] The law accomplishes this by holding that engaged couples have a "confidential relationship."[3] As stated by one court, "This relationship is one of extreme mutual confidence and, thus, presents a unique situation unlike the ordinary commercial contract situations where the parties deal at arm's length."[4]

The confidential relationship places upon the parties a deliberately vague "fiduciary duty" to deal with each other in a "fair" manner. Of course, "fairness" cannot always be measured in purely material terms, and a spouse does not necessarily breach the fiduciary duty merely by insisting on unequal terms as a precondition of marriage.[5]

---

2. *In re* Marriage of Bonds, 5 P.3d 815, 830 (Cal. 2000) (there are "obvious distinctions between premarital agreements and ordinary commercial contracts"); MacFarlane v. Rich, 567 A.2d 585 (N.H. 1989) (the state has a special interest in the subject matter of prenuptial agreements and courts tend to scrutinize them more closely than ordinary commercial contracts); Stoner v. Stoner, 819 A.2d 529, 533 (Pa. 2003) (parties stand in a closer relationship beyond that of professional acquaintances negotiating a commercial contract); *In re* Estate of Smid, 756 N.W.2d 1, 14 (S.D. 2008) (relationships between husbands and wives cannot be likened unto commercial transactions among operatives who deal at arm's length). *See also* AM. LAW INST., PRINCIPLES OF FAMILY DISSOLUTION: ANALYSIS AND RECOMMENDATIONS § 7.04 cmt. b (2002) (burden shifting reflects appropriate "heightened scrutiny" of bargaining process leading to marital agreements as compared with bargaining process leading to commercial contracts).

3. *See, e.g., Ex parte* Brown, 26 So. 3d 1222 (Ala. 2009); *In re* Estate of Harber, 449 P.2d 7 (Ariz. 1969); Burnes v. Burnes, 157 S.W.2d 24 (Ark. 1942); Linker v. Linker, 470 P.2d 921 (Colo. App. 1970); Friezo v. Friezo, 914 A.2d 533 (Conn. 2007); Posner v. Posner, 257 So. 2d 530 (Fla. 1972); *In re* Estate of Hopkins, 520 N.E.2d 415 (Ill. Ct. App. 1988); Parr v. Parr, 635 N.E.2d 124 (Ind. Ct. App. 1994); Christians v. Christians, 44 N.W.2d 431 (Iowa 1950); Cannon v. Cannon, 865 A.2d 563, 584 (Md. 2005); Ansin v. Craven-Ansin, 929 N.E.2d 955 (Mass. 2010); Rockwell v. Estate of Rockwell, 180 N.W.2d 498 (Mich. Ct. App. 1970); Estate of Serbus v. Serbus, 324 N.W.2d 381 (Minn. 1982); Christiansen v. Christiansen, 393 N.W.2d 207 (Minn. Ct. App. 1986); *In re* Estate of Hollett, 834 A.2d 348 (N.H. 2003); DeLorean v. DeLorean, 511 A.2d 1257 (N.J. Super. Ch. Div. 1986); Beverly v. Parilla, 848 N.E.2d 881 (Ohio App. 7th Dist. 2006); *In re* Cobb's Estate, 305 P.2d 1028 (Okla. 1957); White v. White, 313 A.2d 776 (Pa. Super. 1973); *Smid*, 756 N.W.2d 1; Baker v. Baker, 142 S.W.2d 737 (Tenn. Ct. App. 1940); Black v. Powers, 628 S.E.2d 546 (Va. Ct. App. 2006); Button v. Button, 388 N.W.2d 546 (Wis. 1986). *Cf. In re* Estate of Malchow, 172 N.W.2d 915 (Minn. 1919) (where parties discussed marriage as business proposition at their first meeting ever, no confidential relationship imposed); *In re* Koeffler's Estate, 254 N.W. 363 (Wis. 1934) (where marriage is one of convenience, there is no confidential relationship).

Some cases have called the relationship a "fiduciary relationship." This is more common in community property states where the fiduciary relationship exists during the marriage. *See, e.g.,* Smith v. Smith, 860 P.2d 634, 643 (Idaho 1993); Williams v. Waldman, 836 P.2d 614, 618 (Nev. 1992); Sidden v. Mailman, 563 S.E.2d 55, 58 (N.C. Ct. App. 2002); *In re* Estate of Lutz, 563 N.W.2d 90, 98 (N.D. 1997); Cohen v. Estate of Cohen, 491 N.E.2d 698, 699 (Ohio 1986); *In re* Estate of Gab, 364 N.W.2d 924, 925 (S.D. 1985); Miller v. Ludeman, 150 S.W.3d 592, 597 (Tex. App. 2004).

4. Benker v. Benker, 331 N.W.2d 193, 196 (Mich. 1982). *Accord In re* Vallish's Estate, 244 A.2d 745 (Pa. 1968).

5. *E.g.,* Reizfeld v. Reizfeld, 125 Conn. App. 782, ___ A.3d ___ (gross disparity in parties' assets did not render antenuptial agreement unconscionable), *cert. denied*, 300 Conn. 915, 13 A.3d 1103 (2011); Adams v. Adams, 603 S.E.2d 273 (Ga. 2004) (antenuptial agreement that allowed wife $10,000 for each year of marriage, up to maximum of $100,000, was not unconscionable, even though agreement may have perpetuated already existing disparity between parties' estates); *In re*

The duty instead focuses on procedural fairness, which might best be translated as complete and informed honesty. When such honesty is present, the other party is given clear notice that the transaction is one of self-interest rather than mutual welfare, and is given reason to protect his or her own interest. Of course, the confidential relationship is in addition to the normal contractual requirement of good faith and fair dealing.[6]

A few isolated decisions have held that parties to an antenuptial agreement should receive no special protection.[7] These decisions are clearly in the minority. Engaged persons need some degree of special protection, because their tendency to think in terms of mutual interest rather than self-interest. This tendency makes engaged persons of both sexes uniquely vulnerable to overreaching. A majority of courts have found that the special protection given to engaged persons benefits both spouses equally.

Because of the confidential relationship, the courts insist that the agreement be "voluntary" in a way that is somewhat different from and more difficult to define than the common law contract doctrines of duress and undue influence. Courts considering the question of voluntariness have avoided any precise definition, but there are several factors that may indicate involuntariness. One court advised that the following factors be considered: "[t]he bargaining position of the parties, sophistication of the parties, presence of independent advice, understanding of the legal consequences and rights, and timing of the agreement juxtaposed with the wedding date."[8] None of these factors alone is likely to invalidate an agreement, but the combined effect of all the factors may eventually make the agreement sufficiently involuntary that the court will not enforce it.

For purposes of this chapter, discussion of cases on voluntariness include only situations in which a spouse's will was overcome through some form of direct or indirect

---

Marriage of Shanks, 758 N.W.2d 506 (Iowa 2008) (when considering the enforceability of a premarital agreement, courts must resist the temptation to view disparity between the parties' financial circumstances as requiring a finding of substantive unconscionability); DeMatteo v. DeMatteo, 762 N.E.2d 797 (Mass. 2002) (agreement valid even if settlement was "less than modest" for wife); *Sumpter*, 419 N.W.2d 463 (mere disparity of provisions does not invalidate antenuptial agreement); Webb v. Webb, 851 N.Y.S.2d 828 (N.Y. Sup. Ct. 2007) (prenuptial agreement will be deemed unconscionable if it is so unequal in its effect that it shocks the conscience and confounds the judgment of any person of common sense); *In re* Marriage of Krejci v. Krejci, 667 N.W.2d 780 (Wis. Ct. App. 2003) (premarital or marital agreement fair at execution is not unfair at divorce merely due to the fact that its application results in an unequal property division or one that the court might not order under marital property division statute).

6. Estate of Draper v. Bank of Am., N.A., 205 P.3d 698 (Kan. 2009); Colello v. Colello, 780 N.Y.S.2d 450 (N.Y. App. Div. 2004); Reese v. Reese, 984 P.2d 987 (Utah 1999).

7. *E.g.*, Mallen v. Mallen, 622 S.E.2d 812 (Ga. 2005) (there is no confidential relationship between persons engaged to be married so as to impose special contractual duties); Eckstein v. Eckstein, 514 N.Y.S.2d 47 (N.Y. App. Div. 1987) (stating without authority that engaged persons should receive no special protection); Marsh v. Marsh, 949 S.W.2d 734 (Tex. Ct. App. 1997) (fiduciary relationship exists between parties to midnuptial agreement that is *not* present between prospective spouses); *In re* Geyer, 533 A.2d 423, 430 (Pa. 1987) (Nix, J., dissenting) (special protection is no longer necessary because inexperienced women no longer need protection from overreaching men).

8. Zawahiri v. Alwattar, 2008 WL 2698679 (Ohio Ct. App. 10th Dist. July 10, 2008).

pressure. If the spouse was instead deceived or misled into signing the agreement, the case review is included in **chapter 11** on knowledge.

§ 10.02 Time Given to Sign

The most common factor seen in voluntariness cases is a short time period between offer and acceptance. There are actually two separate time periods that must be considered: the period of informal notification and discussion preceding the offering of a draft, and the period between execution of the agreement and the wedding.

§ 10.021 Sufficient Time

Where the parties have discussed the agreement for a considerable amount of time before its execution, the agreement is likely to be considered voluntary, even if the period of formal negotiations after a written draft was presented was relatively short.[9] Some states even require a minimum amount of time between execution of the agreement and the marriage.[10]

The operative facts for finding sufficient time are whether the party to whom the agreement is presented had sufficient time to read and understand the agreement, and sufficient time to consult with an attorney if he or she so chose.[11]

---

9. *E.g.*, Lee v. Lee, 816 S.W.2d 625 (Ark. Ct. App. 1991) (agreement enforceable although it was presented one hour before wedding; being "rushed" does not amount to duress); Francavilla v. Francavilla, 969 So. 2d 522 (Fla. Dist. Ct. App. 2007) (no duress where negotiations stretched over months); *In re* Marriage of Van Horn, 2002 WL 1428491 (Iowa Ct. App. 2002) (unreported) (although the agreement was signed just two days before the wedding, wife acknowledged discussing the agreement in advance, was given an opportunity to read the document, and was advised to obtain independent counsel); *In re* Adams, 729 P.2d 1151 (Kan. 1986) (agreement discussed for a week before the wedding and presented to the wife one hour before wedding not void); *In re* Estate of Arbeitman, 886 S.W.2d 644 (Mo. Ct. App. 1994) (wife could not establish duress where, although agreement was presented to her on the day of the wedding, she had seen the agreement and knew its contents well before the wedding); Howell v. Landry, 386 S.E.2d 610 (N.C. Ct. App. 1989) (agreement presented one day before wedding, but informally discussed for some time before; wife actually negotiated changes in agreement; brevity of signing period alone not sufficient to invalidate agreement); *In re* Leathers, 779 P.2d 619 (Or. Ct. App. 1989) (agreement was presented the evening before the marriage but discussed in general terms for an "extended period" beforehand), *cert. denied*, 789 P.2d 263 (Or. 1990); Williams v. Williams, 720 S.W.2d 246 (Tex. Ct. App. 1986) (parties discussed agreement informally for six months before marriage; even though wife saw the actual agreement for the first time one day before the wedding, the agreement was deemed voluntarily executed).

10. *E.g.*, CAL. FAM. CODE § 1615 (seven days); DEL. CODE ANN. tit. 13, § 301 (10 days); MINN. STAT. ANN. § 519.11 (one day). *See In re* Marriage of Cadwell-Faso & Faso, 119 Cal. Rptr. 3d 818 (Cal. Ct. App. 2011) (parties did not run afoul of California's seven-day rule, which requires that parties sign agreement at least seven days before wedding, where both parties were represented at outset of negotiations, and execution within seven days was only an addendum to already executed agreement).

11. Brown v. Brown, 26 So. 3d 1210 (Ala. Civ. App. 2007) (antenuptial agreement was valid, even though it was signed by the parties one day before their wedding and wife failed to read the entire document; wife was not prevented from reading the agreement, as a real estate agent

§ 10.022 Insufficient Time

Where the agreement was not even discussed informally until days or hours before the marriage, courts have been more reluctant to enforce the agreement. For example, in *Zimmie v. Zimmie*,[12] the wife first learned of the agreement one day before the wedding. The court found the agreement was not voluntary. Similarly, in *Norris v. Norris*,[13] the wife refused to sign an antenuptial agreement during the weeks before the marriage. The husband allowed the wedding plans to proceed, and then presented the agreement to the wife again one hour before the wedding ceremony. The court found the agreement involuntary.[14]

---

wife was familiar with the import of reading a legal document, wife knew husband was a "millionaire" before they married, and, thus, was aware of the general extent of his assets at the time she signed the agreement, and wife attempted to seek legal advice, but when she was advised that her attorney was unavailable she declined to seek other counsel); Friezo v. Friezo, 914 A.2d 533 (Conn. 2007) (wife had sufficient time to review prospective husband's financial disclosure, so that prospective wife knowingly and voluntarily executed premarital agreement, for purposes of enforceability under Connecticut Premarital Agreement Act, where copy of schedule to agreement, listing prospective husband's assets and liabilities, was faxed from prospective husband's attorney to prospective wife's attorney six days before she executed the agreement); Gordon v. Gordon, 25 So. 3d 615 (Fla. Dist. Ct. App. 2009) (trial court did not abuse its discretion by declaring that a period of 10 days prior to the marriage was sufficient time for one to exercise the opportunity to review prenuptial agreement, and, if one so chose, to seek the advice of legal counsel); *Shanks*, 758 N.W.2d 506 (Iowa 2008) (agreement executed 10 days prior to wedding date was not procedurally unconscionable based on husband's superior bargaining position as attorney, where he twice urged wife to obtain independent legal counsel, wife was encouraged by Nebraska attorney to seek counsel from attorney licensed to practice in Iowa, but wife elected not to seek independent counsel, and wife had sufficient time to seek advice from counsel); Binek v. Binek, 673 N.W.2d 594 (N.D. 2004) (two days before wedding sufficient time to review agreement); Millstein v. Millstein, 2002-Ohio-4783, 2002 WL 31031676 (Ohio Ct. App. 2002) (wife entered into prenuptial agreement freely and without fraud, duress, coercion, or overreaching; wife independently retained one of the foremost domestic relations attorneys at that time, the attorney participated in negotiating the agreement, wife did not sign the agreement until eight days after she received the final draft and she therefore had ample time to pursue changes, to retain new counsel, or to refuse to sign it, and wife could have postponed the wedding without undue embarrassment if she chose to further negotiate terms in the prenuptial agreement). *See also In re* Yannalfo, 794 A.2d 795 (N.H. 2002) (although agreement was presented one day before wedding, court would not presume wife did not have opportunity to consult with counsel).

12. 464 N.E.2d 142 (Ohio 1984).

13. 419 A.2d 982 (D.C. 1980).

14. *Accord* Roberts v. Roberts, 802 So. 2d 230 (Ala. Civ. App. 2001) (agreement presented one day before wedding); Faiman v. Faiman, 2008 WL 5481382 (Conn. Super. Ct. 2008) (antenuptial property agreement was invalid where wife had not known that the husband's attorney was putting together the agreement and wife was brought to an attorney's office to sign it three days before the wedding, wife had never met the counsel who had been picked for her by her husband's attorney, and both attorneys noted she seemed surprised by the agreement); Juliano v. Juliano, 20 Conn. L. Rptr. 249, 1997 WL 576544 (Conn. Super. Ct. 1997) (premarital agreement presented and signed three hours before wedding unenforceable); Simzer v. Simzer, 514 So. 2d 372 (Fla. Dist. Ct. App. 1987)(contract signed a few hours before ceremony, no mention of prior discussions); Lutgert v. Lutger, 338 So. 2d 1111 (Fla. Dist. Ct. App. 1976) (agreement first presented to wife on day before

If the parties disagree on when the agreement was presented, the trial court does not abuse its discretion by accepting a longer time period.[15] For example, in *Lee v. Lee*,[16] the wife claimed that she didn't see the antenuptial agreement until one hour before the wedding, when the husband's attorney called her and told her she needed to come to his office to sign the agreement. There was ample evidence, however, that the parties had been prepared several days prior to the wedding, the wife knew about the agreement and its contents, and the wife was fully aware of the nature and extent of the husband's assets. The court upheld the agreement.

Further, if the shortness of time did not affect the attacking party's willingness to sign, the agreement may still be enforceable.[17] The general experience of the attacking party and his or her ability to consult with counsel may be important factors in determining whether the short time period actually inhibited review of the contract.[18]

---

wedding while parties were picking up wedding rings from jeweler); Pattison v. Pattison, 283 P. 483 (Kan. 1930) ("tactless, if not manifestly unfair," for husband to present agreement to wife on wedding day); Hoag v. Dick, 799 A.2d 391 (Me. 2002) (agreement presented on wedding day unenforceable, as wife had no opportunity to consult counsel); Pember v. Shapiro, 794 N.W.2d 435 (N.D. 2011) (premarital agreement executed by spouses on their wedding day was unenforceable, based on lack of consent; very little planning preceded creation of premarital agreement, drafting lawyer did not receive any information regarding spouses' property until the morning of the wedding, husband was not advised to seek independent legal advice and there was not time to do so, husband told the court he did not understand the agreement when it was signed or when asked about it at divorce trial, and terms apparently were inflexible); Peters-Riemers v. Riemers, 644 N.W.2d 197 (N.D. 2002) (wife did not see agreement until three days before wedding and did not have independent counsel); Fletcher v. Fletcher, 628 N.E.2d 1343 (Ohio 1994) (execution of agreement on wedding day raises presumption of overreaching and coercion that may be rebutted); Postiy v. Postiy, 2003-Ohio-2146, 2003 WL 1962410 (Ohio Ct. App. 5th Dist. 2003) (wife testified that she first saw prenuptial agreement two days before the wedding, she sought legal advice but was unable to see an attorney before wedding, and she had to work on day before wedding; husband testified that he insisted they get the agreement signed on day before wedding, and wife signed agreement before notary at bank before going to her job; agreement held unenforceable); In re Marriage of Rudder, 217 P.3d 183 (Or. Ct. App. 2009) (agreement unenforceable where parties first discussed premarital agreement a few weeks before wedding and then only in general terms and first time wife saw the agreement or had any indication of its specific terms was the day before parties were scheduled to fly out of town for their wedding); In re Bernard, 204 P.3d 907 (Wash. 2009) (wife's attorney lacked sufficient time to review final draft of agreement that was not provided to wife until a few days before wedding, and wife was busy with guests, wedding details, and honeymoon preparations); In re Matson, 730 P.2d 668 (Wash. 1986) (wife first learned of contract three days before signing; wife received no copy of agreement).

15. Simeone v. Simeone, 581 A.2d 162 (Pa. 1990).

16. 816 S.W.2d 625 (Ark. Ct. App. 1991).

17. Pajak v. Pajak, 385 s.E.2d 384 (W. Va. 1984) (agreement presented one day before marriage, but wife did not even try to read it or ask for independent counsel); Lebeck v. Lebeck, 881 P.2d 727 (N.M. Ct. App. 1994) (shortness of time between presentation of agreement and wedding does not compel finding of duress or undue influence, especially where party had her own attorney who explained the agreement).

18. DeLorean v. DeLorean, 511 A.2d 1257 (N.J. Ch. Div. 1986) (agreement presented a few hours before marriage, but wife had business experience and also consulted independent counsel, who told her not to sign; agreement was enforceable).

§ 10.03 Ability to Consult Independent Counsel

Another common fact seen in cases challenging antenuptial agreements is the lack of independent counsel.[19] When attacking an agreement due to lack of independent counsel, however, it must be remembered that it is not the actual presence or lack of counsel that is the focus, but rather the ability and opportunity to consult independent counsel in a meaningful way.[20] No state makes consultation with independent counsel an absolute requirement for validity.

If a spouse had an opportunity to consult independent counsel but failed to exercise it, the agreement is not involuntary. This most commonly occurs when one party's counsel directly tells the other party to seek independent counsel. For example, in *Greenwald v. Greenwald*,[21] the husband's attorney advised the wife to employ her own attorney, but she refused his advice and signed the agreement. The court found the agreement was voluntary.[22]

---

19. *In re* Estate of Lutz, 563 N.W.2d 90 (N.D. 1997) (lack of advice to obtain independent counsel is significant factor in weighing voluntariness of agreement).

20. Rhyne-Morris v. Morris, 671 So. 2d 748 (Ala. Civ. App. 1995) (presence of independent counsel is not absolutely necessary to render agreement valid); Nanini v. Nanini, 802 P.2d 438 (Ariz. Ct. App. 1990) (fact that wife was not advised by counsel did not vitiate the agreement, where wife could have been advised by counsel); Friezo v. Friezo, 914 A.2d 533 (Conn. 2007) (a reasonable opportunity to consult with independent counsel, as required under the Connecticut Premarital Agreement Act for enforceability of prenuptial agreement, does not require that a party actually seek or obtain the advice of counsel, only that he or she be afforded a reasonable opportunity to do so); Binek v. Binek, 673 N.W.2d 594 (N.D. 2004) (husband did not prevent wife from consulting an attorney or asking questions prior to signing agreement, so agreement could not be vitiated on basis of lack of counsel). *Cf.* Ware v. Ware, 687 S.E.2d 382 (W. Va. 2009) (where one party to a prenuptial agreement is represented by counsel while the other is not, the burden of establishing the validity of that agreement is on the party seeking its enforcement), *overruling* Gant v. Gant, 329 S.E.2d 106 (W. Va. 1985).

21. 454 N.W.2d 34 (Wis. Ct. App.), *rev. denied*, 454 N.W.2d 806 (Wis. 1990).

22. *Accord* Strait v. Strait, 686 So. 2d 1230 (Ala. Civ. App. 1996) (wife had opportunity to consult counsel, but chose not to); Martin v. Martin, 612 So. 2d 1230 (Ala. Civ. App. 1992); Woolwine v. Woolwine, 519 So. 2d 1347 (Ala. Civ. App. 1987); *In re* Marriage of Bonds, 5 P.3d 815 (Cal. 2000); Gordon v. Gordon, 25 So. 3d 615 (Fla. Dist. Ct. App. 2009) (wife understood the significance of the document she was about to sign and chose not to seek the advice of a lawyer though she had sufficient time); Liebelt v. Leibelt, 801 P.2d 52 (Idaho Ct. App. 1990); Warren v. Warren, 523 N.E.2d 680 (Ill. App. Ct. 1988); *In re* Marriage of Shanks, 758 N.W.2d 506 (Iowa 2008) (agreement executed 10 days prior to wedding date was not procedurally unconscionable based on husband's superior bargaining position as attorney, where he twice urged wife to obtain independent legal counsel, wife was encouraged by Nebraska attorney to seek counsel from attorney licensed to practice in Iowa, and wife had sufficient time to seek advice from counsel); *In re* Marriage of Van Horn, 2002 WL 1428491 (Iowa Ct. App. 2002) (wife advised to obtain independent counsel); Ferry v. Ferry, 586 S.W.2d 782, 787 (Mo. Ct. App. 1979); Baer v. Cabiran-Baer, 44 So. 3d 840 (La. Ct. App. 2010) (husband was told by wife to seek counsel, but he did not do so in order to save money); Herget v. Herget, 550 A.2d 382 (Md. Ct. Spec. App. 1988); *In re* Estate of Garbade, 633 N.Y.S.2d 878 (N.Y. App. Div. 1995); *In re* Marriage of Foran, 834 P.2d 1081 (Wash. Ct. App. 1992). *See also* Robinson v. Robinson, 64 So. 3d 1067 (Ala. Civ. App. 2010) (husband knew he had opportunity to consult attorney where he himself was attorney).

A party has had sufficient opportunity to consult counsel if the agreement was drafted by the party's attorney at the party's own request,[23] or if the agreement was actively negotiated by the party himself or herself.[24]

Conversely, if a spouse never had an opportunity to obtain independent counsel, the agreement is deemed involuntary. The clearest cases are those in which the disadvantaged party had absolutely no chance to consult with independent counsel. For example, in *In re Estate of Crawford*,[25] the wife first learned of the agreement at her husband's attorney's office three days before the wedding. Even though she had no attorney and she said she did not understand the agreement, the husband insisted the wife sign the agreement at that time. The court found the agreement to be involuntary.[26]

The agreement is also considered involuntary if the disadvantaged spouse had an opportunity to consult with counsel, but counsel had no reasonable opportunity to give independent advice.[27] If the attorney had an opportunity to give advice, the agreement is not involuntary if the advice is bad (although it might be grounds for a malpractice action).[28] The agreement is also not involuntary if independent counsel gave advice but

---

23. *In re* Byrne, 535 N.E.2d 14 (Ill. App. Ct. 1989) (where agreement was drafted by wife's attorney at her request, agreement was voluntary, even though attorney did not explain provisions of agreement to wife); Hill v. Hill, 356 N.W.2d 49 (Minn. Ct. App. 1984) (wife requested her former attorney to draft agreement as representative of both parties; even though attorney did not give wife "independent" advice, agreement was held voluntary); Edwards v. Edwards, 16 Neb. App. 297, 744 N.W.2d 243 (2008) (although wife was not represented by counsel when signing agreement, she was represented by counsel when terms of agreement were negotiated until immediately prior to execution of agreement, and original draft was altered at request of her attorney).

24. Matuga v. Matuga, 600 N.E.2d 138 (Ind. Ct. App. 1992) (where agreement was proposed by wife and achieved ends purportedly desired, the agreement was enforceable although wife did not consult counsel; wife was high school graduate and husband was attorney); Pollack-Halvarson v. McGuire, 576 N.W.2d 451 (Minn. Ct. App. 1998); Simeone v. Simeone, 581 A.2d 162 (Pa. 1990); B.J.D. v. L.A.D., 23 S.W.3d 793 (Mo. Ct. App. 2000) (agreement was voluntary where it was drafted by husband's attorney, but wife's attorney negotiated changes).

25. 730 P.2d 675 (Wash. 1986).

26. *Accord* Hjortaas v. McCabe, 656 So. 2d 168 (Fla. Dist. Ct. App. 1995) (agreement set aside where it was presented to wife two days before wedding and she did not have adequate time to consult an attorney); *In re* Marriage of Gonzalez, 561 N.W.2d 94 (Iowa Ct. App. 1997) (agreement set aside where wife did not review agreement with independent counsel before signing); McMullin v. McMullin, 926 S.W.2d 108 (Mo. Ct. App. 1996) (wife not given enough time to consult counsel); Chaplain v. Chaplain, 682 S.E.2d 108 (Va. Ct. App. 2009) (agreement held unfair where wife could not read or write English when she signed agreement, was not given opportunity to have agreement reviewed by independent counsel, was taken to husband's attorney's office and presented signature page of agreement to sign, and thought she was signing "marriage paper"); Pember v. Shapiro, 794 N.W.2d 435 (N.D. 2011) (husband was advised not to seek counsel, and was given no time to do so before wedding).

27. Orgler v. Orgler, 568 A.2d 67 (N.J. App. Div. 1998) (wife unable to meet with her attorney for even an hour before signing agreement).

28. Casto v. Casto, 508 So. 2d 330 (Fla. 1987).

that advice was not heeded. For example, if counsel advises against signing the agreement, but the party signs anyway, the agreement is not invalid.[29]

It is also important that the counsel consulted be "independent," that is, counsel of one's choice. "Advice" to sign the agreement, or an explanation of the terms of the agreement, by the other spouse's attorney does not constitute the opportunity to consult independent counsel.[30] Two cases offer contrasting views of whether this requirement has been satisfied. In *In re Matson*,[31] the wife was advised by the husband's attorney, who had also represented the wife previously in her divorce case, concerning the antenuptial agreement he had drafted on the husband's behalf. The court held that she had a reasonable expectation that her husband's attorney would protect her interests, since he had previously represented her, but he had not represented her at all during the course of negotiations concerning the antenuptial agreement. The agreement was therefore invalid.[32] In a case with almost identical facts, however, the court in *Fletcher*

---

29. Tyler v. Tyler, 990 So. 2d 423 (Ala. Civ. App. 2008) (wife signed agreement against advice of her attorney); *In re* Estate of Cobb, 91 P.3d 1254 (tbl.) (Kan. Ct. App. 2004); DeLorean v. DeLorean, 511 A.2d 1257 (N.J. Ch. Div. 1986) (wife did not choose her own attorney but the attorney chosen for her told her not to sign and she signed anyway; agreement not involuntary); Darr v. Darr, 950 S.W.2d 867 (Mo. Ct. App. 1997) (wife signed agreement despite attorney's advice not to); Sailer v. Sailer, 764 N.W.2d 445 (N.D. 2009); Gardner v. Gardner, 190 Wis. 2d 217, 527 N.W.2d 701 (1994) (wife was advised by attorney not to sign, but she did so anyway five days before wedding; agreement upheld).

30. Lutgert v. Lutgert, 338 So. 2d 1111 (Fla. Dist. Ct. App. 1976) (wife given advice by husband's attorney by telephone); Ware v. Ware, 687 S.E.2d 382 (W. Va. 2009) (prenuptial agreement was invalid because attorney inappropriately purported to represent both wife and husband in the formation of the agreement, thereby interfering with wife's opportunity to consult with independent counsel). *Cf. Tyler*, 990 So. 2d 423 (although counsel for wife was chosen by husband, counsel was independent and not deficient in his representation of wife).

31. 730 P.2d 668 (Wash. 1986).

32. *See also Casto*, 508 So. 2d 330 (wife's counsel told her not to sign, and husband threatened wife into hiring less experienced attorney, who allowed wife to sign; agreement held invalid); *In re* Marriage of Richardson, 606 N.E.2d 56 (Ill. App. Ct. 1992) (husband tried to find substitute counsel for wife when wife's counsel recommended wife not sign agreement); Furer v. Furer, 2010 WL 3271504 (Nev. June 10, 2010) (where husband purported to represent wife's interest in marital agreement, wife was not represented by independent counsel); Sogg v. Nev. State Bank, 832 P.2d 781 (Nev. 1992) (wife not afforded meaningful consultation with independent counsel where husband interrupted their meeting, canceled the wedding, and then did not present new agreement until day of rescheduled wedding); Rowland v. Rowland, 599 N.E.2d 315 (Ohio Ct. App. 1991) (wife not given opportunity to consult counsel when she was pressured to sign by husband's counsel in husband's counsel's office); Carpenter v. Carpenter, 449 S.E.2d 502 (Va. Ct. App. 1994); *In re* Marriage of Bernard, 155 P.3d 171 (Wash. Ct. App. 1st Div. 2007) (attorney hired by wife at time of drafting of prenuptial agreements was not independent counsel, where attorney's role was limited to commenting on unfair provision and advising wife whether or not to sign document as written, and wife and attorney did not believe that entire prenuptial agreement was open for negotiation during amendment discussions); Ware v. Ware, 687 S.E.2d 382 (W. Va. 2009) (prenuptial agreement was invalid because attorney inappropriately purported to represent both wife and husband in the formation of the agreement, thereby interfering with wife's opportunity to consult with independent counsel). *Cf.* Strong v. Durbin, 851 N.Y.S.2d 428 (N.Y. App. Div. 1st Dep't 2008) (attorney who represented wife at time she signed prenuptial agreement did not have conflict of interest or

v. Fletcher[33] reached the opposite result. In *Fletcher*, when the husband and wife met, they were married to other parties. In their respective divorces from their spouses, husband had Attorney A of the firm A & B represent him, while wife had Attorney B of that same firm represent her. Attorney A then drafted an antenuptial agreement for husband and wife, and then presented the agreement to the wife in Attorney A's office. Attorney A did not explain to the wife what her rights were under the agreement. The wife, believing that Attorney A was representing her interests as well, since he was Attorney B's partner, signed the agreement. Indeed, the court noted that the wife, by virtue of her prior relationship with the firm, placed undue trust in the firm to protect her interests.[34] Nevertheless, the Ohio Supreme Court held that since the wife had the opportunity to consult independent counsel, but did not, she could not attack the validity of the agreement on that basis. The dissent pointed out that the wife did not consult independent counsel because she believed she *had* counsel representing her interests. The *Fletcher* case is very hard to understand.

Equally baffling is *Friezo v. Friezo*.[35] In that case, the majority found "fair and reasonable disclosure" where the husband's disclosure document simply listed 31 ambiguously labeled assets, giving no indication of how they were valued or, in some cases, what they truly were; indicated the value of the husband's holdings as "Estimated Value: $000"; and failed to list any income for the defendant. The wife was also steered to her future husband's sister-in-law's law firm, where the attorney failed to give the wife any advice or counsel or make even the most rudimentary discovery requests. Nonetheless, the court concluded the wife understood what she was signing and the agreement was enforceable.

§ 10.04 Lack of Understanding

Assuming that the contract was reasonably clear and that the parties had the opportunity to consult with independent counsel, the agreement is not invalid merely because one party failed to understand it. Courts have been particularly strong on this point where the party attacking the agreement failed to read it. For example, in *Laird v. Laird*,[36] the court summarily found the contract valid. "It is negligence as a matter of law to not read a contract before signing it."[37] Likewise, in *In re Estate of Garbade*,[38] the wife claimed that even though she had the opportunity to consult independent counsel but did not do so, the agreement was invalid because she could not understand

---

exercise undue influence over her, although husband's counsel recommended attorney after wife said she did not have one, and attorney had worked in husband's counsel's office as an intern during college).

33. 628 N.E.2d 1343 (Ohio 1994).
34. *Id.* at 1358.
35. 914 A.2d 533 (Conn. 2007).
36. 597 P.2d 463 (Wyo. 1973).
37. *Id.* at 467.
38. 633 N.Y.S.2d 878 (N.Y. App. Div. 1995).

it. The court disagreed, and held that the wife established "nothing more than her own dereliction in failing to acquaint herself" with the agreement's provisions.[39]

As charmingly stated in *Busch v. Busch*,[40]

Wife listed all her stocks and other property,

and estimated what their value might be.

Now he says her figures were stale and too low,

their worth was much higher, and he'd the right to know.

This is true in so far as his reasoning goes,

but this right was waived, the moment he chose

not to look at her assets; in his blissful condition

he never relied on the list's composition.[41]

The only exception to this rule is when the agreement is in a foreign language that the attacking spouse cannot understand, and the other spouse did not provide a translation.[42]

---

39. *Id.* at 880. *Accord* Brown v. Brown, 26 So. 3d 1210 (Ala. Civ. App. 2007); *In re* Marriage of Kloster, 469 N.E.2d 381 (Ill. App. Ct. 1984) (one who has had an opportunity to read a contract before signing, but signs before reading, cannot later plead lack of understanding or that the contract misled him); Ware v. Ware, 7 So. 3d 271 (Miss. Ct. App. 2008); Pulley v. Short, 261 S.W.3d 701 (Mo. Ct. App. W.D. 2008); *In re* Estate of Robertson, 60 S.W.3d 686 (Mo. Ct. App. S.D. 2001); Wiley v. Iverson, 985 P.2d 1176 (Mont. 1999) (wife's self-serving testimony that she did not understand antenuptial agreement was not credible evidence that agreement was invalid, given the strong evidence that wife was a relatively experienced businesswoman, was well educated, had more than a cursory understanding of the English language, and could have read the agreement but declined to do so); Kornegay v. Robinson, 637 S.E.2d 516 (N.C. 2006); Gartrell v. Gartrell, 908 N.E.2d 1019 (Ohio Ct. App. 5th Dist. 2009) (husband's negligence in failing to read antenuptial agreement before he signed it rose above ordinary negligence, and thus husband's unilateral mistake as to the terms of the agreement could not support rescission of the agreement); Barth v. Barth, 2010 WL 453548 (Ohio Ct. App. 4th Dist. 2010); Busch v. Busch, 732 A.2d 1274 (Pa. Super. 1999) (any defects in antenuptial agreement were waived when husband signed agreement without reading it or questioning wife's word); Cantrell v. Estate of Cantrell, 19 S.W.3d 842 (Tenn. Ct. App. 1999) (lack of interest does not vitiate agreement); Marsh v. Marsh, 949 S.W.2d 734 (Tex. Ct. App. 1997) (agreement would not be set aside at request of husband where he failed to read it and as a result did not understand the tax consequences; such a failure will not excuse a mistake of fact or law).

40. 732 A.2d 1274, 1277 (Pa. Super. 1999).

41. West's headnote to this part of the discussion summarizes:
   Former husband waived his right to assert
   that the pre-nup he signed didn't give just deserts;
   his counsel's advice he failed to heed,
   when the prenuptial he chose not to read,
   so the values alleged in the words of the plan
   would forever be binding on this man.

42. *In re* Marriage of Gonzalez, 561 N.W.2d 94 (Iowa Ct. App. 1997); *In re* Estate of Halmaghi, 457 N.W.2d 356 (Mich. Ct. App. 1990) (contract was in German, a language in which the wife had limited command, and husband knew this but failed to provide translation); *In re* Marriage of Shirilla, 319 Mont. 385, 89 P.3d 1 (2004) (wife did not sign voluntarily when she spoke only

§ 10.05 Fraud or Misrepresentation

A lack of independent counsel, in and of itself, can be particularly significant when it is combined with misrepresentations by the opposing party on the effect of the agreement. Contracts signed under these conditions are often found involuntary.[43]

Material misrepresentation may take place even in the presence of counsel. For example, in *Fagan-Massello v. Massello*,[44] the court held that the husband's failure to disclose his drug abuse and severe addiction constituted a material misrepresentation that made the antenuptial agreement invalid.

§ 10.06 Duress

The traditional contract defense of duress is available against an antenuptial agreement. Duress is but a subspecies of the "involuntariness" that has been discussed up to this point. The following cases in this subsection are more traditional contract "duress" cases than those above.

§ 10.061 Pregnancy

The cases are split on whether a threatened refusal to marry a pregnant woman constitutes duress or undue influence. Many cases hold that such a threat is *not* duress. In *Hamilton v. Hamilton*,[45] the wife was 18 years old, pregnant, and unemployed. She was informed by the husband that there would be no wedding unless she signed the

---

Russian, the attorney provided to her by the husband did not speak Russian, and any advice given was without the benefit of a translator); Holler v. Holler, 364 S.C. 256, 612 S.E.2d 469 (Ct. App. 2005) (Ukranian wife did not understand contents of agreement, and tried to translate agreement into Russian but had no money to do so); *In re* Marriage of Obaidi & Qayoum, 226 P.3d 787 (Wash. Ct. App. 3rd Div., 2010) (Islamic antenuptial agreement, *mahr*, was in Farsi, which husband did not read or understand). *Cf. Wiley*, 985 P.2d 1176 (wife's self-serving testimony that she did not understand antenuptial agreement was not credible evidence that agreement was invalid, given the strong evidence that wife was a relatively experienced businesswoman, was well educated, had more than a cursory understanding of the English language, and could have read the agreement but declined to do so); Chaplain v. Chaplain, 2011 WL 134104 (Va. Ct. App. 2011) (unreported) (although wife claimed she could not read or understand English, the evidence showed wife had read English menus and newspapers and wrote various business letters in English).

43. Mixon v. Mixon, 550 So. 2d 999 (Ala. Ct. App. 1989) (wife signed agreement on evening before wedding noting at bottom that contract would be rewritten later to incorporate new terms on husband's representations; the contract was not rewritten; agreement set aside); Ferry v. Ferry, 586 S.W.2d 782 (Mo. Ct. App. 1979) (wife signed agreement without independent counsel two days before wedding in reliance on husband's promise to change certain terms; terms were not changed; agreement set aside).

Cases considering fraud and misrepresentation as to the disclosure of assets and income is considered in **chapter 11**.

44. 1997 WL 89091 (Del. Ch., Feb. 24, 1997).

45. 591 A.2d 720 (Pa. 1991).

agreement. Despite this pressure, the court found there was no duress, because she had signed the agreement despite her attorney's advice not to do so.[46]

On the other hand, some cases have held that a threat not to go through with the wedding when the bride is in a family way *does* constitute duress. For example, in *Ex parte Williams*,[47] the wife was pregnant at the time the husband presented the agreement to her. The husband said he would not marry her unless she signed. The court held that the husband's conditioning of the marriage on the signing of the antenuptial agreement, coupled with her moral objection to abortion and the importance of legitimacy in a small town, created a material issue of fact of whether a coercive atmosphere existed.[48]

---

46. *See also* Kilborn v. Kilborn, 628 So. 2d 884 (Ala. Civ. App. 1993) (fact of pregnancy is not duress, especially where wife had contacted two attorneys and husband made full and complete disclosure); *In re* Marriage of Dawley, 551 P.2d 323 (Cal. 1976); Margulies v. Margulies, 491 So. 2d 581 (Fla. Dist. Ct. App. 1986) (wife felt pressured to marry husband to legitimate child; held not duress); Mallen v. Mallen, 622 S.E.2d 812 (Ga. 2005) (prospective husband's insistence on execution of prenuptial agreement as a condition of marriage did not constitute duress that would void agreement, even though prospective wife was pregnant at the time); Biliouris v. Biliouris, 852 N.E.2d 687 (Mass. App. Ct. 2006) (fact that wife found herself, single and pregnant, presented with antenuptial agreement shortly before her scheduled wedding date and being told that if she did not sign the agreement there would be no wedding, did not establish that execution of antenuptial agreement was a product of coercion or duress); *Hamilton*, 591 A.2d 720 (antenuptial agreement pursuant to which wife expressly waived right to spousal support in event of divorce was enforceable absent showing that agreement was entered into under duress; though wife was 18, pregnant, unemployed, and probably frightened at the time she signed the agreement, and was told that without agreement there would be no wedding, she was represented by counsel and signed agreement despite counsel's contrary advice); Osorno v. Osorno, 76 S.W.3d 509 (Tex. Ct. App. 2002) (husband had no legal duty to marry his wife, and, thus, their premarital agreement was not unenforceable on ground that wife's decision to sign agreement as she was 40, unmarried, and pregnant was involuntary); Bassler v. Bassler, 593 A.2d 82 (Vt. 1991) (although wife felt pressured into signing agreement because she was pregnant, claim of duress for this reason must fail).

47. 617 So. 2d 1033 (Ala. 1992).

48. *See also* Rowland v. Rowland, 599 N.E.2d 315 (Ohio Ct. App. 4th Dist. 1991) (antenuptial agreement was unenforceable due to overreaching; agreement was prepared entirely by husband's counsel without any input from wife, husband's counsel was unaware that wife was pregnant at time agreement was signed, counsel failed to advise wife of rights she was giving up in agreement and her right to independent counsel, and wife's signature was obtained only after being advised in husband's counsel's office, procedure in clear violation of Canons of Ethics); Holler v. Holler, 364 S.C. 256, 612 S.E.2d 469 (Ct. App. 2005) (premarital agreement was invalid and unenforceable as result of being signed under duress, where Ukrainian wife did not understand contents of agreement, she unsuccessfully attempted to translate agreement into Russian to better comprehend it, husband was aware that wife's visa was set to expire and he told wife to sign agreement if she wanted to be married prior to expiration of visa, wife was in United States with no means to support herself, wife had no money to retain attorney or translator, if wife was not able to marry she would be forced to return to Ukraine, and because she was pregnant with husband's child, she sought to ensure his continued support and to remain in United States).

These cases may be reconcilable by looking at evidence other than the pregnancy. Where pregnancy is essentially the only evidence of duress or undue influence, the cases tend to find the agreement valid. Where there are other aggravating factors in addition to pregnancy, however, the agreement is more questionable. In *Williams*, for instance, the wife's strong opposition to abortion combined with her pregnancy to make the agreement unenforceable. Viewed in this light, *Hamilton* seems to be an aberration, as the wife's pregnancy combined with her young age and complete lack of ability to support the child arguably should have made the agreement invalid. The court may have paid too much attention to the fact that the wife had counsel and ignored the overwhelming economic pressure that prevented her from objecting to the agreement.

§ 10.062 Physical Threats

There is not a great deal of case law dealing with agreements signed under the pressure of threatened physical abuse. Where such threats overcome the will of the innocent spouse, however, the agreement is invalid.[49]

In a stinging rebuke to domestic violence, one court invalidated an antenuptial agreement on the grounds of duress based on evidence of physical abuse during the marriage—abuse that occurred after the antenuptial agreement was signed. In *In re Marriage of Foran*,[50] the court held that the manner in which the wife was treated, both before and after the marriage, was relevant to determining the procedural fairness of the agreement and its ultimate validity. Logically, this principle should be extended to matters beyond duress. For example, a party's behavior during the marriage can be relevant to the issue of full and fair disclosure as well.[51]

§ 10.063 Threat to Call Off the Wedding

Apart from the factors considered thus far—time to sign, ability to consult counsel, lack of understanding, misrepresentation, and specific threats—other attempts to show involuntariness have generally failed. Courts generally toss out the claim that the

---

49. Casto v. Casto, 508 So. 2d 330 (Fla. 1987) (husband threatened that he would blow up the house and throw bleach over the wife's clothes unless she found an attorney who would let her sign the agreement).

50. 834 P.2d 1081 (Wash. Ct. App. 1992).

51. *See* Parr v. Parr, 635 N.E.2d 1124 (Ind. Ct. App. 1994) (where husband dominated wife during their first marriage and wife relied on husband to take care of her needs, wife's consultation of independent attorney prior to execution of antenuptial agreement before parties' second marriage did not obviate her lack of voluntariness).

agreement is invalid because one party refused to proceed with the marriage unless the agreement was signed before the wedding,[52] or that the agreement is invalid because it was signed at a hectic time.[53] The reasoning of the courts is that the threat is really no threat at all: One is always free to cancel a wedding.[54]

---

52. *E.g., Ex parte* Walters, 580 So. 2d 1352 (Ala. 1991) (no duress shown where husband told wife they would not get married unless she signed agreement, and wife had independent counsel); Liebelt v. Liebelt, 801 P.2d 52 (Idaho Ct. App. 1990) (duress not shown where husband told wife he had to have agreement prior to marriage); *In re* Marriage of Barnes, 755 N.E.2d 522 (Ill. App. Ct. 4th Dist. 2001); Rose v. Rose, 526 N.E.2d 231 (Ind. Ct. App. 1988) (where husband told wife they would not marry unless wife signed agreement, duress not shown as wife insisted on signing and insisted she did not want independent counsel); *In re* Marriage of Adams, 729 P.2d 1151 (Kan. 1986) (husband told wife to sign agreement one hour before wedding or wedding would be canceled; no duress because wife had seen agreement before, knew contents, and had consulted an attorney); Lebeck v. Lebeck, 881 P.2d 727 (N.M. Ct. App. 1994); Weinstein v. Weinstein, 830 N.Y.S.2d 179 (N.Y. App. Div. 2d Dep't 2007); Colello v. Colello, 780 N.Y.S.2d 450 (N.Y. App. Div. 4th Dep't 2004); *In re* Estate of Heric, 669 N.Y.S.2d 791 (N.Y. Sur. Ct. 1998) (incarcerated husband's subjective fear that wife would not marry him unless he signed agreement was not duress); Taylor v. Taylor, 832 P.2d 429 (Okla. Ct. App. 1991) (no duress shown where, although husband threatened to call off wedding unless wife signed, evidence showed wife had antenuptial agreement for months before wedding and had consulted with independent counsel); Greenwald v. Greenwald, 454 N.W.2d 34 (Wis. Ct. App. 1990), *rev. denied*, 454 N.W.2d 806 (Wis. 1990).

53. Herget v. Herget, 550 A.2d 382 (Md. Ct. Spec. App. 1988), *rev'd on other grounds*, 573 A.2d 798 (Md. 1990).

54. *E.g., In re* Marriage of Miller, 2002 WL 31312840 (Iowa Ct. App. 2002) (unreported) (fact that husband presented wife with prenuptial agreement on day before wedding, and wife knew that husband would not marry her unless she signed it, did not establish duress, where wife could have canceled wedding and husband's insistence that wife sign prenuptial agreement as condition of marriage was not a threat or unlawful).

Procedural Fairness: Knowledge of Rights

11

As stated in § **8.01**, in all states the parties must have had reasonable knowledge of the value of the rights they were waiving under the agreement. In order to have that knowledge, each party must have had some understanding of the financial situation of the other. There are two ways in which this understanding can be obtained: full and fair disclosure, or independent knowledge.[1]

§ 11.01 Full and Fair Disclosure

Financial knowledge is most frequently obtained when one spouse makes a full and fair disclosure of assets and income. Generally, due to the confidential relationship of the parties, the burden is to disclose, not to inquire.[2] Even though the burden is to disclose and not to inquire, there is

---

1. *See generally* Annotation, *Failure to Disclose Extent or Value of Property Owned as Ground for Avoiding Premarital Agreement*, 3 A.L.R.5th 394 (1992). In Florida, however, no disclosure of assets is required for an antenuptial agreement to be valid in the probate context. FLA. STAT. ANN. § 732.702(2).

2. *In re* Estate of Lebsock, 618 P.2d 683 (Colo. App. 1980); Friezo v. Friezo, 914 A.2d 533 (Conn. 2007); Hjortaas v. McCabe, 556 So. 2d 168 (Fla. Dist. Ct. App. 1995); Blige v. Blige, 656 S.E.2d 822 (Ga. 2008); Cannon v. Cannon, 865 A.2d 563 (Md. 2005); DeMatteo v. DeMatteo, 762 N.E.2d 797 (Mass. 2002); Rosenberg v. Lipnick, 389 N.E.2d 385 (Mass. 1979); Mabus v. Mabus, 890 So. 2d 806 (Miss. 2003); DeLorean v. DeLorean, 511 A.2d 1257 (N.J. Super. 1986); *In re* Marriage of Bowers, 922 P.2d 722 (Or. Ct. App. 1996); Ryken v. Ryken, 461 N.W.2d 122 (S.D. 1990); *In re* Estate of Beesley, 883 P.2d 1343 (Utah 1994). The burden to disclose might be less, however, when the party complaining of nondisclosure is the one who sought the agreement. Rostanzo v. Rostanzo, 900 N.E.2d 101 (Mass. Ct. App. 2009); *In re* White, 718 S.W.2d 185 (Mo. Ct. App. 1986) (where parties had discussed their

split of authority on whether the disadvantaged party must affirmatively introduce evidence of lack of disclosure[3] or whether the burden of proof regarding disclosure is on the party relying on the agreement.[4] Regardless of where the burden of proof lies, it is clear that the mere allegation that a spouse failed to disclose the value of his or her assets does not, standing alone, constitute fraud or overreaching sufficient to vitiate the agreement.[5]

Disclosure must contain not only the assets, but the reasonable value of those assets as well.[6] The disclosure need not be exact, but it must be reasonably accurate.[7] Thus, if

---

finances in general terms and wife was motivating party in obtaining agreement, wife's attack on agreement was rejected). *But see* Porreco v. Porreco, 811 A.2d 566 (Pa. 2002) (wife's reliance on husband's misrepresentation of the value of engagement ring, which was included as wife's asset in prenuptial agreement, was not reasonable, for purposes of determining whether prenuptial agreement could be voided due to fraudulent misrepresentation, where wife had possession of ring at time of agreement, could have obtained an appraisal, and had sufficient opportunity to inform herself of the nature and extent of her own assets).

3. *In re* Marriage of Bonds, 5 P.3d 815 (Cal. 2000); *In re* Estate of Lopata, 641 P.2d 952 (Colo. 1982); Matuga v. Matuga, 600 N.E.2d 138 (Ind. Ct. App. 1992); *Cannon*, 865 A.2d 563; *In re* Estate of Benker, 331 N.W.2d 193 (Mich. 1982); *In re* Estate of Peterson, 381 N.W.2d 109 (Neb. 1986); *In re* Estate of Zach, 536 N.Y.S.2d 774 (N.Y. App. Div. 1989) (husband claimed no memory of circumstances under which agreement was signed; not sufficient to show lack of disclosure); Paroly v. Paroly, 876 A.2d 1061 (Pa. Super. Ct. 2005).

4. Debolt v. Blackburn, 159 N.E. 790 (Ill. 1927); *In re* Marriage of Sokolowski, 597 N.E.2d 675 (Ill. App. Ct. 1992); Lawson v. Loid, 896 S.W.2d 1 (Ky. 1995) (burden of proof regarding disclosure is on party relying on agreement); Ortel v. Gettig, 116 A.2d 145 (Md. 1955); *In re* Estate of Serbus, 324 N.W.2d 381 (Minn. 1982); Hook v. Hook, 431 N.E.2d 667 (Ohio 1982); *In re* Estate of Davis, 213 S.W.3d 288 (Tenn. Ct. App. 2006).

5. Freiman v. Freiman, 680 N.Y.S.2d 797 (N.Y. Sup. Ct. 1998).

6. Stemler v. Stemler, 36 So. 3d 54 (Ala. Civ. App. 2009); Casto v. Casto, 508 So. 2d 330 (Fla. 1987) (mere listing of assets without values is insufficient); Fern v. Fern, 207 So. 2d 291 (Fla. 1968) (husband disclosed ownership of stock but not its value; contract invalid); *In re* Estate of Shinn, 925 A.2d 88 (N.J. Super. App. Div. 2007); McMullin v. McMullin, 926 S.W.2d 108 (Mo. Ct. App. 1996) (full disclosure was lacking where there were no values for assets listed); Orgler v. Orgler, 568 A.2d 67 (N.J. App. Div. 1989) (even though wife knew husband was "wealthy," she had no idea of his net worth; agreement set aside); *In re* Marriage of Bernard, 204 P.3d 907 (Wash. 2009). *But see* Robinson v. Robinson, 64 So. 3d 1067, 2010 WL 5030120 (Ala. Civ. App. 2010) (failure to disclose values of properties did not void agreement, especially given that listing of those properties put parties on notice of their existence, and husband was aware that wife's family possessed large amount of real property); *Friezo*, 914 A.2d 533 (disclosure that contained assets but assigned value to each asset as $0 deemed sufficient).

7. Tyler v. Tyler, 990 So. 2d 423 (Ala. Civ. App. 2008) (a spouse does not have to have an exact knowledge of the other spouse's separate estate in order for an antenuptial agreement to be enforceable; a general knowledge of the extent of the other party's estate is all that is necessary); Lemaster v. Dutton, 694 So. 2d 1360 (Ala. Civ. App. 1996) ("general knowledge" of assets is all that is required in light of full disclosure requirement); Nanini v. Nanini, 802 P.2d 438 (Ariz. Ct. App. 1990); *Estate of Lopata*, 641 P.2d 952 (fair disclosure is not synonymous with detailed disclosure); Del Vecchio v. Del Vecchio, 143 So. 2d 17 (Fla. 1962) (while disclosure should be full, fair, and open, it need not be minutely detailed or exact); Gordon v. Gordon, 25 So. 3d 615 (Fla. Dist. Ct. App. 4th Dist. 2009); *Matuga*, 600 N.E.2d 138 (disclosure need not be exact); Davis v. Miller, 7 P.3d 1223 (Kan. 2003); Hartz v. Hartz, 234 A.2d 865 (Md. 1967) (disclosure need not be drastically

a party fails to disclose a small fraction of the total estate, the disclosure will be deemed sufficient.[8] Where, however, disclosure is not made or is misleading, courts will find the antenuptial agreement invalid.[9] Further, while most cases focus on disclosure of

---

sweeping); Harbom v. Harbom, 760 A.2d 272 (Md. 2000); Rostanzo, 900 N.E.2d 101 (husband's failure to list the mortgages on his real estate holdings set out in a schedule of assets appended to the prenuptial agreement did not give rise to grounds for invalidating the agreement after husband's death; husband's error in estimating his worth and his resources was an error in wife's favor, and there was no indication that disclosure of information reducing the husband's net worth would have materially affected wife's decision to sign the agreement); Miles v. Werle, 977 S.W.2d 297 (Mo. Ct. App. 1998) (while detailed disclosure is preferable, lack of detail does not invalidate agreement; general knowledge of the nature, extent, and amount of assets is sufficient); In re Marriage of Yager, 963 P.2d 137 (Or. Ct. App. 1998); In re Estate of Geyer, 533 A.2d 423 (Pa. 1987) (disclosure need not be exact); Wilson v. Moore, 929 S.W.2d 367 (Tenn. Ct. App. 1996) (due to confidential relationship between parties, there must be disclosure of assets that is reasonable, although it need not be exact; inadvertent nondisclosure that does not render disclosure as a whole insufficient will not render agreement invalid); Estate of Beesley, 883 P.2d 1343 (disclosure need not be exact as to every item; general disclosure of worth is sufficient). See also Waton v. Waton, 887 So. 2d 419 (Fla. Dist. Ct. App. 2004) (disclosure that husband owned 25 percent of company was reasonable disclosure, although no value was stated). But see De Lorean, 511 A.2d 1257 (full and complete disclosure means detailed disclosure).

8. In re Hopkins, 520 N.E.2d 415 (Ill. App. Ct. 1988) (husband failed to disclose $24,000 of estate worth over $300,000; agreement upheld); Herget v. Herget, 550 A.2d 382 (Md. Ct. Spec. App. 1988), rev'd on other grounds, 573 A.2d 798 (Md. 1990) (although undisclosed pension was worth $71,700, it was only a "small fraction" of husband's total net worth); Heady v. Heady, 766 S.W.2d 489 (Mo. Ct. App. 1989) (disclosure omitted personal items of nominal value); Sasarak v. Sasarak, 586 N.E.2d 172 (Ohio Ct. App. 1991) (wife understood disclosure of assets); Gula v. Gula, 551 A.2d 324 (Pa. Super. 1988) (contract stated husband's worth as $90,000 to $130,000; disclosure sufficient). But see Barnett v. Lovely, 2010 WL 1133249 (Ky. Ct. App. Mar. 26, 2010) (although husband listed his assets as totaling $1.8 million, and husband's representation was understated by $2.7 million, the understatement did not invalidate the agreement; "We fail to see how the knowledge that some of Donnie's assets were worth $4 million rather than $1.8 million would have caused Andrea to refuse to sign the agreement.").

9. Stemler, 36 So. 2d 54 (although husband said wife had a general knowledge of what his assets were, based on the parties' cohabitation prior to marriage, there was no valuation of husband's assets listed in the agreement, wife lacked financial sophistication to convert the information in the agreement to an apprised value, and the agreement contained no information regarding husband's income); Wylie v. Wylie, 459 S.W.2d 127 (Ark. 1970) (husband told wife he was worth $200,000, when he was actually worth $455,000); Anttila v. Sinikka, 611 So. 2d 565 (Fla. Dist. Ct. App. 1992) (lack of financial disclosure vitiates agreement); Blige v. Blige, 656 S.2d 822 (Ga. 2008) (husband failed to disclose a fact material to the parties' antenuptial agreement, i.e., the $150,000 in cash he had hidden away, and therefore he did not make a full and fair disclosure of his financial status before the signing of the antenuptial agreement); Alexander v. Alexander, 610 S.E.2d 48 (Ga. 2005) (antenuptial agreement for lack of full disclosure where husband did not disclose a $40,000 investment account); Estate of Stack v. Venzke, 485 N.E.2d 907 (Ind. Ct. App. 1985) (husband failed to disclose $44,000 of $149,000 estate); In re Marriage of Richardson, 606 N.E.2d 56 (Ill. App. Ct. 1992) (husband undervalued stock on balance sheet); In re Marriage of Lewis, 808 S.W.2d 919 (Mo. Ct. App. 1991); Fick v. Fick, 851 P.2d 455 (Nev. 1993) (husband's failure to disclose assets rendered agreement unenforceable where assets were of such magnitude the wife could not have known or guessed their worth); Jacobitti v. Jacobitti, 623 A.2d 794 (N.J. Super. App. Div. 1993) (husband failed to disclose net worth); Rivera v. Rivera, 243 S.W.3d 1148 (N.M. Ct. App.

assets, the parties may also be required to disclose their incomes.[10] This is not, however, a universal rule.[11]

It is possible that a party may fail to make full and accurate financial disclosure, but the agreement will be upheld anyway because the lack of disclosure caused no prejudice. For example, in *Hill v. Hill*,[12] the husband disclosed only $300,000 to $400,000 of his $750,000 net worth. The error was a good-faith underestimation of value, how-

---

2010) (agreement invalid where wife did not disclose extent of her assets); Postiy v. Postiy, 2003 WL 1962410 (Ohio Ct. App. 5th Dist. 2003) (where husband omitted from his financial statement an airplane and gold assets amounting to $150,000 of his aggregate worth of $1.5 million, valued his business based on an insurance amount of $700,000 though actual value was $1 million, and utilized a value for his oil wells that was three years old, disclosure insufficient); *In re* Mize, 611 N.E.2d 460 (Ohio Ct. App. 1992) (disclosure insufficient where there was no description or listing of properties, and merely a vague reference to "assets"); Mormello v. Mormello, 682 A.2d 824 (Pa. Super. 1996) (agreement failed for lack of disclosure where the agreement obscured the husband's financial resources, sources of income, pensions, and salaries); *Estate of Geyer*, 533 A.2d 423 (husband failed to disclose real estate and store, which together were 50 percent of net worth); *Estate of Davis*, 213 S.W.3d 288 (wife did not make a full and fair disclosure of the nature, extent, and value of her holdings to husband, where individual who typed list of wife's assets for attachment to agreement, which list could not be located, testified she could not recall there being any values on the list, husband testified there was some property he did not even know wife owned, and as to the property of which he knew, he did not know its value save for real property he sold to wife prior to their marriage); Carpenter v. Carpenter, 449 S.E.2d 502 (Va. Ct. App. 199); *In re* Estate of Hansen, 892 P.2d 764 (Wash. Ct. App. 1995) (parties must disclose amount, character, and value of property).

10. Ashton v. Ashton, 6 Conn. Super. Ct. Rep. 1001 (1991) (husband failed to disclose income); Corbett v. Corbett, 628 S.E.2d 585 (Ga. 2006) (husband's failure to disclose his income to wife rendered antenuptial agreement unenforceable; income was material fact since wife waived right to seek alimony as part of agreement, and parties' standard of living before marriage did not put wife on notice that husband had failed to disclose material facts); *Orgler*, 568 A.2d 67 (financial disclosure was inadequate when wife knew only that husband was a man of substance; wife must be made aware of true net worth, including income); *DeLorean*, 511 A.2d 1257 (in order for the requirement of full disclosure to be satisfied, the parties must provide a written list of assets and income); Marschall v. Marschall, 477 A.2d 833 (N.J. Super. Ch. Div. 1984) (disclosure must include the nature and extent of assets, the parties' incomes, and anything else that might bear on the parties' conclusion that the agreement is fair; failure to disclose husband's $250,000 income warranted setting aside the agreement). Nitkiewicz v. Nitkiewicz, 535 A.2d 664 (Pa. Super. Ct. 1988), *allocatur denied*, 551 A.2d 216 (Pa. 1988) (husband failed to disclose second source of income; exact amount of income unclear, because husband invoked the Fifth Amendment when asked about it; disclosure not sufficient); *Estate of Geyer*, 533 A.2d 423 (full disclosure is made only when the parties reveal all their financial resources); Schumacher v. Schumacher, 388 N.W.2d 912 (Wis. 1986) (adequate disclosure means complete disclosure of financial status).

11. Smith v. Walsh-Smith, 887 N.Y.S.2d 565 (N.Y. App. Div. 1st Dep't 2009) (husband's failure to disclose income was not in and of itself sufficient to vitiate agreement, where there was no evidence that husband used wealth as leverage to coerce wife to sign agreement); King v. King, 66 S.W.3d 28 (Mo. Ct. App. 2001) (antenuptial agreement not rendered invalid by husband's failure to disclose all sources of income, where nondisclosure did not adversely affect wife's ability to make an informed decision regarding her marital rights).

12. 356 N.W.2d 49 (Minn. Ct. App. 1984).

ever, and the wife testified that she would have signed the agreement even if accurate disclosure had been made. The agreement was upheld.[13]

Obviously, the best way to prove financial disclosure is by an attached appendix to the agreement. Contracts containing accurate financial disclosure by way of an appendix have almost always been found to have made adequate financial disclosure,[14] unless, obviously, the financial disclosure statement is false, or there is a statement in the antenuptial agreement stating that a financial disclosure statement is attached to the agreement but there is no such financial disclosure statement.[15] A statement in the antenuptial agreement itself that the necessary information has been disclosed is also good evidence that disclosure has been made.[16] Courts, however, have not hesitated to ignore a full disclosure statement and find the disclosure inadequate when the financial disclosure is not attached to the agreement or there is other evidence that disclosure has not been made.[17] One court even held that lack of financial disclosure in the face of a full disclosure clause constituted a breach sufficient to rescind the contract.[18]

---

13. *Accord* Kolflat v. Kolflat, 636 So. 2d 87 (Fla. Dist. Ct. App. 1994) (wife testified she would have signed agreement even if husband had been worth $100 million); Hiers v. Estate of Hiers, 628 S.E.2d 653 (Ga. Ct. App. 2006) (misstatements in husband's financial documents attached to prenuptial agreement could not establish that the agreement was obtained by fraud or misrepresentation of material fact, so as to invalidate agreement and enable wife to claim year's support from husband's estate, where there was no evidence wife inquired into husband's financial condition or relied on the financial documents before signing agreement); Colonna v. Colonna, 791 A.2d 353 (Pa. Super. Ct. 2001) (husband's overvaluation of his closely held business did not render antenuptial agreement unenforceable; overvaluation did not induce wife to enter the contract or the marriage); Schutterle v. Schutterle, 260 N.W.2d 341 (S.D. 1977) (wife admitted that she did not need to get married for support, and that she was interested in her husband and not in what he had, and that she would have married him even if he had been a poor man); Greenwald v. Greenwald, 454 N.W.2d 34 (Wis. Ct. App.) (wife admitted she would have signed the contract regardless of the husband's worth; lack of knowledge did not invalidate contract), *review denied*, 454 N.W.2d 806 (Wis. 1990).

14. McKee-Johnson v. Johnson, 444 N.W.2d 259 (Minn. 1989) (attaching statement to contract is an appropriate and practical way in which to comply with the disclosure requirement); Estate of Hensley v. Estate of Hensley, 524 So. 2d 325 (Miss. 1988) (enforcing contract containing disclosure statement); *In re* Adelman's Estate, 377 S.W.2d 549 (Mo. Ct. App. 1964); Simeone v. Simeone, 581 A.2d 162 (Pa. 1990). *Cf. DeLorean*, 511 A.2d 1257 (suggesting prophylactic rule that agreement be per se unenforceable unless financial statement is attached).

15. Brees v. Cramer, 586 A.2d 1284 (Md. 1991); Reed v. Rope, 817 S.W.2d 503 (Mo. Ct. App. 1991); Sogg v. Nev. State Bank, 832 P.2d 781 (Nev. 1992); *Estate of Geyer*, 533 A.2d 423.

16. Dornemann v. Dornemann, 850 A.2d 273 (Conn. Super. Ct. 2004) (parties' premarital agreement was not rendered unenforceable because written financial disclosures were not attached, where wife acknowledged that husband provided full and detailed financial disclosure to wife's attorney before the execution of the premarital agreement); Estate of Serbus v. Serbus, 324 N.W.2d 381 (Minn. 1982); Day v. Vitus, 792 P.2d 1240 (Or. Ct. App. 1990); Paroly v. Paroly, 876 A.2d 1061 (Pa. Super. 2005).

17. Fick v. Fick, 851 .2d 445 (Nev. 1993); Orgler v. Orgler, 568 A.2d 67 (N.J. Super. App. Div. 1989); *DeLorean*, 511 A.2d 1257; *In re* Mize, 611 N.E.2d 460 (Ohio Ct. App. 1992); *Estate of Geyer*, 533 A.2d 423.

18. *Id.* 533 A.2d 423.

§ 11.02 Independent Knowledge

The knowledge requirement may be satisfied if the party has independent knowledge of the other party's estate. In such a situation, some courts have held that a general recitation in the antenuptial agreement that one party is "wealthy" may be sufficient, obviating the need for more exact figures.[19] Other cases, however, have held that mere knowledge of a reputation as to wealth is not sufficient.[20]

One common source of knowledge is through personal exposure to the other spouse's property, as when the parties live together or visit each other's property.[21]

---

19. Nanini v. Nanini, 802 P.2d 438 (Ariz. Ct. App. 1990); Warren v. Warren, 523 N.E.2d 680 (Ill. App. Ct. 1988) (contract noted husband was multimillionaire and gave general recital of wealth); *In re* Adams, 729 P.2d 1151 (Kan. 1986) (wife knew husband was multimillionaire but didn't know net worth); *DeLorean*, 511 A.2d 1257 (wife knew husband was man of substantial means); Taylor v. Taylor, 832 P.2d 429 (Okla. Ct. App. 1991) (full and fair disclosure requirement is satisfied by general knowledge of worth).

20. Watson v. Watson, 126 N.E.2d 220 (Ill. 1955); Schumacher v. Schumacher, 388 N.W.2d 912 (Wis. 1986). *But see In re* Marriage of Sokolowski, 597 N.E.2d 675 (Ill. App. Ct. 1992) (friend telling wife that husband was "probably worth more than $100,000" was sufficient independent knowledge).

21. Ruzic v. Ruzic, 549 So. 2d 72 (Ala. 1989) (parties owned property together, lived together for six years); *Ex parte* Walters, 580 So. 2d 1352 (Ala. 1991) (parties lived together); Lemaster v. Dutton, 694 So. 2d 1360 (Ala. Civ. App. 1996) (prospective wife had general knowledge of fiancé's estate where they had lived together for a year and she knew of his ownership of major assets); Martin v. Martin, 612 So. 2d 1230 (Ala. Civ. App. 1992) (parties lived together for two years prior to marriage, and wife frequently visited husband's properties); Hughes v. Hughes, 471 S.W.2d 355 (Ark. 1971) (parties knew each other for nine years, visited properties); Newman v. Newman, 653 P.2d 728 (Colo. 1982); Winchester v. McCue, 882 A.2d 143 (Conn. App. Ct. 2005) (parties dated for several years before marriage, became knowledgeable as to each other's standard of living and spending habits, and thereby acquired independent knowledge of each other's financial circumstances); Doig v. Doig, 787 So. 2d 100 (Fla. Dist. Ct. App. 2d Dist. 2001); Lawrence v. Lawrence, 286 Ga. 309, 687 S.E.2d 421 (2009) (evidence of wife's familiarity, garnered over the course of a lengthy premarital relationship including over two years of cohabitation, with husband's business dealings and personal financial condition, which included husband's successful real estate practice, ownership of two homes, a boat, and several vehicles, along with the absence of any evidence of material income or assets of husband of which wife was unaware, was sufficient to support trial court's finding that there was full and fair disclosure of husband's financial condition prior to execution of antenuptial agreement); Mallen v. Mallen, 280 Ga. 43, 622 S.E.2d 812 (2005) (since wife had lived with prospective husband for four years and was aware from standard of living they enjoyed that he received significant income from his business and other sources, lack of financial disclosure did not render agreement void); *In re* Estate of Brosseau, 531 N.E.2d 158 (Ill. App. Ct. 1988) (husband acquired independent knowledge of wife's land by farming it for a number of years); Fleming v. Fleming, 406 N.E.2d 879 (Ill. App. Ct. 1980) (parties dated for two years, wife knew nature of husband's portfolio); Parr v. Parr, 644 N.E.2d 548 (Ind. 1994) (sufficient disclosure of assets to support validity of antenuptial agreement signed before couple's remarriage, although parties discussed their property for three to four minutes and wife's attorney was not present; parties lived together for 17 of preceding 18 years and wife opted to forgo having her attorney examine instrument); Matuga v. Matuga, 600 N.E.2d 138 (Ind. Ct. App. 1992) (wife could not maintain she was unaware of husband's professional corporation); *In re* Marriage of Miller, 2002 WL 31312840 (Iowa Ct. App. 2002); *In re* Estate of Ascherl, 445 N.W.2d 391 (Iowa Ct. App.

Another common way for a party to obtain independent knowledge is by working in the other spouse's business before marriage. The employee spouse's position, however, must be one that gives that spouse some degree of exposure to financial information.[22]

A few cases have held that knowledge obtained *after* the marriage, along with acceptance of the benefits of the agreement, constitutes knowledge sufficient to uphold

---

1989) (wife had visited husband's farm, and had observed its machinery and general condition); *In re* Palmira, 513 N.E.2d 1223 (Ind. Ct. app. 1987) (husband's disclosure was incomplete, but wife already knew of omitted assets; agreement valid); *Marriage of Adams*, 729 P.2d 1151 (wife knew husband for 20 years, had worked for him for part of that time); *In re* Estate of Martin, 938 A.2d 812 (Me. 2008) (wife had independent knowledge of husband's finances, where wife had access to husband's detailed financial records, husband routinely left his financial statements in plain sight on kitchen counter, premarital agreement stated that each of the parties had made a full disclosure to the other party of all of his or her property and assets, and wife declared to the notary public that she had read the premarital agreement and had no questions); Pollack-Halverson v. McGuire, 576 N.W.2d 451 (Minn. Ct. App. 1998) (although disclosure not complete, wife had independent knowledge having lived in husband's home for six years); Darr v. Darr, 950 S.W.2d 867 (Mo. Ct. App. 1997) (agreement valid despite husband's failure to disclose 12 percent of his monthly income, where wife was husband's social director before marriage, was exposed to husband's finances and income, and received a $500 per week stipend and gifts worth over $100,000); *In re* Estate of Reinsmidt, 897 S.W.2d 73 (Mo. Ct. App. 1995) (wife demonstrated sufficient independent knowledge of husband's assets where she stated, "I know more about [husband's] finances than he does"); *In re* Estate of Thies, 903 P.2d 168 (Mont. 1995) (requirement of fair disclosure was met where wife had knowledge of husband's assets); Panossian v. Panossian, 569 N.Y.S.2d 127 (N.Y. App. Div. 1991) (wife knew nature and extent of husband's property by cohabitation); Binck v. Binek, 673 N.W.2d 594 (N.D. 2004) (wife was sufficiently aware of husband's financial situation where she knew husband owned coal mine and equipment thereon, guessed he owned his house, and had been told by her family that he was worth over a million dollars); *In re* Estate of Burgess, 646 P.2d 63 (Okla. 1982) (wife had independent knowledge of husband's assets, where they had dated for 18 months and had visited property); *Taylor*, 832 P.2d 429 (wife knew husband owned cattle business, stocks, real property, and service station, and wife assisted husband in business and personal matters); Paroly v. Paroly, 876 A.2d 1061 (Pa. Super. Ct. 2005) (when a spouse is fully engaged in the couple's financial affairs and is familiar with a business owned by the other spouse, appellate court will uphold marital settlement agreement even when it contains neither disclosure nor an affirmation that disclosure was made); Greenwald v. Greenwald, 454 N.W.2d 34 (Wis. Ct. App. 1990). *Cf.* Wylie v. Wylie, 459 S.W.2d 127 (Ark. 1970) (wife had seen husband's farms, but was not qualified to determine their value; husband's failure to disclose 50 percent of estate vitiated contract); Linker v. Linker, 470 P.2d 921 (Colo. App. 1970) (wife too unsophisticated to understand what she was waiving, although she had general knowledge of husband's assets); *In re* Marriage of Norris, 624 P.2d 1345 (Or. Ct. App. 1981) (although wife visited husband's home and manufacturing plant, she could not have reasonably known even general worth of assets).

22. *Newman*, 653 P.2d 728 (wife worked as bookkeeper for husband before marriage); Lawson v. Loid, 896 S.W.2d 1 (Ky. 1995) (wife was husband's bookkeeper for his business); *In re* Estate of Arbeitment, 886 S.W.2d 644 (Mo. Ct. App. 1994) (independent knowledge gained where wife worked in husband's business); *Greenwald*, 454 N.W.2d 34 (wife kept husband's financial books before marriage). *Cf.* Luck v. Luck, 711 S.W.2d 860 (Ky. Ct. App. 1986) (although wife worked in husband's automotive store for three years, she did not know extent of his assets); *In re* Marriage of Lewis, 808 S.W.2d 919 (Mo. Ct. App. 1991) (wife's position as employee of hospital did not give her knowledge of husband's assets).

the antenuptial agreement.[23] These are very old cases, however, and should not be relied upon.

Like full and fair disclosure, independent knowledge must include at least a rough inventory of the other spouse's assets and an approximate knowledge of their value.[24] The knowledge need not, however, be precise.[25]

§ 11.03 Knowledge of Legal Rights

Some of the knowledge cases include as a factor whether each spouse has reasonable knowledge of his or her legal rights under the agreement.[26] Despite case law mentioning this element, however, there are no cases that have invalidated an agreement solely because a party did not understand his or her legal rights under the contract. In fact, some states have eliminated all knowledge requirements in a deliberate step toward making antenuptial agreements easier to enforce.[27] Because prospective spouses are vulnerable to overreaching during the months before marriage, however, most states have not taken this position.

---

23. Brown v. Brown, 160 N.E. 149 (Ill. 1928); Brown v. Brown's Adm'r, 80 S.W. 470 (Ky. 1904).

24. Orgler v. Orgler, 568 A.2d 67 (N.J. App. Div. 1989) (even though wife knew husband was "wealthy," she had no idea of his net worth; agreement set aside).

25. Day v. Vitus, 792 P.2d 1240 (Or. Ct. App. 1990) (husband knew wife did not have to work and owned a business, a home, a motor home, and substantial investments; contract upheld); Pajak v. Pajak, 385 S.E.2d 384 (W. Va. 1984) (wife knew husband was successful businessman with substantial real estate holdings; contract valid).

26. E.g., Del Vecchio v. Del Vecchio, 143 So. 2d 17 (Fla. 1962); Harbom v. Harbom, 760 A.2d 272 (Md. Ct. App. 2000); Eyster v. Pechenik, 887 N.E.2d 272 (Mass. App. Ct. 2008); *In re* Estate of Kinney, 733 N.W.2d 118 (Minn. 2007); Simeone v. Simeone, 581 A.2d 162 (Pa. 1988); *In re* Marriage of Bernard, 204 P.3d 907 (Wash. 2009). *Cf.* Friezo v. Friezo, 914 A.2d 533 (Conn. 2007) (parties do not need a detailed understanding of Connecticut law on marriage and divorce to knowingly waive their statutory rights in a prenuptial agreement).

27. FLA. STAT. ANN. § 732.02(2). *See* Eckstein v. Eckstein, 514 N.Y.S.2d 47 (N.Y. App. Div. 1987) (seeming to hold that nondisclosure, as distinct from misrepresentation, is never a basis for finding an agreement invalid); Trapani v. Gagliardi, 502 So. 2d 957 (Fla. Dist. Ct. App. 1987).

Substantive Fairness | 12

§ 12.01 Substantive Sufficiency

In those states that adopted the Uniform Premarital Agreement Act (UPAA), the party seeking to avoid enforcement of the agreement carries the burden of proof to show that the agreement was reached involuntarily, that is, it either was the result of fraud or duress, or is unconscionable and resulted from lack of disclosure. Thus, if the agreement is fair, the inquiry ends, and the agreement will be upheld. Therefore, an examination of the provisions of the agreement is always important when attacking and defending an antenuptial agreement.

It should be noted at the outset of this chapter that "substantive sufficiency" should not be confused with "consideration." For antenuptial agreements, the marriage itself is sufficient consideration to avoid an attack for lack of mutuality. As stated by many courts, an antenuptial agreement is an agreement made by prospective spouses in contemplation of *and in consideration of* marriage.[1] Consequently, if the marriage does not take place, the agreement that is dependent on the marriage is of no force and effect.[2]

Instead, the sufficiency analysis focuses on whether the property awarded to each party under the contract meets some mandatory mini-

---

1. *See* § **8.041**.

2. UPAA § 4; Hurt v. Hurt, 433 S.E.2d 493 (Va. Ct. App. 1993). Similarly, since marriage is the consideration for the agreement, a marriage subsequently declared void renders the agreement void as well. *E.g.*, Lang v. Reetz-Lang, 488 N.E.2d 929 (Ohio Ct. App. 1985). *See generally* Wade R. Habeeb, Annotation, *Enforcement of Antenuptial Contract or Settlement Conditioned Upon Marriage Where Marriage Was Subsequently Declared Void*, 46 A.L.R.3d 1403 (1972).

mum amount. If property awarded is less than the minimum amount, the sufficiency test is not met.

§ 12.02 Measure of Sufficiency

There are two measures of sufficiency that courts have adopted. One line of cases holds that because of the confidential relationship between the parties, the contract fails the sufficiency test if it is "unfair."[3] Another line of cases stresses the parties' freedom to contract, and holds that the contract fails the sufficiency test only if it is "unconscionable."[4] This is the position of the UPAA.[5]

The difference between "unfair" and "unconscionable" is one of degree; agreements that are unfair may not be unconscionable.[6]

§ 12.03 Time of Measurement

Before turning to cases considering whether an agreement is unfair or unconscionable, we must examine when the sufficiency test should be applied: at the time the agreement is signed (before the marriage), or when the agreement is implemented (at the time of the divorce)? The decisions are split. One line of authority holds that the test should be applied only at the time the agreement was signed.[7] Indeed, one case held that the test

---

3. Ruzic v. Ruzic, 549 So. 2d 72 (Ala. 1989); Burtoff v. Burtoff, 418 So. 2d 1085 (D.C. 1980); Casto v. Casto, 508 So. 2d 330 (Fla. 1987); Warren v. Warren, 523 N.E.2d 680 (Ill. App. Ct. 1988); Button v. Button, 388 N.W.2d 546 (Wis. 1986); *In re* Matson, 730 P.2d 668 (Wash. 1986).

4. Lewis v. Lewis, 748 P.2d 1362 (Haw. 1988); *In re* Estate of Ascherl, 445 N.W.2d 391 (Iowa Ct. App. 1989); Rose v. Rose, 526 N.E.2d 231 (Ind. Ct. App. 1988); Gant v. Gant, 329 S.E.2d 106 (W. Va. 1985).

5. UPAA § 5(a).

6. *See In re* Marriage of Murphy, 834 N.E.2d 56 (Ill. App. Ct. 3d Dist. 2005) (trial court employed an incorrect standard when determining the validity of the parties' antenuptial agreement, which was entered into before enactment of the UPAA, when, instead of finding the agreement fair and reasonable, the trial court found that the terms were "not unconscionable," which was the standard for determining the validity of antenuptial agreements under the Act); Upham v. Upham, 630 N.E.2d 307 (Mass. App. Ct. 1994) (conscionable is not the same as fair and reasonable, although the two overlap); *In re* Marriage of Bernard, 204 P.3d 907 (Wash. 2009) (while there is nothing unfair about two well-educated working professionals agreeing to preserve the fruits of their labor for their individual benefit, a prenuptial agreement that is disproportionate to the respective means of each spouse, and that also limits the accumulation of one spouse's separate property while precluding any claim to the other spouse's separate property, is substantively unfair). Moreover, the court may use the term "fair" but may really be setting out a test of unconscionability. *See* Rostanzo v. Rostanzo, 900 N.E.2d 101 (Mass. App. Ct. 2009) (it is only where the contesting party is essentially stripped of substantially all marital interests that a judge may determine that a prenuptial agreement is not fair and reasonable and therefore not valid).

7. Barnhill v. Barnhill, 386 So. 2d 749, 751 (Ala. Civ. App. 1980); Del Vecchio v. Del Vecchio, 143 So. 2d 17 (Fla. 1962); *In re* Marriage of Shanks, 758 N.W.2d 506 (Iowa 2008); *In re* Marriage of Gonzalez, 561 N.W.2d 94 (Iowa Ct. App. 1997); Herget v. Herget, 550 A.2d 382 (Md. Ct. Spec.

for substantive sufficiency must be whether the agreement was unconscionable under the circumstances at the time of execution, despite a drastic reversal of fortune suffered by the husband.[8] A second line of authority holds that the test of sufficiency should be applied at the time of divorce.[9]

A recent trend is to apply the two tests together, by examining the entire agreement to determine if the circumstances have so changed that to enforce the agreement at the time of the divorce would work a substantial injustice.[10] This is often

---

App. 1988), *rev'd on other grounds*, 550 A.2d 382 (Md. 1988); Austin v. Austin, 839 N.E.2d 837 (Mass. 2005); *In re* Yannalfo, 794 A.2d 795 (N.H. 2002); *In re* Marriage of Rudder, 217 P.3d 183 (Or. Ct. App. 2009); Perkinson v. Perkinson, 802 S.W.2d 600 (Tenn. 1990); Rogers v. Yourshaw, 448 S.E.2d 884 (Va. Ct. App. 1994); *Marriage of Bernard*, 204 P.3d at 912 ("He urges us to alter our analysis and evaluate substantive fairness at the time of enforcement, as opposed to at the time of execution, of an agreement. We refuse. To do so would change the test from one of fairness to fortuity."). UPAA § 205 (agreement invalid if, inter alia, it is unconscionable at time of execution).

    8. Justus v. Justus, 581 N.E.2d 1265 (Ind. Ct. App. 1991).

    9. Rider v. Rider, 648 N.E.2d 661 (Ind. Ct. App. 1995); Edwardson v. Edwardson, 798 S.W.2d 941 (Ky. 1990); Lewis v. Lewis, 748 P.2d 1362 (Haw. 1988); Darr v. Darr, 950 S.W.2d 867 (Mo. Ct. App. 1997) (reasonableness of agreement was to be determined by reference to wife's financial status at time of divorce).

    10. *See* Newman v. Newman, 653 P.2d 728 (Colo. 1982) (review entire agreement for fairness at execution, and review alimony provisions for unconscionability at divorce); Crews v. Crews, 989 A.2d 1060 (Conn. 2010) (trial court should examine circumstances of parties at time marriage was dissolved and determine if they are so beyond contemplation of parties at time agreement was entered into as to cause its enforcement to work injustice); Scherer v. Scherer, 292 S.E.2d 662 (Ga. 1982) (review for unconscionability at execution, and for unfairness at divorce; review at time of divorce should consider only changed circumstances); Rider v. Rider, 669 N.E.2d 160 (Ind. 1996) (test of whether waiver of spousal support is unconscionable is to be determined by comparing situations of parties at time of dissolution); Spencer v. Estate of Spencer, 313 S.W.3d 534 (Ky. 2010) (unlike other contracts, antenuptial agreements are often negotiated and entered into when the parties are not truly bargaining at arm's length, and they are often sought to be enforced long after their creation when the parties' circumstances may have changed substantially; for these reasons, courts retain broad discretion to modify or invalidate all or part of an antenuptial agreement where enforcement is unconscionable); Edwardson v. Edwardson, 798 S.W.2d 941 (Ky. 1990) (agreement will be reviewed for unconscionability at time of execution and unfairness at time of enforcement); Austin v. Austin, 839 N.E.2d 837 (Mass. 2005) (when an antenuptial agreement is valid at the time of execution, a judge must take a second look at its provisions at the time of divorce); Woodlington v. Shokoohi, 792 N.W.2d 63 (Mich. Ct. App. 2010) (a prenuptial agreement may be avoided when the facts and circumstances are so changed since the agreement was executed that its enforcement would be unfair and unreasonable); Hutchison v. Hutchison, 2009 WL 2244522 (Mich. Ct. App. July 28, 2009) (trial court did not err in determining that prenuptial agreement was unenforceable due to unforeseeable change in wife's circumstances; evidence indicated that husband and wife entered into a prenuptial agreement, but that after they were married, husband abused wife at work and insisted that she quit her employment, and that she subsequently became financially dependent upon husband); Lentz v. Lentz, 721 N.W.2d 861 (Mich. Ct. App. 2006) (antenuptial agreements, though otherwise valid, could be invalidated if circumstances changed since the agreement was executed, so as to make its enforcement unfair and unreasonable); Booth v. Booth, 194 Mich. App. 284, 486 N.W.2d 116 (1992) (agreement will be reviewed for unconscionability at time of execution and unfairness due to unforeseen circumstances at time of enforcement); McKee-Johnson v. Johnson, 444 N.W.2d 259 (Minn. 1989) (review for unfairness at execution, and for unsconsciona-

referred to as the "second look" doctrine, and is particularly appropriate to spousal support.[11]

The hybrid test, although fair on its face, has the effect of ratifying many agreements, because it cannot be said that the circumstances have so changed during the marriage as to be beyond the parties' comprehension or expectations. For example, in *Reed v. Reed*,[12] the court stated that an agreement can be void when the facts and circumstances are so changed since the agreement was executed that its enforcement would be unfair and unreasonable. The court then concluded that the 25-year marriage of the parties did not constitute a change in facts or circumstances that would justify departing from the prenuptial agreement, since a long marriage was easily foreseen by the parties, the tremendous growth of the parties' assets during the course of the marriage was foreseeable, and the wife admitted she signed the agreement.

Likewise, in *Blue v. Blue*,[13] even though the husband's business increased in value from $5 million to $77 million during the marriage, the court held that the agreement limiting the wife to $650,000 in the event of divorce was not unconscionable, since the values of the parties' respective estates were already disparate at the time of the marriage, and the parties could only expect the estates to grow more disparate.

§ 12.04 The General Factors of Unfairness or Unconscionability

Neither the unfairness test nor the unconscionability test can be reduced to a mathematical formula. An agreement is not unfair or unconscionable merely because one of the parties drove a hard bargain, or one of the parties made an "error in judgment" when it came time to sign.[14]

---

bility at divorce); *In re* Estate of Lutz, 620 N.W.2d 589 (N.D. 2000); Gross v. Gross, 11 Ohio St. 3d 99, 464 N.E.2d 500 (1984) (review property division provisions at execution and support provisions at divorce, using unfairness standard at both stages); Sailer v. Sailer, 764 N.W.2d 445 (N.D. 2009) (remand was required for specific findings to support determination as to whether premarital agreement was so one-sided that enforcement of the agreement would be unconscionable); *In re* Marriage of Bracken, 2010 WL 3734057 (Wash. Ct. App. Div. 1, Sept. 27, 2010) (court reviewed agreement for fairness at time of divorce after 20-year marriage); Gant v. Gant, 174 W. Va. 740, 329 S.E.2d 106 (1985) (review for unconscionability at execution, but contract is unenforceable if unforeseen changed circumstances make it unconscionable at divorce); Button v. Button, 131 Wis. 2d 84, 388 N.W.2d 546 (1986) (review for unfairness at both execution and divorce; review at divorce should consider only changed circumstances beyond the parties' reasonable expectations).

11. *In re* Marriage of Barnes, 755 N.E.2d 522 (Ill. App. Ct. 4th Dist. 2001); Colello v. Colello, 780 N.Y.S.2d 450 (N.Y. App. Div. 2004) (court has no authority to determine if prenuptial agreement regarding property division is unconscionable at time of divorce, although it can so determine with regard to spousal support).

12. 693 N.W.2d 825 (Mich. Ct. App. 2005).

13. 60 S.W.3d 585 (Ky. Ct. App. 2001).

14. Hawxhurst v. Hawxhurst, 723 A.2d 58 (N.J. Super. 1999); Fazakerly v. Fazakerly, 996 S.W.2d 260 (Tex. Ct. App. 1999). Similarly, regret at an unwise decision does not vitiate an agree-

Nonetheless, under both tests, the court must consider a number of different factors that bear on the relationship between what each spouse gets under the agreement and what each spouse would have received had there been no agreement. Factors identified by the courts include[15]

- duration of the marriage
- stated purpose of the agreement
- assets owned by each party
- income and earning capacity of each party
- property each party brings to the marriage
- any obligations owed by each party to other family members, such as children by prior marriages
- any anticipated contributions by one spouse to the earning capacity of the other
- future support needs of each party
- age and health of each party
- intelligence and level of education of each party
- parties' standard of living during the marriage
- each party's contribution to the marriage, including homemaker and child care contributions

Regardless of which test applies, the sufficiency element clearly does *not* require the parties to divide their property in the exact same manner that a divorce court would. Such a rule would effectively make all property division contracts meaningless.[16]

§ 12.05 Unfairness

States applying the unfairness test frequently require some reasonable relationship between the total of the spouses' estates and the amount of property a spouse receives on divorce or death. This relationship is frequently found lacking where one spouse receives no property at all from the pot that would otherwise be considered marital. For example, in *In re Matson*,[17] the wife received no property after a 13-year marriage. The court held that the fairness inquiry must be made "zealously and scrupulously" where the wife receives no property. Similarly, in *Norris v. Norris*,[18] the contract waived all of the wife's rights to the husband's property; the husband was wealthy, but the wife had next to nothing. The court again found the agreement to be unfair.

---

ment, Fletcher v. Fletcher, 628 N.E.2d 1343 (Ohio 1994), nor does the realization one has made a bad bargain, Webb v. Webb, 851 N.Y.S.2d 828 (N.Y. Sup. Ct. 2007).

15. Del Vecchio v. Del Vecchio, 143 So. 2d 17 (Fla. 1962); *In re* Marriage of Shanks, 758 N.W.2d 506 (Iowa 2008); *In re* Estate of Hildegass, 244 A.2d 672 (Pa. 1968); *Button*, 131 Wis. 2d 84, 388 N.W.2d 546.

16. McKee-Johnson v. Johnson, 444 N.W.2d 259, 268 (Minn. 1989); *Button*, 131 Wis. 2d 84, 388 N.W.2d 546.

17. 730 P.2d 668 (Wash. 1986).

18. 419 A.2d 982 (D.C. 1980).

The agreement may also be unfair when one spouse receives substantially less under the agreement than he or she would have received in the absence of an agreement.[19] In *Casto v. Casto*,[20] the wife received only $225,000 of a marital estate worth $10 million. The court found the agreement unfair, given the disparity between the total marital estate and the portion that would be due the wife.[21]

This is not to say, however, that an agreement is unfair merely because it is disproportionate. Thus, mutual waivers of property rights are generally not considered

---

19. *But see* Lemaster v. Dutton, 694 So. 2d 1360 (Ala. Civ. App. 1996) (fairness of antenuptial agreement is not to be judged upon a comparison of what the spouse takes under the agreement and what he or she would have taken without the agreement).

20. 508 So. 2d 330 (Fla. 1987).

21. *See also* Stemler v. Stemler, 36 So. 3d 54 (Ala. Civ. App. 2009) (antenuptial agreement, which provided that after a marriage of 10 years, the wife would receive $50,000, any property that was titled in her name, and a share of any property titled jointly with the husband, was unfair or inequitable to the wife and disproportionate to the means of the husband, where none of the parties' real property was titled in the wife's name, only the marital home had been jointly titled in the parties' names, and, at the time of the marriage, the husband had a net worth of approximately $2 million, which had increased to between $5 million and $10 million at the time of the divorce); Kolflat v. Kolflat, 636 So. 2d 87 (Fla. Dist. Ct. App. 1994) (agreement not fair and reasonable where wife waived support, but parties lived extravagantly during marriage, wife had not worked in 10 years, and wife had little practical job experience); *In re* Marriage of Richardson, 606 N.E.2d 56 (Ill. App. Ct. 1992) (agreement unfair where wife received only 7.55 percent of assets); Cannon v. Cannon, 865 A.2d 563 (Md. 2005) (an antenuptial agreement that provides valuable consideration, other than the marriage itself, in exchange for a waiver, or where the parties agree to a mutual waiver of the marital rights, is more likely not to be found unfairly disproportionate); Hill v. Hill, 356 N.W.2d 49 (Minn. Ct. App. 1984) (wife received $20,000 in exchange for all rights to husband's estate, which was worth $750,000 when the agreement was signed; contract unfair; property division ultimately found valid because wife had voluntarily agreed to it; waiver of alimony invalid); Pulley v. Short, 261 S.W.3d 701 (Mo. Ct. App. W.D. 2008) (husband's and testator's mutual waiver of rights to other's assets was sufficient consideration to support antenuptial agreement, despite considerable disparity in relative wealth of parties); *In re* Estate of Hartman, 582 A.2d 648 (Pa. Super. Ct. 1990) (antenuptial agreement was not invalid due to failure of consideration where agreement contained mutual promises of parties to waive claims in each other's estate); Bateleman v. Rubin, 199 Va. 156, 98 S.E.2d 519 (1957) (wife gave up rights in $248,000 estate in return for $20,000 to be paid at time of husband's death; contract found unfair and therefore invalid); *In re* Marriage of Bernard, 165 Wash. 2d 895, 204 P.3d 907 (2009) (prenuptial agreement as amended by side letter was substantively unfair to wife; agreement made provisions for wife that were disproportionate to the means of husband, and limited wife's ability to accumulate her separate property while precluding her common law or statutory claims on husband's property); Friedlander v. Friedlander, 494 P.2d 208 (Wash. 1972) (mutual waivers contained therein constitute adequate consideration for a prenuptial agreement); *In re* Marriage of Krejci v. Krejci, 266 Wis. 2d 284, 667 N.W.2d 780 (2003) (prenuptial agreement that excluded any appreciation in value of resort from property division in a divorce was inequitable and thus unenforceable; parties operated resort for 18 years as a partnership, and wife's efforts were beyond those of customary spousal obligations).

unfair.[22] This result is especially appropriate when the parties marry late in life and have children from previous marriages.[23] And at least one court has held that when the marriage is of short duration, the agreement is fair if it returns the parties to the status quo before the marriage.[24]

There is a definite trend, however, to minimize the extent to which a court will inquire into the fairness of an agreement. In *In re Marriage of Spiegel*,[25] the court noted that there are "inherent difficulties" in assessing any agreement for fairness. The court adopted what it termed a "liberal" approach to the substantive fairness test, and held that an agreement is substantively fair if its obligations and waivers are mutual or the economically disadvantaged spouse receives a financial improvement in his or her premarital circumstances.[26]

Finally, when fairness is reviewed at the time of the divorce, the contract may be unfair if changed circumstances make the future support provisions unreasonable. The

---

22. *See* Francavilla v. Francavilla, 969 So. 2d 522 (Fla. Dist. Ct. App. 4th Dist. 2007) (agreement was not unfair where at time agreement was signed, wife was 33 and husband was 31, this was high-risk marriage as wife had left him twice before, agreement provided for alimony even if marriage was short, wife was entitled to $25,000 cash payment after filing of petition for dissolution of marriage but before she vacated marital home, and agreement did not address child support, which would be based on respective incomes of parties); Snedaker v. Snedaker, 660 So. 2d 1070 (Fla. Dist. Ct. App. 1995) (mutual waivers of all interest in property of the other and alimony on a sliding scale was substantively fair); *In re* Hopkins, 166 Ill. App. 3d 652, 520 N.E.2d 415 (1988); Herget v. Herget, 550 A.2d 382 (Md. 1988) (where wife had substantial estate of at least $500,000 and husband had voluntarily supported and adopted wife's children from prior marriage, mutual property waivers not unfair, even though husband's estate was worth $1,435,000), *rev'd on other grounds*, 573 A.2d 798 (Md. 1990); Ware v. Ware, 7 So. 3d 271 (Miss. Ct. App. 2008) (antenuptial agreement wherein wife agreed that husband's interest in his family's business and other interests would be considered nonmarital assets was enforceable; nothing in record suggested that wife was forced to sign agreement, since she had not read the contract she could not complain it provided she had obtained advice from attorney when she had not done so, agreement did not cover entire marital estate, and wife received 40 percent of marital assets); Schutterle v. Schutterle, 260 N.W.2d 341 (S.D. 1977) (husband was worth around $125,000 and wife was worth around $50,000 when contract signed; wife received $65,000 in personal property on husband's death, but each party waived all rights in the other's real property; contract fair).

23. *See* Gant v. Gant, 329 S.E.2d 106 (W. Va. 1985) (noting role of parties' ages and expectations in apply fairness test).

24. Burtoff v. Burtoff, 418 So. 2d 1085 (D.C. 1980).

25. 553 N.W.2d 309 (Iowa 1996).

26. *See also* McNamara v. McNamara, 40 So. 3d 78 (Fla. Dist. Ct. App. 5th Dist. 2010) (Florida public policy does not protect a spouse from making a bad bargain where the contract is entered into freely and voluntarily, with full disclosure); *In re* Estate of Cooper, 2010 WL 844778 (Tenn. Ct. App. Mar. 9, 2010); Simeone v. Simeone, 581 A.2d 162 (Pa. 1990) (court will decline to inquire into fairness of agreement when parties have voluntarily and freely executed its provisions); Chiles v. Chiles, 779 S.W.2d 127 (Tex. Ct. App. 1989) (parties should be free to execute agreements as they see fit and whether they are fair is not material to their validity).

Ohio Supreme Court, in *Gross v. Gross*,[27] gave several examples of situations in which a waiver of alimony would be unfair:

> an extreme health problem requiring considerable care and expense; change in employability of the spouse; additional burdens placed upon a spouse by way of responsibility to children of the parties; marked changes in the cost of providing necessary maintenance of the spouse; and changed circumstances of the standards of living occasioned by the marriage, where a return to the prior living standard would work a hardship upon a spouse.[28]

Consequently, a contract can be fair in its property provisions but unfair in its alimony provisions.[29]

§ 12.06 Unconscionability

The test for unconscionability is harder to meet than the test for unfairness. Accordingly, if the evidence is sufficient to prove that the agreement is fair, then the agreement is not unconscionable.

Although unconscionability clearly requires more than mere unfairness, the test for unconscionability is different in the antenuptial agreement setting than in the business setting. In this respect, the use of the term "unconscionable" is unfortunate. The comments to the UPAA make this problem even worse by expressly referring to the unconscionability test under the Uniform Commercial Code.[30] As other commentators have noted, the drafters did not intend by this reference to incorporate into antenuptial agreements the same standard of unconscionability used in commercial cases.[31] All antenuptial agreement cases dealing with unconscionability recognize that because of the parties' confidential relationship, they are entitled to more protection against overreaching than parties in commercial cases. The debate between unfairness is not a debate over whether special protection is appropriate, but rather over how much special protection should be given.

The courts have held agreements unconscionable only when there is a substantial and gross disparity between the provisions for one spouse and the share of the marital

---

27. 464 N.E.2d 500, 509–10 n.11 (Ohio 1984).

28. *See supra* note 10.

29. *See supra* note 11.

30. UNIF. PREMARITAL AGREEMENT ACT § 6, cmt.

31. Thomas J. Oldham, *Premarital Agreements Are Now Enforceable, Unless . . .* , 21 HOUS. L. REV. 757, 774–77 (1984).

estate that spouse would have otherwise been entitled to.[32] The disparity must be of such dimension as to almost shock the conscience of the court.[33]

Courts are more willing to find unconscionability in alimony provisions than in property division provisions. For example, in *Hill v. Hill*,[34] the wife received $20,000 in exchange for waiving all rights in a marital estate worth $750,000 at the time of signing. Because the wife signed the contract voluntarily and admitted that the husband's wealth was not a factor in her decision to sign, the court upheld the property division provisions of the agreement. The wife was in poor physical and mental health, how-

---

32. McGilley v. McGilley, 951 S.W.2d 632 (Mo. Ct. App. 1997) (agreement is unconscionable when inequality is so strong, gross, and manifest that it must be impossible to state it to one with common sense without producing exclamation at the inequality of it). *See also* Cosh v. Cosh, 847 N.Y.S.2d 136 (N.Y. App. Div. 2d Dep't 2007) (an unconscionable bargain is regarded as one such as no person in his or her senses and not under delusion would make on the one hand, and as no honest and fair person would accept on the other).

33. DeLong v. DeLong, 24 Fam. L. Rep. (BNA) 1148 (Mo. Ct. App. Jan. 20, 1998) (where effect of agreement was to exclude the wife from receipt of any financial benefit of marriage, agreement was unconscionable); Tremont v. Tremont, 827 N.Y.S.2d 309 (N.Y. App. Div. 3d Dep't 2006) (an agreement is not unconscionable merely because some terms may seem improvident; to be set aside, it must shock the conscience); Bloomfield v. Bloomfield, 712 N.Y.S.2d 490 (N.Y. App. Div. 2000) (premarital agreement that provided for no division of property at end of marriage and no right of election on husband's death was unconscionable); Thomas v. Thomas, 145 A.D.2d 477, 535 N.Y.S.2d 736 (1988) (where wife received 10 times as much property under the agreement as husband, contract was unconscionable); Marsocci v. Marsocci, 911 A.2d 690 (R.I. 2006) (premarital agreement purporting to prevent a marital interest from arising from income produced as result of husband's ownership of real property was unconscionable when executed, as element for being unenforceable under UPAA; husband's business when agreement was executed, and during the marriage, involved selling one property and purchasing another and mortgaging one to obtain another, using rent derived from those properties to pay his personal and marital debt, and income therefrom composed the majority of husband's earnings throughout the marriage); Holler v. Holler, 364 S.C. 256, 612 S.E.2d 469 (2005) (agreement unconscionable that provided both parties were responsible for paying on property leased to husband, that required husband to have interest in increase in value during marriage of homestead real estate proportionate to contribution of household expenses and child care/household duties performed by husband, but agreement did not contain similar provision for wife, and husband had net worth over $150,000 with $30,000 in annual income, while Ukrainian wife had no assets or net worth and earned $1,400 per year in Ukraine); Chaplain v. Chaplain, 682 S.E.2d 108 (Va. Ct. App. 2009) (wife made prima facie showing that premarital agreement was unconscionable where, under agreement, husband received entire net worth of approximately $20 million and wife received nothing except the right to $100,000 upon husband's death provided they were married and living together at time of death; wife was from Morocco and left her job there to marry husband, wife remained unemployed during marriage, wife had limited knowledge of English and could not read or write it at time she signed agreement, wife was not given opportunity to have agreement reviewed by independent counsel, but was taken to husband's attorney's office and presented signature page of agreement to sign, wife thought she was signing "marriage paper," and she was not given copy of agreement to review either before or after she signed it); UPAA §6(b) (agreement is invalid to the extent it would make either party eligible for public assistance).

34. 356 N.W.2d 49 (Minn. Ct. App. 1984).

ever, and was a long-term homemaker with few job skills. Because she lacked sufficient income to support herself, the court found the waiver of alimony unconscionable.
The Colorado Supreme Court noted unconscionability exists "when enforcement of the
terms of the agreement results in a spouse having insufficient property to provide for
his reasonable needs and who is otherwise unable to support himself through appropriate employment."[35]

Where no gross disparity exists, antenuptial agreements have generally been
found to be conscionable,[36] even when circumstances have changed during the mar-

---

35. Newman v. Newman, 653 P.2d 728, 735 (Colo. 1982). *See also* Lane v. Lane, 202 S.W.3d
577 (Ky. 2006) (antenuptial agreement in which parties waived spousal maintenance was unconscionable, where marriage was the first for both parties who were in their 20s when they married,
two children were born of marriage and wife quit her job to care for children while husband rapidly
progressed in his career, significant disparity in parties' incomes at time of marriage grew expo-
nentially during marriage in large part because husband was able to concentrate on his career while
wife stayed home to care for the children and home, and parties maintained an affluent lifestyle
during marriage); Rivera v. Rivera, 243 P.3d 1148 (N.M. Ct. App. 2010) (prenuptial agreement was
unconscionable and thus unenforceable as it pertained to husband's right to seek spousal support
in divorce proceedings); Rogers v. Gordon, 961 A.2d 11 (N.J. Super. Ct. App. Div. 2008) (because
agreement was unconscionable, court would set aside portion preventing wife from receiving alimony); Jacobitti v. Jacobitti, 623 A.2d 794 (N.J. Super. Ct. App. Div. 1993) (agreement unconscionable where wife was left penniless after divorce); Gross v. Gross, 464 N.E.2d 500 (Ohio 1984)
(where enforcing contract would have substantially reduced wife's standard of living, alimony provisions of contract were unconscionable); Maloof-Wolf v. Wolf, 2011 WL 550116 (Ohio Ct. App.
8th Dist. Feb. 17, 2011) (antenuptial agreement's clause waiving spousal support was unconscionable to wife at time of divorce and thus was unenforceable, even though wife was an attorney; wife
and her family invested large amount of money in husband's business ventures, wife had relied on
husband for financial support throughout marriage, wife did not work but rather raised children,
and husband and wife enjoyed significant and substantial lifestyle during the marriage). *But see*
Rider v. Rider, 669 N.E.2d 160 (Ind. 1996) (wife's waiver of alimony was not unconscionable even
though wife became disabled and unable to support herself during the marriage).

36. Adams v. Adams, 603 S.E.2d 273 (Ga. 2004) (agreement that allowed wife $10,000 for
each year of marriage, up to maximum of $100,000, was not unconscionable, even though agree-
ment may have perpetuated already existing disparity between parties' estates); Rose v. Rose, 526
N.E.2d 231 (Ind. Ct. App. 1988) (husband received over $1 million while wife received only the
household furniture and an outdated automobile; contract enforced; agreement not unconscionable
merely because one spouse receives little); MacFarlane v. Rich, 567 A.2d 585 (N.H. 1989) (where
wife owned $450,000 in retirement benefits, contract was not unconscionable); Binek v. Binek, 673
N.W.2d 594 (N.D. 2004) (premarital agreement was not unconscionable at time it was executed or
at time of enforcement, despite wife's alleged failure to receive full financial disclosure, and despite
agreement's alleged effect of placing wife on public assistance; agreement provided means for wife
to keep her own assets and allow them to grow, husband was obligated to support wife throughout marriage, agreement did not govern parties' rights regarding spousal support, parties' assets
decreased throughout marriage, and there was no convincing evidence of economic fault by either
party).

riage.[37] Further, mutual waivers of property rights are always conscionable, even if the spouses' estates are substantially unequal.[38]

---

37. Winchester v. McCue, 882 A.2d 143 (Conn. 2005) (change not beyond contemplation of parties, even if husband's estate increased by 430 percent over the course of the marriage); Mallen v. Mallen, 622 S.E.2d 812 (Ga. 2005) ($14 million increase in husband's net worth during marriage did not constitute changed circumstances from time of execution of prenuptial agreement so as to render enforcement of agreement unfair and unreasonable); *In re* Marriage of Shanks, 758 N.W.2d 506 (Iowa 2008) (premarital agreement that provided that each party would retain assets acquired prior to marriage as separate property, that the only assets subject to division in event of death or divorce were marital home and joint bank account, and that parties would mutually waive alimony, and that provided formula to allocate marital property in different percentages based on nature of property and years of marriage, was not substantively unconscionable; although provisions contemplated that husband would receive greater portion of marital assets in event of divorce, terms were consistent with parties' financial conditions at time of marriage, and agreement contemplated leaving both parties substantially in same financial condition as they were before marriage with some potential financial benefits to wife); Blue v. Blue, 60 S.W.3d 585 (Ky. Ct. App. 2001) (significant increase in value of husband's nonmarital property did not make prenuptial agreement unconscionably one-sided to husband so as to invalidate agreement, although husband's company was worth about $5 million at time of agreement and could be worth $77 million at time of dissolution); *In re* Yannalfo, 794 A.2d 795 (N.J. 2002) (husband's use of marital assets for unsuccessful litigation and unwise business ventures, his unemployed and underemployed status, his erratic change in behavior, and wife's and wife's parent's contributions to household expenses were not changes in circumstances so far beyond the contemplation of the parties when antenuptial agreement was executed that its enforcement would work an unconscionable hardship).

38. Hiers v. Estate of Hiers, 628 S.E.2d 653 (Ga. Ct. App. 2006) (wife who sought to invalidate prenuptial agreement and claim year's support from husband's estate failed to establish that prenuptial agreement was unconscionable, despite wife's contention that she was left with no visible means of support, car, or place to live; wife entered marriage with $2,500 and no property and left marriage with approximately $100,000, wife remained in marital home for several months after husband's death and drove cars belonging to the estate, wife was employed by husband's company until she chose to leave, and fact that prenuptial agreement perpetuated existing disparity of wealth did not render it unconscionable); *In re* Estate of Ascherl, 445 N.W.2d 391 (Iowa Ct. App. 1989) (mutual property waivers are not unconscionable); Lewis v. Lewis, 748 P.2d 1362 (Haw. 1988) (mutual waivers of rights to inherited and premarital property are not unconscionable); Kornegay v. Robinson, 625 S.E.2d 805 (N.C. App. 2006) (prenuptial agreement signed by wife, in which the parties waived all marital rights including intestacy rights, was not unconscionable, where waivers were reciprocal). *See supra* note 22.

Breach or Waiver 13

§ 13.01 Breach

When one party materially breaches an antenuptial agreement, the other party may, at his or her option, rescind the agreement. For example, in *In re Estate of Geyer*,[1] the majority held that an antenuptial contract was invalid because the husband failed to disclose his assets. A concurring justice noted that the contract contained a clause stating that both parties had fully disclosed their assets, and opined that even if the contract was initially valid, the husband's material breach of the disclosure clause allowed the wife to rescind the contract.[2]

---

1. 533 A.2d 423 (Pa. 1987).

2. *Id*. at 430. *Accord* Estate of Lampert *ex rel*. Thurston v. Estate of Lampert *ex rel*. Stauffer, 896 P.2d 214 (Alaska 2005); Prather v. Cox, 689 S.W.2d 623 (Ky. Ct. App. 1985); Reed v. Rope, 817 S.W.2d 503 (Mo. Ct. App. 1991). *But see* Brees v. Cramer, 586 A.2d 1284 (Md. 1991) (breach of a covenant in a prenuptial or separation agreement does not "ipso facto" excuse performance of another covenant by the other party).

Most cases, however, find that breaches of the contract are not sufficiently "material" to permit rescission.[3] In addition, a material breach cannot be committed by someone who is not a party to the agreement.[4]

---

3. *In re* Marriage of Hadley & Levine, 2003 WL 1870955 (Cal. Ct. App. 1st Dist. 2003) (husband's breach of his obligation under premarital agreement, providing that parties agree to make every reasonable effort to invest a minimum annual amount of $20,000 in a community property asset each calendar year during the marriage, was not sufficiently material to justify rescission of premarital agreement, especially where rescission would award to wife one half of all of husband's earnings during marriage); Burtoff v. Burtoff, 418 A.2d 1085 (D.C. 1980) (husband breached promise to keep $3,000 in joint checking account; breach not material); Gridley v. Galego, 698 So. 2d 273 (Fla. Dist. Ct. App. 1997) (husband's bequest of annuity instead of trust fund for support did not constitute breach of antenuptial agreement allowing wife to claim agreement was rescinded); Wales v. Wales, 422 So. 2d 1066 (Fla. Dist. Ct. App. 1982) (partial compliance belied claim of breach); Morris v. Master, 182 N.E. 406 (Ill. 1932) (failure to make provision for payment as required by contract was not breach); Estate of Gillilan v. Estate of Gillilan, 406 N.E.2d 981 (Ind. Ct. App. 1980) (husband's will gave wife conditional right to income during period between his death and establishing testamentary trust, instead of absolute right as agreement required; breach not material); *In re* Estate of Johnson, 452 P.2d 286 (Kan. 1969) (failure to make will as contemplated in agreement was not material breach); *In re* Estate of Martin, 938 A.2d 812 (Me. 2008) (husband's failure to designate wife as the beneficiary of his life insurance policy, as he agreed to do in the premarital agreement, did not warrant rescission of the agreement, especially in light of partial performance); Doster v. Doster, 853 So. 2d 147 (Miss. Ct. App. 2003) (wife's failure to make payments on family home for 11 out of 24 months of parties' married life did not amount to material breach of prenuptial agreement as to provision allowing her to receive first $25,000 equity in family home in event of divorce); Johnson, 2011 WL 345671 (Ohio Ct. App. 2d Dist. 2011) (will and trust provisions of the prenuptial agreement, which required that husband maintain a trust for wife's benefit for the rest of her life and fund the trust through his will, were not intended to be enforceable after divorce, and thus husband did not breach prenuptial agreement by altering the provisions of his will and trust after he filed for divorce); Nicholson v. Nicholson, 2009 WL 3518172 (Tenn. Ct. App. 2009) (wife did not breach agreement by filing for divorce on fault grounds, where agreement stated, "to the extent feasible the divorce shall be filed on a non-fault basis, such as irreconcilable differences"); Shepard v. Shepard, 876 P.2d 429 (Utah Ct. App. 1994) (wife's failure to execute deed did not constitute material breach of antenuptial agreement where husband enjoyed benefit of home and he was not prejudiced by wife's failure to execute deed).

4. *In re* Estate of Barilla, 535 A.2d 125 (Pa. Super. Ct. 1987) (contract gave wife a life estate in deceased husband's property, but heirs refused to let her take possession; their acts could not constitute breach of agreement because they were not parties to agreement).

Marital misconduct is not considered a breach of the agreement.[5] In *Noto v. Buffington*,[6] the court explained that the premarital agreement whereby the parties waived any claims of alimony and assignment of property in the event of a divorce was not unconscionable and would be enforced, despite the wife's adultery. The husband argued that because the wife committed adultery and deserted the marriage, enforcing the agreement would offend generally accepted standards of marital fidelity, rendering the agreement unconscionable. The court rejected that argument, reasoning that the parties entered into the agreement knowing that it specifically provided for the possibility of a future dissolution and, thus, it was reasonable to infer that they contemplated some form of marital discord or misconduct. If such misconduct were to render the agreement unenforceable, the purpose for the agreement would have been undermined.

Damages are available for breach of an antenuptial agreement.[7]

§ 13.02 Abandonment/Revocation/Rescission

Antenuptial agreements, like other contracts, may be abandoned if the parties mutually intend to do so.[8] The general contract law test for abandonment of contracts has been expressed as follows:

---

5. Maloy v. Maloy, 362 So. 2d 484 (Fla. Dist. Ct. App. 1978) (fact that wife committed adultery did not invalidate agreement); Moss v. Moss, 589 N.Y.S.2d 683 (N.Y. App. Div. 1992) (even if provision in antenuptial agreement requiring wife to carry out her marriage vows were enforceable on its face, husband failed to show that wife breached vows in any way other than by seeking divorce, which could be a violation of requirement that she remain his wife for as long as they both live, and thus husband could not rely on such alleged breach to avoid agreement upon divorce; by requesting wife to sign separation agreement, husband effectively forced wife into situation where if she signed agreement, she would cease to be "loving wife" as long as they both live, and if she refused to sign, she could be accused of failing to "respect" his wishes as required by vows); Gross v. Gross, 464 N.E.2d 500 (Ohio 1984); Perkinson v. Perkinson, 802 S.W.2d 600 (Tenn. 1990) (enforcement of antenuptial agreement cannot be denied because of marital fault). *Cf.* Britven v. Britven, 145 N.W.2d 450 (Iowa 1966) (husband's failure to fulfill marriage vows by kicking wife out of bed when she refused to commit sodomy constituted breach of agreement).

6. 2010 WL 1565554 (Conn. Super. Ct. Mar. 22, 2010).

7. Dutton v. Marshall, 729 So. 2d 860 (Ala. Civ. App. 1998) ($29,000 in damages for widow whose $35,000 house was supposed to devolve to her); Reed, 817 S.W.2d 503; Harllee v. Harllee, 565 S.E.2d 678 (N.C. Ct. App. 2002). *Cf.* Williamson v. Bullington, 534 S.E.2d 254 (N.C. Ct. App. 2000) (former wife of testator was not entitled to have testator's widow transfer testator's interest in golf course leases to her as remedy for testator's breach of property settlement agreement in which testator agreed to convey his interests in leases by will to former wife, where agreement specifically provided that former wife's remedy for testator's breach was for former wife, her father, or her brother to have option to purchase testator's interest in leases for fair market value).

8. *See generally* Annotation, *Parties' Behavior During Marriage as Abandonment, Estoppel, or Waiver Regarding Contractual Rights*, 56 A.L.R.4th 998 (1987).

[A] contract may be abandoned by mutual consent and . . . such consent may be implied from the acts and conduct of the parties. . . . A contract will be treated as abandoned when the acts of one party, inconsistent with its existence, are acquiesced in by another. . . . Where acts and conduct are relied upon to constitute abandonment, however, they must be positive, unequivocal, and inconsistent with intent to be further bound by the contract.[9]

This general rule applies with full force to antenuptial and postnuptial agreements, that is, an agreement executed during the marriage. As the court stated in *O'Dell v. O'Dell,*[10] when determining whether an agreement has been abandoned, the court should not apply different principles simply because the parties who made the agreement are about to marry:

Antenuptial contracts . . . are in no way different from any other ordinary contracts. They are to be considered, construed, and treated as are contracts in general. Any executory contract, when the rights of others are not involved, may be rescinded all together or modified, by the mutual consent of the parties. Either party may waive any right thereunder. Those who are qualified to make an antenuptial or other contract are likewise qualified, by the mutual consent to eliminate or modify any part hereof, or to unmake the contract all together, or to substitute a new contract. . . . A claim that the parties could make such a contract, and then not, as between themselves unmake or change it, would involve a legal absurdity.

Therefore, because parties to antenuptial agreements should be allowed to modify or abandon their agreements in the same manner as parties to garden-variety commercial contracts, courts have generally accepted the idea that parties to antenuptial agreements may mutually abandon their contracts.

One way for parties to abandon their agreement is to act inconsistently with the terms of the agreement. For example, in *In re Pillard,*[11] the parties agreed to waive their rights in each other's property. They then commingled their funds untraceably during the marriage and generally treated all their property as jointly owned. The court found this course of conduct sufficient to abandon the agreement. Some courts have reached the same result on an unfairness theory.[12]

---

9. H.T.C. Corp. v. Olds, 486 P.2d 463 (Colo. App. 1971).

10. 26 N.W.2d 401 (1947).

11. 448 N.W.2d 714 (Iowa Ct. App. 1989).

12. *See* Compton v. Compton, 902 P.2d 805 (Alaska 1995) (court would not enforce antenuptial agreement where parties' conduct during marriage would make enforcement unfair and unreasonable); Brandt v. Brandt, 427 N.W.2d 126 (Wis. Ct. App. 1988) (where parties commingled their estates after promising to keep them separate, antenuptial agreement failed fairness test due to changed circumstances). *See* § **12.03**, discussion of "second look."

It is difficult to discern from court opinions when parties have abandoned the agreement by their actions,[13] and when they have not abandoned the agreement,[14] except to

13. *In re* Marriage of Zimmerman, 714 P.2d 927 (Colo. App. 1986) (although agreement stated parties would maintain separate assets, parties pooled assets into joint business); *In re* Marriage of Young, 682 P.2d 1233 (Colo. App. 1984) (parties abandoned agreement to keep separate assets by pooling assets through 28-year marriage); *In re* Marriage of Zimmer, 714 P.2d 927 (Colo. App. 1986) (wife invested time and her credit in husband's separate corporation); *In re* McMullen, 185 So. 2d 191 (Fla. Dist. Ct. App. 1966) (parties agreed to hold property as tenants by the entireties, but through marriage wife treated property as hers alone, and insisted that one property be conveyed to her in her sole name; agreement abandoned); Liebelt v. Liebelt, 870 P.2d 9 (Idaho Ct. App. 1994) (parties abandoned antenuptial agreement where they freely transferred their properties in disregard of the agreement); Lung v. Lung, 655 N.E.2d 607 (Ind. Ct. App. 1995) (parties showed intent to modify antenuptial agreement when husband deeded his separate property to himself and wife as tenants by the entirety); Fredericks v. Fredericks, 2009 WL 2633228 (Ky. Ct. App. Aug. 28, 2009) (where provisions of antenuptial agreement provided that separate assets were to be purchased with nonjoint funds and that the parties' joint residence was to be purchased with each party contributing an equal amount, but parties instead chose to commingle their assets in joint accounts and did not invest in equal amounts in the joint residence, agreement was waived); Prather v. Cox, 689 S.W.2d 623 (Ky. Ct. App. 1985) (agreement to maintain separate property abandoned by husband when he took control of all property after marriage and combined tobacco and farming operations); Englund v. Englund, 175 N.W.2d 461 (Minn. 1970) (claim of separate property waived as to property placed into joint tenancy); Tweeten v. Tweeten, 772 N.W.2d 595 (N.D. 2009) (divorcing parties had destroyed parties' separate ownership of ranch and farmland by transferring the properties to themselves as joint tenants); *In re* Estate of Pate, 459 S.E.2d 1 (1995) (no intent to abandon agreement where parties signed agreement, broke up, reconciled, and then married); Simoni v. Simoni, 657 N.E.2d 800 (Ohio Ct. App. 1995) (evidence showed that parties intended agreement to be rescinded, where there was no copy produced at trial, the husband told his attorney to destroy the agreement in consideration of the wife paying off the husband's corporate loans, and the parties' estate planner testified that the parties never mentioned the existence of the agreement); *In re* Marriage of Baxter, 911 P.2d 343 (Or. Ct. App. 1996) (where husband and wife worked together to convert husband's separate property golf course into profitable business to support both parties, using wife's separate property retirement account, parties showed mutual intent to abandon agreement); Hurt v. Hurt, 433 S.E.2d 493 (Va. Ct. App. 1993) (prenuptial agreement repudiated where husband called off wedding when wife refused to sign agreement, wedding was rescheduled, and husband told wife marriage was "with no strings attached"); *In re* Marriage of Fox, 795 P.2d 1170 (Wash. Ct. App. 1990) (conduct supported finding that parties rescinded agreement where they put their inheritances in joint accounts and spent all separate funds on a community home).

14. *In re* Marriage of Dawley, 551 P.2d 323 (Cal. 1976) (reference to "our house" and filing of joint tax returns did not rescind agreement); Carnell v. Carnell, 398 So. 2d 503 (Fla. Dist. Ct. App. 1981) (no intent to abandon when wife's failure to pay for remodeling work was de minimis); *In re* Marriage of Burgess, 462 N.E.2d 203 (Ill. Ct. App. 1984) (agreement not abandoned when wife funded husband's retirement plans through her personal loans); Ryan v. Ryan, 659 N.E.2d 1088 (Ind. Ct. App. 1995) (evidence failed to show parties commingled assets to such an extent that antenuptial agreement was abandoned); *In re* Marriage of Elam, 680 N.W.2d 378 (Iowa Ct. App. 2004) (table op., unreported) (parties did not abandon antenuptial agreement; parties' commingling of funds and properties during marriage was not inconsistent with agreement's continuing validity, agreement provided for each party to have full control over his or her own property, and parties led their marital life as if marriage would continue indefinitely, which did not serve to abandon contract); *In re* Marriage of Van Brocklin, 468 N.W.2d 40 (Iowa Ct. App. 1991) (there was no abandonment of antenuptial agreement by making reciprocal wills at variance with agreement); *In*

note that in those cases finding no abandonment, the actions taken at variance with the agreement were de minimis with regard to the obligations under the agreement.

Finally, with regard to mutual intent to abandon an agreement by action, it is essential to remember that the intent to abandon the agreement must be mutual. One party's intent is insufficient.[15]

Another way for parties to abandon their agreement is to physically destroy the agreement,[16] or execute a document that revokes the previous antenuptial agreement.[17]

To revoke an existing agreement, the parties must have sufficient mental capacity to make a contract. Further, the revocation must not be the result of undue influence. In short, the act of revocation must meet all the requisites of entering a contract. In *In re Will of Goldberg*,[18] the issue before the court was whether the testator had the capacity to release his wife from their antenuptial agreement, in which she had waived her right to elect against his will. The court first determined that it was incumbent upon the testator's estate to prove that the testator did not have the requisite capacity to release his wife. After applying the traditional contract standard to determine capacity, that is, whether the person was able to understand the nature and consequences of the transaction and make a rational judgment concerning it, the court determined that the estate

---

re Marriage of Christensen, 453 N.W.2d 915 (Iowa Ct. App. 1995) (antenuptial agreement was not abandoned where the parties' conduct, although inconsistent with ownership of marital property, was not inconsistent with terms of agreement); Cline v. Graves, 641 S.W.2d 151 (Mo. Ct. App. 1982) (failure to make will did not constitute abandonment of agreement); *Estate of Pate*, 459 S.E.2d 1 (no abandonment of agreement though parties broke up for six months and called off wedding in between signing of agreement and marriage ceremony); *In re* Marriage of Bowers, 900 P.2d 1085 (Or. Ct. App. 1995) (antenuptial agreement whereby corporation was husband's separate property was not subsequently modified orally by the actions of the parties, whereby the wife worked for the corporation and she was compensated as an employee and husband executed no documents evidencing an ownership interest by the wife); Rubino v. Rubino, 765 A.2d 1222 (R.I. 2001) (wife did not abandon agreement by accepting $5,000 as advance of distribution of assets, where wife made unequivocal and specific attempts to enforce agreement).

15. *In re* Estate of Catto, 944 P.2d 1052 (Wash. Ct. App. Div. 2, 1997); *In re* Greulich, 243 P.3d 110 (Or. Ct. App. 2010).

16. Gustafson v. Jensen, 515 So. 2d 1298 (Fla. Dist. Ct. App. 1987) (husband tore up agreement in consideration of wife's promise to reconcile; agreement abandoned); *Simoni*, 657 N.E.2d 800 (evidence showed that parties intended agreement to be rescinded where there was no copy produced of the agreement, husband told his attorney to destroy the agreement in consideration of wife paying off husband's corporate loans, and parties' estate planner testified that parties never mentioned the existence of the agreement). *But see* Felkner v. Felkner, 652 S.W.2d 174 (Mo. Ct. App. 1983) (court held agreement not abandoned when husband tore it up and burned it in the fireplace; claim showed lack of mutual agreement necessary to rescind or cancel bilateral agreement).

17. Martello v. Martello, 960 So. 2d 186 (La. Ct. App. 1st Cir. 2007); Chappelow v. Savastano, 758 N.Y.S.2d 782 (N.Y. Sup. Ct. 2003).

18. 582 N.Y.S.2d 617 (N.Y. Sur. Ct. 1992).

had not met its burden in demonstrating that the husband did not understand the nature of the transaction. The estate also challenged the revocation as having been procured by the wife's undue influence. The court found no evidence of undue influence, holding that motive and opportunity to exercise undue influence is not sufficient.

When an antenuptial agreement is clearly revoked by the later act of the parties, that same agreement may nonetheless be revived. In *In re Estate of Shore*,[19] the parties entered into an antenuptial agreement. After the marriage, the parties then entered into a postnuptial agreement, by which the parties clearly intended to replace and revoke their prior agreement. In their postnuptial agreement, however, the parties failed to make property financial disclosure as required by section 732.702(2) of the Florida Statutes. Relying on the *Restatement (Second) of Contracts* § 279, the court held that when the substitute agreement was voided, the earlier contract was then revived and enforceable.

The Uniform Premarital Agreement Act (UPAA) changed the common law rule that an antenuptial agreement can be revoked by the mere acts of the parties. Section 5 of the UPAA provides:

> After marriage, a premarital agreement may be amended or revoked only by a written agreement signed by the parties. The amended agreement or the revocation is enforceable without consideration.

The Comment to the section indicates that the intent of the section was to require the same formalities of execution for an amendment or revocation of an antenuptial agreement as are required for its original execution. Thus, states the Comment, inconsistent acts alone will not suffice to amend or revoke an agreement.[20]

Where the agreement itself, however, provides that revocation must be in writing, then the courts generally hold that acts are insufficient to revoke the agreement.[21]

---

19. 605 So. 2d 951 (Fla. Dist. Ct. App. 1992).

20. *See also* Muchmore v. Trask, 666 S.E.2d 667 (N.C. Ct. App. 2008) (trial court did not err in not making findings of fact regarding the alleged tearing of parties' premarital agreement; California's Uniform Premarital Agreement Act required that a premarital agreement may be amended or revoked only by a written agreement signed by the parties, and neither party claimed that a subsequent writing to rescind or revoke the agreement was executed, and therefore, allegations surrounding the purported physical revocation of agreement were immaterial); Huntley v. Huntley, 538 S.E.2d 239 (N.C. Ct. App. 2000) (provision of premarital agreement, by which husband agreed to convey to wife a one-half interest in his home following their marriage, could not be rescinded by the parties' conduct after their marriage, even if husband failed to execute the conveyance or the parties orally agreed to contrary terms, where there was no written amendment or revocation); *see also In re* Marriage of Bowers, 900 P.2d 1085 (Or. Ct. App. 1995) (antenuptial agreement whereby corporation was husband's separate property was not subsequently modified orally by the actions of the parties by the fact that wife worked for corporation, where she was otherwise compensated and husband executed no documents evidencing an ownership interest by wife).

21. Johnson v. Johnson, 2011 WL 345671 (Ohio Ct. App. 2d Dist. 2011).

§ 13.03 Modification

The parties to an antenuptial agreement can modify it by mutual consent.[22] For example, in *Jensen v. Jensen*,[23] the parties agreed that their respective salaries would be their separate property. They worked for the same employer, however, and they subsequently agreed to take a single salary in the husband's name only for both their efforts. The salary was placed in a joint checking account, and used for community purposes. The court found that the parties had modified their agreement by mutual consent so that the single salary was community property. The remaining portions of the agreement remained valid.

As in the case of abandonment or revocation, the UPAA requires that modifications be in writing. Further, where the agreement itself requires that modifications be in writing, the requirement will be upheld.[24]

Finally, it must be remembered that while marriage is sufficient consideration for an antenuptial agreement, when the agreement is modified after marriage, the modification requires new consideration.[25]

---

22. Rupert v. Rupert, 667 N.Y.S.2d 537 (N.Y. App. Div. 4th Dep't 1997); Webb v. Webb, 851 N.Y.S.2d 828 (N.Y. Sup. Ct. 2007); Boyer v. Boyer, 925 P.2d 82 (Okla. Ct. App. 1996); Gamache v. Smurro, 904 A.2d 91 (Vt. 2006); Lund v. Lund, 849 P.2d 731 (Wyo. 1993).

23. 753 P.2d 342 (Nev. 1988).

24. *Johnson*, 2011 WL 345671 (plain language of prenuptial agreement provided that the agreement could not be changed or terminated orally, and thus any oral agreement by parties that wife quit her job to become a homemaker did not constitute modification or waiver of the prenuptial agreement); Bradley v. Bradley, 164 P.3d 537 (Wyo. 2007). *But see* Compton v. Compton, 902 P.2d 805 (Alaska 1995) (provision in prenuptial agreement that required that all modifications or amendments of agreement be in writing did not preclude transmutation of parties' separate property by virtue of parties' subsequent actions).

25. Schneider v. Schneider, 824 S.W.2d 942 (Mo. Ct. App. 1992); *Boyer*, 925 P.2d 82. *See* **chapter 16**.

Construction | 14

§ 14.01 General Rules of Construction

As a general rule, antenuptial agreements are interpreted under the same rules of construction that apply to any other contract.[1] As with any other contract, the court looks first to the four corners of the agreement to carry out the intention of the parties.[2] The court must consider the contract's clear provisions, and should not use the recitals to change the meaning of the contract itself.[3]

---

1. *E.g., In re* Marriage of Garrity/Bishton, 226 Cal. Rptr. 485 (Cal. Ct. App. 1986); *In re* Marriage of Fiffe, 140 P.3d 160 (Colo. App. 2005); Reizfeld v. Reizfeld, 125 Conn. App. 782, ___ A.3d ___, *cert. denied* 125 Conn. 182 (2011); Herpich v. Estate of Herpich, 994 So. 2d 1195 (Fla. Dist. Ct. App. 5th Dist. 2008); *In re* Estate of Parker, 525 N.E.2d 1149 (Ill. App. Ct. 1988); *In re* Marriage of Connor, 713 N.E.2d 883 (Ind. Ct. App. 1999); Irvine v. Irvine, 685 N.E.2d 67 (Ind. Ct. App. 1997); *In re* Marriage of Spiegel, 553 N.W.2d 39 (Iowa 1996); Spencer v. Estate of Spencer, 313 S.W.3d 534 (Ky. 2010); McIntyre v. McIntyre, 654 S.E.2d 798 (N.C. Ct. App. 2008); Howell v. Landry, 386 S.E.2d 610 (N.C. Ct. App. 1989); *In re* Estate of Zimmerman, 579 N.W.2d 591 (N.D. 1998) (prenuptial agreement is a contract, and its interpretation is primarily a question of law for the court); *In re* O'Brien, 898 A.2d 1075 (Pa. Super. Ct. 2006); Hardee v. Hardee, 558 S.E.2d 264 (S.C. Ct. App. 2001); Soloman v. Murrey, 103 S.W.3d 431 (Tenn. Ct. App. 2002); D'Aston v. D'Aston, 794 P.2d 500 (Utah Ct. App. 1990); Seherr-Thoss v. Seherr-Thoss, 141 P.3d 705 (Wyo. 2006).

2. *In re* Marriage of Van Regenmorter, 587 N.W.2d 493 (Iowa Ct. App. 1998); *In re* Marriage of Gonzalez, 561 N.W.2d 94 (Iowa Ct. App. 1997); Estate of Draper v. Bank of Am., N.A., 205 P.3d 698 (Kan. 2009); *Estate of Spencer*, 313 S.W.3d 534; DelDuca v. DelDuca, 758 N.Y.S.2d 145 (N.Y. App. Div. 2003); Levin v. Carlton, 213 P.3d 884 (Utah Ct. App. 2009).

3. Johnson v. Johnson, 725 So. 2d 1209 (Fla. Dist. Ct. App. 3d Dist. 1999).

If the contract is unambiguous, the court must construe it as written.[4] Courts are reluctant to hold that promises in antenuptial agreements are too vague to be enforced.[5] A court may decline, however, to enforce an agreement that is too ambiguous.[6] Where the contract is ambiguous, the court may look to extrinsic evidence of the parties' intent and to rules of construction.[7]

An agreement may be construed against the drafter.[8] An agreement will not be construed against either party where the agreement so provides.[9]

---

4. Hubbard v. Bentley, 17 So. 3d 652 (Ala. Civ. App. 2008); *Reizfeld*, 125 Conn. App. 782, ___ A.3d ___, *cert. den.* 125 Conn. 182 (2011); *Johnson*, 725 So. 2d 1209 (Fla. Dist. Ct. App. 1999); MacKaravitz v. MacKaravitz, 710 So. 2d 57 (Fla. Dist. Ct. App. 1998); Holland v. Holland, 700 S.E.2d 573 (Ga. 2010) (term "net profits" is unambiguous); In re Marriage of Best, 901 N.E.2d 967 (Ill. App. Ct. 2d Dist. 2009); Prevatte v. Prevatte, 411 S.E.2d 386 (N.C. Ct. App. 1991); Rhodes v. Rhodes, 692 N.W.2d 157 (N.D. 2005) (only if the prenuptial agreement is ambiguous or if it does not reflect a spouse's intent because of fraud, mistake, or accident can a court employ parol evidence to clarify the terms of the contract or to find the intent of the parties); Davis v. Davis, 391 S.E.2d 255 (Va. 1990); McGilley v. McGilley, 951 S.W.2d 632 (Mo. Ct. App. 1997); *Levin*, 213 P.3d 884.

5. *E.g.*, In re Lemoine-Hoffman, 827 P.2d 587 (Colo. App. 1992) (where the contract unambiguously stated that the parties were to support each other through college, the court held that such a promise was not too vague to be enforced); Winter v. Winter, 658 N.E.2d 38 (Ohio Ct. App. 1995) (modifications made to antenuptial agreement after the parties were married did not render agreement ambiguous as a whole).

6. Golden v. Golden, 695 A.2d 1231 (Md. Ct. Spec. App. 1997) (oral agreement between parties that their property would remain "separate" was not specific enough to waive equitable distribution; parties had to provide that property was "non-marital" to opt out of statute); Moss v. Moss, 589 N.Y.S.2d 683 (N.Y. App. Div. 1992) (promise to "fulfill marriage vows" was unenforceable as too ambiguous).

7. Tuthill v. Tuthill, 763 A.2d 417 (Pa. Super. 2000); Webb v. Webb, 434 N.W.2d 856 (Wis. Ct. App. 1988) (looking at parol evidence to help determine whether agreement applied upon divorce).

8. Levitz v. Levitz, 481 So. 2d 1319 (Fla. Dist. Ct. App. 4th Dist. 1986); *In re* Estate of Taris, 2005 WL 736627 (Ohio Ct. App. 10th Dist. 2005).

9. Montoya v. Montoya, 909 A.2d 947 (Conn. 2006) (court improperly considered prenuptial agreement's drafter in construing agreement, where agreement provided that "the parties agree that for purposes of construction neither party is deemed to be the draftsman thereof"); Johnson v. Johnson, 2011 WL 345671 (Ohio Ct. App. 2d Dist. 2011) (agreement specifically provided under "Interpretation of Agreement" that "[n]o provision in this Agreement is to be interpreted for or against any party because that party or that party's legal representative drafted the provision"). *But see In re* Marriage of Weiss, 357 Mont. 320, 239 P.3d 123 (2010) (court would construe marital property distribution ambiguity in premarital agreement, drafted by wife's attorney, against wife, even though agreement provided that "No provision of this Agreement is to be interpreted for or against any party because that party or that party's legal representative drafted the provision," as that provision was contrary to statute).

§ 14.02 Rights Arising from the Marital Relationship; Separate Property

Most states permit parties to an antenuptial agreement to waive any and all rights arising out the marital relationship,[10] including rights arising out of the marital relationship as a result in a change in the law.[11]

Nevertheless, not all marital rights are waived in every contract. Thus, the courts must consider which "marital rights" are waived in the contract. Generally, waivers of marital rights apply only to the rights that fairly fit within the scope of the waiver itself. If an interest in property is not waived, then the court is free to equitably divide that property.[12]

For example, many courts have held that a waiver of rights arising out of the marriage does not encompass a waiver of attorney's fees or spousal support pendente lite, and in some instances, alimony.[13]

---

10. *E.g.*, Rose v. Rose, 526 N.E.2d 231 (Ind. Ct. App. 1988) (where contract on its face applies to all assets, courts would not construe it to exclude assets acquired during the marriage); *In re* Estate of Spurgeon, 572 N.W.2d 595 (Iowa 1998); Berman v. Berman, 749 P.2d 1271 (Utah Ct. App. 1988) (waiver of rights in all property, specifically including husband's business, applies to all assets other than business as well). *See* § **8.02.**

11. Beatty v. Beatty, 555 N.E.2d 184 (Ind. Ct. App. 1990); Herget v. Herget, 573 N.E.2d 798 (Ind. Ct. App. 1990); Gula v. Gula, 551 A.2d 325 (Pa. 1988); Rogers v. Yourshaw, 448 S.E.2d 884 (1994); Prevatte v. Prevatte, 411 S.E.2d 386 (N.C. Ct. App. 1991).

12. Langworthy v. Preston, 975 S.W.2d 249 (Mo. Ct. App. 1998); McKissick v. McKissick, 497 S.E.2d 711 (N.C. Ct. App. 1998) (if premarital agreement does not completely dispose of marital property, then party can come in and invoke equitable distribution for what is not covered); Hardee v. Hardee, 355 S.C. 382, 585 S.E.2d 501 (2003) (agreement did not bar wife from receiving an equitable division of the property acquired during the parties' marriage where agreement stated that disposition of property provisions "shall in no way affect the property, whether real, personal or mixed which shall be acquired by the parties, whether titled separately or jointly, subsequent to the date of this Agreement"); Wilson v. Wilson, 987 S.W.2d 555 (Tenn. Ct. App. 1998).

13. Worley v. Worley, 855 So. 2d 632 (Fla. Dist. Ct. App. 2d Dist. 2003) (prenuptial agreement that did not specifically mention alimony or support did not result in waiver by wife of her right to seek future support following dissolution of marriage); *In re* Cullman, 541 N.E.2d 1274 (Ill. App. Ct. 1989); Bamberger v. Hines, 2009 WL 1025122 (Ky. Ct. App. Apr. 17, 2009) (trial court did not err in finding that an antenuptial agreement did not prohibit temporary maintenance where agreement stated that the rights regarding maintenance would only be assessed "upon termination of their marriage" or "upon legal separation"); Ackerman v. Yates, 847 A.2d 418 (Me. 2004) (agreement where husband waived "any claim or rights to a share of the personal property or estate of [wife] . . . , specifically waiving any and all claims that [accrued] to him by reason of the marriage" did not waive spousal support); Hawley by Cordell v. Hawley, 904 S.W.2d 584 (Mo. Ct. App. 1995) (although antenuptial agreement contained waiver of claims arising out of marriage, because parties did not expressly waive support, husband could sue wife for support). *See also In re* Marriage of Best, 9d N.E.2d 967 (Ill. Ct. App. 2d Dist. 2006) (antenuptial agreement's bar on support applied when the parties were separated, which referred to when the parties were legally separated, and thus antenuptial agreement allowed the provision of support while a dissolution action was pending until parties had legally separated); Seherr-Thoss v. Seherr-Thoss, 141 P.3d 705 (Wyo. 2006) (although the divorce proceedings had commenced, the parties remained legally married during that time and, as such, husband was obligated to pay $10,000 to wife each year during this

Another common scenario in waiver of marital rights clauses arises when the parties waive all rights to the estate of the other. Specific designations as beneficiary or specific bequests will take precedence over the general waiver.[14]

Another common construction issue is whether particular property (and its appreciation) is separate when the agreement provides that a party's separate property shall remain that party's separate property.[15]

---

time period pursuant to parties' prenuptial agreement requiring husband to pay to wife the sum of $10,000 per year for so long as the parties were married to each other).

14. *E.g.*, Taylor v. Taylor, 1 So. 3d 348 (Fla. Dist. Ct. App. 1st Dist. 2009) (prenuptial agreement unambiguously waived wife's right to elective share of husband's estate, intestate share, family allowance, and all other rights generally afforded to surviving spouses, where agreement provided that husband's property would "forever remain his personal estate," and that such property would be "forever free" of any claim by wife); *In re* Estate of Anderson, 552 N.E.2d 429 (Ill. App. Ct. 1990) (husband died without naming beneficiary of certain life insurance policy, making wife beneficiary by operation of law; antenuptial agreement contained general waiver clause but reserved to each spouse the right to give gifts to the other; since wife's rights can arise by law and not by voluntary gift, general waiver applied); Boetsma v. Boetsma, 768 N.E.2d 1016 (Ind. Ct. App. 2002) (general waiver includes statutory survivors' rights); *Estate of Spurgeon*, 572 N.W.2d 595 (no claims against estate of other, including dower, statutory right, right of support, right of inheritance, and homestead, operated to waive wife's right to elect against will); King v. Estate of King, 962 P.2d 1118 (Kan. Ct. App. 1998) (prenuptial agreement providing that one-half interest in parties' house would eventually devolve to husband's heirs, rather than joint tenancy deed signed by husband and wife, controlled disposition of house following husband's death); Affiliated Banc Group, Ltd. v. Zehringer, 527 N.W.2d 585 (Minn. Ct. App. 1995) (wife waived right to elect against will in antenuptial agreement that waived all survivor's rights); *In re* Estate of Kilbourn, 898 S.W.2d 583 (Mo. Ct. App. 1995) (waiver of claims as "surviving spouse, heir, or otherwise" barred husband's claim against wife's estate as creditor for services rendered to wife's rental properties); Brown v. Ginn, 640 S.E.2d 787 (N.C. Ct. App. 2007) (wife waived her rights to federal tobacco transition payments derived from husband's farm after his death pursuant to antenuptial agreement, in which each party was entitled to retain all rights in his or her separate property, farm was husband's separate property, and wife waived statutory rights in the property of husband or his estate) *In re* Estate of Lutz, 563 N.W.2d 90 (N.D. 1997) (spouse who waives rights in property of other may still make gifts or bequests in will); Kinkle v. Kinkle, 699 N.E.2d 41 (Ohio 1998) (antenuptial agreement in which husband and wife released all rights to other's property and in which husband listed his IRA as an asset operated to cut off wife's beneficiary status); *In re* Estate of Uzelac, 110 P.3d 177 (Utah App. 2005) (antenuptial agreement entitled wife to all property acquired during marriage and held at husband's death, not merely property jointly acquired during marriage and held by husband and wife at time of husband's death, where relevant clause stated that all property would go to survivor in event of death of the other); Pysell v. Keck, 263 Va. 457, 559 S.E.2d 677 (2002) (general waiver did not include statutory right to renounce will and claim portion of estate).

15. *In re* Marriage of Spaletta, 2003 WL 23439 (Cal. Ct. App. 2003) (unpublished, noncitable) (farming partnership was husband's separate property under prenuptial agreement, where agreement identified the stock in the husband's first ranch as husband's separate property, and his separate property interest did not evaporate when he reorganized as a farming partnership); Starbuck v. Starbuck, 2006 WL 894440 (Conn. Super. 2006) (unreported) (engagement ring became wife's separate property at time of marriage, under terms of prenuptial agreement defining "separate property" as all property, including jewelry, acquired by a party prior to contemplated marriage); Irwin v. Irwin, 857 So. 2d 247 (Fla. Dist. Ct. App. 2d Dist. 2003) (prenuptial agreement did not limit wife to receiving only property titled solely in her name, where agreement did not specifically

The types of waivers parties can include in their agreement are limitless, and so case law on construction of agreements comprises many different types of waivers.[16]

---

reserve husband's marital earnings as his separate property and thus did not exclude wife's claim to share in value of assets purchased with those earnings); Timble v. Timble, 616 So. 2d 1188 (Fla. Dist. Ct. App. 1993) (waiver of interest in husband's securities encompassed waiver of appreciation of those securities); Grissom v. Grissom, 647 S.E.2d 1 (Ga. 2007) (under provision of prenuptial agreement stating that the ownership of any real or personal property acquired by the parties in the future would be determined in reference to legal title, former wife did not acquire ownership interest in former husband's separate real property and brokerage account when the real estate was refinanced and conveyed to husband and wife as joint tenants with right of survivorship and when wife was listed as coaccount holder upon transfer of brokerage account; the provision applied only to properties acquired "in the future," i.e., during the marriage); *In re* Marriage of Box, 968 S.W.2d 161 (Mo. Ct. App. 1998) (antenuptial agreement provided that separate bank accounts were separate, but that did *not* include marital funds deposited into husband's account after the marriage); *In re* Marriage of Weiss, 357 Mont. 320, 239 P.3d 123 (2010) (transfer of funds from wife to husband did not transmute funds to marital property, but would be construed as loan of wife's separate property); Kalousdian v. Kalousdian, 35 A.D.3d 669, 827 N.Y.S.2d 250 (2d Dep't 2006) (prenuptial agreement did not accord wife the right to a share in the appreciation in value of husband's separate property, and thus, husband should not have been compelled to disclose to wife the amount of that appreciation in an action for divorce); Parker v. Parker, 2 Misc. 3d 484, 773 N.Y.S.2d 518 (2003) (wife's lottery proceeds, won during marriage, were her separate property where parties' prenuptial agreement stated that the only property subject to equitable distribution was property held in joint name, and lottery proceeds were not held in joint name); Stewart v. Stewart, 541 S.E.2d 209 (N.C. Ct. App. 2000) (separate property retained by husband included husband's interest in medical clinic, medical license, and any appreciation therein whether active or passive); Brummond v. Brummond, 785 N.W.2d 182 (N.D. 2010) (renunciation of interest in separate property included appreciation of that property); Rothrock v. Rothrock, 765 A.2d 400 (Pa. Super. Ct. 2000) (property held by the parties meant only jointly owned property); Bufkin v. Bufkin, 2003 WL 22725522 (Tex. App. Nov. 20, 2003) (increase in value of stock was community property under prenuptial contract, although stock itself was husband's separate property, where contract stated that "any income or increases in kind or value that are yielded by the separate property of either party shall become the community property of the parties provided that it is acquired or produced" after fifth anniversary date), *aff'd in part, rev'd in part*, 259 S.W.3d 343 (Tex. App.—Dallas 2008); Brough v. Brough, 2009 WL 4263534 (Utah Ct. App. Nov. 27, 2009) (where agreement stated that the wife was in "no way associated" with the personal property and business of the husband and that she had no claim against the property, the lack of association became predicate of the disclaimer of interest; thus, where the court found that the wife had become associated with the business by working for the business, jointly taking out a loan for business expansion and the intermingling of business and personal funds, wife had become "associated" with the listed properties, she had gained an interest in them); Carr v. Hancock, 216 W. Va. 474, 607 S.E.2d 803 (2004) (antenuptial agreement preserving as parties' separate property real and personal property owned prior to marriage had no application to property acquired during marriage, and such after-acquired property was properly subjected to equitable distribution).

    16. Murley v. Wiedamann, 25 So. 3d 27 (Fla. Dist. Ct. App. 2d Dist. 2009) (plain language of parties' prenuptial agreement excluded wife's stock and stock options from marital estate such that the assets were not subject to equitable distribution upon divorce; agreement expressly and unambiguously stated that all interests acquired from an employee benefit plan, including stock options, were to be regarded as nonmarital property, and a plain interpretation of the language was consistent with the parties' intent to protect their assets should the parties choose to terminate the marriage); Katz v. Katz, 666 So. 2d 1025 (Fla. Dist. Ct. App. 1996) (clause in antenuptial agreement

Waivers directed at claims other than ones arising out of the particular marriage, that is, rights independent of the marriage, have not been applied to divest a party of those rights.[17] Consequently, a waiver of prior claims does not apply to rights that arise after the antenuptial agreement has been executed.[18]

---

giving wife right to be supported from husband's "income" does not give wife right to portion of unspent income in husband's IRAs and stocks); Tadlock v. Tadlock, 660 S.E.2d 430 (Ga. Ct. App. 2008) (where clause provided that "monies coming in" to husband would be solely the husband's and would demise to husband's son after husband's death, wife waived her right to her share of survival claim for worker's predeath pain and suffering under Federal Employers Liability Act); Mitchell v. Mitchell, 693 N.Y.S.2d 351 (N.Y. App. Div. 3d Dep't), *lv. denied*, 723 N.E.2d 89 (N.Y. 1999) (wife waived interest in husband's business, and so she should not receive lump sum award of percentage gain realized in sale of interest in corporation, even though same was characterized as child support in later separation agreement); Williams v. Williams, 246 S.W.3d 207 (Tex. App.— Houston [14 Dist.] 2007) (agreement did not address the wages and salaries earned by the parties during marriage, and therefore, they retained their status as community property); Levin v. Carlton, 213 P.3d 884 (Utah Ct. App. 2009) (when determining what assets constituted community property subject to distribution in event of divorce, term "earnings" in unambiguous prenuptial agreement meant salary accumulated or derived from employment, and specifically excluded any profits from husband's investments, which were explicitly designated in agreement as husband's separate property).

17. Kubian v. Alexian Bros. Med. Ctr., 651 N.E.2d 231 (Ill. App. Ct. 1995) (antenuptial agreement did not bar wife from bringing loss of consortium claim against hospital, because she did not waive right to bring claim against third parties in agreement); Weber v. Weber, 142 P.3d 338 (Kan. Ct. App. 2006) (premarital agreement in which wife agreed to make no claim on husband's property in the event of a divorce did not serve to waive insurance coverage for wife's loss of personal property following a fire at the couple's home that occurred prior to the couple's divorce, even though the insurance policy was held by husband; anything in the premarital agreement that related to the division of property was effective only upon the couple's divorce); Walsh v. Young, 660 A.2d 1139 (N.H. 1995) (wife did not waive ownership rights to bank accounts held by joint tenancy by waiving claims arising by virtue of marriage; claims arise by contract, not by marital status); Liptrap v. Coyne, 675 S.E.2d 693 (N.C. Ct. App. 2009) (surviving spouse who had made payments pursuant to a guaranty agreement on a note executed by her deceased husband was not barred, by prenuptial agreement relinquishing her rights to husband's separate property, from seeking reimbursement from husband's estate, since agreement was not an intentional waiver of her statutory right to sue for reimbursement of payments made as surety for husband's debt); *In re* Leathers, 779 P.2d 619 (Or. Ct. App. 1989) (general waiver applies to all marital claims, but does not prevent wife from claiming half of husband's business under partnership law), *cert. denied*, 789 P.2d 263 (Or. 1990); Davis v. Davis, 391 S.E.2d 255 (Va. 1990) (contract gave each party the right to manage his or her property free from any claims "made by the other party by reason of their marriage"; waiver covered only right to property and did not apply to alimony); *In re* Wakefield, 763 P.2d 459 (Wash. Ct. App. 1988) (waiver of claims to other's estate did not apply to claim of equitable reimbursement for community contributions to separate estates).

18. Luppino v. Luppino, 521 N.Y.S.2d 34 (N.Y. App. Div. 1987); Wilson v. Wilson, 987 S.W.2d 555 (Tenn. Ct. App. 1998) (antenuptial agreement could apply only to separate property owned at time of agreement; phase in agreement "property owned partially or wholly" by parties could not overcome statutory definition of marital property of property acquired during marriage).

§ 14.03 Second Marriage, One Agreement

There is a split as to whether, when the same parties have been married twice, a prenuptial agreement signed before the first marriage is still effective upon the termination of the second marriage. On the one hand, there are cases that unequivocally hold that where parties enter into an antenuptial agreement, marry, divorce, then remarry, and then one party dies, the provisions of the antenuptial relating to a release of inheritance rights remain in full force and effect. In *In re Wynne's Estate*,[19] the widow of the deceased elected to take against the will. The evidence revealed that the testator and the widow had been married in 1942, divorced in 1943, remarried in 1944, divorced in 1946, and remarried in 1947. Twelve days after the first marriage, the widow executed a postmarital agreement whereby she waived all claims to participate as a spouse in the estate of the deceased. The court found it significant that she specifically waived any rights in the estate as a widow at the time of the testator's death. The waiver, the court held, was extant when the testator died.

> The contention that because the parties were thereafter divorced and then remarried the agreement fails is a claim which runs counter to the very text of the agreement which speaks of a lifetime and not of a marriage period. The parties contracted in their characters as husband and wife. There is no limitation on the purport of the agreement and none upon its future effectiveness.[20]

On the other hand, there are cases that very clearly hold that because the first, original marriage is the consideration for the waiver of rights, when the parties enter into a second marriage, the original waiver of rights cannot be applied because the original consideration no longer exists. In *Seuss v. Schukat*,[21] Johanna Wolfrum married Otto Schukat in 1912. Prior to this marriage, they entered into an antenuptial agreement, whereby Otto waived his rights as surviving widower. The parties divorced in 1919, and they remarried in 1921. Johanna died intestate in 1931, and Otto claimed an estate in homestead and his right of dower. The court recognized the validity of the original antenuptial agreement, but held it applied only to the first marriage. The court stated that after the divorce, the former husband and wife were strangers to each other and their marital rights and duties were at an end. The marriage contemplated by their antenuptial agreement, the very consideration for the agreement, was at an end. During the interval between the marriages, they could have contracted again with each other, but did not elect to do so. Thus, when they entered into a second marriage, new rights

---

19. 194 Misc. 459, 85 N.Y.S.2d 743 (Sur. Ct. 1948).

20. 85 N.Y.S.2d at 747. *See also* Application of Liberman, 167 N.Y.S.2d 158, 165 (N.Y. App. Div. 1957) (wife and husband number two were married in a civil ceremony, then wife divorced husband number one, then wife married husband number two in a religious ceremony; premarital agreement between wife and husband number two, executed before first civil ceremony, wherein wife waived rights as "widow," was applicable when husband number two died; parties regarded marriage number one and marriage number two as the same marriage, and so the antenuptial agreement applied to both marriages).

21. 358 Ill. 27, 192 N.E. 668 (1934).

and duties attached, including inheritance rights. The court concluded unequivocally, "An existing antenuptial agreement made in contemplation of the particular marriage is, after its dissolution, without any purpose or effect and necessarily is terminated."[22]

A more recent case reached a similar result. In *Stevenson v. U.S. National Bank*,[23] David and Alberta executed an antenuptial agreement prior to their marriage in 1979. In 1981, the parties were divorced. In connection with the divorce, the parties entered into a property settlement agreement, and the husband wrote a new will. That separation agreement provided that it superseded all other written or oral agreements relating to the settlement of the parties' property rights. The parties remarried in March 1982, and the husband died shortly thereafter.

The court held that the antenuptial agreement governed the rights of David and Alberta until the time of the first divorce, at which time it was expressly superseded and replaced by the terms of the property settlement agreement. The prenuptial agreement had no further force and effect once a judgment was entered incorporating the property settlement agreement.

Clearly, while the holding of this case is that the prenuptial agreement did not govern the parties' rights at the time of the husband's death, this case is distinguishable because the parties had entered into a property settlement agreement that was intended to supersede the antenuptial agreement.[24]

§ 14.04 Particular Assets

Courts have refused to extend to other assets or rights a waiver of the right to share in one particular asset or right.[25] When the assets in which a party waives rights are not

---

22. 192 N.E. at 673. *Accord* Fern v. Fern, 355 A.2d 672 (N.J. App. Div. 1976); *In re* Broadhurst, 737 S.W.2d 504 (Mo. Ct. App. 1987); Busekist v. Busekist, 398 N.W.2d 722 (Neb. 1987).

23. 695 P.2d 77 (Or. Ct. App. 1985).

24. *See also* Barham v. Barham, 202 P.2d 289 (Cal. 1949) (parties executed antenuptial agreement October 1, 1928; married October 8, 1929; executed subsequent property settlement agreements June 28, 1935, November 16, 1936, December 16, 1936, November 1, 1937, and December 2, 1937; divorced January 13, 1942; executed amendment to property settlement agreement August 24, 1943; remarried May 11, 1945; held, original antenuptial agreement did not apply to second marriage, as subsequent property settlement agreements were intended to supersede antenuptial agreement).

25. *See* Schlaefer v. Fin. Mgmt. Serv., Inc., 996 P.2d 745 (Ariz. Ct. App. 2000) (where agreement provided that debts incurred during marriage shall remain the debt of the person incurring the debt except "joint obligations," "joint obligations" referred only to obligations signed or authorized by both spouses); Tolar v. Tolar, 639 So. 2d 399 (La. Ct. App. 1994) (agreement applied only to property listed and did not purport to establish a separate property regime); Deschamps v. Deschamps, 223 P.3d 324 (Mont. 2009) (parties' prenuptial agreement governed only the parties' respective property at the time of the agreement, and the agreement was silent as to future improvements, contributions, or appreciation, in divorce proceeding; the agreement stated that the parties would each "retain all property that they presently own as separate property," and nothing in the agreement referred to the increase in value of either parties' respective property); Davis v. Davis, 391 S.E.2d 255 (Va. 1990) (contract gave each party the right to manage his own property free

particularized, but the waiver is to "separate property" or "marital property," the court then must determine exactly which assets are separate or marital, much as it must do in an ordinary equitable distribution case. For example, in *Pardieck v. Pardieck*,[26] the court held that the agreement providing that stock in husband's name was his separate property precluded wife from claiming an interest in the profits, earnings, and capital assets accumulated by the corporation.[27]

In another case, *Mitchell v. Mitchell*,[28] the court held that when the wife waived any interest in the husband's corporation, she was not entitled to a lump sum award representing a percentage of the gain realized when the husband sold his interest in that corporation.

§ 14.05 Death versus Divorce

Quite a number of cases have stressed that when the contract on its face mentions only death and not divorce, any waivers in the estate of the other are limited to death.[29] Con-

---

from any claims "made by the other party by reason of their marriage"; waiver covered only rights to property, and did not apply to alimony); *In re* Wakefield, 763 P.2d 459 (Wash. Ct. App. 1988) (waiver of claims to separate property did not apply to claim of equitable reimbursement for community contributions to separate estate). *See also supra* note 16.

26. 676 N.E.2d 359 (Ind. Ct. App. 1997).

27. *See also* Katz v. Katz, 666 So. 2d 1025 (Fla. Dist. Ct. App. 1996) (clause in antenuptial agreement giving wife right to portion of husband's unspent income did not give wife right to portion of husband's IRA and stocks).

28. 693 N.Y.S.2d 351 (N.Y. App. Div. 1999).

29. Friedman v. Friedman, 384 S.E.2d 641 (Ga. 1989); *In re* Marriage of Homann, 658 N.E.2d 492 (Ill. Ct. App. 1995); Bressler v. Bressler, 601 N.E.2d 392 (Ind. Ct. App. 1992); Moldofsky v. Moldofsky, 842 N.Y.S.2d 505 (N.Y. App. Div. 2d Dep't 2007) (agreement in which wife purportedly waived her interest in husband's estate did not waive wife's right to equitable distribution in divorce action); Busekist v. Busekist, 398 N.W.2d 722 (Neb. 1987); Stokes v. Stokes, 648 N.E.2d 83 (Ohio Ct. App. 1994); Smetana v. Smetana, 726 N.W.2d 887 (S.D. 2007) (agreement was unenforceable in divorce proceeding where the agreement failed to mention divorce or separation); Roth v. Roth, 565 N.W.2d 782 (S.D. 1997); Schuman v. Schuman, 2010 WL 1539955 (Va. Ct. App. 2010); Levy v. Levy, 388 N.W.2d 170 (Wis. 1986). *But see* Gillette v. Gillette, 835 N.E.2d 556 (Ind. App. 2005) (agreement applied to divorce, although it did not specifically mention divorce, where agreement stated that each party shall separately retain all rights in his or her own property, whether now owned or hereafter acquired, and each of them shall have the absolute and unrestricted right to dispose of such separate property free of any claim that may be made by the other by reason of their marriage, and with the same effect as if no marriage had been consummated between them); Woodington v. Shokoohi, 792 N.W.2d 63 (Mich. Ct. App. 2010) (prenuptial agreement providing that "the parties specifically agree and state that agreement is intended to waive rights upon death and is not made in contemplation of divorce" was ambiguous, requiring remand to trial court for reconsideration of its ruling that parties did not intend for the agreement to apply to a divorce and resolution of the ambiguity in the agreement, as at least two interpretations of agreement were possible, i.e., that the agreement was not intended to govern the division of assets in a divorce, or the agreement should govern, or at least guide, the division of assets in a divorce if such provisions were legally enforceable). Fletcher v. Fletcher, 628 N.E.2d 1343 (Ohio 1994) (although agreement did not mention divorce or termination of marriage, because agreement mentioned "division of

versely, when part of the contract does deal with divorce, courts have generally construed the general provisions to apply to divorce as well.[30] Of course, if neither death nor divorce occurs, a court is without authority to divide property pursuant to the terms of an antenuptial agreement.[31]

The result of the failure to mention divorce can obviously have unintended consequences when there is a divorce. For example, in one case, the parties agreed that in the event one party predeceased the other, the surviving spouse would have a life estate in a particular condominium.[32] There was no mention of what was to happen in the event of divorce. The court held that the agreement did not prevent the parties from partitioning the property, even though they intended one spouse to remain in possession.

§ 14.06 Conditional Waivers

The parties can agree to make their waivers conditional upon some future event. Courts will construe these conditions according to their language and the parties' intent. For example, in *Harland v. Harlan*,[33] the agreement provided that the wife waived her rights in the husband's business for the first five years of the marriage, and if the marriage lasted more than five years, the waiver had no effect. The agreement was upheld, and the wife was able to share in the business.

Such "sunset" provisions are more common with waivers of maintenance, and the courts have not hesitated to enforce the agreement. Query, though, whether a sunset provision can be considered violative of public policy for promoting divorce, since the supporting spouse may time the divorce to become effective before the waiver of alimony becomes ineffective.[34]

---

property," agreement applied to divorce); Webb v. Webb, 434 N.W.2d 856 (Wis. Ct. App. 1988) (contract contained both general waiver and specific waiver of rights on death; if contract were limited to death only, general waiver would be superfluous; contract therefore applied to death and divorce).

30. McGilley v. McGilley, 951 S.W.2d 632 (Mo. Ct. App. W.D. 1997); Sabad v. Fessenden, 825 A.2d 682 (Pa. Super. 2003). *See also In re* Marriage of Best, 886 N.E.2d 939 (Ill. 2008) (the term "separate" in premarital agreement that waived spousal support and insurance coverage in the "event the parties separate or the marriage" was dissolved required that there be a legal separation); Ryken v. Ryken, 440 N.W.2d 300 (S.D. 1989) (contract applying upon "death or legal proceedings" applies to divorce, since divorce is a legal proceeding).

31. Smith v. Smith, 656 So. 2d 1153 (Miss. 1995).

32. *Marriage of Homann*, 658 N.E.2d 492.

33. 544 N.E.2d 553 (Ind. Ct. App. 1989).

34. *See* § **9.01**.

Procedure $\Big|$ 15

§ 15.01 Burden of Proof/Standard of Proof

The law is a gallimaufry of rules concerning burden of proof.

In most states, the burden of proof is on the party attacking the agreement, that is, the party seeking to invalidate the agreement.[1] Section 6 of the Uniform Premarital Agreement Act (UPAA) places the burden of proof on "the party against whom enforcement is sought."[2] When the burden is on the party seeking to prevent enforcement of the agreement, invalidity is an affirmative defense that can be lost if not properly pled.[3]

---

1. *In re* Marriage of Pownall, 5 P.3d 911 (Ariz. Ct. App. Div. 1 2000); *In re* Marriage of Bonds, 5 P.3d 815 (Cal. Ct. App. 2000); Parr v. Parr, 644 N.E.2d 548 (Ind. 1994); Boetsma v. Boetsma, 768 N.E.2d 1016 (Ind. Ct. App. 2002); Blue v. Blue, 60 S.W.3d 585 (Ky. Ct. App. 2001); Davis v. Miller, 7 P.3d 1223 (Kan. 2000); Reed v. Reed, 693 N.W.2d 825 (Mich. Ct. App. 2005); Rinvelt v. Rinvelt, 475 N.W.2d 478 (Mich. Ct. App. 1991); Potts v. Potts, 303 S.W.3d 177 (Mo. Ct. App. W.D. 2010); *In re* Marriage of Thomas, 199 S.W.3d 847 (Mo. Ct. App. S.D. 2006); Wiley v. Iverson, 985 P.2d 1176 (Mont. 1999); *In re* Estate of Peterson, 381 N.W.2d 109 (Neb. 1986); McFarlane v. Rich, 567 A.2d 585 (N.H. 1989); *In re* Estate of Shinn, 925 A.2d 88 (N.J. Super. App. Div. 2007); Lebeck v. Lebeck, 881 P.2d 727 (N.M. Ct. App. 1994); First Am. Bank W. v. Michalenko, 501 N.W.2d 330 (N.D. 1993); *In re* Marriage of Rudder, 217 P.3d 183 (Or. Ct. App. 2009); *In re* Estate of Geyer, 533 A.2d 423 (Pa. 1987); Paroly v. Paroly, 876 A.2d 1061 (Pa. Super. Ct. 2005); Marsocci v. Marsocci, 911 A.2d 690 (R.I. 2006); Nesmith v. Berger, 64 S.W.3d 110 (Tex. App.—Austin 2001); Marsh v. Marsh, 949 S.W.2d 734 (Tex. App.—Houston [14 Dist.] 1997); Ware v. Ware, 687 S.E.2d 382 (W. Va. 2009).

2. Unif. Premarital Agreement Act, 9C U.L.A. 35, 48 (2001).

3. Howell v. Landry, 386 S.E.2d 610 (N.C. Ct. App. 1989).

In some states, the burden of proof is on the party defending the agreement, that is, the party seeking enforcement.[4]

When an antenuptial agreement provides disproportionately less than the party challenging it would have received under an equitable distribution, the burden is on the one claiming the validity of the contract to show that the other party entered into it with the benefit of full knowledge or disclosure of the assets of the proponent. The burden of proving fraud, duress, coercion or overreaching, however, remains with the party challenging the agreement.

In some states, the burden is on the attacker to demonstrate that the agreement is substantively unfair; then the burden shifts to the defender to show that the agreement was obtained in a procedurally fair manner.[5]

The standard of proof is generally a preponderance of the evidence,[6] but some states have stated the standard as clear and convincing evidence.[7]

§ 15.02 Choice of Law

Premarital agreements and property settlement agreements, as contracts, are subject to the same rules of construction as any other contract.[8] Thus, the choice of law rules that apply to contracts apply to premarital agreements.

§ 15.021 No Choice of Law Clause

In the absence of an express choice of law clause, the court will look to the forum's choice of law rules.[9] In most states, this means that the law of the state where the con-

---

4. Barnhill v. Barnhill, 386 So. 2d 749 (Ala. Civ. App. 1980), *cert. denied*, 386 So. 2d 752 (Ala. 1980); Lutgert v. Lutgert, 311 So. 2d 1111 (Fla. Dist. Ct. App. 1976); Dove v. Dove, 680 S.E.2d 839 (Ga. 2009); Cannon v. Cannon, 865 A.2d 563 (Md. 2005); Randolph v. Randolph, 937 S.W.2d 815 (Tenn. 1996); Friedlander v. Friedlander, 494 P.2d 208 (Wash. 1971).

5. Norris v. Norris, 419 A.2d 982 (D.C. 1980); *In re* Marriage of Drag, 762 N.E.2d 1111 (Ill. App. Ct. 3d Dist. 2002); *In re* Palamann, 513 N.E.2d 1223 (Ind. Ct. App. 1987); *In re* Estate of Martin, 938 A.2d 812 (Me. 2008); Ansin v. Craven-Ansin, 929 N.E.2d 955 (Mass. 2010); *In re* Estate of Kinney, 733 N.W.2d 118 (Minn. 2007); McKee-Johnson v. Johnson, 444 N.W.2d 259 (Minn. 1989); *In re* Greiff, 703 N.E.2d 752 (N.Y. 1998); Strong v. Dubin, 851 N.Y.S.2d 428 (N.Y. App. Div. 1st Dep't 2008); Weinstein v. Weinstein, 830 N.Y.S.2d 179 (N.Y. App. Div. 2d Dep't 2007); Benker v. Benker, 331 N.W.2d 193 (Mich. 1982); Fletcher v. Fletcher, 628 N.E.2d 1343 (Ohio 1994); Griffin v. Griffin, 94 P.3d 96 (Okla. Ct. App. Div. 3, 2004).

6. *Ansin*, 929 N.E.2d 955.

7. *In re* Estate of Harber, 449 P.2d 7 (Ariz. 1969); Marsocci v. Marsocci, 911 A.2d 690 (R.I. 2006); N.J. Stat. Ann. § 37:2-38.

8. *See* § **14.01**.

9. *In re* Estate of Halmaghi, 457 N.W.2d 356 (Mich. Ct. App. 1990) (court can apply its own law if neither party argues otherwise).

tract is entered into, or the lex loci contractus, governs a contract as to its nature, interpretation, validity, obligation, and effect.[10] This rule has also been applied in a variety of jurisdictions to premarital agreements executed in foreign countries.[11]

Some states have adopted a hybrid rule that the law of the place of execution will govern procedural fairness, that is, voluntariness, and the law of the forum will govern substantive fairness.[12]

Finally, some states have adopted the *Restatement (Second) of Conflict of Laws* rule, which holds that the law of the state with the "most significant" relationship to the

10. Rhyne-Morris v. Morris, 671 So. 2d 748 (Ala. Civ. App. 1995); Victor v. Victor, 866 P.2d 899 (Ariz. Ct. App. 1993) (court will apply law of place of execution as to procedural validity); Hill v. Hill, 262 A.2d 661 (Del. Ch. 1970), *aff'd*, 269 A.2d 212 (Del. 1970) (antenuptial agreement executed in Maryland would be enforced in Delaware, where it was executed in conformance with laws of Maryland); *In re* Estate of Davis, 184 S.W.3d 231 (Tenn. Ct. App. 2004); Gamache v. Smurro, 904 A.2d 91 (Vt. 2006) (law of the state in which a prenuptial agreement is made governs the validity and interpretation of the agreement); Padova v. Padova, 183 A.2d 227 (Vt. 1985) (contract executed in Connecticut enforced according to law of Connecticut in divorce proceedings in Vermont); Black v. Powers, 628 S.E.2d 546 (Va. Ct. App. 2006) (under Virginia choice of law rules, validity of prenuptial agreement executed in Virgin Islands was governed in divorce action filed in Virginia by laws of Virgin Islands; parties did not clearly intend for Virginia law to govern validity of agreement, and neither party argued that substantive law of Virgin Islands regarding prenuptial agreements was contrary to Virginia's established public policies). *See generally* 41 C.J.S. *Husband and Wife* § 101 (1971) (validity, interpretation, and effect of the marriage settlement are governed by the law of the jurisdiction in which the contract of settlement was made, and are not affected by the subsequent removal of the parties to another state).

11. *See* Fernandez v. Fernandez, 15 Cal. Rptr. 374 (Cal. Ct. App. 1961) (where contract was executed in Mexico but would be enforced in California, California court must look to law of Mexico at time of marriage to determine validity of execution); Van Kipnis v. Van Kipnis, 840 N.Y.S.2d 36 (N.Y. App. Div. 1st Dep't 2007) (French prenuptial agreement adopting "separation of estates" property regime, i.e., opting out of community property regime customary under Civil Code, was enforceable in subsequent divorce); Chaudry v. Chaudry, 388 A.2d 1000 (N.J. Super. Ct. App. Div. 1978), *cert. denied*, 395 A.2d 204 (N.J. 1978) (contract executed in Pakistan would be enforced in New Jersey according to law of Pakistan); Sapir v. Stein-Sapir, 382 N.Y.S.2d 799 (N.Y. App. Div. 1976) (contract executed in Mexico would be enforced in New York according to law of Mexico, where there was no evidence of fraud, duress, or coercion). *Cf.* Gustafson v. Jensen, 515 So. 2d 1298 (Fla. 3d Dist. Ct. App. 1987) (declining to apply law of Denmark to agreement when parties knew they would be moving to Florida).

12. Victor v. Victor, 866 P.2d 899 (Ariz. Ct. App. 1993) (court will apply law of place of execution as to procedural validity); *Hill*, 262 A.2d 661 (antenuptial agreement executed in Maryland would be enforced in Delaware where it was executed in conformance with the laws of Maryland); Rivers v. Rivers, 21 S.W.3d 117 (Mo. Ct. App. 2000) (Missouri would apply its own law regarding validity of agreement executed in sister state).

parties will apply.[13] Public policy questions, however, are always decided according to the law of the forum state.[14]

§ 15.022 Choice of Law Clause

The UPAA specifically provides that parties may contract as to the law that governs the agreement.[15] A contractual choice of law clause will be enforceable so long as the parties have some reasonable contacts with the forum of choice.[16] This general rule, however, is not without exception. *Restatement (Second) of Conflict of Laws* provides that the court shall apply the law of the state chosen by the parties in most cases, unless that state has no substantial relation to the contract or unless the law of that state offends a fundamental policy of a state having a greater interest in the particular issue.[17]

In the context of antenuptial agreements, the *Restatement* rule was explained thus:

Where the issue is the formal requisites for an antenuptial agreement, or the validity of the disclosure made by a party, it would seem that the law of the

---

13. *In re* Estate of Santos, 648 So. 2d 27 (Fla. Dist. Ct. App. 1995) (court applied lex loci contractus rule, and certified to supreme court question of which state had more significant relationship to parties); Gordon v. Russell, 561 So. 2d 603 (Fla. Dist. Ct. App. 1990) (applying Florida's "most significant relationship" test: Florida has closer connection to case although agreement was signed in New Jersey); *Gustafson*, 515 So. 2d 1298 (contract signed in Denmark, but parties lived in Florida during marriage; because parties had closer connection to Florida, that law would apply); Lewis v. Lewis, 748 P.2d 1362 (Haw. 1988) (applying Hawaii's "most significant relationship" test: parties resided in Hawaii and owned property there, so Hawaii law would control, although parties signed agreement in New York); *Rivers*, 21 S.W.3d 117; DeLorean v. DeLorean, 511 A.2d 1257 (N.J. Super. Ct. Ch. Div. 1986) (New Jersey applied California law as state having greatest interest in estate of parties); Sabad v. Fessenden, 825 A.2d 682 (Pa. Super. Ct. 2003) (law of New York where parties negotiated and executed prenuptial agreement before marriage there, rather than Pennsylvania where husband sought divorce, governed the validity of the antenuptial agreement; New York had the more significant contacts and was one of many places of anticipated performance, and voiding the agreement would have no effect on integrity of the divorce decree).

14. McNamara v. McNamara, 988 So. 2d 1255 (Fla. 5th Dist. Ct. App. 2008); Scherer v. Scherer, 292 S.E.2d 662 (Ga. 1982); *Lewis*, 748 P.2d 1362; Muchmore v. Trask, 666 S.E.2d 667 (N.C. Ct. App. 2008).

15. UPAA § 3(7).

16. Nanini v. Nanini, 802 P.2d 438 (Ariz. Ct. App. 1990) (choice of law of Illinois would be upheld although parties were divorced in Arizona); Montoya v. Montoya, 909 A.2d 947 (Conn. 2006); Norris v. Norris, 419 A.2d 982 (D.C. 1980) (enforcing provision that contract would be governed by Florida law); Davis v. Miller, 7 P.3d 1223 (Kan. 2000); Lupien v. Lupien, 891 N.Y.S.2d 785 (N.Y. App. Div. 4th Dep't 2009); Steiner v. Steiner, 23 Fam. L. Rep. (BNA) 1242 (N.Y. Sup. Ct. Mar. 5, 1997) (forum selection provision was enforceable; parties could not seek a divorce in England when they agreed they would litigate only in New York); Franzen v. Franzen, 520 S.E.2d 74 (N.C. Ct. App. 1999); Bradley v. Bradley, 164 P.3d 537 (Wyo. 2007). *Cf. Scherer*, 292 S.E.2d 662 (court can ignore choice of law clause if neither party relies on it in enforcement proceedings).

17. RESTATEMENT (SECOND) OF CONFLICT OF LAWS §§ 187, 188 (1971 & Supp. 1989)

place of execution of the agreement ought to be the governing law. The reason for this is that the parties presumably acted with reference to that law. But where the issue is whether the antenuptial agreement may validly control alimony or the division of property on divorce, the state having the most significant relationship to the controversy would seem to be that of the parties' domicile at the time of the divorce, and therefore the law of that state should apply. It is that state which will have the greatest interest in the welfare of the parties and the support of the spouses.[18]

Thus, the law of the place of execution will determine the validity of the execution and will generally apply to the enforceability of the contract, except that the law of the state with the greater interest in the issue may apply its own law where a fundamental public policy will be violated by enforcement according to the law of the place of execution.[19]

§ 15.03 Limitations

Courts have generally been reluctant to apply statutes of limitations and the doctrine of laches to antenuptial agreements. If the limitations clock is ticking while the parties are married, the disadvantaged spouse would be forced to sue on the agreement during the marriage. This would encourage marital discord and result in useless litigation. Thus, while the few cases on the subject find limitations defenses available in theory, especially in New York,[20] the limitations period is generally tolled during the marriage.[21]

A related issue is whether a party can bring an action for declaratory judgment as to the validity of an antenuptial agreement during a presumably happy, intact marriage, as opposed to during divorce proceedings or at death, when the agreement would be enforced.[22] The few cases on the issue have held that such an action is not viable, because the issue is not ripe.[23]

---

18. 1 HOMER C. CLARK, THE LAW OF DOMESTIC RELATIONS IN THE UNITED STATES § 1.9, at 48 (2d ed. 1988).

19. *In re* Marriage of Proctor, 229 P.3d 635 (Or. Ct. App. 2010).

20. *E.g.*, DeMille v. DeMille, 774 N.Y.S.2d 156 (N.Y. App. Div. 2d Dep't 2004).

21. Hosseiniyar v. Alimehri, 852 N.Y.S.2d 338 (N.Y. App. Div. 2d Dep't 2008) (tolling limitations because of continuing duress); Zipes v. Zipes, 599 N.Y.S.2d 941 (N.Y. Sup. Ct. 1993) (six-year limitations period did not apply to unconscionability); Miller v. Miller, 983 A.2d 736 (Pa. Super. Ct. 2009); *In re* Estate of Crawford, 730 P.2d 675 (Wash. 1986).

22. *E.g.*, Holland v. Holland, 700 S.E.2d 573 (Ga. 2010); Barber v. Barber, 38 So. 3d 1046 (La. Ct. App. 1st Cir. 2010); Strong v. Dubin, 901 N.Y.S.2d 214 (N.Y. App. Div. 1st Dep't 2010).

23. Martin v. Martin, 287 S.W.3d 260 (Tex. App.—Dallas 2009). *Cf.* Moore v. Moore, 25 A.2d 130 (Pa. 1942) (controversy was ripe because of need to quiet title).

§ 15.04 Statute of Frauds

When a statute does not require that an antenuptial agreement be in writing, an oral antenuptial agreement is enforceable.[24] A number of state statutes, however, provide that antenuptial agreements must be in writing.[25] The UPAA takes this position.[26]

While a number of separate writings together can form a contract,[27] the intent to contract must be clear, and the court will not imply an agreement from informal arrangements.[28]

When the agreement must be in writing, and thus the statute of frauds is applicable, the effect of the writing requirement is no different from any other statute of frauds. The statute of frauds is an affirmative defense that is lost if not properly pled.[29] Further, partial performance is an affirmative defense to the writing requirement.[30]

The contract need not be reduced to writing before the marriage. A postnuptial transcription of a prenuptial oral agreement is enforceable as an antenuptial agreement.[31]

Some states also require special formalities before the signing of an antenuptial agreement.[32] Failure to adhere to these requirement may result in nonenforceability.[33]

---

24. Marcoux v. Marcoux, 507 N.Y.S.2d 458 (N.Y. App. Div. 1986).

25. *E.g., Strong*, 901 N.Y.S.2d 214; Tietjen v. Tietjen, 853 N.Y.S.2d 118 (N.Y. App. Div. 2d Dep't 2008).

26. UPAA § 2. *E.g., In re* Marriage of Shaban, 105 Cal. Rptr. 2d 863 (Cal. Ct. App. 2001); Hall v. Hall, 271 Cal. Rptr. 773 (Cal. Ct. App. 1990) (construing UPAA § 2 as a statute of frauds, subject to the normal common law exceptions such as part performance).

27. Pulver v. Pulver, 837 N.Y.S.2d 369 (N.Y. App. Div. 3d Dep't 2007).

28. Bridgeman v. Bridgeman, 391 S.E.2d 367 (W. Va. 1990) (refusing to imply antenuptial agreement from parties' courtship letters).

29. *Marcoux*, 507 N.Y.S.2d 458.

30. *Hall*, 271 Cal. Rptr. 773 (construing UPAA § 2 as a statute of frauds, subject to the normal common law exceptions, such as part performance); Dewberry v. George, 62 P.3d 525 (Wash. Ct. App. 2003) (oral premarital agreement whereby each party would treat income each would earn as separate property was enforceable where parties fully performed during marriage).

31. Trapani v. Gagliardi, 502 So. 2d 957 (Fla. Dist. Ct. App. 1987), *cert. denied*, 508 So. 2d 13 (Fla. 1987); Beatty v. Beatty, 555 N.E.2d 184 (Ind. Ct. App. 1990).

32. Dunagan v. Dunagan, 213 P.3d 384 (Idaho 2009) (requiring notarization); Succession of Haydel, 529 So. 2d 856 (La. Ct. App. 1988) (requiring that agreement be notarized and signed by two witnesses), *cert. denied*, 533 So. 2d 363 (La. 1988); Ritz v. Ritz, 666 So. 2d 1181 (La. Ct. App. 1995) (agreement not valid when it was not executed with proper formalities); Bradley v. Bradley, 164 P.3d 537 (Wyo. 2007). *See generally* Annotation, *Noncompliance with Statutory Requirements Concerning Form of Execution or Acknowledgement as Affecting Validity or Enforceability of Written Antenuptial Agreement*, 16 A.L.R.3d 370 (1967).

33. Siewert v. Siewert, 691 N.W.2d 504 (Minn. Ct. App. 2005) (agreement unenforceable where statute required antenuptial agreements to be executed in the presence of two witnesses, and hus-

§ 15.05 Estoppel and Ratification

Parties can be estopped from challenging the validity of an antenuptial agreement if they have accepted the benefits of the agreement.[34] For example, in *In re Palamara*,[35] the wife accepted benefits under the agreement, and failed to return them with interest before the case was tried. The court found her estopped from attacking the agreement. Similarly, in *Schutterle v. Schutterle*,[36] the contract contained mutual waivers of each spouse's rights in the other's real property. The wife sold her real property during the marriage, and treated the proceeds as hers alone. The court found this treatment of the proceeds sufficient to ratify the contract. Thus, it is possible that even though an antenuptial agreement may initially fail the voluntariness test, the agreement may nonetheless be enforceable due to subsequent ratification by the disadvantaged party.[37]

---

band and wife executed their antenuptial agreement in the presence of only one witness, a notary public); Matisoff v. Dobi, 659 N.Y.S.2d 209 (N.Y. 1997) (unacknowledged agreement was unenforceable). *Cf.* Weinstein v. Weinstein, 36 A.D.3d 797, 830 N.Y.S.2d 179 (2d Dep't 2007) (prenuptial agreement's acknowledgment substantially complied with requirements of real property law, and thus minor discrepancy in date on which agreement was executed was not, in itself, basis to set aside agreement, where agreement was in writing and was subscribed by both parties).

34. *See generally* Annotation, *Antenuptial Agreements: Parties' Behavior During Marriage as Abandonment, Estoppel, or Waiver Regarding Contractual Rights*, 56 A.L.R.4th 998 (1987).

35. 513 N.E.2d 1223 (Ind. Ct. App. 1987).

36. 260 N.W.2d 341 (S.D. 1977).

37. *See* Bakos v. Bakos, 950 So. 2d 1257 (Fla. Dist. Ct. App. 2 Dist. 2007) (antenuptial agreement that was the result of undue influence or overreaching by husband was not void ab initio but, rather, was voidable only by wife at her option, and thus agreement could be ratified by postnuptial agreement executed by the parties six years into their marriage); Curry v. Curry, 392 S.E.2d 879 (Ga. 1990); Rosenblatt v. Kazlow-Rosenblatt, 655 N.E.2d 640 (Mass. App. Ct. 1995) (wife ratified antenuptial contract by reexecuting after marriage); Webb v. Webb, 851 N.Y.S.2d 828 (N.Y. Sup. Ct. 2007) (modification of agreement ratified by wife by her acceptance of benefits); Nesmith v. Berger, 64 S.W.3d 110 (Tex. App.—Austin 2001) (evidence was sufficient to support finding that postnuptial agreement was valid contract between husband and wife, despite wife's testimony that she never saw appendices attached to document; husband testified that document was complete at signing and wife had ratified the agreement each year by performing according to its terms). *Cf.* Estate of Murphy, 661 S.W.2d 657 (Mo. Ct. App. 1983) (absent knowledge of rights in spouse's property, spouse cannot ratify marital agreement relinquishing right in spouse's property or be estopped to claim it is invalid).

Postnuptial Agreements 16

§ 16.01 Standard for Enforceability

A postnuptial agreement is a contract between a husband and wife executed after the marriage ceremony, and entered into for a reason other than an anticipated divorce or separation.[1] Most states have held that postnuptial agreements do not violate public policy,[2] and the standard of

---

1. Thus, if parties sign an agreement contemplating divorce but do not then divorce, the agreement cannot be used many years later as a postnuptial agreement. *In re* Marriage of Grossman, 338 Or. 99, 106 P.3d 618 (2005).

2. *Contra* OHIO REV. CODE § 3103.06 ("A husband and wife cannot, by any contract with each other, alter their legal relations, except that they may agree to an immediate separation and make provisions for the support of either of them and their children during the separation."). There are two exceptions to this rule: postnuptial agreements that are executed pursuant to separation and those that memorialize in writing oral antenuptial agreements.

validity and enforceability of postnuptial agreements is the same as that governing antenuptial agreements.[3] They are subject to the same rules of contract construction, and will not be enforced if they are too vague.[4]

Consequently, the party against whom enforcement is sought must have entered into the agreement voluntarily, free of circumstances involving fraud, duress or undue influence;[5] and the agreement must appear fair and reasonable

---

3. *E.g.*, Tibbs v. Anderson, 580 So. 2d 1337 (Ala. 1991); Simmons v. Simmons, 98 Ark. App. 12, 249 S.W.3d 843 (2007); *In re* Estate of Lewin, 595 P.2d 1055 (Colo. App. 1979); Bedrick v. Bedrick, 300 Conn. 691, 17 A.3d 17 (2011); Casto v. Casto, 508 So. 2d 230 (Fla. 1987); Epp v. Epp, 905 P.2d 54 (Haw. Ct. App. 1995); *In re* Marriage of Richardson, 606 N.E.2d 56 (Ill. App. Ct. 1992); Flansburg v. Flansburg, 581 N.E.2d 430 (Ind. Ct. App. 1991); *In re* Estate of Loughmiller, 629 P.2d 156 (Kan. 1981); McAlpine v. McAlpine, 679 So. 2d 85 (La. 1996); Ansin v. Craven-Ansin, 457 Mass. 283, 929 N.E.2d 955 (2010); Bell v. Bell, 2011 WL 1217246 (Mo. App. S.D., Mar. 31, 2011); Bronfman v. Bronfman, 645 N.Y.S.2d 20 (N.Y. App. Div. 1996); Dawbarn v. Dawbarn, 175 N.C. App. 712, 625 S.E.2d 186 (2006); Stoner v. Stoner, 572 Pa. 665, 667, 819 A.2d 529 (2003); *In re* Estate of Gab, 364 N.W.2d 924 (S.D. 1985); Bratton v. Bratton, 136 S.W.3d 595 (Tenn. 2004); Minor v. Minor, 863 S.W.2d 51 (Tenn. Ct. App. 1993); *In re* Estate of Beasley, 883 P.2d 1343 (Utah 1994); Button v. Button, 388 N.W.2d 546 (Wis. 1986). *See also* Davis v. Miller, 269 Kan. 732, 7 P.3d 1223 (2000) (parties free to incorporate standards of Uniform Premarital Agreement Act into postnuptial agreement).

4. Doe v. Doe, 712 A.2d 132 (Md. Ct. Spec. App. 1998) (agreement to vague to be enforced).

5. Cases finding duress: Chait v. Chait, 681 N.Y.S.2d 269 (N.Y. App. Div. 1998) (wife threatened to take children away from husband, and with her family's wealth she had the means to do it); Barchella v. Barchella, 44 A.D.3d 696, 844 N.Y.S.2d 78 (2d Dep't 2007) (postnuptial agreement between husband and wife, pursuant to which wife surrendered her interest in significant assets in exchange for husband's agreement to purchase a home for her with a maximum value of $600,000, was unfair because of husband's overreaching, so as to warrant setting aside the agreement, where wife had signed the agreement against the advice of her attorney, while she was undergoing treatment and suffering from mental and physical effects of complications arising from a surgery); Sanders v. Sanders, 2010 WL 4056196 (Tex. App.—Fort Worth, Oct. 14, 2010) (unreported) (wife did not voluntarily execute postnuptial agreements with husband, and thus the agreements were not enforceable under the marital property agreement statute, where wife lacked the mental capacity to voluntarily enter into the agreements); Izzo v. Izzo, 2010 WL 1930179 (Tex. App.—Austin, May 14, 2010) (postmarital property agreement, which was executed prior to divorce, was invalid because it was entered into involuntarily by wife, where husband threatened to dissolve the marriage unless the wife signed the agreement).

Cases finding no duress: Zoldan v. Zohlman, 915 So. 2d 235 (Fla. 3d Dist. Ct. App. 2005) (evidence in proceeding to invalidate postnuptial agreement between husband and wife, pursuant to which husband agreed to treat wife's daughter from earlier marriage equally to his three sons from earlier marriage in his estate plan, was insufficient to establish that agreement was product of

on its face,[6] or not unconscionable.[7] The question of whether an agreement is fair or unconscionable is a question of law for the court.[8]

---

undue influence; wife's only allegedly improper conduct was becoming upset upon learning that husband intended to favor sons, threatening to divorce husband, and requesting that daughter and son-in-law recommend an attorney, daughter and son-in-law's only conduct was to recommend and set up meetings with attorney, and none of this conduct amounted to duress or destroyed husband's free agency); *In re* Marriage of Tabassum & Younis, 377 Ill. App. 3d 761, 881 N.E.2d 396 (2d Dist. 2007) (postmarital agreement was not produce of duress on basis that wife was out of the country with parties' daughter as they negotiated the terms and husband perceived an implied threat to remain out of country and thus restrict his ability to meaningfully parent unless agreement was reached, where parties made changes to agreement between first draft and version they ultimately signed, husband did not sign agreement until two days after wife had returned with daughter, husband was represented by counsel, and he subsequently hired same law firm to represent him in dissolution proceedings); Garner v. Garner, 46 A.D.3d 1239, 848 N.Y.S.2d 741 (3d Dep't 2007) (record did not support husband's contentions that postnuptial agreement, entered into when parties agreed to stay married after husband disclosed drug addiction and affair, on division of marital assets, child support, and maintenance in the event of divorce was the product of duress and overreaching; the record revealed that the husband suggested the idea of such an agreement and dictated many of its terms, the wife found a lawyer to draft it by consulting the yellow pages, and the husband read the agreement as drafted by that lawyer and made handwritten changes before signing it, and no medical proof supported the husband's allegation that drug withdrawal symptoms at the time he entered into the agreement compromised his state of mind).

6. *Ansin*, 457 Mass. 283, 929 N.E.2d 955 (2010); Pacelli v. Pacelli, 725 A.2d 56 (N.J. Super. Ct. App. Div. 1999) (midnuptial agreement must be fair and just, both when executed and when enforced); Ebersole v. Ebersole, 713 A.2d 103 (Pa. Super. 1998) (full and fair disclosure required in postnuptial agreement unless there is clear evidence that the other spouse possesses the information).

7. *Bedrick*, 300 Conn. 691, 17 A.3d 17; *Bell,*, 2011 WL 1217246; McKeon v. McKeon, 78 A.D.3d 667, 911 N.Y.S.2d 93 (2d Dep't 2010); Infante v. Infante, 76 A.D.3d 1048, 908 N.Y.S.2d 263 (2d Dep't 2010).

8. O'Malley v. O'Malley, 41 A.D.3d 449, 836 N.Y.S.2d 706 (2d Dep't 2007) (postnuptial agreement entered into by husband and wife was not fair on its face, requiring a hearing to determine whether the agreement was unconscionable in substance; the husband received no benefit from the agreement, other than a promise to receive $50,000 years in the future, which in all likelihood he would have been entitled to as part of his equitable share of marital property, and husband relinquished a primary asset of the marriage, along with his inheritance rights, without a reciprocal waiver of inheritance rights by the wife).

There must be full and fair disclosure.[9] Each spouse must have an opportunity to consult counsel.[10] The agreement must not be against public policy.[11] This standard is the same standard as that contained in the Uniform Premarital Agreement Act.

In *Ansin v. Craven-Ansin*,[12] however, the court opined that the obligation to disclose each party's financial circumstances is *greater* with respect to marital agreements than premarital agreements, because each spouse owes a duty of absolute fidelity to the other. This case held that the requirement of full disclosure of a spouse's financial circumstances may be satisfied if, prior to signing a marital agreement, the spouse seeking to enforce it provided the other spouse with a written statement accurately listing (1) his or her significant assets, and their total approximate market value; (2) his or her approximate annual income; and (3) any significant future acquisitions, or changes in income, to which the spouse has a current legal entitlement or that the spouse reasonably expects to realize in the near future.[13]

---

9. Nelson v. Estate of Nelson, 53 So. 3d 922 (Ala. Civ. App. 2010); *Ansin*, 457 Mass. 283, 929 N.E.2d 955 (before a marital agreement is sanctioned by a court, careful scrutiny by the judge should determine at a minimum whether (1) each party has had an opportunity to obtain separate legal counsel of each party's own choosing; (2) there was fraud or coercion in obtaining the agreement; (3) all assets were fully disclosed by both parties before the agreement was executed; (4) each spouse knowingly and explicitly agreed in writing to waive the right to a judicial equitable division of assets and all marital rights in the event of a divorce; and (5) the terms of the agreement were fair and reasonable at the time of execution and are fair and reasonable at the time of divorce); *Bell*, 2011 WL 1217246 (evidence was insufficient to support finding that a valid postnuptial agreement existed between husband and wife, in dissolution action in which wife challenged the court's finding that she validly waived her interest in parcels of real property owned by husband; wife signed documents that stated she was waiving any claim to the properties and that the properties were husband's separate property, there was no evidence of any disclosure of what wife's legal rights were to any of the properties, there was no evidence that wife had access to independent counsel, and there was no evidence that wife received any consideration to waive her rights); Darius v. Darius, 665 N.Y.S.2d 447 (N.Y. App. Div. 1997) (postnuptial agreement premised on specific property in schedules, schedules never included; agreement unenforceable); Matisoff v. Dobi, 663 N.Y.S.2d 526 (N.Y. App. Div. 1997) (postnuptial agreement has to be acknowledged like other agreements). *See also* Schwartz v. Schwartz, 67 A.D.3d 989, 890 N.Y.S.2d 71 (2d Dep't 2009) (wife failed to demonstrate that deed constituted valid postnuptial agreement).

10. *Compare Nelson*, 53 So. 3d 922 (wife not prevented from seeking counsel), *and Garner*, 46 A.D.3d 1239, 848 N.Y.S.2d 741 (husband encouraged to seek counsel), *with* Furer v. Furer, 2010 WL 3271504 (Nev. 2010) (unreported) (wife prevented from seeking counsel).

11. Snell v. Snell, 2010 WL 2010899 (Ohio App. 5th Dist., May 14, 2010) (postnuptial agreement entered into between husband and wife was unconscionable, and thus unenforceable, to extent that it purported to prevent wife from seeking civil protection order or other relief from domestic violence; agreement could not prevent person from seeking protection from potentially violent situation).

12. 457 Mass. 283, 929 N.E.2d 955 (2010).

13. *See also In re* Grossman, 191 Or. App. 294, 82 P.3d 1039 (2003) (statute providing legislative framework for enforcement of premarital agreements did not apply to postnuptial agreements, and premarital agreements were inherently more arm's length in nature than were settlement agreements made after marriage).

Because the consideration for a prenuptial agreement is the marriage itself, in the context of a postnuptial agreement there must be consideration other than just the marriage.[14] Reconciliation in the face of an impending separation or divorce may constitute adequate consideration.[15] A release by one spouse of his or her interest in the estate of the other spouse, in exchange for a similar release by the other spouse, may constitute adequate consideration for a postnuptial agreement.[16]

By way of example, the issue of the validity and enforceability of a postnuptial agreement was specifically addressed in *In re Estate of Harber*.[17] In that case, the court noted that it had never addressed the issue of the validity of postnuptial agreements:

> The validity of postnuptial agreements not related to separation or divorce and which attempt to prevent, prospectively, the acquisition of community property has never been expressly ruled upon by this Court. Antenuptial contracts are not covered by Sec. 25-201, A.R.S., and are not involved in this case.[18]

---

14. Simmons v. Simmons, 98 Ark. App. 12, 249 S.W.3d 843 (2007) (husband and wife's 25-year marriage was not adequate legal consideration to support postnuptial agreement whereby husband stated his intention to convey to wife marital interest in property that he inherited from his parents, as past consideration would not support current promise); Whitmore v. Whitmore, 8 A.D.3d 371, 778 N.Y.S.2d 73 (2d Dep't 2004) (postnuptial agreement in which wife waived her right to any business property owned by husband, regardless of whether it was acquired before or after marriage, lacked consideration; husband did not relinquish any rights to any of wife's property or give wife anything in return for her release of her claims on husband's business property, and continuation of the marriage did not provide adequate consideration); Peirce v. Peirce, 994 P.2d 193 (Utah 2000) (postnuptial agreement under which wife agreed to give intestate husband all her future paychecks in return for husband's promise to leave his estate to her at his death, contained implied restriction on husband's ability to give away substantial portions of his estate during his lifetime; otherwise, husband would essentially have given no consideration, and his promise to leave estate to wife would be illusory). *Contra* Zagari v. Zagari, 191 Misc. 2d 733, 746 N.Y.S.2d 235 (Sup. Ct. 2002) (continuation of marriage provided consideration for postnuptial equitable distribution agreement). *Cf. Nelson*, 53 So. 3d 922 (record established that adequate consideration was provided for postnuptial agreement, in action challenging the validity of the agreement, where agreement was signed eight months after the wedding, and, thus, the marriage between husband and wife was not so far removed from the date of execution for the agreement as to prevent the marriage from serving as partial consideration for the postnuptial agreement, and the parties relinquished any claims they may have had to each other's separately owned property, which also constituted valid consideration for the agreement).

15. Ah You v. Ah You, 2008 WL 4890246 (Alaska, Nov. 17, 2008) (unreported); Gaskell v. Gaskell, 900 N.E.2d 13 (Ind. Ct. App. 2009); *In re* Marriage of Tabassum & Younis, 377 Ill. App. 3d 761, 881 N.E.2d 396 (2d Dist. 2007); *Garner*, 46 A.D.3d 1239, 848 N.Y.S.2d 741 (and cases cited therein); Dawbarn v. Dawbarn, 175 N.C. App. 712, 625 S.E.2d 186 (2006); Bratton v. Bratton, 136 S.W.3d 595 (Tenn. 2004).

16. Stewart v. Combs, 368 Ark. 121, 243 S.W.3d 294 (2006); Bedrick v. Bedrick, 300 Conn. 691, 17 A.3d 17 (2011).

17. 449 P.2d 7 (Ariz. 1969).

18. *Id*. at 14.

After discussing the Married Women's Property Act, the court concluded:

We feel that in view of the relatively equal status of women to men under the law, that married couples should not be deprived of the right to contract to divide their property as they please, both presently and prospectively, *assuming the contract is voluntary, free from fraud and is fair and equitable.*[19]

The court concluded:

We adopt the proposition that marital partners may in Arizona validly divide their property presently and prospectively by a postnuptial agreement, even without its being incident to a contemplated separation or divorce. We also feel that this rule should include the built-in safeguards that the agreement *must be free from any taint of fraud, coercion or undue influence; that the wife acted with full knowledge of the property involved and her rights therein, and that the settlement was fair and equitable.*[20]

Thus, it is the burden of the person seeking enforcement of the contract to prove by clear and convincing evidence that the agreement was not fraudulent or coerced, or that it was not unfair or inequitable.

The general rules of construction applicable to antenuptial agreements are applied to postnuptial agreements.[21] Thus, when a spouse waives an interest in an asset, the scope of the waiver is determined according to the same principles outlined previously.[22]

Because postnuptial agreements are entered into for reasons *other* than divorce or separation, when one party negotiates with the secret intent of divorcing, the agreement is not enforceable.[23]

§ 16.02 Postnuptial Agreement for Gift

Perhaps the most common postnuptial agreement cases before the courts are those in which a party makes a midnuptial gift to the other spouse. This has been called "reverse transmutation," but it is really an agreement to convert one party's separate property or both parties' marital property into the other party's separate property.

In its most common form, the doctrine of transmutation provides that under certain circumstances, an existing item of property can change its classification from separate to marital. Transmutation of property from separate to marital occurs in one of two

---

19. *Id.* at 15 (emphasis added).

20. *Id.* at 16 (emphasis added).

21. *E.g.*, Kelln v. Kelln, 515 S.E.2d 789 (Va. Ct. App. 1999).

22. *In re* Marriage of Gurda, 711 N.E.2d 339 (Ill. App. Ct. 1999) (in case concerning construction of wife's waiver of beneficiary designation on IRA during marriage, court held she waived her right as beneficiary, but not her interest in IRA itself).

23. Blaising v. Mills, 374 N.E.2d 1166 (Ind. Ct. App. 1978); Fogg v. Fogg, 409 Mass. 531, 567 N.E.2d 921 (1991); Wright v. Wright, 279 Mich. App. 291, 761 N.W.2d 443 (2008); Church v. Church, 630 P.2d 1243 (N.M. Ct. App. 1982).

ways: transmutation by commingling, and transmutation by gift.[24] Transmutation by commingling occurs when separate and marital property are mixed together to such a degree that the separate and marital property components cannot be traced. This may occur by adding separate property to marital property, by adding marital property to separate property, or by mixing separate and marital property together in a new asset. The result can be that separate property may transmute into marital property even though the parties did not intend that result, because the separate property is so mixed with the marital property that the separate portion cannot be identified.[25]

Transmutation by gift (also called transmutation by intent or transmutation by agreement)[26] occurs when the spouse owning separate property gifts property to the marital estate. The gift to the marital estate is proven just like any other gift: by statements or conduct showing an intent to make a gift of separate property to the marital estate and the delivery of the gift to the marital estate.[27] Thus, the gift may be either express or implied.

Obviously, marital property cannot transmute into separate property by commingling. The basis of transmutation by commingling is that the separate and marital portions are no longer identifiable, like the white and yellow parts of an egg being mixed together for an omelet. An omelet cannot unscramble itself and divide itself into its component parts once the parts have become unidentifiable. On the other hand, marital property certainly can transmute into separate property under the principle of transmutation by gift. In order for marital property to transmute into separate property, there must be clear and convincing evidence that *both* parties, not just one party, intended that the marital asset become separate property. This is because both parties have an interest in marital property. As stated by one author, "[T]he court should recognize this form of reverse transmutation only where both parties acted voluntarily and completely understood the consequences of their actions."[28]

Reverse transmutation by gift can be by express gift, as when parties enter into a midnuptial agreement whereby property that otherwise would be marital is given to one party only. For example, in *Barner v. Barner,*[29] the husband confronted the wife about her extramarital affair. In return for the husband's forgiveness, the wife agreed that certain marital assets would be the husband's sole property. The court found that the parties had intended not only to convey title to the assets to the husband alone, but also that in the event of divorce, the conveyed assets were the husband's separate property. Thus, where there is an unambiguous document showing the intent of the parties

---

24. *See generally* Brett R. Turner, Equitable Distribution of Property § 5.24, at 275 (2d ed. 1994).

25. *E.g., In re* Davis, 576 N.E.2d 44 (Ill. App. Ct. 1991); Harriman v. Harriman, 710 A.2d 923 (Me. 1998) (husband failed to prove what portion of investment account was nonmarital).

26. J. Thomas Oldham, *Tracing, Commingling, and Transmutation,* 23 Fam. L.Q. 219, 233 (1989).

27. Turner, *supra* note 24, at 277–78.

28. *Id.* at 286. *See, e.g.,* Fuqua v. Fuqua, 765 S.W.2d 640 (Mo. Ct. App. W.D. 1989) (stating that both parties must intend for marital property to become the separate property of one spouse).

29. 527 A.2d 122 (Pa. Super. 1987).

to transfer marital property to one party only, the midnuptial agreement is proven, and the transmutation by express gift is complete. The clearest evidence of an intent to transmute marital property into separate property is a deed whereby both parties convey property to one party as his or her "separate property."[30]

Reverse transmutation by gift may also occur by an implied gift: the gift is implied by the conduct of the parties. For example, in *DeHaven v. DeHaven*,[31] the court noted that funds may transmute from marital to separate property if the parties together intend and act as though the property is separate property. The actions of one party alone, however, cannot effect the transmutation, and the fact that title may be in one person's name alone does not effect the transmutation:

> "Property which is initially separate may become marital property either by express agreement, or by the manner in which it is maintained." McDavid, 19 Va. App. at 410–11, 451 S.E.2d at 716 (citations omitted). "Great consideration should be given to the actions, or non-action, of the parties with regard to exercising control over the property in question." Stainback, 11 Va. App. at 21, 396 S.E.2d at 691. *The mere fact that husband maintained a separate bank account for the funds to be used in the home's initial construction does not in and of itself transmute the marital property into husband's separate property.*[32]

As the *DeHaven* case makes clear, the intent of the parties may be gleaned from their actions. Thus, in *Beener v. Beener*,[33] where the parties agreed that each would receive a separate royalty check instead of one check to both parties for their joint interest in an invention, the parties evinced an intent to create separate property, and the check to each party was that party's separate property. Likewise, in *Perkins v. Perkins*,[34] the parties informally divided certain joint property during the marriage. The wife then used her share to purchase a farm. In a creditor's proceeding against the husband, he denied any interest in the farm, claiming it was the wife's separate property. Hence, on divorce, the court correctly determined that the farm was the wife's separate property, based on the parties' intent.[35]

Where there is no mutual intent to transmute marital property into separate property, then there can be no reverse transmutation by implied gift. For example, in *Sorrell*

---

30. *E.g.*, McDavid v. McDavid, 451 S.E.2d 713 (Va. Ct. App. 1994) (husband and wife jointly conveyed real estate and stock into sole name of husband; real estate conveyance indicated property would be husband's separate estate); Bliss v. Bliss, 898 P.2d 1081 (Idaho 1995) (community asset conveyed to wife by deed that referred to asset as wife's separate property); Pettry v. Pettry, 610 N.E.2d 443 (Ohio Ct. App. 1991) (husband quitclaimed half interest in marital home to wife, and quitclaim gave up husband's equitable distribution rights; thus at least 50 percent of home was wife's separate property).

31. No. 0097-96-4 (Va. Ct. App. Apr. 8, 1997) (unpublished).

32. *Id.*

33. 619 A.2d 713 (Pa. Super. Ct. 1992).

34. 641 N.Y.S.2d 396 (N.Y. App. Div. 1996).

35. *See also* Husband R.T.G. v. Wife G.K.G., 410 A.2d 155 (Del. 1979) (interspousal transfer can be evidence of an implied midnuptial agreement; remanding for further findings on the question).

v. Sorrell,[36] the parties transferred real property into the wife's sole name during the marriage. The wife testified the transfer was a gift, but the husband testified the transfer was for insurance purposes only. The trial court did not thus err in classifying the real estate as marital property. The same result was reached in *Pfleiderer v. Pfleiderer.*[37] In that case, during the parties' 57-year marriage, the parties acquired a cabin and lakefront property. They converted the property from a joint tenancy to the wife's sole title for estate planning purposes. "Transferring joint property into one party's name for estate planning purposes does not convert marital property into nonmarital property."[38]

Consequently, when one party does not participate in the decision to transfer marital property to separate property, then the mere fact that the property is in one party's name alone will not suffice to create separate property. This was well stated in *In re Marriage of Box.*[39] In that case, the husband's premarital bank account was separate property, but the interest earned on the premarital bank account during the marriage was determined to be marital property, even though the parties had agreed in an antenuptial agreement that the funds in the bank account were separate property. The court stated that the wife never intended that the *increase* in the account be separate property as well:

> [T]o the extent that the increase in [the husband's] account constituted marital property, [the wife] had no opportunity to participate with [the husband] in a transaction whereby the increase was transmuted from marital property into the husband's separate property.[40]

In sum, both parties must intend marital property to transmute into separate property in order for there to be a reverse transmutation by gift. The burden of proof is on the party seeking to prove the transmutation from marital to separate property.

---

36. 650 N.Y.S.2d 237 (N.Y. App. Div. 1996).
37. 591 N.W.2d 729 (Minn. Ct. App. 1999).
38. *Id.* at 732
39. 968 S.W.2d 161 (Mo. Ct. App. S.D. 1998).
40. *Id.* at 165.

Bibliography

Barbara Ann Atwood, *Ten Years Later: Lingering Concerns about the Uniform Premarital Agreement Act*, 19 J. LEGIS. 127 (1993)

Brian Bix, *Bargaining in the Shadow of Love: The Enforcement of Premarital Agreements and How We Think About Marriage*, 40 WM. & MARY L. REV. 145 (1998)

Brian H. Bix, *Premarital Agreements in the ALI Principles of Family Dissolution*, 8 DUKE J. GENDER L. & POL'Y 231 (2001)

Lindsey E. Blenkhorn, Note, *Islamic Marriage Contracts in American Courts: Interpreting Mahr Agreements as Prenuptials and Their Effect on Muslim Women*, 76 S. CAL. L. REV. 189 (2002)

Comment, *Marriage as Contract and Marriage as Partnership: The Future of Antenuptial Agreement Law*, 116 HARV. L. REV. 2075 (2003)

Amberlynn Curry, Comment, *The Uniform Premarital Agreement Act and Its Variations Throughout the States*, 23 J. AM. ACAD. MATRIM. LAW. 355 (2011)

Jonathan E. Fields, *Forbidden Provisions in Prenuptial Agreements: Legal and Practical Considerations for the Matrimonial Lawyer*, 21 J. AM. ACAD. MATRIM. LAW. 413 (2008)

Jens-Uwe Franck, *"So Hedge Therefore, Who Join Forever": Understanding the Interrelation of No-Fault Divorce and Premarital Contracts*, 23 INT'L J.L. POL'Y & FAM. 235 (2009)

Laura P. Graham, *The Uniform Premarital Agreement Act and Modern Social Policy: The Enforceability of Premarital Agreements Regulating the Ongoing Marriage*, 28 WAKE FOREST L. REV. 1037 (1993)

Michelle Greenberg-Kobrin, *Civil Enforceability of Religious Prenuptial Agreements*, 32 COLUM. J.L. & SOC. PROBS. 359 (1999)

Leah Gugenheimer, *A Modest Proposal: The Feminomics of Drafting Premarital Agreements*, 17 WOMEN'S RTS. L. REP. 147 (1996)

P. André Katz & Amanda Clayman, *When Your Elderly Clients Marry: Prenuptial Agreements and Other Considerations*, 16 J. AM. ACAD. MATRIM. LAW. 445 (2000)

Allison A. Marston, *Planning for Love: The Politics of Prenuptial Agreements*, 49 STAN. L. REV. 887 (1997)

Julia Halloran McLaughlin, *Premarital Agreements and Choice of Law: "One, Two, Three, Baby, You and Me,"* 72 MO. L. REV. 793 (2007)

Faun M. Phillipson, Note, *Fairness of Contract vs. Freedom of Contract: The Problematic Nature of Contractual Obligation in Premarital Agreements*, 5 CARDOZO WOMEN'S L.J. 79 (1998)

Nancy R. Schembri, *Prenuptial Agreements and the Significance of Independent Counsel*, 17 St. John's J. Legal Comment. 313 (2003)

Alexandra Selfridge, *Challenges for Negotiating and Drafting an Antenuptial Agreement for the Religious Upbringing of Future Children*, 16 J. Contemp. Legal Issues 91 (2007)

Joline F. Sikaitis, *A New Form of Family Planning? The Enforceability of No-Child Provisions in Prenuptial Agreements*, 54 Cath. U. L. Rev. 335 (2004)

Jocelyn E. Strauber, *A Deal Is a Deal: Antenuptial Agreements Regarding the Religious Upbringing of Children Should Be Enforceable*, 47 Duke L.J. 971 (1998)

Judith Younger, *Perspectives on Antenuptial Agreements*, 40 Rutgers L. Rev. 1059 (1988)

Appendix

A Mini-Encyclopedia of Ambiguous Marital Agreement Provisions and Their Construction by the Courts

Abandons
A separation agreement provided that the wife would lose certain benefits if she "abandons" or "deserts" the marital home. The wife did not lose her benefits when the court gave the husband exclusive use of home, because leaving under court order was neither abandonment nor desertion. Lang v. Lang, 551 So. 2d 547 (Fla. Dist. Ct. App. 1989).

Adjusted Gross Income
Where an agreement allocated college expenses in proportion to "adjusted gross income" as listed on each spouse's federal income tax return, the trial court properly used actual income rather than earning capacity. Albrecht v. Albrecht, 19 Conn. App. 146, 562 A.2d 528 (1989), *cert. denied*, 212 Conn. 813, 565 A.2d 534 (1989).

Age of Majority
A separation agreement provided that support would continue until the "age of majority." This clause meant that support would stop at the statutory age of majority, which was 18. The result was not changed by another statute providing that the duty of support at law extends until the child graduates from high school. If postmajority support was payable under

this statute, the proper plaintiff was the child and not the mother. There was a strong dissenting opinion. *In re* Lazar, 59 Ohio St. 3d 201, 572 N.E.2d 66 (1991).

All Sums Necessary or Desirable
"All sums necessary or desirable" for support of child included college expenses. Smith v. Smith, 159 A.D.2d 929, 553 N.Y.S.2d 243, 244 (1990).

Annual Net Income
The husband agreed to pay the wife one-third of his "annual net income" over $20,000. The phrase included contributions made by the husband's employer to the husband's pension and profit-sharing plans. Rosenthal v. Rosenthal, 172 A.D.2d 198, 568 N.Y.S.2d 603 (1991).

Any State University
The parties agreed that the husband would pay the child's college tuition at "any state university in South Carolina." The parties were South Carolina residents at the time the agreement was signed, but the wife and children subsequently moved to North Carolina. Thus, when the child chose to attend a South Carolina university, she was charged the out-of-state tuition. The court held that under the plain language of the agreement, the husband was required to pay the entire tuition, regardless of whether it was the in-state or out-of-state amount. *In re* White, 299 S.C. 406, 385 S.E.2d 211 (Ct. App. 1989).

Apprise
An agreement stated that the husband would "apprise" the wife when he obtained medical insurance on the children. The agreement placed upon the husband a legal duty to provide notification when insurance was obtained. Agee v. Agee, 551 N.W.2d 804, 805 (S.D. 1996).

Approved
An agreement required the husband to obtain a life insurance policy to be "approved" by the wife. The trial court held that the husband violated the provision by failing to send the wife a copy of the policy. The appellate court reversed, holding that the plain meaning of "approved" did not automatically require the husband to send such a copy. (The wise wife might refuse to approve the policy without seeing it, but the wife apparently never requested a copy, and the husband did not violate the agreement by failing to send one.) The husband was held in contempt, however, for failing to take any steps to obtain the wife's approval of the policy he selected. Wilson v. Collins, 27 Va. App. 411, 499 S.E.2d 560 (1998).

Arising
A separation agreement allowed the husband to deduct from the wife's monetary award all "claims, debts, or other expenses related to that property arising before May 1, 2001." The deduction was limited to the unpaid balance of debt on the stated date, and did not include debt payments that became due only after that date. Colorio v. Marx, 72 Mass. App. Ct. 382, 388, 892 N.E.2d 356, 362 (2008).

Assessed

An agreement required the wife to share in any tax liability "assessed" to the parties by the federal government. In the year in question, the parties owed tax, but it was covered by certain carry-forward tax benefits earned by the husband in previous years. Because no actual payment of taxes was required, the court held that no liability had been "assessed" against the parties. The decision expressly construed the agreement in light of the technical usage of terms in federal income tax law, and the result could be different in other contexts. Smith v. Smith, 15 Va. App. 371, 423 S.E.2d 851, 852 (1992).

Bonus

Where an agreement required the husband to pay the wife a portion of any "bonus," the obligation did not apply to dividends received on corporate stock. *In re* Marriage of Olsen, 229 Ill. App. 3d 107, 593 N.E.2d 859 (1992).

Camp Expenses

An agreement to pay "comparable camp" expenses did not require the father to pay the costs of his daughter's summer trip to tour and study in France. Rich v. Rich, 234 A.D.2d 354, 651 N.Y.S.2d 107 (1996).

Cohabitation

An agreement provided that the wife pay the husband the value of his interest in the marital home upon sale of the home or the wife's "cohabitation." The word "cohabitation" included remarriage. Kurtz v. Jackson, 859 S.W.2d 609, 611 (Tex. Ct. App. 1991). *See* § **6.034**.

College

See § **6.044**.

Commissions

An agreement called for division of certain "sale proceeds less commissions paid to any broker or Trustee reasonably necessary to procure a buyer." The property at issue was real property in Portugal, and under Portuguese law, all real property owned by nonresidents had to be titled in the name of a resident trustee. The trustee holding the property demanded a fee in order to permit sale, and without this trustee's consent, sale was impossible. The court held that the fee was not a "commission" paid "to procure a buyer," and refused to subtract the fee in determining net proceeds. Osborn v. Osborn, 159 Vt. 95, 614 A.2d 390, 392 (1992).

Consumer Price Index

A surprising number of agreements call for support to increase proportionally with the "consumer price index." The agreements are problematic, for the federal government publishes many different consumer price indexes. Where the agreement does not specify which one is intended, the contract is incomplete and the court must look to extrinsic evidence. *See* Nisbet v. Nisbet, 102 N.C. App. 232, 402 S.E.2d 151 (1991) (remanding the issue for a full hearing).

Conveyed

An agreement provided that if certain real property was "conveyed" by the wife, the husband would receive a lump sum monetary award of $75,000. The wife conveyed the property to herself and her second husband as joint tenants. "Clearly, the joint tenancy warranty deed 'conveyed' an interest 'by' Kim to a third party," and the $75,000 award became due. Strunk v. Chromy-Strunk, 270 Neb. 917, 940, 708 N.W.2d 821, 841 (2006).

Costs Incurred for Education

"Costs and expenses incurred for and in connection with such education" includes child's college room and board expenses, but not the expense of special foods required because of medical problems. Allyn v. Allyn, 163 A.D.2d 665, 558 N.Y.S.2d 983, 984 (1990).

Day Camp

An agreement to pay "day camp expenses" did not justify the trial court's decision that the father must pay the expenses of overnight camp. Verasco v. Verasco, 225 A.D.2d 616, 639 N.Y.S.2d 132, 132 (1996).

Death Benefits

The husband promised in a separation agreement to name the child as beneficiary of "any and all retirement plan[s], pension plans, and death benefits." *In re* Estate of Trevino, 381 Ill. App. 3d 553, 554, 886 N.E.2d 530, 532 (2008). "We do not read this language as limiting its application to only the death benefits of retirement and pension plans." Rather, "the phrase 'death benefits' is [also] commonly used to describe the proceeds of a life-insurance policy." *Id.* at 556, 886 N.E.2d at 533–34.

Defined Benefit Retirement Plan

A separation agreement awarded the wife "[o]ne-half of the [plaintiff's] defined benefit retirement plan." The plan had "two components: an annuity savings account and a monthly pension paid for life." Both components were divided by the agreement. Dougherty v. Dougherty, 109 Conn. App. 33, 35, 950 A.2d 592, 594 (2008).

Dental Expenses

The term "dental expenses" includes orthodontics. Arnold v. Fernandez, 184 A.D.2d 805, 584 N.Y.S.2d 231, 231 (1992).

Departure with Intent to Establish a Separate Residence

A separation agreement provided that the husband's duty to provide postmajority support ended with the child's "departure [from the wife's home] with intent to establish a separate residence." This standard was not met when the child left home to attend college. Fetherston v. Fetherston, 172 A.D.2d 831, 569 N.Y.S.2d 752 (1991).

Dependent

A separation agreement provided that the husband's support obligation stopped when the child was emancipated and no longer "dependent." A "dependent" is any person who looks to another for support. Where the child's physical disabilities had limited his earning capacity and forced him to postpone plans for future education, the child was still dependent, even though he was past the age of majority. The husband's support obligation therefore continued. Oblizalo v. Oblizalo, 54 Wash. App. 800, 776 P.2d 166 (1989).

Deserts
See **abandons**.

Dissolution
A provision permitting recovery of attorney's fees "associated with this dissolution" did not permit recovery of fees incurred in a postjudgment support modification action. "Dissolution" referred only to the initial divorce proceedings, and not to proceedings on subsequent motions. Tanner v. Tanner, 57 Cal. App. 4th 419, 67 Cal. Rptr. 2d 204, 207 (1997).

Education beyond the High School Level
The phrase "education beyond the high school level" includes both college and medical school. Allyn v. Allyn, 163 A.D.2d 665, 558 N.Y.S.2d 983, 984 (1990).

Educational Expenses
A contract to pay half of a child's "educational expenses" for college is not too vague to be enforced. *In re* Pierce, 95 B.R. 154 (Bankr. N.D. Cal. 1988).

An obligation to pay "educational and related expenses" includes college expenses. Nash v. Yablon-Nash, 61 A.D.3d 832, 833, 878 N.Y.S.2d 382, 384 (2009). *See* § **6.044**.

Educational Needs
The husband agreed to use the proceeds from sale of certain stock for his children's "educational needs." This obligation "was intended to include the costs associated with a college education," including "transportation expenses enabling Kyle to attend classes." Nicholson v. Nicholson, 378 S.C. 523, 536–37, 663 S.E.2d 74, 81 (Ct. App. 2008).

Eligible
A separation agreement required the husband to pay spousal support until the wife was "eligible to receive Social Security benefits." Slorby v. Slorby, 760 N.W.2d 89, 92 (N.D. 2009). "The plain language of the second amended judgment does not require Maureen Slorby to be sixty-five years old or to be eligible to receive full social security benefits. The second amended judgment does not even require Maureen Slorby to receive the social security benefits. The only requirement of the second amended judgment is that Maureen Slorby be eligible to receive any social security benefits," even partial ones. *Id.* at 93. A dissenting opinion would have held that the wife was not eligible for social security benefits until she actually began to receive them.

Employment
An agreement provided the wife with nonmodifiable maintenance, which was to terminate upon her "employment." The wife then worked for a local farmer for a period of five weeks, driving a truck and helping him harvest his crop. She earned $6 per hour for 140

hours, for a total income of $840. The trial court held that the wife's support did not terminate, and the appellate court affirmed. "[T]he word "employment" was a reference to full-time employment, or at least substantial regular employment which would take the place of the maintenance." Hughes v. Hughes, 23 S.W.3d 838, 841 (Mo. Ct. App. 2000).

Enforce

A separation agreement awarded attorney's fees to the prevailing party in any future action to "enforce" the agreement. The provision applied in an action to construe the agreement. Badell v. Badell, 122 Idaho 442, 835 P.2d 677, 684 (1992).

Equity

The husband promised to hold seven percent of the "equity" in certain real property in trust for the parties' children. Extrinsic evidence showed that seven percent was chosen because funds borrowed from the children constituted roughly seven percent of the purchase price of the property at issue. The obligation applied to the total value of the property, and not only to the difference between total value and the mortgage lien. Murphy v. Murphy, 694 A.2d 932, 934 (Me. 1997).

Exceeds

A separation agreement required that the husband pay 25 percent of the difference by which $1,400 "exceeds [the wife's] actual psychiatry bills." The wife incurred no such bills, but argued that that she should received 25 percent of the difference between $1,400 and zero. The court disagreed. The agreement clearly required the husband to make payments only if the wife's actual psychiatry bills were greater than $1,400. Scott v. Mohr, 191 Ga. App. 825, 383 S.E.2d 190, 191 (1989).

Extraordinary Expenses

A father promised pay his child's "extraordinary medical and dental expenses." This phrase did not include attorney's fees incurred defending the child after he murdered the father. *In re* Marriage of Braun, 222 Ill. App. 3d 178, 583 N.E.2d 633, 639 (1991).

Financially Able

A father with net annual income of $23,500 was "financially able" to pay $21,500 in college expenses spread out over six years, but payment of interest on this amount would be unduly burdensome. Stefani v. Stefani, 166 A.D.2d 577, 560 N.Y.S.2d 862, 863 (1990).

For Life

An agreement to pay the wife the net income from certain properties "for life" gave her the right to receive those payments during her entire lifetime, and not for any shorter period. *In re* Marriage of McKeon, 252 Mont. 15, 826 P.2d 537 (1992).

Forthwith

An obligation to pay a sum "forthwith" is inherently ambiguous; it might mean immediately, or it might mean within a reasonable time. On the basis of extrinsic evidence, the trial court did not err by choosing the second definition. *In re* Marriage of Sloane, 255 Ill. App. 3d 653, 628 N.E.2d 1198, 1200 (1993).

Good Faith

A child's mother agreed to contribute toward the child's college expenses "whatever contribution she determines in good faith she is able to provide." She then borrowed $100,000 to invest in a questionable business. The court found that the mother was obligated to contribute to the child's college expenses. Whelan v. Frisbee, 29 Mass. App. Ct. 76, 557 N.E.2d 55, 57 (1990). *See generally* § **5.08**.

Graduates from High School

Under an agreement providing for child support until the child "graduates from high school," support terminated when the child received general education development (GED) certificate. *In re* Marriage of Hahn, 324 Ill. App. 3d 44, 754 N.E.2d 461 (2001).

Gross Earnings

Where the agreement used the phrase "gross earnings," it was error to subtract business expenses from total income. Fishkin v. Fishkin, 201 A.D.2d 202, 615 N.Y.S.2d 899 (1994).

The husband promised to pay alimony equal to 15 percent of his "gross earnings." The provision applied to the husband's total real estate commissions. It did not apply to either the husband's total taxable income or his total commissions less business expenses. Vellinga v. Vellinga, 442 N.W.2d 472 (S.D. 1989).

Gross Income

The term "gross income" did not include income distributed to the husband from his corporation solely for the purpose of purchasing a corporate office. The corporation received substantial tax benefit from the arrangement. The court essentially held that the husband had neither legal nor beneficial ownership of the funds. C.D. v. N.M., 160 Vt. 495, 631 A.2d 848 (1993).

A separation agreement awarded the wife alimony equal to 15 percent of the husband's "gross income" over $95,000. The husband acquired stock options as consideration for employment and used them to purchase stock at less than fair market value. The difference between the value and the purchase price was not "income" under the agreement. The court relied significantly on the fact that in the original divorce action, earlier options had been listed on both parties' financial statements as "assets" rather than "income." Baldwin v. Baldwin, 19 Conn. App. 420, 562 A.2d 581 (1989).

A separation agreement awarded the wife part of the husband's "current gross income." This provision entitled the wife to part of the husband's $117,000 retirement incentive. Keene v. Keene, 175 A.D.2d 666, 572 N.Y.S.2d 592, 593 (1991).

Income

The phrase "income from all sources" includes capital gains. The language at issue appeared immediately after a provision requiring exchange of federal tax return, and the court held that the parties intended to adopt the federal tax law definition of "income." Keller v. Keller, 877 S.W.2d 192, 194 (Mo. Ct. App. 1994). *See* § **6.031**. *See generally* Annotation, *Separation Agreement—Alimony—"Income,"* 79 A.L.R.2d 609 (1961).

Income Earned Outside Place of Employment

A separation agreement stated that income earned "outside [the husband's] primary place of employment" would not be treated as a source for future support. The clause did not prevent the court from considering the husband's retirement benefits in setting support. Keffer v. Keffer, 852 P.2d 394, 395 (Alaska 1993).

Inheritance

Where an agreement waived the right to receive an "inheritance," the parties intended to waive the right to take as beneficiary of a trust. Flynn v. Flynn, 615 A.2d 119 (R.I. 1992).

The word "inheritance" is inherently ambiguous. It might be used in a narrow sense to mean direct descent upon death, or it might be used in a broader sense to mean any passage of title associated with death. On the basis of extrinsic evidence, the court held that the term included funds received from upon the decedent's death from an inter vivos trust. Wedin v. Wedin, 57 Ark. App. 203, 944 S.W.2d 847 (1997).

Insurance Program

An "insurance program" includes not only a policy purchased from a private insurer, but also insurance provided as a fringe benefit of employment. The term also includes any policy purchased as a replacement for the exact policy owned when the agreement was signed. Kruse v. Todd, 260 Ga. 63, 389 S.E.2d 488 (1990).

Intention

A child's father stated in a separation agreement his "intention" to pay college expenses in an amount to be agreed upon by father and child. This language was sufficient to create an enforceable obligation, and it was not an unenforceable agreement to agree. Stevens v. Stevens, 798 S.W.2d 136, 137 (Ky. 1990).

Intrical

An agreement that provided that spousal support was an "intrical" part of the parties' overall bargain was not an integrated bargain agreement. A search through dictionaries revealed no listing for this word, and there was no clear extrinsic evidence that the parties meant to say "integral." Williams v. Williams, 120 N.C. App. 707, 463 S.E.2d 815, 820 (1995), aff'd mem., 343 N.C. 299, 469 S.E.2d 553 (1995).

Matriculated

An agreement required support past age 21 if the child had "matriculated in a full time course of study." The child enrolled shortly before age 21, but the first semester of courses did not begin until 10 days after the child's 21st birthday. The court held that the requirement of the agreement was not met. ("Matriculate" is a synonym of "enroll," and the child was unquestionably enrolled on his 21st birthday, so the court's holding seems questionable.) Lawrence v. Lawrence, 180 A.D.2d 619, 579 N.Y.S.2d 162, 163 (1992).

Matrimonial Action

The parties agreed to waive all rights to recover attorney's fees in any future "matrimonial action." Two years later, the husband moved to reopen the judgment and set aside the agreement on grounds of duress, fraud, and unconscionability. The motion was a "matrimonial action," and neither party could recover attorney's fees. Healy v. Healy, 167 A.D.2d 687, 562 N.Y.S.2d 880 (1990).

Medical Expenses

An agreement required the husband to pay a portion of the wife's medical expenses. The wife was then admitted to a nursing home. The costs of care were medical expenses to the extent that they were compensation for services provides or supplies required by health care providers. The costs of care were not medical expenses to the extent that they were compensation for providing the wife with room and board. Franklin v. Franklin, 262 Ga. 218, 416 S.E.2d 503 (1992).

An agreement to pay "medical expenses" includes both dental and ophthalmological expenses. C.F. v. R.F., 176 Misc. 2d 82, 671 N.Y.S.2d 925 (1998).

Movable Property

It is unclear whether the phrase "movable property" includes retirement benefits. On the basis of extrinsic evidence, the court held that under the facts, retirement benefits were included. McCarroll v. McCarroll, 680 So. 2d 681 (La. Ct. App. 1996).

Net Earnings

"Net earnings" meant earnings after deduction of business expenses, even though the only deductions expressly listed in the agreement were taxes, hospitalization insurance, and disability care. Bottitta v. Bottitta, 194 A.D.2d 510, 598 N.Y.S.2d 304 (1993).

Net Income after Taxes

The phrase "net income after taxes" refers to the federal tax definition of adjusted gross income, minus the amount of taxes paid. It does not refer to the federal tax definition of taxable income, which includes a number of artificial deductions. Paul v. Paul, 235 Ga. 382, 219 S.E.2d 736 (1975).

Net of Tax

A promise to pay a certain amount of alimony "net of tax" means that the amount of alimony minus the taxes incurred on that alimony should equal the stated amount. In computing the best way to achieve this goal, the trial court has discretion to accept any reasonable tax expert's opinion. Sadur v. Ellison, 553 A.2d 651 (D.C. 1989).

Net Pay

The father agreed to pay 12.5 percent of his "net pay" per child in child support. "Net pay" includes not only the face amount of the husband's paycheck, but also the amount of any income tax refund he receives for the year in question. Donato v. Lucarelli, 109 A.D.2d 741, 486 N.Y.S.2d 58 (1985).

Net Profits

In determining the "net profits" of the husband's business, the court should not allow deductions for the husband's personal health insurance or for his retirement plan. A deduction should be allowed for the one-half of federal self-employment tax paid by the employer, but not for the other half paid by the employee. Where the amount of support was to be "based on" the husband's federal tax return, it was error to limit the proper deductions to those listed on Schedule C; instead, the husband should be permitted to take any deduction permitted on the entire return, absent evidence of a contrary intention. *In re* Marriage of Yaxley, 259 Ill. App. 3d 544, 631 N.E.2d 252, 253 (1994).

Net Recovery after Attorney's Fees

The husband was injured by medical malpractice during the marriage, and the separation agreement awarded the wife one-fourth of the "net recovery to him after attorney's fees." The husband settled the claim for $50,000 and paid $20,000 to his attorney, but he claimed the right to subtract additional expenses as well. The court held that by specifically mentioning attorney's fees, the parties had intended to exclude all other expenses from the definition of "net recovery." The wife's share was therefore one-fourth of $30,000, or $7,500. Harrington v. Perry, 103 N.C. App. 376, 406 S.E.2d 1 (1991).

No Sooner Than

An agreement called for de novo review of spousal support "no sooner than" 36 months after the first payment. "We believe that the use of the phrase, 'no sooner than,' indicates that the parties contemplated that a review would in fact occur at some time after the 36 months passed," upon motion filed by either spouse. *In re* Marriage of Golden, 358 Ill. App. 3d 464, 472, 831 N.E.2d 1177, 1184 (2005).

Normal Retirement Date

"Under its plain and ordinary meaning, the husband's "normal retirement date" is when he is eligible to retire under his pension plan," and not his date of actual retirement. Andrukiewicz v. Andrukiewicz, 860 A.2d 235, 238 (R.I. 2004).

Permanent Resident

Under the parties' agreement, the wife's support ceased if an unrelated male became a "permanent resident" of her household. Where her paramour visited her frequently but had his own residence and kept no clothes at the wife's home, the support did not terminate. Phillips v. Phillips, 555 So. 2d 698 (Miss. 1989).

Pharmaceutical Expenses

Where one spouse was required to pay the other's "pharmaceutical expenses," the provision covered only medications that require a prescription, plus any peripheral items necessary to administer them (e.g., hypodermic syringes). It did not cover over-the-counter medications, even if prescribed by a physician. Stewart v. Stewart, 190 Misc. 2d 438, 738 N.Y.S.2d 536 (City Ct. 2002).

Possession

The wife waived in an agreement her right to property in "possession" of the husband. The husband was at the time the sole resident of jointly titled real property. The word "possession" meant ownership and not mere residence, so that the wife did not waive her joint ownership rights in the property. Newborn v. Clay, 263 Ga. 622, 436 S.E.2d 654, 655 (1983).

An agreement awarded to the husband all real property in his "possession." Possession meant physical occupation and not legal title, so that the wife was not entitled to a share of property that was jointly titled, but occupied by the husband. Soto v. Soto, 936 S.W.2d 338, 339 (Tex. Ct. App. 1996).

An agreement awarded the husband all property in his "possession." "[S]ettlement clauses encompassing property within the 'possession' of a spouse do not affect intangible property, that is, property not subject to physical control or immediate enjoyment or disposition." Thus, the award did not apply to the husband's retirement benefits, which were subject to partition as an undivided community asset. *In re* Marriage of Malacara, 223 S.W.3d 600, 602 (Tex. Ct. App. 2007).

Prevailing Party
See § **6.053**.

Private and/or Parochial School
A promise to pay the expenses of "private and/or parochial school" includes the expenses of college. The failure to specify which expenses would be paid made the agreement too broad. The proper remedy was a court order specifying the expenses, however, and the contract was not unenforceable. Glassberg v. Obando, 791 S.W.2d 486 (Mo. Ct. App. 1990).

Proceeds
The husband agreed to give the wife part of the "proceeds" of any "sale" of certain corporate stock. The corporation then sold its assets, and the husband exchanged his stock in the seller corporation for stock in the buyer corporation. This transaction constituted a "sale." Because the wife's interest in the "proceeds" attached to whatever the husband received in exchange for the old stock, the wife should receive stock in the new corporation and not a monetary award. Braswell v. Braswell, 574 So. 2d 790 (Ala. 1991).

Publicly Traded Stocks
"[T]he trial court correctly held that the parties intended the term 'publicly traded stocks' to refer only to those stocks held in the non-retirement accounts." The term was used in a provision involving capital gains, which are not payable upon stock held in a retirement account. Kreimer v. Kreimer, 274 Ga. 359, 552 S.E.2d 826 (2001).

Remarriage
Under the parties' agreement, the wife's support terminated on death or "remarriage." After the divorce, the wife started a new relationship, and sought a religious annulment of her first marriage. She was unable to obtain such an annulment, and her religious convictions prevented her from marrying again. She nevertheless began cohabiting with her new partner, and even had a priest bless the new relationship. Despite these indicia of marriage, the wife's support did not terminate. "Remarriage" as used in the contract requires a legal remarriage, the court held, and not merely religious or social remarriage. Buchan v. Buchan, 550 So. 2d 556 (Fla. Dist. Ct. App. 1989).

Resided and Resides
See § **6.034**.

Resided on a Substantially Continuous Basis
A separation agreement provided that the wife's support would terminate if she "resided on a substantially continuous basis" with another man. The wife's paramour spent three to four nights per week at the wife's home, but kept his belongings at a separate residence. In addition, there was no financial interdependency between the couple. The contractual standard was not met, and the wife's support therefore continued. Emrich v. Emrich, 173 A.D.2d 818, 571 N.Y.S.2d 49 (1991).

Resides without Benefit of Marriage
An agreement provided for termination of support if the wife "resides with any unrelated man without benefit of marriage." The court held that this phrase required a marriage-like relationship, and not mere joint residency. The court noted that a contrary construction would permit the husband to harass the wife, in violation of a provision stating that the parties would live separate lives. Gordon v. Gordon, 342 Md. 294, 675 A.2d 540 (1996).

Retirement
An agreement called for an automatic reduction in spousal support upon the husband's "retirement." The husband retired at age 69, but several months later returned to work, doing the same job as the same hospital as before his retirement. The husband was not entitled to the automatic reduction for months in which he worked, even after his brief retirement. Kim v. Kim, 173 Vt. 525, 790 A.2d 381 (2001).

Retirement Benefits
See § **6.021**.

Salary
"Both interpretations of the term 'salary'—to include or to not include bonuses—are plausible." Isham v. Isham, 292 Conn. 170, 184, 972 A.2d 228, 237 (2009). A trial court decision excluding bonuses was reversed, and the case was remanded with instructions to consider extrinsic evidence.

Sale
Where the parties agreed to split the proceeds of sale of their home, and the mortgagee foreclosed, leaving a surplus, the foreclosure was held to be a sale. Thus, the surplus was properly divided between the parties. Troy Sav. Bank v. Calacone, 209 A.D.2d 777, 617 N.Y.S.2d 995 (1994).

The husband agreed to make monthly housing payments if the wife "sold" the marital home. This provision did not require sale to a third party, and it was triggered when the parties agreed that the husband would buy out the wife's interest. Webster v. Webster, 566 So. 2d 214 (Miss. 1990).

The husband agreed to give the wife part of the proceeds of any "sale" of certain corporate stock. The corporation then sold its assets, and the husband exchanged his stock in the seller corporation for stock in the buyer corporation. This transaction constituted a "sale," and the husband was obligated to give part of his new stock to the wife. Braswell v. Braswell, 574 So. 2d 790 (Ala. 1991).

The parties owned a trailer park. Their separation agreement provided that the husband would retain the park, but that he could sell it for a price not less than $180,000. If he did so, the wife received part of the proceeds; and if he died owning the trailer park, the husband was required to devise part of it to the wife. Shortly before his death, the husband sold the trailer park to his second wife for exactly $180,000, even though its fair market value was $970,000. The court held that the transaction was not a "sale," because the term "sale" implies a price determined by arm's-length negotiation. The husband therefore did not comply with the agreement merely by giving the wife her share of the $180,000 stated sale price. Cravero v. Holleger, 566 A.2d 8 (Del. Ch. 1989).

So Long As . . . And
A separation agreement provided that the child would attend public school "so long as he maintains a C or better average and does not need disciplinary intervention," and would otherwise be enrolled in private school. Both conditions had to be for the child to remain in public school. If only one condition was met, the agreement required the child to attend private school. Afkari-Ahmadi v. Fotovat-Ahmadi, 294 Conn. 384, 391, 985 A.2d 319, 324 (2009).

So Long As . . . Or
A separation agreement required the husband to pay child support "so long as" the children were dependent or unemancipated. When a promise applies "so long as" certain conditions are met, the promise becomes unenforceable only when none of the listed conditions is met. By contrast, if the contract had used "until," the promise would have become unenforceable when any one of the listed conditions was met. Where one of the children was emancipated but still dependent, the husband's support obligation continued. Oblizalo v. Oblizalo, 54 Wash. App. 800, 776 P.2d 166 (1989).

Substantially Similar to a Marriage Relationship
An agreement between the parties provided that alimony would cease if the payee wife entered into a relationship that was "substantially similar to a marriage relationship." This provision was triggered only where the wife entered into an emotional and physical relationship with some degree of financial interdependency. Where the relationship was emotional and physical but the wife was entirely financially independent, the support did not terminate. In re Marriage of Winningstad, 99 Or. App. 682, 784 P.2d 101 (1989).

Successful
An agreement gave the wife a right to an additional monetary award if the husband was "successful" in a certain lawsuit. The husband prevailed at trial of the lawsuit, but settled for a lesser amount to avoid an appeal. The husband was still "successful" overall, so that the additional award was payable. Reiman v. Goldstein, 252 A.D.2d 486, 675 N.Y.S.2d 137 (1998).

Tax Consequences

An agreement set forth certain tax rules, and required renegotiation of spousal support if "these tax consequences are changed." The agreement was ambiguous as to whether renegotiation was required when the stated rules remained the same, but a change in overall federal income tax rates materially changed the tax consequences of the provision. The case was remanded to consideration of extrinsic evidence. Bondy v. Levy, 121 Idaho 993, 829 P.2d 1342 (1992).

Taxes

"Net income after taxes" means net income minus the actual taxes paid by the husband in the year in question. It does not mean the amount of taxes the husband would have paid if he had remained single instead of remarrying. Paul v. Paul, 235 Ga. 382, 219 S.E.2d 736, 739 (1975).

Taxes Deriving from Permanent Alimony

The husband promised to pay permanent alimony, plus all "taxes . . . deriving from . . . permanent alimony." The taxes should be computed as if the wife had no income other than the alimony. Taxes paid because the wife's other income put her in a higher tax bracket were not within the scope of the provision. O'Hara v. O'Hara, 564 So. 2d 1230 (Fla. Dist. Ct. App. 1990).

Terminate

A contract that called for "termination" of spousal support did not suspend that support during appeal. Unkel v. Unkel, 699 So. 2d 472 (La. Ct. App. 1997).

Unrelated

An agreement provided that spousal support would terminate if the wife cohabited with an "unrelated" male. She then cohabited with her second cousin. Her support did not terminate. "[T]he term "unrelated" cannot include second cousins because second cousins are related." Tarafa v. Takach, 934 So. 2d 524, 526 (Fla. Dist. Ct. App. 2005).

Until

See **So Long As ... And**; **So Long As ... Or.**

Wages

In an agreement to pay alimony based upon "wages," the term "wages" is ambiguous, and extrinsic evidence must be considered. On the facts, the parties intended that "wages" include retirement income. Dube v. Horowitz, 258 A.D.2d 724, 684 N.Y.S.2d 689 (1999).

Appendix B

Discovery Materials on the Validity of Marital Agreements

Overview

The purpose of this appendix is to suggest questions that can be asked in determining the underlying facts of a case in which the validity of a marital agreement is at issue. The questions are not necessarily intended to be used as interrogatories; in fact, some of the questions may be too direct, or may suggest an answer that would be in the opposing party's interest. Rather, the questions are intended to assist the reader in framing deposition questions, interrogatories, requests for production other discovery materials, questions for counsel's own client, and even questions for direct and cross-examination. Many of the questions will be inapplicable to specific cases where certain legal theories (e.g., duress) are not argued by the attacking spouse. In all cases, the reader should use the questions only as a general guide, and not as a comprehensive list of questions that must be asked in every case.

General Questions

1. When did you first see the separation agreement at issue?
2. Who drafted the agreement?

3. Did you read the agreement before signing it?
4. Did you want to sign the separation agreement? If not, explain why you signed it.
5. At the time you signed, did you understand what a separation agreement is? Did you understand the terms of the agreement? If not, which specific terms did you not understand?[1]
6. When you and your spouse signed the agreement, were either of you under the influence of medication, alcohol, or drugs? If so, did the other spouse know of this fact?[2]
7. How long had you been married before you signed the agreement?
8. What was the state of your marriage at the time of signing?
9. Were you separated at the time you signed the agreement?
10. If the answer to the previous question is yes:
   A. Which of you first left your former home?
   B. Who was responsible for the separation?
   C. Did you continue to see each other or do activities together after the separation? If so, describe your contacts with each other.[3]

Questions Regarding Negotiation of the Agreement

11. Did you discuss the provisions of the agreement with your spouse before signing?
12. If the answer to the previous question is yes:
   A. What did each of you say during the course of the discussions?
   B. What were the states of mind of you and your spouse during the discussions? Where you friendly? Were the discussions hostile?
   C. Were either of you under the influence of medication, alcohol, or drugs during the discussions? If so, did the other spouse know this fact?
   D. How long did the discussions last? Were they conducted in a single setting, or in a series of separate conversations?
   E. During the discussions, did either of you make statements to the other regarding your property or income? If so, describe the statements.
   F. During the discussions, did either of you make statements to the other regarding the legal effect of any portion of the agreement? If so, describe the statements.
   G. If the answer to either of the above two questions was yes:
      (1) With regard to each statement, was the statement correct, to the best of your present knowledge?

---

1. This question is of obvious importance in determining the extent to which the agreement was a product of mistake. *See* **§ 4.054.** The answer may also suggest areas in which one spouse may have made fraudulent misrepresentations to the other.

2. This question obviously points in the direction of undue influence. *See* **§ 4.052.**

3. The questions on the nature of the parties' relationship are aimed mostly at determining whether the parties had a confidential relationship when the agreement was signed. *See* **§ 4.03.** When dealing with one's own client, counsel can ask bluntly about the degree to which a relationship of trust was involved. In seeking discovery from the other spouse, the issue is best approached more indirectly.

(2) With regard to each statement, did you rely upon the truth of the statement when you signed the agreement?

H. Were any persons present during the discussions, other than you and your spouse? If so, what role did they play in the discussions?

I. Were any changes made in the original draft of the agreement, as a result of the discussions?[4]

13. Did your spouse, at any point before you signed the agreement, provide you with documents regarding his or her assets and income, or your assets and income, or the meaning of the agreement, or any other matter involving the agreement? If so, please provide a copy of all such documents.

14. If one or more such documents were provided:

A. Was the information stated in each document correct, to the best of your present knowledge?

B. Did you rely upon the accuracy of each document when you signed the agreement?

15. Did your spouse tell you that any specific consequences would occur if you failed to sign the agreement?

16. Did you at any point refuse to sign a draft of the agreement? If so, how did your spouse react to your refusal?[5]

Questions Regarding Counsel and Other Advisors[6]

17. At any point between the time you first saw or discussed the agreement and the time you signed it, did you ever discuss the agreement with an attorney?

18. If the answer to the previous question is yes:

A. Name all attorneys with whom you discussed the agreement.

B. How did you come to know each of these attorneys? Did you know them personally? Were they recommended by others? If so, who recommended them?

C. State the conditions under which each discussion occurred. Did you pay the attorney a retainer? Did you consult the attorney without actually hiring him or her?

D. State the content of each discussion.

19. If you did not speak to an attorney:

A. Did anyone ever suggest that you should speak with an attorney? If so, who made the suggestion, and under what circumstances?

---

4. All of these questions bear obvious relevance to the possibility of fraud. *See* § **4.053**. They also bear at points upon the issues of duress and undue influence. *See* § **4.051–4.052**. The last question bears particularly upon duress, as the negotiation of changes suggests a reasonable measure of control over the content of the agreement.

5. The last two questions point at the heart of a claim of duress. *See* § **4.051**.

6. The presence of counsel is relevant to all of the various grounds upon which an agreement can be attacked, but particularly to the defense of undue influence. *See* § **4.052**.

  B. Did you make a conscious decision not to speak with an attorney, or did the thought of retaining an attorney never occur to you?

  C. If you did make a conscious decision not to speak with an attorney, why did you make that decision?

20. To your knowledge, did your spouse at any point ever retain counsel or discuss the agreement with an attorney?

21. If the answer to the previous question is yes, did you ever discuss the agreement with your spouse's attorney? If so, what was said during that discussion?

22. At any point between the time you first saw or discussed the agreement and the time you signed it, did you discuss the agreement with any person other than an attorney?

23. At any point between the time you first saw or discussed the agreement and the time you signed it, did you discuss the agreement with any person other than an attorney?

24. If the answer to the previous question is yes:

  A. Name all such persons with whom you spoke.

  B. How did you come to know each of these people?

  C. State the content of each discussion with each of these persons.

Questions Regarding Performance of the Agreement

25. Have you and your spouse attempted to reconcile since the agreement was signed? If so, please state the nature of the attempt, the duration of any reconciliation, and the reasons for its success or failure.[7]

26. Has your spouse ever failed to comply with any provision of the agreement? If so, did you complain about the violation? How and when did you do so?

27. Have you ever failed to comply with any provision of the agreement? If so, did your spouse complain about the noncompliance? How and when did the complaint occur?[8]

Unconscionability and Unfairness

The above questions address primarily the voluntariness of the agreement, and the possibility of a subsequent reconciliation or abandonment. A voluntary agreement can still be invalid, however, if its substantive provisions are sufficiently unfair to the attacking party. *See* § **4.06**.

  As a general rule, to determine the substantive sufficiency of a separation agreement, the court must compare the property and support provisions of the agreement with the property and support awards that the attacking spouse would have received if

---

  7. The doctrine of reconciliation is discussed at length in § **4.073**.

  8. These questions are aimed at uncovering any possible claim of abandonment or laches. *See* §§ **4.072, 4.075**.

the agreement had never been signed. In most cases, the terms of the agreement will be apparent from the face of the document. To determine the award that the attacking spouse would have received absent the agreement, counsel must ask the same sort of discovery questions that would be asked in a case that failed to settle. Thus, discovery must be used to identify, classify, and value assets; to determine the parties' incomes; and to identify any particular equitable factor suggesting an unequal division or a deviation from a guidelines amount of support. Discovery on these questions is well addressed in other works on the substantive areas of law involved.[9] The subject will therefore not be covered here.

---

9. *See, e.g.*, BRETT R. TURNER, EQUITABLE DISTRIBUTION OF PROPERTY ch. 4 (3d ed. 2005); LAURA W. MORGAN, CHILD SUPPORT GUIDELINES: INTERPRETATION AND APPLICATION ch. 6 (Supp. 2008).

Appendix C

Discovery for Premarital Agreements

General Questions

1. During the period of time before you were married to _____, did you two ever discuss the possibility of entering into a prenuptial agreement, that is, an agreement concerning your property after you were married?
2. Was the subject discussed more than once?
3. Over what period of time did these discussions take place? When was the first discussion?
4. Can you describe the substance of the conversations?
5. Did you discuss why you (or your spouse) wanted a prenuptial agreement? What was the stated reason?

Questions Concerning Counsel

6. Who prepared the prenuptial agreement?
7. Were you represented by counsel? If not, why? If not, did your spouse and/or his/her attorney recommend that you be represented by counsel?

8. If you were represented by counsel, did your spouse select your lawyer? Did you select your lawyer? How did you select your lawyer?
9. Who paid your lawyer?
10. Was your spouse represented by counsel?
11. If your spouse was represented by counsel, who was that? Who paid your spouse's counsel?
12. If your spouse was represented by counsel, did your spouse's counsel negotiate any changes? Did he or she recommend that your spouse sign or not sign? Was your spouse's counsel present at the execution?
13. If your spouse was not represented by counsel, do you know why?
14. If your spouse was not represented by counsel, do you know if you or your attorney suggested that your spouse engage counsel?
15. If you were both represented by counsel, were there any meetings about the prenuptial agreement between you and your attorney regarding the agreement? Between your spouse and your spouse's counsel, if you know?
16. How many meetings were there between you and your counsel? Between your spouse and your spouse's counsel, if you know?
17. How many days before the wedding was the agreement executed?
18. Did your counsel explain the provisions of the agreement to you at any time before the execution of the agreement?
19. Did you read the agreement?
20. Is this the agreement? Is this your signature? Is this your spouse's signature?

Questions Concerning Misrepresentation, Fraud, Duress

21. Did your spouse tell you what the agreement provided? Did that differ from what your attorney told you about the agreement?
22. At the time the agreement was executed, did you or your spouse state that there would be no wedding unless the agreement was signed?
23. Did you or your spouse make any promises not contained in the agreement?
24. Did you or your spouse warn of any consequences that would ensue if the agreement were not signed?
25. Is there any history of domestic violence between you and your spouse?

Questions Concerning Full and Fair Disclosure

26. When was the first time, relative to your wedding date, that you had a draft agreement in hand to review?
27. When was the first time you had disclosure of your spouse's financial circumstances?
28. What opportunities were given to you to verify the representations made by your spouse as his/her financial circumstances?

29. Did you or your spouse attach to the agreement a schedule of assets and/or income?
30. Is the schedule complete? Does it contain the values of assets as well as the assets themselves?
31. Was the schedule discussed with your spouse? With your attorney? With your spouse's attorney?
32. If there is not a schedule, did you otherwise have knowledge of your spouse's assets? Did you live together? Did you work for your spouse in any capacity?
33. Did you and your spouse ever discuss the legal effect of the agreement?
34. Did you and your attorney or you and your spouse's attorney ever discuss the legal effect of the agreement?

Questions Concerning Substantive Sufficiency

35. At the time of the marriage, what was your net worth? Your spouse's net worth?
36. Has your net worth or your spouse's increased or decreased since that time? By how much?
37. Have you and your spouse acquired any assets that are jointly owned? What are they?

Questions Concerning Abandonment/Modification

38. After you and your spouse were married, did you abide by the agreement?
39. Did you and/or your spouse carry out its provisions that were to be carried out during your marriage?
40. Were your premarital assets ever used for marital expenses? Were they ever mixed with your spouse's marital assets?

Table of Cases

Index